KARL MARX
FREDERICK ENGELS
COLLECTED WORKS
VOLUME
46

KARL MARX
FREDERICK ENGELS

COLLECTED
WORKS

INTERNATIONAL PUBLISHERS

NEW YORK

KARL MARX
FREDERICK ENGELS

Volume
46

MARX AND ENGELS: 1880-83

INTERNATIONAL PUBLISHERS

NEW YORK

This volume has been prepared jointly by Lawrence & Wishart Ltd., London, International Publishers Co. Inc., New York, and Progress Publishing Group Corporation, Moscow, in collaboration with the Russian Independent Institute of Social and National Problems (former Institute of Marxism-Leninism), Moscow.

Editorial commissions:
GREAT BRITAIN: Eric Hobsbawm, John Hoffman, Nicholas Jacobs, Monty Johnstone, Martin Milligan, Jeff Skelley, Ernst Wangermann, Ben Fowkes.
USA: Louis Diskin, Philip S. Foner, James E. Jackson, Leonard B. Levenson, Victor Perlo, Betty Smith, Dirk J. Struik.
RUSSIA: for Progress Publishing Group Corporation— Yu. V. Semyonov, Ye. N. Vladimirova; for the Russian Independent Institute of Social and National Problems—L. I. Golman, M. P. Mchedlov, V. N. Pospelova, G. L. Smirnov

Library of Congress Cataloging in Publication Data

Marx, Karl, 1818-1883.
    Karl Marx, Frederick Engels: collected works.
1. Socialism — Collected   works.   2. Economics — Collected   works.   I. Engels,   Friedrich,   1820-1895.
Works. English. 1975. II. Title
HX 39. 5. A 16 1975   335.4   73-84671
ISBN 0-7178-0546-8 (v. 46)

Printed in the USA

Contents

KARL MARX AND FREDERICK ENGELS
LETTERS
January 1880-March 1883

1880

APPENDICES

NOTES AND INDEXES

ILLUSTRATIONS

TRANSLATORS:

RODNEY LIVINGSTONE: Letters 8, 9, 19, 20, 25, 32, 83, 84, 115, 118, 131, 164, 193, 255, Appendix 5
STANLEY MITCHELL: Letters 100, 123
PETER and BETTY ROSS: Letters 1, 3-7, 10, 11, 13, 14, 16, 17, 23, 24, 26, 27, 29-31, 34, 35, 38, 39, 42, 45-53, 61, 63, 65-72, 74, 76, 78-81, 85-93, 95-98, 101-14, 116, 117, 120-22, 124, 126-28, 130, 132-46, 149-63, 165-75, 177-82, 184-89, 191, 192, 194-99, 201-17, 219, 220, 222-29, 231-35, 238-41, 243-46, 250-54, 257
STEPHEN SMITH: Letter 99

Preface

Volume 46 of the *Collected Works* of Karl Marx and Frederick Engels contains letters dating from January 1880 to March 1883. It was during these last few years of Marx's life that Engels assumed the main burden of corresponding with leaders of the international working-class movement.

Marx concentrated on his economic research; he also studied the history and culture of primitive society, world history, agriculture and peasant conditions in different countries, notably socio-economic relations and the state of the peasant commune in Russia after the abolition of serfdom. He also pursued his interest in higher mathematics and collected new facts for *Capital*. His plans to complete *Capital*, however, were not destined to be realised by him. His health deteriorated rapidly, compelling him to devote much time to medical treatment and often live out of London. Deprived of his library, he could not work on the second and third volumes of *Capital* (see this volume, pp. 158, 161) and even failed to finish reading the proofs of the third German edition of the first volume (pp. 425, 434). All this is reflected in this volume.

Responding to Paul Lafargue's request and prompted by the vital need of the workers' movement, Engels in this period wrote *Socialism: Utopian and Scientific* (see present edition, Vol. 24, pp. 281-325), destined to become the most widely read Marxist book alongside the *Manifesto of the Communist Party*.

Socialism: Utopian and Scientific, produced in the spring of 1880, was based on three chapters of *Anti-Dühring*. The introduction to the

French edition was written by Marx and published over the signature of Paul Lafargue (see pp. 16, 332). The pamphlet played a conspicuous role in imparting the Marxist outlook to the French socialists. '... I have seen what a regular revolution the thing has wrought in the minds of many of the better people in France,' wrote Engels (p. 300). This encouraged Engels to prepare a separate German edition (1882). To make it more comprehensible to factory workers (pp. 335, 352, 369), he revised the text, added a few new passages, and wrote a special preface (p. 331). An essay on the history of landownership in Germany from the ancient commune to the 1870s, 'The Mark' (see present edition, Vol. 24, pp. 439-56), was appended.

The essay, which later appeared under separate cover, entitled, *Der deutsche Bauer. Was war er? Was er ist? Was könnte er sein?*, completed Engels' research of 1881-82 into the social system of the ancient Germans. Its inclusion as a supplement in the German-language edition of *Socialism: Utopian and Scientific* was meant to arouse the German Social-Democrats' interest in the peasantry as the working class's potential ally. The importance Marx and Engels attached to this is reflected in Engels' letter of 23 September 1882, urging Bebel to read up on the subject, thus gaining 'solid foundations to go on in any debate [in the Reichstag] about landownership or agrarian questions' (p. 336).

Engels tried to resume his study of the philosophy of natural science he had begun in 1873 and dropped owing to his work on *Anti-Dühring* (see present edition, Vol. 25). But only short spells of time were available to him, though, as he put it, the book (*Dialectics of Nature*), 'has also long been pending' (p. 350). He managed to write a few fragments in 1880-82 (see Vol. 25, p. 660). The problems raised in *Dialectics of Nature*, and the history of primitive society which Engels studied in the early 1880s, were only partly reflected in his letters of that period.

By the 1880s, socialist workers' parties had sprung up in Austria, France, Denmark, Spain, Portugal, Belgium, and the United States of America. The emergence of national working-class parties was an objective trend that had begun in the 1860s. The letters in this volume produce a fairly good cumulative picture of the help that Marx and especially Engels had given them in drawing up their programme and in their strategy and tactics.

Marx and Engels took the emergence of self-dependent national working-class parties as a sign of the times. They were critical of the untimely attempts at re-establishing the International and working out a single legislative political and economic programme for all countries where socialists could come to power. Since the matter had been put on the agenda of the impending international congress in Switzerland, called on the initiative of the Belgian socialists, the Dutch Social-Democrat Ferdinand Domela Nieuwenhuis requested Marx in January 1881 to give his opinion on this score.

The reply to Nieuwenhuis (see p. 61) and Engels' letter to Johann Philipp Becker of February 10, 1882, stressed it would be not only useless but also harmful to restore the International or hold international congresses at the time 'in so far as they do not relate to the immediate, actual conditions obtaining in this or that specific nation' (p. 67). The formation of mass socialist parties was still far from completed. Indeed, it had only just begun in some countries, so that a new, 'reorganised International ... would only give rise to fresh persecution' (p. 196). As Marx and Engels saw it, international contacts between socialist organisations were then, in fact, maintained through the socialist and workers' press, and through contacts between recognised workers' leaders (see p. 197). This meant new ways of consolidating the workers' international unity were coming to the fore. Not until later, when the workers' movement attained a higher level and the ideas of scientific socialism spread, would the ground be ready for 'the establishment of an *official*, formal International' (p. 198).

Marx's and Engels' contacts with the German working-class movement were especially strong. The Socialist Workers' Party of Germany was then the largest proletarian political organisation in the world. It had proved its viability despite the difficult climate created by the Anti-Socialist Law of October 1878. Continuously persecuted, it managed to maintain its membership, establish an underground organ, the newspaper *Sozialdemokrat*, in Switzerland, and to keep alive its contacts with the masses.

The letters in this volume give a good idea of the diversity of Marx's and Engels' aid to the German Social-Democrats. They urged them to combat the reformist sentiment introduced by bourgeois intellectuals who, admitted to the party before the enactment of the

Anti-Socialist Law, opposed the revolutionary tactics of the left wing, and tried, as Engels wrote, 'to get rid of the Anti-Socialist Law at any cost and to do so ignominiously by means of moderation and meekness, tameness and toadyism' (p. 279).

Engels countered this by examining the situation in the party and in Germany, and stressing that this course of action had no hope of succeeding. 'After 3 years of unprecedented persecution...,' he wrote to Eduard Bernstein on 30 November 1881, 'our lads have returned, not only in all their former strength, but actually stronger than before' (p. 153). And he amplified: 'the movement ... from being restricted to a few local centres, has *only now come to be a national movement. And that is what frightens the bourgeois most of all*' (p. 154).

Engels had deep faith in the perseverance of the German workers. Bismarck's policy, which amounted to war against the workers (a state of siege had been declared in a number of cities, and the like), he noted, only helped the German Social-Democrats' influence to grow. 'The infamies to which socialist workers everywhere have been subjected,' Engels wrote Sorge on 20 June 1882, 'have everywhere made them much more revolutionary than they were even 3 years ago' (p. 279). Not submission, as suggested by the right-wing leaders (Blos, Hasenclever, and others), but workers' pressure, Engels held, could force the government to repeal the Anti-Socialist Law.

The clash with the reformist elements in the party and division on fundamental and tactical issues were objectively unavoidable, because the right and left wings of the German Social-Democratic movement reflected the interests of different social groups. In principle, Marx and Engels considered a break with the reformists desirable because, as Engels wrote Bebel on 21 June 1882, the schism would 'serve to elucidate the situation and we shall be rid of an element that in no way belongs to us' (pp. 281-82). But considering the Anti-Socialist Law, Engels advised against needless haste, because in the circumstances the workers might think the break would weaken the party and augur loss of its gains. Division over controversial issues, he held, called for a public discussion, which, however, was practically impossible owing to the Anti-Socialist Law. All the same, Marx and Engels promised the party's revolutionary leaders public support if matters should come to 'a show-down with these gentry and the party's left wing declares itself' (p. 282).

Engels wrote a large number of letters to Bernstein, editor of the *Sozialdemokrat*, the party's central organ. He offered advice as to the tactics the paper should follow to suit the conditions of that time. Engels commended the paper's opposition to the reformist stance of the right-wing Social-Democratic deputies in the Reichstag (pp. 173, 203, 244), and advised its editors to seek workers' support and apply for help to correspondents 'from amongst the genuine workers—not those who have become "leaders"' (p. 188). This tactic, worked out jointly by Marx and Engels (see, e. g., p. 393), proved successful. 'I am delighted,' Engels wrote Bernstein on 22 February 1882, 'that subscriptions should have passed the 4,000 mark and that the paper should find regular distribution in Germany, despite the police, etc. It is an *incredible* feat for a German paper that is *banned*' (p. 203).

At a difficult time for the German Social-Democrats, Marx and Engels undertook to represent the party in the international workers' movement, explaining its political tactics. In their letters to various countries, they called on the working class to give its moral and material aid to the German Social-Democrats. Marx started collecting funds for victims of the Anti-Socialist Law, addressing himself, among others, to Friedrich Adolph Sorge and journalist John Swinton, who was close to the socialists in the United States. 'Even if the monetary result were not important,' he wrote Swinton on 4 November 1880, 'denunciations of Bismarck's new *coup d'état* in public meetings held by you, reported in the American press, reproduced on the other side of the Atlantic—would sorely hit the Pomeranian *hobereau* [Junker] and be welcomed by all the socialists of Europe' (p. 41).

The letters in this volume show the part Marx and Engels played in organising the French Workers' Party. They established contact with Jules Guesde and the editors of the *Égalité* through Paul Lafargue. This gave them an opportunity to influence the French labour movement. A big role here, as we have said, was played by Engels' *Socialism: Utopian and Scientific*. In March 1880, Engels contributed an article, 'The Socialism of Mr Bismarck', to the *Égalité*. It struck out against the Bonapartist social demagogy of that time. At the request of Benoît Malon, Marx drew up a *Workers' Questionnaire* (see present edition, Vol. 24). More important still, he participated in drawing up the Workers' Party programme, whose theoretical part he simply dictated to Guesde in the presence of Engels and Lafargue (see pp. 43-44). Later, Engels commented: 'A masterpiece of cogent reasoning, calculated to explain things to the masses in a few words;

I have seldom seen its like and, even in this concise version, found it astonishing' (p. 148). This, indeed, was the programme the Workers' Party congress adopted in the autumn of 1880 in Le Havre. Its adoption, Marx pointed out, opened an entirely new stage in the French workers' struggle. This was when *'the first real workers' movement'* began in France, he said (p. 44).

The theoretical views of the members of the newly formed Workers' Party, however, were still immature. The revolutionary wing headed by Guesde and Lafargue (Collectivists) and the reformist followers of Malon and Brousse (Possibilists) were entangled in a controversy. It had begun before the congress and was especially heated after it. Contrary to any revolutionary transformation of society, the Possibilists advanced the idea of the workers' gradually winning a majority in the municipalities, thus paving the way for broader public services (*services publics*) and the gradual transfer of the means of production into the possession of the municipal authorities (municipal socialism).

In letters to Bebel and Bernstein, Engels predicted that a conflict within the Workers' Party was objectively unavoidable. 'It would seem,' he wrote, 'that *any* workers' party in a large country can develop only through internal struggle, as indeed has been generally established in the dialectical laws of development.... Such being the case, it would be sheer folly to advocate unification. Moral homilies are of no avail against teething troubles which, circumstances being what they are today, are something that has got to be gone through' (p. 343).

Marx and Engels sided with the Collectivists, who controlled the *Égalité* (p. 173). In his letters, Engels informed socialists in different countries of the reasons for the turmoil within the French Workers' Party, and stressed the fundamental nature of the controversy (see pp. 196-97, 332-33, 370). The argument concerned diametrically opposite attitudes to the party's political programme: whether the struggle against the bourgeoisie should be fought as a class struggle or whether the class nature of the movement and the revolutionary programme should be opportunistically renounced in all cases where such renunciation would win it more followers and more votes in elections. Engels pointed out that the Possibilists were 'sacrificing the proletarian class character of the movement' (p. 350).

In addition, Marx and Engels also called attention to the Guesdists' theoretical faults and the many tactical mistakes they made in the heat of the struggle. To begin with, Guesde and Lafargue negated reforms in bourgeois society. They denied the need of fighting for democratisation, and of combining struggle for society's social reorganisation with struggle for democratisation. In the absence of insight, Engels pointed out, 'party politics cannot be pursued with success' (p. 333). Engels therefore faulted Guesde's utterances against the Radicals (Clemenceau) (ibid.), who had in the early 1880s worked for democratisation of the French Republic and thereby furthered the vital tasks of the working-class movement in the country.

Engels deplored the Guesdists' lack of political skill. He censured them for having involved themselves in a polemic on personal grounds which only obscured the fight for fundamental aims, and also for their contentiousness, quick temper, failure to wait for the right time of action, and for phrase-mongering (pp. 181, 154-55 et seqq.). These blunders prevented Marx and Engels from giving their full support publicly to the Collectivists.

All the greater was the importance that Marx and Engels attached to correct coverage in the socialist press of Germany of the state of affairs in the French Workers' Party. They called on the French and German socialists regularly to exchange their newspapers—*Égalité* and *Sozialdemokrat* (pp. 360-61). In his many letters to the leaders of the German Socialist Workers' Party, Engels never failed to refer to the struggle inside the French party. This was doubly necessary, because, having failed to grasp its substance, the editors of the *Sozialdemokrat* had initially backed the Possibilists (pp. 386-87). His letters to Bernstein, Bebel, and others, showing the social and political similarity of possibilism and reformist currents in the workers' and socialist movements in other countries, finally prompted the editors of the *Sozialdemokrat* to back the Guesdists.

Marx and Engels were aware that the two distinct currents could no longer coexist within one party, it was time the Guesdists and Possibilists parted ways (see pp. 343, 350-51). At the St-Étienne congress in September 1882 the Possibilists had not only emasculated, but in effect totally rejected, the Havre programme by proclaiming local party branches fully autonomous as concerned programme issues (p. 341). That was why neither Engels nor Marx were discouraged by the fact that only a minority followed Guesde and Lafargue as a result of the split. Engels observed: 'The whole of the "workers' party", both factions included, constitutes only a small and dwindling portion of the Parisian working-class masses' (p. 333). The party, he said, was in the first stage of the internal struggle that the socialists in Germany had already passed (p. 351).

Marx and Engels believed that being champions of revolutionary principles, the Guesdists had a far better future than the Possibilists, even though the latter were in the majority. 'To be momentarily in the minority — *quoad* [as to] organisation — and have the right programme,' Engels wrote to Bernstein in November 1882, 'is at least better than having no programme and a large, though almost entirely nominal and bogus, following' (p. 389). Years later, he was proved right.

The correspondence of Marx and Engels in 1880-83 is evidence of their unflagging interest in the British labour movement, which was experiencing change, however slow, due to Great Britain's changing economic situation. The prolonged depression had shaken the Empire's industrial monopoly. The condition of the working people deteriorated. Radical workers' clubs sprang up in London. This was a new symptom, Marx wrote to Pyotr Lavrov at the end of January 1882 (p. 185), and evidence of the appeal socialist ideas had won among a section of the working class which began to oppose the Liberal Party, Gladstone's government, and '*official* trades-unionism' (ibid.).

The labour movement's vitalisation in the early 1880s also stimulated interest in scientific socialism among a part of the democratic intelligentsia. 'The English,' Marx wrote to Sorge in December 1881, 'have latterly begun to take rather more notice of *Capital*' (p. 162). He had been asked for permission to translate it into English or to translate it himself (ibid.). In letters to his friends, Marx said the first honest reviews had appeared in the British press. He commended young English philosopher Belfort Bax's article, 'Karl Marx', in the journal *Modern Thought* of December 1881, and described it as the first English publication 'pervaded by a real enthusiasm for the new ideas themselves' and standing up boldly against British philistinism (p. 163).

Engels' letters contain the story of his association with *The Labour Standard*, a trades union newspaper, in 1881. The attempt at addressing trades union members directly, setting forth the basics of the Marxian political economy and propagating the ideas of scientific socialism, proved unsuccessful. In letters to the *Labour Standard* editor George

Shipton of August 10 and 15, 1881, Engels deplored that the impact his
articles had made on readers was very weak (pp. 123 and 121). He explained: 'The British working man just doesn't want to advance; he has
got to be galvanised by events, the loss of industrial monopoly' (p. 121).

Despite its various setbacks, Marx and Engels noted, the British
bourgeoisie was able to offer more favourable conditions to more
highly qualified workers thanks to Britain's enormous colonial possessions and its supremacy in the world market. They saw this as the reason for the weakness of the British labour and socialist movement, the
slow spread of socialist ideas in the labour movement, and the protracted formation of an independent labour party. But Engels' contributions to *The Labour Standard* had not passed without influence.
George MacDonald, a British socialist with Marxist leanings, pointed
out, among others, that it had been Engels' articles in *The Labour
Standard* that prompted him to accept scientific socialism (see *How I
Became a Socialist*, London, 1896, pp. 61-62).

Letters showing Marx's and Engels' relationship with Henry
Mayers Hyndman, a prominent English radical, are of considerable
interest. Marx tried to explain what factors he thought created possi-
bilities for power to pass peacefully into the hands of the British working class. In December 1880, he wrote: 'If you say that you do not
share the views of my party for England I can only reply that that
party considers an English revolution not *necessary*, but — according
to historic precedents — *possible*. If the unavoidable evolution turn into a revolution, it would not only be the fault of the ruling classes, but
also of the working class. Every pacific concession of the former
has been wrung from them by "pressure from without"' (p. 49).

Marx's letter to Hyndman of 2 July 1881 shed light on the reasons
for their estrangement. Hyndman had put out a pamphlet, *England
for All*, as a kind of commentary on the programme of the Democratic
Federation he had founded the month before, in which he set out the
content of a number of sections from the first volume of *Capital*
without crediting Marx. The latter objected to this publication, chiefly because the Federation's bourgeois democratic goals conflicted
with the ideas borrowed from *Capital*. The pamphlet would have made
sense, Marx pointed out, 'for the foundation of a distinct and independent Working Class Party' (p. 103). Later, however, even though
he was strongly critical of Hyndman (pp. 161-62, 234, 347), Marx
admitted the objective usefulness of Hyndman's pamphlet because it
propagated the ideas of *Capital* (p. 163).

Numerous letters from 1880 to 1883 show Marx's and Engels' continual interest in Ireland. At the end of 1880 in a letter to John Swinton, Marx stressed the connection between the land questions in Ireland and England. Defeat of English landlordism in Ireland, he believed, would bring about the collapse of the land system in England (p. 40). But the Land League's peasant war against English landlordism and Gladstone's rule, and the heightened activity of Irish M.P.s under Charles Parnell, led Marx to conclude that Home Rule was the only possible solution of the Irish problem. This he wrote to Jenny Longuet at the end of April 1881 (see p. 90) and Eduard Bernstein in July 1882. 'In the absence of a foreign war or the threat thereof,' he wrote, 'an Irish uprising has not the remotest prospect of success' (p. 287), and amplified: 'The only recourse remaining to the Irish is the constitutional method of gradual conquest, whereby one position is taken after another' (pp. 287-88).

The letters also show that Marx and Engels followed events in North America. Engels noticed 'the colossal speed with which the concentration of capitals' was taking place there (p. 251). The two friends were aware that the labour movement in the United States followed a specific and anything but easy road. Apart from objective conditions (free land in the West, and so on), the spread of socialist ideas was hindered by strong sectarian tendencies imparted by German socialist immigrants, on the one hand, and the dissociation of socialist propaganda from the daily struggle of the workers, on the other, leaving the stage free for the spread of various radical bourgeois theories. Highly popular, for example, were the ideas of the radical economist Henry George. Nationalisation of landed property, which he considered the lever of social reconstruction, found a following among farmers and those workers who still dreamed of returning to the land and were angered by the plunderous ways of real estate profiteers, railroad companies, and the like. Marx, however, thought the attempt at blaming all social evils on private landownership wholly groundless. Contrary to George's theory, cheap land in the United States was contributing to the growth of the capitalist system at a rate unheard of in Europe. In June 1881, writing of George's ideas to Swinton and Sorge, Marx described them as 'merely an attempt, tricked out with socialism, to *save the capitalist régime* and, indeed, *to re-establish it on an even broader basis* than at present' (p. 101).

Marx's and Engels' ties with Russian revolutionaries and public leaders continued to expand. Their letters of 1880 to 1883 to Lavrov, Vera Zasulich, Danielson, Hartmann, Minna Gorbunova and others, reflect their lasting interest in the social-economic and political processes underway in Russia and in the life of their Russian acquaintances. Revolution was in the air in Russia. Marx and Engels held that the country stood 'on the threshold of a world historical crisis' (p. 18). As before they believed that events in Russia would create a revolutionary situation in Europe (see p. 209). And even though they were wrong about the time the crisis would break out, Engels predicted quite correctly in 1882 that the collapse of the Russian Empire would be a long process that would 'go on for years' (p. 208).

Intensive ideological search was under way within the Narodnik (Populist) movement, leading to its split and the emergence of two groups, Narodnaya Volya (People's Will) and Chorny Peredel (General Redistribution), whose members (Georgi Plekhanov and Vera Zasulich) founded the Emancipation of Labour group, the first Russian Marxist group, in 1883, after Marx's death. The future of the peasant commune and its place in the social reorganisation, that is, the idea of non-capitalist development in Russia, was the central problem that occupied the Russian revolutionary movement at that time. Marx's works, notably *Capital*, were fairly well known in Russia (see p. 45), and he was repeatedly asked to give his views on the matter (see, e.g., pp. 71-72).

The volume contains Marx's letter to Vera Zasulich, outlining his ideas about the future of the peasant commune in Russia. The analysis in *Capital*, he observed, 'does not adduce reasons either for or against the viability of the rural commune', and added that it might become 'the fulcrum of social regeneration in Russia' provided 'the deleterious influences which are assailing it from all sides' are eliminated, and it is ensured normal conditions for spontaneous development (pp. 71-72). To be sure, the letter did not speak of the long reflections that led up to this answer. This we see from the drafts of the letter examining the development of the peasant commune after the abolition of serfdom in 1861 (see Vol. 24).

Marx had ties with the Executive Committee of Narodnaya Volya, which he and Engels considered a revolutionary party 'of exceptional devotion and vigour' (p. 18). They had always opposed terrorism as a means of political struggle, but regarded its terrorist acts in Russia's specific conditions of the time as a reaction to governmental terrorism and the absence of elementary democratic freedoms for open political struggle.

The volume contains a number of letters concerning the question of national independence and the views of Marx and Engels on concrete independence struggles of oppressed peoples. Engels pointed out in a letter to Kautsky in February 1882 that 'it is historically impossible for a great people to discuss this or that internal question in any way seriously so long as national independence is lacking' (p. 191).

Marx and Engels considered the work of setting the West European proletariat free a priority, at least for Europe, with everything else being subordinate to that aim (see p. 205). They took the example of the liberation struggle of the Slav peoples to show that the value of any movement of oppressed nations in the historical setting of the time depended on whether it clashed with the interests of the working class. They were convinced that only 'the victory of the proletariat will liberate them [the oppressed nations] in reality and of necessity' (ibid.).

Until the end of his life, Marx followed developments in India. In February 1881, in a letter to Danielson, he observed that serious complications had arisen there for the British government, if not a general outbreak, caused by merciless exploitation of the indigenous population (see p. 63). It was the duty of the proletariat of Europe, Marx and Engels held, to back the liberation struggles of the oppressed peoples. Marx commended the meetings organised by the French followers of Guesde in defence of the popular movement in Egypt (see p. 297).

At the same time, Marx and Engels warned the European socialists against indiscriminate acceptance of national movements and their leaders, calling attention to the intrinsic contradictions of social processes. 'As I see it,' Engels wrote in reference to the National Party of Egypt and its leader Arabi Pasha in August 1882, 'we can perfectly well enter the arena on behalf of the oppressed fellaheen without sharing their current illusions (for a peasant population has to be fleeced for centuries before it learns from experience), and against the brutality of the English without, for all that, espousing the cause of those who are currently their military opponents' (p. 302).

Reflecting on the future of the colonies, Engels said he was sure they would all become independent. But he refused to predict how exactly this would occur. As he saw it, revolutions could win in India and Algeria and Egypt. That, he added, 'would certainly suit *us* best' (p. 322), meaning the revolutionary proletariat in the advanced countries. Engels assumed, however, that the proletarian revolution would first occur in Europe, and the colonial countries would 'have to be temporarily taken over by the proletariat and guided as rapidly as possible towards independence' (ibid.).

Marx's and Engels' letters to each other in the last few years of their joint activity produce an inspiring picture of intellectual collaboration and intimacy. Engels, naturally, saw to it that Marx had the best doctors and the best health resorts in Europe, and even Algeria. 'Your altruistic concern for me is unbelievable,' Marx wrote in September 1882 (p. 326). But bereavements occurred one after the other: Marx's wife died in 1881, and his eldest daughter Jenny in January 1883. This was a blow Marx could not survive. He passed away on 14 March 1883.

'Mankind is the poorer for the loss of this intellect — the most important intellect, indeed, which it could boast today,' wrote Engels (p. 462), who was destined to outlive his friend and carry on the cause to which they had both devoted their lives.

* * *

Volume 46 contains 257 letters by Marx and Engels, of which 138 are published in English for the first time and 119 were published in this language earlier, 45 of them in part only. Those previously published in English are indicated in the notes. The Appendices present four letters of Jenny Longuet's and one of Jenny Marx's. They contain thoughts expressed by Marx at one time or another and show his attitude towards various events. All the letters in the Appendices appear in English for the first time.

Obvious slips of the pen have been silently corrected. Proper and place names and separate words the authors had abbreviated, are given in full. Defects in the manuscripts are indicated in the footnotes, while passages of lost or illegible texts are indicated by omission points. Texts crossed out by the authors are reproduced in footnotes only where they substantially affect the meaning.

Foreign words and expressions are retained in the form in which they were used by the authors, with a translation where necessary in the footnotes, and are italicised (if underlined by the authors, they are given in spaced italics). English words and expressions used by Marx and Engels in texts written in German and French are printed in small caps. Longer passages written in English in the original are placed in asterisks.

The numbers of notes relating to the same facts and events given in the texts of different letters, are duplicated.

The texts of the letters and the notes were prepared by Alexander Zubkov. He also wrote the preface. The volume was edited by Valentina Smirnova. The name index and the indexes of quoted and mentioned literature and of periodicals were prepared by Victoria Reznikova (Institute of the History and Theory of Socialism).

The translations were made by Rodney Livingstone, Peter and Betty Ross and Stanley Mitchell and edited by Nicholas Jacobs (Lawrence & Wishart), K. M. Cook, Stephen Smith, Margarita Lopukhina, Andrei Skvarsky and Yelena Vorotnikova (Progress Publishers) and Norire Ter-Akopyan (USSR Academy of Sciences).

The volume was prepared for the press by the editor Margarita Lopukhina (Progress Publishers).

KARL MARX
and
FREDERICK ENGELS

LETTERS

January 1880-March 1883

1880

1

ENGELS TO WILHELM LIEBKNECHT

IN LEIPZIG

London, 10 January 1880

Dear Liebknecht,

Your letter arrived slap in the middle of the festive hurly-burly which, in view of the multiplication of the Marx family [1] and also because two of our friends[a] from Manchester were staying with us, assumed pretty formidable proportions. In order to forward your letter I had to consult the *latest* POST OFFICE DIRECTORY which was not to be had except at some distance from this house. *Enfin*[b] I laid my hands on it at the beginning of this week and sent your letter to

Alexander Macdonald Esq. M.P.
Well Hill (according to the DIRECTORY, Well hl.)
by Hamilton, North Britain (N. B.)

Macdonald is the bigger scoundrel of the two [2] but more deeply involved officially with the coal miners. Maybe you will get his reply before mine. As soon as Parliament opens, you can address your letters simply: Alexander Macdonald, House of Commons.

Since you say you have asked Macdonald for the documents mentioned in the main body of your letter, I shall of course do nothing further on this score until I hear from you again.

The silver and/or bimetallism [3] affair is the chimera of a few cotton speculators in Liverpool. Since it is virtually only silver that circulates among the Indian and Chinese traders, and silver has fallen from $^1/_{15.5}$ to $^1/_{17.5}$-$^1/_{18}$ of the value of gold over the past 10 years, this circumstance has, of course, further accentuated the crisis in the said article brought about by the over-export of cotton goods to the Far East. In

---

[a] Probably Carl Schorlemmer and Samuel Moore - [b] Finally

the first place, prices fell as the result of increased supply, and then, on top of that, these depressed prices represented an even lower gold value than hitherto so far as the English exporter was concerned. The crafty men of Liverpool, to whom it was quite inconceivable that cotton could ever fall in price as well, now blamed everything on the difference in the currency and thought that all would be in order and the Indo-Chinese trade would flourish, once it had been decreed here that silver should again be $^1/_{15.5}$ of the value of gold; i. e. that the British public must put up with silver at 13%-15% above its value so that cotton goods exporters might profit by that amount. That's all there is to the swindle, and a few more CROTCHET-MONGERS have latched on to it. It was never of any significance. Not long ago *The Times* was philanthropic enough to opine that gold currency was unsuited to so poor a country as Germany and that it would be preferable to revert to the more convenient silver currency—in the unspoken hope of creating an outlet for the London money market where the latter could dispose of its depreciated silver at a price higher than its value. Again a pious hope, of course, just like our friend Bismarck's childish fancy not long since to go back to bimetallism and reissue the taler as good for all payments, although it is worth 15% less than the amount it is supposedly good for. However, the German money chaps have grown *so* crafty under friend Bismarck that this no longer proved an attraction and the talers that had been issued came hurtling back at lightning speed into the Bank and the imperial treasuries.

I, too, wish you and all the others success in the New Year, as I do *the Russian revolution* which will surely get under way in the course of it and at once impose a quite different character upon Europe. For this too we are largely indebted to our friend Bismarck. With his ostentatious trip to Austria and the alliance he concluded there [4] he presented the Russian government at precisely the right moment (*for us!*) with the alternative: war or revolution. *Quel génie!*[a]

Your
F. E.

First published, in Russian, in *Marx-Engels Archives*, Vol. I (VI), Moscow, 1932

Printed according to the original

Published in English for the first time

---

[a] What a genius!

2

MARX TO CHARLES WALSTONE (WALDSTEIN) [5]

IN LONDON

[London,] 26 January 1880

Dear Waldhorn,[a]

If I don't find you in, I shall leave this note for you. I am prepared to come at 7 o'clock on Wednesday evening, WIND AND WEATHER PERMITTING. THAT IS TO SAY, IF IT BE NOT TOO COLD FOR THE PRESENT CONDITIONS OF MY *corpus delicti*.[b] For in this world all promises are relative.

Meanwhile, *salut*
Your
Moor

First published in: Marx and Engels, *Works*, Second Russian Edition, Vol. 50, Moscow, 1981

Printed according to the original

Published in English for the first time

3

ENGELS TO CARL HIRSCH

IN LONDON

[London,] 17 February 1880

Dear Hirsch,

Many thanks for the banker's letter which I return herewith. But I have not the faintest idea what can be meant by 'negotiated *à 340ᶜ*'. I can discover no rational connection whatever between this figure and German or Austrian currency. If the man would tell us how many marks he thinks he will be able to get for 200 Austrian gulden,

---

[a] Waldhorn (French horn) is a jocular name given to Walstone by Marx. - [b] A pun on *corpus* (body) and *corpus delicti* (substance of the offence).

Borkheim could decide what to do, and I think he would probably send them to him for realisation.

Your

F. E.

First published in Marx/Engels, *Werke*, Bd. 39, Berlin, 1968

Printed according to the original

Published in English for the first time

4

MARX TO BERNHARD KRAUS [6]

IN LONDON

[Copy]

[London,] 26 March 1880

Dear Dr Kraus [Kranz?],

I had quite forgotten that today was Good Friday; hence found the Café Royal shut on arriving there with my daughter Eleanor at 12 o'clock, waited until 1 o'clock and, not seeing you arrive, [proceeded?] to your hotel. Would you be so kind as to write to me today — so that I have your reply tomorrow — and let me know whether you might honour us with your company at dinner this Sunday at 5 o'clock (not 2).

With best wishes from Miss Eleanor.

Yours,

Karl Marx

First published in: Marx and Engels, *Works*, First Russian Edition, Vol. XXVII, Moscow, 1935

Printed according to a copy in an unknown hand

Published in English for the first time

5

ENGELS TO JOHANN PHILIPP BECKER [7]

IN GENEVA

London, 1 April 1880

Dear Old Man,

This is to notify you that I have taken out a money order for you at the post office for four pounds sterling — should amount to 100 frs 80 cts — and hope it will reach you safely. I trust that your health and that of your wife has improved now that the bitter winter is happily behind us. Here things are so-so. Mrs Marx is still not quite up to the mark and Marx, too, could be better. When winter's over, he always has his worst time; his coughing fits prevent him from sleeping.

For the rest, things have reverted to what they were in 1850. The Workers' Society has split up into a multitude of parties [8] — Most here, Rackow there — and it is as much as we can do not to get drawn into this maelstrom.[a] So many storms in a teacup, which may have an altogether salutary effect on some of the participants in that they contribute to their development but, so far as the march of events is concerned, whether 100 German working men here declare themselves for this side or for that is pretty immaterial. If they could exert any influence on the English — but there's no question of that. In his thirst for action Most cannot keep still but nor, for that matter, can he get anything done; people in Germany just won't see that, because Most has been statutorily slung out of the country, the moment of revolution is at hand. The *Freiheit* is to become, by hook or by crook, the most revolutionary paper in the world, but this cannot be achieved simply by repeating the word 'revolution' in every line. Luckily it matters very little what's in the paper and what isn't. The same thing applies to the Zurich organ,[b] which advocates revolution one day, only to declare on the next that a violent upheaval is the greatest of misfortunes, which is afraid on the one hand of being outdone by Most's rhetoric and fears on the other that the workers may take its own rhetoric to heart. Well, take your pick between the empty rantings of the *Freiheit* and the narrow philistinism of the *Sozialdemokrat*.

---

[a] See this volume, p. 9. - [b] *Der Sozialdemokrat*

I fear that our friends in Germany are deluding themselves as to the kind of organisation that ought to be maintained under present circumstances. That elected members of parliament should wish to place themselves in the van because there would otherwise be no leadership—to that I have no objection. But they can neither demand nor impose the implicit obedience that could be demanded by the former party leadership, *specifically* elected for the purpose. Least of all under present circumstances, without a press, without mass meetings. The more loose-knit the organisation now seems to be, the more tightly-knit it is in reality. Instead of this, the old system is to be retained, the party leadership is to have the final say (although there is no congress to discipline or, if necessary, dismiss it), and anyone who attacks one of its members is branded a heretic. At the same time, the best of them are themselves aware that they have in their midst all sorts of incapable and otherwise not very savoury persons, and they must be obtuse indeed if they fail to see that it is not they who are in control of their organ, but Höchberg, thanks to his money-bags, and with him his fellow philistines Schramm and Bernstein. In my view, the *old* party, together with its former organisation, is finished. When, as may be expected, the European movement shortly gets going again, then it will be joined by the vast mass of the German proletariat, of which the 500,000 men of 1878 [9] will form the trained and educated nucleus, and then, too, the old 'rigorous organisation' deriving from the Lassallean tradition will become a brake which, though it might hold back a waggon, no one could hope to apply to an avalanche.

At the same time, these men are doing a number of things which may wholly disrupt the party. First, the party is to go on maintaining its former agitators and editors by saddling itself with a mass of papers which contain nothing more than may be found in any middle-class local rag. And the workers are supposed to tag along with that indefinitely! Secondly, their bearing in the Reichstag and in the Saxon Diet is for the most part so meek as to discredit both them and the party in the eyes of the whole world; they make 'positive' suggestions to the existing government as to how it might do better in minor questions of detail, etc. And the workers, who have been declared outside the law and delivered up, bound hand and foot, to the tender mercies of the police, are expected to regard this as adequate representation! Thirdly, there is their tolerance of the philistine petty bourgeoiserie of the *Sozialdemokrat*. In *every* letter we are told that we must on no account believe any reports of splits or differences of opinion within the party, but everyone who comes here from Germany assures us that our people are completely bewildered by this conduct on the part of their leaders and that they by no means agree with it. Nor could it be otherwise, given the character of our workers which has so splendidly stood the test. It is a peculiarity of the German movement that all the mistakes committed by the leadership are invariably put right by the masses, and no doubt such will again be the case this time.[10]

Well, keep your pecker up and drop us a line occasionally. Borkheim is still in pretty well the same helpless condition as before.[a]

Your
F. E.

First published in: F. Engels, *Vergessene Briefe (Briefe Friedrich Engels' an Johann Philipp Becker)*, Berlin, 1920

Printed according to the original

Published in English in full for the first time

6

ENGELS TO H. MEYER

IN LONDON

[London,] 3 April 1880
122 Regent's Park Road, N. W.

Mr H. Meyer,

Your favour of 25 March[11] did not come into my hands until late at night on Saturday, 27 March, and hence, if only for that reason, I could not accept your invitation.

In view of the rifts and differences of opinion that have recently occurred among German Social-Democrats here and elsewhere, I am unable for the time being to declare myself in favour either of one party or of the other, especially as I cannot but reprobate, not only the policy of the Zurich *Sozialdemokrat*, but also and no less that of the London *Freiheit*.[b]

---

[a] See present edition, Vol. 45, p. 349.-[b] See this volume, p. 7.

I would request you to be good enough to convey this to the executive, and meanwhile remain

Yours very truly,

F. Engels

First published in: Marx and Engels, *Works*, First Russian Edition, Vol. XXIX, Moscow, 1946

Printed according to the original

Published in English for the first time

7

ENGELS TO AUGUST BEBEL

IN LEIPZIG

[London, after 27 April 1880] [12]

[...][a] so as to make the whole thing impossible without actually prohibiting it.

Mr Hasselmann will soon become harmless if you people bring to light *really* compromising facts about him and take the wind out of his sails in the Reichstag, i. e. proceed in a frankly revolutionary way, which can be done by using quite temperate language, as you yourself did in exemplary fashion in your speech on the persecutions.[13] If, however, a person is constantly afraid of being thought by the philistine, as often happens, to be a bit more extreme than he really is, and if in fact the enclosed cutting from the *Kölnische Zeitung* is correct in reporting that the Social-Democrats have brought a motion intended to restore the *guild privilege* of trading in home-made goods, then the Hasselmanns and Mosts will have an easy task.

None of this, however, is really of much consequence. What is now keeping the party alive is unobtrusive, spontaneous activity on the part of individuals; like its organisation, it is kept going by their irrepressible journeyings. In Germany we have fortunately reached the stage when every action of our adversaries is advantageous to us; when all historical forces are playing into our hands, when nothing,

---

[a] The beginning of the letter is missing.

absolutely nothing, can happen without our deriving advantage from it. For that reason we can quietly allow our adversaries to work for us. Bismarck is working for us like a real Trojan. He has now won Hamburg for us [14] and will shortly also make us a present, first of Altona, and then of Bremen. The National Liberals [15] are working for us, even though all they do is submit to kicks and vote taxes. The Catholics are working for us, even though they voted first against, and then *for*, the Anti-Socialist Law,[16] in return for which they, too, have simply been delivered by Bismarck over to the tender mercies of the government, i. e. also placed outside the law. Anything we can do is a mere drop in the ocean compared with what events are doing for us at this moment. Bismarck's feverish activity, which is throwing everything into disorder and putting everything out of joint without achieving anything of a remotely positive nature; which is stretching the philistine's tax-paying potential to the utmost limit, and this for nothing and worse than nothing; which wants one thing one day and the opposite the next and is forcibly driving into the arms of the revolution the philistine who would so gladly grovel at his feet — this is our strongest ally, and I'm delighted at your being able to confirm from actual observation that there has in fact been a shift to the left, as was inevitable in the circumstances.

In France, too, things are progressing well. Our communist viewpoint is breaking new ground everywhere and the best of those advocating it are all of them former anarchists who have come over to us without our raising a finger.[a] Unanimity has thus been established among European socialists; any who are still shilly-shallying aren't worth mentioning now that the last remaining sect, the anarchists, has melted away. There, too, we find increasingly a general shift to the left among the bourgeois and peasants, as you have already remarked; but there's one snag here: this shift to the left is primarily tending towards *a war of retribution* and that must be avoided.

The victory of the Liberals here has at least *one* good aspect in that it puts a spoke in the wheel of Bismarck's foreign policy.[17] Since he might just as well dismiss the Russian war from his mind now, he will, as usual, doubtless sell his ally — Austria — to the first comer. After all, the bitter experiences of 1864-66 have already shown the Austrians that Bismarck seeks allies only to betray them [18] — but they're too stupid and will again fall into the trap.

---

[a] Engels probably means, above all, Paul Brousse and Benoît Malon.

In Russia, too, everything is proceeding splendidly, despite judicial murder, banishments and an appearance of calm. You can't banish sheer lack of money. *Not one banker will make a loan* without a guarantee from the Imperial Assembly. Hence the present desperate recourse to an *internal* loan. *On paper* it will be a success, in reality a total failure. And then they will have to convene some assembly or other if only to obtain cash — always supposing something else doesn't happen in the meantime.

Kindest regards to you and Liebknecht from Marx and

Yours

F. E.

First published, in Russian, in *Marx-Engels Archives*, Vol. I (VI), Moscow, 1932

Printed according to the original

Published in English for the first time

8

ENGELS TO PAUL LAFARGUE [19]

IN LONDON

London, 4 May 1880

My dear Lafargue,

What are we to do about the introduction Malon has submitted? [20] Grateful as I am for his good intentions, what is needed here are facts, and where would he get them from? The history of German socialism from 1843 to 1863 is not yet in print, and Malon's German friends in Zurich know hardly anything about that period, which preceded their entry into political life. So it is natural enough that Malon's introduction should omit the most important facts while going into details which can hardly interest the French reader and should, besides, be riddled with mistakes of a fairly serious kind. To mention only one — Lassalle was never editor of the *Neue Rheinische Zeitung*. He never so much as contributed to it, if one excepts a feuilleton in a single issue — a feuilleton which was, moreover, completely rewritten by the editorial staff. At that time Lassalle was almost wholly taken up with the adulteries and divorce proceedings of Countess Hatzfeldt and her

Bibliothèque de la REVUE SOCIALISTE

I.

SOCIALISME UTOPIQUE

ET

SOCIALISME SCIENTIFIQUE

PAR

FRÉDÉRIC ENGELS

Traduction française par

PAUL LAFARGUE

Prix: 50 centimes

PARIS

DERVEAUX LIBRAIRE-ÉDITEUR

32, Rue d'Angoulème, 32

1880

husband [21]; and had he offered to join the editorial department, we should have refused outright to associate ourselves with a man up to his eyes in the filth necessarily arising from the conduct of such a scandalous case. Neither Marx nor I have ever collaborated with Lassalle. In about 1860 he suggested we should join him in founding a big daily newspaper in Berlin, but the conditions we laid down were such that he was bound to find them unacceptable.[22]

Come to that, if someone is needed to introduce me to the French public, as is very possible, it seems to me that it could only be you, who have taken the trouble to translate my articles[a] and who *alone* are in a position to get hold of the necessary information which I have asked Marx to let you have. To my mind, I owe it to you as much as to myself to take on no one else.

Yours ever,
F. Engels

First published in F. Engels, P. et L. Lafargue, *Correspondance*, t. I, Paris, 1956

Printed according to the original

Translated from the French

9

MARX TO PAUL LAFARGUE [23]

IN LONDON

[London, circa 4-5 May 1880]

Dear Lafargue,

Here is the fruit of my consultation (of yesterday evening) with Engels. Polish the phrases, leaving the gist intact.

Yours ever,
Karl Marx

First published as a facsimile in: Marx and Engels, *Works*, Second Russian Edition, Vol. 19, Moscow, 1961

Printed according to the original

Translated from the French

Published in English for the first time

---

[a] F. Engels, 'Le Socialisme utopique et le socialisme scientifique', *La Revue socialiste*, Nos. 3, 4 and 5, 20 March, 20 April and 5 May 1880.

10

MARX TO FERDINAND DOMELA NIEUWENHUIS [24]

IN THE HAGUE

London, 27 June 1880
41 Maitland Park Road, N. W.

Dear Sir,

At the urgent insistence of my doctor I must refrain from work of any kind for some time to come; [indeed] [a] I should already have left London on a recuperative trip to the seaside or mountains had I not been prevented from doing so by the very serious illness of my wife. Letters sent to the above address, however, will always find me, as they will be forwarded.

But my present state of health apart, I could not have complied with your request, [25] if only because I don't know enough Dutch to be able to judge whether this or that expression is appropriate.

Nevertheless, to go by the essays of yours I have read in the *Jahrbuch der Sozialwissenschaft* (Volume I, Second Half),[26] I have not the slightest doubt that you are the right man to provide the Dutch with a résumé of *Capital*—I would also mention *en passant* that Mr Schramm (C. A. S., p. 81) [b] *misconstrues my theory of value*. From a note in *Capital* to the effect that A. Smith and Ricardo are mistaken in *lumping together value* and *price of production* [27] (let alone *market prices*, therefore)—he could already have gathered that the connection between 'value' and 'price of production', hence also between 'value' and the market prices that oscillate about the 'price of production', has no place whatever in the theory of value as such, still less can it be anticipated by cliché-ridden, scholastic generalisations.

Under present circumstances the 2nd part of *Capital* [28] cannot appear in Germany, which I am quite glad of inasmuch as certain economic phenomena are, at this precise moment, entering upon a new phase of development and hence call for fresh appraisal.

With kindest regards,

Yours sincerely,

[Karl Marx]

First published, in Russian, in the magazine *Istorik-marksist*, Vol. 6 (40), Moscow, 1934

Printed according to the original

Published in English in full for the first time

---

[a] Manuscript damaged. - [b] [C. A. Schramm,] 'Zur Werttheorie', signed 'C.A.S.', *Jahrbuch für Sozialwissenschaft und Sozialpolitik*, 1880.

11

ENGELS TO MINNA GORBUNOVA

IN BIARRITZ

London, 22 July 1880
122 Regent's Park Road, N. W.

Dear Madam,

After a number of vagaries, your letter from Biarritz [29] has safely reached me here, where I have been living for the past 10 years, and I hasten to let you have such information as it is within my power to give.

I have talked over the matter with my friend Marx, and we both take the view that no better sources on the English industrial school system are to be had over here than the official reports [a] you already possess. The content of other non-official literature on the subject amounts to little more than window-dressing, where it is not expressly designed to provide an advertisement for some humbug or other. I shall have a look round and see if I can find anything that might interest you among the reports of the SCHOOL BOARDS and the Education Department in recent years, and shall send you further details if you would be so kind as to let me know to what address I should write or send packages, either within the next fortnight or so, or else in the autumn (since I shall be away from London for some time [30]). The industrial education of young people is in an even worse state here than in most countries on the Continent and what is being done, is done mostly for appearances' sake. You will have seen from the actual reports that the 'INDUSTRIAL SCHOOLS' are by no means on a par with continental industrial schools, but are a kind of penal institute where neglected children are committed for a given number of years by order of court.

On the other hand, the efforts made in America might perhaps be of greater interest to you. The United States has sent a wealth of material connected with this to the Paris Exhibition, [31] material which must be lodged in the big library in the rue Richelieu [32] and of which

---

[a] *Reports of the Commissioners Appointed to Inquire into the State of Popular Education in England* and *Reports of Reformatory and Industrial School.*

you will find details in the catalogue of the exhibition at the said library.

I am further endeavouring to find out for you the address of a Mr Da Costa[a] in Paris; his son[b] played a part in the Commune in 1871, and the father is himself employed in education, is passionately interested in his profession and would be more than willing to be of assistance to you.

Again, the schools for the further education of adult working men over here are not as a rule up to very much. Where anything worth while is done, it is usually thanks to special circumstances and individual personalities, i.e. local and temporary. In all such matters, the only element that systematically recurs here is humbug. The best of establishments relapse after a short while into a stultifying routine and the avowed purpose increasingly becomes a pretext for the employees to earn their keep as comfortably as possible. So much is this the rule that even establishments for the education of the children of the middle classes — bourgeoisie — form no exception. Indeed I have latterly come across a number of notable instances of this very kind.

I am sorry that at this stage I should not myself be able to place any fresh material at your disposal; for a number of years it has unfortunately been impossible for me to follow the course of public education in any detail. Otherwise I should have been only too delighted to be able to offer you more. Everything that furthers public education and hence the movement, however indirectly, in a country such as Russia, which stands on the threshold of a world historical crisis, and has produced a dynamic party of exceptional devotion and vigour — everything of this nature commands our most ardent sympathy.

I am, Madam,

Yours truly,
F. Engels

First published in Russian and in the language of the original (German) in the book *Neizdanniye pisma F. Engelsa* (F. Engels' Unpublished Letters), Leningrad, 1924

Printed according to the original

Published in English for the first time

---

[a] Eugene François Da Costa - [b] Charles Nicolas Da Costa

12

MARX TO PHILIP STEPHEN KING [33]

IN LONDON

[London,] 27 July 1880
41 Maitland Park Road, N. W.

Dear Sir,

Please send me:

Part IV of *Reports from Her M's Consuls.*

Yours truly,
Karl Marx

First published in the language of the
original (English) in *Marx-Engels Jahrbuch*,
Nr. 8, Berlin, 1985   Reproduced from the original

13

ENGELS TO MINNA GORBUNOVA

IN BIARRITZ

London, 2 August 1880
122 Regent's Park Road, N. W.

Dear Madam,

In all haste — for several days my house has been full of friends,
come on a visit from the provinces — herewith the address:

M. Da Costa, 40 rue Gay-Lussac, Paris. Since I have only seen the
old gentleman once and very briefly, he will certainly not remember
me. But all you need say by way of introduction is that Marx obtained the address expressly for you through his son-in-law Longuet
— who is a friend of young Da Costa's. [a]

---

[a] Charles Nicolas Da Costa

In the course of this week I shall have time to write to you at greater length, and shall address my letter to Paris, *poste restante.* Meanwhile I remain,

Yours faithfully,

F. Engels

First published in Russian and in the language of the original (German) in the book *Neizdanniye pisma F. Engelsa* (F. Engels' Unpublished Letters), Leningrad, 1924

Printed according to the original

Published in English for the first time

14

ENGELS TO MINNA GORBUNOVA [34]

IN PARIS

London, 5 August 1880
122ª Regent's Park Road, N. W.

Dear Madam,

Further to my brief note sent to Biarritz,[b] all I can tell you is that I don't in fact know of any documents or reports I could recommend to you other than those first enumerated by yourself in your previous esteemed letter.[35] However, after the school holidays, when the various people I'm acquainted with return, I shall make further inquiries, and if I find anything new, shall send it to you in Moscow [36] or report to you further. In order that such correspondence should appear perfectly innocuous, I shall write in English and sign myself E. Burns. When communicating with me from there, you could address your letters: Miss E. Burns, 122 Regent's Park Road, N. W., London. An inner envelope is unnecessary; she is my niece.

I was most interested to hear about your activities in Moscow and about the prospect of your setting up an industrial school with the help of the president of the земство [c][37]; we, too, have the statistical reports of all the Russian земства over here, as in general quite excel-

---

[a] 112 in the manuscript. - [b] See previous letter. - [c] Zemstvo

lent material on economic conditions in Russia, but unfortunately I cannot look it out at this moment as it is at Marx's house and he and all his family are away at the seaside.[38] However it wouldn't be much help to me in answering your inquiry,[39] since this calls for a knowledge of the relevant branches of the cottage industry, its operation, products and competitiveness, and that can only be acquired on the spot. All in all it seems to me that most, at any rate, of the branches of industry you mentioned would probably be capable of competing with large-scale industry for some time yet. Industrial revolutions such as these progress extremely slowly; even the handloom has not yet been entirely superseded in some branches in Germany, whereas in England those same branches did away with it 20 or 30 years ago. In Russia that process might well be even slower. After all, the long winter provides the peasant with a great deal of spare time, and even if he only earns something during the day, that is still so much gain. Admittedly these primitive forms of production cannot escape their ultimate demise, and in a highly developed industrial country, as here, for example, one might claim that it would be more humane to accelerate this process of dissolution rather than prolong it. In Russia the situation may well be different, especially as there is some prospect there of violent changes in the political situation as a whole. The minor palliatives which have proved virtually useless in Germany, as you yourself have of course discovered, and also elsewhere, might in Russia help the people on occasion to surmount the political crisis and keep their industry going until such time as they also have a say. The schools, however, might perhaps enable them to get at least some idea of *what* they ought to say. And all genuine educative elements that are dispersed among the people will, to a greater or lesser extent, contribute to that end. Technical instruction might perhaps best achieve its aim if it sought, on the one hand, to organise the operations at any rate of the more viable branches of traditional industry in a more rational way and, on the other, to provide the children with sufficient training in general technology to facilitate their transition to other industries. Aside from such generalisations there is, at this distance, little to be said. Except that this much seems pretty clear to me: The Moscow *gouvernement* is unlikely to become a seat of large-scale industry in the near future, since it is remote from the coal-mining areas, and wood fuel is already in short supply. Cottage industry in some, if not always the same, form might persist there for a bit longer even if protective tariffs were to make feasible the introduction of this or that large enterprise, such as the cotton industry of Shuya and Ivanovo in the Vladimir *gouvernement*. And, after all, the only way one can really help the peasants is to see that they get more land and cultivate it in associations.

Your report about the incipient decay of the община[a][40] and the artel[41] confirms news that has also come to us from another quarter. Nevertheless this process of disintegration may go on for a very long time. And since the general current in Western Europe is flowing in precisely the opposite direction and, with the next convulsion, must acquire a strength of a quite different order, it may be expected that in Russia, too, which has certainly produced a great many critical minds over the past 30 years, this current will still be strong enough to make a timely appeal to the people's innate, millennial urge to associate before that urge is completely extinguished. For this reason, productive associations and other means of promoting the associate system among the people in Russia should also be looked at from an aspect other than the Western one. Admittedly they still remain no more than minor palliatives. I remain,

Yours most respectfully,

F. Engels

First published in Russian and in the language of the original (German) in the book *Neizdanniye pisma F. Engelsa* (F. Engels' Unpublished Letters), Leningrad, 1924

Printed according to the original

15

MARX TO JOHN SWINTON

IN LONDON

[Postcard]

Ramsgate, 15 August 1880
10 Cumberland Road

Dear Sir,

I got only today your letter.[42] I am staying here with my family,

---

[a] obshchina

and, if your time allows, shall be very glad to see you in Ramsgate.[43]

Yours truly

Karl Marx

[On the side reserved for the address]

John Swinton, Esq.
12 Norfolk Street, Strand, London

First published in the language of the origi-   Reproduced from the original
nal (English) and in Japanese in: Suzuki
Koichiro, *Sihonron hekireki*, Tokyo, 1971

16

ENGELS TO JOHANN PHILIPP BECKER [44]

IN GENEVA

Ramsgate, 17 August 1880

Dear Old Man,

Your postcard was not forwarded to me here [30] until today and I immediately took out a money order for you for two pounds sterling, i. e. 50 frs and a few centimes (on which I wrote my *London* address). It goes without saying, of course, that we wouldn't let you be thrown out of your house while we were restoring our health at the seaside here. There's no need for you to make such a to-do about a few pence; that sort of thing is a matter of course between old comrades-in-arms who have been fighting under the same flag for forty years and who hearken to the same trumpet-calls.

We are all here — Marx, his wife and his daughters, together with husbands and children,[a] and the visit is proving especially beneficial to Marx, who, I hope, will be completely refreshed. His wife has unfortunately been ailing for some time, but is as cheerful as could be expected. I shall be returning to London next week but Marx ought to stay here as long as he possibly can.

---

[a] Laura and Paul Lafargue; Jenny and Charles, Jean, Henri and Edgar Longuet

Apropos, I should perhaps add that there's been a great muddle over the letters. Marx has never had letters of yours for safe-keeping, whereas Borkheim was supposed to have had some of yours and, when Mrs Marx was still in Geneva with you, you got her to ask Marx to get Borkheim to give them to him.[a] But now Borkheim denies ever having got any from you; so what the actual facts of the case are, we over here are unable to fathom.

Well, I hope that, for the time being at least, you have extricated yourself from the worst of your predicament and will get a bit of peace. Kindest regards from us all, and in particular from,

Your

F. Engels

First published in: F. Engels, *Vergessene Briefe* (*Briefe Friedrich Engels' an Johann Philipp Becker*), Berlin, 1920

Printed according to the original

Published in English in full for the first time

17

MARX TO FRIEDRICH ADOLPH SORGE

IN HOBOKEN

[Ramsgate,] 30 August 1880

Dear Sorge,

I am writing from Ramsgate, where I now am with my wife [38]; before that I took her up to Manchester for a consultation with my friend Dr Gumpert. She is suffering from a *dangerous* liver complaint.

In consequence of our wanderings I only got your letter very belatedly. I am entirely of your opinion. If you can't get hold of any money — i. e. $ 200 — in YANKEELAND, the matter will have to be dropped.[45] What the position is here will be evident to you if only from the fact that the *Égalité* went under for want of 3,000 francs.[46] I will, for form's sake, let Liebknecht know about the affair.

The article from *The Sun* received with many thanks.[47] Though he

---

[a] See present edition, Vol. 45, p. 443.

may have the best of intentions, the man nevertheless shows that he doesn't understand the first rudiments of the matter about which he writes.

De minimis non curat lex,[a] and among those minima I number, inter alia, the priestly Douai.[48]

With warmest regards,

Your
Karl Marx

First published in Briefe und Auszüge aus Briefen von Joh. Phil. Becker, Jos. Dietzgen, Friedrich Engels, Karl Marx u. A. an F. A. Sorge und Andere, Stuttgart, 1906

Printed according to the original

Published in English for the first time

18

ENGELS TO LAURA LAFARGUE [49]

IN LONDON

[Bridlington Quay,] 3 September 1880

My dear Laura,

I have only a few minutes to reply to your amiable letter—we have been inspecting a geological amateur's collection this evening and to-morrow we are off to an excursion to Flamboro' Head. The weather here continues grand: regular Rhenish October weather, that is the acme of fine weather as far as I know, not a cloud on the sky, hot sun, cool bracing air at the same time. Why cannot you and Lafargue come for a week, the place is getting empty, plenty of apartments and accommodation of every sort.

I have not heard from Pumps since the letter I had at Ramsgate dated, I believe, 15th August. I wrote her at once, and since then, on arrival in London, last Friday[b] this day week, a postcard, but no re-ply. Now I am almost certain that she has written to Sarah or her mother Mrs Nicholls who stays in our house during my absence.

___

[a] The law does not concern itself with trifles. - [b] 27 August

Would it be too much trouble for you to call there and inform me of the result of your inquiries as I am getting rather anxious and as I am sure there is some misunderstanding abroad by which I am kept without news?

It is now half past nine at night, all windows wide open and yet the fine cool air outside will not come in rapidly enough to enable me to keep my coat on. The beer—oh the beer, it would be worth your while to come here only in order to drink one glass of beer at the Pier refreshment rooms, a nice little café—such splendid beer!

Moore and Beust are off to the 'Parade' (such a thing you know is *de rigueur*[a] at every seaside place) to hear the music and hunt *backfishes*, of which there are excellent specimens here; you know the *backfish*[b] lives on dry land. At all events before leaving they wished to be kindly remembered to both of you.[c]

Yours affectionately
F. Engels

First published in the language of the original (English) in: F. Engels, P. et L. Lafargue, *Correspondance*, t. I, Paris, 1956

Reproduced from the original

19

ENGELS TO PAUL LAFARGUE [50]

IN LONDON

Bridlington Quay, Yorkshire,
3 September 1880
7 Burlington Place

My dear Lafargue,

Why Geneva? [51] The seat of the Swiss Federal Government is Berne and, besides, any other Swiss town would do as well as Geneva. Unless you have specific objections, of which I may be unaware, the

---

[a] the form - [b] See this volume, p. 29. Engels puns on the German *Backfisch* (Anglicised here) which means both 'adolescent girl' and 'fried fish'. - [c] Laura and Paul Lafargue

stuff might just as well be deposited in Zurich where someone could undoubtedly be found to take charge of the business. If it suits you, send the things to me here and we will readdress them to someone who will immediately attend to them.

> May the soil rest lightly
> On the egalitarian *Égalité*.[46]

Yours ever,
F. Engels

First published in F. Engels, P. et L. Lafargue, *Correspondance*, t. I, Paris, 1956

Printed according to the original

Translated from the French

20

ENGELS TO PAUL LAFARGUE[19]

IN LONDON

Bridlington Quay, 9 September 1880

My dear Lafargue,

I had to write to you in haste the day before yesterday[52] because we were due to leave at 9.30 for an excursion to Flamboro' Head where our two naturalists[a] botanised in the sea. In case I didn't express myself clearly enough, let me summarise.

The more serious aspect of Grant's scheme is that he alone has the right to raise or lower the value of your shares, if not make them virtually worthless. To begin with, he is deducting 12% per annum for the first 4 guides. If the gross profit amounts to 15%, that leaves a net profit, the shareholders' dividend, of only 3%; if 20% it leaves 8%, etc. But with the generous salaries Grant proposes to pay the local directors, can one count on such profits? That seems to me exceedingly doubtful.

Let us suppose, however, that the gross profit amounts to 20% or even 25%. What will Grant do then? He will propose to borrow yet

---

[a] Samuel Moore and Adolph Beust

more money so as to launch the remainder of the guides. And he will claim that he can only obtain that money at 15% or 20%. Since he will have a ready-made majority, the vote will go his way. And since you and Jervis won't be able to obtain the money at a cheaper rate, you will get nowhere at all by opposing him. Well then, £ 3,000 at 12%, £ 3,000 at 20%, gives an average of 16% — just imagine how a business can function if it is saddled with interest at that rate before so much as a thought can be paid to dividends.

There is nothing to prevent Grant providing you with funds, as soon as there is a further need of them, at still higher interest, the rate of which will depend upon him alone. Since it is he who pockets the interest, at least the greater part thereof, it is in his interest to approach as closely as possible the rate of gross profit generated by the firm. He shares the interest only with the man who advances this money — the net profit he shares with all the other shareholders.

So in fact the value of your PAID UP shares goes down and down and Grant alone has the right to reduce it to nothing. In other words he pays the two of you for your literary property 1. £ 400; 2. £ 300 each the moment it suits him to get rid of you; 3. in virtually worthless shares carrying no dividend; total £ 500 each, always provided Grant does not find a way of avoiding payment of the £ 300 — which wouldn't be too difficult — by accusing you of breach of contract, in which case there would be a fine old lawsuit costing you much more than £ 300, even if you won.

Grant cannot invoke your letter. Even if it contains what he alleges, that letter ceases to be valid after the month during which you were bound by it.

Jervis' interest is not identical with yours. If he has neglected his affairs and is prepared to sacrifice the lot of them for £ 300 a year, that goes to show that they weren't worth the trouble of discussing. Jervis is staying in London. Once launched by Grant on this enterprise, it is in his interest to be launched by him on other enterprises, to act as his UNDERSTRAPPER until such time as he has enough money and enough financial contacts to do without him. You have an entirely different interest. You are going to Paris, you hope to find an assured existence in this enterprise. Ask yourself if such is to be found under the terms proposed by Grant.

It is likewise in the interests of your SOLICITOR, evidently another underling, to pay court to Grant. And this applies to everyone save yourself. All the more reason not to conclude anything in haste.

Jervis has undertaken to find the necessary capital; well and good, but this must obviously be on terms acceptable to you, and not on such as would deliver you over bound hand and foot to a money-lender of the first water.

You would do well to sound Bradshaw. The latter has a twofold interest in coming to an arrangement with you in respect both of this country and of the Continent. If only as a means of putting pressure on Grant. It would be better still to have a choice between the two. And Bradshaw cannot allow himself to go in for the sharp practices that are the other man's stock-in-trade. Unfortunately you can no longer have full confidence in Jervis, once he claims to have tired of the matter and advises you to accept forthwith.

That is, of course, the gloomier aspect of the affair. Grant may possibly have more generous intentions, but once the contract has been signed you will be at his mercy, of that you may be certain.

With a man like Grant I see no means of safeguarding oneself. You could insert a condition that all net profits must be used to pay off the £3,000 and that no dividends are distributed so long as the company is paying interest of more than 6% — they would either not accept it or find a way of deleting if at the first shareholders' meeting. And that would merely safeguard the first £3,000; as regards subsequent borrowings it would do nothing of the kind; it would be nonsensical to repay with one hand and borrow with the other.

My advice is *try to manage without Grant* and, if you can't, at least try to make him fear that you can do without him, so that he robs you a little less UNMERCIFULLY than he intended. He will rob you anyhow.

The weather here continues magnificent, sunshine all the time, bracing air, north-east breeze, sea-bathing already somewhat bracing, but this evening I fear I shall have to wear an overcoat as at Ramsgate. The visitors are quite different from those at Ramsgate. Here we have the SHOPKEEPER, the small manufacturer, the TRADESMAN from Leeds, Sheffield, Hull, etc., an atmosphere decidedly more provincial yet at the same time more solid than at Ramsgate; no 'ARRYS. What strikes you most is the fact that all the young girls are *backfish* [a] between 14 and 17 years — what you call the ugly age, although there are some very pretty ones here. Of young girls fashioned to perfection there are none or virtually none. No sooner have they ceased to be backfish than they're put into long skirts and, so it would seem,

---

[a] Properly *Backfische* — adolescent girls

get married. All the women of 18 and over that one sees are accompanied by their husbands and even by children. Nor did poor Beust, who casts tender glances at the backfish, succeed in initiating any amorous exchanges, however brief. Papa and mama, like the Prussians of Frederick II, are 'constantly on sentry go'. My best wishes to Laura. The two herbalists [a] send their compliments. The thing has been sent to Beust's father [b] in Zurich. The newspapers will be returned to you. I don't know Marx's whereabouts, for I have not had word from him.

Yours ever,
F. Engels

First published in F. Engels, P. et L. Lafargue, *Correspondance*, t. I, Paris, 1956

Printed according to the original

Translated from the French

21

MARX TO NIKOLAI DANIELSON [53]

IN ST PETERSBURG [54]

Ramsgate, 12 September 1880

My dear Sir,

I need not tell you that I should feel only too happy to do anything you consider useful,[55] but a short statement of the circumstances in which I find myself at this moment will convince you that I am at present unfit for theoretical labour. Having been sent here by the medical men in order to 'do nothing' and to restore my nervous system by the *'far niente'*,[c] an illness of my wife, under which she suffered long time since, has suddenly been aggravated to a degree which menaces to tend to a *fatal* termination. Whatever little time I may snatch for work, is necessarily limited to things which I *must* get rid of.

However, the most important part for the *public in general* is that

---

[a] Moore and Beust - [b] Friedrich Beust - [c] Abbreviated from *dolce far niente* (sweet doing nothing), which originates from a similar Latin expression used by Pliny the Younger in Epistle VIII.

which you have already performed — the drawing up of the statistical tables and the interpretation of the *facts* which they imply. It would be a pity if you delayed the publication which I expect myself with the greatest impatience.[56]

Whatever you may have found useful in my letters for that purpose, you may freely dispose of. Only I fear it is not much, since I sent you only a few fragmentary scraps.

The present crisis was the greatest England has passed through with regard to duration, extent and intensiveness,[57] but despite the failures of some Scotch and English provincial banks — the crowning of the past English great periodical crises, I mean the financial crash in London, shone by its absence. This most extraordinary incident — the absence of the *monetary panic* properly so called, was due to a concatenation of circumstances the analysis of which would lead me too far at present. One of the most decisive circumstances was, however, this: The heavy bullion drain of 1879 was to a great extent met by the cooperation of the Banque de France and the Imperial Bank of Germany. On the other hand, the sudden revival in the United States — since the spring of 1879 — reacted on England like a *deus ex machina*.[a]

As to the agricultural crisis, it will gather strength, develop itself, and, by the bye, come to a head, carrying with it quite a revolution in the relations of landed property,— quite independent of the cycles of the commercial-industrial crises. Even such optimists as Mr Caird have commenced 'to smell a rat'. Most characteristic of English blockheadedness is this: since two years there have been published letters of farmers — in *The Times* as well as in agricultural papers — giving the items of their expenses in cultivating their farms, comparing them with their returns at present prices, and winding up with a positive *deficit*. Would you believe that not one of the specialists — expatiating upon these accounts — has thought of considering *how these accounts* would stand if *the item of rent* was struck out in many cases or reduced 'most feelingly' in many other cases? But this is a delicate point which must not be touched. The farmers themselves, though become unbelievers in the *nostrums* proposed by their landlords or the *'plumitifs'* [b] of the latter, dare not yet assume attitudes of bold vi-

---

[a] *deus ex machina* — a god from the machine (by which in ancient theatre gods were shown in the air); a power or an event that comes in the nick of time to solve a difficulty -
[b] hired scribblers

rility, considering that they, on their part, are denounced by the rustic 'labouring class'. A nice pickle it is altogether.

I hope there will be no general war in Europe. Though, ultimately, it could not check, but would rather intensify, the social, I mean thereby the *economical*, development, it would certainly produce a useless exhaustion of forces for some longer or shorter interval.

Please to send your letters as before to my London address, from where I shall always receive them even in case of momentary absence.

Yours most sincerely
A. Williams[a]

<table>
<tr><td>First published, in Russian, in the magazine Minuvshiye gody, No. 1, St Petersburg, 1908</td><td>Reproduced from the original

Published in English for the first time</td></tr>
</table>

22

ENGELS TO PAUL LAFARGUE [58]

IN LONDON

Bridlington Quay, 12th September 1880

My dear Lafargue,

How can I advise you on business if you give me all the information afterwards? If you had sent me the draft articles [59] before, I should have known better what to say. Do not say that you had not got it; it was your business to have had it as soon as printed. *Mais on dirait que vous brûlez de vous faire voler.*[b]

You say the articles *forbid* to borrow at more than 10%. Whoever told you that, reckoned upon your credulity. Article 74 says distinctly that the directors can raise money *upon such terms and conditions in all respects as they think fit.* Now I do not know and cannot be expected to know whether the acts of parliament forbid limited companies to raise money at more than 10%. I doubt it. But if it be the fact, you have before your eyes the proof that that is no use whatever. Have

---

[a] Marx's pseudonym - [b] But anyone would think you were begging to be robbed.

you not written to me that Grant wanted to raise £ 3,000 — at 10% and a bonus of 20% at the end of five years? 20% divided by 5 is 4, and 10 + 4 are 14; thus, you pay really 14% for your money. Why do you not speak of that when people want to make you believe that Grant cannot get more than 10% out of your company in interest?

Then you say, Jervis and Mason had pris des garanties contre Grant, en ce que rien de nouveau pouvait être décidé sans qu'on ait au moins le vote des 4/5 des actionnaires, et que Grant n'avait que 55% et que par conséquent il ne pouvait rien faire sans votre consentement.

Décidément on se moque de vous.[a] In the whole agreement *not a word* about 4/5 of the shareholders. All resolutions by *simple majorities*. It may be in the acts of parliament that 4/5 are required *to alter the original deed of association*. But that is not the question. I have shown you the way how Grant by his system of loans at 10% and any bonus he likes, can suck all the profits out of the company. And Article 74 gives him the right to do so, without even consulting anybody but his directors who, whatever they may be, are sure to be his puppets.

Secondly. All the capital being subscribed you have
1) 5,000 votes for original capital — £ 5,000.-
2) 3,000 votes for preference shares 3,000 at £ 5 each (Art. 49).
8,000 votes in all. Out of these you, Jervis and Mason have together 2,250 votes, that is to say not 45% against 55%, but 28% against 72%. Still more than 1/5, but not very far off. Let a few shares be sold by one of you, and the power to stop even alterations of deed of association is lost by you. You will be told that it is not intended to issue all the preference shares. But how long that remains so, will depend upon Grant.

There is another article which may affect you and alter the case. Art. 21 says that for calls not yet made, but paid up by the shareholder voluntarily, interest up to 10% shall be paid. I should presume that this applies to your *paid up* shares, only, if it was so, Jervis and Mason would have pointed it out to you; at least I should think so. If that be the case and you can secure 10% on the greater part of your shares that would be so much in your favour. *See whether it is so or not.*

_____

[a] safeguarded themselves against Grant in that no new decision could be taken without the consent of at least 4/5 of the shareholders and that Grant had only 55% and hence could do nothing without your consent.— They're having you on, no doubt about that.

Upon the whole I think, after your last letter, a little more favourably of the business. If the money raised at such ruinous interest can be limited to the first £ 3,000 .- and these repaid after the 5 years or before, the thing may work well. But it strikes me that it will require very large profits indeed to pay all these lavish expenses. £ 50.- to each director, £ 100.- to the Chairman, £? to the Manager, £ 300.- to the directors in London and Paris and so forth. All that with a working capital of £ 3,000.-, less than three times the salaries named above! And 14% interest besides.

I cannot write to you about Jervis as you say you read my letters to him and Mason. Else I should have something to say to that. Anyhow, the honesty of a financier is different from that of some people, be it ever so honest in its own way.

I must conclude; dinner is going to be laid. Si vous ne voyez pas d'autre voie, naturellement vous vous êtes trop avancé pour reculer tout seul. Mais réfléchissez bien, et rassurez-vous sur les points indiqués ci-dessus.

Je n'ai que l'argent absolument nécessaire pour mon voyage et même peut-être pas cela. Mon CHEQUE-BOOK est à Londres où je serai de retour samedi soir [30]; jusque là, je ne pourrai rien faire.

Si vous pouvez retarder l'affaire G. jusqu'à mon arrivée, on pourrait peut-être avoir plus de renseignements.

Bien des choses à Laura de la part de nous tous.

Bien à vous
F. E.

Je rapporterai les articles d'association à moins que vous n'en avez un besoin immédiat.[a]

First published, in the languages of the original (English and French), in F. Engels, P. et L. Lafargue, *Correspondance*, t. I, Paris, 1956

Reproduced from the original

---

[a] Unless you can see some other way out you have, of course, gone too far to withdraw all on your own. But think it over carefully and make sure about the points outlined above.

I only have such money as is absolutely essential for my journey, and maybe not even that. My cheque-book is in London, whither I shall return on Saturday evening [30]; until then I shall be unable to do anything.

23

ENGELS TO MARX

IN LONDON

Bridlington Quay, 13 September 1880
7 Burlington Place

Dear Moor,

Have received the enclosed from Liebknecht. I am writing to tell him that, provided he hears nothing to the contrary within the next few days, we shall be back in London again from next Sunday, 19 September,[30] and shall be expecting them (him and Bebel).[60] So if you should be prevented in any way, kindly let me know.

I haven't had an answer to a postcard sent from here to your address in Ramsgate[38] on 29 August; no doubt it didn't arrive. Yesterday I heard from Lafargue, who said you would be returning to London today.

We shall be returning at the end of this week; wet weather since the day before yesterday, before which the weather was splendid.

I hope your wife is better.

Warmest regards to all, likewise from Moore and Beust.

Your
F. E.

First published in MEGA, Abt. III, Bd. 4, Berlin, 1931

Printed according to the original

Published in English for the first time

If you can postpone the Grant business until my arrival, it might be possible to obtain more information.

Best wishes to Laura from us all.

Yours ever,
F. E.

I shall bring the articles of association with me unless you need them at once.

24

MARX TO FERDINAND FLECKLES

IN KARLSBAD

[London,] 29 September 1880

My Dear Friend,

My best thanks for your letter.[61] Ladies have their own ideas about things. Which is why my wife[a] didn't want to reply on this side of the form, nor indeed, in accordance with any formula, but after her own fashion. Not having read her letter, I don't know whether her answer is appropriate; however, women will have their way.[b] Eleanor sends her kind regards.

Tout à vous,[c]

Karl Marx

First published in *Beiträge zur Geschichte der deutschen Arbeiterbewegung*, Nr. 1, Berlin, 1966

Printed according to the original

Published in English for the first time

25

ENGELS TO EUGEN OSWALD
AND AN UNKNOWN CORRESPONDENT [62]

IN LONDON

[London,] 5 October 1880
122 Regent's Park Road

Dear Oswald,

Many thanks for the recommendations for Beust,[d] which have all been attended to. As regards Kaulitz, I got an identical letter —

---

[a] Jenny Marx - [b] Marx paraphrases the German proverb 'Des Menschen Wille ist sein Himmelreich' corresponding to the English 'The will of man is the arbiter of his fortune'. - [c] All yours - [d] Adolf von Beust

my reply on the reverse. As regards Br.,ᵃ we are unlikely to quarrel.

Ever yours

F. Engels

[On the reverse of the letter]

* (Copy) Confid.

Sir,

Mr Kaulitz was introduced to me on his arrival in England last spring, by a letter from an old friend in Germany. The letter stated that Mr Kaulitz was of a very good family, his father being one of the first notaries in Brunswick (a position of much importance and great trust in Germany), and recommended him warmly to me. From what I have seen of him since, he appears to be a man of very great business abilities and to have succeeded very well, so far, in the scholastic line; but on this point no doubt the professional gentleman to whom Mr K. may have referred you, will be able to give you more satisfactory information.

I am etc.

F. E.*

First published in: Marx and Engels, *Works*, Second Russian Edition, Vol. 34, Moscow, 1964

The letter to Oswald is printed according to a typewritten copy and that to the unknown correspondent reproduced from a photocopy of the original

Published in English for the first time

ᵃ Presumably Bennet Burleigh (cf. this volume, p. 38).

38 26. Engels to Becker. 12 October 1880

26

ENGELS TO JOHANN PHILIPP BECKER

IN GENEVA

London, 12 October 1880

Dear Old Man,

I've heard from Liebknecht that you're still short of cash but that they can't help you just now. By a lucky chance I was on the point of putting a five pound note on one side for you and have lost no time in changing it into a money order for 126 frs. I trust it reaches you safely and soon and will tide you over your initial difficulties until such time as the Leipzigers can do something for you. And so they damned well ought. You're certainly as much a victim of the Exceptional Law[16] as the agitators in Germany who have been deprived of their livelihood.

Liebknecht was here[60] and promised that the Zurich paper[a] would adopt a different attitude in keeping with the party's former attitude. If that is done, it's all we ask.

Adieu and keep your pecker up.

Your old friend

F. Engels

First published in: F. Engels, *Vergessene Briefe (Briefe Friedrich Engels' an Johann Philipp Becker)*, Berlin, 1920

Printed according to the original

Published in English for the first time

27

ENGELS TO HARRY KAULITZ

IN LONDON

[Draft]

[London,] 28 October 1880

Mr H. Kaulitz

I return herewith Mr Burleigh's letter.

As to the matter of Mr Lafargue, you concede the chief point,

[a] *Der Sozialdemokrat*

namely that you have given his name as a reference without his permission. The rest is beside the point.

With regard to Beust,[a] I do not propose to go into the question of *when* you offered to give the said lessons elsewhere. This much is certain: that after our return from Bridlington Quay [30] you again offered to give lessons to Beust, that you promised, in the presence of myself and Schorlemmer, to set about the thing in the manner stipulated, that you did the opposite of what you had promised, and that Beust, far from attacking his 'very dear friend Kaulitz' behind his back, told him in Trafalgar Square exactly what he thought of him, adding quite rightly that all three of us had been convinced from the outset that you wouldn't do a single thing you had promised. I should have written you off there and then had it not been for the fact that I avoid making *private* matters a cause for breaking with people with whom I have been in any way connected *politically*.

Concerning the tittle-tattle in the Central News, I will not labour the point as to whether it was you or Most who disseminated it, since I am not permitted to divulge my sources, and since, on the other hand, I lay no store at all by the agent's letter.

If one is compelled to make a decision such as mine in regard to yourself, one bases it not on this or that particular indiscretion, but rather on the other's whole mode of behaviour, observed over a considerable period. And in any case your almost daily intercourse with Most and Co., which you freely admit, is quite enough to supply, in place of the fact you contest, another that is no less convincing.

Yours very truly

First published in: Marx and Engels, *Works*, First Russian Edition, Vol. XXVII, Moscow, 1935

Printed according to the original

Published in English for the first time

---

[a] Adolf von Beust

28

MARX TO JOHN SWINTON

IN NEW YORK

London, 4 November 1880
41 Maitland Park Road, N. W.

My dear Sir,

I have sent you today a copy of the French edition of the *Capital*. [63] I have at the same time to thank you for your friendly article in *The Sun*. [43]

Apart Mr Gladstone's 'sensational' failures abroad [64] — political interest centres here at present on the Irish 'Land Question'. And why? Mainly because it is the harbinger of the English *'Land Question'*.

Not only that the great landlords of England are also the largest landholders of Ireland, but having once broken down in what is ironically called the 'Sister'-island, the English landed system will no longer be tenable at home. There are arrayed against it the British farmers, wincing under high rents, and — thanks to the American competition — low prices; the British agricultural labourers, at last impatient of their traditional position of ill-used beasts of burden, and — that British party which styles itself *'Radical'*. The latter consists of two sets of men; first the *ideologues* of the party, eager to overthrow the political power of the aristocracy by mining its material basis, the semi-feudal landed property. But behind these principle-spouters, and hunting them on, lurks another set of men — sharp, close-fisted, calculating *capitalists*, fully aware that the abolition of the old land laws, in the way proposed by the ideologues, cannot but convert land into a commercial article that must ultimately concentrate in the hands of capital.

On the other side, considered as a national entity, John Bull has ugly misgivings lest the aristocratic English landed garrison in Ireland once gone — England's political sway over Ireland will go too!

Liebknecht has to enter prison for 6 months.— The *Anti-Socialists' Law* [16] having failed to overthrow or even to weaken the German Social-Democratic organisation, Bismarck clings the more desperately to his panacea, and fancies that it *must* work, if only applied on a larger scale. Hence he has extended the *state of siege* [65] to Hamburg, Altona, and 3 other Northern towns. Under these circumstances the German friends have written me a letter of which one passage runs thus:

'The Socialist Law, though it could not break and never will break our organisation, does impose pecuniary sacrifices almost impossible to bear. To support the families ruined by the police, to keep alive the few papers left to us, to keep up the necessary communications by secret messengers, to fight the battle on the whole line—all this requires money. We are nearly exhausted and forced to appeal to our friends and sympathisers in other countries.'

So far this extract.

Now, we, here at London, Paris, etc., will do our best. At the same time, I believe that a man of your influence might organise a subscription in the United States. Even if the monetary result were not important, denunciations of Bismarck's new *coup d'état* in public meetings held by you, reported in the American press, reproduced on the other side of the Atlantic—would sorely hit the Pomeranian *hobereau* [a] and be welcomed by all the socialists of Europe. More information you might get from Mr Sorge (Hoboken). Any money forthcoming to be sent over to Mr *Otto Freytag, Landtagsabgeordneter,* [b] *Amtmannshof, Leipzig.* His address ought of course not to be made public; otherwise the German police would simply *confiscate.*

À propos. My youngest daughter [c]—who was not with us at Ramsgate—just tells me that she has cut my portrait from the copy of the *Capital* I sent you, on the pretext that it was a mere caricature. Well, I shall make up for it by a photogram to be taken on the first fine day.

Mrs Marx and the whole family send you their best wishes.

Yours most sincerely,

Karl Marx

First published in *Science and Society*, Vol. II, No. 2, New York, 1938

Reproduced from the original

---

[a] Junker - [b] deputy to the Provincial Diet - [c] Eleanor Marx

29

MARX TO FRIEDRICH ADOLPH SORGE [63]

IN HOBOKEN

[London,] 5 November 1880
41 Maitland Park Road, N.W.

Dear Sorge,

You must excuse my long silence on the grounds 1. of excessive pressure of work, 2. of my wife's exceedingly grave illness which has now lasted for something over a year.

You have yourself seen what JOHN Most has blossomed out into and, on the other hand, how wretchedly the so-called party organ, the Zurich *Sozialdemokrat* (not to mention the *Jahrbuch*[a] of that place) — *duce*[b] Dr Höchberg, has been run. As a result Engels and I have been constantly engaged in acrimonious exchanges with the Leipzigers in the course of which many a hard word has been said.[c] But we have eschewed any kind of *public* intervention. It does not befit those who are peacefully — *comparativement parlant*[d] — ensconced abroad to contribute to the gratification of government and bourgeosie by doing anything to aggravate the position of those who are operating in the homeland under the most difficult circumstances and at considerable personal sacrifice. Liebknecht was here a few weeks ago [60] and promised 'improvement' in every respect. The party organisation has been revived, something that could only be done by secret means, i.e. in so far as 'secret' denotes secret from the police.

It was, believe it or not, in a *Russian* socialist paper[e] that I first discovered what a blackguard Most is. He has never dared print in *German* what is to be read here in the *Russian* VERNACULAR. This isn't just an attack on individual persons but a dragging-through-the-mire of the *entire German workers' movement*. At the same time *his utter incomprehension* of the doctrine in which he used to traffic is grotesquely in evidence. It's idle chatter, so silly, so illogical, so abysmal that it finally dissolves into *the inane*, namely into Johannes Most's unbounded personal vani-

---

[a] *Jahrbuch für Sozialwissenschaft und Sozialpolitik* - [b] chief - [c] See present edition, Vol. 45, pp. 366-68, 379-80, 394-408, 416-21, 423-26, 429-31. - [d] comparatively speaking - [e] *Черный передѣлъ* (Cherny Peredel)

ty. [a] Having failed, for all his caterwauling, to achieve anything in
Germany — save, perhaps, among certain hoodlums in Berlin — he
has allied himself with the Parisian successors of the Bakuninists, the
group which publishes the *Révolution Sociale* (its circulation = 210
EXACTLY, but possesses allies in the shape of *Pyat's Commune*. *Pyat*, that
cowardly, melodramatic farceur — in whose *Commune* I figure as *Bismarck*'s right-hand man — has a grudge against me for having always
treated him with the utmost contempt and frustrated all his attempts
to use the *International* for his sensation-mongering). At all events
there's one good thing Most has done, namely to bring together in
one group all the brawlers — Andreas Scheu, Hasselmann, etc., etc.

In view of *Bismarck*'s new emergency decrees [65] and the persecution
of our party members, it is absolutely essential that there should be
a *whip-round* for the party. Yesterday I wrote and said as much to *John
Swinton* [b] (for a well-disposed bourgeois is best suited to this job), at
the same time telling him that he should refer to you for further information about conditions in Germany.

Apart from the inanities mentioned on the previous page — and
during our long years of exile how many of the same have we not seen
explode like squibs and then fizzle out again! — things in general are
going splendidly (I mean the course of events in Europe as a whole),
as they are within the confines of the genuinely revolutionary party
on the Continent.

You will probably have noticed that the *Égalité*, in particular,
(thanks *en première instance* [c] to *Guesde's* having come over to us and to the
efforts of my son-in-law, Lafargue) has become the first 'French' *workers' paper* in the true sense of the term. Even *Malon* — albeit with the
inconsistencies inseparable from his eclectic nature — has felt bound,
in his *Revue socialiste*, (we used to be enemies, he being one of the
original co-founders of the *Alliance* [67]) to espouse *le socialisme moderne
scientifique*, [d] i. e. the *German* variety. I drew up a '*questionneur*'[sic] [e] for
him which was first published in the *Revue socialiste* and then reprinted
in quantity for distribution throughout France. Shortly afterwards
Guesde came to London to collaborate with us (MYSELF, Engels and
Lafargue) in drafting an electoral programme [68] for the use of the
workers in the forthcoming general elections. With the exception of

---

[a] [J. Most] [I. Мостъ,] *Нѣмецкая соціаль-демократія* in *Черный передѣлъ*, No. 2,
September 1880, pp. 11-13. - [b] See previous letter. - [c] in the first place - [d] B.Malon,
'Les Débuts du Parti ouvrier', *La Revue socialiste*, No. 11, 5 August 1880. - [e] K. Marx,
'Workers' Questionnaire'

some foolishnesses such as *minimum wages* fixed by law, etc., which despite our protests Guesde thought fit to dole out to the French workers (I told him that if the French proletariat was so puerile as to require these sops SO IS IT NOT WORTH WHILE DRAWING UP ANY PROGRAMME WHATEVER), the economic section of this very short document consists (apart from some introductory words which define the communist aim in a few lines) solely of demands that have, in fact, arisen spontaneously out of the workers' movement itself. To bring the French workers down to earth out of their verbal cloud-cuckoo land was a tremendous step forward, and therefore aroused much resentment among all those French intellectual frauds who make a living as 'cloud-assemblers'. The programme was first adopted, after most vigorous opposition on the part of the anarchists, in the *Région centrale*—i. e. Paris and all its purlieus, and later in many other working-class areas. The simultaneous formation of opposing workers' groups—which (*sauf les anarchistes*,[a] not made up of genuine workers, but of déclassé people with a few misguided workers for their rank-and-file) nevertheless adopted most of the 'practical' demands in the programme—as also the ventilation of the most diverse points of view in relation to other matters, is to my mind proof that this is *the first real workers' movement* in France. Hitherto there have been nothing but sects there which, of course, received their *mot d'ordre*[b] from their founders, while the bulk of the proletariat followed the radical or pseudo-radical bourgeois and fought for them when the day came, only to be slaughtered, deported, etc., on the morrow by the very laddies they had placed at the helm.

The *Émancipation*, which first came out a few days ago at Lyons, will be the organ of the *'parti ouvrier'*[c]—a party that has arisen on the basis of German socialism.

Meanwhile we have also had—and still have—our pioneers in the very camp of the enemy—i. e. in the radical camp. *Theisz* has taken on the workers' question in the *Intransigeant*, Rochefort's organ; after the defeat of the 'Commune' he, like all 'thinking' French socialists, came to London as a Proudhonist and, while there, changed completely as a result of personal intercourse with myself and of a conscientious study of *Capital*. My son-in-law,[d] for his part, gave up his teaching post at King's College,[69] went back to Paris (his

---

[a] save for the anarchists - [b] word of command - [c] workers' party - [d] Charles Longuet

family, I'm glad to say, is remaining here for the time being), where he became one of the most influential editors of *Justice*, owned by Clemenceau, the leader of the extreme left. He has laboured to such good purpose that Clemenceau who, only last April, publicly entered the arena as the opponent of socialism and the advocate of the American-democratic-republican viewpoint, recently made an anti-Gambetta speech[a] at Marseilles, in which, to judge by its general tenor no less than its references to the most essential points in the *minimum programme*, he came over to our side. Whether he sticks to what he promised doesn't really matter. At all events, he has introduced an element of ours into the radical party whose organs, comically enough, now admire as SOMETHING WONDERFUL, on Clemenceau's lips, what had been ignored or sneered at by them when merely a catchword emanating from the '*parti ouvrier*'.

I need hardly tell you—for you know what *French chauvinism* is like—that the secret strings whereby the LEADERS—from Guesde-Malon to Clemenceau—have been set in motion, must remain *e n t r e n o u s. Il n'en faut pas parler. Quand on veut agir pour Messieurs les Français, il faut l e f a i r e a n o n y m e m e n t, pour ne pas choquer le sentiment 'national'.*[b] *As it is, the Anarchists denounce our co-operators already as Prussian agents, under the dictatorship of the 'notorious' Prussian agent *—Karl Marx.

In Russia—where *Capital* is more widely read and acclaimed than anywhere else—our success is even greater. On the one hand, we have the *critics* (mostly young university professors, some of them personal friends of mine,[c] SOME also *littérateurs*), on the other, the *terrorist Central Committee*,[70] whose recent *programme*, clandestinely printed and published in St Petersburg,[71] aroused considerable ire among the anarchist Russians in *Switzerland*, who bring out *The Black Redistribution*[d] (to translate literally from the Russian) in Geneva. Unlike the terrorists, who risk life and limb, these men—most of whom (but not all) left Russia *of their own accord*—constitute the so-called Propaganda Party. (In order to disseminate *propaganda in Russia*—they remove *to Geneva*! What a *quid pro quo*!) These gentry are all of them opposed to politico-revolutionary action. Russia is to leap

---

[a] 'Discours de M.Clémenceau', *La Justice*, No. 291, 1 November 1880. -[b] *between ourselves.* You mustn't talk about it. If one wants to act on behalf of *Messieurs les Français*, this must be *done anonymously* so as not to offend 'national' sentiment. -[c] N. I. Sieber, M. M. Kovalevsky -[d] Черный передѣлъ

head-over-heels into the anarchist-communist-atheist millennium! Meanwhile they pave the way for that leap by tedious doctrinarianism of which the self-styled *principes courent la rue depuis le feu Bakounine*. [a] Well, that's enough for now. Let us [hear] from you soon. Warmest regards from my wife.

Totus tuus, [b]

Karl Marx

I should be most grateful if you could unearth for me some sound stuff (meaty) on economic conditions in *California*, OF COURSE AT MY EXPENSE. California is of great moment to me because in no other place has revolution by capitalist centralisation been effected with such effrontery at such great speed.

First published in *Briefe und Auszüge aus Briefen von Joh. Phil. Becker, Jos. Dietzgen, Friedrich Engels, Karl Marx u. A. an F. A. Sorge und Andere*, Stuttgart, 1906

Printed according to the original

30

MARX TO FRIEDRICH ADOLPH SORGE

IN HOBOKEN

[London,] 5 November 1880
IN HASTE

Dear Sorge,

I had just sent off a longish letter to you [c] when, after the event — *post festum* but not before the post office closed — another point occurred to me in connection with that poor devil Borkheim. Last summer, when I went from Ramsgate [38] to see him in Hastings, where I found him ill in bed, he requested me to ask you to dun a certain *Francis Murhard* (215 Washington Street, Hoboken). This man owes our

---

[a] principles have been current since the late Bakunin's time. - [b] Ever yours - [c] See previous letter.

friend Borkheim some money — £10 if I remember aright — which he lent Murhard for the journey to America and in respect of which he possesses a promissory note.

Salut.

Your
K. M.

First published in *Briefe und Auszüge aus Briefen von Joh. Phil. Becker, Jos. Dietzgen, Friedrich Engels, Karl Marx u. A. an F. A. Sorge und Andere*, Stuttgart, 1906

Printed according to the original

Published in English for the first time

31

MARX TO FERDINAND FLECKLES

IN CARLSBAD

[London,] 12 November 1880
IN HASTE

Dear Friend,

Herewith a card of introduction to my son-in-law Longuet who is to introduce you to Rochefort.

No doubt you will by now have received the letter my wife eventually sent off; like all female invalids, she always despairs of the doctors who happen to be attending her.

With kindest regards,

Yours very sincerely,
Karl Marx

[Address on the envelope in Marx's hand]

Dr. F. Fleckles, Carlsbad (Austria)

First published in full in: Marx and Engels, *Works*, Second Russian Edition, Vol. 50, Moscow, 1981

Printed according to the original

Published in English for the first time

32

MARX TO ACHILLE LORIA [72]

IN MANTUA

London, 13 November 1880
41 Maitland Park Road, N. W.

Dear Mr Loria,

Domestic upsets resulting from my wife's very dangerous illness have delayed my reply to your letter of 14 September. [73] I regret that my lack of personal means does not allow me to provide for your stay in London, the more so since I have the highest opinion of your talent, your learning and your scientific future. [74]

Being of a somewhat solitary disposition and eschewing as I do all contact with the English press, I have very little influence and few connections to place at your disposal. I know from experience that Italian competition, as regards both contributions to the press and private lessons, is OVERDONE in London, as in every other sphere of the struggle for existence.

Nevertheless, on the re-opening of Parliament — until which time everyone, i. e. THE UPPER TEN THOUSANDS, deserts the metropolis — I shall consult SOME WELL-MEANING AND INFLUENTIAL MEN. In the meantime, perhaps you would be so kind as to let me know whether you speak French and a modicum of English.

Yours very faithfully,

Karl Marx

First published abridged in A. Loria, *Ricordi di uno studente settuagenario*, Bologna, 1927 and in full in: Marx and Engels, *Works*, Second Russian Edition, Vol. 34, Moscow, 1964

Printed according to the original

Translated from the French

33

MARX TO HENRY MAYERS HYNDMAN [75]

IN LONDON

[London,] 8 December 1880

My dear Sir,

Mrs Marx, like most sickly people whose illness has assumed a chronic character, becomes sometimes suddenly unable to leave her bedroom and then fit again for social intercourse. Believing she could within a few days pay a visit to Mrs Hyndman, she did not write to her at once, but as we are this week inundated with visitors from the Continent, she begs me to write you that she will give herself the pleasure to call upon Mrs Hyndman next week.

I welcome the prospect of the journal you speak of. If you say that you do not share the views of my party for England I can only reply that that party considers an English revolution not *necessary*, but — according to historic precedents — *possible*. If the unavoidable evolution turn into a revolution, it would not only be the fault of the ruling classes, but also of the working class. Every pacific concession of the former has been wrung from them by 'pressure from without'. Their action kept pace with that pressure and if the latter has more and more weakened, it is only because the English working class know not how to wield their power and use their liberties, both of which they possess legally.

In Germany the working class were fully aware from the beginning of their movement that you cannot get rid of a military despotism but by a Revolution. At the same time they understood that such a Revolution, even if at first successful, would finally turn against them without previous organisation, acquirement of knowledge, propaganda, and [word illegible]. Hence they moved within strictly *legal* bounds. The illegality was all on the side of government, which declared them *en dehors la loi.* [a] Their crimes were not *deeds*, but *opinions* unpleasant to their rulers. Fortunately, the same government — the working class having been pushed to the background with the help of the bourgeoisie — becomes now more and more unbearable to the

---

[a] beyond the law

latter, whom it hits on their most tender point — the pocket. This state of things cannot last long.

Please to present my compliments to Mrs Hyndman.

Yours very truly,
Karl Marx

First published in: H. M. Hyndman, *The Record of an Adventurous Life*, London, 1911

Reproduced from the book

34

ENGELS TO JOHANN PHILIPP BECKER

IN GENEVA

London, 24 December 1880

Dear Old Man,

This is to advise you in all haste that I have taken out a money order for you for five pounds sterling = 126 frs, which I trust you will receive.

When Liebknecht was here [60] I hauled him over the coals for having failed so much as to consider you when distributing the relief fund. I told him you were just as much, if not more, a victim of the Anti-Socialist Law [16] as many of the Berliners, amongst whom there are some notorious blackguards. Now he has written to say: *Becker will be cared for.* So make sure this is done and, if not and supposing it embarrasses you to dun them, drop me a line and I'll see to it for you.

Better luck in the New Year.

Your old friend,
F. Engels

First published in: F. Engels, *Vergessene Briefe (Briefe Friedrich Engels' an Johann Philipp Becker)*, Berlin, 1920

Printed according to the original

Published in English for the first time

35

MARX TO CARL HIRSCH

IN LONDON

[London,] 29 December 1880

Dear Hirsch,

You would oblige me by coming here next Friday evening (*7 o'clock*) to dine with us and to celebrate the New Year. *Salut.*

K. M.

First published in: Marx and Engels, *Works*, Second Russian Edition, Vol. 39, Moscow, 1966

Printed according to the original

Published in English for the first time

1881

36

MARX TO CHARLES LONGUET

IN PARIS

[London,] 4 January 1881

Dear Longuet,

With the immense agglomerate of old newspapers it would take me too much time to find out *The Eastern Post* which contains the controversy of the General Council (inclus. its Communard members) with the illustrious Bradlaugh. [a][76] However, I suppose Lessner will have the *Post* ready at hand. This, however, is for you the least important thing. That Bradlaugh denounced the Communards, that he reproduced the worst calumnies, as you told him then in the *Post*, [b] of such papers as the *Liberté*, the *Soir*, that he fell foul of the manifesto of the General Council on 'The Civil War in France', [c] etc., this will hardly damage him in the eyes of the Paris bourgeoisie. Still the thing may be shortly hinted at as characteristic of the man. In an answer of the General Secretary of the General Council (it was *Hales*, but that man must not be honoured by naming him) to Bradlaugh (in *The Eastern Post, September 1871*), he said amongst other things:

'...The wanton destruction of private dwellings (by Thiers' bombardment) was the work of Mr Bradlaugh's friends... Rochefort has been sentenced under the Republic to transportation for life for a press offence. Fancy Mr Bradlaugh being transported for life for his utterances!' [d]

The important thing is that Bradlaugh was denounced by the General Council (extracts of whose sittings were reported by *The*

---

[a] 'Mr Bradlaugh and the International', *The Eastern Post*, No. 173, 20 January 1872. - [b] 'Mr Bradlaugh and the Communists', *The Eastern Post*, No. 168, 16 December 1871. - [c] K. Marx, *The Civil War in France. Address of the General Council of the International Working Men's Association.* - [d] J. Hales, 'To the Editor of *The Eastern Post*', *The Eastern Post*, No. 158, 7 October 1871.

Eastern Post) as a Courtesan of Plon-Plon (he was at London then) and because of his suspect relations in Paris.[a] In the sitting of the General Council of *December 19, 1871* I (informed by the Frenchman, who wrote under the name Azamouth or another Turkish name, and who was informed by a lady—probably the Brimont, present at social gathering later on referred to) denounced a recent trip of Bradlaugh's to Paris, where he associated with Détroyat and Émile de Girardin. In his honour the latter gave a dinner where equivocuous, i. e. *Bonapartist,* ladies assisted and where Bradlaugh rendered himself ridiculous by the boastful display of his pretended London influence.

If Bradlaugh says that the Brimont was a great patriot, at the time he made her acquaintance, he may be fully believed. Before the battle of Sedan all Bonapartists were so far patriots that they wished victory to their Emperor.[b] After the battle of Sedan they still remained patriots, because, from their standpoint, *France could only be saved* by Louis Bonaparte's restauration, even if that restauration must be accomplished by the aid of Bismarck.

It is self-understood that you must *not name* me. As to the details of Bradlaugh's intimacy with the Brimont, Blanc (*le vieux*)[c] is the man to furnish them.

In his controversy with the General Council Bradlaugh got the help—of the *Soir* (Paris journal). In the Council's sitting of *January 2, 1872* Serraillier communicated:

'He had read an article in *Le Soir* written in defence of Bradlaugh. It said he (Bradlaugh) *had honoured the Journal (Le Soir) by contributing to it* and was a safe governmental man, and had nothing to do with demagogic intrigues.'

When Gladstone dissolved Parliament (the occasion on which he was overthrown by Disraeli), Bradlaugh's lecturing room was decorated by immense placards with the inscription 'Farewell to Iconoclast, the People's Redeemer! Welcome to the great dreadnaught of St Stephen's!'[77] But he had counted without his host. He was not elected member of Parliament, despite his public begging letters (for a good testimonial) to Bright and other leaders of the 'great liberal party', who replied in a very cool way. It was also no use boasting of having dined with a life-Bishop (of the church of England).

---

[a] 'International Working Men's Association', *The Eastern Post*, No.169, 23 December 1871.-[b] Napoleon III-[c] old man

In the last election [a] Bradlaugh was happier for this reason: He was one of the noisiest demagogic supporters of Gladstone's pro-Russian campaign against Disraeli — in fact one of the most turbulent tools of the Party who wanted to get in 'Place and Pelf' again, *coûte que coûte*. [b] Moreover, no constituency was to be hazarded in the impending, decisive electoral battle. The prudery of the Whig and radical party had to be thrown overboard. Now Bradlaugh's election at Northampton was not safe, despite the strong contingent of shoemakers in that town who belong to his 'sect'; but these shoemakers had before voted for him like one man, and he had failed. But then there was another liberal candidate, difficult to place, because notorious for his *'affaires véreuses en matière de finances'* [c] and moreover damaged by some scandals of another sort (*des gifles reçus*). [d] This man was Labouchere. He is one of the three proprietors of *The Daily News*, hence the partner of that *gros bonnet* [e] of the liberal party — the *pietist* capitalist *Samuel Morley*. Difficult as it was to carry through either Bradlaugh or Labouchere, it was feasible to do so by making a *couple* of them. Samuel Morley's — the pietist's — public recommendation (by printed letter) of the atheist Bradlaugh secured him the religious element of Northampton, while Bradlaugh secured to Labouchere the infidel shoemakers of that town. Thus both together passed as members for Northampton.

The utter meanness of Bradlaugh shines most in the manoeuvres by which he has succeeded to oust all the other popular preachers of free thought (the scientific preachers address themselves to other *couches sociales* [f]) such as Mrs Law, who wanted not to be his personal *séides*, [g] by appropriating to himself all the funds of the party. He even succeeded to have all lecturing halls in London shut to them, while he built out of the party's funds a lecturing hall for his own personal use. Mrs Law etc. were so confined to lecturing in the provinces. If it interests you (but I think it is not worth while entering into details), you can have full information on this point from the persons concerned.

Salut

K. M.

(*Verte*) [h]

---

[a] in 1880 - [b] at any cost - [c] shady dealings in financial matters - [d] slaps in the face - [e] bigwig - [f] social strata - [g] henchmen - [h] (Turn over)

Can you give me some information on a person named *E. Fortin* who has written me several letters addressing me as: '*Mon cher maître.*' His demand is very 'modest'. While he studies the *Capital* he proposes to make monthly *résumés* which he is kind enough to be willing to send over to me monthly, whereupon I shall correct them monthly, elucidating the points he might have misunderstood. In this quiet way, when he had done with the last monthly résumé, and I sent it back corrected—he would have a manuscript ready for publication and—as he says—inundate France with torrents *de lumière.* [a]

Now I shall—even for mere want of time—not answer to his call, but at all events I must reply to his letter. He may be a well-intentioned man. Before writing him I should like to have some information. He resides at present at Beauvais, 22, rue de la Porte de Paris.

First published, in Russian, in the magazine *Voinstvuyushchiy materialist*, Book IV, Moscow, 1925

Reproduced from the original

Published in English for the first time

37

MARX TO AN UNKNOWN CORRESPONDENT [78]

IN LONDON

[London,] 31 January 1881
41 Maitland Park Road, N. W.

Dear Sir,

Please to forward me the papers etc. enumerated in the enclosed list. At the same time you would greatly oblige me by the information whether there exists a short compendium of the Factory and Workshops' Acts?

I possess myself the several Acts, but a member of the French Chamber of Deputies has asked me to procure him such a compendium where he might find the whole matter together. Has not been

---

[a] of light

something of the sort been published by Mr Redpath, Factory Inspector?[a]

Yours truly,

Karl Marx

First published in: Marx and Engels, *Works*, Second Russian Edition, Vol. 35, Moscow, 1964

Reproduced from the original

Published in English for the first time

38

ENGELS TO KARL KAUTSKY [79]

IN VIENNA

London, 1 February 1881
122 Regent's Park Road, N. W.

Dear Mr Kautsky,

Having been long prevented, I am at last able to reply to your letter. [80]

Now, in view of the fact that you intend to come here shortly, it would be a somewhat unnecessary labour to let you have a detailed critique *in writing* of the book you have been good enough to send me; since I shall, in all probability, have the pleasure of discussing it with you in person, I shall confine myself to just a few points.

1. What you say on p. 66 etc. is invalidated by the fact that other, real differences exist between surplus value and profit on capital besides the percentage estimate based on the variable or total capital. The main passages from *Capital* relating to this are summarised in *Anti-Dühring*, p. 182. [81]

2. Even if the armchair socialists [82] persist in demanding that we proletarian socialists should help them solve the problem of how to avoid what looks like imminent over-population and the threat of collapse this poses to the new social order, that is very far from being a reason why I should do them such a favour. To resolve all the

---

[a] Presumably A. Redgrave, *The Factory and Workshop Act, 1878*, London, 1879.

doubts and scruples of these chaps which they owe to the excess of
their own muddle-headed wisdom, or even to refute, for example, all
the monstrous twaddle which Schäffle alone has assembled in his
many fat tomes,[83] is, in my opinion, a sheer waste of time. It would
fill a fair-sized book were one merely to attempt to put right all the
misquotations from *Capital* inserted by these gentlemen between invert-
ed commas.They should first learn to read and copy before demanding to have their questions answered.

Moreover, I do not regard the question as in any way a burning
one at a moment when American mass production, as yet only in its
infancy, and *really* large-scale agriculture are threatening to all but
suffocate us by the sheer volume of the means of subsistence produced; on the eve of an upheaval of which one of the first consequences must be to *populate the globe*—what you say on the subject
on pp. 169-70, skates too lightly over this point—and which, moreover, will *of necessity call for* considerable demographic growth in
Europe.

Euler's calculation[84] has about as much merit as the one concerning the kreutzer which, invested at compound interest in the year dot,
doubles every 13 years and therefore now amounts to some
$\frac{1 \times 2^{144}}{60}$ gulden, a silver nugget larger than the earth. When you
say on p. 169 that social conditions in America are not very different
from those in Europe, this holds good only so long as you consider
nothing but the large coastal cities, or even the outward legal forms
those conditions assume. There can be no doubt that the vast mass of
the American people live in conditions that are exceedingly favourable to demographic growth. The stream of immigrants is proof of
this. And yet it has taken more than 30 years to double itself. Alarm-
ism doesn't come into it.

The abstract possibility that mankind will increase numerically to
such an extent that its propagation will have to be kept within
bounds does, of course, exist. But should communist society ever find
itself compelled to regulate the production of humans in the same
way as it has already regulated the production of things, then it, and
it alone, will be able to effect this without difficulty. In such a society
it would not, or so it seems to me, be particularly difficult to obtain
deliberately a result which has already come about naturally and
haphazardly in France and Lower Austria. At all events, it's for those
chaps to decide whether, when and how it's to be done and what

means they wish to use. I don't consider myself qualified to supply them with suggestions and advice about this. Indeed, these chaps will, presumably, be every bit as clever as we are. Incidentally, as early as 1844 I wrote (*Deutsch-Französische Jahrbücher*, p. 109): 'For even if Malthus were completely right, this' (socialist) 'transformation would have to be undertaken straight away; for only this transformation, only the education of the masses which it provides, makes possible that moral restraint of the propagative instinct which Malthus himself presents as the most effective and easiest remedy for over-population.'[a]

That must suffice until I am able to discuss the other points with you in person. You are quite right to come over here. You are one of the few among the younger generation who really tries to learn something, and hence it will do you a lot of good to get out of the atmosphere of non-criticism in which all the historical and economic literature currently being produced in Germany is going to wrack and ruin.

With sincere regards,

Yours,

F. Engels

First published, in Russian, in *Marx-Engels Archives*, Vol. I (VI), Moscow, 1932

Printed according to the original

Published in English in full for the first time

39

ENGELS TO EDUARD BERNSTEIN

IN ZURICH

London, 2 February 1881

Dear Mr Bernstein,

Enclosed a letter to Kautsky,[b] which kindly forward; I don't know whether the Vienna address I was given is still the right one.

---

[a] F. Engels, *Outlines of a Critique of Political Economy* (present edition, Vol. 3, p. 439). -
[b] See previous letter.

The 5 nos. of the *Sozialdemokrat* since the year began testify to a significant step forward. Gone are the melancholy, despairing tones of a 'beaten man', the complementary grandiloquence of stuffy respectability, the incessant revolutionary rhetoric *à la* Most alternating with philistine tameness, finally the constant preoccupation with Most. The tone has become lively and purposeful. The paper will no longer act as an opiate if it stays like this; rather it will put new heart into our people in Germany. As you have the *Neue Rheinische Zeitung* you would do well to take a look at it occasionally. The mockery and contempt with which we treated our opponents were precisely what brought us in almost 6,000 subscribers in the 6 months prior to the state of siege [85] and, although we started again from scratch in November, we again had the full tally and more by May '49. The *Kölnische Zeitung* has now admitted that in those days it *only had 9,000*.

As it seems that you are short of material for your feuilleton, you might, sometime, reprint the poem from No. 44 of 1848: 'This morning I went to Düsseldorf'; possibly with the title 'A Socialist-Eater of 1848' (feuilleton to the *Neue Rheinische Zeitung* of 14 July 1848) and, under it, the author: Georg Weerth (died Havana, 1856). [86] So just keep it up!

Yours,
F. E.

'Thou shalt not steal' and the apology for the execution of Louis XVI [87] are very good.

First published, in Russian, in *Marx-Engels Archives*, Book I, Moscow, 1924

Printed according to the original

Published in English for the first time

40

MARX TO CARL PEARSON [88]

IN LONDON

[London,] 15 February 1881
41 Maitland Park, N. W.

My dear Sir,

I should have answered before but for great pressure of work during the last days.

Will you give me the pleasure to call on me on Thursday next,[a] 8 o'clock p. m.?

Yours truly,
Karl Marx

First published in *Neues Deutschland*, 15./16. Dezember 1984 as a facsimile and in German translation

Reproduced from the original

41

MARX TO NIKOLAI DANIELSON [7]

IN ST PETERSBURG

London, 19 February 1881

My dear Sir,

In all haste these few lines in answer to your friendly letter.

Since my return from Ramsgate [38] my health was generally improving, but the detestable weather, lasting for months, we are passing through, has blessed me with a perpetual cold and coughing, interfering with sleep, etc. But the worst is that Mrs Marx's state becomes daily more dangerous notwithstanding my resort to the most celebrated medical men of London, and I have besides a host of

―――――――
[a] 17 February

domestic troubles, which it would be tedious entering upon. On the other hand, I had and have to struggle through an immense lot of blue books[89] sent to me from different countries, above all from the United States, so that my working time is hardly sufficient for the task, since all night labour has for many years absolutely been interdicted by my medical advisers. Hence an awful correspondence-indebtedness starts me in the face. Just now my whole family is in a hubbub because of the removal of my eldest daughter, Madame Longuet, with her children,[a] from London to Paris, where her husband[b] — (since the amnesty; he was in the interval Professor of King's College, London)[69] — has become one of the editors of the *Justice* (he inspired Clemenceau's semi-socialistic speech at Marseilles[c]). You understand how painful — in the present state of Mrs Marx — this separation must be. For her and myself our grandchildren, three little boys, were inexhaustible sources of enjoyment, of life.

Now first as to the enclosed manuscript.[90] Its author, Mr Lafargue, is the husband of my second daughter,[d] and one of my direct disciples. He has requested me to try whether through your interference he could become a contributor to a Petersburg Review, the *Отечественныя Записки* or the *Слово*. (I think they are the only ones where he might have a chance.) If so, you would be empowered to change or suppress anything not suitable to the St Petersburg Meridian. As to his 'name', the initials would do. At all events it will interest you to read the manuscript.

I have read with the greatest interest your article[56] which is in the best sense of the word 'original'. Hence the Boycotting. If you break through the webs of routine thought, you are always sure to be 'boycotted' in the first instance; it is the only arm of defence which in their first perplexity the *routiniers* know how to wield. I have been 'boycotted' in Germany for many many years, and am still so in England, with that little variation that from time to time something so absurd and asinine is launched against me that I would blush to take any public notice of it. But try on: The next thing to do — in my opinion — is to take up the wonderfully increasing *indebtedness of the landlords*, the upper class representatives of agriculture, and show them how they are 'crystallised' in the retort under the control of the 'new pillars of society'.

---

[a] Jean, Henri and Edgar -[b] Charles Longuet -[c] 'Discours de M. Clémenceau', *La Justice*, No. 291, 1 November 1880. -[d] Laura

I am very anxious to see your polemics with the *Слово*. [91] As soon as I shall sail in more quiet waters I shall enter more fully upon your *Esquisse*. [a] For the present I cannot omit one observation. The soil being exhausted and getting not the elements — by artificial and vegetable and animal manure, etc.— to supply its wants, will with the changing favour of the seasons, of circumstances independent of human influence — still continue to yield harvests of very different amounts, though, summing up a period of years, as f. i. from 1870-80, the stagnant character of the production presents itself in the most striking character. Under such circumstances the favourable climatic conditions pave the way to a *famine year* by quickly consuming and setting free the mineral fertilizers still latent in the soil, while *vice versa* a *famine year*, and still more a series of bad years following it, allow the soil-inherent minerals to accumulate anew, and to work efficiently with returning favour of the climatic conditions. Such a process goes of course everywhere on but *elsewhere* it is checked by the modifying intervention of the agriculturist himself. It becomes *the only regulating factor* where man has ceased to be a 'power' — for want of means.

So we have *1870* an excellent harvest in your country, but that year is a *climax year*, and as such immediately followed by a very bad one; the year *1871*, the very bad harvest, must be considered as the starting point for a new little cycle, till we come to the new climax year 1874, which is immediately followed by the famine year 1875; then the upwards movement begins again, ending in the still worse famine year 1880. The summing up of the years during the whole period proves that the average annual production remained the same and that the mere natural factors have alone produced the changes comparing the single years and the smaller cycles of years.

I wrote you some time ago, [b] that if the great industrial and commercial crisis England has passed through went over without the culminating financial crash at London, this *exceptional* phenomenon was only due to — French money. This is now seen and acknowledged even by English *routiniers*. Thus *The Statist* (January 29, 1881) says:

'The money market has only be[en] so easy as it has been during the past year *through an accident*. The *Bank of France* in the early autumn permitted its stock of gold

---

[a] [N. F. Danielson,] *Очерки нашего пореформеннаго общественнаго хозяйства*. Signed: *Николай — онъ*. - [b] See this volume, p. 30.

bullion to fall from £ 30 Millions to £ 22 Millions... *Last autumn undoubtedly there was a very narrow escape.*' (!)

The *English railway system* rolls on the same inclined plane as the European *Public Debt system.* The ruling magnates amongst the different railway-nets directors contract not only — progressively — new loans *in order to enlarge their networks*, i. e. the 'territory', where they rule as absolute monarchs, but they enlarge their respective networks *in order to have new pretexts for engaging in new loans* which enable them to pay the interest due to the holders of obligations, preferential shares, etc., and also from time to time to throw a sop to the much ill-used common shareholders in the shape of somewhat increased dividends. This pleasant method must one day or another terminate in an ugly catastrophe.

In the *United States* the railway kings have become the butt of attacks, not only, as before this, on the part of the farmers and other industrial '*entrepreneurs*' of the *West*, but also on the part of the grand representative of commerce — the *New York Chamber of Commerce.* The octopodus railway king and financial swindler *Gould* has, on his side, told the New York commercial magnates:

> You now attack the railways, because you think them most vulnerable considering their present unpopularity; but take heed: after the railways *every sort of corporation* (means in the Yankee dialect *joint stock company*) will have its turn; then, later on, *all forms of associated capital*; finally, *all forms of capital*; you are thus paving the way to — *Communism* whose tendencies are already more and more spreading among the people.

M. Gould '*a le flair bon*'. [a]

In *India* serious complications, if not a general outbreak, is in store for the British government. What the English take from them annually in the form of rent, dividends for railways useless to the Hindoos, pensions for military and civil servicemen, for Afghanistan and other wars, etc. etc.— what they take from them *without any equivalent* and *quite apart* from what they appropriate to themselves annually *within* India, speaking only of the *value of the commodities* the Indians have *gratuitously* and annually to send *over* to England, it amounts to *more than the total sum of income of the 60 millions of agricultural and industrial labourers of India!* This is a bleeding process, with a vengeance! The famine years are pressing each other and *in dimensions* till

---

[a] has a good nose

now not yet suspected in Europe! There is an actual conspiracy going on wherein Hindus and Mussulmans cooperate; the British government is aware that something is 'brewing', but this shallow people (I mean the governmental men), stultified by their own parliamentary ways of talking and thinking, do not even desire to see clear, to realize the whole extent of the imminent danger! To delude others and by deluding them to delude yourself—this is: *parliamentary wisdom* in a nutshell! *Tant mieux!* [a]

Can you tell me whether Prof. Lankester's '*Chapter on Deterioration*' [92] (I have seen it quoted in your article) is translated into Russian? He is a friend of mine.

Last month we had here Russian visitors, amongst others Prof. Sieber (now settled at Zurich) and Mr Kablukoff (Moscow). They were all day long studying at the British Museum.

No news of our 'mutual' friend [b]?

Apropos. *Janson*'s last statistical work [c]—comparing Russia with Europe—has made much sensation. I should be glad to see it. [93]

With best compliments

Yours very truly,

Karl Marx

Should Lafargue's article find no 'home' in Petersburg, be so kind as to return it to me. [94]

First published, in Russian, in *Minuvshiye gody*, No. 1, St Petersburg, 1908

Reproduced from the original

Published in English in full for the first time

---

[a] All the better! - [b] Hermann Lopatin - [c] [Janson] Ю. Э. Янсонъ, *Сравнительная статистика Россіи и западно-европейскихъ государствъ*, т. 1-2, С.-Петербургъ, 1878-1880.

42

MARX TO FERDINAND DOMELA NIEUWENHUIS [95]

IN THE HAGUE

London, 22 February 1881
41 Maitland Park Road, N. W.

Dear Comrade,

My prolonged silence is due to the fact that I wished to enclose in my reply to your letter of 6 January a conspectus of the amendments that you might care to make in the event of a 2nd edition of *Kapitaal en Arbeid*. [96] As a result of domestic disturbances, unforeseen labours and other disruptions, I have not yet got this done and shall therefore be sending off this letter without the enclosure for the present, lest my continued silence be misconstrued by you. The amendments I consider necessary relate to details; the main thing, the spirit of the thing, is there already.

I have to thank you for the kind dedication, [97] since you, personally, have thereby thrown down the gauntlet before our bourgeois antagonists.

The author[a] of *Mannen van beteekenis*, [98] an inspector of schools OR SOMETHING OF THAT SORT, wrote to me requesting material for a biographical memoir and, in addition, got his publisher to approach my brother-in-law, Juta, with a view to his persuading me to accede to a request of the kind I habitually turn down. The gentleman — the author of *Mannen* — wrote to me saying he did not share my views but recognised their importance, protested his esteem, etc. The selfsame individual subsequently had the effrontery to embody in his pamphlet a libellous fabrication by that notorious Prussian spy, Stieber, and likewise, — on the inspiration, no doubt, of one of the armchair socialists [82] in Bonn, — to accuse me of deliberate misquotation, nor, in so doing, did the estimable fellow even go to the trouble of reading up my polemic against the worthy Brentano in the *Volksstaat*, [99] where he would have seen that Brentano, who had originally denounced me in the *Concordia* (manufacturers' sheet) for 'formal and substantive falsification', later extricated himself with the lie that he

---

[a] Arnold Kerdijk

had misunderstood me, etc. A Dutch journal proposed to open its columns to me for the chastisement of the 'inspector of schools', but *on principle* I do not reply to pin-pricks of this kind. I have never, even in London, taken the slightest notice of such literary yapping. Any other course would mean wasting the better part of my time on making rectifications all over the place, from California to Moscow. In my younger days I sometimes did some hard hitting, but wisdom comes with age, at least in so far as one avoids useless DISSIPATION OF FORCE.

The forthcoming Zurich Congress's 'question' which you mention would seem to me a mistake. [100] What is to be done, and done *immediately* at any given, particular moment in the future, depends, of course, wholly and entirely on the actual historical circumstances in which action is to be taken. But the said question, being posed *out of the blue*, in fact poses a fallacious problem to which the only answer can be a *critique of the question* as such. We cannot solve an equation that does not comprise within its terms the elements of its solution. Come to that, there is nothing specifically 'socialist' about the predicaments of a government that has suddenly come into being as a result of a popular victory. On the contrary. Victorious bourgeois politicians immediately feel constrained by their 'victory', whereas a socialist is at least able to intervene without constraint. Of one thing you may be sure — a socialist government will not come to the helm in a country unless things have reached a stage at which it can, before all else, take such measures as will so intimidate the mass of the bourgeoisie as to achieve the first desideratum — time for effective action.

You may, perhaps, refer me to the Paris Commune but, aside from the fact that this was merely an uprising of one city in exceptional circumstances, the majority of the Commune was in no sense socialist, nor could it have been. With a modicum of COMMON SENSE, it could, however, have obtained the utmost that was then obtainable — a compromise with Versailles beneficial to the people as a whole. The appropriation of the Banque de France alone would have rapidly put an end to the vainglory of Versailles, etc., etc.

The general demands of the French bourgeoisie before 1789 were, *mutatis mutandis*,[a] just as well-defined as are today, with a fair degree of uniformity, the primary, immediate demands of the proletariat in all countries where there is capitalist production. But could any 18th-

---

[a] the necessary changes being made

century Frenchman, *a priori*, have the least idea of the manner in which the demands of the French bourgeoisie would be implemented? A doctrinaire and of necessity fantastic anticipation of a future revolution's programme of action only serves to distract from the present struggle. The dream of the imminent end of the world inspired the struggle of the early Christians against the Roman Empire and gave them confidence in victory. Scientific insight into the inevitable disintegration, now steadily taking place before our eyes, of the prevailing social order; the masses themselves, their fury mounting under the lash of the old governmental bogies; the gigantic and positive advances simultaneously taking place in the development of the means of production — all this is sufficient guarantee that the moment a truly proletarian revolution breaks out, the conditions for its immediate initial (if certainly not idyllic) *modus operandi*[a] will also be there.

My own conviction is that the critical conjuncture for a new international working men's association has not yet arrived; hence I consider all labour congresses and/or socialist congresses, in so far as they do not relate to the immediate, actual conditions obtaining in this or that specific nation, to be not only useless but harmful. They will invariably fizzle out in a host of rehashed generalised banalities.

Yours most cordially,

Karl Marx

First published, in Russian, in *Pravda*, No. 62, 14 March 1928   Printed according to the original

43

ENGELS TO JENNY LONGUET [101]

IN PARIS

[London,] 24 February 1881

My dear Jenny,

Well may the illustrious Regnard recommend his factum to your 'charity'.[102] This Jacobin defending English respectable Protestant-

---

[a] mode of operation

ism and English vulgar Liberalism with the historical *appareil* of that same vulgar Liberalism is indeed an object of deepest charity. But to his 'facts'.

1) The 30,000 protestants' massacre of 1641. The Irish Catholics are here in the same position as the Commune de Paris. The Versaillais massacred 30,000 Communards and called that the horrors of the Commune. The English protestants under Cromwell massacred at least 30,000 Irish and, to cover their brutality, *invented* the tale that this was to avenge 30,000 protestants murdered by the Irish Catholics.

The facts are these.

Ulster having been taken from its Irish owners who at that time 1600-1610 held the *land in common*, and handed over to Scotch protestant military colonists, these colonists did not feel safe in their possessions in the troublous times after 1640. The puritan English Government officials in Dublin spread the rumour that a Scotch Army of Covenanters [103] was to land in Ulster and exterminate all Irish and Catholics. Sir W. Parsons, one of the two Chief Justices of Ireland, said that in a 12-month there would not be a Catholic left in Ireland. It was under these menaces, repeated in the English Parliament, that the Irish of Ulster rose on 23rd October 1641. But no massacre took place. All contemporaneous sources ascribe to the Irish merely the intention of a general massacre, and even the two protestant Chief Justices (proclam. 8th February 1642) declare that 'the chief part of their plot, and amongst them a general massacre, had been *disappointed*.' The English and Scotch however, 4th May 1642, threw Irish women naked into the river (Newry) and massacred Irishmen. (Prendergast, *Cromwellian Settlement of Ireland*, 1865.)

2) *L'Irlande la Vendée de l'Angleterre.* [104] Ireland was Catholic, Protestant England Republican, therefore Ireland — English Vendée. There is however this little difference that the French Revolution intended to *give* the land to the people, the English Commonwealth intended, in Ireland, to *take* the land from the people.

The whole Protestant reformation, as is well known to most students of history save Regnard, apart from its dogmatical squabbles and quibbles, was a vast plan for a confiscation of land. First the land was taken from the Church. Then the Catholics, in countries where Protestantism was in power, were declared rebels and their land confiscated.

Now in Ireland the case was peculiar.

'For the English,' says Prendergast, 'seem to have thought that god made a mistake in giving such a fine country as Ireland to the Irish; and for nearly 700 years they have been trying to remedy it.'

The whole agrarian history of Ireland is a series of confiscations of Irish land to be handed over to English settlers. These settlers, in a very few generations, under the charm of Celtic society, turned more Irish than the aborigines. Then a new confiscation and new colonization took place, and so *in infinitum*.

In the 17th century, the whole of Ireland except the newly Scotchified North, was ripe for a fresh confiscation. So much so, that when the British (puritan) Parliament accorded to Charles I an army for the reduction of Ireland, it resolved that the money for this armament should be raised *upon the security of 2,500,000 acres to be confiscated in Ireland*. And the 'adventurers' [105] who advanced the money should also appoint the officers of that army. The land was to be divided amongst those adventurers so that 1,000 acres should be given them, if in Ulster for £ 200.- advanced, in Connaught for £ 300, in Munster for £ 450, in Leinster for £ 600. And if the people rose against this beneficent plan they are Vendéens! If Regnard should ever sit in a National Convention, he may take a leaf out of the proceedings of the Long Parliament, [106] and combat a possible Vendée with these means.

The Abolition of the Penal Laws [107]! Why the greater part of them were repealed, not in 1793 but in 1778, when England was threatened by the rise of the American Republic, and the second repeal, 1793, was when the French Republic arose threatening and England required all the soldiers she could get to fight it!

The Grant to Maynooth by Pitt. [108] This pittance was soon repealed by the Tories and only renewed by Sir R. Peel in 1845. But not a word about the other *c a d e a u que faisait à l'Irlande ce grand homme (c'est la première fois qu'il trouve grâce devant les yeux d'un Jacobin)*, [a] that other *'dotation'* not only *'considérable'* but actually lavish — the 3 Million £ by which the Union of Ireland with England [109] was bought. The parliamentary documents will show that the one item of the purchase money of rotten and nomination boroughs alone cost no less a sum than £ 1,245,000 (O'Connell, *Memoir on Ireland addressed to the Queen*).

---

[a] *present* this great man gave to Ireland (it is the first time that grace has been bestowed upon him in the eyes of the Jacobins)

Lord Derby instituted *le système des écoles nationales.* [110] *Very true* but why did he? Consult Fitzgibbon, *Ireland in 1868,* the work of a staunch Protestant and Tory, or else the official Report of Commissioners on Education in Ireland, 1826. The Irish, neglected by the English government, had taken the education of their children into their own hands. At the time when English fathers and mothers insisted upon their right to send their children to the factory to earn money instead of to the school to learn, at that time in Ireland the peasants vied with each other in forming schools of their own. The school-master was an ambulant teacher, spending a couple of months at each village. A cottage was found for him, each child paid him 2d. a week and a few sods of turf in winter. The schools were kept, on fine days in summer, in the fields, near a hedge, and then known by the name of hedge-schools. There were also ambulant scholars, who with their books under the arm, wandered from school to school, receiving lodging and food from the peasants without difficulty. In 1812 there were 4,600 such hedge-schools in Ireland and that year's report of the Commissioners says that such education

was 'leading to evil rather than good', 'that such education *the people are actually obtaining for themselves,* and though we consider it practicable to correct it, *to check its progress appears impossible*: it may be improved *but it cannot be impeded'.*

So then, these truly *national* schools did not suit English purposes. To suppress them, the *sham* national schools were established. They are *so little secular* that the reading-book consists of extracts both from the Catholic and Protestant Bibles, agreed upon by the Catholic and Protestant Archbishops of Dublin. Compare with these Irish peasants the English who howl at compulsory school attendance to this day!

First published, in Russian, in the collection *Sredniye veka* (Middle Ages), Book XIX, Moscow, 1961

Reproduced from the original

Published in English in full for the first time

44

MARX TO VERA ZASULICH[111]

IN GENEVA

London, 8 March 1881
41 Maitland Park Road, N. W.

Dear Citizen,

A nervous complaint which has assailed me periodically over the last ten years has prevented me from replying any sooner to your letter of 16 February. I am sorry that I cannot provide you with a concise exposé, intended for publication, of the question you have done me the honour of putting to me. Months ago I promised the St Petersburg Committee to let them have a piece on the same subject.[112] I hope, however, that a few lines will suffice to dispel any doubts you may harbour as to the misunderstanding in regard to my so-called theory.

In analysing the genesis of capitalist production I say:

'At the core of the capitalist system, therefore, lies the complete separation of the producer from the means of production ... the basis of this whole development is the *expropriation of the agricultural producer*. To date this has not been accomplished in a radical fashion anywhere except in England... But *all the other countries of Western Europe* are undergoing the same process' (*Capital*, French ed., p. 315).

Hence the 'historical inevitability' of this process is *expressly* limited to the *countries of Western Europe*. The cause of that limitation is indicated in the following passage from Chapter XXXII:

'*Private property*, based on personal labour ... will be supplanted by *capitalist private property*, based on the exploitation of the labour of others, on wage labour' (l. c., p. 341).

In this Western movement, therefore, what is taking place is the *transformation of one form of private property into another form of private property*. In the case of the Russian peasants, *their communal property* would, on the contrary, have to be *transformed into private property*.

Hence the analysis provided in *Capital* does not adduce reasons either for or against the viability of the rural commune, but the special study I have made of it, and the material for which I drew from original sources, has convinced me that this commune is the fulcrum of social regeneration in Russia, but in order that it may function as such, it would first be necessary to eliminate the deleterious influences which are assailing it from all sides, and then ensure for it the normal conditions of spontaneous development.

I have the honour to be, dear Citizen,

Yours very faithfully,

Karl Marx

First published, in Russian, in *Marx-Engels Archives*, Book I, Moscow, 1924

Printed according to the original

Translated from the French

45

ENGELS TO S. F. KAUFMANN

IN LONDON

[Draft]

[London,] 11 March 1881
122 Regent's Park Road, N. W.

Dear Mr Kaufmann,

In reply to your esteemed note of the 9th inst. I regret that I am unable to fall in with your wishes regarding the guarantee. My experiences with guarantees have been such that I have resolved once and for all to advance the money straight away myself, if I can, rather than give a guarantee. However the money is not available; if I had it and could do without it, I should regard it as my prime duty to hand it over to the party in Germany to whom we now owe every penny we can spare. [a]

---

[a] Here Engels deleted the following passage: 'There is, however, another reason. Over the past 10 years I have seen all too often how rapid is the turnover here of the people who go to make up the local German working men's associations and, such being the case, it might well come about that the Society [8] adopted a line quite different from its present one before my guarantee expired and that in the last resort I was standing guarantee for Mr Most, which surely cannot be asked of me.'

Trusting that you will find elsewhere the means of obtaining the funds you need,

I remain,
Yours very truly

First published in: Marx and Engels, *Works*, First Russian Edition, Vol. XXVII, Moscow, 1935

Printed according to the original

Published in English for the first time

46

ENGELS TO EDUARD BERNSTEIN [113]

IN ZURICH

London, 12 March 1881

Dear Mr Bernstein,

Herewith some material on the anti-adultery commandment. [114] Whether you'll be able to use it, I confess I don't know. It's a ticklish subject and you must know whether more harm than good will be done by touching on it. At all events I wanted to show you one way of dealing with this commandment without relapsing into moral philistinism, and it may be useful to you anyway to have the historical material on the case, in so far as it was available to me.

For the rest, the paper [a] is doing very well on the whole and some of the nos. are very good; rather less doctrinaire articles, like the one on state socialism, [b] would do no harm. How can one lump together Turgot, one of the leading economists of the 18th century, with Necker, that highly practical man of *haute finance*, [c] precursor of your Laffittes and Péreires and, worse still, the wretched Calonne, the man of hand-to-mouth expedients, who was a genuine *après moi le déluge* [d] [115] aristocrat? How can one place these — Turgot in particular and even Necker — cheek by jowl with Bismarck who, at the most, wants money regardless, *à la* Calonne, and the said Bismarck in his turn quite summarily cheek by jowl with Stoecker on the one hand and Schäffle and Co. on the other, every one of whom in his turn pursues quite different lines? If the bourgeois lump them all together,

---

[a] *Der Sozialdemokrat* - [b] [K. Kautsky,] 'Der Staatssozialismus und die Sozialdemokratie', signed: Symmachos, *Der Sozialdemokrat*, No. 10, 6 March 1881. - [c] high finance - [d] after me the deluge

that is no reason why we should proceed as uncritically. Here, precisely, are the roots of doctrinairism, in that one *believes* the self-interested and narrow assertions of one's opponent and proceeds to construct on those assertions a system which naturally stands or falls with them. With Bismarck it is a case of money, money and again money, and the pretexts he gives change in accordance with purely external considerations. Give him a differently composed majority in the Reichstag and he'll jettison all his present plans and prepare conflicting ones. That's why one can never ever infer a declaration of modern society's bankruptcy from anything that is done by an animal as irrational in theory and inconsistent in practice as Bismarck. Still less from the intellectual St Vitus dance of a fool like Stoecker. Nor yet from the twaddle of 'thinking men' *à la* Schäffle. Their 'thinking' (and this is pretty well all they do 'think') is not directed towards declaring modern society bankrupt. On the contrary, they are, of course, simply living in the hope of patching it up again. But what kind of a thinking man is e. g. Schäffle? In his *Quintessenz* [a] the silly Swabian admits that he pondered one of the (simplest) points in *Capital* for ten years before getting to the bottom of it; in fact the bottom he got to was pure nonsense. [116]

It is nothing but self-interested misrepresentation on the part of the Manchester bourgeois to describe as 'socialism' all interference by the state with free competition: protective tariffs, guilds, tobacco monopoly, nationalisation of branches of industry, the Overseas Trading Company, [117] royal porcelain factory. That is something we should *criticise*, but not *believe*. If we do the latter and base a theoretical argument thereon, this will collapse together with its premises,— simply upon it's being proved, that is, that this alleged socialism is nothing but feudal reaction on the one hand and, on the other, a pretext for extortion, its secondary object being to turn as many proletarians as possible into officials and pensioners dependent on the state, and to organise, alongside the disciplined army of officials and military, a similar army of workers. Compulsory suffrage imposed by senior functionaries instead of by factory overseers—fine socialism that! This is where you get if you believe what the bourgeois himself doesn't believe but only pretends to, namely that the state = socialism.

Otherwise I find that your views on the attitude to be adopted by

---

[a] [A. Schäffle,] *Die Quintessenz des Socialismus*, Gotha, 1875.

the paper coincide entirely with my own, and I'm also glad that of late there has no longer been such liberal use of the *word* revolution as there was at the outset. That was quite all right earlier on, after the sorry opiate-mongering of 1880, [118] but it would be preferable, and this, too, with an eye to Most, to be wary of high-flown rhetoric. One may express revolutionary thoughts without forever harping on the *word* revolution. The pitiful Most is, by the way, quite beside himself; he's at a loss where to pull in and now, on top of that, the success of Fritzsche and Viereck in America [119] has taken the last bit of wind out of his sails.

The paper can now really serve to encourage and cheer up our people in Germany, something a number of them, or at least their so-called leaders, are much in need of. I've received a few more jeremiads and answered them in accordance with their deserts. Viereck was very down in the mouth at the start, but a few days in the fresh air of London were enough to restore his resilience. The paper must import that fresh air into Germany and by far the best way of doing so is to mock our adversaries, treat them with contempt. Once the people learn to laugh at Bismarck & Co. again, much will have been gained. But it mustn't be forgotten that this is the first time such a thing has happened to the people, at any rate the vast majority, or, more especially, that a large number of agitators and editors will have the discomfort of being jolted out of their very comfortable berths. Such being the case, it is just as necessary to cheer people up as it is constantly to remind them that Bismarck & Co. are still the same jackasses, the same scoundrels and the same poor wretches, impotent in face of the historical movement, as they were before the attempted assassinations. [120] So any joke at the expense of this rabble is of value.

As regards Ireland, only this much: The people are far too canny not to know that an uprising would spell their ruin; it would stand no chance save in the case of war between England and America. [121] Meanwhile the Irish have forced Gladstone to introduce continental standing orders in Parliament, [122] thus undermining the whole of the English parliamentary system. They have further forced Gladstone to forswear all his cant and to become more Tory than even the worst of Tories. The Coercion Bills [123] have gone through, the Land Bill [124] will either be thrown out by the Upper House, or else it will be castrated, and then the fun will begin, in other words, the covert disintegration of the parties will become overt. Since Gladstone's nomination, the WHIGS and moderate TORIES, i. e. the big landowners generally, have been secretly combining to form a big landed property party. As soon as this comes to fruition, and family and personal interests have been adjusted, or as soon as the new party is driven out into the open in consequence of, say, the Land Bill, the administration and the present majority will disintegrate. Then the new bourgeois-radical party will come out in opposition to the new conservative party, but with nothing to fall back on save the workers and the Irish peasants. And so that there may be no recurrence of bilking and trickery here, a proletarian-radical party is in process of formation under the leadership of Joseph Cowen (M. P. for Newcastle), an old Chartist who is half, if not wholly, communist and a very worthy chap. Ireland is responsible for all this, Ireland is the driving force in the realm. This for your private information. More on the subject anon.

Regards,

Yours
F. E.

Since Kautsky — will you give him my regards? — will be coming over here soon, there's no point in answering him at length. My regards to Beust should you see him.

First published, in Russian, in *Marx-Engels Archives*, Book I, Moscow, 1924

Printed according to the original

Published in English in full for the first time

47

ENGELS TO JOHANN PHILIPP BECKER [125]

IN GENEVA

London, 28 March 1881
122 Regent's Park Road, N. W.

Dear Old Man,

I shall send you some money the instant you put me in a position to do so by letting me have *your new address*. For I have to produce this, and such addresses as I find in the *Précurseur* do not seem to me really fit to be produced if they are not to create difficulties. The moment I have had a reply you will at once get 100 frs and a lengthy reply from

Your

F. Engels

First published in: F. Engels, *Vergessene Briefe (Briefe Friedrich Engels' an Johann Philipp Becker)*, Berlin, 1920

Printed according to the original

Published in English for the first time

48

ENGELS TO AUGUST BEBEL

IN LEIPZIG

London, 30 March 1881

Dear Bebel,

Viereck (a postcard from whom I enclose) wants me to give you an account of the Boston meeting; but here too, as commonly in combined operations, there has been hitch after hitch; 1. Harney wrote a week later; 2. he forgot to enclose the newspaper report which I did not get till yesterday. Today I gave this to Kautsky, who is over here, for him to work on for the *Sozialdemokrat.* [126]

The meeting in Boston was first-rate; ill-advertised but nevertheless attended by 1,500 people, $1/3$ German. The first speaker was Swinton, an American communist who came to visit us here last summer [43] and is the proprietor of a big New York paper. [a] Then Fritzsche. Finally, Wendell Phillips, the great anti-slavery man who, with the exception of John Brown, did more than anyone else for the abolition of slavery and the prosecution of the war, and is the foremost speaker in America — maybe in the world. He returned thanks to the Germans and gave them credit for the fact that in 1861, in every large city, it was the German gymnasts who shielded him with their own bodies from the American mob, and who kept St Louis in the Union. [127] To give you just one example of how he spoke:

---

[a] *The Sun*

'Being as far as I am away from the field of battle, I would not presume to criticise the method of combat. I look at Russia, 4,000 miles away, and see what a nightmare weighs on the shoulders of the people there. I only hope that someone will be found to relieve them of it. And if the dagger alone can do it, I say: Welcome to the dagger! Is there any American here who would disapprove? If he would, then he should look (pointing to a picture on the wall) at Joe Warren who died at Bunkers Hill.'[a]

That was on the 7th of March. On the 13th a bomb did what the dagger had been unable to do.[128]

According to today's *Standard*, *Most* is to be prosecuted by the British government because of the article on the assassination attempt![129] If the Russian Embassy and Gladstone are absolutely intent on making a great man out of the silly nincompoop, no one can stop them. At the same time, it's far from certain that Most will be found guilty. The moral indignation about the bomb in the big newspapers was largely a matter of observing the proprieties, something your bourgeois here never omits to do, if only for appearances' sake. The humorous papers, which reflect public opinion far more faithfully, have taken an altogether different view of the case and, by the time the trial draws to a close, much may have changed in this respect, so that it's far from certain whether the 12 jurymen will reach the unanimous verdict that is called for.

To return to our American friends, Wendell Phillips' championship (induced by a young American journalist, Willard Brown, who was over here last year, when he consorted much with Marx and generally did his utmost for them with the American press and gave them the boosting they needed) is of the first importance. Their success has altogether exceeded my expectations and shows that Bismarckery has fallen greatly in the esteem of the Germans, even middle-class Germans, in America. However ☐ 's[b] hopes of a *second* trip with Liebknecht would hardly seem practicable; it is inadvisable to turn up twice in rapid succession. Moreover, such a trip — anyhow inadmissible before next year — ought to have been rendered unnecessary by the great event in Petersburg and its inevitable consequences. Alexander III, whether he wants to or not, will have to take some decisive step to get things moving, but before that there might be a short period of intensive persecution, and Switzerland will no doubt soon embark on mass expulsions. Meanwhile old William,[c] if not actually on his last legs, becomes dottier and dottier, Bismarck

---

[a] Retranslated from the German. - [b] Viereck in German means quadrangle. - [c] William I

grows daily more rabid and seems absolutely intent on playing the part of a rampaging Prussian Roland, the bourgeois parties go further off the rails every day, while the government's taxation mania sees to the rest. Even if we all sat with our hands in our laps, events would forcibly propel us to the fore and pave the way for victory. It is a real pleasure to see a revolutionary world situation we have long predicted mature into a general crisis, blinkered opponents do our work for us, and the inexorability of a development that is heading for universal collapse prevail in, and as a result of, the general confusion.

Regards from Marx and from your
F. E.

First published, in Russian, in *Marx-Engels Archives*, Vol. I (VI), Moscow, 1932

Printed according to the original

Published in English for the first time

49

ENGELS TO GOTTLIEB LEMCKE

IN LONDON

[London,] 2 April 1881
122 Regent's Park Road, N. W.

Dear Mr Lemcke,

I have just heard that one of my brothers[a] will be passing through London with his family this evening, and this will mean my spending with them the few hours they will be pausing here. I therefore greatly regret that I shall be unable to take advantage of your kind invitation to the opening ceremony of the new club-house. [130] Hoping that the club will prosper and flourish, I remain

Yours very truly,
F. Engels

First published in the journal *Internationale wissenschaftliche Korrespondenz zur Geschichte der deutschen Arbeiterbewegung*, Nr. 10, Berlin (West), 1970

Printed according to the original

Published in English for the first time

---

[a] Apparently Hermann Engels

50

ENGELS TO JOHANN PHILIPP BECKER [131]

IN GENEVA

London, 4 April 1881

Dear Old Man,

I am writing to you just before the post goes, having only this moment got the money order, four pounds sterling = 100 frs 80 cts, which I trust will be paid over to you without delay. Your address was indispensable,[a] as the post office here *insists* on it, otherwise no money order. I shall press Liebknecht about his false promises[b]; those fellows *must* do something for you. I'm glad, by the way, that our people have plucked up courage again; for a time most of them were suffering from a bad attack of *cold feet*; the paper,[c] too, is giving a good account of itself. That philistine Most is definitely in luck; his *Freiheit* was on its last legs, whereupon the British government felt impelled to give it a helping hand, and did so in the most brilliant manner.[129] Such colossal stupidity passes all belief, but it so happens that we have the liberals at the helm and they are capable of any stupidity, any dirty trick. They went ahead in such a hurry that so far they don't even know under which Act they will charge Most! But Bismarck needed this coup for his socialist debate in the Reichstag[132] and, since Gladstone, our premier, is an enthusiastic admirer of the bumped-off Alexander,[d] there was no difficulty about the thing. It will be all the more difficult for them to draw up an indictment, let alone produce a jury that will find Most guilty. So Most will become famous on the cheap, even if only for a brief spell, while Bismarck, even though he, too, may be gently rubbing his hands just now, will ultimately find himself discredited yet again.

Kindest regards from Marx and your

F. Engels

First published in: F. Engels, *Vergessene Briefe (Briefe Friedrich Engels' an Johann Philipp Becker)*, Berlin, 1920

Printed according to the original

Published in English for the first time

---

[a] See this volume, p. 76. - [b] Ibid., p. 50. - [c] *Der Sozialdemokrat* - [d] Alexander II

51

MARX TO JENNY LONGUET [133]

IN ARGENTEUIL

[London,] 11 April 1881

My dear Jennychen,

It's been boring ever since you left — without you and Johnny and Harra! and Mr 'Tea!' [a] Sometimes I hurry across to the window when I hear children's voices which sound like those of our children, momentarily oblivious of the fact that the little chaps are on the other side of the Channel!

One comfort is that you have found a nice place to live and that it suits the children; otherwise everything seems to be RATHER WORSE than in London, with the exception, however, of the climate, whose beneficial effect — beneficial also to asthma — you will discover BY AND BY.

I have found yet another doctor for Mama, one recommended to me by Prof. Lankester, namely Dr Donkin; HE SEEMS A BRIGHT AND INTELLIGENT MAN; but for Mama's complaint it does indeed strike me that ONE MAN [is] AS GOOD, AND PERHAPS BETTER, THAN ANOTHER MAN. However, the CHANGE OF MEDICAL ADVISERS serves to distract her and, during the initial period — which doesn't usually last long — she is full of praise for the new Aesculapius. Longuet's eyeglass turned up immediately after his departure; it was, in fact, tucked away in your bedroom. Hirsch has been selected to bring it to you, but that gossip-hunter seems hardly able to tear himself away from London at a moment when there is so much to be smelt out. The 'great' Most affair [129] alone is an inexhaustible source of fresh water (if by no means a 'cooling stream') for the said hart. [b] Now he threatens to postpone his departure till 18 April. Then, too, he has found a kindred spirit in Kautsky — on whom he had frowned so grimly; even Engels takes a much more tolerant view of this joker [c] since the latter gave proof of his considerable drinking ability. When the charmer — the little joker, [c] I mean — first came to see me, the first question that rose to my lips was — are you

_____

[a] Marx' grandsons: Jean, Henri and Edgar Longuet - [b] A pun on the name Hirsch — hart. ('As pants the hart for cooling streams / When heated in the chase'.) - [c] *Kautz* (diminutive Käutzchen), an untranslatable pun on the name Kautsky.

like your mother[a]? Not in the least, he exclaimed, and silently I congratulated his mother. He's a mediocrity, narrow in outlook, overwise (only 26 years old), a know-all, hard-working after a fashion, much concerned with statistics out of which, however, he makes little sense, by nature a member of the philistine tribe, for the rest, a decent fellow in his own way; I unload him onto *amigo*[b] Engels as much as I can.

The day before yesterday the Dogberry CLUB[134] was here; yesterday, besides the 2 Maitland girls[c] — and, briefly, Lankester and Dr Donkin — we were invaded by Hyndman and his wife,[d] both of whom have too much staying-power. I quite like the wife on account of her brusque, unconventional and determined manner of thinking and speaking, but it's amusing to see how admiringly she hangs on the lips of her complacent chatterbox of a husband! Mama grew so weary (it was close on half past ten at night) that she withdrew. But there was some BYPLAY which tickled her. For Tussy has discovered a new infant prodigy amongst the Dogberries — one Radford; this youth is already a BARRISTER-AT-LAW, yet looks down upon the *jus*[e] and works in the same LINE as Waldhorn. HE LOOKS WELL, CROSS between Irving and the late Lassalle (but has nothing in common with the latter's cynical, smarmily importunate mannerisms *à la* marquis-cum-Jew), AN INTELLIGENT AND SOMEWHAT PROMISING BOY. WELL, that's him in a nutshell. So shockingly did Dolly Maitland pay court to *him* that during supper Mama and Tussy were constantly exchanging signals. Finally, Mr Maitland also turned up, pretty well sober, and began a verbal duel with his instructive neighbour, Hyndman, on the subject of Gladstone in whom Maitland, a spiritualist, believes. *I — rather annoyed by a bad throat — felt glad when the whole lot vanished. It is a strange thing that one cannot well live altogether without company, and that when you get it, you try hard to rid yourself of it.*

Hartmann is working hard in Woolwich as a COMMON WORKMAN; it is becoming increasingly difficult to converse with him in any language. The Russian REFUGEES in Geneva insist that he should disavow Rochefort and do so publicly. This he neither will nor can, even had this not been made impossible by the immoderate letter sent to Rochefort by the Petersburg Committee and published by him in the *Intransigeant*.[135] The Genevans have, indeed, long been trying to convince

---

[a] Minna Kautsky - [b] friend - [c] Dolly and Clara Maitland - [d] Mathilda Hyndman - [e] law

Europe that it was, in fact, *they* who were directing the movement in Russia; now that the *lie* they themselves had disseminated has been taken up by Bismarck *et cie* and constitutes a threat to them, they assert the opposite and vainly endeavour to convince the world of their innocence. In fact, they are mere doctrinaires, muddle-headed anarcho-socialists, and their influence on the Russian 'theatre of war' is ZERO.

Have you been following the course of the legal proceedings against the assassins in St Petersburg?[136] They are sterling chaps through and through, *sans pose mélodramatique,*[a] simple, matter-of-fact, heroic. Shouting and doing are irreconcilable opposites. The Petersburg Executive Committee,[70] which took such vigorous action, issues manifestoes of exquisite 'moderation'. It is remote indeed from the bungling way in which Most and other puerile ranters advocate TYRANNICIDE as a 'theory' and 'PANACEA' (the same thing was done by ENGLISHMEN as innocent as Disraeli, Savage Landor, Macaulay and Mazzini's friend, Stansfeld); they, on the other hand, are at pains to teach Europe that their *modus operandi*[b] is a specifically Russian and historically inevitable mode of action which no more lends itself to moralising — for or against — than does the earthquake in Chios.[137]

In this connection there was a fine old scandal in the House of Commons (as you know, so as to oblige Bismarck and Gorchakov these miserable Gladstonites are making an onslaught, in the person of the pitiful Most,[129] on the freedom of the press in England, in which they are unlikely to succeed). Lord Churchill, a bumptious Tory youth, and member of the Marlborough FAMILY, questioned Sir Charles Dilke and Brassey, both UNDERSTRAPPERS in the CABINET, about the financial support afforded to the *Freiheit*. This was flatly denied and Churchill was compelled to name his authority. He named the ubiquitous Mr Maltman Barry! I enclose a cutting about this affair from the *Weekly Dispatch* (the Dilkes' paper, edited by the 'PHILOSOPHICAL RADICAL', Ashton Dilke, brother of the great 'Dilke'), and a statement by Maltman Barry in *The Daily News*. Clearly Dilke is lying. How pitiful that this braggart, the self-appointed future 'President of the English republic' should, for fear of losing his post, allow Bismarck to dictate upon what journals he ought or ought not to bestow £ 1! Only suppose it became known that, immediately after Hart-

---

[a] without melodramatic posturing -[b] way of going about things

mann's arrival in London, Ashton Dilke invited him to a LUNCHEON! But Hartmann turned this down, not wanting to 'exhibit' himself.

Apropos the Comtist renegade Maxse. This laddie is done far too great an honour in *La Justice* which handles him with kid gloves. In the eyes of this peculiar clique — ENGLISH LIBERALS and their even worse subspecies, the SO CALLED RADICALS — it is indeed a crime on the part of *La Justice* that, flouting all tradition and contrary to agreement, it fails to treat these SHAMS AND HUMBUGS in the accepted manner, to perpetuate the legend that is current about them in the liberal press on the Continent! If one considers the enormous effrontery with which the London press attacks socialist parties in all European countries, and how difficult it is for anyone who thinks it worth the trouble to say a word in return or even to get a brief answer into that press — it is really a bit too much to have to recognise the principle that, should a Paris newspaper venture to criticise that arch-hypocrite and CASUIST of the old-fashioned school, the 'great' Gladstone, it is duty-bound to put entire columns at the disposal of Mr Maxse and his prose, in order that he might repay Gladstone IN KIND for the *avancement*[a] provided by the latter!

Assuming the policy adopted by Gladstone (man of the COERCION[123] and ARMS ACT[138]) vis-à-vis Ireland to be as right as it is in fact wrong, would this constitute any reason to talk of that man's '*générosité*' and '*magnanimité*'? As though there was any question of *any* such things between England and Ireland! Maxse really ought to be told that, while such Pecksniffian expressions may have free currency in London, they do not have it in Paris!

Get Longuet to read *Parnell*'s speech in Cork in *today*'s *Times*.[b] He will find in it the substance of *what ought to be said about Gladstone's new* LAND ACT[124]; in this connection it should not be forgotten that Gladstone, by his disgraceful preliminary measures (incl. abolishing the freedom of speech of members of the Lower House),[122] has brought about the conditions under which *mass* EVICTIONS *are now taking place in Ireland*, while the ACT is pure humbug, seeing that the LORDS who can get anything they want from Gladstone, and no longer have to tremble before the Land League[139] — will DOUBTLESS throw it out or else so castrate it that the Irish themselves will end up by voting *against* it.

---

[a] advancement - [b] 'Cork, 10 April', *The Times*, No. 30165, 11 April 1881.

Give the children a hundred kisses from me; regards to Longuet. Write and tell me, DEAR CHILD, about the state of your health. *Adio.*

Your

OLD NICK [a]

DEAR JOHNNY, HOW DO YOU LIKE FRANCE?[b]

First published abridged, in Russian, in the magazine *Nachalo*, No. 5, St Petersburg, 1899 and in full in *Bolshevik*, No. 5, Moscow, 1931

Printed according to the original

52

ENGELS TO EDUARD BERNSTEIN [140]

IN ZURICH

London, 14 April 1881

Dear Mr Bernstein,

Very many thanks for the excerpt—for numerous reasons, however, it is desirable that we should read the full text of the relevant speeches. Kautsky will already have asked you to let us have the shorthand report [141] for a day or two. So much has been said in the Reichstag and Landtags that would have been better left unsaid that we cannot express an opinion on such matters unless we are fully acquainted with the case.

Your announcement that you wished to resign from the paper[c] came as a most unpleasant surprise. We can see absolutely no reason for it and it would give us *great pleasure* if you were to reconsider your decision. You have edited the paper ably from the outset, have given it the right tone, at the same time developing the humorous side it needed. Erudition in a newspaper editor is far less important than the ability speedily to interpret things from the aspect that matters, and

---

[a] Marx's jocular nickname.-[b] Written in large block letters at the beginning of the letter-[c] *Der Sozialdemokrat*

this you have nearly always done. Kautsky, for example, would never be able to do that; he always has too many secondary viewpoints, which is perfectly all right for longish articles in a *revue*, but in the case of a paper, where rapid decisions are called for, frequently makes it impossible to see the wood for the trees, and that mustn't happen in a party organ. Alongside you, Kautsky would be quite all right, but on his own he would, I'm afraid, be all too often prevented by qualms of conscience over theory from following up a crucial advantage as unswervingly as is required by the *Sozialdemokrat*. I don't see who could take your place at this juncture, so long as Liebknecht remains in jail [142] and doesn't go to Zurich, which would be senseless except in an emergency, since there's much more need of him in the Reichstag. So you'll have to stay on after all whether you like it or not.

If we have not yet come forward directly and *by name* in the *Sozialdemokrat*, the fault, I do assure you, does not lie with your editorship of this paper up till now. On the contrary. It lies with the very statements made in *Germany* I alluded to at the beginning. Admittedly, we have been promised that this won't recur and that the revolutionary nature of the party is to be plainly spelled out and adhered to. But we should like to see evidence of it first, nor do we have any great confidence (rather the reverse) in the revolutionary bent of certain of these gentlemen, and that is precisely why it is most desirable that we should have the stenographic reports of the speeches made by *all* our deputies. *After* you have used them you can easily send them over here for a day or two; I guarantee their prompt return. That will help to clear away the last obstacles that still exist — through no fault of our own — between ourselves and the party in Germany. *This in confidence.*

It would seem that Gladstone has paved the way for the triumph of Most. It's hardly likely that 12 jurors will be found who will *unanimously* find Most guilty, and, if only one finds him innocent, the case will fall to the ground. Admittedly, he can be brought before another jury, but this hardly ever happens. On top of that, however, the 1861 Act, [143] under which Most is being charged, has never been applied before and by and large it is the opinion of jurists that the wording is inapplicable to the case.

Argyll's resignation from the Ministry because the Irish LAND BILL [124] confers on tenants a measure of co-ownership of the land is an ill omen for the fate of the BILL in the Upper House. Meanwhile Parnell has made a successful start in Manchester to his *English* agitational tour. The position of the grand liberal coalition is becoming ever more critical. But then over here everything moves slowly, if the more surely for that.

So don't be deterred by the initial difficulties; don't lose heart but carry on editing just as before. If the worst comes to the worst, you could write to Leipzig and ask them to send you an assistant. That would probably be the best way of overcoming the difficulties you have to contend with. Then, when you have taught the new man the ropes, there will still be time enough to talk of resigning.

Kindest regards.

Yours

F. Engels

First published, in Russian, in *Marx-Engels Archives*, Book I, Moscow, 1924

Printed according to the original

Published in English in full for the first time

53

ENGELS TO AUGUST BEBEL

IN LEIPZIG

London, 28 April 1881

Dear Bebel,

In response to your inquiry I asked my source (a stockbroker) whether the person concerned would do better to continue paying the GREAT BRITAIN MUTUAL & Co. (Office 101, Cheapside, it's the same surely? GREAT BRITAIN MUTUAL INSURANCE?) or to stop payment of the calls, and received the reply:

* 'We fear there is no alternative but to keep on paying the calls as they are made.' *[a]

Ede [b] has sent us the stenographic reports of the Reichstag debates on the state of siege and the Accident Insurance Bill. [144] We congra-

---

[a] Engels supplies this English text in parentheses after the German translation of this sentence.- [b] Eduard Bernstein

tulate you on both your speeches. The one on the Accident Bill pleased us particularly. It strikes the right note—high-minded, yet based on a real knowledge of the facts, and ironically superior. Your criticism of the Bill was all that could have been said or desired. I have been expressly asked to tell you all this on Marx's behalf as well as my own. It was the best speech of yours we have ever read, and the debate gave one the impression that the turner, Bebel, was the only educated man in the whole of the Reichstag.

At the 2nd reading you might possibly include the following: You might perhaps ask us, gentlemen, how we can prevail upon our consciences to grant *money* to this government, even though it be for the relief of workers who have met with an accident? Gentlemen, after what the Prussian Landtag and you yourselves have done in the matter of subventions, the power of the Reichstag in financial affairs, its ability to wring concessions from the government by virtue of the fact that it holds the purse-strings, has gone by the board. The Reichstag and Landtag have thrown away their entire budgetary authority with nothing to show for it in return, and here it is certainly no longer a case of a paltry million or two.—All those subventions, moreover, were for purposes of exploitation (protective tariffs, purchase of the railways at 30% above their value—Rhenish Rail were standing at less than 120, rose to 150 as a result of the government's offer to purchase, now 160!), and *this time* it is, after all, at least *supposed* to be for the workers.

For the rest, the terms of acceptance you proposed fully protect you to your rear.

But what a typically inflated, maliciously stupid, Prussian Junker-cum-bureaucrat Brother von Puttkamer is! [145]

Your
F. E.

Marx sends kindest regards.

Ede writes to say that he is staying on for the time being. [a]

First published, in Russian, in *Marx-Engels Archives*, Vol. I (VI), Moscow, 1932

Printed according to the original

Published in English for the first time

---

[a] See this volume, p. 85.

54

MARX TO JENNY LONGUET [146]

IN ARGENTEUIL

[London,] 29 April 1881
41 Maitland Park, N. W.

My dear Jenny,

I congratulate you upon the happy delivery; at least I presume that everything is right from your taking the trouble to write. My 'womankind' expected the 'newcomer' to increase 'the better half' of the population; for my own part I prefer the 'manly' sex for children born at this turning point of history. They have before them the most revolutionary period men had ever to pass through. The bad thing now is to be 'old' so as to be only able to foresee instead of seeing.

The 'newcomer'[a] steps in pretty closely to your own birthday, Johnny's, and mine. He, like ourselves, patronizes the merry month of May. I am of course charged by Mama (and Tussy, though she finds perhaps yet the time to write herself) to wish you all possible good things, but I do not see that 'wishes' are good for anything except the glossing over one's own powerlessness.

I hope by and by you will find the servants you want and get your '*ménage*'[b] into some quiet routine. I felt rather anxious about the too many troubles weighing upon you just now, at such a critical moment.

Johnny, according to your last letter, is recovering his health. He is in fact the most delicate of the three boys[c] whom I have the honour to know personally. Tell him that while walking yesterday through the park — our own Maitland Park — that glorious person, the park-keeper, suddenly approached, asked for news about Johnny, and at last communicated me the important fact that he will 'retire' from his office and make place to a younger 'force'. With him one of the pillars of the 'Lord Southampton' disappears. [147]

There is little going on in 'our circle' as Beesly daubed it. Pumps still awaits 'news' from Beust; has in the meanwhile thrown an eye

---

[a] Marcel Longuet - [b] house-keeping - [c] Jenny Longuet's sons: Jean, Henri and Edgar

upon 'Kautsky' who, however, did not yet 'declare'; and she will always feel grateful to Hirsch for having not only virtually 'declared', but, after a refusal, renewed his 'declaration', just before his trip to Paris. This Hirsch becomes more and more a nuisance. My 'opinion' of him grows less and less.

The last London craze was the Disraeli exaltation which gave John Bull the satisfaction of admiring his own magnanimity. Is it not 'grand' to act the sycophant with regard to a dead man whom just before his kicking the bucket you had saluted with rotten apples and foul eggs? At the same time this teaches the 'lower classes' that however their 'natural superiors' may fall out amongst each other during the struggle for 'place and pelf', death brings out the truth that the leaders of the 'ruling classes' are always 'great and good men'.

It is a very fine trick of Gladstone — only the 'stupid party' does not understand it — to offer at a moment when landed property in Ireland (as in England) will be depreciated by the import of corn and cattle from the United States — to offer them at that very moment the public Exchequer where they can sell that property at a price it does no longer possess! [148]

The real intricacies of the Irish land problem — which indeed are not especially Irish — are so great that the only true way to solve it would be to give the Irish Home-rule and thus force them to solve it themselves. But John Bull is too stupid to understand this.

Engels comes just, sends you his best compliments, and as it is almost post-time, so that I cannot afterwards finish this letter, I must abruptly end it.

With my compliments to Johnny, Harry and the 'good' Wolf[a] (who is indeed an excellent boy) and also to father Longuet.

Yours,

Old Nick

First published, in Russian, in the magazine *Nachalo*, No. 5, St Petersburg, 1899

Reproduced from the original

Published in English in full for the first time

---

[a] Edgar Longuet

55

ENGELS TO JENNY LONGUET

IN ARGENTEUIL

London, 31 May 1881
122 Regent's Park Road, N. W.

My dear Jenny,

Many thanks for your kind letter, it is really too good of you to sit down and write to us in the midst of the trouble you have to pass through. But let me at once pass to the main thing. I have every reason to hope that unless unforeseen accidents occur, you still will soon have your Mama [a] with you. Mohr told me on Sunday that the doctor [b] thinks she is getting strong enough for the journey. There are great changes in her state from time to time, sometimes she goes about in the day and even to theatres in the evening, but at other times she suffers from very bad pains and scarcely leaves her bed for a couple of days. But these attacks seem to pass off as they come and not to leave her visibly worse. Still she is upon the whole losing flesh and this seems to be the only constant symptom which if not arrested may turn out serious. What the nature of the complaint is I am totally ignorant of and am apt to conclude that the doctors are equally in the dark, anyhow they don't seem to agree at all about it. When Tussy wrote to you, your Mama was just suffering from one of these attacks, and I believe there was a slight misunderstanding about what the doctor said, namely that she was *then* temporarily not in a fit state to travel. The doctor himself wishes her very much to go, as he anticipates a good effect from the change.

Now about Mohr's Turkish baths, they need not frighten you, he is taking them merely for the sake of his rheumatically stiff leg which bothers him in walking. As to his cold, the present warm weather will soon reduce it to an infinitesimal quantity and a change to the seaside will finish it off—that is my opinion. I have just taken him up to Hampstead Heath, I hope the walk will do him good. Your Mama was out, so she cannot be so very bad just now.

I am glad that amidst all the *petites misères de la vie de campagne* [c] you still are well pleased with house, garden and climate which after all

---

[a] Jenny Marx - [b] Donkin - [c] petty inconveniences of country life

are the main thing, to the rest you will either gradually find remedies or — get used to them. My especial envy is directed of course to the wine cellar and the cellars generally for which we may sigh in vain here in London.

You must indeed have risen tremendously in the eyes of old Collett since you and Longuet have got Clemenceau round to the only 'correct' view about Tunis. [149] I can very well imagine the old man's enthusiasm at seeing the truly orthodox policy preached in a large Paris daily. Fancy the old buffer, who all his life has defended the power of the *Crown*, now talking of a saviour of the *Republic*.

We are going on here much in the usual way, excepting that we have Mrs Pauli here who brings her eldest step-daughter to Manchester where she is going to stay some time with an old friend of Pauli's. She is not quite so stout as she was but quite as lively. Last Sunday by a godsend we got some *waldmeister*, [a] and with the help of a dozen of Moselle we brewed three bowls of *Maitrank* [b] which were duly emptied by a — rather numerous — company. There were fourteen of us, and they were very jolly. Lenchen was there also and told me this morning it had not very well agreed with her: 'she never had such a *Katzenjammer* [c] in her life' (please don't let it out!). Mrs Pauli is very sorry she cannot see you here this time and wishes to be most kindly remembered to you.

Hartmann called yesterday with the news that he is off to America, it is a good thing for him, he could never settle down here properly until he got work for a short time in Siemens' electric factory in Woolwich but that is at an end now too. He talks of coming back in a few months.

Pumps is going on as usual, suffers now and then from headaches, my only complaint is an increasing left-ear deafness, I hope the summer may cure it.

Kind regards to you and Longuet. Pumps sends her love and I join her in it.

Yours affectionately,

F. Engels

First published in: Marx and Engels, *Works*, Second Russian Edition, Vol. 35, Moscow, 1964

Reproduced from the original

Published in English for the first time

---

[a] woodruff, Lat. *Asperula odorata* - [b] wine flavoured with sweet woodruff - [c] hangover

56

MARX TO JOHN SWINTON

IN NEW YORK

London, 2 June 1881
41 Maitland Park Road, N. W.

Dear Mr Swinton,

I need hardly recommend you the bearer of these lines, my excellent friend, Mr Hartmann. I send you through him a photogram of mine; it is rather bad, but the only one left to me.

As to the book of Mr Henry George,[a] I consider it as a last attempt — to save the capitalistic regime. Of course, this is not the meaning of the author, but the older disciples of Ricardo — the radical ones — fancied already that by the public appropriation of the rent of land everything would be righted. I have referred to this doctrine in the *Misère de la Philosophie* (published in 1847 against Proudhon).[b]

Mrs Marx sends you her best compliments. Unfortunately her illness assumes more and more a fatal character.

Believe me, dear Sir,

Yours most sincerely,

Karl Marx

The 'Viereck' was so stultified at his arrival in the US that he confounded my friend Engels with myself and transformed my compliments to you in those of Engels; he did the same with regard to another American friend of mine[c] by whose letter I was informed of the *quid pro quo*.

First published in *A Souvenir from Jimmie Higgins Book Shop*, New York, 1923   Reproduced from the original

---

[a] H. George, *Progress and Poverty: an inquiry into the cause of industrial depressions and of increase of want with increase of wealth. The Remedy*, New York, 1880.- [b] See present edition, Vol. 6, p. 203. - [c] G. J. Harney

57

MARX TO FRIEDRICH ADOLPH SORGE [150]

IN HOBOKEN

London, 2 June 1881

Dear Sorge,

I recommend to you most heartily the bearer of this card, my friend Hartmann.

First published in *The New-York Herald*, No. 16455, 10 September 1881

Reproduced from the newspaper

58

ENGELS TO FRIEDRICH ADOLPH SORGE

IN HOBOKEN

London, 2 June 1881

My dear Sorge,

In the person of the bearer I introduce to you our friend Leo Hartmann, of Moscow celebrity. To recommend him specially to your attention could be superfluous. If during his stay in America you can in any way be of service to him you will by that render a service to the common cause and a personal favor to Marx and myself.

Yours truly,
Fr. Engels

First published in *The New-York Herald*, No. 16455, 10 September 1881

Reproduced from the newspaper

59

MARX TO JENNY LONGUET

IN ARGENTEUIL

[London,] 6 June 1881

My dearest Don Quixote,

I am really wrong to have not written before this, but you know my good intentions and weak doings in this line. There passes, however, no day, when my thoughts are not with you and the lovely children. [a] As to my health you need not trouble you[rself]; I had a nasty cold, almost as sempiternal as was the *Stockschnupfen* [b] of Seguin *selig* [c] — but it is now rapidly passing away.

As to Möhmchen, you are aware that there is no cure of the illness she suffers from, and she gets indeed weaker. Fortunately the pains are not such as they mostly are in such cases, the best proof of which is that she attends still several times during the week at London theatres. She keeps in fact wonderfully up, but travelling to Paris is quite out of the question. I consider it a most happy event that Lina Schoeler surprised us yesterday and is to stay about a month.

Has Johnny got Reineke or rather Renard the Fox[d] I sent him? and has the poor fellow somebody to read it for him?

To-day (Bank Holiday) [151] and yesterday infernal rainy and cold weather, one of the bad tricks the celestial father has always in store for his London plebeian cattle and sheep. Yesterday he spoiled by the rain the Hyde Park Demonstration of Parnell's. [152]

Hartmann has on Friday last left for New York and I am glad that he is out of harm's way. But foolishly, a few days before his departure, he *asked the hand of Pumps from Engels* — and this by writing, telling him at the same time that he believed he committed no mistake in doing so, *alias*, he (Hartmann) believed in his (Hartmann's) acceptance on the part of Pumps — the which girl had indeed rather hardly flirted with him, but only to stir Kautsky. I learn now from Tussy that the same Hartmann had offered himself to her before her voyage to Jersey. But the present case is the worse as the distinguished

---

[a] Jean, Henri, Edgar and Marcel - [b] chronic cold in the nose - [c] the late - [d] J. W. v. Goethe, *Reineke Fuchs*.

Perovskaya, the victim of the Russian movement, had lived with Hartmann in 'free' marriage. And she has hardly died on the gallows. [153] From Perovskaya to Pumps — rather too bad this, and Mama is quite disgusted with it and the whole male sex! Longuet's article on Ireland was good. We all thought there had something happened seeing that for some time he seemed more and more to disappear from the columns of the *Justice*. Have you seen or heard anything of the illustrious Hirsch? He sent me today two New York papers.

There is only one news worth reporting. A Yankee [a] is said to have invented a coal-cutting machine which would do away with the greatest part of the present labour of the colliers — viz. the 'hewing' of coal in the coal-measures and mines, leaving to the miners only the task of *breaking* the cut of coal and loading it into trucks. If this invention prove successful — as there is every reason to believe — it will give an immense stir in Yankeeland and do great damage to John Bull's industrial supremacy.

Mama also asks me to tell you that the pretext for Lina's [Schoeler] presence is the wedding of Lisa Green, daughter of the [b] successful admirer of Martin Tupper.

Laura does everything to amuse and cheer Möhmchen.

Helen [c] sends you her love.

And now kiss many many times for me Johnny, Harra and the noble Wolf [d]. As to the 'great unknown' one, [e] I dare not make so free with him.

How is your asthma? Does it still cling to you? I hardly understand how you manage to get breathing time with 4 children and only nominal servants.

Farewell, my dear child,

Old Nick

First published, in Russian, in the magazine *Nachalo*, No. 5, St Petersburg, 1899

Reproduced from the original

Published in English for the first time

---

[a] Jeffrey - [b] This part of the sentence is in German in the original.- [c] Demuth - [d] Edgar Longuet - [e] Marcel Longuet

60

ENGELS TO JENNY LONGUET

IN ARGENTEUIL

London, 17 June 1881
122 Regent's Park Road, N. W.

My dear Jenny,

I hasten to reply to your letter of the 15th received this morning only. When I wrote to you last, [a] the doctor [b] *insisted* upon your Mama going to Paris and it was herself who resisted, saying she did not feel strong enough for the journey. A few days later the doctor found that she had indeed become so much weaker that he could no longer advise her to go to Paris. She is indeed getting extremely thin and emaciated and complained to me today a great deal about increasing weakness, especially when dressing, she has begun to stay the greater part of the day in bed and the doctor made her get up and go out for a walk while I was there. He has now told Mohr that the best thing to do is for *both of them* to go to Eastbourne, and that at once. We tried to persuade her, but of course she offered all kinds of resistance: now she ought to go to Paris if anywhere, and so forth, so we told her that a fortnight's stay at Eastbourne would perhaps restore her forces sufficiently to enable her to go to Paris afterwards, etc., etc. I left them at it, and you will probably hear the result in a day or two from Tussy who said she would write to you soon.

Whatever the nature of the complaint may be, this constant and increasing loss of flesh and strength seems a very serious feature, especially as it does not seem to come to a stop — most of the doctors said that this was not in itself a dangerous symptom unless it went beyond a certain point; that they had known cases where the weakening all of a sudden had been arrested and strength recovered. I hope the seaside will have that effect, if we only had her there already.

To Mohr the change will be equally favourable, he wants a bit of bracing up too, his cough is not so bad at nights and he sleeps better, that is one thing.

---

[a] See this volume, pp. 91-92. - [b] Donkin

A very great piece of good luck has been the arrival of Lina Schoeler who is now staying at your house, as lively and good-natured as ever, and a good deal more deaf. Her presence cheers your Mama up a good deal, I hope she will stay for some time.

Sam Moore has passed his final examination as Barrister successfully last week.

I hear from Tussy that you have got a fresh servant and that she seems to suit you, so your household troubles bid fair to diminish too.

I close this letter so as to send it by early mail in the morning, hoping thus it may reach you to-morrow night. Miss Parnell's letter I shall return in a few days. Kind regards to Longuet and Johnny from yours affectionately

F. Engels

First published in: Marx and Engels, *Works*, Second Russian Edition, Vol. 35, Moscow, 1964

Reproduced from the original

Published in English for the first time

61

MARX TO FRIEDRICH ADOLPH SORGE [154]

IN HOBOKEN

[London,] 20 June 1881

Dear Sorge,

Today I had broken off some other work I was doing, meaning to embark at long last on a lengthy letter to you and now, as ill luck would have it, I've had one visitor after another and thus hardly have time enough left to drop you a few lines before the post goes. Hence a *brief* survey.

Your son [a] pleases everyone he meets here. Since I have been suffering continuously for 6 months and more from a cough, cold, sore throat and rheumatism, which only seldom permit me to go out and keep me out of society, he and I have an hour or so of private conver-

---

[a] Adolph Sorge

sation ABOUT ONCE A WEEK and I find that he has, *au fond*,[a] absorbed rather more of our views than would appear. He is an altogether capable, decent lad with, moreover, cultivated manners and a pleasant temperament. He is, besides, and that is all-important, FULL OF ENERGY. My last visitors, only just gone, were Viereck and his newly married wife, also née Viereck.[b] I had not seen the gentleman since he came back from America.[119] A few days ago he sent Kautsky to see me with sundry scraps of paper for me to *sign* (one written by Liebknecht and also signed by him in his own and Bebel's names). All of them related to certain agreements respecting the Lingenau legacy[45] negotiated by Viereck with the '*New Yorker Volkszeitung*' *et cie*. I *refused to sign* since, in this matter, I am obliged, as I explained, to deal only with our chief executor, Sorge. At the same time I gave Viereck to understand that, in my view, the first thing to be done was to pay you the 120 dollars for the lawyer in St Louis out of what still remained of the American fund in New York. Viereck now tells me today that — upon my accepting responsibility vis-à-vis the Leipzigers — he at once sent off instructions to that effect to New York. He arrived IN THE NICK OF TIME, for otherwise a *formal protest* would have gone off from me to Leipzig tomorrow, a protest against the *modus operandi*[c] of the Leipzig party leaders who had hitherto conducted themselves in this matter as if the decision rested *solely with them*.

Now, *post festum*,[d] Viereck has mentioned your claim in respect of an advance of 80 dollars. I told him that, after the court decision, should this be unfavourable, we, the executors, would indemnify you, as we damned well ought.

Before getting your copy of Henry George,[e] I had already had 2 others, one from Swinton and one from Willard Brown. I therefore gave one to Engels and one to Lafargue. Today I shall have to confine myself to a very brief assessment of the book. Theoretically, the man is totally *arrière*.[f] He has understood nothing of the nature of *surplus value* and hence, after the English pattern, but lagging far behind the English, he loses himself in speculations about those portions of surplus value that have become independent — about the relations between profit, rent, interest, etc. His basic tenet is that *everything* would be *in order* were rent to be paid to the State. (You will also find payment of this kind among the transitional measures in the *Commu-*

---

[a] basically -[b] Laura Viereck -[c] way of going about things -[d] after the event -[e] See this volume, p. 93.-[f] stick-in-the-mud

nist Manifesto. [a]) This view owes its origin to the bourgeois economists; it was first advanced (if we disregard a similar postulate in the late 18th century) by the earliest *radical* disciples of Ricardo immediately after the latter's death. In 1847, in my anti-Proudhon book, I commented on it thus: '*Nous concevons que des économistes, tels que Mill'* (senior, not his son John Stuart who repeats the same thing in somewhat modified form), '*Cherbuliez, Hilditch et autres, ont demandé que la rente soit attribuée à l'État pour servir à l'acquittement des impôts. C'est la franche expression de la haine que le* capitaliste industriel *voue au* propriétaire foncier, *qui lui parait une inutilité, une superfétation, dans l'ensemble de la production bourgeoise.'* [b]

As already mentioned, we ourselves adopted the appropriation of rent by the State amongst many other *transitional measures* which, as is likewise indicated in the *Manifesto*, are and cannot but be contradictory in themselves.

But making a *socialist* PANACEA of this desideratum of the English *radical* bourgeois economists, declaring this procedure to be a solution of the antagonisms inherent in today's mode of production — this was the prerogative of *Colins*, a native of Belgium and on old, retired officer of Napoleon's Hussars who, in the latter days of Guizot and the early ones of *Napoleon le petit*, [155] sent out into the world from Paris bulky volumes on the subject of this, his 'discovery', [c] likewise making the further discovery that, while there is indeed no God, there is an '*immortal*' human soul, and that animals have 'no sensitivity'. For had they any sensitivity, i. e. soul, we would be cannibals and a kingdom of righteousness could never be set up on this earth. His 'anti-landed property theory', along with his soul, etc., theory, has for years been advocated month after month in the Paris journal *Philosophie de l'Avenir* by his few remaining disciples, mostly Belgians. They call themselves '*collectivistes rationnels*' and have applauded Henry George.

In the same vein as them, and at much the same time, one Samter, amongst others, a shallow-pated Prussian banker and lottery collec-

---

[a] See present edition, Vol. 6, p. 505.- [b] 'We understand such economists as Mill, Cherbuliez, Hilditch and others demanding that rent should be handed over to the State to serve in place of taxes. That is the frank expression of the hatred the *industrial capitalist* bears towards the *landed proprietor*, who seems to him a useless thing, an excrescence upon the general body of bourgeois production.' See K. Marx, *The Poverty of Philosophy*, present edition, Vol. 6, p. 203. - [c] J. G. Colins, *L'économie politique. Source des révolutions et des utopies prétendues socialistes*, vols I-III, Paris, 1856-57.

tor from East Prussia, distended this 'socialism' to fill a hefty tome.[a]
All these 'socialists' since Colins have this in common — they allow
wage labour and hence also *capitalist production* to subsist, while endeavouring to delude themselves and the world into believing that
the transformation of rent into taxation paid to the State must bring
about the automatic disappearance of *all the abuses* of capitalist production. So the whole thing is merely an attempt, tricked out with socialism, to *save the capitalist régime* and, indeed, to *re-establish it on an even
broader basis* than at present.

Again, this cloven hoof, which is at the same time an ass's hoof, is
unmistakably in evidence in the declamations of Henry George. It is
all the more inexcusable in his case in that he ought, on the contrary,
to have asked himself the question: How comes it that in the United
States, where the land was relatively — i. e. by comparison with civilised Europe — accessible to the great mass of the people and TO A CER-
TAIN DEGREE (again relative) still is, the capitalist economy and the corresponding enslavement of the working class have developed more *rapidly* and *brazenly* than in any other country?

On the other hand, George's book, like the sensation it created in
your midst, is significant in being a first, if unsuccessful, attempt at
emancipation from orthodox political economy.

H. George, by the by, seems to know nothing of the history of the
earlier *American Anti-Renters* [156] who were men of practice rather
than theory. In other respects he is a talented writer (talented, too, in
the matter of boosting the Yankees), as is shown by, e. g., his article
on California in the *Atlantic*. [157] He also has the revolting presump-
tiousness and arrogance that is the unmistakable hallmark of all such
Panacea-mongers.

Between ourselves, my wife's illness is, alas, incurable. In a few
days' time I shall be taking her to the seaside at Eastbourne.
Salut fraternel.[b]

Your

K. Marx

First published abridged in *Die Neue Zeit*,
Bd. 2, Nr. 33, 1891-92 and in full in the
book *Briefe und Auszüge aus Briefen von Joh.
Phil. Becker, Jos. Dietzgen, Friedrich Engels,
Karl Marx u. A. an F. A. Sorge und Andere*,
Stuttgart, 1906

Printed according to the original

Published in English in full for the
first time

---

[a] A. Samter, *Social-Lehre. Ueber die Befriedigung der Bedürfnisse in der menschlichen
Gesellschaft*, Leipzig, 1875. -[b] Fraternal greetings.

62

MARX TO HENRY MAYERS HYNDMAN

IN LONDON

[Draft]

Eastbourne, Sussex, 2 July 1881
43 Terminus Road

My dear Sir,

The state of Mrs Marx's health which becomes daily more critical and demands my continual attendance upon her, will account for my belated reply to your letter d. d. June 5.

I confess to some astonishment at the discovery that, during your stay at London, you should have so closely kept the secret of your plan, then matured and executed, to publish, with certain modifications, the rejected article of *The Nineteenth Century* as chapters II and III of *England for All*, that is to say of your *comments on the Federation's Foundation Program*. [158]

In your letter which does not at all refer to the surprise thus kept in store for me, you say:

'If you think I ought to acknowledge your book by your name, etc.'

That question, it seems to me, ought to have preceded your publication instead of coming behind it.

You favour me with two reasons for freely using the *Capital*, a work not yet Englished, without mentioning the book itself or its author.

One reason is, that 'many (Englishmen) have an horror of Socialism and that name'. Was it with a view to assuage this 'horror' that you evoked [on] p. 86 '*the demon of Socialism*'?

Your second and last reason is, that '*the* Englishmen have a dread of being taught by a foreigner'!

I have not found it so during the times of the 'International', nor of Chartism. [159] But let that pass. If this dread of 'the' Englishmen frightened you, why tell them in the preface p. VI that the 'ideas' etc. of chapters II and III, whatever else they may be, bear at all events the stigma of being no home-make? The Englishmen you have to deal with can hardly be so dense as to fancy that the above-said passage points to an — *English* author.

Apart, however, from your rather humorous reasons, I am decidedly of opinion that to have named the *Capital* and its author, would have been a big blunder. Party programs ought to keep free of any apparent dependence upon individual authors or books. But allow me to add that they are also no proper place for new scientific developments, such as those borrowed by you from the *Capital*, and that the latter are altogether out of place in a commentary on a Program with whose professed aims they are not at all connected. Their introduction might have had some fitness in the *Exposé* of a Program for the foundation of a distinct and independent Working Class Party.

You are good enough to inform me that your brochure 'though marked "price half-a crown" is not published', but 'merely' to be 'distributed to members of the Democratic Federation, etc.' I am quite sure that this was your intention, but I know that it is not opinion of your printer. A friend of mine saw your brochure in my study, wanted it, copied its title and place of printing, ordered it through his booksellers Williams and Norgate on the 13th of June and got it by them with their account note d. d. 14th June.

And this brings me to the only point of practical import. In case the public press should pounce upon your brochure, I might be obliged to speak, considering that chapters II and III consist in part of passages simply translated from the *Capital*, but separated by no marks of quotation from a remainder, much of which is not exact or even implies misunderstandings.

I have written with that full frankness which I consider the first condition of friendly intercourse.

Best compliments of Mrs Marx and myself to Mrs Hyndman.

Yours very truly,
K. M.

First published, in the language of the original (English), in *Annali*, an. III, Milano, 1960

Reproduced from the original

63

ENGELS TO MARX

IN EASTBOURNE [160]

[London,] 7 July 1881
122 Regent's Park Road, N. W.

Dear Moor,

In my last letter I quite forgot to mention money; owing to Schorlemmer's presence I have been somewhat restricted in my movements. You can now have £100 à £120, and it's simply a question of whether you want it all at one go and how much is to be sent there and how much is for here. When you get this letter, make up your mind *straight away* so that I get your answer by *tomorrow*. For Schorlemmer and Pumps are going to the theatre tomorrow evening, while I shall remain at home. I can then at once make out a CHEQUE in favour of Lenchen and take it to her. You or your wife can of course decide what is to be done with the money.

Tussy and Dolly Maitland acted very well; the girl showed a great deal of SELF POSSESSION and looked quite charming on the stage. Tussy was very good in the emotional scenes, though it was somewhat apparent that she had taken Ellen Terry for her model, as Radford had Irving, but she'll soon wean herself from that; if she really wants to make her mark in public she must unquestionably STRIKE OUT A LINE OF HER OWN, and she'll do that all right.

I hear that the sea air has not yet had the desired effect on your wife; that often happens in the early days; it may, and I trust will, come later.

Pumps is going to Manchester with Schorlemmer on Monday[a] to bring back little Lydia; I hear you have written to Tussy asking her to join you. I may perhaps come later when Pumps is back. We shall probably be going to Bridlington Quay [161] shortly and then to Jersey with Schorlemmer when he returns from Germany; at any rate that's what we've planned to date.

Best wishes from us all to your wife and yourself.

Your
F. E.

First published in *Der Briefwechsel zwischen F. Engels und K. Marx*, Bd. 4, Stuttgart, 1913

Printed according to the original

Published in English for the first time

___

[a] 11 July

64

ENGELS TO NORRIS A. CLOWES

IN NEW YORK

[Draft]

London, 22 July 1881
122 Regent's Park Road, N. W.

Norris A. Clowes Esq. [162]

Dear Sir,

I am sorry my time will not allow me to write to you the statement you desire.[a] However, if you wish to make yourself acquainted with the present state of the Labour Movement in Great Britain, you will find the necessary information in the weekly *Labour Standard* published at 2 Whitefriars St. of which twelve numbers have up to now been issued. Most of the non-signed leaders are written by me. [163]

If you wish to enter into communication with Mr Most, you had better write to the Editor of the *Freiheit*,[b] 252 Tottenham Court Road, W., London, who will be able to tell you whether such communication will be possible under present circumstances.

I shall be glad to see you in case you should come to London.

I remain
Yours very truly,
F. E.

First published in: Marx and Engels, *Works*, First Russian Edition, Vol. XXVII, Moscow, 1935

Reproduced from the original

Published in English for the first time

---

[a] In the manuscript the following passage is crossed out here: 'as it would require entering into the history of the British working class and its action since at least 1824, if not since the industrial revolution caused by steam, and to that my time will not allow'.-[b] Karl Schneidt

65

MARX TO JENNY LONGUET

IN ARGENTEUIL

[London,] 22 July 1881

*My dear Jenny,

The doctor[a] has just left Mama, and we shall start on Tuesday or Wednesday next. You will be informed by telegram of the exact day.

Please *write at once*, because Mama will not get away from London before you have written her which things from London may be required by you. You know she is fond of that sort of commission-business.*

I enclose £5, since you will have to pay cash for the hire of bed-linen etc.; the remainder will be paid when I arrive. Only on these terms will I agree to the arrangement you have suggested.

As *to the story Hirsch has told you with respect to Lafargue, it is a mere *lie*. Lafargue, as I was sure from the beginning, has never written anything of the sort to his Paris correspondents.

Adio, dear child, with 1000nd kisses to the children

Old Nick*

First published, in Russian, in the magazine *Nachalo*, No. 5, St Petersburg, 1899

Printed according to the original

Published in English for the first time

---

[a] Donkin

66

MARX TO ENGELS [72]

IN LONDON

Argenteuil [164], 27 July 1881
11 Boulevard Thiers

Dear Engels,

I can't write at any greater length today as I have a mass of letters to get off and on this, our first day, the little ones[a] have rightly laid claim to me.

The journey from London to Dover went off as well as could be expected, i. e. my wife, who was most unwell when we set out from Maitland Park, did not notice any change for the worse as a result of the journey. On the boat she at once went to the ladies' cabin where she found an excellent sofa to lie on. The sea was quite calm and the weather couldn't have been finer. She landed in Calais in better shape than when she had left London and decided to carry on. The only stations where our TICKETS allowed us to break the journey to Paris were Calais and Amiens. She thought the latter place (ABOUT 2 HOURS' journey from Paris) too close to stop at. Between Amiens and Creil she felt diarrhoea coming on, and the griping pains also grew more violent. At Creil the train stopped for only 3 minutes, but she had just enough time to do what was necessary. In Paris, where we arrived at 7.30 in the evening, we were met at the station by Longuet. However the direct train from this station to Argenteuil left too late for us to wait for it. So, after the *douaniers*[b] had examined our trunks, by CAB to St Lazare station and from there, after waiting some while, by RAILWAY to our destination which we did not reach, however, until ABOUT 10 O'CLOCK. She was in very poor shape, but this morning (at any rate now, ABOUT 10 O'CLOCK) feels better than she used to do in London at a similar hour. At all events, the return journey will be made in much easier stages.

Longuet is introducing me to his doctor[c] today, so that we can act immediately in the event of the diarrhoea recurring.

---

[a] Marx's grandsons: Jean, Henri, Edgar and Marcel Longuet - [b] customs officers - [c] Dourlen

We found everyone well here, except that Johnny and Harry had slight colds as a result of the change of temperature (all the children, especially Johnny, had been affected by the days of extreme heat). As a *summer residence* the house is first-class, must obviously have once served as such for a *richard*.[a]

WITH BEST COMPLIMENTS TO Pumps.

Your
Moor

It would seem that Tussy has written to her correspondent over there[b] telling him of my arrival and hence, or so Longuet tells me, this is already an open secret. The 'anarchists', he says, will impute to me the malicious intention of swinging the vote.[165] Clemenceau told him that I had absolutely nothing to fear from the police.

First published abridged in *Der Briefwechsel zwischen F. Engels und K. Marx*, Bd. 4, Stuttgart, 1913 and in full in *MEGA*, Abt. III, Bd. 4, Berlin, 1931

Printed according to the original

67

ENGELS TO MARX

IN ARGENTEUIL

Bridlington Quay, Yorkshire
29 July 1881
1 Sea View

Dear Moor,

I got your letter[c] yesterday morning before we left[161] and was very glad to hear that you did, after all, have a reasonably good journey. But you are right in proposing to break the return journey; it's far too risky, letting such an invalid remain on the go for 12 hours.

---

[a] very rich man - [b] Carl Hirsch - [c] See previous letter.

I only hope that the change of air and scene doesn't fail to produce the desired effect.

We left at 10.30 and arrived here at 5.5, minus my trunk, which had gone astray, but turned up before evening. After perhaps a quarter of an hour's search we found lodgings that were first-rate and not too dear (2 doors away from last year's, but a great improvement in every way). We had some rain yesterday, but today it seems to be slowly clearing up. The day before yesterday, by way of insuring myself against rainy weather such as we have again become familiar with lately in London, I went to fetch the Skaldin and the first two volumes of Maurer's *Fronhöfe* [a] from Tussy.

Our present plan is to remain here for 3 weeks or, perhaps, 4, depending on the weather and other circumstances. I have got some CHEQUES with me, so if you need anything, don't hesitate to let me know roughly how much you want. Your wife must not and shall not want for anything; if there's something she would like to have or something you know would give her pleasure, then have it she must.

Tussy dropped in to see us the day before yesterday, so I accompanied her home to fetch the books and drink the inevitable glass of Pilsener with her. Here one can pretty well do without German beer, for the BITTER ALE in the little café on the pier is excellent, and has a head on it like German beer.

Write again soon and tell me how things are.

Warm regards from all of us to your wife and Jenny. Pumps sends her special love to Johnny, as do I. Our regards, too, to Longuet.

Your

F. E.

First published abridged in *Der Briefwechsel zwischen F. Engels und K. Marx*, Bd. 4, Stuttgart, 1913 and in full in *MEGA*, Abt. III, Bd. 4, Berlin, 1931

Printed according to the original

Published in English for the first time

---

[a] [Skaldin] Скалдинъ, *Въ захолустьи и въ столицѣ*, Санкт-Петербургъ, 1870 and G. L. Maurer, *Geschichte der Fronhöfe, der Bauernhöfe und der Hofverfassung in Deutschland*, vols I-II, Erlangen, 1862.

68

MARX TO ENGELS [166]

AT BRIDLINGTON QUAY

Argenteuil, 3 August 1881
11 Boulevard Thiers

DEAR FRED,

Drawing so heavily on your EXCHEQUER is a great embarrassment to me, but the anarchy which has wrought havoc with the housekeeping over the past 2 years and given rise to all sorts of arrears has been oppressing me for some considerable time. On the 15th of this month I have £30 to pay in London, and this has been a weight on my mind since the day we left.

When we shall return is far from clear. Every day we experience the same ups and downs here as we did in Eastbourne, [160] only with the difference — as for instance yesterday — that there are sudden and frightful bouts of pain. Our Dr Dourlen, who is an excellent doctor and fortunately lives quite close by, immediately intervened and used one of the powerful opiates which Donkin had been deliberately keeping up his sleeve. After that she[a] had a good night and today feels so well that she got up for once as early as 11 o'clock and is finding distraction in the company of Jenny and the children.[b] (The diarrhoea was STOPPED on the 2nd day after our arrival. From the start Dourlen had said that if it was merely an ACCIDENT, it didn't matter; but it might also be a symptom of an actual intestinal infection. Fortunately this was not the case, therefore.)

The temporary 'improvements' do not, of course, inhibit the natural course of the disease, but they delude my wife and fortify Jenny — despite my objurgations — in the belief that our stay in Argenteuil should last as long as possible. I know better how things stand, and my anxiety is all the greater for that. Last night, IN FACT, was the first occasion on which I had anything like a decent sleep. My thoughts, they are so dull and dead as turned a mill-wheel in my head.[c] And this is why I have so far remained exclusively in Argenteuil, neither

---

[a] Mrs Marx - [b] Jenny Longuet and her sons Jean, Henri, Edgar and Marcel - [c] A paraphrase from Goethe's *Faust* (Der Tragödie Erster Teil, 'Studierzimmer').

visiting Paris nor writing so much as a line to anybody there encouraging them to come and visit me. Longuet has already heard Hirsch,[a] in the office of *La Justice*, express legitimate surprise at this 'abstention'.

And, INTO THE BARGAIN, a Kotzebue-like drama has been played out here during the past 5 days.

Jenny had, for cook, A VERY LIVELY YOUNG GIRL FROM THE COUNTRY with whom she was satisfied in every respect, since she also behaved most amiably towards the children. Her only testimonial from her last MIS-TRESS, wife of Dr Reynaud (another Argenteuil doctor), was a 'negative' one to the effect that she had quitted her service *voluntarily*. Old MOTHER Longuet who, so far as she is able, exercises a dictatorship over Jenny, was by no means satisfied with this, nor could she think of anything better to do than to go and write, off her own bat, to Madame Reynaud.

Madame Reynaud is a pretty coquette and her husband a dissolute jackass; hence things happen in this couple's house that are much gossiped about in Argenteuil. *They didn't know that their former maid had again taken service in the same locality*, and with none other than Mr Longuet, an intimate friend of Dr Dourlen's whose wife was an intimate enemy of Madame Reynaud's! THIS WAS TO BE LOOKED AFTER.

So one fine morning along comes Madame Reynaud—not, hitherto, personally acquainted with Jennychen—, tells the latter that the girl had had improper affairs with men (*et Madame?*) and, what is worse, is a thief having, *dans l'espèce*,[b] stolen a gold ring of hers; she assures Jenny that she means to settle the matter *en famille*,[c] without appealing to the '*autorités*' etc. Well and good, Jennychen SUMMONS THE GIRL, Madame Reynaud chats with and AT THE SAME TIME threatens her, the girl confesses, returns the ring—whereat Dr Reynaud denounces the unfortunate creature to the *juge de paix*.[d] UPSHOT: yesterday she was brought before the *juge d'instruction*[e] at Versailles. As you know, the *Code*,[167] being a relic of Roman Law whereby *familia = servi*,[f] refers to Assizes petty crimes which would ordinarily come before a police court.

In the meantime Jenny had made every imaginable representation to the *juge de paix*, an excellent man, but the matter had ceased to rest

---

[a] Carl Hirsch - [b] Here: in this particular case.- [c] Here: in private.- [d] police court magistrate - [e] examining magistrate - [f] slaves

with him the moment he had been officially notified of it. Nevertheless, Jenny's statements, which he wrote down, and *la* Reynaud's extra-judicial procedure, which she also placed on record, will be of some benefit to the girl.

Jenny's defence of the girl surprised the *juge de paix*, but he took it all in a very light vein. *Mais vous ne voulez pas défendre le vol?* he asked her.— *Mais non, Monsieur, commencez par arrêter tous les grands voleurs d'Argenteuil, et de Paris par dessus le marché!* [a]

The immediate upshot is that she has no cook. The stupid GIRL from London — sister of our one-time Carry — IS GOOD FOR NOTHING IN THAT LINE and in any case has her hands full with the 4 children.

Apropos. Nordau — who is taking Hirsch's place on the *Vossische Zeitung* — was awarded a French order! Whereupon Hirsch denounced him to *La Justice*! The latter attacked the government for decorating such a traducer of France (he is a German-Hungarian Jew who attacked Tissot on Bismarck's behalf in his *le vrai pays des milliards* [168]), likewise Bleichröder who wished to encumber *la belle France* with indemnities of 10 rather than 5 milliards. [169]

That jackass Nordau, presently in Paris, replied to *La Justice*, in a letter in which he made himself out to be the CHAMPION of France. Whereupon he was unmasked in *La Justice* and, the day after, in *La République française*.

Salut.

Your
Moor

First published abridged in *Der Briefwechsel zwischen F. Engels und K. Marx*, Bd. 4, Stuttgart, 1913 and in full in *MEGA*, Abt. III, Bd. 4, Berlin, 1931

Printed according to the original

Published in English in full for the first time

---

[a] You're not proposing to stand up for theft? — No, monsieur, but start off by arresting all the big thieves of Argenteuil, not to mention those of Paris.

69

ENGELS TO MARX

IN ARGENTEUIL

Bridlington Quay, Yorkshire
6 August 1881
1 Sea View

Dear Moor,

Your letter arrived on the evening of the day before yesterday, to all intents open, thanks to the envelope. A trip to Flamborough Head had been arranged for yesterday, so I haven't got round to replying to you until today.

As regards the paltry £30, don't let it give you any grey hairs. Unless I hear to the contrary I shall send off *in plenty of time* a CHEQUE for that amount to Tussy whom you will be instructing. Should you need *more*, however, let me know and I shall make the CHEQUE larger. For I only brought a few CHEQUE forms with me and have to be economical with them.

Very many thanks for the news of the patient.[a] If I were you, I would stick as closely as possible to the period laid down by Donkin; I'm sure the local doctor[b] will also back you up there. Should the bouts of pain grow more frequent, they might well occur while you were en route and that could land you in a very serious predicament.

The business with the maid is at any rate funnier for us than for poor Jennychen. How fortunate that she should at least have Lenchen there just now. It is impossible to know which of the two French *bourgeoises* is the more admirable, old Mother Longuet who, on the pretext of finding Jennychen virtuous maids, sees to it that she is perpetually maidless, or the good doctor's wife[c] who gives her word (without which she would never have got her ring back) only to break it in the interests of public morality as soon as the ring is returned to her.

Up here everything follows its usual somewhat dreary SEASIDE course, except that I've unfortunately had to give up bathing, as it

_____

[a] Mrs Marx - [b] Dourlen - [c] Madame Reynaud

was making me deafer and deafer. I find this most disagreeable, but there's nothing else for it if I'm not prematurely to go about Allsop-fashion. I am writing to Laura today, inviting her to spend some time here; she can then so arrange things that she will be back in London at the time of your return, or at any rate shortly afterwards. [170]

Enclosed a letter from Gumpert which will surprise you. I need hardly say that the person concerned is the sister, resident in Manchester, of Berta Böcker of London. [a]

The award of an order to Nordau is really incomprehensible. It was only a short while ago that I saw his vile book, *Aus dem wahren Milliardenlande*, reviewed with the utmost satisfaction in the *Kölnische Zeitung*. [b] But it agrees in one respect with Bleichröder as also with Nordau's conclusions, namely that there is still a remarkable amount to be got out of the country. Of this the starving Prussian Junkers will take mental note.

My ink is running out; there is still just enough left for Laura, so I shall close, with warm regards to you all from

Your
F. E.

You're quite right not to bother about Paris any more than you think fit, whatever Hirsch and all the rest may say.

First published abridged in *Der Briefwechsel zwischen F. Engels und K. Marx*, Bd. 4, Stuttgart, 1913 and in full in *MEGA*, Abt. III, Bd. 4, Berlin, 1931

Printed according to the original

Published in English for the first time

---

[a] See this volume, p. 117. - [b] 'Aus dem wahren Milliardenlande', *Kölnische Zeitung*, No. 189, 10 July 1881.

70

MARX TO CARL HIRSCH

IN PARIS

Argenteuil, 6 August[a] 1881
11 Boulevard Thiers

Dear Hirsch,

I have been here for nearly a fortnight [164]; haven't visited Paris or any of my acquaintances. My wife's condition has permitted neither the one nor the other.

Because of her growing weakness, it is possible that I shall have to leave much earlier than I originally planned and I therefore intend (if NO ACCIDENT INTERFERES) to come to Paris TOMORROW MORNING with Lenchen and Johnny. I shall take a cab to your house and, if your time permits, count on your accompanying us. [171]

Regards to Kaub.

Your
K. Marx

First published in: Marx and Engels, *Works*, Second Russian Edition, Vol. 50, Moscow, 1981

Printed according to the original

Published in English for the first time

71

MARX TO ENGELS

AT BRIDLINGTON QUAY

[Argenteuil,] 9 August 1881

DEAR FRED,

Have just received your letter. I am registering this one; Longuet says that, while there can be no question of Stieberian tampering

---

[a] July in the ms.

with letters, registered ones, especially at little places like Argenteuil, are handled with greater despatch.

On Satuday[a] we took my wife to Paris; she watched it go by from an open carriage, which pleased her much (on myself it made the impression of a *foire perpétuelle*[b]). A few pauses, of course, and SITTING DOWN BEFORE cafés. On the way back she felt momentarily sick, but wants to go there again.

Her condition is, as usual, sometimes too much to bear, sometimes better for hours on end. She grows steadily thinner and at the same time weaker. Yesterday there was slight cutaneous bleeding which the doctor[c] considers a symptom of debility. I told him we must seriously consider going home; he said we could wait a day or two before finally deciding. She herself, after I had spoken to her about leaving at the end of this week, played a trick on me by sending out a mass of washing which will *not be returned until the beginning of next week*. At all events I shall let you know by telegraph when we are leaving (should there not be time SIMPLY to notify you beforehand by letter). Oddly enough, though I get damned little rest at night and my days are racked with worry, everyone tells me how well I look — as is, indeed, the case.

Jennychen's asthma is bad, the house being a very draughty one. The child is heroic, as always.

On Sunday I was to show Helen[d] round Paris. I wrote and advised Hirsch[e] of it beforehand — and IN THE NICK OF TIME. He was just on the point of *leaving* for Germany (to the intense annoyance of Kaub and the chagrin of his wife). He wants to show the party leaders in Germany that there's nothing out of the way about exposing oneself to apprehension by the police. He made off yesterday.

A pleasant couple, Jaclard and his Russian wife,[f] came to *déjeuner*[g] here yesterday. Today we expect, for the same PERFORMANCE, Lissagaray and our doctor's wife (along with her sister).

From Jaclard we learned that he had attended an election meeting at Batignolles where the following put themselves up as candidates: *Henry Maret*, our *Dr Regnard* and — *Pyat*, who turned up — SELF-UNDERSTOOD *with the permission of the police* — suddenly and unexpectedly. Pyat was frightfully jeered at. When he mentioned the

---

[a] 6 August - [b] perpetual fair - [c] Dourlen - [d] Helene Demuth - [e] Carl Hirsch (see previous letter). - [f] Anna Korvin-Krukovskaya - [g] luncheon

Commune there was a general cry of '*Vous l'avez lâchée!*' ᵃ Regnard
fared no better. In order to appear paradoxical and profound, the
idiot opened with the declaration: '*Je suis contre la liberté!*' ᵇ GENERAL
HOWLING! His subsequent declaration that it was '*liberté des congréga-
tions*' ᶜ he had meant availed him nothing. The champion of anti-
clericalism ¹⁷² was a flop, likewise Henry Maret.

It may be that the extreme left will slightly increase its numbers,
but the chief upshot of this will PROBABLY be victory for Gambetta.
Things being what they are in France, the shortness of the election
period will decide the issue in favour of *faiseurs* ᵈ with numerous
'strongholds' in their possession, prospective bestowers of places in the
machinery of government, and the men who control the 'exchequer',
etc. The 'Grévystes' ᵉ could have licked Gambetta if, after the latter's
recent FAILURES, they had had the energy to throw his appendages, Cazot, Constans and Farre, out of the cabinet. Since they didn't, the
place-hunters, speculators on the Bourse, etc., etc., are saying to
themselves, 'GAMBETTA IS THE MAN!' THEY HAVE NOT DARED TO ATTACK HIM IN
HIS STRONGHOLDS, YOU CANNOT RELY UPON THEM. The general onslaughts
daily made upon him in the radical and reactionary press CONTRIBUTE
TO ENHANCE HIM DESPITE ALL HIS TOMFOOLERIES. On top of which the
peasants regard Gambetta as the *nec plus ultra* ᶠ in *possible* repub-
licanism.

At the same time as this letter, another will go off to Tussychen, telling her what to do. I shall need a little more money, since this time
the journey is going to cost a lot (the doctor thinks, moreover, that
a few days in Boulogne might do the patient good because of the
sea air), we shall have to meet a large doctor's bill and also make
some compensation to Jennychen for all the expenses we have put
her to.

So Gumpert is founding a 3rd (or is it 2nd?) family? Good luck
to him. It seems a sensible thing for a doctor to do. My wife has
heard a number of people extolling the Böcker woman of Manchester.

Salut.

                                                    Your
                                                    Moor

ᵃ You deserted it.- ᵇ I am against liberty. - ᶜ liberty of the congregation -
ᵈ humbugs - ᵉ Jules Grévy's followers - ᶠ the last word

Beesly is making ever more of an ass of himself. Weiler ought to put a stop to the glorification of Max Hirsch in *The Labour Standard.*[173]

First published abridged in *Der Briefwechsel zwischen F. Engels und K. Marx*, Bd. 4, Stuttgart, 1913 and in full in *MEGA*, Abt. III, Bd. 4, Berlin, 1931

Printed according to the original

Published in English for the first time

72

MARX TO LAURA LAFARGUE[72]

IN LONDON

[Argenteuil,] 9 August 1881

Dear Laurachen,

I can only write you a line or two as the post is about to go.

Mama is in a serious condition as a result of her growing weakness. It was therefore my intention (as we shall only be able to travel by easy stages this time) to set off at all costs at the end of the week, and I informed the patient accordingly. Yesterday, however, she thwarted my plan by sending out our washing. So there can be no question of our leaving before the beginning of next week.

We may — depending on the state she is in — stop in Boulogne *for a few days*. The doctor[a] thinks that (given favourable conditions) the sea air might momentarily have an invigorating effect.

Next time (but for this purpose you must write *at once* giving me your latest address) I shall send you a fuller report. Best wishes to Paul.[b]

Your

OLD NICK

First published in: Marx and Engels, *Works*, Second Russian Edition, Vol. 35, Moscow, 1964

Printed according to the original

---

[a] Probably Dourlen - [b] Lafargue

73

ENGELS TO GEORGE SHIPTON

IN LONDON

[Draft]

Bridlington Quay,
10 August 1881

Dear Mr Shipton,

I return the proof-sheet [174] altered as you wish. The first passage you seem to me to have misunderstood and the second alteration is merely formal.[a] Anyhow, I do not see what good such alterations can do if asked for on Tuesday, received here on Wednesday, to arrive again in London on Thursday after the publication of the paper.[b]

But there is another thing. If such *very* mild and innocent things as these begin to appear to you too strong, it must occur to me that this must be the case, in a far higher degree, with my own articles, which are generally far stronger. I must therefore take your remarks as a symptom, and conclude that it will be better for both of us if I discontinue sending you leading articles. It will be far better than going on until, upon some inevitable point, we come to an open rupture. Moreover my time will certainly not allow me to go on writing leaders regularly,[163] and on this ground alone I had come to some similar resolution to be executed, as I then thought, after the Trades Union Congress.[175] But the sooner I stop the better will be perhaps your position before that Congress.

There is another point: I consider you ought to have sent me before publication the copy or proof of the article on the Max Hirsch Trades Unions in Germany,[c] as to the only man on your staff who knew anything of the matter and could make the necessary notes to it. Anyhow it will be impossible for me to remain on the staff of a paper which, without consulting me, lends itself to writing up these Trades Unions, comparable only to those worst English ones which allow themselves to be led by men openly sold to, or at least paid by the middle class.

---

[a] See this volume, pp. 120-21.- [b] *The Labour Standard*.- [c] See this volume, pp. 117-18.

I need not add that otherwise I wish every success to *The Labour Standard* and if desired shall now and then contribute occasional information from the continent.

Yours truly
F. E.

First published in: Marx and Engels, *Works*, First Russian Edition, Vol. XXVII, Moscow, 1935

Reproduced from the original

Published in English for the first time

74

ENGELS TO MARX

IN ARGENTEUIL

Bridlington Quay, Yorkshire
11 August 1881
1 Sea View

Dear Moor,

Your registered letter arrived yesterday evening but it, too, was open, this time *completely*. I enclose the envelope for you to see; it just wasn't stuck down.

I've this moment sent Tussy a CHEQUE for £ 50, REGISTERED. If you want all or part of the remaining £ 20 (over and above the £ 30 you spoke about) sent to Paris, Tussy can arrange things more quickly than if payment was made by a CHEQUE on London posted straight to you over there. She can easily get hold of a money order on Paris.

As regards the French elections I am entirely of your opinion. This Chamber won't continue sitting much longer anyway; once the *scrutin de liste*[a] has come through, it will soon be dissolved again.

Yesterday morning I informed Mr Shipton that he wouldn't be getting any more leading articles from me.[b] Kautsky had sent me an insipid thing on international factory legislation in a poor translation which I corrected and sent to Shipton.[174] Yesterday the proof and a letter arrived from Shipton who thought 2 of the passages 'too strong', having, what's more, misconstrued one of them; he asked me

---

[a] Here: result of the poll.- [b] See previous letter.

whether I would be prepared to tone them down. I did so and replied as follows:

1. What did he mean by submitting me the request for amendments on Tuesday [a]— i. e. Wednesday up here — when my reply couldn't have reached London until Thursday, *after* the paper[b] had come out.

2. If he thought *this* too strong, how much more so my own far stronger articles? Accordingly it would be better for us both if I gave up.

3. My time no longer permitted me to write a leading article regularly each week and I had already planned to inform him of this *after* the TRADE UNION CONGRESS (September).[175] Under the circumstances, however, it would no doubt improve his position vis-à-vis that congress were I to give up then and there.

4. He damned well ought to have shown me the Max Hirsch article *before* it was printed.[173] I couldn't remain * on the staff of a paper which lends itself to writing up these German Trade Unions, comparable only to those very worst English ones which allow themselves to be led by men sold to, or at least paid by the middle class *.[c] Apart from that I wished him the best of luck, etc. He will get my letter this morning.

I didn't tell him the most vital reason of all, namely, the total ineffectiveness of my articles so far as the rest of the paper and its readers are concerned. Any effect there may be takes the form of an invisible response on the part of unavowed apostles of FREE TRADE. The paper remains the same old omnium-gatherum of probable and improbable CROTCHETS; in matters of politics it is ±,[d] but if anything more Gladstonian. The RESPONSE, which once showed signs of awakening in one or 2 nos., has died away again. The BRITISH WORKING MAN just doesn't want to advance; he has got to be galvanised by events, the loss of industrial monopoly. *En attendant, habeat sibi.*[e]

We have been here for a fortnight now, weather changeable, mostly cold and often threatening, but not very often actually wet. We shall stay at least another week, perhaps a fortnight, but certainly no longer.

Since I've been here I have been taking *The Daily News* instead of the *Standard*. It is even more stupid, if that's possible. Preaches antivivisectionism! Also as deficient in news as the *Standard*.

---

[a] 9 August - [b] *The Labour Standard* - [c] See this volume, p. 119.- [d] more or less - [e] In the meantime let him do as he likes.

Hirsch[a] may suffer for his pleasure jaunt. But he can't help being what he is.

Best wishes to everyone.

Your

F. E.

First published in *Der Briefwechsel zwischen F. Engels und K. Marx*, Bd. 4, Stuttgart, 1913

Printed according to the original

Published in English for the first time

75

ENGELS TO GEORGE SHIPTON

IN LONDON

[Draft]

Bridlington Quay,
15 August 1881

Dear Mr Shipton,

I cannot make it out, how you could so strangely misunderstand Mr Kautsky's article.[174] To the first passage you objected because State interference went against the grain of 'many prominent men in the Unions'. Of course it does, because they are at heart Manchester School[176] men and so long as their opinions of such are taken into account, no working-class paper is possible. But my addition to the passage in question must have convinced you, that the State interference here alluded to, was such, and such only, as has been in England the law of the Land for years: factories and workshops' acts,[177] and nothing further: things not objected to by even your 'prominent men'.

As to the second passage, Mr Kautsky says: an international regulation of the *war of competition* is as necessary as that of *open warfare*; we demand a *Geneva Convention*[178] for the workpeople of the world. The 'Geneva Convention' is an *agreement* entered into by the various *Governments* for the protection of wounded and ambulances in battle. What therefore Mr Kautsky demands, is a similar agreement between the various *Governments* for the protection of the workpeople not of one state only, but of all, against overwork especially of women and

---

[a] Carl Hirsch

children. How out of that you can make an appeal to the *workpeople* of the world to *meet in a Convention of delegates at Geneva,* I am utterly at a loss to understand.[a]

You will own that the occurrence of such misunderstanding on your part cannot at all encourage me to alter my resolution.[b]

As to the Hirsch article,[173] I do know Mr Eccarius and only too well for a traitor to the cause and it will be utterly impossible for me to write for a paper which opens its columns to him.

Moreover, I do not see any progress. *The Labour Standard* remains the same vehicle of the most various and mutually contradictory views on all political and social questions which it was, perhaps unavoidably, on the first day of its existence, but which it ought no longer to be by this time, if there was an undercurrent among the British working class tending towards emancipation from the liberal Capitalists. Such undercurrent not being shown itself up to now, I must conclude it does not exist. If there were unmistakable signs of its existence, I might make an extra effort to assist it. But I do not think that one column a week drowned as I might say amongst the remaining multifarious opinions represented in *The Labour Standard* could do anything towards producing it.

And as I told you, I had resolved to stop writing after the Trade Unions Congress,[175] because of want of time; so whether I write a few articles more till then, would make no difference.

So waiting and hoping for better times, I remain

Faithfully yours,

F. E.

First published in: Marx and Engels, *Works,* First Russian Edition, Vol. XXVII, Moscow, 1935

Reproduced from the original

Published in English for the first time

---

[a] In the manuscript the following passage is crossed out here: 'If you had understood the drift of the article, you must have at once seen that here was a measure of an immediately practical nature, so easy of execution that one of the existing governments of Europe (the Swiss Government) had been induced to take it in hand; that the proposal to equalize the hours of labour in all manufacturing countries by making factory and workshop's legislation a matter of international state agreement, was one of the greatest immediate interest to the working people. Especially to those of England who, besides the Swiss, are the best protected of all against overworking and therefore are exposed to an unfair competition on the part of Belgian, French and German workpeople whose hours of work are much longer.'- [b] See this volume, p. 119.

76

MARX TO ENGELS

AT BRIDLINGTON QUAY

[Argenteuil,] 16 August 1881

Dear Engels,

We shall have to leave tomorrow, as I have received a letter from Miss Maitland[a] saying that Tussy is * *very ill*, will not allow Miss Maitland to attend her any longer, has called no doctor,* etc. Lenchen will possibly, indeed probably, have to accompany Mama to London; I shall have to set off at once (i. e. TO-MORROW and then carry on non-stop).

Your
K. M.

I at once wrote to Dr Donkin about Tussy; however he may no longer be in London.

First published in *Der Briefwechsel zwischen F. Engels und K. Marx*, Bd. 4, Stuttgart, 1913

Printed according to the original

Published in English for the first time

77

MARX TO PYOTR LAVROV

IN PARIS

[Argenteuil,] 16 August 1881

My dear Lavroff,

I must leave to-morrow and will therefore have no occasion to see

---

[a] Dolly Maitland

you again for this time. But having once found my way to Paris, I shall put in my appearance from time to time.

En attendant au revoir

Tout à vous [a]

K. Marx

First published, in Russian, in the magazine *Letopisi marksizma*, Book V, Moscow, 1928

Reproduced from the original

Published in English for the first time

78

ENGELS TO MARX

IN LONDON

Bridlington Quay, Yorkshire
17 August 1881
1 Sea View

Dear Moor,

Your telegram just received. I hope your wife managed the journey all right and conclude from the above that you evidently arrived by the night boat. Drop me a line to say how things are going.

As regards our departure, we ourselves were very much in the dark. Owing to a variety of circumstances we were unable to make preparations for tomorrow when our week expires. On receiving your telegram we arranged with the LANDLADY that we should pay another half week's rent and shall now be arriving back in London on Monday [b] evening if nothing crops up in the meantime. The weather: pretty well continuously overcast, threatening and cold; since yesterday it has been decidedly wet and in conditions like that Bridlington Quay becomes a downright bore.

---

[a] Meanwhile, good-bye, All yours - [b] 22 August

Gambetta HOOTED DOWN *très-bien*[a] in Charonne.[179]

Your
F. E.

First published in *Der Briefwechsel zwischen F. Engels und K. Marx*, Bd. 4, Stuttgart, 1913

Printed according to the original

Published in English for the first time

79

ENGELS TO EDUARD BERNSTEIN [180]

IN ZURICH

Bridlington Quay, Yorkshire,
17 August 1881

Dear Mr Bernstein,

Having spent the past 3 weeks at the seaside here,[161] I am making the most of the bad weather that has set in to drop you a few lines before I leave for home on Monday, the 22nd. If I have time, I shall also write to Kautsky,[b] but he will in any case very shortly be getting a reply and a copy of his article in *The Labour Standard*.[174]

I presume the anti-Semitica got back to you all right; I sent them to Kautsky as you hadn't let me have a more precise address.[181] Never have I seen anything so stupid and puerile. This movement is of importance *only* in the sense that in Germany — thanks to the cowardice of the bourgeoisie — *any* movement instigated from above is of importance, namely as an electioneering ploy to obtain a conservative majority. As soon as the elections are over, or even earlier if the movement (as now in Pomerania) overshoots the mark set by those in higher places, it will, on orders from above, collapse like a pricked balloon and 'never more be seen'[c]. Movements of this kind cannot be treated with too much contempt and I am glad that the *Sozialdemokrat* did so.[182] I have, by the way, heard from C. Hirsch who, acting on a sudden whim, took a jaunt to Berlin, whence he writes [183]:

'The anti-Semitic movement has been organised entirely — one might almost say

---

[a] very nicely - [b] See this volume, pp. 140-42.- [c] Goethe, 'Der Fischer'.

on orders—from above. I have gone into the poorest of haunts and no one has taken exception to my nose; nowhere, either in omnibuses or trains, have I heard a word spoken against the Jews. The semi-official papers, which hawk round anti-Semitic goods, have very few readers. Germans have a natural aversion to Jews, but I notice that the hatred felt for the government by working men as well as by petty-bourgeois and philistine progressives is far more virulent.'

Of the thousand and one secret police in Berlin, he says that everyone is aware who they are and

'in consequence they know nothing. They are so naive that they always frequent the same pubs and sit at the same tables'.

Your articles on the subject of 'intellects'[184] are *very good*. Again, your treatment of Bismarck's mania for nationalisation as something we should not endorse but which, like everything else that happens, nevertheless turns out *nolens volens*[a] in our favour, is quite outstanding, and likewise your treatment of 'intellects' as being those of people who, in so far as they are worth anything, come to us of their own accord but, in so far as we have first to recruit them, can only do us harm through what remains of the old leaven. There is much else of equal merit, though anyone could, of course, find occasional fault with the way things are put. The last number, too, was very good as a whole—the right kind of tone, brisk, assured, which the leaders had lost after the assassination attempts[128] and the exceptional law,[16] is back again and makes up for what Frederick William IV used to call 'trouser trumpetings'. You've given Bradlaugh a first-class drubbing.[b]

A few notes as to detail:

1. There's no need to be so complimentary about Vallès.[185] He is a wretched man of letters, or rather, literatus, an absolutely worthless peddlar of stock phrases who, for want of talent, took up with extremists so as to dabble in tendencies—so-called isms—and thus find a market for his indifferent belletristic wares. During the Commune he did nothing but pontificate and, if he exerted any kind of influence, it was for the worse. Don't allow Parisian cliquishness (for which Malon also has a great proclivity) to mislead you about this *drôle de fanfaron*.[c] What kind of politician he is may be seen from his letter to Grévy[186] when the latter became president, advising him to introduce the socialist republic *par ordre du mufti*[d], etc., a letter which retarded the amnesty by many months.

---

[a] willy-nilly -[b] *Der Sozialdemokrat*, No. 33, 11 August 1881.-[c] big-mouthed rascal -[d] by ukase

2. The Spaniards are by no means a bunch of anarchists. There's a quite outstanding nucleus in Madrid (the erstwhile nueva federación madrileña [187]) and, in addition, some very good elements, notably in Valencia and in certain of the smaller Catalonian industrial towns, not to mention others dispersed elsewhere. The most energetic and clear-sighted is our friend José Mesa, presently in Paris, a quite excellent fellow who also collaborates with Guesde and the rest of them over there, and keeps them in touch. If you want news about Spain, write to him in French (Malon will be able to forward the letter direct or through Guesde — I haven't got his address up here). You can mention my name.

On the whole I consider that a young man who is doing so well in and by his post as you, ought by rights to stick to that post. It is, I think, most questionable whether Kegel, who in any case is still in jug, would prove equally adaptable. What his theoretical standpoint is, I do not know, and in any case there is nothing to show that his qualifications are suited to anything more than a local paper, and a humorous one at that. LET WELL ALONE, as the English say; don't try and improve on what is good. I must confess that the thought of any change fills me with mistrust and uneasiness.

Well, now for the Revolutionary Congress.[188] Lafargue has got hold of an Italian who was a delegate but — why I don't know — was thrown out. In addition, Lafargue has met various other members of that gang, likewise anarchists, at the house of a French wine and provisions merchant. It appears that:

1. The congress consisted of *twenty-odd* people, mostly *resident in London* with mandates from elsewhere. Also a few Frenchmen and Italians and one Spaniard. They held their sessions *in public*. But not a soul turned up, neither dog, nor cat, nor reporter. After this vain wait for a public had lasted 3 or 4 days and still continued in vain, they took an heroic resolution and declared the sessions were to be *secret*!

2. The first thing that was noted was the general disappointment caused by the ineffectuality of the anarchist movement as a whole, and the certain knowledge that nowhere at all was there anyone at all behind the vociferous few. Everyone knew this to be true of himself and his own locality and, although everyone had hoodwinked everyone else into believing the most colossal lies about the colossal strides made by the movement in his *own* district, everyone had none the less believed the lies told by *everyone else*. So colossal was the collapse of

their illusions that, even in the presence of strangers, they were unable to suppress their astonishment at their own ineffectuality.
3. The congress was retrieved up to a point, first by the meeting to which, of course, they invited reporters, and next by the silly questions asked in Parliament by idiotic Tories and even more idiotic Radicals. In view of the present plague of nihilists, it was only to be expected that the press should make capital out of a meeting attended by at most 700 men.

So when the *Freiheit* speaks of delegate No. 63, etc.,[189] this refers to the number of the *mandate* made out by 1, 2 or 3 men, either in blank or in the name of a man wholly unknown to them and resident in London, or by 10-20 in the name of a delegate travelling to London. The number of delegates actually present was nearer 20 than 30, and of those who actually went there from elsewhere, certainly below 10.

NB. All this to be used with circumspection, as I have it *third-hand*. E. g. your allusion to it might take the form of a question — whether that was how it happened.[190] The gentlemen always fasten on *one* inaccurate word. It's the same old story as in the case of *all* anarchist congresses. You should read in *Fictitious Splits in the International* what the fellows wrote about their own Congress of the Fédération Jurassienne, or the account in the *Alliance of Socialist Democracy* of the first congress after the split.[191] With those chaps, the first form anarchy assumes is that all want to be officers, and none rankers. Take, for instance, that raging anarchist Adhémar Schwitzguébel (*quel nom!*ᵃ) whose objection to acceptance of office from the state as a betrayal of the cause doesn't prevent him from being a lieutenant *dans l'armée fédérale suisse*ᵇ!

Kindest regards to yourself and also to Kautsky who will get a letter when next it rains.

Yours,
F. Engels

First published, in Russian, in *Marx-Engels Archives*, Book I, Moscow, 1924

Printed according to the original

Published in English in full for the first time

ᵃ what a name!-ᵇ in the Swiss Federal Army

80

ENGELS TO MARX

IN LONDON

Bridlington Quay,
18 August 1881
1 Sea View

Dear Moor,

Not until last night did I get your Argenteuil letter explaining your sudden arrival. I trust Tussy's indisposition is of no real significance—she wrote me a cheery letter only the day before yesterday; at all events, I shall presumably hear further details tonight or tomorrow morning, and also whether your wife accompanied you as far as Boulogne or Calais or whether she stopped off before that.

Yesterday, then, I at last plucked up the courage to make a thorough study of your mathematical mss. [192] without any reference to manuals and was glad to find I had no need of them. I offer you my congratulations. The thing is so crystal clear that one can only marvel at the obstinacy with which mathematicians insist on shrouding it in mystery. But that is what comes of those gentry's one-sided mentality. To write firmly and categorically $\frac{dy}{dx} = \frac{0}{0}$ could never enter their heads. And yet it is obvious that $\frac{dy}{dx}$ can only be the pure expression of a process undergone by x and y when the last trace of the *terms* x and y has disappeared and all that remains is the expression, free from all quantity, of the process of variation they are undergoing.

There is no need to fear that some mathematician may have anticipated you in this. The above method of differentiating is, after all, much simpler than any other—so much so that I myself have just used it to deduce a formula that had momentarily slipped my mind, afterwards verifying it in the usual way. The process would undoubtedly create a great stir, especially since it clearly demonstrates that the usual method, ignoring dx dy, etc., is *positively wrong*. And the particular beauty of it is that *only* when $\frac{dy}{dx} = \frac{0}{0}$ is the operation absolutely correct mathematically.

So old Hegel was quite right in supposing that the basic premiss for differentiation was that both variables must be of varying powers and at least one of them must be to the power of at least 2 or $^1/_2$.[a] Now we also know why.

When we say that in $y = f(x)$, x and y are variables, this is an assertion which, so long as we continue to maintain it, has no implications whatsoever and x and y still remain, *pro tempore*,[b] factual constants. Only when they *really* change, i. e. *within the function*, do they become variables in fact, nor does the relationship implicit in the original equation—not of the two quantities as such, but of their variability—come to light till then. The first derivate $\dfrac{\Delta y}{\Delta x}$ shows this relation as it occurs in the course of true variation, i. e. in any *given* variation; the final derivate $= \dfrac{dy}{dx}$ shows it purely and simply in its generality and hence, from $\dfrac{dy}{dx}$ we can arrive at any $\dfrac{\Delta y}{\Delta x}$ we choose, while this itself never covers more than the particular case. But in order to proceed from the particular case to the general relation, the particular case as such has to be eliminated. Hence, after the function has gone through the process from x to x′ with all this implies, one can simply let x′ revert to x; it is no longer the old x, a variable only in name; it has undergone *real variation*, and the *result* of that variation remains, even if we again eliminate that variation itself.

Here at last we are able to see clearly what has long been maintained by many mathematicians who were unable to produce rational grounds for it, namely that the differential *quotient* is the prototype, while the differentials dx and dy are derived: the derivation of the formula itself requires that the two so-called irrational factors should originally constitute one side of the equation and only when one has reduced the equation to this, its original form, $\dfrac{dy}{dx} = f(x)$, can one do anything with it, is one rid of the irrational factors, replacing them with their rational expression.

The thing has got such a hold over me that it not only keeps going round in my head all day, but last night I actually had a dream in

---

[a] G. W. F. Hegel, *Wissenschaft der Logik*, Book I, Section II, Chapter 2. Note: Der Zweck des Differentialkalkuls aus seiner Anwendung abgeleitet.- [b] temporarily

which I gave a fellow my studs to differentiate and he made off with the lot.

Your

F. E.

First published in *Der Briefwechsel zwischen F. Engels und K. Marx*, Bd. 4, Stuttgart, 1913

Printed according to the original

Published in English for the first time

81

MARX TO ENGELS

AT BRIDLINGTON QUAY

[London], 18 August 1881

DEAR FRED,

No doubt you will by now have had the brief note I wrote you day before yesterday from Argenteuil and have gathered from it that I am here without my wife (not *with her* as you necessarily supposed in your letter).

On hearing the news of Tussy's condition I resolved to leave that very same day if possible; my wife, on the other hand, was to set off *to-day* with Helen[a] and travel FIRST CLASS, first to Amiens and spend the night there; then, the next day, to Boulogne and rest there for at least a day, but 2 or 3 days if she wished; thence to Folkestone and, depending on circumstances, from there straight on to London or else (and this seemed to me best), by a later train of her own choosing. It was, of course, distressing to part from her, but the REAL SUPPORT FOR HER IS Helen; MY OWN PRESENCE wasn't absolutely necessary. Moreover, my departure compelled her finally to make up her mind to tear herself away from Argenteuil, which after all had got to happen in view of her growing weakness.

So I left Paris on Tuesday[b] evening at 7.45 by EXPRESS TRAIN via Calais, and arrived in London at ABOUT 6 O'CLOCK (MORNING).

I at once telegraphed Dr Donkin who was here by 11 o'clock and

---

[a] Demuth - [b] 16 August

had a long consultation with Tussy. HER STATE IS ONE OF UTTER NERVOUS DEJECTION. She has been eating next to nothing for weeks, less than Dr Tanner during his experiment.[193] Donkin says there's no organic trouble, HEART SOUND, LUNGS SOUND, etc.; fundamentally the whole condition is attributable to a PERFECT DERANGEMENT OF ACTION OF STOMACH which has become unaccustomed to food (and she has made matters worse by drinking a great deal of tea: he *at once* forbade her *all tea*) and a DANGEROUSLY OVERWROUGHT NERVOUS SYSTEM. Hence SLEEPLESSNESS, NEURALGIC CONVULSIONS, etc. It was a miracle, he said, that a COLLAPSE of this kind hadn't happened before. He intervened at once and, what is most important of all in this little person's case, brought it home to her that, if she was an obedient patient, *there would be no danger, but that if she insisted on having her own way, all would be p e r d u.*ª (Indeed he is convinced that this is so.) Fortunately she promised to do as he said, and when she makes a promise she keeps it. Later on, he says, she will have to go away in order to distract herself.

Another reason for hastening my departure was the knowledge that Donkin intended to take his HOLIDAYS in the Hebrides from 17 August. He is staying here until Saturday on Tussy's account and will then leave a *remplaçant*ᵇ for her and my wife.

At the latest meeting of *électeurs* Mr Gambetta learnt something inside the MEETING-HALL [179] that he had learnt only at the hands of the crowd outside the meeting-hall at the first Belleville MEETING.[194] This second meeting also consisted solely of people who had been invited by his own COMMITTEE, and none of them was admitted except after a twofold *triage*ᶜ by the stewards appointed by the *comité*. Hence the uproar was all the more significant. On both occasions *Galliffet!* was the *cri* that predominated. Thus Gambetta learnt the lesson that effrontery of the *Italian* variety is out of place in Paris. Had Rochefort been able to speak in public and had he thus been enabled to offer himself then and there as a competing candidate, Gambetta would certainly have been defeated. As a result of what happened at the time of the Commune, the Belleville working-class population lost about 20,000 men, most of whom have been replaced by lower middle-class philistines. And even the remaining or newly arrived working-class population of Belleville (both *arrondissements*) is one of *arriérés*, stick-in-the-muds, whose ideal, if it goes beyond Gambetta, stops at Rochefort; both were returned as deputies there in 1869.

ª lost - ᵇ locum - ᶜ screening process

As to the state of the *parti ouvrier*[a] in Paris, someone who is wholly impartial in this respect, namely Lissagaray, admitted to me that, although only existing *en germe*,[b] *it alone* counts for anything vis-à-vis the bourgeois parties OF ALL NUANCES. Its organisation, though still tenuous and *plus ou moins fictive*,[c] is nevertheless sufficiently disciplined for it to be able to put up candidates in every *arrondissement* — to make its presence felt at MEETINGS and annoy the OFFICIAL SOCIETY PEOPLE. I myself have been following this aspect in Paris papers of every complexion and there's not one that doesn't grind its teeth at that GENERAL NUISANCE — *le parti ouvrier collectiviste.*[d] [195]

As regards the latest splits among the leaders of the *parti ouvrier*, it would be best if I told you about this in person later on.

With best wishes to Pumps and Mrs Rendstone.

Your

Moor

First published in *Der Briefwechsel zwischen F. Engels und K. Marx*, Bd. 4, Stuttgart, 1913

Printed according to the original

Published in English for the first time

82

MARX TO JENNY LONGUET

IN ARGENTEUIL

[London,] 18 August 1881

My dear sweet child,

I came to London, i. e.[e] in Maitland Park about 7 o'clock.

Tussychen is looking pale and thin, since weeks she eats almost nothing (literally); her nervous system is in a state of utter dejection; hence continuous sleeplessness, trembling of the hands, neuralgic convulsions of the face, etc.

I telegraphed at once to Dr Donkin; he put in his presence at 11 o'clock (yesterday morning), had a long consultation with and examination of Tussy. He says that there is no organic disease, heart

---

[a] workers' party - [b] in embryo - [c] more or less a fiction - [d] collectivist workers' party -
[e] The beginning of the letter is in German.

sound, lungs sound, etc., but only action of stomach quite deranged by her foolish way of living, and nervous system fearfully overwrought.

He has succeeded to frighten her into obedience to his prescriptions, and you know, if she once gives way and promises, she will keep her promise. With all that, her recovery cannot but be slow, and I arrived in the very nick of time. There was the greatest danger in case of any further delay.

Donkin was about — as he had informed me before our departure — to leave this day London for the Hebrides. Because of Tussy, and hoping still to hear something of Maman, he will now stay till the end of the week.

Tell me about the state of Maman, whether she has left you, etc. How is Longuet and Harra[a]? and yourself and the other dear children[b]?

How do you go on with your new servant?

Apropos. Sarah[c] (Engels' Sarah), now for some hours daily the helpmate of Tussy, a girl of the best character and *fitness for every thing*, told Tussy that she had nothing liked better than to go with you, but Pumps did never tell her about Lizzy's having left you and about your want of a *remplaçant*[d] for her. She has also told Tussy and again myself, that she *is still ready* to come over to you. Only she dares not travel alone to France, but this matters little. I myself can bring her over later on.

And now *adio*, dear child. The pleasure to be with you and the dear children has given me a more substantial satisfaction than I could have found anywhere else.

My compliments to that excellent Dr Dourlen.

With 1000 kisses for the children

Yours,

Old Nick

Tussy sends her best wishes to Wolf[e] and the whole family.

First published, in Russian, in the magazine *Nachalo*, No. 5, St Petersburg, 1899

Reproduced from the original

Published in English for the first time

---

[a] Henri Longuet - [b] Jean, Edgar and Marcel - [c] Parker - [d] locum - [e] Edgar Longuet

83

MARX TO ENGELS

AT BRIDLINGTON QUAY

[London,] 19 August 1881,
11.30 p. m.

Mama and Helen[a] have JUST arrived via Folkestone, after stopping at Boulogne.

What I didn't write and tell you — Longuet and little Harry are very ill. Nothing but misfortune in the family at the moment. *Salut.*

K. M.

First published in *Der Briefwechsel zwischen F. Engels und K. Marx*, Bd. 4, Stuttgart, 1913

Printed according to the original

Translated from the French

Published in English for the first time

84

MARX TO JENNY LONGUET [196]

IN ARGENTEUIL

[London,] 20 August 1881
41 Maitland Park Road, N. W.

My Sweetheart,

You may find it difficult to make head or tail of the above scrawl. But in effect, Mama and Helen arrived safely last night.

First published in: Marx and Engels, *Works*, Second Russian Edition, Vol. 50, Moscow, 1981

Printed according to the original

Published in English for the first time

---

[a] Demuth

85

ENGELS TO AUGUST BEBEL

IN LEIPZIG

London, 25 August 1881

Dear Bebel,

I would have replied sooner to your letter of 13.5.[197] But, after the Leipzig 'local', [198] I waited to see whether you might perhaps send me another forwarding address; as you haven't I am using the old one, and also enclosing a letter from Tussy Marx to Mrs Liebknecht, for whom we haven't got an address either.

Bernstein still writes to say he wants to leave the *Sozialdemokrat*, and now proposes that Kegel be taught the ropes and, once he knows them, appointed in his place. My view is that any change would be for the worse. Bernstein has made good, so greatly exceeding our expectations (for instance, his articles on 'intellects'[184] were, trifles apart, quite excellent and written along exactly the right lines) that it would be hard to find anyone better. Kegel hasn't proved himself, at any rate in *this* sphere, and, as things stand now, all experimentation should be avoided. I have urgently requested Bernstein to stay,[a] and believe you could do no better than give him similar advice. In his hands the paper is getting better and better, and so, too, is he. He has genuine tact and is quick on the uptake — just the reverse of Kautsky, who is an exceptionally good chap, but a born pedant and hair-splitter in whose hands complex questions are not made simple, but simple ones complex. Like all the rest of us, I am very fond of him as a person and, in longer articles of the review type, he might occasionally do something pretty good, but even with the best will in the world he can't go against the grain, *c'est plus fort que lui*.[b] On a newspaper, a doctrinaire of this kind is a real disaster; even Ede[c] was forced to append a critical note to one of his articles in the last *Sozialdemokrat*. On the other hand, he has written a fly-sheet for the consump-

---

[a] See this volume, pp. 85-86 and 128.- [b] it's too much for him - [c] Eduard Bernstein

tion of peasants in Austria ᵃ in which he gives proof of something of his mother's ᵇ gift for short story writing; aside from one or two erudite expressions, it's really good and should be effective.

I wrote to Liebknecht about the speeches in the Landtag, and in reply [199] was told that these had been a matter of 'tactics' (but I had pointed out that it was precisely those tactics that prevented us from siding openly with him) and that speeches of a different kind would shortly be made in the Reichstag. True, this has now been done by you [200]— but what is one to think of Liebknecht's unfortunate and wholly unnecessary remark about the 'Reich Chancellor's honesty' [201]? It may have been *meant* ironically, but that's not evident from the report, and what capital the bourgeois press made out of it! I have sent no further reply — it does no good, after all. But Kautsky, too, has told us not only that Liebknecht is writing letters all over the place — e. g. to Austria — saying Marx and I are in complete agreement with him and had sanctioned his 'tactics', but also that people *believe* him. This really can't go on indefinitely! Again, the *Freiheit* has got a lot of fun of Hartmann's ᶜ speech on the Accident Bill [202] which, if the passage they quote is genuine, was certainly a pretty wretched affair.

In France, working-class candidates obtained 20,000 votes in Paris and 40,000 in the provinces [203] and, if their leaders hadn't perpetrated one stupidity after another since setting up the collectivist workers' party, things would have gone even better. But there, too, the masses are better than most of their leaders. For instance, several Parisian candidates lost thousands of votes through using empty revolutionary verbiage (as much part of the business in Paris as patter is of trade) in the provinces as well where it was taken seriously and people asked: 'How can you make a revolution without weapons and organisation?' For the rest, developments in France are taking their regular, normal and very necessary course along peaceful lines, and that is a very good thing just now, for otherwise the provinces could not be swept earnestly into the movement.

I understand very well that your fingers should itch, when everything's going so nicely for us in Germany and you, having your hands tied, cannot reap the fruits of victories that are all but falling into your laps. But this does no harm. Many people in Germany have set

---

ᵃ [K. Kautsky,] *Der Vetter aus Amerika, eine Erzählung für Landleute, erbaulich zu lesen.* - ᵇ Minna Kautsky - ᶜ Georg Wilhelm Hartmann

too much store by overt propaganda (Viereck, who was completely cast down by the impossibility of making overt propaganda, is just one striking example of this), and too little by the real impetus of historical events. It can do nothing but good if experience acts as a corrective in this case. The fact that we cannot reap the fruits of our victories *at the moment* in no way means that they are lost to us. The galvanising of the indifferent, inert masses can only be effected by actual events and even if, in present circumstances, those thus galvanised are left in a state of some considerable bewilderment, the word of deliverance will, when the time comes, strike home with all the more force; the effect upon state and bourgeoisie will be all the more drastic when the 600,000 votes [204] are suddenly multiplied threefold, when, besides Saxony, *all* the big towns and industrial districts fall to us and even rural workers are, for the first time, so situated as to be intellectually accessible to us. To take the masses by storm in this way is of far greater value than to win them over gradually by *overt* propaganda which, under present circumstances, would in any case quickly be stamped on. As things are now, the Junkers, clergy and bourgeois *cannot* allow us to cut the ground from under their feet and hence it is better to let them take care of this themselves. For a time will surely come when a different wind will blow. Meanwhile it's you people who must in person go through the mill, it's you who must endure the infamies of the government and the bourgeoisie, and that's no laughing matter. But mind you don't forget any of the dirty tricks played on yourselves and on all our people; the day of retribution is nigh and it must be exploited to the full.

Your
F. E.

Viereck is in Copenhagen. Address *poste restante*, Copenhagen.

First published, in Russian, in *Marx-Engels Archives*, Vol. I (VI), Moscow, 1932

Printed according to the original

Published in English for the first time

86

ENGELS TO KARL KAUTSKY

IN ZURICH

London, 27 August 1881

Dear Mr Kautsky,

In a day or two you will be getting by post 1. *The Labour Standard* containing your article,[a] in connection with which there have been sundry comic interludes, 2. a *Nature* of 18 August, 3. your ms. back. After I had somewhat revised what was an altogether bungled translation, I sent it to Shipton for a leading article. However, the worthy Shipton got it all wrong and complained to me,[b] but as usual too late. God knows what the man took the bit about 'State interference' in favour of the workers to mean—certainly not what it said, nor that such State interference has long *existed* in England in the shape of FACTORIES AND WORKSHOPS ACTS.[177] Still worse: into the words WE DEMAND A GENEVA CONVENTION [178] FOR THE WORKING CLASSES he read a demand by you for *the convening of a conference of delegates in Geneva* to settle the matter!! What can one do with such an oaf? I made this business the occasion to go ahead with my decision and break with *The Labour Standard*, as that paper is getting worse rather than better.

In *Nature* you will find a speech made by John Simon[c] before the international Medical Congress here [205] in which *the bourgeoisie is virtually put on the mat by medical science.* J. Simon is MEDICAL OFFICER TO THE PRIVY COUNCIL,[206] virtual head of Britain's entire public health inspectorate, and the same who is so frequently and approvingly quoted by Marx in *Capital*, a man—perhaps the last of the old really professional and conscientious officials of the 1840-60 period who, in the performance of his duty, everywhere found that bourgeois interests were the first obstacle he was obliged to combat. Hence, his instinctive hatred of the bourgeoisie is as violent as it is explicable. Now he, a doctor, finding his own special field invaded by the Church-led bourgeoisie and their anti-vivisection movement, has turned the tables on them. Instead of preaching dull and colourless sermons like

---

[a] [K. Kautsky,] 'International Labour Laws', *The Labour Standard*, No. 15, 13 August 1881. - [b] See this volume, pp. 122-23. - [c] J. Simon, 'State Medicine', *Nature*, No. 616, Vol. XXIV, 18 August 1881.

Virchow, he goes into the attack comparing the *few scientific* experiments made by doctors on *animals* with the *vast commercial* experiments made by the bourgeoisie upon the *popular masses*, thereby placing the question for the first time in its true perspective. An extract from this would make a splendid feuilleton for the *Sozialdemokrat*. [207]

The Congress, by the way, declared unanimously that vivisection was essential to science.

Your fly-sheet [a] shows that you have inherited something of your mother's [b] gift for short story writing. It pleased me more than anything you have written hitherto. A little more polishing might have enabled you to improve one or two expressions and turns of speech, and I would advise you to do this in the case of a second edition. Literary German is a very clumsy idiom for narrative prose and erudite words such as reaction, which mean nothing to the peasant, ought to be avoided. The thing is worthy of being seriously revised by you along these lines. It is the best fly-sheet I have ever seen.

Your Mostian chaps in Austria will have to learn by painful experience; there are no two ways about it. It's a process during which many otherwise good elements come to grief, but if those elements are positively intent on conspiring for the fun of it and with no particular purpose in mind, there's no helping them. Luckily the proletarian movement has an enormous reproductive capacity.

Viereck and wife [c] had an awful lot of bad weather in Scotland, after which they left for Copenhagen where they have now arrived. They will be remaining there for the time being—address *poste restante*, Copenhagen.

Our French friends, it seems, are still not satisfied with the many stupidities perpetrated over the past 2 years out of officiousness, cliquism, an itch for oratory, etc. *Le Citoyen* has, it seems, been sold to the Bonapartists who have not yet unceremoniously kicked our men out, but have stopped their pay and otherwise treated them *en canaille*, [d] as though trying to push them into striking and so get rid of them. On top of that, all our chaps have fallen out with one another, as so often happens when things go wrong. One of the most unhappy is Brousse, a thoroughly honest chap but a consummate muddle-head and one who positively insists that the entire movement should de-

---

[a] [K. Kautsky,] *Der Vetter aus Amerika, eine Erzählung für Landleute, erbaulich zu lesen*.- [b] Minna Kautsky - [c] Laura Viereck - [d] like dirt

vote itself to converting erstwhile anarchist friends. It was he, too, who was originally responsible for the crazy resolution concerning the rejection of candidature.[208] For the rest, the steady, peaceful course of events in France can, in the long run, only prove favourable to us. Not until the provinces have been drawn into the movement, as has been happening since 1871, and emerge, as they are increasingly doing, as a power in the land — along normal legal lines, that is,— can an end be put in the interests of us all to the spasmodic form hitherto assumed by developments in France, derived from coups in Paris and for years retarded by reaction in the provinces. *Then, when* the time has come for Paris to act, it will not have the provinces against it, but behind it.

Kindest regards from all,

Yours

F. Engels

First published, in Russian, in *Marx-Engels Archives*, Vol. I (VI), Moscow, 1932

Printed according to the original

Published in English for the first time

87

MARX TO KARL KAUTSKY[209]

IN ZURICH

[London,] 1 October 1881
In great haste

Dear Mr Kautsky,

I enclose a line to your mother[a] together with the enclosed note for my daughter.[b][210] It would have saved time if you had sent me your mother's Paris address.

I would have asked your mother to spend a few days at my house and at the same time take a look round London with me. *My wife's*

---

[a] Minna Kautsky, see next letter.- [b] Jenny Longuet

fatal illness, which day by day *is drawing closer to its consummation,* prevented this. I am her *garde malade.*[a]

I get the *Arbeiterstimme* regularly; it edifies but does not surprise me, for I've known my Swiss for decades.

With regard to Mr McGuire, it would appear from your letter that he is in London. How comes it that none of our New York friends gave him letters of recommendation? I have, *prima facie,*[b] always been somewhat suspicious of YANKEE socialists and know in particular that the kind that Shipton keeps in touch with are *very crotchety and sectarian. With all that, Mr McGuire may be an excellent party man.*

Yours very sincerely,
Karl Marx

My wife and daughter[c] send you their compliments.

First published, in Russian, in *Marx-Engels Archives,* Vol. I (VI), Moscow, 1932

Printed according to the original

Published in English for the first time

88

MARX TO MINNA KAUTSKY

IN PARIS

London, 1 October 1881
41 Maitland Park Road, N. W.

Dear Madam,

I enclose herewith a note for my daughter.[210] Argenteuil is quite close to Paris, about 20 minutes from the Gare[d] St Lazare.

I would have taken the liberty of inviting you to stay at my house in London — and your son will have told you how greatly everyone in the family admires your works — had not my wife's shocking and,

---

[a] nurse - [b] Here: from the outset. - [c] Eleanor Marx - [d] Station

I fear, *fatal* illness put a stop, as it were, to our intercourse with the outside world.

With sincerest wishes for your future prosperity,

Yours very truly,

Karl Marx

First published in the yearly, *Das Jahr*, Wien, 1929

Printed according to the original

Published in English for the first time

89

ENGELS TO EDUARD BERNSTEIN [211]

IN ZURICH

London, 25 October 1881

Dear Mr Bernstein,

I am most grateful to you for having written to me about the *Égalité* business.[212] Aside from the point at issue, this provides me with an opportunity of letting you know what is Marx's attitude, and hence also my own, towards the French movement. And from this one instance you will be able to gauge our attitude towards other non-German movements, in so far as these are in sympathy with us and we with them.

I am glad that you are not at present in a position to give financial support to the *Égalité*. Lafargue's letter was another of those *coups de tête*[a] which the French, in particular those south of the line Bordeaux-Lyons, now and again find themselves unable to resist. So certain was he of perpetrating a stroke of genius and a blunder rolled into one, that he didn't even tell his wife[b] (who has prevented many such things) about it until after the event. With the exception of Lafargue, who is always in favour of 'something being done', *n'importe quoi*,[c] we over here were unanimously against *Égalité* No. 3.[d] I confidently

---

[a] impulsive actions - [b] Laura Lafargue - [c] no matter what - [d] Engels means the third series of *L'Égalité*.

predicted that, with their 5,000 frs (*if* as much), they would last out for 32 numbers. If Guesde and Lafargue are intent on acquiring the reputation in Paris of *tueurs de journeaux,*[a] we can't stop them, but nor shall we do anything else. If, contrary to all expectation, the paper improves again, and if it gets really good, we shall always be able to see what can be done if it finds itself in a predicament. But it's absolutely essential that these gentlemen should learn at last how to stand on their own feet.

The fact of the matter is that, during the past 12 or 15 months, our French friends, who are trying to set up the *parti ouvrier,*[b] have made one blunder after another, and this applies to all of them without exception. The first was committed by Guesde when, for absurdly purist reasons, he prevented Malon from accepting the editorship of the labour department on the *Intransigeant* at a salary of 12,000 frs. *That was when the whole squabble began.* This was followed by the unpardonable folly over the *Émancipation,* when Malon allowed himself to be misled by the false promises of the Lyonnais (the worst working men in France), while Guesde showed himself no less feverishly anxious to have a daily paper *à tout prix.*[c] Next came the hair-splitting over the matter of candidature,[208] in which connection it is more than probable that Guesde was guilty of the solecism you reprobate, though it is obvious to me that Malon was *seeking* to pick a quarrel. Finally, the ingress into, followed by the egress from, the *Citoyen français,* of Mr Bourbeau, alias Secondigné, an adventurer of the worst repute—his egress being due simply to non-payment of salary, *not to any political motive.* Next, Guesde, in very mixed company, joined the most recent *Citoyen,* and Malon and Brousse the miserable *Prolétaire* which they—or Malon at any rate—had always secretly opposed as a vulgar loutish rag.

The *Prolétaire* was the organ of the very narrowest clique of the most inveterate scribblers among the Parisian workers. It was axiomatic that access could be had and contributions made only by genuine manual workers. The most bigoted Weitlingian 'scholar'-baiting was the order of the day. The sheet was in consequence quite without substance, while preening itself on being *la plus pure expression*[d] of the Parisian proletariat. Hence, for all its apparent cordiality, it always secretly looked upon other papers, including the 2 *Égalités,* as mortal enemies and intrigued against them.

---

[a] killers of newspapers -[b] workers' party -[c] at all costs -[d] the purest expression

When Malon now maintains that the French workers' party is endeavouring to create an organ for itself in the *Prolétaire*, and questions the need for a competing *Égalité*, no one is better aware than Malon, 1. that the two first *Égalités* also existed alongside the *Prolétaire* simply because 2. nothing could be made of the *Prolétaire*, and Malon knows the *Prolétaire* people just as well as Guesde does, and 3. that the few blockheads on the *Prolétaire*, together with Malon and Brousse, don't by any means make up the whole of the French workers' party. Hence he knows that all this is a red herring and that it is *he* who is seeking to create an organ for *himself* in the *Prolétaire*, having made things too hot for himself everywhere else.

But the link that binds Malon and Brousse to this potty little sheet is their common jealousy of Marx. To the majority of French socialists it is an anathema that the nation which confers upon the world the boon of *idées françaises* [a] and has a monopoly of ideas — that Paris, *centre des lumières* [b] — must now all of a sudden import its socialist ideas ready-made from a German, Marx. But there's no denying the fact and, what is more, Marx's genius, his almost excessive scientific scrupulousness and his incredible erudition place him so far above all the rest of us that anyone who ventures to criticise his discoveries is more likely to burn his fingers than anything else. That is something which must be left to a more advanced epoch. If, then, French socialists (i. e. the majority) are obliged, whether they like it or not, to bow to the inevitable, it will not happen without a certain amount of grumbling. It is the *Prolétaire* people who say, of both Guesde and Lafargue, that they are Marx's mouthpieces or, translated into more familiar idiom, that *ils veulent vendre les ouvriers français aux Prussiens et à Bismarck.* [c] And in everything M. Malon writes, this grumbling is most plainly audible and, what's more, in most ignoble form: Malon is at pains to find or impute other progenitors (Lassalle, Schäffle and actually De Paepe!) on whom to father Marx's discoveries. Now it is, of course, perfectly in order to disagree with party members, no matter whom, as to their mode of procedure in this or that case, or to dispute or differ on a point of theory. But thus to contest the right of a man like Marx to his own achievements is to betray a pettiness such as is found, one might almost say, only in a compositor,— a race of whose self-conceit you will surely have had ample experience. I sim-

---

[a] French ideas - [b] centre of enlightenment - [c] they want to sell the French workers to the Prussians and Bismarck

ply cannot understand how anyone can be envious of genius; it's something so very special that we, who have not got it, know it to be unattainable right from the start; but to be envious of anything like that one must have to be frightfully small-minded. The furtive way Malon goes about it, doesn't improve matters. The fact that it is *he* who eventually comes out worst, betraying his lack of knowledge and discernment at every turn, is something of which he might at some time be made unpleasantly aware, should it at any time become necessary to scrutinise Malon's goodly *Histoire du Socialisme 'depuis les temps les plus reculés'* [a] (!!) and other productions with an eye to their substance.

Brousse is, I think, the most hopelessly muddle-headed man I have ever known. He has dropped the anarchy — i. e. opposition to political activity and voting — out of anarchism, while at the same time retaining all its other catchwords and, more notably, its tactics. Thus, in tedious articles in the *Prolétaire* directed against Guesde (but not naming him), he is currently brooding on the insoluble question of how to set up an organisation in such a way as to preclude a dictatorship (Guesde's!!). If this consummate literary and theoretical ignoramus, whose forte, however, is cliquism, is again able to play a part, the blame must be shared by Lafargue, Guesde and Malon.

Lastly Guesde. In matters of theory this man is by far the most lucid thinker amongst the Parisians, and one of the few who takes no exception at all to the German origins of present-day socialism. *Hinc illae lacrimae.* [b] Which is why the gentlemen of the *Prolétaire* are letting it be known that he is merely Marx's mouthpiece, a rumour which, with lugubrious mien, Malon and Brousse carry further afield. Outside that clique no one dreams of such a thing. What there is to it, we shall see anon. That he is domineering may well be true. Every one of us is domineering in the sense that he would like to see his views predominate. If Guesde seeks to do this by direct and Malon by tortuous means, it says much for Guesde's character and for the superiority of Malon's worldly wisdom — especially in dealing with people like the Parisians who obstinately dig their heels in if you try to dictate to them but are only too delighted to let you lead them by the nose. Come to that, whenever I have heard anyone who is worth his salt described as domineering, I have only been able to conclude that

---

[a] from the earliest times. See B. Malon, *Histoire du socialisme depuis les temps les plus reculés jusqu'à nos jours.* - [b] Hence those tears (Terence, *Andria*, I, 1, 99).

there was nothing that could really be said against the man. Guesde's failings are of quite a different kind. First, the Parisian superstition that the word revolution is something one must continually bandy about. And secondly, boundless impatience. He is suffering from a nervous complaint, believes he has not much longer to live and is absolutely determined to see something worthwhile happen before he goes. That, and his morbid excitability, provide the explanation for his exaggerated and sometimes destructive thirst for action.

If, in addition, you take the inability of the French, especially the Parisians, to conceive of differences that are other than *personal*, and it is obvious enough how it was that these gentry, as soon as they had scored a few small successes, saw themselves already at the goal, sought to divide as yet inexistent spoils, and fell out with each other in the process.

Guesde's pamphlets and articles, by the way, are the best to have appeared in the French language, and he is, moreover, one of the best speakers in Paris. Also, we have always found him forthcoming and reliable.

Now for ourselves. We, i. e. Marx and I, do not even correspond with Guesde. We have only written to him for specific reasons of business. We have no more than a general idea of what Lafargue says in his letters to Guesde, nor have we by any means read everything Guesde writes to Lafargue. Heaven only knows what plans the two of them have exchanged of which we have no inkling. Every now and again Marx, like myself, has transmitted advice to Guesde via Lafargue, but it has hardly ever been taken.

It is true, however, that Guesde came over here when the question arose of *drafting* a programme for the French workers' party.[68] The *considérants* to this was dictated to him by Marx,[a] here in my own room, in the presence of Lafargue and myself: the worker is free only when he is the owner of his instruments of labour — this may assume either individual or collective form — the individual form of ownership is being daily and increasingly superseded by economic developments, hence, all that remains is that of communal ownership, etc.— a masterpiece of cogent reasoning, calculated to explain things to the masses in a few words; I have seldom seen its like and, even in this concise version, found it astonishing. The remaining contents of the programme were then discussed; we added this and took out that, but

---

[a] See K. Marx, 'Preamble to the Programme of the French Workers' Party'.

as for Guesde being Marx's mouthpiece, how little this holds water is evident from the fact that he insisted on including his nonsense about the *minimum du salaire*[a] and since not we but the French were responsible for the thing, we eventually gave him his head, although he admitted that, theoretically, it was absurd.

Brousse was in London at the time and would have liked to join us. But Guesde was short of time and anticipated, not incorrectly, that Brousse would engage in tedious arguments about ill-digested anarchist terms; he therefore insisted that Brousse should not attend this meeting. *C'était son affaire.*[b] But Brousse has never forgiven him for it and it's to that time that his intrigues against Guesde go back.

This programme was subsequently discussed by the French and accepted with a few alterations, including Malon's which were by no means improvements.

Then, too, I wrote 2 articles for the *Égalité* No. II on *Le socialisme de M. Bismarck*[c] and that, so far as I'm aware, is the sum total of our active participation in the French movement.

But what mainly annoys the small-minded carpers who count for nothing, yet like to think themselves all-important, is the fact that Marx, thanks to his theoretical and practical achievements, has attained a position in which he enjoys the complete trust of the best people in all the labour movements in the various countries. At *critical junctures* it is to him they turn for advice, when they generally find that his advice is the best. He occupies that position in Germany, in France, and in Russia, not to speak of the smaller countries. Hence it is not Marx who imposes his opinion, let alone his will, on these people; rather it is these people who come to him of their own accord. And it is precisely on this that Marx's peculiar influence rests, an influence of the utmost importance to the movement. Malon also wished to come here, but to procure a special invitation from Marx through Lafargue, which naturally he didn't get. We were as prepared to deal with him as we are with anybody else *de bonne volonté*,[d] but invite him! Why? Who has ever had an invitation of that kind from us?

Marx's attitude, and hence also my own, towards the French is the same as towards the other national movements. We are constantly in touch with them in so far as it is worth our while and opportunities

---

[a] minimum wage - [b] It was his business.- [c] F. Engels, 'The Socialism of Mr Bismarck, I-II', *L'Égalité*, Nos. 7 and 10, 3 and 24 March 1880 (see present edition, Vol. 24). - [d] willingly

present themselves, but any attempt to influence people against their will would only do us harm, destroy the old trust that dates from the International. And we have, after all, too much experience *in revolutionaribus rebus*[a] to do that.

Now for two more FACTS.

1. It was Guesde, and with him Lafargue, who, in the *Égalité*, brought quite undeserved fame to Malon, turned him, as it were, into a legend, and this simply because Guesde thought, in typically French fashion, that as a writer one had to have a *working man* beside one.

2. And here is something the recipient of the letter has authorised me to tell you: Lissagaray, who was the chairman of the meeting at which Malon arraigned that blackguard Lullier, writes to say that, just as the meeting was supposed to begin, Lullier sent word to Malon requesting a short discussion. Malon departed, didn't return, and finally *his Comité* went in search of him (Lissagaray was the chairman of the *Comité* and the meeting) only to find him toping most jovially and on the brink of a peaceable understanding with Lullier, the man he had (rightly) described as the dirtiest of blackguards. Had not Malon had to leave at 9 o'clock for the congress at Zurich,[213] there would have been the risk of a full reconciliation. And he describes himself as a man of politics!

Mesa's address is: J. Mesa, 36 Rue du Bac, Paris.

Marx knows nothing about this letter. He has been in bed for the past 12 days with bronchitis and all kinds of complications, but since Sunday[b] — due precautions having been taken — there has no longer been any danger. I've been anxious enough, I can tell you. Now things are looking up and tomorrow, 27 October, we shall, I trust, show the world that we are still there as large as life.[214] Kindest regards to Kautsky.

Your
F. E.

As regards the *Égalité*, I think it would be best if our people were *not* to found a new paper for the time being, at any rate until the state of affairs within the party has become a little less obscure. If they do want to start one, however, neither we nor anyone else can stop them, though I don't see how it's going to be managed this time without

---

[a] in revolutionary matters - [b] 23 October

a row between the *Égalité* and the *Prolétaire*. This wouldn't be a major disaster, but it would still be a perhaps unnecessary case of teething trouble.

What kind of operation is Kautsky having? — I trust he won't let himself be cut up into a complete Malthusian!

First published, in Russian, in *Marx-Engels Archives*, Book I, 1924

Printed according to the original

Published in English in full for the first time

90

ENGELS TO JOHANN PHILIPP BECKER

IN GENEVA

[London,] 4 November 1881
122 Regent's Park Road, N. W.

Dear Old Man,

Your postcard re the congress [215] arrived too late for me to write to you about it. Since then we have also had sundry calamities over here. Mrs Marx has been in bed for months, critically ill, and then Marx went down with bronchitis accompanied by all sorts of complications which, at his time of life and considering the general state of his health, was certainly no laughing matter. Fortunately the worst is over and, so far as Marx is concerned, all danger has been completely eliminated for the time being, though he has to spend the greater part of the day in bed and is greatly weakened.

Herewith money order for 4 pounds sterling = 100 frs 80 c. which is what I have to send you this time. I trust it will come in handy for, delighted though I am to hear that you have been able to make a start at earning a living, it is after all only a start and I'm only sorry that of late I myself have been somewhat short and therefore unable to step into the breach any sooner.

I'm always glad when a so-called international congress passes off, as it did on this occasion, without anyone making an ass of himself in public. You always get such a hotchpotch of people attending these affairs, some of whom have no other object than to look important in public and who for that very reason are capable of any stupidity. Well, this time it went off without any mishap.

Our people in Germany have given a splendid account of themselves at the elections.[216] In 23 or 27 constituencies (I can't find out the exact number) they were in the second ballot, despite the fact that on this occasion all the other parties turned out to the very last man. And this under the stress of the exceptional law [16] and state of siege,[65] without a press, without meetings, without any means of public agitation and in the certain knowledge that by way of return the livelihood of some thousands within the party would again be sacrificed. It is altogether splendid and the impression it has made throughout Europe, and particularly here in England, has been quite tremendous. How many seats we get is neither here nor there. Enough anyway to say what is necessary in the Reichstag. But the fact that we have gained ground in the larger towns instead of losing it — that is first rate and here's three cheers for our lads in Germany!

Your old friend,

F. E.

First published in: F. Engels, *Vergessene Briefe (Briefe Friedrich Engels' an Johann Philipp Becker)*, Berlin, 1920

Printed according to the original

Published in English for the first time

91

ENGELS TO EDUARD BERNSTEIN [217]

IN ZURICH

London, 30 November 1881

Dear Mr Bernstein,

If any one outside event has contributed to putting Marx more or less to rights again, then it is the elections.[216] Never has a proletariat conducted itself so magnificently. In England, after the great defeat of 1848,[218] there was a relapse into apathy and, in the end, resignation to bourgeois exploitation, with the proviso that the TRADES UNIONS fought individual battles for higher wages. In France the proletariat disappeared from the stage after the 2nd December.[219] In Germany, after 3 years of unprecedented persecution and unrelenting pressure, during which any form of public organisation and even communication was a sheer impossibility, our lads have returned, not only in all their former strength, but actually stronger than before.[16] And stronger in one crucial respect, in that the movement's centre of gravity has shifted from the semi-rural districts of Saxony to the *large industrial towns*.

The bulk of our people in Saxony consist of hand-loom weavers, who are doomed to obsolescence by the power-loom and are only just enabled to keep going by starvation wages and secondary occupations (gardening, toy carving, etc.). These people find themselves in an economically reactionary situation and represent an obsolescent stage of production. So they are not born representatives of revolutionary socialism — not, at any rate, to the same degree as are the workers in large-scale industry. Hence they are not reactionary by nature (as, for instance, the remaining hand-loom weavers eventually became *over here* — the hard core of the 'CONSERVATIVE WORKING MEN') but cannot be relied upon in the long run. This is also very largely due to their appallingly miserable condition, which means that they have far less power of resistance than townsmen, and also to their dispersion, which makes them easier to enslave politically than the inhabitants of large towns. The facts reported in the *Sozialdemokrat*[a] fill one with admiration for the heroism with which so many of those poor devils continued to stand firm.

But they are not the right kind of nucleus for a great national movement. In certain circumstances — as in 1865-70 — their poverty renders them more readily receptive to socialist views than the inhabitants of large towns. But this same poverty also makes them unreliable. A drowning man clutches at any straw, nor can he wait for a boat to push off from the bank and come to his rescue. The boat is socialist revolution, the straw, protective tariffs and state socialism. It is significant that there, in our old constituencies, it was almost only conservatives who stood any chance against us. And if, on a previous occasion, Kayser could talk such rubbish about protective tariffs[220] without anyone's venturing any real objection, whose was the

---

[a] 'Warum sind wir in Glauchau (Sachsen) unterlegen?', *Sozialdemokrat*, No. 47, 17 November 1881.

blame — as Bebel himself remarked in a letter to me [221] — if not the constituents', and Kayser's in particular? Now everything's different. Berlin, Hamburg, Breslau, Leipzig, Dresden, Mainz, Offenbach, Barmen, Elberfeld, Solingen, Nuremberg, Frankfurt am Main, Hanau, *as well as* Chemnitz and the Erzgebirge districts — that's backing of quite a different order. A class that is revolutionary by reason of its economic situation has come to be the nucleus of the movement. Aside from that, the movement is evenly distributed over the entire industrial area of Germany and, from being restricted to a few local centres, has *only now come to be a national movement*. And that is what frightens the bourgeois most of all.

As regards those who have been elected, we shall have to hope for the best, although I find it very difficult to do so where some of them are concerned. But it would be a disaster if, this time, Bebel were not to be returned. [222] For there will be many new elements — each armed, no doubt, with his own little schemes — whom Bebel alone, with his unerring tact, would be able to keep in order and prevent from making asses of themselves.

As regards the French, it would now be best simply to let Messrs Malon and Brousse have their head, and show what they can do. But it's unlikely to come to that. One of these days the *Égalité* will appear; Brousse will, as before, be guardedly libellous, launching attacks in the *Prolétaire* without naming names, while the others, falling headlong into the snare, will, in their attacks, name names from the outset, whereupon they will be hailed as disturbers of the peace, sectarians, spreaders of dissension and budding dictators. Nothing can be done to stop this. The fellows are completely incapable of waiting until their opponents have got into a mess of their own contriving, but must perforce take issue with them and thus give them a longer lease of life. Left to their own devices Malon and, more especially, Brousse would scupper themselves (and probably each other) within 6 months. But as things are, it may take longer.

Like almost all such congresses, the Congress of Rheims [223] served to impress the outside world but, seen in the cold light of day, was a swindle. Of the 'federations' represented there, only the Centre, Nord and Est really exist; the others exist only on paper. The Algerian federation had elected the *bourgeois* Henry Maret (*radical deputy*) as its delegate!!, which just shows what kind of allies Malon has got. Guesde had wanted only *properly organised* federations to be represented on the *Comité national* — but his proposal was turned down. This was *misrepresented*, i. e. *suppressed*, in the official account in the *Prolétaire*.[a] Thus, half the delegates to the congress and on the *Comité national* represent *nothing at all*, or at best only castles in Spain. The haste to declare the *Prolétaire*, already completely taken over by Malon and Brousse, an official gazette was due solely to the desire to steal a march on the forthcoming *Égalité*. As usual, none of the resolutions on organisation were determined by expediency but by the opportunist considerations of the parties concerned.

Here is something that will give you an idea of Malon's Marxophobia: last spring he asked Lafargue, when the latter was in Paris, to obtain from *Marx a foreword* to the new edition of Malon's *Histoire du Socialisme*; needless to say, Lafargue laughed in his face and told him he must have a very poor idea of Marx if he thought him capable of lending himself to such humbug.

G. Howell, luckily not returned as 'labour candidate' for Stafford, is undoubtedly the biggest blackguard of all the *politicanti*[b] ex-working men here. He was until recently secretary of the TRADES UNIONS PARLIAMENTARY COMMITTEE (needless to say, a salaried post) and took occasion to cook the books, this being only hushed up with some difficulty; however, he was given the sack.

Within the next few days I shall write to K. K. of Käsburg[c] about the Polish affair.[224] In the meantime, give him my best regards.

Marx is still very run down, isn't allowed to leave his room or engage in any serious occupation, but he is visibly gaining weight. His wife is growing ever weaker.

With best regards,

Yours,

F. E.

First published, in Russian, in *Marx-Engels Archives*, Book I, Moscow, 1924

Printed according to the original

Published in English in full for the first time

---

[a] 'Cinquième congrès national ouvrier socialiste de Reims. Compte rendu analytique', *Le Prolétaire*, Nos. 162 and 163, 5 and 12 November 1881. - [b] politicising - [c] Karl Kautsky's jocular nickname (*Käse* = cheese).

92

MARX TO JENNY LONGUET [140]

IN ARGENTEUIL

London, 7 *Décembre* 1881

My dear, sweet Jennychen,

You will, assuredly, find it quite natural that I should not feel in the mood for 'writing' at the moment and hence only now be sending you this brief note. Since I haven't yet even left the sick room, there was no gainsaying the doctor's interdict on my attending the funeral. Moreover I resigned myself, for only the day before her death our dear departed [a] had told her NURSE, apropos some neglected formality: 'WE ARE NO SUCH *EXTERNAL* PEOPLE!'

Schorlemmer came up from Manchester of his own accord.

I still have to paint my chest, neck, etc., with iodine and, when regularly repeated, this produces a somewhat tiresome and painful inflammation of the skin. The said operation, which is only being performed to prevent a relapse during convalescence (now complete apart from a slight cough), is therefore doing me sterling service just at this moment. There is only one effective antidote for mental suffering, and that is physical pain. Set the end of the world on the one hand against a man with acute toothache on the other.

It now gives me extraordinary happiness to recall that, despite numerous misgivings, I ventured on the trip to Paris. Not only because of the time itself that she, of undying memory, spent with you and the little ones [b] — 'barely' marred by the image OF A CERTAIN DOMESTIC BULLY *et Mirabeau de la cuisine*,[c] but also the reliving of that time during the final phase of her illness. There can be no doubt that during that phase the presence of you and the children could not have distracted her to such good purpose as her mental preoccupation with you all!

Her resting-place is fairly close to that of dear 'Charles'.[d]

It is a comfort to me that her strength gave out before it was too late. Because of the highly unusual location of the growth — which meant that it was moveable, not static — the really typical and unbearable pain did not set in until the very last days (and even then

---

[a] Jenny Marx - [b] Jean, Henri, Edgar and Marcel Longuet - [c] and kitchen Mirabeau - [d] son of Charles and Jenny Longuet

could still be kept within limits by the injection of morphine which the doctor had intentionally held in reserve for the end, since with protracted use it ceases to have any effect). As Dr Donkin had predicted, the course of the illness assumed the form of a gradual decline, as in the weakness that comes of old age. Even during *her last hours*, there were no death agonies, a gradual falling asleep, her eyes larger, lovelier, more luminous than ever.

Apropos. Engels — as always the truest of friends — has sent you at my request a copy of the *Irish World* in which an Irish bishop *declares himself against landownership* (private). This was *one of the last items of NEWS* I passed on to *your mamma*, and she thought you might get it into A FRENCH PAPER so as to horrify *the French clericals*. At all events it shows that such gentlemen are able to pipe any tune they like.

(In *La Justice* of 2 December 1881 a certain laddie by the name of B. Gendre[a] seeks, under the title '*Le catholicisme socialiste en Allemagne*', to assuage his chauvinism by taking *au sérieux*,[b] like Laveleye before him, the *fanciful statistics* of our friend R. Meyer (in his book *Emancipationskampf des 4. Standes*). The fact is that, since the German Empire came into being, the so-called *Catholic socialists* have *only once* elected a deputy to the Reichstag and that, from the moment of his election, he 'figured' only as a 'member of the Centre'.[225] As to the *numerical strength of the Catholic labour unions*, on the other hand, our R. Meyer accords *France* a number disproportionately greater even than that he accords Germany.)

Have just received *La Justice* of *7 Décembre* and see that, under the rubric *Gazette du jour*, there is an obituary, which says inter alia:

'*On devine que son*' (*il s'agit de votre mère*) '*mariage avec Karl Marx, fils d'un avocat de Trèves, ne se fit pas sans peine. Il y avait à vaincre bien des préjugés, le plus fort de tous était encore le préjugé de race. On sait que l'illustre socialiste est d'origine israélite.*'[c]

Toute cette histoire[d] IS A *SIMPLE INVENTION*, THERE WAS *NO préjugés à vaincre*.[c] * I suppose, I am not mistaken in crediting Mr Ch. Longuet's inventive genius with this literary * '*enjolivement*'.[f] * The same writer when speaking of the limitation of the working day and the factory acts,

---

[a] real name Varvara Nikitina - [b] seriously - [c] 'One may suppose that her' (this refers to your mother) '*marriage* to Karl Marx, son of a Trier barrister [Heinrich Marx], *did not take place without difficulties. A great many prejudices* had to be overcome, *the strongest of all being racial prejudice.*The illustrious socialist is known to be of Jewish origin.' - [d] The whole thing - [e] prejudices to be overcome - [f] embellishment

mentioned in another number of the *Justice*—'Lassalle and Karl Marx', the former having never printed or spoken a syllable on the matter in question. Longuet would greatly oblige me in never mentioning my name in *his* writings.

The allusion to your Maman's occasional anonymous correspondence (in fact in behalf of Irving) [226] I find indiscreet. At the time she wrote to the *Gazette de Francfort* (she never wrote to the *Journal de Francfort*—as the *Justice* calls it—, a simply reactionary, and philistine paper) the latter (the *Gazette*) was still on more or less friendly terms with the socialist party.

As to the '*von Westphalen[s]*', they were not of Rhenish, but of* Brunswickian origin. *The father of your mother's father[a] was the factotum of the* notorious *Duke of Brunswick[b] (during the 'seven years' war'). As such he was also overwhelmed with favours on the part of the British government and married a near relative of the Argyll's.[c] His papers relative to the war and politics have been published by the Minister v. Westphalen.[d] On the other hand,* '*par sa mère*,'[e] *your mother descends from a small *Prussian* functionary[f] and was actually born at Salzwedel in the Mark. All these things need not be known, but knowing nothing of them, one ought not to pretend correcting* *d'autres*[g] ·BIOGRAPHIES·.

*And now, my dear child, send me a long description of the doings of Johnny et Co. I still regret that Henry was not left to us at the time he went on so well. He is a child who wants a whole family's attendance being singly, exclusively concentrated upon him. As it is, with so many other little ones requesting your care, he is rather an impediment.

With many kisses to you and your 'little men'[h]

Your devoted father,

K. M.

I was rather disagreeably affected by Meissner's communication, that a new third edition of the *Capital* Vol. I has become necessary. I wanted indeed to apply all my time—as soon as I should feel myself able again—exclusively to the finishing of the 2nd volume.[227]

---

[a] Christian Heinrich Philipp von Westphalen -[b] Ferdinand -[c] Jeanie Wishart of Pittarow -[d] Ch. H. Ph. von Westphalen, *Geschichte der Feldzüge des Herzogs Ferdinand von Braunschweig-Lüneburg*.-[e] through her mother -[f] Julius Christoph Heubel -[g] other -[h] Jenny Longuet's four sons

Please write a few words in my name to *Reinhardt*. I could not find his address. He was an acquaintance of Mama's.* [a]

First published, in Russian, in the magazine *Nachalo*, No. 5, St Petersburg, 1899

Printed according to the original

Published in English in full for the first time

93

MARX TO JOHANN PHILIPP BECKER [72]

IN GENEVA

[Postcard]

London, 10 December 1881

Dear Friend,

You may have already learned from the papers of my wife's death (she breathed her last on 2 December). You will find it natural enough that, during the first days following upon this irreplaceable loss, I should have been in no state to write letters; in fact, apart from her brother, Edgar von Westphalen, in Berlin you are the *only one* whom I have so far informed in person; other friends and acquaintances have been notified by my youngest daughter.[b]

To the last my wife remained your loyal friend and was rightly incensed by the party's failure to help you — a man who has, for so many years, been a staunch and heroic standard bearer — and your loyal spouse[c] in your struggle for existence.

I myself am still an invalid, but on the road to recovery; so serious a grip had pleurisy combined with bronchitis gained over me that for a time, i. e. several days, the doctors doubted whether I would pull through.

Farewell, dear friend. Regards to your wife.

K. M.

---

[a] The last two paragraphs were added by Marx at the beginning of the letter. - [b] Eleanor Marx - [c] Elisabeth Becker

[On the side reserved for the address]

M.J.Ph. Becker, Chemin des Vollandes, Eaux Vives.
Genève (Switzerland)

First published in: Marx and Engels,   Printed according to the original
Works, First Russian Edition, Vol. XXVII,
Moscow, 1935

94

MARX TO NIKOLAI DANIELSON

IN ST PETERSBURG

London, 13 December 1881

My Dear Friend,

On the second of this month, after a long and painful malady, I lost my wife. I had been with her during the autumn months—as her *garde-malade*,[a] first to the English seaside (Eastbourne), afterwards to Argenteuil (about 20 minutes from Paris) where she and myself enjoyed together the great pleasure to be with our eldest daughter (Madame Longuet) and her 4 little boys[b] (the eldest about 5 years), all exceedingly attached to their grandparents.

It was a very risky affair, on my part, to undertake this voyage to Paris, considering the enfeebled state of my dear wife. But trusting to my excellent friend, Dr Donkin, I dared it in order to procure her this last satisfaction!

Unfortunately, my own health having been more or less shaky during all this time, I suddenly underwent—after our return to London—an attack of bronchitis complicated by a pleurisy, so that during 3 out of the last 6 weeks of her life, I could not see my wife, although we were in two rooms contiguous to each other.

Till now I was not yet able to leave my house. I was very near 'leaving this bad world'. The doctors want to send me to the south of France or even to Algeria.

_____
[a] nurse - [b] Jean, Henri, Edgar and Marcel

The letters of condolence I have received from all sides were so far a great source of consolation for me, as there rang through them (except a single *Russian* letter) a true ring of sympathy, of true acknowledgment and understanding of the rare qualities of my dear wife. My German editor [a] informs me that a third edition of the *Capital* has become necessary. This comes at a moment anything but opportune. In the first instance I must first be restored to health, and in the second I want to finish off the 2nd vol.[227] (even if to be published abroad) as soon as possible. I have now the additional interest to have it ready in order to inscribe in it a dedication to my wife.

However that may be, I will arrange with my editor that I shall make for the 3d edition only the fewest possible alterations and additions, but, on the other hand, that he must this time only draw off 1,000 copies, instead of 3,000, as was his want. When these 1,000 copies forming the 3d edition are sold, then I may change the book in the way I should have done at present under different circumstances.

Believe me always

Your true friend

A. Williams [b]

First published, in Russian, in *Minuvshiye gody*, No. 1, St Petersburg, 1908

Reproduced from the original

Published in English for the first time

95

MARX TO FRIEDRICH ADOLPH SORGE [228]

IN HOBOKEN

[London,] 15 December 1881

Dear Sorge,

Having heard our news from over here by word of mouth from your son,[c] you must surely have been prepared to learn of the death of my wife, my unforgettable and beloved partner (on 2 December).

[a] Otto Meissner - [b] Marx's pseudonym - [c] Adolph Sorge

I myself had not recovered sufficiently to pay her my last respects. Indeed, I have so far been confined to the house, but am to go to Ventnor (Isle of Wight) next week.

I am emerging from this last illness doubly handicapped, emotionally by the loss of my wife, physically in that I am left with a thickening of the pleura and increased sensitivity of the bronchial tubes.

I shall, alas, have to fritter away a certain amount of time on schemes for restoring my health.

Another edition of the German text of *Capital* [227] has now become necessary. Most inopportune so far as I'm concerned.

Your Henry George is increasingly revealing himself to be a humbug.

I trust Sorge jun. arrived in good shape; give him my regards.

Your
K. Marx

The English have latterly begun to take rather more notice of *Capital*, etc. For instance, in last *October's* (or November's, *I am not quite sure *) issue of the *Contemporary*, there was an article by *John Rae* on GERMAN SOCIALISM. [a] (Very inadequate, full of mistakes, but ʹFAIRʹ, as one of my ENGLISH FRIENDS remarked to me day before yesterday.) And why FAIR? *Because John Rae does *not suppose* that for the forty years I am spreading my pernicious theories I was being instigated by ʹ*bad*ʹ motives.* ʹI must praise his magnanimity!ʹ *The fairness of making yourself at least sufficiently acquainted with the subject of your criticism seems a thing quite unknown to the penmen of British philistinism.

Before this, in the beginning of June, there was published by a certain *Hyndman* (who had before intruded himself into my house) a little book: *England for All*. It pretends to be written as an *exposé* of the programme of the ʹ*Democratic Federation*ʹ [158]— a recently formed association of different English and Scotch radical societies, half bourgeois, half *prolétaires*.[b] The chapters on Labour and Capital are only literal extracts from, or circumlocutions of, the *Capital*, but the fellow does neither quote the book, nor its author, but to shield himself from exposure remarks at the end of his preface:

---

[a] J. Rae, ʹThe Socialism of Karl Marx and the Young Hegeliansʹ, *The Contemporary Review*, Vol. XL, October 1881.- [b] See this volume, pp. 102-03.

'For the ideas and much of the matter contained in chapters II and III, I am indebted to the work of a great thinker and original writer, etc., etc.'

Vis-à-vis myself, the fellow wrote stupid letters of excuse, for instance, that 'the English don't like to be taught by foreigners', that 'my name was so much detested, etc.' With all that his little book — so far as it pilfers the *Capital* — makes good propaganda, although the man is a 'weak' vessel, and very far from having even the patience — the first condition of learning anything — of studying a matter thoroughly. All these amiable middle-class writers — if not specialists — have an itching to make money or name or political capital *immediately* out of any new thoughts they may have got at by any favourable windfall. Many evenings this fellow has pilfered from me, in order to take me out and to learn in the easiest way.

Lastly, there was published on the 1st December last (I shall send you a copy of it) in the monthly review *Modern Thought* an article: '*Leaders of Modern Thought*: No. XXIII — *Karl Marx. By Ernest Belfort Bax.*'

Now this is the first English publication of that kind which is pervaded by a real enthusiasm for the new ideas themselves and boldly stands up against British philistinism.This does not prevent that the biographical notices the author gives of me are mostly wrong, etc. In the exposition of my economic principles and in his translations (i. e. quotations of the *Capital*) much is wrong and confused, but with all that the appearance of this article, announced in large letters by placards on the walls of West End London, has produced a great sensation. What was most important for me, I received the said number of *Modern Thought* already on the 30th of November, so that my dear wife had the last days of her life still cheered up. You know the passionate interest she took in all such affairs.*

First published in *Briefe und Auszüge aus Briefen von Joh. Phil. Becker, Jos. Dietzgen, Friedrich Engels, Karl Marx u. A. an F. A. Sorge und Andere*, Stuttgart, 1906

Printed according to the original

96

MARX TO JENNY LONGUET [72]

IN ARGENTEUIL

London, 17 December 1881
41 Maitland Park Road, N. W.

My Dear Child,

Tussy, SUPPORTED BY Engels, is this moment taking the Christmas hamper for our little ones by CAB to the PARCEL COMPANY. *Helen*[a] wants me to point out specially that 1 little jacket for Harry, 1 for Eddy,[b] and a woollen bonnet for Pa[c] are *from her*; again for the selfsame Pa, a 'little blue frock' from *Laura*; from myself a SAILOR'S SUIT for MY DEAR Johnny. On one of the last days of her life, Möhmchen[d] laughed so merrily when telling Laura how you and I took Johnny to Paris, and chose a suit for him there in which he looked like a little *bourgeois gentilhomme*.[e]

The letters of condolence I get from near and far, and from people of such various nationalities, professions, etc., etc., are, in their appreciation of Möhmchen, all of them animated by a spirit of truth and a depth of feeling rarely found in what are as a rule merely conventional tributes. I ascribe this to the fact that everything about her was natural and genuine, unforced and without affectation. Hence the impression she made on others was one of vivaciousness and lucidity; even Mrs Hess writes:

'In her, Nature has destroyed its own masterpiece, for never in my life have I met so witty and loving a woman.'[229]

Liebknecht writes to say that, without her, he would have succumbed to the wretchedness of exile,[230] etc., etc.

How exceptionally healthy she was by nature, for all her delicate constitution, is evident from the fact that, despite being bed-ridden for so long, she did not have a sore spot on her body, much to the astonishment of the doctors; during my recent illness I already had a number of sore places after only two weeks of being confined to bed.

---

[a] Demuth - [b] Edgar Longuet - [c] Marcel Longuet - [d] Pet name for Jenny Marx. -
[e] a bourgeois with pretensions to gentility (from the title of a play by Molière)

The weather has been very bad since I got over my illness, so I have been under house arrest up till now, but next week, on doctors' orders, I am to go to Ventnor (Isle of Wight) and from there, later on, somewhere further south. Tussy will accompany me.

You will be getting (posted at the same time as this) an article about me in the monthly review *Modern Thought*.[a] It's the first time an English critic has gone into the matter with such enthusiasm. It arrived in time to cheer Möhmchen up. Where the QUOTATIONS from the German 'text' are too bad (I MEAN too badly DONE INTO ENGLISH), I have got Tussy to write in corrections on such few copies as we are reserving for friends. The mistakes that occur under the heading 'LIFE' are indifferent.

And now, my dear child, the best service you can do me is to keep your chin up! I hope that I shall spend many more happy days with you and worthily fulfil my functions as a GRANDPA.

With a thousand kisses to you and the little ones,

Your loving
OLD NICK

I could have written much more about Vivanti, etc., but believe that Tussy has bagged this for herself.

First published, in Russian, in the magazine *Nachalo*, No. 5, St Petersburg, 1899   Printed according to the original

97

ENGELS TO KARL KAUTSKY

IN ZURICH

London, 18 December 1881

Dear Mr Kautsky,

I got the telegram from you and Bernstein at 3.50 this afternoon and am glad to be able to inform you that Marx has now recovered to

---

[a] See this volume, p. 163.

the extent that he can be sent—initially—to the south coast of England. He will be going there in the course of this week; as soon as he has grown a little more accustomed to the open air and there is no further fear of a relapse, he will then probably move on to the south of Europe and spend some time there.

I couldn't reply to you by telegram, as it would have meant going to the CENTRAL OFFICE and, as usual, I had Pumps, her husband[a] and Sam Moore (all of whom send you their best wishes) here for a meal and later on, as you can imagine, more people dropped in. There would hardly be any point in telegraphing tomorrow as this letter will doubtless arrive just as soon ($\pm$).[b]

About the Poles, something presently [224]; things here have been rather at sixes and sevens of late.

So the *Égalité* is appearing again. Almost all the articles in No. 1 begin quite splendidly and end up most disappointingly.[231] I haven't seen No. 2 yet.

Best wishes to Bernstein.

Yours

F. Engels

First published, in Russian, in *Marx-Engels Archives*, Vol. I (VI), Moscow, 1932

Printed according to the original

Published in English for the first time

98

ENGELS TO FERDINAND DOMELA NIEUWENHUIS

IN THE HAGUE

London, 29 December 1881
122 Regent's Park Road, N. W.

Dear Comrade,

I am glad to be able to inform you that the news according to which Karl Marx is mortally sick is wholly false and fictitious. He has

---

[a] Percy Rosher - [b] more or less

MAYALL'S PHOTOGRAPHIC STUDIO, 224, REGENT ST LONDON.

Herr Roland Daniels

mit freundschaftlichem Gruss

31, December, 1881.   Karl Marx

Ventnor (Isle of Wight)

Dies Photogram hatte meine Tochter zufällig
mitgebracht bei unserer Abreise von London;
Sie theile ich damit, nachdem meine Briefe an
Ihre Frau Mutter und Sie selbst bereits
expedirt waren, daher diese Nachsendung.

now got over his illness (bronchitis and pleurisy) and, on the advice of his doctors, has today left for Ventnor (the Isle of Wight); they hope that the warm climate and dry air there will rapidly complete his recovery. I will forward your letter to him.

Yours sincerely,
F. Engels

First published, in Russian, in the magazine *Istorik-Marksist*, Vol. 6 (40), Moscow, 1934

Printed according to the original

Translated from the Dutch

Published in English for the first time

99

MARX TO ROLAND DANIELS [232]

IN COLOGNE

To Mr Roland Daniels
     with compliments

Karl Marx

Ventnor (Isle of Wight),
31 December 1881

My daughter[a] happened to bring this photogram with her when we left London; she told me of this when my letters to your esteemed mother[b] and yourself[233] had already been despatched. Hence this is being sent later.

First published in German and in Russian in: Karl Marx, Frederick Engels, *Collection of Photographs*, Moscow, 1976

Printed according to the copy of the original

Published in English for the first time

---

[a] Eleanor Marx - [b] Amalie Daniels

100

ENGELS TO LEV HARTMANN

IN LONDON

[Draft]

[London, end of December 1881]

I have a letter from America for you, but I am instructed to hand it to you personally.

Can you come and receive it?

Your[a]

First published in: Marx and Engels, *Works,* First Russian Edition, Vol. XXVII, Moscow, 1935

Printed according to the original

Translated from the Russian

Published in English for the first time

---

[a] Unsigned

1882

101

MARX TO LAURA LAFARGUE [72]

IN LONDON

Ventnor, 4 January 1882
1 St Boniface Gardens

Dear Laurachen,

Today is our first sunny and tolerable day in Ventnor. The weather is said to have been excellent — up till the time of our arrival.[234] Thereafter GALES EVERY DAY, wind raging and howling throughout the night, in the morning THE SKY OVERCAST, LEADEN, LONDONLIKE. Temperature significantly lower than in London and, on top of that, and most tiresome of all, a great deal of rain. (The air itself was of course 'purer' than in London.)

In the circumstances it was only natural that my cough, IN FACT my bronchial catarrh, should have got worse rather than better. But for all that I have progressed to the extent that for part of the night I sleep naturally, without opium, etc. However my general condition is not such as to render me fit for work. Today, ABOUT the end of the first week of our stay, it looks as though a change is setting in. Given warmer weather this would certainly be a splendid health resort for convalescents of my description.

My companion[a] (this *strictly between ourselves*) eats practically nothing; suffers badly from nervous tics; reads and writes all day long, when not engaged in buying the necessary provisions or taking short walks. She is very taciturn and, INDEED, seemingly endures staying with me simply out of a sense of duty, as a self-sacrificing martyr.

Has there been no more news from Jenny about the arrival of the CHRISTMAS BOX[b]? I'm worried about the thing.

---

[a] Eleanor Marx - [b] See this volume, p. 164.

You will understand, dear child, if I have nothing positive to report to you from here, my experiences hitherto having been purely negative, unless it be the great discovery that local literature here is represented by 3 newspapers, and that there is even A SCHOOL OF ART and SCIENCE INSTITUTION where a big lecture is to be given next Monday evening ON THE CASTES AND 'MÉTIERS' OF INDIA.

Today I received a letter from Reinhardt in Paris in which he speaks of our sad bereavement[a] in the MOST SINCERE and MOST SYMPATHETIC manner. The vehemence with which the bourgeois papers in Germany have announced either my demise, or at any rate the inevitable imminence thereof, has tickled me hugely, and the 'man at odds with the world' will have to get fit for action again, if only to oblige them.

Willard Brown has written to Tussy from New York; he has entrusted the business of your house to a very intimate and competent friend of his in new Orleans[235]; the latter has written to say that AT FIRST SIGHT there has been a great deal of underhand work but that he must first make further investigations in order to obtain actual proof.

I enclose, as a curiosity for Paul,[b] a cutting from the *MONEY ARTICLE* in *The Times* (29 December 1881) which was obviously inserted by Messrs Say and Rothschild.[c](Regards to Paul and Helen.[d])

Adio, MY DEAR CHILD, write soon.

Your

OLD NICK

First published in the language of the original (German) in *Annali,* an. I, Milano, 1958

Printed according to the original

---

[a] the death of Jenny Marx - [b] Lafargue - [c] 'Money-Market and City Intelligence', *The Times,* No. 30390, 29 December 1881.- [d] Demuth

102

MARX TO ENGELS[140]

IN LONDON

Ventnor, 5 January 1882
1 St Boniface Gardens

Dear FRED,

Cold and wet during the day, raging winds at night; that, by and large, is the kind of weather and climate we've been experiencing here up till today.[234] — The exception was yesterday, when it was dry with brilliant sunshine.— According to letters received by Tussy, it has been the same everywhere on the south coast of England; disappointment everywhere on the part of the not inconsiderable number of convalescing, etc., rabble. *Qui vivra verra.*[a] Perhaps there will be a change for the better.

I now wear — (*au cas de besoin*[b]) — a muzzle, alias RESPIRATOR; this makes one less dependent on the caprices of the weather when taking one's obligatory walk.

I still have a tiresome and persistent cough and bronchial catarrh; but it's an undoubted step forward that I should get a few hours sleep at night without recourse to artificial remedies, and this despite the roar of the wind across the sea close by; on the contrary, the noise helps to send me to sleep.

My companion, Tussy, is sorely plagued with nervous tics and insomnia, etc. However I hope that her frequent excursions in the fresh air — for she goes into 'town' every day to attend to this and that — will have a beneficial effect on her.

What has tickled me greatly was the announcement by the LIBERAL ASSOCIATION — I no longer recall where, Birmingham perhaps[236] — that, in celebration of some ANNIVERSARY or other, not only will OLD Bright and THE ILLUSTRIOUS VESTRYMAN AND CAUCUSMAN Chamberlain be speaking, *but that also old Obadiah's 'son', Mr Jacob Bright jun.[237] and several 'Miss' Cobden, are to put in their appearance. It is not said whether one of the 'Miss' Cobden or all of them will be given away to the young Obadiah, so as to perpetuate in the most appropriate and safest way the Bright-Cobden stock.*

---

[a] Who survives will see.- [b] in case of need

A different picture is presented by the 3,000 LANDLORDS' MEETING AT Dublin,[238] *duce*[a] Abercorn, the sole aim of which is *'to maintain... contracts and *the freedom between man and man in this realm'.* The laddies' rage at the ASSISTANT COMMISSIONERS is comical. Their attacks on Gladstone are, by the by, fully justified, but it is only the latter's COERCITIVE [sic] MEASURES and his 50,000 men,[123] not counting the police, that permit these gentlemen to confront him in so critical and threatening a manner. All this uproar is, of course, merely aimed at getting John Bull ready to pay 'compensation costs'. SERVES HIM RIGHT.

You will see from the enclosed letter from Dietzgen that the unhappy fellow has 'progressed' backwards and safely 'arrived' at the *Phänomenologie.*[239] I regard the case as an incurable one.

I have also had a very kind letter of condolence from Reinhardt in Paris who asks me to give you, amongst others, his kindest regards. He always had a soft spot for my beloved partner.

I wish I were fit for action again; not yet reached that stage, alas. With best wishes from Tussy.

Your

Moor

First published in *Der Briefwechsel zwischen F. Engels und K. Marx,* Bd. 4, Stuttgart, 1913

Printed according to the original

Published in English in full for the first time

103

ENGELS TO EDUARD BERNSTEIN

IN ZURICH

London, 6 January 1882

Dear Mr Bernstein,

I am writing to you in haste today in order to shed some light on the peculiar expressions that occur in the last number of the *Égalité*

---

[a] under the leadership of

on the subject of the *Sozialdemokrat*. The point is that, out of the goodness of his heart, Guesde engaged for the German section of the paper a person known to be the mortal enemy of everything appertaining to 'Zurich',[a] and the said person was unable to refrain from thus expressing his displeasure that the *Sozialdemokrat* should survive and not the *Laterne*. You would oblige us and serve the cause by taking no notice of this. If it happens again, we shall at once put a stop to it. By contrast, we were delighted that the *Sozialdemokrat* should not have hesitated to accuse the deputies of downright cowardice, thus bringing matters to a head, something which many of them, had Bebel not been there, would doubtless have sooner avoided.[240]

The *Égalité* people, by the way, have been luckier than, *au fond*,[b] they deserved. Malon and Brousse made horrible fools of themselves in connection with Joffrin's candidature by putting forward a watered-down programme — in defiance of the congressional resolution passed at Rheims,[223] and quite simply suppressed one of the points discussed there, just because it happened not to suit their book (*Égalité*, No. 4, p. 7, Paris).[c] In this way they put the *Égalité* in the right which, in the circumstances and on tactical grounds, was absolutely imperative — not Guesde and Co., but Malon and Co., were the real '*autoritaires*',[d] the strivers after dictatorship.[e] And, now that the struggle has come out into the open, I need hardly say that our sympathies lie wholly with Guesde and his friends. Moreover, the *Égalité* is, and always has been, infinitely superior to the *Prolétaire* as far as content is concerned. Malon and Brousse are again behaving like true Bakuninists: they accuse others of hankering for dictatorship and, under pretence of maintaining their 'autonomy', want to rule the roost themselves without regard for party resolutions.

Marx is at Ventnor in the Isle of Wight, but writes to say that the weather is atrocious,[f] worse than here. Well, it will soon change, no doubt; at all events, there would now seem to be no real danger of a relapse. The haste the bourgeois press was in to disseminate the news of his confidently anticipated demise did him no end of good: 'Now I must live to a ripe old age, if only to spite the damned rascals.'

---

[a] Carl Hirsch - [b] really - [c] 'Allemagne', *L'Égalité*, 3rd series, No. 4, 1 January 1882.- [d] authoritarians - [e] 'Paris', *L'Égalité*, 3rd series, No. 4, 1 January 1882.- [f] See this volume, p. 171.

Kautsky will have to be patient for a few more days. Schorlemmer is still here, which means that the most that I can do is dabble in natural science; on top of that, there's all the coming and going which won't be over until next week. Then, when time's no object, as Schorlemmer says Darmstadt-fashion, I'll write to him about the Poles.[a]

Kindest regards to him and you,

from yours

F. Engels

First published, in Russian, in *Marx-Engels Archives*, Book I, Moscow, 1924

Printed according to the original

Published in English for the first time

104

ENGELS TO MARX

IN VENTNOR

London, 8 January 1882

Dear Moor,

We were glad to hear that there was no reason for yours and Tussy's silence and, even though you couldn't be expected to make very much progress in view of the adverse weather, you have at least benefited to the extent that the danger of a relapse has now been pretty well eliminated, which was, after all, the main reason why you were sent to Ventnor.

The festive season here ends tomorrow. Schorlemmer will be returning to Manchester, and then it's back to the grindstone. I am looking forward to it; things were really getting too much. Tuesday with Lenchen, Friday with Pumps, yesterday with the Lafargues, today here at my house — and every morning the eternal Pilsener; it couldn't go on indefinitely. Lenchen was always one of the party, of course, and still is, so she hasn't felt too lonely.

---

[a] See this volume, pp. 191-95.

By the time you get this note you will have been edified by old William's[a] magnificent proclamation in which he avows his solidarity with Bismarck and declares all this to be the free expression of his own opinion.[241] I also liked the bit about the inviolability of the person of the monarch having persisted in Prussia since time immemorial. Particularly when one considers the shots fired by Nobiling.[120] How comforting for Alexander II and III that their persons should be inviolable! One might, by the way, imagine that one was living under a travesty of Charles X when one reads that sort of drivel.

There has been yet another nice item in *The Standard*, a letter from a Russian general about the situation and the Nihilists,[242] just like what used to be said and written by the Prussian generals of 1845 about demagogues,[243] liberals, Jews, the bad principles of the French, and the universal and undying loyalty to the king felt by the sound core of the nation. Which didn't, of course, set the revolution back one day. You will have seen that the *zemstvos*[37] have rebelled against Ignatiev, partly via the medium of petitions, partly by an outright refusal to convene.[244] That is a most important step, the first to be taken by official bodies under Alexander III.

Like you, we hope for better weather. Yesterday was very fine with a north-wester from which you will have been sheltered. Schorlemmer and I were on the go the whole day and it was not until half past midnight that we accompanied Lenchen home from Laura's, covering the whole distance on foot. Today it's been beastly and wet, though during a brighter spell we got out and about for an hour or so with Sam Moore who turned up again the day before yesterday. It's blowing good and hard again outside. How is Tussy actually? Regards to her and to you from us all.

Your
F. E.

First published in *Der Briefwechsel zwischen F. Engels und K. Marx*, Bd. 4, Stuttgart, 1913

Printed according to the original

Published in English for the first time

---

[a] William I

105

MARX TO ENGELS [166]

IN LONDON

Ventnor, 12 January 1882
1 St Boniface Gardens

Dear Engels,

I am going to try spending one more week here (the 3rd as from today); so far there's been no improvement in the weather — if anything the reverse. On Monday, Tussy is going up to London for a theatrical performance she is taking part in, after which she will come back here.

By the time I left London, I had to pay out SOMEWHAT LESS THAN £ 20 of the £ 40 you gave me on unavoidable expenses. Here my lodgings cost me 2 GUINEAS a week and with coal and gas but excluding other EX-TRAS, ABOUT £ 2 15s.; remaining weekly expenditure ABOUT 4 GUINEAS. Considering the climatic performance this hole has put up, it's a tidy sum. Including travelling expenses, I have spent ABOUT £ 17 and have still got £ 5. This will not suffice for the last week (incl. Tussy's INCI-DENTAL London TRIP and our probable return together next week). So I'd be grateful if you could let me have SOME £ by Monday NEXT, if it can be done.

As for future plans, the first consideration must be to relieve Tussy of her role as my companion (when I again set forth I shall be able to dispense with an escort altogether). The girl is under such MENTAL PRESSURE that it is undermining her health. Neither travelling, nor CHANGE OF CLIMATE, nor PHYSICIANS CAN DO ANYTHING IN THIS CASE. All one can do for her is to do as she wishes, and let her take a course of theatrical LESSONS with Madame Jung. She has an ardent desire to open up a ca-reer for herself, or so she imagines, as an independent, active artist and, once this has been conceded, she is undoubtedly right in saying that, at her age, there's no more time to be lost. Not for anything in the world would I have the girl think she is to be sacrificed as an old man's 'nurse' on the altar of family. In fact, I am convinced that *pro nunc* [a] Madame Jung is the only doctor for her. She is not open

---

[a] for the time being

with me; what I say is based on observation, not on her own statements. Nor is the above assertion in any way incompatible with the
fact that the most disquieting symptoms, which notably occur at
night, are of an alarmingly hysterical nature, or so Miss Maitland[a]
told me (she spent 2 days here). But for this, too, no remedy is available just now save an absorbing and congenial pursuit. I have certain conjectures about her affairs of the 'heart', but that is too delicate a subject to admit of discussion in black and white.

I have had a letter from the Sorge family,[245] written by the old
man, countersigned by Mrs Sorge and Sorge jun.,[b] in which they
invite me TO TURN OVER A NEW LEAF, i. e. go and settle with them in
New York. Well meant, at any rate!

In the *Arbeiterstimme* in which C. Schramm, invoking myself, attacked Karl Bürkli,[c] Bürkli now attacks Schramm, [d] for whose benefit he demonstrates that everything he [Schramm] has adduced is
quite beside the point since I nowhere consider the kind of money he,
Bürkli, proposes, namely 'interest-bearing mortgage bank certificates'.
Bürkli does, however, express surprise that I should make no mention
of the Pole, August Cieszkowski (*Du crédit et de la circulation*, Paris,
1839), although in his *Système des contradictions économiques* that 'rough
diamond Proudhon' frequently, if respectfully, takes issue with Cieszkowski (the 'prior inventor' of Bürkli's bank certificates). The said
Cieszkowski — a count, as Bürkli, NATIVE of Switzerland, remarks, and
a ['doctor of philosophy' and 'Hegelian'][e] INTO THE BARGAIN, if not actually a *'fellow-countryman* of Marx', i. e. as 'deputy for Posen' in the
'Prussian' National Assembly — the said count, etc., did in fact once
call on me in Paris (at the time of the *Deutsch-Französische Jahrbücher*),
and such was the impression he made on me that I neither wanted
nor would have been able to read anything whatever of his contriving. Nevertheless, it's a notable fact that the inventors of 'real' credit
money, which was meant to serve as a means of circulation at the
same time, as opposed to what they call 'personal' credit money (e. g.
present-day bank-notes), should have chanced their hand — albeit
in vain — as far back as the founding of the Bank of England, and
this in the interests and at the behest of the landed aristocracy.[f] At

---

[a] Dolly Maitland - [b] Friedrich Adolph, Katharina and Adolph Sorge - [c] C. Schramm,
'Karl Bürkli und Karl Marx', *Arbeiterstimme*, Nos. 52 and 53, 24 and 31 December
1881.- [d] K. Bürkli, 'Abschüttelungs halber', *Arbeiterstimme*, 7 and 14 January 1882.-
[e] manuscript damaged - [f] See K. Marx, *Capital*, Vol. III, Part V, Ch.XXXVI (present edition, Vol. 37).

all events, Bürkli is under a delusion as to the 'historical' date of birth of the Cieszkowskian 'idea', independently rediscovered by himself.

What has struck me from the first about the Bismarck-William manifesto [241] is the confusion as between Prussian king and German emperor! In the latter capacity, the laddie has, after all, no historical antecedents whatsoever, nor yet Hohenzollern traditions (on which a start has now been made with the 'Prince of Prussia's' ostentatious trip to England — to study the Constitution! [246]). After the nauseous protestations, expiring in submissive love, of your Mommsens, Richters, Hänels [247] *et tutti quanti*,[a] it was charming of Bismarck to play this card — however silly his manner of doing it. With any luck we shall yet see something happen.

Your
K. M.

First published in *Der Briefwechsel zwischen F. Engels und K. Marx*, Bd. 4, Stuttgart, 1913

Printed according to the original

Published in English in full for the first time

106

ENGELS TO EMIL ENGELS

IN ENGELSKIRCHEN

London, 12 January 1882

Dear Emil,

After sundry disturbances and unforeseen events, among which the eating and drinking that goes with the festive season, I have composed myself sufficiently to send you, Lottchen, Elisabeth and her fiancé[b] my heartiest congratulations on their engagement. I would never have thought, when travelling to Manchester with August Erbslöh in the late autumn of 1842 [248] (I've only seen him once or

---

[a] and all the rest - [b] Charlotte and Elisabeth Engels, Carl Alexander Erbslöh

twice since then in Barmen), that his son would marry a niece of mine. Admittedly, neither of the two young people had been so much as thought of at that time. It is a subject that lends itself to all kinds of suitable and unsuitable remarks — which, however, I shall refrain from making since anyone can easily do that for himself and the young couple will in any case be much too preoccupied with present and future to have time for utterly useless comments on a past that is antecedent to their births.

Apart from that, I shall soon be moved to hope that engagements in our family, along with their more immediate and more remote consequences, will come at rather less frequent intervals, though admittedly in a family as numerous and prolific as ours these cases multiply proportionately to the square of the distance in time from a starting-point that lies over 60 years behind us, and there's no going against a natural law such as that.

I'm keeping quite well on the whole, except that I'm rather deaf in my left ear and regularly catch cold during the winter, but I got used to that years ago. At all events, the mild winter will help you shake off the effects of pneumonia, or at any rate alleviate them. Today it turned so warm again that I had to take my greatcoat off, despite a bit of SCOTCH MIST.

Love to you all, especially to Lottchen and the happy couple.

Your
Friedrich

I shall be glad to see Emil[a] here.

First published in: Marx and Engels, *Works*, First Russian Edition, Vol. XXVII, Moscow, 1935

Printed according to the original

Published in English for the first time

---

[a] Emil Engels jun.

107

MARX TO AMALIE DANIELS

IN COLOGNE

[Ventnor,] Isle of Wight, 12 January 1882
1 St Boniface Gardens

My dear Mrs Daniels,

On the same day as I wrote to you,[233] my daughter[a] found an even earlier photograph of mine among the papers she had brought with her from London. I at once sent it to Cologne[b] in the enclosed envelope, the same in which it was returned to me by the 'Imperial Post Office'.

Perhaps you would be so good as to send me *your exact address.* I shall then despatch the *corpus delicti*[c] anew.[249]

Best regards.

Yours very sincerely,
K. Marx

First published in: Marx and Engels, *Works*, First Russian Edition, Vol. XXVII, Moscow, 1935

Printed according to the original

Published in English for the first time

108

ENGELS TO MARX

IN VENTNOR

London, 13 January 1882

Dear Moor,

First, I enclose £20 in 4 bank-notes à 5 GK 53969, 70, 71, 72. London, 7 October 1881. I have in addition given Lenchen £10 so

---

[a] Eleanor Marx - [b] See this volume, p. 167.- [c] exhibit

that she can pay the RATES and still have something in hand. Next week, larger amounts will become available and then, after your return, we shall be able to make further plans.

I'm very glad that you should feel strong enough to be able to travel alone in future.

I skimmed through part of the Schramm-Bürkliade[a] and was greatly tickled by it. Even before 1842, Cieszkowski had already written a book on natural philosophy (botany)[b] and, if I am not mistaken, also contributed to the *Deutsche*, if not actually the *Hallische Jahrbücher*.[c]

Our Parisian friends have reaped what they had sown. What we had both of us told them would happen has actually come to pass. They have, by their impatience, ruined what was a first-rate position which, if they were to have made the most of it, called precisely for discretion and the ability to wait and see. For Malon and Brousse had set a trap for them in true old Alliance style [67] — calumny in the form of mere hints, no open naming of names, and supplemented on the sly by word of mouth; they went straight into it like so many schoolboys (Lafargue in the van), inasmuch as they counterattacked *by name* and were then dubbed disturbers of the peace. Moreover, their argument is so utterly puerile; as soon as one reads their opponents' retort, this leaps to the eye. Thus Guesde suppresses important qualificative passages of Joffrin's because they don't suit his book, and *fails to mention* the fact that, despite his opposition, the Comité national [250] declared Joffrin's programme to be *more radical* than the *programme minimum*,[251] thus giving Joffrin the party's *blessing*. A fact which he, of course, triumphantly parades before Guesde.[d] Then Lafargue words his articles in such a way as to enable Malon to say in reply: 'But have we ever maintained that the struggles of the medieval *communiers*[e] against the feudal aristocracy were anything but *class struggles* — and do you, Mr Lafargue, contest this?' — And now we get jeremiad after jeremiad from Paris, saying that they have been hopelessly defeated and, at the next meeting of the Comité national, would even be set upon physically, and Guesde is as despairing as he was uppish 4 weeks ago, and can see no salvation in anything short of secession by

---

[a] See this volume, p. 177.- [b] A. von Cieszkowski, *Prolegomena zur Historiosophie*, Berlin, 1838.- [c] *Deutsche Jahrbücher für Wissenschaft und Kunst* and *Hallische Jahrbücher für deutsche Wissenschaft und Kunst* - [d] J. Joffrin, 'A M. Jules Guesde, rédacteur de *l'Égalité*', *Le Prolétaire*, No. 171, 7 January 1882.- [e] commoners

the minority. And *now*, finding to their astonishment that they are having to lie on the bed they have made,—now they come to the laudable conclusion that they must eschew all personalities!

I am sending you an old *Kölnische Zeitung* which, however, contains a very interesting article on Russia.[252]

Incidentally, the factum (anti-Guesde) in the *Prolétaire*, written by Malon and Brousse and signed by Joffrin, is a splendid example of Bakuninist polemics and very much in the style of the 'Sonvillier circular',[253] but ruder.

So the ukase has been issued *re* the reduction of *vykup*[a] payments.[254] Having regard to the colossal *nedoimki*,[b] the paltry per cent or two will, no doubt, make a great deal of difference! But every million it doesn't get makes a difference to the Russian Treasury.

Bismarck, by the way, has had better luck than might have been expected: the Reichstag has endorsed his pilgrimage to Canossa by a $^2/_3$ majority.[255] But that would seem to be about the only thing upon which this Reichstag is able to agree. A fine majority: feudalists, ultramontanes, particularists, Poles, Danes, Alsatians, a few men of Progress,[256] demoscratchers and socialists!

Ad vocem[c] pilgrimages, this morning I met Furnivall wearing a blue ulster, belted at the waist, and a broad-brimmed hat—he looked exactly like a pilgrim going to the Holy Land on a quest for St Anthony's beard.

Kindest regards to Tussy.

Your
F. E.

First published abridged in *Der Briefwechsel zwischen F. Engels und K. Marx*, Bd. 4, Stuttgart, 1913 and in full in *MEGA*, Abt. III, Bd. 4, Berlin, 1931

Printed according to the original

Published in English for the first time

---

[a] redemption - [b] deficit - [c] As to

109

MARX TO ENGELS

IN LONDON

[Ventnor,] 15 January 1882

DEAR FRED,

BEST THANKS FOR THE £ 20.

I have resolved to leave tomorrow as the weather is getting progressively 'colder', which does my swollen cheek no good. So I shall lose only 2 days, and this will also save Tussy the double journey. Though repeatedly warned, our people in Paris have got themselves into a nice mess[a] (SERVES Lafargue AND Guesde RIGHT); however, since they possess two papers,[b] they may, with a little ingenuity, nevertheless gain command of the field.

I regard it as a major victory, not only in Germany itself but vis-à-vis the outside world GENERALLY, that Bismarck should *admit* in the Reichstag that the German workers have to some extent 'given the thumbs down' to his state socialism.[257] London's rascally bourgeois press always sought to disseminate the opposite.

I have received an extraordinarily kind letter from OLD Frankel from the 'state prison', ditto a letter from Wróblewski who was *évidemment*[c] writing on behalf of his Polish party in Geneva[258]; but in his haste he forgot to append not only the party's name but also his own.

If, as Joffrin relates in his factum in the *Prolétaire*,[d] he once staged *a pro-Guesde demonstration* in London against the 'International' there, it was at all events such a *platonic* demonstration that no one knew anything about it apart from Joffrin himself and perhaps a few of his closest accomplices, i. e. it was carried out entirely in 'private'.
Salut.

Your
Moor

First published abridged in *Der Briefwechsel zwischen F. Engels und K. Marx*, Bd. 4, Stuttgart, 1913 and in full in *MEGA*, Abt. III, Bd. 4, Berlin, 1931

Printed according to the original

Published in English for the first time

---

[a] See this volume, pp. 181 - 82. - [b] *L'Égalité* and *Le Citoyen* - [c] evidently - [d] See previous letter.

110

MARX TO PYOTR LAVROV [72]

IN PARIS

London, 23 January 1882
41 Maitland Park Road, N. W.

Dear Friend,

I enclose a few lines for the Russian edition of the Communist *Manifesto*[a]; as these are to be *translated* into Russian they have not been polished to the degree that would be necessary if they were to be published IN THE GERMAN VERNACULAR.

I have only been back in London for a few days. For as a result of pleurisy and bronchitis, from which I had recovered, I was left with chronic bronchial catarrh which my doctor[b] hoped to clear up by sending me to Ventnor (Isle of Wight), a place that is usually warm, even in winter. On this occasion, however, — during the 3 weeks of my stay there — Ventnor was invaded by cold, wet, dull, misty weather while at the same time in London the weather turned almost summery, only to change again, however, on my return.

The intention now is to send me somewhere in the south, possibly Algiers. It is a difficult choice, because Italy is barred to me (a man was arrested in Milan for having a name like mine); I can't even go from here to Gibraltar by STEAMER, as I have no passport and even the English demand a passport there.

Despite all the urging on the part of doctors and those closest to me, I would never have agreed to such a time-wasting operation were it not for the fact that this accursed 'English' disease impairs one's intellect. Moreover a relapse, even if I pulled through, would take up still more time. All the same I intend to carry out some further experiments here first.

*I send you a number of *Modern Thought* with an article on myself[c]; I need not tell you that the biographical notice of the author is altogether wrong. My daughter — your correspondent Eleanor, who sends you her love — has in the copy forwarded to you taken upon herself to correct the English misquotations from the *Capital*. But

---

[a] See present edition, Vol. 24. - [b] Donkin - [c] See this volume, p. 163.

however badly Mr Bax—I hear he is quite a young man—may translate, he certainly is the first English critic who takes a real interest in modern socialism. There is a sincerity of speech and a ring of true conviction about him which strike you. A certain John Rae—I think he is lecturer of Political Economy at some English University—has, some months ago, published in *The Contemporary Review* an article on the same subject,[a] very superficial (though he affects to quote many of my writings he has evidently never seen), and full of that pretence of superiority which the true Briton is inspired with thanks to a peculiar gift of stolid blockheadedness. Still he tries hard to be so condescending as to suppose, that from conviction, and not from interested motives, I am, for almost 40 years, misleading the working class by unsound doctrines! Generally speaking, people here commence to yearn for some knowledge of socialism, nihilism, and so forth. Ireland and the United States on the one hand; on the other, the impending struggle between farmers and landlords, between agricultural labourers and farmers, between capitalism and landlordism; some symptoms of revival among the industrial working class, as f. i. at some late partial elections for the House of Commons, where the official workingmen's candidates (especially the renegade of the International, miserable Howell [259]), proposed by the acknowledged leaders of Trades' Unions and publicly recommended by Mr Gladstone, 'the people's William'—were disdainfully rejected by the workmen; the demonstrative radical clubs forming in London, mostly composed of workmen, English and Irish intermingling, dead against the 'great liberal party', *official* trades-unionism, and the people's William, etc. etc.—all this induces the British philistine to want just now some information on Socialism. Unfortunately, the reviews, magazines, journals, etc., exploit this 'demand' only to 'offer' the public the expectorations of venal, ignorant, and sycophantic penny-a-liners (suppose even that they are shilling-a-liners).

There appears a 'weekly', called *The Radical*, full of good aspirations, bold in language (the boldness is in the *sans gêne*,[b] not in the vigour), trying to break through the trammels of the British press, but, with all that, of feeble performance. What the paper lacks, are intelligent editors. Many months ago these people wrote to me, I was then at Eastbourne [160] with my dear wife, then at Paris,[164] etc., so that they had not yet any interview with me. I consider it in fact useless.

---

[a] Ibid., p. 162. - [b] nonchalance

The more I have read of their paper, the more I feel convinced that it is incurable.

My daughter[a] reminds me that it is high time to finish this letter, the last minutes for letter delivery being near.*

Salut,
Karl Marx

First published, in Russian, in the maga-   Printed according to the original
zine *Letopisi marksizma*, Book V, Moscow-
Leningrad, 1928

111

ENGELS TO EDUARD BERNSTEIN [260]

IN ZURICH

London, 25 January 1882

Dear Mr Bernstein,

Not until today have I been able to get round to answering your letter of the 12th. Marx is home from the Isle of Wight with his youngest daughter,[a] both considerably better, and Marx strong enough to go walking with me yesterday for 2 hours without a break. Since he isn't working yet and the Lafargues as often as not also drop in before dinner (i. e. 5 o'clock) when a bottle of good Pilsener is served up, my hours of daylight are usually frittered away and I have never liked writing by lamplight after the warning (chronic conjuctivitis) that was given to my left eye 3 years ago.

Just now I happen to be at Marx's, so would you be so good as to thank Höchberg very much on Marx's behalf for his kind offer which, however, he is unlikely to be able to make use of; all that he knows for certain about his journey south is that he is *not* going to the Riviera or to any part of Italy, if only on account of the police. The first proviso where convalescents are concerned is that there should be no harass-

---

[a] Eleanor

ment by the police, in which respect Italy can hold out fewer guarantees than anywhere else — save, of course, Bismarck's empire. We were greatly interested by what you told us of the goings-on among the 'leaders' in Germany. I have never made a secret of my opinion that the masses in Germany have been far better than their leaders, particularly since the press and agitation combined to turn the party into the latter's milch cow and butter purveyor, only to see the said cow abruptly slaughtered by Bismarck and the bourgeoisie. [261] For the thousands instantly ruined thereby, it is a personal disaster not to have been placed in an immediately revolutionary situation, i. e. exile. Otherwise not a few who are now bemoaning their fate would have gone over to Most's camp or at any rate found the *Sozialdemokrat* far too moderate. The majority of our people remained in Germany, as they needs must, for the most part going to fairly reactionary places, where they remained social outcasts dependent for their living on philistines and became, to a great extent, themselves tainted with philistinism. For them, everything soon began to turn on the hope that the Anti-Socialist Law would be repealed. Small wonder that, under pressure from the philistine establishment, some of them became obsessed with the idea — in reality an absurd one — that this could be attained by the exercise of moderation. Germany is a truly infamous country for people without much willpower. The narrowness and pettiness of prevailing conditions, both civil and political, the provincial character of even the cities, the petty but cumulative harassment in the running battle with police and bureaucracy — all this enervates instead of stimulating resistance, and in this way many of those in the 'great nursery' [a] grow childish themselves. Petty conditions engender a petty outlook, so that a great deal of intelligence and vigour is called for if anyone living in Germany is to look beyond the immediate future, to keep his eyes fixed on the wider context of world events and not succumb to that complacent 'objectivity' that cannot see beyond its own nose and is therefore the most blinkered subjectivity, even though it be shared by a thousand other such fellow-subjects.

True, the emergence of such a tendency, cloaking its lack of insight and resolution under the mantle of 'objective' wisdom, is natural enough; nevertheless it must be ruthlessly combated. And for this the working masses themselves provide the best purchase. They alone in

---

[a] A paraphrase from Heine's 'Zur Beruhigung'.

Germany live in anything approaching modern conditions, all their misfortunes, great and small, are attributable to the pressure exerted by *capital* and, whereas all other struggles in Germany, both social and political, are petty and paltry and revolve round paltry issues which have long been surmounted elsewhere, the workers' struggle alone is noble, it alone is abreast of the times, it alone does not enervate the participants but is for them a constant source of fresh energy. So the more you are able to draw your correspondents from amongst the genuine workers,— not those who have become 'leaders' — the better will be your chance of counterbalancing the whines of the leadership.

This time it was inevitable that all manner of peculiar people should get into the Reichstag. All the more unfortunate, then, that Bebel should not have been elected. [222] He alone is lucid, politically far-sighted and energetic enough to prevent blunders being committed.

Could you not, *after you have done with them*, let us have for a week or two the 'stenographic reports' of debates[a] in which our deputies have played a serious part? I will vouch for their return. Newspaper reports, as we have often seen, simply cannot be relied on and none of the deputies, not even Liebknecht, could be induced to send us speeches that do them no honour.

31 January

More interruptions. Amongst others, little Hepner has been here, on his way to seek refuge in America, his purse and heart alike empty of content. A poor little chap in every respect, author of a well-intentioned pamphlet on distraint, the law governing bills of exchange, the Jewish question and postal reform, dull as dull can be, all the old Jewish stuff he turned out 10 years ago, [262] completely gone to rack and ruin; I almost felt like advising him to get baptised. Yet he provided me with the opportunity of finding out about the new imperial judicial code. [263] It really is unutterably infamous! All the dirty tricks of Prussian law combined with all the infamies of the Code Napoléon, [264] and without any of the latter's better side. The

---

[a] *Stenographische Berichte über die Verhandlungen des Reichstages.* V. Legislaturperiode. I. Session 1881/82 [Bd. I], Berlin, 1882.

judge has freedom of decision in all spheres, being bound by nothing save—the Disciplinary Law which, in political cases, will undoubtedly, and indeed does, grant him power of 'discretion'. Thus—within the general German context—the judge inevitably becomes the executive official and tool of the police. Incidentally, here is a joke (originating no doubt from Windthorst) about Leonhardt, who is alleged to have said on his death-bed: 'Now I have avenged myself on Prussia; I've given it a legal system that's bound to bring it to its knees.'

Bürkli's interest-bearing mortgage certificates, also supposed to represent money, go back much further than that thoroughly addlepated, old Hegelian Pole, Cieszkowski.[a] Similar schemes for the general good of mankind had already been adumbrated as far back as the founding of the Bank of England. Since there is no mention whatever of credit in the first volume of *Capital* (apart from the conditions governing simple debt), credit money *admits* of consideration here only, if at all, in its very simplest form (token of value, etc.) and in relation to its lowliest monetary functions, while *interest-bearing* credit money does not admit of consideration at all. Hence Bürkli is right in telling Schramm that none of these passages in *Capital* apply to *my* particular monetary paper; and Schramm is right when he proves to Bürkli from *Capital* that he, Bürkli, hasn't the faintest idea of the nature and function of money.[b] This is not to say, however, that Bürkli's own particular monetary proposal is actually reduced to its own absurdity; that would require, besides general proof that this 'money' is incapable of fulfilling the most essential monetary functions, particular proof as to the functions which such paper might really be able to fulfil. Moreover, when Bürkli says, 'What concern have I with Marx? I stick to Cieszkowski'—the whole argument adduced by Schramm against Bürkli falls to the ground.—How fortunate that the *Sozialdemokrat* shouldn't have got mixed up in all this business! No doubt the whole hullabaloo will eventually die down of its own accord.

That crises are one of the most powerful levers of political upheaval has already been pointed out in the *Communist Manifesto* and was expounded in the *Neue Rheinische Zeitung* Review up to and including 1848, not without the rider, however, that a recurrence of prosperity will in turn hamstring the revolutions and pave the way for the

---

[a] See this volume, pp. 177-78. - [b] Ibid.

victory of reaction. [a] Any detailed argument in support of this should take into consideration intermediate crises, some being of a more localised and some of a more specialised character; we are currently experiencing one such intermediate crisis which may be attributed entirely to swindle on the stock exchange; up till 1847 they were recurring middle terms, which is why, in my *Condition of the Working Class*, [b] the cycle is still shown as a five-year one.

In France, there have been gross blunders on both sides. However, in the end Malon and Brousse, in their impatience to bring matters to a head and engineer the suspension of the *Égalité* (which is quite outside the competence of the Union Fédérative [265]), have put themselves so clearly in the wrong that they are likely to suffer for it. Such bungling would be incomprehensible in cabalists as wily as Malon and Brousse, unless they felt that time was against them. For the *Prolétaire* is said to be on its last legs and, if it expires, they will have no paper at all while the others will have two. [c] Hence the issue had to be decided while they still had a paper in which the resolutions ·were published. The scurrilities and pure fabrications they are now disseminating against Guesde, Lafargue, etc., and in particular Joffrin's concoction [d] — not concocted by him, however, but by Brousse and Malon — are altogether in the style of the old Bakuninist Alliance, [67] and have awakened old memories in us. The *Sozialdemokrat* is absolutely right not to get involved until things have cleared up a bit, which they will, I think, before very long.

I had also meant to write to Kautsky about the Poles, [224] but will have to drop that for today. Kindest regards,

Yours,

F. E.

First published, in Russian, in *Marx-Engels Archives*, Book I, Moscow, 1924

Printed according to the original

Published in English in full for the first time

---

[a] See present edition, Vol. 6, pp. 489-90 and Vol. 10, pp. 493-510.- [b] Ibid., Vol. 4, p. 382.- [c] *L'Égalité* and *Le Citoyen*- [d] See this volume, p. 182.

112

ENGELS TO KARL KAUTSKY [140]

IN ZURICH

London, 7 February 1882

Dear Mr Kautsky,

I have at last got round to answering your letter of 8 November. [224]

One of the real tasks of the revolution of '48 (and the *real* as distinct from illusory tasks of a revolution are always carried out on the strength of that revolution) was the restoration of the oppressed and disunited nationalities of Central Europe in so far as these were at all viable and, in particular, ripe for independence. In the case of Italy, Hungary and Germany, this task was carried out by the executors of the revolution, Bonaparte, Cavour and Bismarck, in accordance with the circumstances obtaining at the time. There remained Ireland and Poland. Ireland need not be considered here; it is only very indirectly concerned with conditions on the Continent. But Poland lies in the middle of the Continent and keeping it partitioned is precisely the bond that continually re-cements the Holy Alliance [266] and hence Poland is of great interest to us.

Now it is historically impossible for a great people to discuss this or that internal question in any way seriously so long as national independence is lacking. Prior to 1859 there was no question of socialism in Italy; even the republicans were few in number, although they constituted the most vigorous element. Not until 1861 did the republicans begin to expand, [267] subsequently yielding their best elements to the socialists. Similarly in Germany. Lassalle was on the point of giving up the cause for lost when he was lucky enough to be shot. It was not until 1866, the year that actually decided Little Germany's Greater Prussian unity, [268] that both the Lassallean and the so-called Eisenach parties [269] acquired any significance, and it was not until 1870, when the Bonapartist urge to interfere had been eliminated for good, that the cause gathered momentum. If we still had the old Federal Diet [270], where would our party be now? Similarly in Hungary. It wasn't until 1860 that it was drawn into the modern movement — sharp practice above, socialism below. [271]

Generally speaking an international movement of the proletariat is possible only as between independent nations. What little republican internationalism there was in the years 1830-48 was grouped round the France that was to liberate Europe, and *French chauvinism* was thus *raised* to such a pitch that we are still hampered at every turn by France's mission as universal liberator and hence by its natural right to take the lead (seen as a caricature in the case of the Blanquists but also much in evidence in that of e. g. Malon & Co.). In the International, too, the French not unnaturally took this view. They, and many others, had first to learn from events, and must still do so daily, that international co-operation is possible only among *equals*, and even a *primus inter pares*[a] at most for immediate action. So long as Poland remains partitioned and subjugated, therefore, there can be no development either of a powerful socialist party within the country itself or of genuine international intercourse *between Poles other than émigrés* and the rest of the proletarian parties in Germany, etc. Every Polish peasant and workman who rouses himself out of his stupor to participate in the common interest is confronted first of all with the fact of national subjugation; that is the first obstacle he encounters everywhere. Its removal is the prime requirement for any free and healthy development. Polish socialists who fail to put the liberation of the country at the forefront of their programme remind me of those German socialists who were reluctant to demand the immediate repeal of the Anti-Socialist Law [16] and freedom of association, assembly and the press. To be able to fight, you must first have a terrain, light, air and elbow-room. Otherwise you never get further than chit-chat.

Whether, in this connection, a restoration of Poland is possible *before* the next revolution is of no significance. It is in no way *our* business to restrain the efforts of the Poles to attain living conditions essential to their further development, or to persuade them that, from the international standpoint, national independence is a very secondary matter when it is in fact the basis of all international co-operation. Besides, in 1873, Germany and Russia were on the brink of war [272] and the restoration of *some kind* of Poland, the embryo of a later, real Poland, was therefore a strong possibility. And if these Russian gents don't soon put a stop to their pan-Slav intrigues and rabble-rousing in Herzegovina, [273] they may well find themselves with a war on their hands, a war neither they, nor Austria nor Bismarck will be able to control. The only people who are concerned that the

---

[a] first among equals

Herzegovina affair should take a serious turn are the Russian Pan-Slav Party and the Tsar; no one can really concern himself with the rapacious Bosnian riff-raff any more than with the idiotic Austrian ministers and officials who are presently pursuing their activities there. So even *without* an uprising, as a result, rather, of purely European conflicts, the establishment of an independent Little Poland would be by no means impossible, just as the Prussian Little Germany invented by the bourgeois owed its establishment not to the revolutionary or parliamentary methods they had dreamed of, but to war.

Hence I am of the opinion that *two* nations in Europe are not only entitled but duty-bound to be national before they are international — Ireland and Poland. For the best way they can be international is by being well and truly national. That's what the Poles have understood in every crisis and proved on every revolutionary battleground. Deprive them of the prospect of restoring Poland, or persuade them that before long a new Poland will automatically fall into their laps, and their interest in the European revolution will be at an end.

We, in particular, have absolutely no reason to impede the Poles in their necessary efforts to attain independence. In the first place they invented and put into practice in 1863 the methods of struggle which the Russians are now so successfully imitating (cf. *Berlin und [St] Petersburg*, Appendix 2) [274] and, in the second, they were the only reliable and capable military leaders in the Paris Commune. [275]

Come to that, who are the people who oppose the Poles' national aspirations? First, the European bourgeoisie in whose eyes the Poles have been utterly discredited since the 1846 insurrection with its socialist tendencies [276] and, secondly, the Russian pan-Slavs and those they have influenced, such as Proudhon, who saw this through Herzen's spectacles. But up till today few Russians, even the best of them, are free of pan-Slav tendencies and recollections; they take Russia's pan-Slav vocation for granted, just as the French do France's natural revolutionary initiative. In reality, however, pan-Slavism is an imposture, a bid for world hegemony under the cloak of a non-existent *Slav* nationality, and it is our and the Russians' worst enemy. That imposture will in due course disintegrate into the void, but in the meantime it could make things very awkward for us. A pan-Slav war, as the last sheet-anchor for Russian Tsardom and Russian reaction, is presently in preparation; whether it will actually materialise is a moot

point, but if it does there is one thing of which we may be certain, namely that the splendid progress in the direction of revolution now being made in Germany, Austria and Russia itself will be totally disrupt-
ed and forced into different and quite unpredictable channels. At
best, this would set us back by 3-10 years; in all likelihood it would
mean one last respite for a constitutional 'new era'[277] in Germany
and also, perhaps, Russia; a Little Poland under German hegemony,
a war of retribution with France, renewed racial incitement and, finally, another Holy Alliance. Hence pan-Slavism is now more than
ever our mortal enemy, despite—or perhaps just because of—its
having one foot in the grave. For the Katkovs, Aksakovs, Ignatievs
and Co. know that their empire will be gone for ever the moment
Tsardom is overthrown and the stage taken by the Russian people.
And hence this ardent desire for war at a moment when the treasury
contains less than nothing and not a banker is willing to advance the
Russian government so much as a penny.

That is precisely why the pan-Slavs have a mortal hatred of the
Poles. Being the only *anti*-pan-Slav Slavs, they are consequently
traitors to the sacred cause of Slavdom and must be forcibly incorporated into the Great Slav Tsardom of which the future capital is
Tsarigrad, i.e. Constantinople.

Now you may perhaps ask me whether I have no feeling of sympathy for the small Slav peoples and fragments thereof which have been
split apart by those three wedges—the German, the Magyar and the
Turkish—driven into the Slav domain? To tell the truth, damned
little. The Czecho-Slovak cry of distress:

> *Bože! ... Ach nikdo není na zemi*
> *Kdoby Slavům* (sic) *spravedlivost činil?*[a]

has been answered by Petersburg, and the entire Czech national
movement cherishes the aspiration that the Tsar should *spravedlivost
činiti*[b] them. The same applies to the others—Serbs, Bulgarians, Slo-
venes, Galician Ruthenians (at least some of them). But these are aims
of a kind we cannot support. Only when the collapse of Tsardom frees
the national aspirations of these diminutive peoples from their entangle-
ment in pan-Slav hegemonic tendencies, only then can we let them
do as they please and, in the case of most of the Austro-Hungarian

---

[a] 'O God ... there's no one on earth who would see that justice be done to the Slavs'.
From Jan Kollár's *Slávy dcera*, Part III, 'Dunag', p.287.-[b] see that justice was
done

Slavs, I am sure that six months of independence will suffice to bring them begging for re-admittance. But in no circumstances will these little nationalities be granted the right they are presently arrogating to themselves in Serbia, Bulgaria and East Rumelia — of preventing, that is, the extension of the European railway network to Constantinople.

Now as for the differences that have arisen between the Poles in Switzerland, these are émigré squabbles [224] such as are seldom of any consequence, least of all in the case of an emigration which will be celebrating its centenary in 3 years' time and which, owing to the urge felt by all émigrés to do, or at any rate plan, something, has given birth to plan after plan, one new so-called theory after another. But, as you will see from the foregoing, we are not of the same opinion as the *Równość* people and, indeed, we told them as much in a message sent on the occasion of the 50th anniversary of 29 November 1830, which was read out at the meeting in Geneva.[a] You will find a Polish version of it in the report (*Sprawozdanie*, etc.— Biblijoteka *Równośći*: No. 1, Geneva, 1881), pp. 30 ff. The *Równość* people have apparently allowed themselves to be impressed by the radical-sounding slogans of the Genevan Russians and are now anxious to prove that they are not open to the reproach of national chauvinism. This aberration, of which the causes are purely local and transitory, will blow over without having any appreciable effect on Poland as such, and refuting it in detail would be more trouble than it was worth.

How the Poles, by the way, will sort things out with the White and Little Russians and Lithuanians of the old Poland, or with the Germans as regards the frontier is, for the time being, no concern of ours.

Proof, by the way, of how little the workers, even in allegedly 'oppressed' countries, are tainted by the pan-Slav yearnings of the academics and bourgeois is provided by the splendid accord between German and Czech workers in Bohemia.

But enough for now. Kindest regards from

Yours,

F. E.

First published, in Russian, in *Marx-Engels Archives*, Vol. I (VI), Moscow, 1932

Printed according to the original

Published in English in full for the first time

---

[a] See present edition, Vol. 24, pp. 343-45.

113

ENGELS TO JOHANN PHILIPP BECKER [113]

IN GENEVA

London, 10 February 1882

Dear Old Man,

We had absolutely no idea that you were so seriously ill; all we knew was that you had been suffering from erysipelas and that's something that can be cleared up pretty easily. Had I had an inkling of how matters stood, I should have raised some money for you straight away, even though I myself was very short at the time and calls were being made on me from all sides. However, it's still not too late and I've therefore taken out a money order for you for four pounds = 100 frs 80 cts. of which you will doubtless have already been advised; because of an irregularity that cropped up here I wasn't able to write until today.

Between ourselves, one might almost count it a blessing that Marx should have been so preoccupied with his own illness during his wife's last days as to prevent him being unduly preoccupied with his loss, both when it was impending and when it actually happened. Even though we had known for 6 months or more how matters stood, the event itself still came as a terribly hard blow. Marx left yesterday for the South of France [278]; where he will go from there won't be definitely decided until he gets to Paris. Under no circumstances will he make for Italy first; at the start of his convalescence even the *possibility* of harassment by the police must be avoided.

We have thought about your proposal [279] and take the view that the time has not yet come, though it soon will, to put it into effect. Firstly, a new, formally reorganised International in Germany, Austria, Hungary, Italy and Spain would only give rise to fresh persecution and ultimately leave one with the choice either of giving the thing up, or of carrying on in *secret*. The latter option would be a calamity on account of the inevitable passion for coups and conspiracies and the no less inevitable admittance of *mouchards*.[a] Even in France the renewed application of the law banning the International,[280]

---

[a] informers

a law which has not been repealed — far from it — is by no means impossible. — Secondly, in view of the current wrangles between the *Égalité* and the *Prolétaire*, there's absolutely no counting on the French; we would have to declare ourselves for one party or the other and that, too, has its disadvantages. As individuals we are on the side of the *Égalité*, but shall take good care not to support them publicly *just now* after the succession of tactical blunders they have made, despite our express warnings. — Thirdly, the English are proving more intractable than ever at present. For 5 whole months I tried, through *The Labour Standard*, for which I wrote leading articles,[163] to pick up the threads of the old Chartist movement and disseminate our ideas so as to see whether this might evoke some response. Absolutely nothing, and since the editor,[a] a well-meaning but feeble milksop, ended up by taking fright even at the Continental heresies I introduced into the paper, I called it a day.[b]

Thus, we should have been left with an International confined, apart from Belgium, *exclusively to refugees*, for with the possible exception of Geneva and its environs we couldn't even count on the Swiss — *vide* the *Arbeiterstimme* and Bürkli.[c] It would, however, hardly be worth the trouble to set up a mere refugee association. For the Dutch, Portuguese and Danes wouldn't really improve matters either and the less one has to do with Serbs and Romanians the better.

On the other hand the International does indeed still *exist*. In so far as it can be effective, there *is* liaison between the revolutionary workers of all countries. Every socialist journal is an international centre; from Geneva, Zurich, London, Paris, Brussels and Milan the threads run criss-cross in all directions and I honestly don't see how at this juncture the grouping of these small centres round a large main centre could give added strength to the movement — it would probably only lead to greater friction. But once the moment comes for us to concentrate our forces, it will, for that very reason, be the work of a moment, nor will any lengthy preparation be called for. The names of the pioneers in one country are known in all the others and a manifesto signed and supported by them all would make a tremendous impact — something altogether different from the largely unknown names of the old General Council. But that is precisely why such a manifesto should be saved up for the moment when it can really strike home, i.e. when events in Europe provoke it. Otherwise you will de-

---

[a] George Shipton - [b] See this volume, pp. 119-20. - [c] Ibid., pp. 177-78.

tract from its future effect and will simply have put yourselves out for nothing. But such events are already taking shape in Russia where the avant-garde of the revolution will be going into battle. You should—or so we think—wait for this and its inevitable repercussions on Germany, and then the moment will also have come for a big manifesto and the establishment of an *official*, formal International, which can, however, no longer be a propaganda association but simply an association for action. For that reason we are firmly of the opinion that so splendid a weapon ought not to be dulled and blunted during the comparatively peaceful days on the very eve of the revolution.

I believe that if you think the matter over again you will come round to our view. Meanwhile we both wish you a good and speedy recovery and hope to hear before long that you are quite all right again.

Ever your old friend,

F. E.

First published in: F. Engels, *Vergessene Briefe (Briefe Friedrich Engels' an Johann Philipp Becker)*, Berlin, 1920

Printed according to the original

Published in English in full for the first time

114

MARX TO ENGELS [72]

IN LONDON

Marseilles, 17 February 1882
Hôtel au petit Louvre,
Rue de Cannebière

DEAR FRED,

I presume that Tussy dropped you a line yesterday. I had not originally intended to leave Paris until next Monday[a]; since my *state of health was rather not improving, I took at once the resolution of re-

---

a 20 February

moving to Marseilles, and thence at once, on Saturday, to sail for Algiers*.[278]

In Paris, accompanied by my Johnny,[a] I called upon but one mortal, namely Mesa. (In fact he, Mesa, *sollicitierte*[b] me to chatter too much, in addition to which I returned to Argenteuil somewhat too late, ABOUT 7 O'CLOCK IN THE EVENING. I didn't sleep a wink all night.) I tried to persuade Mesa to ask his friends, notably Guesde, if they would be kind enough to *postpone* a meeting with me *until my return *from Algiers.* But all that in vain. In fact, Guesde is so much on all parts assailed just now, that it was important for him to have an 'official' meeting on my side*. After all, one was bound to concede that much to the party. Hence I arranged a meeting at the Hôtel de Lyon et de Mulhouse, 8 boulevard Beaumarchais, to which Guesde and Deville came with Mesa at ABOUT 5 in the afternoon. I first received them downstairs in the restaurant, having been accompanied there from Argenteuil (on Wednesday[c] afternoon) by Tussy and Jennychen. Guesde was rather embarrassed on Jennychen's account BECAUSE HE HAD JUST [brought out] an acrimonious article against Longuet, ALTHOUGH SHE (Jennychen) DID NOT TAKE NO REGARD WHATEVER TO THAT INCIDENT. As soon as the young ladies had left, I *d'abord*[d] went up to *ma chambre*[e] with them, chatted there for ABOUT 1 HOUR, then DOWN — it being now time for Mesa to be off — to the restaurant where they still had leisure ENOUGH to empty a BOTTLE of Beauve with me. By 7 o'clock they'd 'all' gone. WITH ALL THAT, although I was in bed by 9 o'clock, a fiendish din of traffic without intermission until 1 o'clock, at which time (ABOUT 1 O'CLOCK) I had a *vomissement*,[f] having again got too much engrossed in conversation.

A fine day for the journey to Marseilles, and ALL RIGHT until just beyond the STATION at Lyons. First, 1½ hours *d'arrêt*[g] AT *Cassis* on account of the locomotive's DISTEMPER; then again the same mishap with the engine AT Valence, although this time the *arrêt* wasn't so long. Meanwhile it had turned bitter cold with a nasty BITING WIND. Instead of arriving *some time before* midnight, we did not reach [Marseilles] until after 2 o'clock in the morning; to some extent I was MORE OR LESS FREEZING, despite all my wrappings, the only antidote I found being 'alcohol' and I AGAIN AND AGAIN RESORTED TO IT. During the last quarter of an hour (if not more) in the exposed, cold and windswept *gare de Mar-*

---

[a] Marx's grandson Jean Longuet - [b] incited - [c] 8 February - [d] first - [e] my room - [f] bout of vomiting - [g] stop

seille,ª there was one last *épreuve*ᵇ in the shape of prolonged formalities before obtaining possession of one's LUGGAGE.

Today it's sunny in Marseilles, but the wind itself not yet warm. Dr Dourlen advised me to stay at the above-named hotel, whence I shall leave for Algiers tomorrow (Saturday) at 5 in the afternoon. The office of the Paquebots à vapeur des Postes françaisesᶜ is located here, *in the very hotel* at which I am staying, so that I was able to take a ticket (at 80 frs FIRST CLASS) for the *paquebot*ᵈ *Said* straight away; one's BAGGAGE is likewise ENREGISTERED here, so that everything is as convenient as can be.

Apropos. I [got] hold of a *Prolétaire* (*L'Égalité* is also SOLD here). Lafargue seems to me to be constantly fomenting further USELESS INCIDENTS — though maybe the DETAILS are *far from exact. As to his characterising *Fourier* a 'Communist', he is now that theyᵉ make fun of him obliged to explain in *what sense* he might have called Fourier as a 'Communist'.* Such 'audacities' may be ignored, 'interpreted' or 'differently interpreted'; what is worse is that SUCH small FACTS BE SAVED at all. To my mind, he is far too long-winded.

My best compliments to Laura; I shall write her from Algiers. There is one single man sufficient as patron; it is a long letter written by Longuet to his friend Fermé, who has successfully made his way from being an erstwhile deportee to Algeria (under Napoleon III) to the post of *juge d'appel*ᶠ of Algiers. No question of passports and such like. Nothing is entered on the passengers' tickets save Christian and surnames.

My compliments also to Lenchenᵍ AND THE OTHER FRIENDS. *Addio.*

OLD MOOR

First published abridged in *Der Briefwechsel zwischen F. Engels und K. Marx*, Bd. 4, Stuttgart, 1913 and in full in *MEGA*, Abt. III, Bd. 4, Berlin, 1931

Printed according to the original

ª Marseilles station - ᵇ trial - ᶜ Steam Ferries of the French Post Office - ᵈ steam ferry - ᵉ the editors of the *Prolétaire* - ᶠ appelate judge - ᵍ Demuth

115

ENGELS TO PYOTR LAVROV

IN LONDON

[Postcard]

[London,] 18 February 1882
122 Regent's Park Road

My dear Mr Lavrov,

I am exceedingly sorry to have missed you this afternoon—
however if, as I hope, this note reaches you tonight, I would ask you
to be so good as to come to my house tomorrow, Sunday evening, at
about 7 or 8 o'clock. You will find some friends there and we shall all
be very pleased to see you.

Yours ever,
F. Engels

[On the side reserved for the address]

P. Lavrov, Esq.
13 Alfred Place
Tottenham Court Road
W. C.

First published, in Russian, in the magazine *Letopisi marksizma*, Book V, Moscow-Leningrad, 1928

Printed according to the original

Translated from the French

Published in English for the first time

116

MARX TO ENGELS [72]

IN LONDON

[Postcard, unsigned]

Alger,[a] 21 February 1882
Hôtel d'Orient

Dear Fred,

I left Marseilles on Saturday 18 February at 5 in the afternoon aboard the *Said*, EXCELLENT STEAMER; the PASSAGE was a fast one, so that we had already reached Algiers by half past three in the morning on Monday (20 February).[278] However, it was a chilly crossing and, though the ship was equipped with every comfort, the 2 nights were sleepless ones for me owing to the diabolical noise of the engines, wind, etc., which were disturbing in the cabin.

Here again, I found in store for me the same *quid pro quo, mutatis mutandis*[b] as in the Isle of Wight.[234] This particular SEASON happens to be, for Algiers, exceptionally cold and wet, while Nice and Menton are presently luring away most of its visitors! I had in any case had some misgivings and more than once hinted at the possibility of starting off *d'abord*[c] with the Riviera. However it would seem to be a *fatalité*.[d] The good *juge*[e] gave me a most friendly welcome yesterday; Longuet's letter had forewarned him the day before I arrived; he is calling on me today to consider future moves. Then I shall write at greater length. Kindest regards to all. Letters aren't dispatched every day to France and England.

Write to me under my name, *Aux soins de* Monsieur Fermé, *juge au tribunal civil*,[f] No. 37, Route Mustapha Supérieur, Alger.

[On the side reserved for the address]

Fr. Engels, Esq.
122 Regent's Park Road,
Londres, N. W. Angleterre

First published in *Der Briefwechsel zwischen F. Engels und K. Marx*, Bd. 4, Stuttgart, 1913   Printed according to the original

---

[a] Algiers - [b] topsyturvydom, allowing for different circumstances - [c] first - [d] fatality - [e] judge (Fermé) - [f] Care of Monsieur Fermé, Judge in the Civil Courts.

117

ENGELS TO EDUARD BERNSTEIN [24]

IN ZURICH

London, 22 February 1882

Dear Mr Bernstein,

I am answering your letter straight away, 1. because of the increasing urgency of the pan-Slav business, and 2. because, now that Marx has left,[278] I shall have to set seriously to work again and shall no longer have time for such lengthy dissertations.

The 'short-hand reports'[a] will be returned today. Many thanks. Mostly rather dull, but I'm happy enough if it all passed off without any denial of principles or anything really discreditable happening. I should always be grateful if you could send me further consignments from time to time. I was much gratified to see that the shocking blunders perpetrated earlier in the Saxon Landtag had been retrieved.[118] I imagine the *Sozialdemokrat* is quite satisfied with the result of its intervention. Signing the statement must have been a bitter pill for Blos.[240] I am delighted that subscriptions should have passed the 4,000 mark and that the paper should find regular distribution in Germany, despite the police, etc. It is an *incredible* feat for a German paper that is *banned*. Before '48 such papers got in much more easily through having the support of the bourgeois and the booksellers, but no subscriptions were ever received. But in this case the workers actually *pay* — proof of their discipline and of the extent to which they live and have their being in the movement. I have no misgivings whatever about our German lads when things come to a head. They have stood the test splendidly on every occasion. And it's not *they* who are behaving like philistines but only their leaders who, from the start, have been prompted by the masses, not the masses by them.

That my letter[b] should have failed to convert you is quite understandable, since you were already in sympathy with the 'oppressed' southern Slavs. For after all, everyone of us, in so far as he has first gone through a liberal or radical phase, has emerged from it with these feelings of sympathy for all 'oppressed' nationalities, and I for

---

[a] See this volume, p. 188.- [b] Ibid., pp. 191-95.

one know how much time and study it took me to shake them off—
but then it was for good and all.

Now, however, I must ask you not to ascribe to me opinions I have
never expressed. I am in no way concerned with the official Austrian
viewpoint represented for years by the Augsburg *Allgemeine Zeitung*.
Where it was right, it's out of date, and where it isn't out of date, it's
wrong. I have absolutely no cause for complaint about the centrifugal
movement in Austria. A 'bulwark against Russia' becomes superfluous the moment revolution breaks out in Russia, i. e. when some sort
of representative assembly meets. As from that day, Russia will be
busy with its own affairs, pan-Slavism will collapse like the nonentity
it is and the Empire will begin to crumble. Pan-Slavism is simply an
artificial product of the 'educated classes', of the towns and universi-
ties, the army and the civil service; it is unknown in the country and
even the landed aristocracy is in such a fix that it would execrate any
kind of war. From 1815-59, cowardly and foolish though its policy
may have been, Austria *was* indeed a bulwark against Russia. To afford it yet another opportunity—now, on the eve of revolution in
Russia—of setting itself up as a 'bulwark' would be tantamount to
giving Austria a new lease of life, a new historical justification for its
existence, and postponing the disintegration which inevitably awaits
it. And in allowing the Slavs to come to power, Austria has, with true
historical irony, itself declared that what has hitherto been its sole *rai-
son d'être* has ceased to exist. Come to that, a war with Russia would,
within 24 hours, put paid to Slav domination in Austria.

You say that, as soon as the Slav peoples (always excepting the
Poles!) have no further grounds for looking to Russia as their only liberator, pan-Slavism will be checkmated. That's easily said and it
sounds plausible. But in the first place the danger of pan-Slavism, in
so far as it exists, does not lie at the periphery but at the centre, not in
the Balkans but in the 80 million slaves upon whom Tsarism draws
for its army and its finances. Hence it is there that the greatest effort
must be made and, indeed, *has been* made. And is it to be blighted by
a war?

Again, I do not propose to go into the question of how the smaller
Slav nations have come to look to the Tsar as their only liberator. Let
it suffice that they do so; we cannot alter the fact and it will rest at
that until Tsarism has been smashed; if there's a war, all these interesting little nations will be on the side of Tsarism, the enemy of all
bourgeois progress in the West. So long as this remains the case, I can

take no interest in their *immediate* liberation here and now; they are as much our declared enemies as their ally and patron, the Tsar.

We must co-operate in the work of setting the West European proletariat free and subordinate everything else to that goal. No matter how interesting the Balkan Slavs, etc., might be, the moment their desire for liberation clashes with the interests of the proletariat they can go hang for all I care. The Alsatians, too, are oppressed, and I shall be glad when we are once more quit of them. But if, on what is patently the very eve of a revolution, they were to try and provoke a war between France and Germany, once more goading on those two countries and thereby postponing the revolution, I should tell them: Hold hard! Surely you can have as much patience as the European proletariat. When they have liberated themselves, you will automatically be free; but till then, we shan't allow you to put a spoke in the wheel of the militant proletariat. The same applies to the Slavs. The victory of the proletariat will liberate them in reality and of necessity and not, like the Tsar, apparently and temporarily. And that's why they, who have hitherto not only failed to contribute anything to Europe and European progress, but have actually retarded it, should have at least as much patience as our proletarians. To stir up a general war for the sake of a few Herzegovinians, which would cost a thousand times more lives than there are inhabitants in Herzegovina, isn't my idea of proletarian politics.

And how does the Tsar 'liberate'? Ask the peasants of Little Russia whom Catherine liberated from 'Polish oppression' (pretext — religion) only to annex them later on. And what does all this Russian pan-Slav imposture amount to? The capture of Constantinople, that's all. Nothing else would act so powerfully on the religious traditions of the Russian peasant, inspire him to defend the holy city of Tsarigrad and give a new lease of life to Tsarism. And once the Russians are in Constantinople, farewell to Bulgarian and Serbian independence and liberty — the little brothers (*bratanki*) would soon realise how much better off they had been even under the Turks. It calls for the most colossal naïveté on the part of the said *bratanki* for them to believe that the Tsar is out for their good rather than his own.

You say that a Greater Serbia would be as good a bulwark against Russia as Austria. As I have already said, the 'bulwark' theory generally has ceased to hold any water for me since a revolutionary movement gained strength in Russia. I have also said that I look forward with pleasure to Austria's disintegration. But this brings us to the *quality* of these exiguous nations which is, after all, a consideration when it comes to sympathising with them.

In 2-4 generations' time and after general European upheavals, Greater Serbia will certainly be feasible; today, having regard to the cultural level of its elements, it as certainly is not.

1. The Serbs are divided into 3 denominations (the figures are taken from Šafařík, *Slovanský Národopis* and are applicable to 1849): Greek Orthodox 2,880,000; Catholic, including the so-called Croats who, however, speak Serbian, 2,664,000, minus the Croats, 1,884,000; Mohammedans 550,000. Where these people are concerned, religion actually counts for more than nationality, and it is the *aim* of each denomination to predominate. So long as there's no cultural advance such as would at any rate make toleration possible, a Greater Serbia would only spell civil war. See enclosed *Standard*.

2. The country has 3 political centres — Belgrade, Montenegro, Agram. Neither the Croats nor the Montenegrins wish to submit to the supremacy of Belgrade. On the contrary. The Montenegrins and your friends, the aborigines in Krivosíje and Herzegovina, would uphold their 'independence' vis-à-vis Belgrade or any other central government — Serbian or otherwise — just as much as they would vis-à-vis the Turks or the Austrians. That independence consists in demonstrating their hatred of the oppressor by stealing cattle and other valuable chattels from their own 'oppressed' Serb compatriots as they have done for the past 1,000 years, and any attack on their right of rapine is regarded as an attack on their independence. I am enough of an authoritarian to regard the existence of such aborigines in the heart of Europe as an anachronism. And even if these little folk had had a standing as high as Sir Walter Scott's vaunted Highlanders, who were also really shocking cattle thieves, the most we could do is condemn the *manner* in which they are treated by present-day society. If we were at the helm, *we too* should have to put an end to the Rinaldo Rinaldini-Schinderhannes business which, by long tradition, these laddies indulge in. And so would the government of Greater Serbia. Here too, then, Greater Serbia would mean a revival of the struggle now being conducted by the Herzegovinians, and hence civil war involving all the highlanders of Montenegro, Cattaro and Herzegovina.

On closer consideration, then, Greater Serbia does not appear anything like as simple and straightforward a matter as pan-Slavs and liberals *à la* Rasch would have us believe.

Well, go on sympathising with these aborigines as much as you like; there's certainly no denying them a sort of poetic radiance and, in fact, they do still produce folk songs that closely resemble the old Serbian ones (which are very fine); I shall even send you an article from *The Standard* by way of proof. But the fact remains that they are the tools of Tsardom, and there's no room in politics for poetical feelings of sympathy. And if the rebellion of these laddies threatens to unleash a general war that would make a complete hash of our revolutionary situation, they and their right of cattle stealing will have to be mercilessly sacrificed to the interests of the European proletariat.

Come to that, if Greater Serbia were to materialise it would only be an enlarged version of the principality of Serbia. And what has the latter achieved? Set up an educated bureaucracy on the Austrian model, consisting of chaps from Belgrade and other towns who have been to university in the West, particularly Vienna, and, knowing nothing of the conditions governing communal ownership among the peasants, make laws after the Austrian pattern that fly in the face of those conditions so that masses of peasants are impoverished and expropriated, whereas in the days of the Turks they enjoyed *full autonomy*, grew rich and paid fewer taxes.

The Bulgarians have depicted themselves in their folk songs, a collection of which, made by a Frenchman, has recently appeared in Paris.[a] Fire plays a major role here. A house burns down, the young woman is burnt to death because, instead of his wife, her husband chooses to save his black mare. Another time a young woman saves her jewellery and leaves her child to burn. If, by way of exception, there is a noble and courageous act, it is invariably performed by a *Turk*. In what other part of the world would you find such a beastly lot?

Incidentally, if you take a look at a passable philological map of the district (e. g. Šafařík's, in the above-mentioned book, or Kiepert's of Austria and the countries of the Lower Danube 1867[b]) you will find that the liberation of these Balkan Slavs is not an altogether simple affair and that, with the exception of Serbian territory, there are pockets of Turks all over the place, and a Greek fringe along the coast, not to mention Salonika which is a Spanish Jewish town. True, the worthy Bulgarians are now rapidly dealing with the Turks in Bulga-

---

[a] [A. Dozon,] *Български народни пѣсни. Chansons populaires bulgares inédites*, Paris, 1875. - [b] H. Kiepert, *Karte von Böhmen, Maehren und Oesterreich*, Berlin, 1866.

ria and East Rumelia by slaughtering them, driving them out and burning down their houses over their heads. Had the Turks adopted the same course, instead of allowing them more autonomy and fewer taxes than they have at present, the world would no longer be troubled with a Bulgarian question.

As regards war, you would seem to me to have *le coeur un peu trop léger*.[a] If war breaks out, it will be easy for Bismarck to make it look as though Russia were the aggressor: he can wait, but the Russian pan-Slavs *can't*. But Germany and Austria once committed in the East, one would have to be a poor judge of Frenchmen, and particularly Parisians, not to anticipate that there would instantly arise a chauvinistic clamour for retribution which would reduce to silence the peaceful majority of the people and cause France to appear yet again as the aggressor; or that the chauvinism then prevailing would very soon demand the left bank of the Rhine. That this would soon involve Germany in a struggle for survival so that there, too, patriotic chauvinism would completely regain the upper hand, seems to me self-evident. So far, all the prospects are against us. But once a war is under way, there is no knowing what will be the outcome of this, the first such European conflict since 1813-15, and I would be the last man to wish for it. If it does come, however, then it can't be helped.

But now for the other side of the coin. In Germany we have a situation that is drifting ever more rapidly towards revolution and must before long push our party to the fore. We ourselves needn't lift a finger, just let our opponents do the work for us. On top of which a new era [277] is impending with a new, liberalising, highly irresolute and wavering Emperor,[b] who is exactly cut out to be a Louis XVI. All that is wanting is a timely impulse from without. This will be afforded by the situation in Russia where the onset of the revolution is only a question of months. Our people in Russia have virtually taken the Tsar prisoner,[281] have disorganised the government and shattered popular tradition. Even without any other major coup, a collapse must ensue in the very near future, and the process will go on for years, as it did between 1789 and '94. Hence it will allow ample time for repercussions in the West, more notably Germany, so that the movement will gradually gather momentum, unlike 1848, when reaction was already in full swing throughout Europe by 20 March. Never, in short, has there been so magnificent a revolutionary situa-

---

[a] to be a bit too light-hearted - [b] William II

tion. Only one thing can spoil it: as Skobelev himself said in Paris, only war with another country could get Russia out of the morass into which it is sinking.[282] That war would repair all the damage our people, at the cost of their lives, have done to Tsarism. It would be enough at any rate to rescue the Tsar from his captivity, to expose the social revolutionaries to the general fury of the mob, to deprive them of the support they now get from the Liberals and undo all they have achieved by their sacrifices; everything would have to be begun all over again under less favourable circumstances. But a play of this kind scarcely admits of a second performance and even in Germany — upon that you may depend — our people will either have to join in the patriotic ululations, or draw down upon their heads a furore by comparison with which the one that followed the assassination attempts[120] was mere child's play; and Bismarck's riposte to the recent elections would be of quite a different order from the one he made then with his Anti-Socialist Law.[16]

If peace is maintained, the Russian pan-Slavs will be bilked and will soon have to retreat. Whereupon the Emperor[a] can at most try one last throw with the old bankrupt bureaucrats and generals who have already once been on the rocks. That could last for a month or two at the outside, after which there would be no recourse save to call on the Liberals — i. e. a National Assembly of some kind and that, if I know my Russia, would mean revolution à la 1789. And then you go and suggest I want war! Not on your life, even if it means the demise of 200 noble robber nations.

But enough of that. And now for Bürkli. I haven't read his pamphlet[b] and have mislaid it, but shall look and see if I can find it in Marx's house or mine. So I can't say exactly what he is after.

(25 February)

I have just been hunting high and low at Marx's and couldn't find it. With our division of labour, specialised questions of this kind fall to Marx's share and, because of his illness, we haven't even been able to discuss the matter.

I assume that Bürkli permits every Zurich real property owner to take out a mortgage of this kind on his property, and that the rele-

---

[a] Alexander III - [b] K. Bürkli, *Demokratische Bank-Reform*, Zurich, 1881.

vant certificate is supposed to circulate as money. In this way the amount of money in circulation is dictated by the amount which the real property in question is worth, and not by the far smaller amount that would suffice for circulation. So even at this stage:
1. Either they are non-redeemable certificates, in which case they depreciate in accordance with the law expounded by Marx [283];
2. Or they are redeemable, in which case the portion over and above what is needed for circulation returns to the bank for redemption and ceases to be money, which, of course, means that the bank must tie up capital.

Now a substitute for money which is interest-bearing and of which, therefore, the value fluctuates day by day is, if only for that reason, an unsuitable means of circulation; not only does one first have to agree the price of the commodity in real money, but also the price of the paper. The people of Zurich would have to be worse businessmen than I suppose if, the certificates being redeemable, they didn't all promptly surrender them to the bank for redemption, and go back to using only the old, convenient, non-interest-bearing money. Which means that the cantonal bank would have tied up in mortgages its own capital as well as everything it could borrow and would have to cast round for new sources of working capital.

But, if non-redeemable, they simply cease to be money. Metallic or good paper money is drawn from the outside world which, luckily, is a little bit larger than the Canton of Zurich, and that's what people use, for no one will accept these dreary certificates as money and in that case they are, as you rightly say, no better than Brandenburg mortgage bonds. And if the government insists on forcing the public to accept them as money, it is in for a surprise.

This between ourselves; if you make use of it, please don't mention *my* name since, as I have said, I have not read the little pamphlet or had time to read up the subject in the classic economic texts; but if one tries to criticise such things out of one's own head, just like that, there's no guaranteeing that one won't make blunders. At all events, the thing is nonsensical.

Marx arrived in Algiers [278] on Monday morning, a place I and the doctors had always wanted him to go to, though he himself wasn't very keen. He has met a judge in the *tribunal civil*[a] there, a former deportee of Bonaparte's, who has made a close study of communal

---

[a] Civil Courts (Fermé)

ownership among the Arabs and has offered to enlighten him on the subject.

Kindest regards both to yourself and Kautsky.

Yours,
F. E.

First published in full, in Russian, in *Marx-Engels Archives*, Book I, Moscow, 1924

Printed according to the original

Published in English in full for the first time

118

ENGELS TO PYOTR LAVROV

IN LONDON

[London,] 23 February 1882
122 Regent's Park Road, N. W.

My Dear Friend,

The *Financial Reform Almanach 1882* gives the following addresses: Dilke, W. Ashton, 1 Hyde Park Gate, S. W.

Ditto Sir Charles, 76 Sloane St, S. W.

When I got home from your place I found a letter from Dr Donkin (the one who treated Hartmann some time ago, and also the Marx family) in which he says:

* 'I had a letter from Hartmann a few days ago (dating from 14 Huntley St, Bedford Sq.) asking me if he might come and see me. I answered his letter directly — giving him the choice of two days — but have heard nothing of him.

'In case my letters have miscarried will you tell me if you know anything about him. If you see him perhaps you will tell him that I will see him any morning here (60 Upper Berkeley St., W.) between 11 and 12 o'clock.' *

Would you be so kind as to pass on the preceding lines to Hartmann? Since Donkin's letter failed to arrive, I fear there may be some mistake as to the *number*, of which I am not sure, since I know of it only from Donkin. Hence it is impossible for me to communicate with Hartmann direct or with any certainty, and that is why I am asking you to act as intermediary, the more so since you say it is quite close to your place.

I am replying to Donkin,[284] saying that I hope to be able to tell him something more precise within the next few days; if possible, could you let me have some further information concerning this matter on Sunday evening?

Yours ever,

F. Engels

First published, in Russian, in the magazine *Letopisi marksizma*, Book V, Moscow-Leningrad, 1928

Printed according to the original

Translated from the French

Published in English for the first time

119

MARX TO JENNY LONGUET

IN ARGENTEUIL

[Postcard]

[Algiers,] 23 February 1882

Dearest Child,

The good weather has set in; live in a most comfortable Villa, out of the fortifications of Algiers, on the hills; only thing I want now is tranquillity, hope soon to be a 'better' man again.

Kisses to all the children; compliments to Longuet.

Yours most devoted

Old Nick

[On the side reserved for the address]

Madame Charles Longuet
11, Boulevard Thiers, Argenteuil
près Paris (France)

First published, in Russian, in the magazine *Nachalo*, No. 5, St Petersburg, 1899

Reproduced from the original

Published in English for the first time

120

MARX TO ENGELS [72]

IN LONDON

Algiers, 1 March 1882
Hôtel Pension Victoria,
Mustapha Supérieur,
Boulevard Bon Accueil

(Letters can now be sent to me
direct at the above address)

DEAR FRED,

The telegram [284] I sent you anticipated my POSTCARD, [a] as the latter would have caused somewhat unnecessary anxiety. The fact is that thanks to an accumulation of unfavourable circumstances of a petty nature (incl. the sea crossing), I have been frozen to the marrow, my *corpus delicti* [b] having landed at Algiers on 20 February.

December was an atrocious month in Algiers, January fine, February cold when not also damp. I struck the 3 coldest days of the said last month, the 20th, 21st and 22nd of February. No sleep, no appetite, a bad cough, somewhat perplexed, not without an occasional bout of *profunda melancolia*, like the great Don Quixote. AT ONCE THEN back to Europe, no go, what with the *faux frais*, [c] on top of which the prospect of another 2 nights in one of the *cabines*, one's brain tortured by the racket from the engines! Or again, certain escape from the *quid pro quo* [d] by setting off at once for Biskra, right next to the Sahara Desert? But difficult, considering the fact that the means of communication or transport demand a further journey of 7 to 8 days and, according to the advice of someone familiar with the conditions, no small undertaking for a *pro nunc* [e] invalid in view of possible INCIDENTS before arrival in Biskra!

Anyway, as the thermometer on the *après-midi* [f] of 22 February indicated fair weather and I had already spied out the Hôtel-Pension Victoria on the day of my arrival in company with the good JUDGE

---

[a] See this volume, p. 202. - [b] Here: offending body - [c] unforeseen expenses - [d] Here: topsyturvydom - [e] temporary - [f] afternoon

Fermé, I left the Grand Hôtel d'Orient (also *sleeping* there THE ABOMIN-
ABLE PHILOSOPHICAL RADICAL Ashton Dilke — BY THE BY, to *le Petit Colon*
and other *petits journaux Algériens*[a] every Englishman IS A LORD, EVEN
Bradlaugh FIGURES HERE AS LORD Bradlaugh) with *bagage* to *une des
collines en dehors de la fortification, du côté de l'Est de la ville*.[b]
Magnificent position here, from my *chambre*[c] the bay of the MEDITER-
RANEAN, the port of Algiers, villas climbing up the *collines* as in an
amphitheatre (*des ravines au dessous des collines, d'autres collines au
dessus*)[d]; further away, *des montagnes,*[e] among those *visibles* being the
snowy crests *derrière Matifou, sur les montagnes de Kabilie, des points
culminants du Djurdjura*.[f] (All the aforementioned *collines* are of lime-
stone.) At 8 o'clock in the morning there is nothing more magical
than the panorama, the air, the vegetation, a wonderful *mélange* of
Europe and Africa. Every morning — at 10 or 9-11 or THEREABOUTS MY
PROMENADE between *des ravines et les collines situées au dessus de la
mienne*.[g]

WITH ALL THAT one lives on nothing but dust. IN FIRST INSTANCE only
FROM 23-26TH FEBR. REALLY EXCELLENT CHANGE; but now (and nevertheless
I'm still *so frozen that EVEN THEN the only difference* between my clothing in the Isle of Wight [234] and my clothing in the city of Algiers is
that in the villa I have up till now simply replaced the rhinoceros
greatcoat with my light *great*coat, no other change having been
made so far) there began (and will doubtless last for some 9 days
reckoned from the 27TH Feb.) the so-called *tempête, c. a. d. le tapage
du vent sans de tonnerre et sans d'éclairs*,[h] DANGEROUS AND TREACHEROUS TIME
MUCH FEARED EVEN BY THE NATIVES. So in fact only 3 really fine days up
till now.

Meanwhile, my cough got worse FROM DAY TO DAY, *le crachement abominable*,[i] little sleep, * above all a certain nasty feeling that my *left side*
is once for all deteriorated by the perish, and my intellectual state
most dejected. Thus I summoned Dr Stephann (best Algiers doctor).
I had two interviews yesterday and to-day. What to do? I am just
go[ing] to Algiers to make prepare his prescriptions given; they are,
after he had very seriously examined me,* 1. *collodion cantharidal*[j]

---

[a] the *Petit Colon* and other little Algerian papers - [b] *one of the hills* outside the fortifications on the eastern side of the city - [c] room - [d] hills (ravines below the hills, other hills
above) - [e] mountains - [f] beyond Matifu of the mountains of Kabylia, the highest peaks
in the Jurjura - [g] ravines and the hills above mine - [h] tempest, in other words a roaring
wind without accompaniment of thunder or lightning - [i] vile expectorations -
[j] cantharidic collodion

applied with a *pinceau*ᵃ; 2. *arseniate de soude*ᵇ in a specific quantity of water; 1 tablespoon of same at every mealtime; 3. *au cas de besoin*,ᶜ especially if the cough comes on at night, a tablespoonful of a MIXTURE *of codéine* and *julep gommeux*.ᵈ He is coming again in a week's time; as to my BODILY EXERCISES, has ordered me * to keep within very moderate limits; no real intellectual work except some reading for my distraction.* So in fact I shan't be back AT London A BIT (RATHER A LESS) sooner! * Hence a man ought never [to] delude himself by too sanguine views! *

I must break off as I have to go to the chemist in Algiers. *By the by, you know that few people more averse to demonstrative pathos; still, it would be a lie [not] to confess that my thought to great part absorbed by reminiscence of my wife, such a part of my best part of life! Tell my London daughtersᵉ to write to Old Nickᶠ instead of expecting him to write himself first.

How is Pumps going on in that serious work of man-creating? Give her my best compliments.

Give my compliments to Helen,ᵍ ditto Moore, Schorlemmer.

Now, old good fellow,

Yours,*

Moor

* Apropos! Dr Stephann, like my dear Dr Donkin, does not forget — the cognac. *

First published abridged in *Der Briefwechsel zwischen F. Engels und K. Marx*, Bd. 4, Stuttgart, 1913 and in full in *MEGA*, Abt. III, Bd. 4, Berlin, 1931

Printed according to the original

ᵃ paint brush - ᵇ arseniate of soda - ᶜ in case of need - ᵈ eucalyptus julep - ᵉ Laura Lafargue and Eleanor Marx - ᶠ Marx's jocular name in the family - ᵍ Demuth

121

MARX TO ENGELS [72]

IN LONDON

[Postcard]

[Algiers,] 3 March 1882

Dear FRED,

Your letter dated 25 February [284] arrived yesterday together with the *Daily News* CUTS (O. N.[a] tragi*comical* secret of politics and passion in England). I trust Tussy will at last stop playing fast and loose with her health; that Cacadou, alias Laurachen, continues to flourish, for she is subjected to a great deal of physical exertion. As yet no reply from Paris.

The *tempête — c'est ici l'expression sacramentale*[b] — has been going on since 26 February though always with VARIABLE ASPECTS.

On 2 March confined to the house FOR THE WHOLE DAY in common with all my fellow-lodgers; pouring rain from EARLY MORNING from a SKY of a colour reminiscent of London, grey as grey; this time however the squalls were accompanied by thunder and lightning; at 4 o'clock in the afternoon an azure sky AGAIN; later on a really lovely moonlit evening. One short spell alternating with another throughout the day, now a rise in temperature, now a drop. Meanwhile I resumed inter alia the painting of my skin; that very night A REMARKABLE IMPROVEMENT SETTING IN.— *This morning*, 3 March, painting first task of the day; despite wind not intimidated, from 9 o'clock to ABOUT quarter TO 11 out for a stroll in the balmy sea air which I found MOST DELIGHTFUL; got back just before the wind worked itself into a fury again. I shall be SUMMONED TO *déjeuner*[c] IN A FEW MINUTES and am making use of this vital moment to send these FEW LINES TO YOU.

Your
Moor

---

[a] Olga Novikova - [b] Tempest — that's the ritual expression here - [c] luncheon

[On the side reserved for the address]

Fr. Engels
122 Regent's Park Road,
London, N. W., Angleterre

First published abridged in *Der Briefwechsel zwischen F. Engels und K. Marx*, Bd. 4, Stuttgart, 1913 and in full in *MEGA*, Abt. III, Bd. 4, Berlin, 1931

Printed according to the original

122

MARX TO JENNY LONGUET [166]

IN ARGENTEUIL

[Algiers,] 16 March 1882
Hôtel Victoria
(Go on writing to me here,
aux soins de [a] Fermé)

My Dear Child,

After receiving *your letter through Fermé*, I sent a messenger to the Hôtel d'Orient to make inquiries there as well; he was handed a letter for me from you dated 24 February.

I shall now give you a short account of the state of my health.

Since my cough had become more persistent, with severe expectoration, insomnia, etc., I sent for Dr Stephann (who also looks after some of my other fellow-lodgers) and have thus been under his care since *26 February* when he first examined me. He is a very shrewd and determined man. He found that, as a result of the unfortunate concatenation of events from the time I left Paris until now, my left side, which had been weakened by pleurisy, was functioning abnormally. The chief antidote consists in *vésicatoires* [b] (the drawing off of fluid by painting the left side of my back and the lefthand side of my chest with cantharidic collodion) which works well in my case, and also a 'soothing' cough mixture; lastly, an arsenical preparation (as tasteless as water) to be taken after every meal. *In so far as the weather permitted*, I was to continue taking a gentle stroll each morning.

Unfortunately (had the weather been more favourable, my violent

---

[a] Care of - [b] vesicatories

coughing would [undoubtedly] ᵃ have gone of its own accord) I began to spit blood on 6 March but, after 8 and 9 March, had a really
serious [haemorrhage] with some residual pain until the 12th, and on
the 13th *all trace of haemorrhage had gone*. So this disagreeable episode
lasted a week; Dr Stephann intervened energetically, forbidding all
movement (walks, needless to say); likewise ALMOST all TALK; hot foot-
baths, etc., along with drastic medicaments. During this time the
treatment with *vésicatoires*, cough TONICS, etc., continued and did, in
fact, reduce the coughing quite amazingly. Also, the weather has gradually begun to change although not yet ALTOGETHER *comme il faut*.ᵇ
From my hill-top villa (Hôtel Victoria) I have before me the prospect
of the bay and, to one side, villas rising in an amphitheatre—, [finest
air], ᵃ even without a stroll, [wafting] past the little balcony in front
of my own and the adjoining *chambres*,ᶜ or again in the verandah, the
latter giving access to the first floor. The doctor will not permit me to
resume my strolls until he has again examined the *corpus delicti*.ᵈ Be it
noted that latterly not only have I regained my appetite, but have at
last managed to *snatch some sleep*. (From the 16th of February, IN FACT
SINCE THE NIGHT IN THE hôtel in Paris, I had suffered from insomnia unre-
mittingly until the moment referred to above.)

   * Take now all in all, the upshot is, as I too reported to London,ᵉ
that in this foolish, ill-calculated expedition, I am now just arrived
again at that standard of health when I possessed it on leaving Maitland Park.ᶠ I must, however, say that many visitors here too passed,
and are passing still through the same trial. Since 10 years Alger had
not such a failure of the winter season. Myself had had some doubts;
there was the experience of the Isle of Wight ²³⁴ and other corners,
but Engels and Donkin fired each other mutually into African furor,
neither one nor the other getting any special information, considering
that in regard to temperature this year was extraordinary. I had now
and again by innuendo given to understand to begin at least by Mentone (or Nizza) as Lavrov had received from Russian friends very favourable news, but all this was ruled down by my sanguine good old
Fred ᵍ who, I repeat it, I say it amongst you and myself, may easily
kill some one out of love.

   I must tell you that in this Villa-Hôtel, the two ladies, its mana-
gers, did everything in my service, no care nor attention neglecting.

ᵃ Difficult to decipher in the ms.- ᵇ as it should be - ᶜ rooms - ᵈ offending body - ᵉ See
this volume, pp. 213-15. - ᶠ Marx's London address - ᵍ Engels

And as to the operations relating to the *vésicatoires*, a young *pharmacien*, Mr Casthelaz (with his mother he is here as a patient ever since December) is so kind as to tattoo me, then open the* blisters filled with fluid, *then put linen on the somewhat rough skin, etc. He does all such things in the most genteel way, and offers these voluntary services in the most delicate manner.*

Nothing could be more magical than the city of Algiers, unless it be the *campagne* [a] outside that city in summertime [and] before; it would be like the *Arabian Nights*, particularly — given good health — with all my dear ones (in particular not forgetting my GRANDSONS [b]) about me. I have been delighted each time you have sent me news of the staunch little fellows; Tussy, too, has written saying that she can't stop thinking about the children, and longs to have them with her again. [It is] hardly likely that I shall be able to leave this place before the month is out, for I must firstly complete the full course of treatment prescribed by Dr Stephann, and not till then (always supposing that ALL THEN AS TO WEATHER ALTOGETHER SETTLED) shall I actually be able to commence the actual fresh air treatment.

I have seen nothing of the *Justice* (polemic with *Citoyen*), nor indeed any of the Paris papers save for the *Égalité*. I was very pleased to learn from your letter that Tussy had found a tactful solution to the catastrophe.[285] If and when Lissagaray launches his *Bataille*, you will, I presume, send me the early numbers; *I do not believe in a great result*; *mais qui vivra verra.*[c]

During my very first days here (while I was still at the Hôtel d'Orient), the GOOD Fermé 'over-walked' me — I mean, set me traipsing *up hill and down dale*, and likewise OVERTALKED me. *All this I put at once an end to this, making him understood that I was an invalid.* But he meant very well, and now he knows rest, SOLITUDE and silence to be duties that are incumbent on me as a citizen.

Kisses to all the children. Regards to Longuet. And many kisses to yourself, dear child,

From your
OLD NICK

First published, in Russian, in the magazine *Nachalo*, No. 5, St Petersburg, 1899

Printed according to the original

Published in English in full for the first time

---

[a] countryside - [b] Jean, Henri, Edgar and Marcel Longuet - [c] Here: We shall see.

123

MARX TO PAUL LAFARGUE [286]

IN PARIS

[Algiers,] Monday, 20 March [1882]

My dear Paul,

Your kind letter of 16 March was delivered to me today (20th) so that it seems to have taken far less time to get here than is usual for letters from London.

First of all, my gallant Gascon, 'what does Mustapha supérieur[a] refer to?' Mustapha is a proper name like John. If you leave Algiers by the rue d'Isly, you see a long street in front of you. On one side of it, in the foothills, rise Mauretanian villas surrounded by gardens (one of these villas is the Hôtel Victoria); on the other side — along the road — houses are spread out in descending terraces. All of this together is called Mustapha supérieur: Mustapha inférieur[b] begins at the incline of Mustapha supérieur and stretches down to the sea. Both Mustaphas form a single commune (Mustapha) whose mayor (this gentleman bears neither an Arab nor a French name but a German one) communicates with the inhabitants from time to time by means of official notices — a very soft regime, as you see. New houses are constantly being constructed in Mustapha supérieur, old ones are being demolished, etc., but although the workers engaged in this activity are healthy people and local residents they go down with fever after the first three days. Part of their wages, therefore, consists of a daily dose of quinine supplied by the employers. The same practice can be observed in various places in South America.

My dear augur. You are so well informed that you write: 'You must be consuming all the French newspapers that are sold in Algiers'; in actual fact I don't even read the few newspapers which the other hotel residents in the Victoria receive from Paris; my political reading is entirely limited to the telegraphic announcements in the *Petit Colon* (a small Algerian paper similar to the Parisian *Petit-Journal*, the *Petite République Française*, etc.). That's all.

Jenny wrote that she was sending Longuet's articles which you

---

[a] Upper Mustapha - [b] Lower Mustapha

mention too, but I still haven't received them. The only newspaper that I receive from London is *L'Égalité*, although you can't call it a newspaper.

What a strange fellow you are, St Paul! Where did you get the idea or who told you that I should 'rub my skin with iodine'? You will interrupt me and say that this is a mere trifle, but it does reveal your method of the 'material fact'. *Ex ungue leonem.*[a] In reality, instead of 'rubbing my skin with iodine' I have to have my back painted with cantharidic collodion to draw out the fluid. The first time I saw my left side (chest and back) treated in this manner, it reminded me of a kitchen garden in miniature planted with melons. Since 16 March when I wrote to Engels [284] there has not been a single dry place either on my back or my chest (the latter is also being treated) on which the operation could be repeated; this cannot happen now before the 22nd.

You say: 'A letter of invitation is enclosed which will make you laugh.' *Es regular.*[b] But how do you expect me to laugh when the 'enclosed' letter is still in your hands? When the opportunity arises, I shall remind Mr Fermé of his former comrade — the Proudhonist Lafargue. At present, while Doctor[c] forbids me to go out, I am using the time to refuse frequent visits and prolonged conversations.

The rains continue as before. The climate is so capricious; the weather changes from one hour to the next, going through every phase or suddenly leaping from one extreme to the other. However, there are signs of gradual improvement, but we shall have to wait. And just to think that from the moment of my departure for Marseilles and right up to the present there has been the finest weather in both Nice and Menton! But there was this insistent idea — for which I was not responsible — of the African sun and the wonder-working air out here!

Last Saturday we buried one of the residents of the Victoria, by the name of Armand Magnadère, in Mustapha supérieur; he was quite a young man sent here by Parisian doctors. He worked in a Paris bank; his employers continued to pay his salary in Algiers. To please his mother they arranged by telegraph to have his body exhumed and sent to Paris — all at their expense. Such generosity is seldom met with even among people charged with 'other people's money'.

---

[a] Judge the lion from his claws. - [b] Of course - [c] Stephann

My sleep is gradually returning; someone who has not suffered from insomnia cannot appreciate that blissful state when the terror of sleepless nights begins to give way.

Greetings to my dear Cacadou[a] and to all the others.

Yours,

K. Marx

First published, in Russian, in the magazine *Nachalo*, No. 5, St Petersburg, 1899

Printed according to the magazine

Translated from the Russian

Published in English in full for the first time

124

MARX TO ENGELS

IN LONDON

[Postcard]

[Algiers,] 23 March, Thursday [1882]

DEAR FRED,

Just now — after BREAKFAST — MY HELP[b] lanced, etc., the dense throng of greatly distended blisters produced on one side of my chest by yesterday's embrocation; after which [he told] me to idle away another hour or two in bed; so here I am scribbling a few lines on this postcard, as there's no time to be lost; for a messenger from this house is leaving for Algiers at an unusually early hour in order to take letters to the post office there, etc. (There's no post to France on Mondays and Wednesdays.)

Ever since Tuesday (21 March) another storm has been raging night and day save for the usual INTERVALS — thunder, not much lightning, downpours in the evening and particularly at night, *today in the morning as well*. As the storm approached on Tuesday afternoon, presaged by a SKY so overcast, pitch-black and lowering, I was

---

[a] Laura Lafargue - [b] Maurice Casthelaz

particularly struck by the rôle the TRULY AFRICAN SIROCCO played in the said storm.— Dr Stephann here yesterday; EXAMINATION *satisfactory*; progress; still *peccans*^a [are] a place at the *very bottom* of one side of my chest and a corresponding place on my back. Next week (i. e. ABOUT Wednesday or Thursday of next week), my HELP is to refrain from embrocating those spots; so Stephann is specially reserving this for himself.

Regards to all.

Your

Moor

[On the side reserved for the address]

Fr. Engels
122 Regent's Park Road,
London, N. W., Angleterre

First published in *Der Briefwechsel zwischen F. Engels und K. Marx*, Bd. 4, Stuttgart, 1913

Printed according to the original

Published in English for the first time

125

MARX TO JENNY LONGUET

IN ARGENTEUIL

[Algiers,] Monday, 27 March 1882

My Dear Child,

I received your letter to-day (27 March); you know how delighted I am always to hear of you. My reports to you did not conceal the worst from you; so you may also feel quite sure that I *simply tell the truth* in announcing you that since the date of my last letter to you^b my state of health is progressively improving. There is no longer insomny (the worst of all), nor want of appetite, nor any violent character of cough, the latter indeed much subdued. Of course the *vésicatoi-*

---

^a at fault - ^b See this volume, pp. 217-19.

res[a] can, because of their intense action, only once a week be renewed; so the process of the healing of the membranes (the essential tissue of the organ has not at all suffered) on the left side wants some time. Of course the most unsteady weather, with sudden changes, storms, heats, colds, rain, in fact only a few good intervals,— the steady *seasonable* air warm and '*sec*'[b] is still the great desideratum. When we just, like yesterday, had caught the decisive turning point — it was a beautiful day, and I had a promenade,— but to-day sky grey (with a *nuance noirâtre*[c]), rain pouring down, wind howling. People here get it quite tired, for, it must not again and again be repeated: this such weather since December (inclus.) quite anormous in Algier. The thing was to inform oneself before starting on such a *chasse aux oies sauvages*.[d]

Entre nous[e]: Though in the Isle of Wight [234] the weather was unfavourable, but still my health improved so greatly that people wondered when myself returning to London. But, then, I had *tranquillity* at Ventnor; at London, on the contrary, Engels' excitement (Lafargue, too, a quack, thought 'walking', free air etc. were all I did want) in fact has upset me: I felt, I could not longer stand it; hence my impatience to get from London away on any condition whatever! People may kill some one out of real most sincere love; with all that nothing more dangerous in such cases for a reconvalescent!

As I told you,[f] dear child, I have had the good chance of having met with well-meaning, kind and unpretending people (French-Swiss and unmixed French, no German nor English in my Villa-Hôtel). Mr Maurice Casthelaz functions as volunteer under the orders of Dr Stephann; no Nym[g] more careful or attentive. Hence, my child, do not worry yourself as to my fancied helpless situation. Enough of male and female helps; and, on the other hand, it is the privilege of a 'patient' to be silent, to withdraw, etc., whenever I prefer the solitude or take no notice of the company.

Generally I have altogether neglected the French, English etc. daily press; I read only the telegraphic news. What I had desired, f. i., was Longuet's articles on the *grève*[h] (Lafargue wrote me greatly praising those articles). As to Massard's *sottise*,[i] I know to that moment nothing save what you have written me.

---

[a] vesicatories - [b] dry - [c] blackish tinge - [d] wild goose chase - [e] Between us - [f] See this volume, p. 219. - [g] Helene Demuth - [h] strike - [i] stupidity

Write to Hirsch to send me his Adam-Contribution.[287] What I would like, to get *durch Wünschenkappe*[a] on a brilliant day here over Johnny; what would my little darling, wonder at *Maures*,[b] Arabs, Berbers, Turks, niggers, in one word this Babel and costumes (most of them poetic) of this oriental world, mixed with the 'civilised' French etc. and the dull Britons. Kiss also my sweet Harry, the noble Wolf, and the grand Pa[c]!

And now farewell, my best child; also my compliments to Longuet.

Yours,

Old Nick

As to any working, is still out of the question; not even the correction of the *Capital* for a new edition.[d]

First published, in Russian, in the magazine *Nachalo*, No. 5, St Petersburg, 1899

Reproduced from the original

Published in English for the first time

126

MARX TO ENGELS [72]

IN LONDON

[Algiers, 28-] 31 March 1882

DEAR FRED,

28 March: A maddeningly wet day early this morning — when I finished writing a short epistle to Tussy.[284] This had already gone off, however, when a storm developed which, for the first time, put on a good performance; not only howling wind, torrents of rain and thunder, but incessant lightning INTO THE BARGAIN. This went on until late at night, accompanied as usual by a considerable drop in temperature. Interesting, the varying colours of the waves in the lovely, almost elliptical bay; the surf snowy white, and the sea beyond changing from blue to green.

---

[a] by magic cap - [b] Moors - [c] Henri, Edgar and Marcel Longuet - [d] Marx is referring to the third German edition of Volume One of *Capital*.

29 March (Wednesday): Maddening drizzle today; no less maddening the moaning gusts of wind; temperature, cold and damp.

Today, shortly before *déjeuner*[a] (takes place at a QUARTER PAST or perhaps half past 11) Dr Stephann arrived for the specific purpose of 'devoting' himself to the painting of those places at the very bottom of my back and chest he had specially signalled out and reserved for his own attack. Beforehand, as on every visit, a thorough examination; by far the largest part of my left side was accorded much better STATUS; the aforementioned *nethermost* spots, presently giving forth no more than a low murmur in place of Helmholtz's musical note, can only be put to rights by slow degrees (anything speedier being hampered by the bad weather). Today, for the first time,— no doubt because he thought me far enough on the road to recovery for him to speak his mind — Stephann told me that I had already suffered a *rechute*[b] of a most serious kind by the time I arrived in Algiers. The *épanchements*[c] could only be controlled by recourse to *vésicatoires*,[d] and I had made better progress than might have been foreseen. He added, however, that I should have to treat myself very carefully for years. When I leave Algiers, he will give me a written diagnosis — intended in particular for my London doctor.[e] People of my age, he said, should be careful not to experiment too often with *rechutes*. A few hours after *déjeuner* the *tableau*[f] on my skin began to come to life in grim earnest; like someone who feels his epidermis has contracted and he himself is seeking to burst out of it; agony all night long; I had been absolutely forbidden to scratch.

30 March: At 8 o'clock in the morning my ASSISTANT-DOCTOR, my helpmate,[g] appeared at my bedside. It transpired that, as a result of spontaneous movements, the blisters GENERALLY had burst; a veritable flood had taken place during the night — linen, flannel, night-shirt soaked. So the painting had had the *desired effect on the places under attack*. My kind HELP at once proceeded to bandage me, not only so as to prevent the flannel's rubbing, but also to draw off what remained of the fluid. This morning (*31 March*) Mr Casthelaz discovered that the SUCTION was at last nearing its end and the process of drying-out almost complete. This being so, I shall probably be able to undergo a second application within the same week (beginning 29 March). *Tant mieux.*[h]

---

[a] lunch - [b] relapse - [c] effusions - [d] vesicatories - [e] Dr Donkin - [f] picture - [g] Maurice Casthelaz - [h] So much the better.

30 March (yesterday), the weather turned nice and warm at about midday, for which reason I strolled out onto the balcony; later I slept a little to make up for the restless night, as I shall also do today, since the strict avoidance of scratching keeps one awake at night even though, as during the night of 30 to 31, it's not agonising.

Weather today (31 March) uncertain; no rain yet, at all events; might turn relatively 'fine' towards midday, as it did yesterday.

There's nothing further to add to the health bulletin; quite satisfactory on the whole.

Have received [a letter] from Tussychen today.

Apropos, a short while ago she sent me the enclosed letter; I can't make out the signature; you will be able to. At all events a strange phenomenon, a Quedlinburg lawyer with a *Weltanschauung* of his own! But one thing I can't make out: Has the copy of the chap's 'book' intended for me arrived at Maitland Park,ᵃ or does he want to have my exact address first so as to ensure that his book gets there safely? If the first, Tussy should acknowledge receipt of his book, if the second, send him my 'safe' address.

Mon cher,ᵇ like other FAMILY MEMBERS, you, too, will have been struck by my mistakes in spelling and syntax, and bad grammar; I never recall these — my absent-mindedness being still very great — until after the event. SHOWS YOU there's something in the saying *sana mens in sano corpore*.ᶜ No doubt this will mend itself BY AND BY.

The *tocsin pour déjeuner* ᵈ has just sounded and this little note must accordingly be got ready for the messenger to Algiers. So my love to one and all.

Your
Moor

First published abridged in *Der Briefwechsel zwischen F. Engels und K. Marx*, Bd. 4, Stuttgart, 1913 and in full in *MEGA*, Abt. III, Bd. 4, Berlin, 1931

Printed according to the original

ᵃ Marx's London address - ᵇ Dear old man - ᶜ a sound mind in a sound body - ᵈ lunch bell

127

ENGELS TO HENRY MAYERS HYNDMAN

IN LONDON

[London, circa 31 March 1882]

Dear Sir,

I thank you for the pamphlet[a] you have sent me. I am very glad that glorious old Tom Spence has been brought out again.

I shall be very happy to make your personal acquaintance as soon as you shall have set yourself right with my friend Marx whom I see you can now afford to quote.

Yours truly,

F. E.

First published in: Marx and Engels, *Works*, First Russian Edition, Vol. XXVII, Moscow, 1931

Reproduced from the original

Published in English for the first time

128

MARX TO ENGELS

IN LONDON

[Postcard]

[Algiers,] Tuesday, 4 April 1882

DEAR FRED,

Have received your postcard [284]; Laurachen's letter dated 29 March has also arrived.

My congratulations to Pumps.[288]

I'm progressing well on the whole but the weather is making an April fool of me.

---

[a] [Th. Spence,] *The Nationalisation of the Land in 1775 and 1882...*, London, Manchester, 1882.

On 31 March, Friday afternoon — a few hours before I DISPATCHED my letter to you[a] — Fermé called; he told me *inter alia* of a secret vouchsafed to him by an Algerian meteorologist, namely that next week the weather would *d'abord*[b] be very wild for 3 days on account of the sirocco, after which there would be 3-4 wet days but finally a normal spring would step into the breach, booted and spurred. And anyone who doesn't believe it is mistaken.

Meanwhile Saturday (1 April), as well as Monday (3 April), was *warm* (a bit 'too' CLOSE) but the wind (no sirocco yet) confined me to my balcony on account of the swirls of dust; by contrast, the morning of 2 April (Sunday) was so fine and inviting that I went for a 2 hours' stroll.

Last night a piping wind; rain at ABOUT 5 o'clock *this morning*; dry since 8 o'clock, sky overcast, continual squalls. Yesterday evening wonderful moonlight on the bay. I can never stop feasting my eyes on the sea in front of my balcony.

Give my best regards to Jollymeyer,[c] ditto the others.

Your
Moor

[On the side reserved for the address]

Fr. Engels
122 Regent's Park Road,
London, N. W. (Angleterre)

First published in *Der Briefwechsel zwischen F. Engels und K. Marx*, Bd. 4, Stuttgart, 1913

Printed according to the original

Published in English for the first time

---

[a] See this volume, pp. 225-27. - [b] at first - [c] Schorlemmer's jocular nickname from the English 'jolly' and the German 'Meier' (farmer).

129

MARX TO JENNY LONGUET

IN ARGENTEUIL

[Algiers,] 6 April 1882

My Sweet Child,

Just now judge Fermé brought me your letter d. d. March 31; I am always delighted at your letters, but whenever, my dear child, did you find the time for writing them? I think often anxiously at your little household, limited to the services of this queer fish of Emily, and the four little boys[a] alone would absorb the whole working time of a superior servant.

Fermé handed me also a few days ago the promised numbers of the *Justice* (*ci-inclus*[b] Hirsch's elucubrations reproduced from Madame Adam's *Revue*[287]). Longuet's articles on the '*grèves*'[c] are very good. *En passant.* He says somewhere that Lassalle did *only* invent the *words* (not the law itself developed by Ricardo, Turgot, etc.[289]). In fact, however, he, Lassalle, borrowed, to German 'cultured' people well known, *expression of Goethe* who himself had modified Sophocles' '*ewige unwandelbare Gesetze*'[d] into '*ewige eherne Gesetze*'.[e]

Fermé had to sit opposite to me in my '*chambre*',[f] silent, reading, until I had finished a letter to Tussy (from her I had the same day received a letter, ditto one from Engels) to be ready for the messenger to Algiers.

I expect Dr Stephann to-day. If he comes, I should be able to report on his examination, before despatching these lines you tomorrow morning. Meanwhile the progress of my health goes on satisfactory, though slowly for somebody eager to be again active and to drop that *invalid's, stupid métier.* All this delay is due to this violent Algerian distemper, altogether quite anormous, never heard of since Fermé's 12 years long sojourn here. The weather remains fidgety, fitful, capricious; *April weather,* from sunny changing suddenly into rainy, from hot to cold, chilly, from a sky *diaphane*[g] to scowling, almost black; from the dry atmosphere to being heavy with aqueous vapours; in

---

[a] Jean, Henri, Edgar and Marcel Longuet - [b] including - [c] 'strikes' - [d] 'eternal immutable laws' (from Sophocles' *Antigone*) - [e] 'eternal iron laws' - [f] room - [g] clear, transparent

one word, the weather far from being 'settled' or having subsided to what here may be considered the average 'normal' Algerian 'spring' character. However, if the wind blows not violently, if there be no rain, the April's early hours were pleasant, so that I could indulge my morning promenades to-day, yesterday, and the day last before yesterday; thus I enjoyed three consecutive morning promenades one or two hours long.

I am just interrupted *by a noise* rising from the little, in terraces mounting little garden (*ein rotblühender Garten*[a]) that forms the avenue to our *Verandah* (behind it the first *étage*[b] of our Villa), while my *chambre* on the second *étage* (and 5 other ones) opens upon the little gallery over the Verandah, both of them looking at the sea before and from all sides to a charming panorama. Well, the noise called me upon the gallery, and how he would laugh, at my side, so heartfully, so delightfully, that little Johnny, below him in the garden a real pitch dark negro, dancing, playing a small fiddle, beating his long iron castagnettes, writhing his body into plastic grimaces and folding his face into broad humorous grins. These Algerian Negroes were formerly in general slaves of Turks, Arabs, etc., but were emancipated under the French régime.

Well, there looks down *behind him*, the negro, another figure, in a dignified manner and rather condescendingly smiling at the blackie's exhibition. This is a *Maure* (*anglice* Moor, *germ.* Mohr); *en passant* the *Maures* are called *the Arabs* in Algeria, a small minority of them, withdrawn from the desert and their communities, dwelling in the towns at the side of the Europeans. They are taller than the average French measure, oval faces, noses aquiline, eyes large and brilliant; hairs and beards black, their skin's colour running over an *échelle*[c] from almost white to darkly bronze. Their costumes — even if in tatters — elegant and graceful, a *culotte*[d] (or a mantle), a rather toga of thin white wool, or a *capot à capuchon*[e]; for their cover of the head (for which *the capuchon* serves also in unfavourable (too hot etc.) weather) a turban or a piece of white *mousseline*, wound round their *culottes*; generally they leave their legs naked, the feet also, but more rarely they wear *pantoufles*[f] of yellow or red maroquin.

Even the poorest *Maure* surpasses the greatest European comedian as to the '*art de se draper*' *dans son capot*,[g] and to show natural, graceful,

---

[a] a garden in red blossom - [b] floor - [c] range - [d] breeches - [e] cape with a hood - [f] shoes - [g] art of draping in his cape

and dignified attitudes, whether walking or standing (*if they ride* on their mules, or asses, or exceptionally on horses,— always throwing their both legs on some side down, instead of a European taking his horse *between* his both legs — then they offer the image of indolence).

Well, the said *Maure* — behind the negro in our garden — cries out for sale of 'oranges' and 'cocks' (incl. hens), a strange combination of these articles vendible. Between the *Maure*, majestical even then, and the dancing grinning nigger there struts an animal — a most vain *paon*[a] (belonging to one of our co-*pensionnaires*[b]) with its wonderfully blue throat and most adorned long tail. At this trio, how my Johnny's laughter I should like to hear ring!

It is now 4 o'clock p. m. (during part of the afternoon, I had of course some conversation with Fermé, having brought me your letter, then later on he removed himself to Algiers). The rain pours down: the sudden lowering of the temperature most disgusting. My best compliments to Dr Dourlen!

7 April 1882

Raining through the whole night; this morning is sky covered, but no rain; pleasant air, but too saturated with watery vapours. I had an hour's promenade (9-10 a. m.), doubtful whether not surprised by rain — but none yet. As Dr Stephann came not yesterday nor the day before, I wrote him to-day morning, but at all events these lines, in order to be despatched still to-day, cannot await the Doctor's examination. He will not appear before 5 o'clock afternoon. You see, it is a good sign, that the Dr neglects me a little; in other words, he is no longer anxious to strictly repeat his visits in court intervals.

How I shall feel happy when returning to my grandsons and their excellent Maman! I am not at all inclined here to prolong my sojourn longer than the Dr considers it absolutely necessary. Many kisses from your

Old Nick

The inclosed cut from a German-American paper Engels sent me; it is an amusing criticism of the newest 'Teutsche Bedientenpoesie'.[c] I hope Longuet tries to understand it.

---

[a] peacock - [b] lodgers - [c] German servile poetry

Dear child, I had already sealed this letter, but was forced to re-open it. Dr Stephann came a bit earlier than expected. The fresh examination led him to conclude — and I am very pleased to be able to tell you this — that my left side has in the meantime healed almost as well as the right one.[290]

First published, in Russian, in the magazine *Nachalo*, No. 5, St Petersburg, 1899

Reproduced from the original

Published in English for the first time

130

MARX TO ENGELS[72]

IN LONDON

[Algiers,] 8 April[a] (Saturday) 1882

DEAR FRED,

At 4 o'clock yesterday afternoon I was examined by Dr Stephann. Despite the changeable weather, which had again brought on a persistent cold, he was very satisfied; found that the *épanchement*[b] low down (to the left of my chest) had almost completely disappeared; the one on my back (low down on the left) being rather more stubborn. Yesterday he gave this a special lambasting by painting it with *collodion cantharidal*.[c] The result was most acute pain and, thanks to the 'painting', a sleepless night (from 7 to 8 April), but this morning there has also been a MOST EFFECTIVE PUMPING OF WATER from the blisters that have formed. So I have no doubt that this offending spot will also capitulate in the very near future. My ASSISTANT-DOCTOR, Mr Casthelaz, had to work away for half an hour in my flourishing watermelon plantation, after which I was made to lie in bed until *déjeuner*[d] at half past eleven; for after bandaging the drawing off, drop by drop, of any residual fluid works best in that position.

On the other hand Stephann found my cough somewhat worse (only *relatively*, however, for the cough had reached a nadir), a con-

---

[a] March in the ms.-[b] effusion-[c] cantharidic collodion-[d] luncheon

sequence of the absurd weather; for 4 days this week the *mornings* were fine enough for walks; since yesterday afternoon it has never stopped raining; in the night and today THE RAIN ASSUMED THE '*caractère torrentiel*'; today there has been a feeble attempt at lighting the fire in the dining-room, but these fireplaces don't in fact seem to exist for that purpose, BUT ONLY FOR SHOW'S SAKE.

After *déjeuner* I retired for a nap AT 2 O'CLOCK to make up in part for last night, but by some infernal chance the *courts are on vacation* this week and next. So my plan was thwarted by the otherwise most amiable JUDGE Fermé who didn't release me until ABOUT 5 p.m. when dinner time was approaching. Fermé told me amongst other things that during his *carrière* on the bench a form of *torture* has been used (and this happens 'regularly') to extract confessions from Arabs; naturally it is done (like the English in India) by the 'police'; the judge IS SUPPOSED TO KNOW NOTHING ABOUT ALL OF IT. On the other hand, he says that when, for example, a murder is committed by an Arab gang, usually with robbery in view, and the actual miscreants are in the course of time duly apprehended, tried and executed, this is not regarded as sufficient atonement by the injured colonist family. They demand INTO THE BARGAIN the 'pulling in' of *at least* half a dozen *innocent Arabs*. But this is resisted by the French judges and particularly the *cours d'appel*,[a] though now and again the life of an *individual*, isolated judge may be threatened by the colonists if he does not provisionally consent (his competence extends no further) to having a dozen innocent Arabs locked up for suspected murder, burglary, etc., and involving them in the investigation. However we are aware that when a European colonist dwells among the 'lesser breeds', either as a settler or simply on business, he generally regards himself as even more inviolable than handsome William I. Still, when it comes to barefaced arrogance and presumptuousness vis-à-vis the 'lesser breeds', to a grisly, Moloch-like obsession with atonement, the British and Dutch outdo the French.

Pumps' FAMILY MISSION shows great promise,[288] as opposed to Hyndman's political mission which might be regarded as problematical. It serves the laddie right that your note[b] should have annoyed him, especially since he took these liberties with me only because he was counting on my own inability, for 'considerations of propaganda', to compromise him in public.[291] He knew that well enough.

---

[a] courts of appeal - [b] See this volume, p. 228.

Scandalmonger Bodenstedt and Friedrich Vischer-Sewer-Aesthete are the Horace and Virgil of William I.[292]

Apropos. The *Kölnische Zeitung*'s article on Skobelev you sent me is most interesting.

This note won't leave today (Saturday), for there are *no 'paquebots'* [a] at all to Marseilles on *Mondays, Wednesdays* or *Saturdays*; but by way of exception a *paquebot* leaves Algiers on a *Sunday* at *1 p. m.* and letters for it must be delivered to the post office by 11 o'clock in the morning (Sunday); the Hôtel Victoria, Algiers, despatches a MESSENGER with the letters *early* on Sunday *mornings*. On the other days, when there is a *paquebot* from Algiers to Marseilles, departure is at 5.30 in the afternoon.

But I wanted to get these lines off by tomorrow, since Dr Stephann's last examination was so especially favourable.

Best wishes to everyone.

Your

Moor

First published abridged in *Der Briefwechsel zwischen F. Engels und K. Marx*, Bd. 4, Stuttgart, 1913 and in full in *MEGA*, Abt. III, Bd. 4, Berlin, 1931

Printed according to the original

131

ENGELS TO PYOTR LAVROV

IN LONDON

[London,] 10 April 1882
122 Regent's Park Road

My dear Lavrov,

I am returning the proofs,[293] for which I thank you. I should have done so earlier had I not hoped to see you last night and to say Христосъ, воскресъ ли онъ? [b]

Would you be so kind as to lend me the German manuscript of the

---

[a] ferry-boats - [b] Engels is using a Russian Easter greeting in an ironical form

preface for a day or two? The *Sozialdemokrat* has asked us to send it to them and, since the thing has appeared in the *Народная воля*[a] (to which we are proud to find ourselves contributors), there can no longer be any objection.

Yours sincerely,
F. Engels

Our ideas seem to me to have been very well rendered.

First published, in Russian, in the magazine *Letopisi marksizma*, Book V, Moscow-Leningrad, 1928

Printed according to the original

Translated from the French

Published in English for the first time

132

ENGELS TO BERTHOLD SPARR [294]

IN LONDON

[Draft]

[London,] 12 April 1882

Dear Sir,

I am not acquainted either with you or with the Mr K. Schmidt you refer to. If you mean Mr K. Schneidt, the anarchist, he will be able to get you into the club in Rose Street [295] and obtain assistance for you. In view of the way in which the people on the *Freiheit* have laid into the Social-Democratic Party in Germany,[296] I hardly feel called upon to give the adherents of that tendency a helping hand. However I do not know which tendency you belong to. The German Club, which sides with the great party in Germany, is, as anyone will tell you, at 49 Tottenham Street [297] and I find it inconceivable that both these clubs should let a fugitive party member starve to death.— In view of the great distress brought about among the members of the great Social-Democratic Party by police persecution in Germany, my resources will scarcely permit me to support, in addition, ad-

---

[a] Narodnaya Volya

herents of other, opposing tendencies. If, however, the Tottenham Street society is prepared to do something for you, I shall be pleased to make a contribution.

Yours very truly

First published in: Marx and Engels, *Works*, First Russian Edition, Vol. XXVII, Moscow, 1935

Printed according to the original

Published in English for the first time

133

ENGELS TO FRIEDRICH ADOLPH SORGE

IN HOBOKEN

[Postcard]

[London, 13 April 1882]

Dear Sorge,

Have posted to you today such *Égalités* as have so far appeared. More to follow. Marx is in Algiers; had a recurrence of pleurisy but has now almost completely got over it. Will have to take very great care of himself next winter. Trust your letter will arrive soon. What is your son[a] doing? Kindest regards.

Your
F. E.

[On the side reserved for the address]

F. A. Sorge, Esq.,
Hoboken, N. Y.
U. S. America

First published abridged in *Briefe und Auszüge aus Briefen von Joh. Phil. Becker, Jos. Dietzgen, Friedrich Engels, Karl Marx u. A. an F. A. Sorge und Andere*, Stuttgart, 1906 and in full in: Marx and Engels, *Works*, First Russian Edition, Vol. XXVII, Moscow, 1935

Printed according to the original

Published in English for the first time

---

[a] Adolph Sorge

134

MARX TO LAURA LAFARGUE [166]

IN LONDON

[Algiers,] Thursday, 13 April 1882

Darling Cacadou,

I reproach myself for not having written to you again until now, not that there's anything special to report from here. How often do I not think of you—at Eastbourne,[298] beside my Jenny's[a] sick-bed, and during your faithful daily visits so cheering to that crosspatch, OLD NICK. But you should know, dear child, that this week and last were Fermé's Easter vacation; he lives in the rue Michelet (as part of the route Mustapha supérieur[b] is called) at the foot of the hill from which the Hôtel Victoria looks down. It's only a stone's throw away for him, although he has to 'clamber' since there's no proper path leading up to it. And in fact he has latterly been visiting me assiduously, thus frustrating the best of resolutions in regard to afternoon letter-writing.— Otherwise not an unwelcome guest, MR Fermé, nor devoid of humour. After I had given him some *Citoyens* and *Égalités* to read, he arrived chuckling not a little over Guesde's 'terrorism of the future' [which is to go on] until—this anticipated in heavy type— the last bourgeois oppressor has been guillotined out of existence. Fermé is not fond of Algiers whose climate doesn't suit either him or his family (often visited by fever, etc.) although its members are all of them '*des indigènes*' *à commencer par Madame l'épouse.*[c] Above all, however, his salary as a judge is hardly sufficient for even the most modest way of life. Living in a colonial capital is always expensive. But one thing he does admit—in no town ELSEWHERE, which is at the same time the seat of the central government, is there such *laisser faire, laisser passer*[d]; police reduced to a *bare minimum*; unprecedented public *sans gêne*[e]; the Moorish element is responsible for this. For Mussulmans there is no such thing as subordination; they are neither 'subjects' nor '*administrés*'[f]; no authority, save in *politica,*[g] something which Europeans have totally failed to understand. Few police in Al-

---

[a] Jenny Marx-[b] Upper Mustapha-[c] 'natives', starting with his lady wife-
[d] easy-going ways-[e] nonchalance-[f] persons under the jurisdiction of others-
[g] political matters

giers, and such as there are for the most part *indigènes*. And yet, with such a medley of national elements and unscrupulous characters, frequent clashes are inevitable, and it is here that the *Catalonians* live up to their old reputation; the white or red belts they wear, like the Moors, etc., outside their coats and not, like the French, beneath their clothing, often conceal 'bodkins' — *long stilettos* which these sons of Catalonia are not slow to 'employ' with equal impartiality against Italians, Frenchmen, etc., and natives alike. Incidentally, a few days ago a gang of forgers was apprehended in the province of Oran, amongst them their chief, a former Spanish officer; their European agency, it now transpires, is in the capital of Catalonia — Barcelona! Some of the laddies were not arrested and escaped to Spain. This piece of news, and others of a similar kind, derives from Fermé. The latter has received 2 advantageous offers from the French government; *firstly*, a transfer to New Caledonia where he would, at the same time, be responsible for introducing a new legal system, salary 10,000 frs (he and family to travel there gratis and, on arrival, be given free official accommodation); or, *secondly*, to *Tunis*, where he would likewise occupy a higher magisterial rank than here, and under far more favourable conditions. He has been given a certain period in which to make up his mind; will accept one or the other.

From Mr Fermé to the *weather* is a natural transition, since he freely heaps imprecations on the same.— Since Easter Monday (incl.) I have not missed a single morning stroll, although only yesterday (12th) and today have been spared the caprices of April. *Yesterday, bien que nous subissions le léger siroco et, par conséquent, quelques coups de vent, ce fut le maximum du beau temps: à 9 heures le matin (le 12) le température à l'ombre fut de 19.5°, et celle au soleil, de 35°.*[a] In spite of having gone for a walk in the morning (12 April), I visited Algiers in the afternoon in order to take a look at the Russian ironclad, *Peter the Great*, which had arrived in the harbour there a few days before.

The official meteorological office has forecast intense atmospheric disturbances for 15-16 April (when there'll be *orage*[b]), 19, 21, 25, 27, 29 and 30 April; nevertheless, the weather during the remainder of April will on the whole be fine; at the same time it is feared that *in May*, to make up for the absence of a *true Algerian spring* (which did

---

[a] although we experienced a slight sirocco and, as a result, some gusts of wind, it was the finest possible weather: at 9 o'clock in the morning (the 12th) the temperature was 19.5° in the shade and 35° in the sun.- [b] a storm

not begin till yesterday), summer will arrive all at once and with it unbearable heat. However that may be, I do not, as *corpus vile*,ᵃ feel inclined to serve as an experimental station for the weather. In view of the altogether abnormal character of the past 4¹/₂ months, God knows what Algeria may have in store. Large numbers of shrewd folk (amongst them *l'illustre*ᵇ 'Ranc') departed from the African shore day before yesterday. I shall only stay until Dr Stephann has declared my left side to be in good order again, apart, of course, from the scar well known to the *doctissimi*ᶜ Drs Donkin and Hume, left by an earlier attack of pleurisy. What has been tiresome here so far is the constant recurrence of my cough, even if within moderate limits; withal, much boredom.

Interruption of the most argeeable kind: Knocks at the door; *Entrez!*ᵈ Madame Rosalie (one of the serving spirits) brings me a letter from you, dear Cacadou, and, from the good Gascon,ᵉ a long letter of which the paper, like the envelope, already bears the official stamp: '*L'Union Nationale*'.²⁹⁹ This time he seems to have pulled it off! *Ce n'est pas une de ces entreprises patronées par Mr Ch. Hirsch!*ᶠ On the other hand, to be sure, the prospect of my Cacadou's departure looms closer! But not just yet, I trust. Also, I regard it as some compensation that aunty Cacadou should represent so great a gain to Jennychen and her childrenᵍ; anyway, with Paris so close, there's no need to spend the whole year in London.— Apropos. *Has Lafargue* sent the next instalment of the article to Petersburg? (I don't know what became of the first consignment.)³⁰⁰ It's most important not to lose the vantage point of Petersburg; it will gain in importance daily! Also for anyone who sends despatches there.

Second interruption: It is 1 o'clock p.m., and I have promised to visit the '*Jardin du Hamma*' ouʰ '*Jardin d'Essai*' with Madame Casthelaz, *son fils*,ⁱ and one of our other fellow *pensionnaires*,ʲ Madame Claude (of Neufchâtel). We have to be back before dinner (6 o'clock p.m.), later than which every effort at writing never as yet dared upon by me. So no more till tomorrow. Simply by way of a supplement * to the useful knowledge of Cacadou I allow myself to remark, that on that very Hamma took place the landing of 24,000 soldiers under the commandment of Charles V, emperor, (or Carlos I, according to the Spaniards) on 23 October 1541³⁰¹; 8 days later he had to ship the * *beaux*

ᵃ a vile body - ᵇ the illustrious - ᶜ most learned - ᵈ Come in.- ᵉ Paul Lafargue - ᶠ It isn't one of those enterprises patronised by Mr Ch. Hirsch.- ᵍ Jean, Henri, Edgar and Marcel Longuet - ʰ or - ⁱ her son - ʲ lodgers

restes de son armée détruite sur les vaisseaux échappés à la tempête du 26, et rallies à grand' peine par Doria, à Matifou. Ce dernier lieu où finit la baie d'Alger c. à. d.— le cap Matifou [a] — OPPOSITE, ON THE EAST, TO ALGIERS, IS TO BE ESPIED, *par des bonnes lunettes,* [b] BY MYSELF FROM Hôtel Victorias GALLERY.

Vendredi, [c] 14 April

*I commence this letter *at the moment* when I have a few lines to be added to the foregoing, that is to say at about *1 o'clock p. m.* The day ended yesterday as fine as that of the 12th. Both *the evenings* 12 and 13 (about 8 hours p. m.) were warm — quite exceptional this — but cool (relatively) at the same time, hence really delightful. This morning the warmth a little more 'heavy', and just since two hours the wind blows violently, probably the *'orage'* predicted yesterday from 14-15.

Yesterday at 1 o'clock p. m. we went down to Inferior Mustapha whence the tram brought us to *Jardin Hamma* or *Jardin d'Essai,* the which used for *'Promenade Publique'* with occasional military music, as *'pépinière'* [d] for the production and diffusion of the indigenous vegetables, at last for the purpose of *scientific botanical experiments* and as a *garden* of *'acclimatation'.* — This all encloses a very large ground, part of which is mountainous, the other belonging to the plain. In order to see more minutely, you would want at least a whole day, and beside being somebody with you a *connaisseur,* f. i. like M. Fermé's friend and old Fourieriste, M. Durando, professor of botanics, who is the leader of a section of the 'Club Alpin Français' on its regular Sunday excursions. (I very much regretted that my bodily circumstances and the Dr. Stephann's strict prohibition till now did not yet allow me to share in these excursions, having 3 times [been] invited thereto.)

Well, before entering the 'Jardin d'Essai' we took coffee, of course in the free air, a Mauresque *'café'.* The Maure prepared it excellently, we were on a bank. On a rough table, in inclined positions, their legs crossed, half a dozen Maure visitors [...] [e] were delighted in their small *'cafétières',* [f] (everyone gets one of his own) and together

---

[a] remnants of his shattered army aboard the vessels which had escaped the storm of the 26th and been rallied with much difficulty by Doria, at Matifu. This latter place, where the Bay of Algiers ends — Cape Matifu - [b] with good glasses - [c] Friday - [d] nursery - [e] Illegible passage in the ms.- [f] coffee pots

playing at cards (a conquest this on them of civilisation). Most striking this spectacle: Some these Maures were dressed pretentiously,
even richly, others in, for once I dare call it *blouses*, sometime of
white woollen appearance, now in rags and tatters — but in the eyes
of a true Musulman such accidents, good or bad luck, do not distinguish Mahomet's children. *Absolute equality in their social intercourse*, not
affected; on the contrary, only when demoralized, they become aware
of it; as to the hatred against Christians and the hope of an ultimate victory over these infidels, their politicians justly consider this
same feeling and practice of absolute equality (not of wealth or position but of personality) a guarantee of keeping up the one, of not giving up the latter.* (Nevertheless, they will go to rack and ruin WITH-
OUT A REVOLUTIONARY MOVEMENT.)

*In regard to the plain part of the *Jardin d'Essai* I remark only: It is
cut by *three great longitudinal 'allées'* ᵃ of a wonderful beauty; opposite to the principal entry is the *'allée' of the platenes* [*platanes*] ᵇ;
then the *'allée des palmiers'*,ᶜ ended by an oasis of immense 72 *'palmiers'*, limited by the railway and the sea; at last the *'allée'* of the
magnolia and a sort of *figues* (*ficus roxburghi*). These three great *'allées'*
are themselves cut by many others crossing them, such as the long
'allée des bambous' astonishing, the *'allée'* of *'palmiers à chanvre'*,ᵈ
the *'dragon[n]iers'*,ᵉ the 'eucalyptus' (blue gum of Tasmania), etc.,
(the latter are of an extraordinarily quick vegetation).

Of course, these sorts of* *allées* cannot be reproduced in European
'Jardins d'acclimatation'.ᶠ

During the afternoon there was a concert of military music in
a large open space encircled by plane trees; the conductor, a non-
commissioned officer, wore ordinary French uniform, whereas the
musicians (common soldiers) wore red, baggy trousers (of oriental
cut), white felt boots buttoning up to the bottom of the baggy trousers; on their heads a red fez.

While on the subject of the garden, I did not mention (though
some of these were very pleasing to the nose) orange trees, lemon —
ditto, almond trees, olive trees, etc.; nor, for that matter, cactuses and
aloes which also grow wild (as do wild olives and almonds) in the
rough country where we have our abode.

Much though this garden delighted me, I must observe that what

---

ᵃ avenues - ᵇ plane trees - ᶜ palm trees - ᵈ hemp palms - ᵉ dragon trees - ᶠ Botanical
Gardens

is abominable about this and similar excursions is the ubiquitous *chalky dust*; though I felt well in the afternoon and after coming home and during the night, my cough was nonetheless rather troublesome, thanks to the irritation caused by the dust.

I am expecting Dr Stephann today, but as I cannot put off the despatch of this missive, I will send a report to Fred [a] later on.

Finally, as Mayer of Swabia used to say, let us take a little look at things from a higher historical perspective. Our nomadic Arabs (who have, in many respects, gone very much to seed while retaining, as a result of their struggle for existence, a number of sterling qualities) have memories of having once produced great philosophers, scholars, etc., which, they think, is why Europeans now despise them for their present ignorance. Hence the following little fable, typical of Arab folklore.

A ferryman is ready and waiting, with his small boat, on the tempestuous waters of a river. A philosopher, wishing to get to the other side, climbs aboard. There ensues the following dialogue:

Philosopher: Do you know anything of *history*, ferryman?

Ferryman: No!

Philosopher: Then you've wasted half your life!

And again: *The Philosopher*: Have you studied mathematics?

Ferryman: *No!*

Philosopher: Then you've wasted more than half your life.

Hardly were these words out of the philosopher's mouth when the wind capsized the boat, precipitating both ferryman and philosopher into the water. Whereupon,

Ferryman shouts: Can you swim?

Philosopher: No!

Ferryman: Then you've wasted your *whole* life.

That will tickle your appetite for things Arabic.

With much love and many kisses.

OLD NICK

(BEST COMPLIMENTS TO ALL)

First published in: Marx and Engels, *Works*, Second Russian Edition, Vol. 35, Moscow, 1964

Printed according to the original

Published in English in full for the first time

---

[a] Engels

135

ENGELS TO EDUARD BERNSTEIN

IN ZURICH

London, 17 April 1882

Dear Mr Bernstein,

As soon as I heard from Lavrov that the preface[a] had appeared in the *Narodnaya Volya*[302] I asked for a copy of the original,[b] but he had left it in his desk in Paris; however, he said he would write. Then I went to Marx's and searched in vain for the *brouillon*.[c] Finally I got Lavrov to let me have a copy of the Russian translation so that, if the worst came to the worst, I could retranslate it myself; I feared, as indeed happened, that some Russian or other would see to this. Lavrov has just sent me the enclosed copy of the original. However, I have only myself to blame for this. For I had meant to send you a postcard, but have got Schorlemmer and Adolf Beust staying with me, and there's quite a lot of gadding about with Mrs Lafargue (whose husband[d] is in Paris) and Tussy Marx, so that the postcard got overlooked. But in order that you may see that good intentions were not wanting, I am belatedly sending you the thing.

Congratulations on your attack upon Geiser's spineless conduct.[303]

Confidential: Marx has been in Algiers since 21 February. On arrival he had a fresh attack of pleurisy as a result of catching cold on the journey; he found wretched weather conditions, but is now pretty well all right again. How long he'll stay there is not yet certain. Has had distinctly bad luck with the weather.

Kindest regards from

Yours,

F. Engels

First published, in Russian, in *Marx-Engels Archives*, Book I, Moscow, 1924

Printed according to the original

Published in English for the first time

---

[a] K. Marx and F. Engels, 'Preface to the Second Russian Edition of the *Manifesto of the Communist Party*' (see present edition, Vol. 24, pp.425-26).- [b] See this volume, pp. 235-36 - [c] draft - [d] Paul Lafargue

136

MARX TO ENGELS[72]

IN LONDON

[Algiers,] Tuesday, 18 April 1882

DEAR FRED,

Got your letter yesterday,[284] likewise Tussy's, together with the 'imperial' remittance.[a]

In my last letter to Laurachen[b] I announced the arrival of our '2 finest days'; but even before I had finished the letter, the sirocco (the official weather bulletins, like other French printed matter, spell it sometimes with one c, sometimes with 2) began to blow and the din served me as an overture to the '*mouvements atmosphériques intenses*'[c] which had been predicted. I admitted to Laura that I was tired of such things — if not, indeed, tired of Africa, and was determined to turn my back on Algiers the moment Dr Stephann DID NO LONGER 'WANT ME'.

From the 14th April (afternoon) to the 17th April, gusts of wind, storms, heavy downpours, burning sunshine, continual ups and downs, now hot now cold (almost from one hour to the next). First thing this morning gloriously fine, but now, at 10 A.M., the wind is already piping its maddening tune.— In its report — or rather forecast — yesterday, the meteorological office announced an '*intense mouvement atmosphérique*' for 3-4 May, but more especially for 7-8 May (not having *pro nunc*[d] probed any further into the future); in addition, for the first week of this self-same May, it has promised us SO CALLED '*seismiques mouvements*'[e] (apparently the periodicity of these '*seismiques*' coincides with latent earth tremors).

Dr Stephann called on the 16th (Sunday), percussed, and declared that there was no longer any trace of '*pleurésie*'[f] (AS FAR AS TO '*rechute*'[g]); on the other hand he was, he said, less satisfied with the bronchial condition (also on the left) than when he last examined me. However, he painted away with great vigour (a vigour I damned well had time to appreciate in the course of Sunday afternoon — 16 April — and

---

[a] Engels had arranged the remittance through the bankers Kayser & Co. *Kaiser* = Emperor.- [b] See this volume, pp. 238-43.- [c] intense atmospheric disturbances - [d] for the time being - [e] seismic disturbances - [f] pleurisy - [g] relapse

night, and right into the small hours of Monday — 17 April!).—
Incidentally, Dr Stephann shares my view that bronchial trouble is
inseparable from this weather and, such being the case, any prolon-
gation of my stay here could only have unfavourable consequences.
He thinks he will be able to let me leave, with a written diagnosis, at
the end of April unless something unforeseen should happen — e. g.
the weather here take a distinct turn for the better or, which seems
unlikely, my health take a turn for the worse. All things being equal,
then, I should leave *on 2 May*, being delivered back to Marseilles *by the
selfsame Said* under the same Captain Mace (very nice chap) who
brought me to Algiers, and from there should go and try my luck at
Cannes, Nice or Menton. So don't send me either letters or anything
in the way of documents or newspapers from London, *unless it be* JUST
AFTER THE RECEIPT OF THESE LINES. But should I change my mind in the
meantime, I shall at once notify you from here.

I am afraid that '*IRON*' may arrive in Algiers after not only I, but
also the Casthelaz FAMILY, have evacuated Africa; all the world's preparing to take flight. You must excuse the meagreness of this MISSIVE.
The night of the 16th to 17th April was sleepless because of the vigour
of the painting; no pain from the 17th to the 18th April because the
ASSISTANT DOCTOR [a] had already attended to me by 7 o'clock yesterday
morning; but the itching due to the formation of new skin banished
sleep for the 2nd night running. Since, in addition, I went for a stroll
(2 whole hours) very early this morning, *üw begrijp* [b] (I can no longer
recall how the Dutch spell it, but I still hear the *ü begreip!* — what it's
got to do with 'concept', God alone knows — as enunciated in the old
days at Zalt-Bommel [304] by Pastor Rothhaus's [c] wife, since divorced
and replaced by my cousin [d]), IN ONE WORD, as you can conceive, I have
got to lay my head on my pillow and make up for some sleep. Meanwhile:— sleep, what would'st thou more? Only first let me tell you
about the rotten trick played by the French authorities on a poor,
thieving Arab, a poor, multiple assassin by profession. Only at the
last minute — ON THE MOMENT, as the infamous COCKNEYS say, 'TO LAUNCH'
the poor sinner 'INTO ETERNITY' did he discover that he wasn't going to
be shot but guillotined! *This, in defiance of prior arrangements!* In defiance of promises! He was guillotined despite what had been agreed.
But that wasn't all. The French having always permitted this hith-

---

[a] Maurice Casthelaz - [b] You [can] conceive - [c] A. Roodhuizen - [d] Antoinette Philips

erto, his relatives had expected the head and body to be handed over to them so that they could sew the former to the latter and then bury the 'whole'. *Quod non!* [a] Howls, imprecations and gnashing of teeth; the French authorities dug their heels in, the first time they had done so! Now, when the body arrives in paradise, Mohammed will ask, 'Where have you left your head? Or, how did the head come to be parted from its body? You're not fit to enter paradise. Go and join those dogs of Christians in hell!' And that's why his relations were so upset.

Your

OLD Moor

On closer inquiry—I hadn't asked him before—Stephann told me that, although he doesn't speak German, he is the son of a German. His father emigrated to Algiers from the Palatinate (Landau).

First published in *Der Briefwechsel zwischen F. Engels und K. Marx*, Bd. 4, Stuttgart, 1913

Printed according to the original

137

ENGELS TO EDUARD BERNSTEIN

IN ZURICH

London, 21 April 1882

Dear Mr Bernstein,

I am sending you a piece from the *Kölner Zeitung* on 'Baron Hirsch'.[305] It is significant that *bourgeois* papers should find it necessary to denounce such a trickster. The whole article is worth reprinting if space is available. It would make a splendid feuilleton, particularly as emanating from the *Kölnische Zeitung*. If you can't reprint it in its entirety, perhaps you would return it to me when you have done with it. You might also return me the ms. of the 'Preface' [b] sometime.

Let me elucidate: Mahmud *Nedim* Pasha is, like Mahmud Damat

---

[a] But no.- [b] K. Marx and F. Engels, 'Preface to the Second Russian Edition of the *Manifesto of the Communist Party*' (see present edition, Vol. 24, pp. 425-26).

Pasha (the Sultan's[a] brother-in-law), Russia's chief paid agent in Constantinople. When the Russian, Poliakov, who was also after the Turkish railway concessions, had failed to get them (for the Russians could not start a war against Turkey and *simultaneously* con the Turks), it was naturally of the utmost concern to the Russians to see to it that the terms imposed upon the Austrian, Hirsch, who was the sole competitor and, what's more, Austria's *protégé*, were of such a kind as to make Hirsch, and with him Austria, hated in Turkey and to prevent Turkey from getting a coherent railway network after all. Besides, anything that weakened Turkey financially was advantageous to Russia — relatively speaking. So Nedim does his deal. Hirsch pays him for selling Turkey to *him* and Russia pays him again just for selling Turkey. The fact is that Russian diplomacy does business in the grand manner, with none of your small shopkeeper's niggardly, envious eye to his competitors and hence, if there's no other way of doing it, it can even permit an adversary like Austria an apparent or momentary advantage and nevertheless turn this to its own account.

Kindest regards to you and Kautsky.

Yours,
F. E.

First published, in Russian, in *Marx-Engels Archives*, Book I, Moscow, 1924

Printed according to the original

Published in English for the first time

138

MARX TO ENGELS [72]

IN LONDON

[Algiers,] Friday, 28 April 1882

Dear FRED,

RECEIVED YOUR LETTER AND THE *Kölnische Zeitungs*.

This note is simply to inform you that I shall be leaving Algiers on

---

[a] Abdul Hamid II

2 May (Tuesday) on the same *Said* and with the same *commandant*[a]
Mr Mace, *'lieutenant de vaisseau'*,[b] as brought me to Algiers. Last
Wednesday I paid a visit to a French squadron of 6 ironclads; naturally I inspected the flagship, *Le Colbert*, where a petty officer,
a handsome, intelligent lad, showed me around and demonstrated
everything in detail. As I took my leave he told me in typically
French fashion that he was sick of his boring duties and hoped to get
his discharge *bientôt*.[c] I and my companions (3 *co-locataires*[d] from the
Hôtel Victoria) were not allowed on board until after 'duties'. So we
watched the manoeuvres of the flagship and the 5 other ironclads
from our boat, alias skiff, as we rowed to and fro. There is to be
a 'ball' on the *Colbert* tomorrow afternoon. I could have got hold of an
invitation card for this, too, through Fermé, but there wasn't time.
For on Tuesday (25 *Avril*) I was given my final examination by
Stephann; no more *tatouement*[e] with collodion; *quo-ad*[f] a recurrence of
pleurisy ALTOGETHER ABSOLVED; however I'm to see him tomorrow (Saturday) at 3 o'clock to get his written diagnosis and take my leave of
him. The weather is now very hot on occasion, but IN FACT a hurri-
cane—with sirocco storms coming and going—has persisted (un-
interruptedly at night, in repeated gusts during the day) throughout
the week (including TO-DAY). That is the reason why my cough has not
responded hitherto; HENCE high time to flee Algiers.
Best wishes to all.

Your
OLD MOOR

Apropos; because of the sun, I have done away with my prophet's
beard and my crowning glory but (in deference to my daughters) had
myself photographed before offering up my hair on the altar of an Algerian barber. I shall receive the photographs next Sunday (30 April). *Specimina* will be sent to you from Marseilles. On inspection you
will observe that, CONSIDERING the 8 whole weeks (during which I did
not in fact have one day of complete repose) of painting with collodion (after the manner of Ludwig of Bavaria [306]), *j'ai fait encore bonne
mine à mauvais jeu*.[g]

First published in *Der Briefwechsel zwischen*   Printed according to the original
F. Engels und K. Marx, Bd. 4, Stuttgart, 1913

[a] captain - [b] Lieutenant Commander - [c] soon - [d] fellow lodgers - [e] painting - [f] as to -
[g] I am still putting a good face on things.

139

MARX TO JENNY LONGUET

IN ARGENTEUIL

[Algiers,] 28 April 1882

Dearest Child,

Only 2 lines: I think only seaside living can help poor Harry. You ought — *if possibly* — lose no time to get him and his brothers [a] to Normandy. It is childish to fancy that in any case I should return to England without a previous visit to you and my grandsons, whether we meet in Normandy, at Paris, or elsewhere.

As to my health, it proceeds favourably; otherwise Dr Stephann would not allow me to leave 'Africa'. I think, 2 weeks or so, will suffice for the 'transitory' stadium at the Riviera.

My best wishes, dearest child,

Old Nick

First published, in Russian, in the magazine *Nachalo*, No. 5, St Petersburg, 1899

Reproduced from the original

Published in English for the first time

140

ENGELS TO EDUARD BERNSTEIN [113]

IN ZURICH

London, 3 May 1882

Dear Mr Bernstein,

Could you not send me some additional offprints of the article on early Christianity [b] or further copies of the relevant issue? I should like to have them very much and they would come in useful for prop-

---

[a] Jean, Edgar and Marcel - [b] F. Engels, 'Bruno Bauer and Early Christianity'.

aganda purposes. I should send them to people who don't otherwise
see the *Sozialdemokrat*; 3 or 4 would suffice.

Encl. a note which is of interest in that it gives evidence of the colossal speed with which the concentration of capitals is taking place in
America. UNITED STATES BONDS are *Staatsschuldscheine der Vereinigten Staa-
ten*. N.Y.C. and H. R. STOCK are the shares of the NEW YORK CENTRAL
and HUDSON RIVER Railroad; REAL ESTATE = *Grundbesitz*.

A dollar is slightly more than 4 marks = roughly 4 marks = 5 frs.

Delighted to see that people everywhere are supporting the *Sozialdemokrat* against the whines of the milksops.

Darwin's letter was of course addressed to Marx and was an extremely kind one.[307] But beware of the article by Lafargue in the
Citoyen of 28 April on '*La sélection darwinienne et les classes régnantes*'
which he concludes with the discovery of a new Amphioxus; it's too
funny for words. Lafargue is in Paris and I have just written to
him [284] pouring frightful scorn on his *Amphioxus Lafargii*.

Best wishes.

Yours,

F. E.

Don't let the Society here [8] mislead you about the DEMOCRATIC FED-
ERATION.[158] So far, the latter has been of no importance at all. Its
leader is an ambitious parliamentary candidate by the name of
Hyndman, a former Conservative; only with the help of the Irish and
with specifically Irish aims in view can he succeed in staging a big
meeting, and when he does he plays third fiddle; otherwise the Irish
would tell him where to get off.

Gladstone has made a dreadful ass of himself—his Irish policy has
failed utterly; is having to drop Forster and the LORD LIEUTENANT of
Ireland, Cowper Temple (whose father was a Palmerston on his mother's side),[a] and say *pater peccavi*[b]; the Irish Members of Parliament
have been released, the Coercion Bill has not been extended, part of
the farmers' rent arrears are to be cancelled, another part to be taken
over by the state against fair amortisation.[308] On the other hand, the
TORIES have now got to the stage of wanting to salvage whatever there
is to be salvaged; thus, before the farmers *take possession* of the land,

---

[a] Engels confuses Francis Thomas Cowper with William Cowper-Temple, who was
the son of the 5th Earl Cowper. After the latter's death his widow married, as her second husband, Lord Palmerston.- [b] Father, I have sinned (Luke 15:18).

they are to discharge their rents with state assistance on the Prussian mode so that the landlords do actually get *something*! The Irish have really made dawdling John Bull get a move on. That's what comes of shooting![309]

First published, in Russian, in *Marx-Engels Archives*, Book I, Moscow, 1924

Printed according to the original

Published in English in full for the first time

141

MARX TO LAURA LAFARGUE

IN LONDON

Monte Carlo, 6 May 1882
Hôtel de Russie

My dear Cacadou,

Only a few hours since I arrived here at Monte Carlo.[310] I even doubt whether I shall find the time enough to indite a letter announced already to Engels (at all events he will but receive it a day later).

For the present I am obliged to run about on different errands. I enclose one photo for you, another for Fred [a]; no art can make the man look worse.

Old Nick

First published in: Marx and Engels, *Works*, Second Russian Edition, Vol. 35, Moscow, 1964

Reproduced from the original

Published in English for the first time

---

[a] Engels

142

MARX TO ENGELS [72]

IN LONDON

Monte Carlo, 8 May 1882
Hôtel de Russie

DEAR FRED,

2 or 3 weeks before I left Algiers (at the beginning of May),[310] the meteorologists had already forecast storms at sea. In fact, during my last days in Africa, the sirocco blew itself out and very hot weather set in, spoilt, however, by gusts of wind, eddies of dust and unexpected, if temporary and often short-lived, drops in temperature. During that same time my bronchial catarrh grew worse and has not yet been properly subdued. The storm at sea (during the night of 4 to 5 May) was such that, even in the cabin, there was an appreciable draught. It was pouring when I arrived in Marseilles (on the morning of 5 May), and continued to rain all the way to Nice. I even imported *one wet day* (yesterday) into Monte Carlo; glorious weather today. So you see how constant I have remained, for until I arrived it hadn't rained for months in Nice or Monte Carlo. But this time it was just badinage, not real earnest as in Algiers.

In Nice, where I spent the 5th and 6th, I soon discovered that the wind could be very capricious and that a uniform, even temperature was by no means to be expected. Today my brief experience was confirmed by Dr Delachaux, *médecin-chirurgien*^a (lives at Interlaken), who is staying at the same hotel here. He has spent his holiday touring Nice and its environs, and the most famous places on the Riviera * generally, so far with an eye to business as to ascertain which places he might best recommend to sufferers of lung diseases, bronchial catarrh of a chronic character, etc. He declared decidedly against Nice, but preferred Monte Carlo even to Menton.* Dr Delachaux returns to his native Switzerland today.

You will know EVERYTHING about the charm exerted by the beauties of nature here, whether from your own observations,[311] or from paintings and printed descriptions. Many of its features vividly recall those of Africa.

---

^a doctor and surgeon

As regards a 'warm, dry atmosphere', it will soon, generally speaking, be available everywhere. The sun-spots indicate that there will be intense activity of the rays, and a drought is feared in France. FOR CONSCIENCE SAKE I shall consult Kunemann, a German doctor, here tomorrow. I have with me Dr Stephann's written diagnosis (only on looking at his visiting card do I see that Stephann is also *Professeur suppléant à l'Ecole de Médecine*[a] at the faculty of Algiers) which will spare me further talkee-talkee.— As soon as Stephann declared that I was rid of my pleurisy, I at once began, as prescribed by him (Stephann), to embrocate with tincture of iodine all the spots on the upper part (left) of my chest and back. Since the time I boarded the ship until TO-DAY I have discontinued these operations which would in any case be 'difficult' for me to carry out in person on my own back, despite Dr Delachaux's advice that I should attempt it with the help of a mirror. *Qui vivra verra.*[b] At all events, I shall speak to Dr Kunemann first. I am anxious to get out and about in the open air as much as I can.

Practically all the Parisian and Italian papers and periodicals are to be found in the reading room of the Monte Carlo Casino; a fair selection of German papers, very few English. I read in the *Petit Marseillais* of today's date about *'l'assassinat de lord Cavendish et de M. Burke'.*[312] The public here, e. g. my table-d'hôte companions in the Hôtel de Russie, is, by contrast, more interested in what goes on in the Casino's *salles de jeu (tables de roulette et de trente-et-quarante).*[c] I was particularly amused by a son of Albion, sulky, ill-tempered and bewildered, AND WHY? Because he had lost a certain number of yellow boys, whereas he had been absolutely intent on 'copping' the same. He couldn't understand that not even British boorishness is able 'TO BULLY' fortune.

These lines must be my last since letters from here have first to be sent to the post office in Monaco by messenger.

Kindest regards to all.

Your
Moor

First published abridged in *Der Briefwechsel zwischen F. Engels und K. Marx*, Bd. 4, Stuttgart, 1913 and in full in *MEGA*, Abt. III, Bd. 4, Berlin, 1931

Printed according to the original

---

[a] Assistant lecturer at the School of Medicine - [b] Here: We shall see. - [c] gaming rooms (roulette and trente-et-quarante tables)

143

MARX TO JENNY LONGUET [72]

IN ARGENTEUIL

Monte Carlo, 8 May 1882
Hôtel de Russie, Monte Carlo

Dear Jennychen,

The said *Monte Carlo*, whence I send you these lines, is one of the 3 places (adjoining one another) whose trinity constitutes the state of 'Monaco' (i. e. Monaco, Condamine and Monte Carlo). A really beautiful situation. Climate preferable to that of Nice or even Menton.

I need hardly say that with comical consistency I imported into the region *the first 2 rainy days* (since January); it would seem that they were only awaiting my arrival from Algiers for this to happen. Apart from that I struck magnificent weather.

As you will have learnt from my last letter,[a] I am quit of my pleurisy; the bronchial catarrh can only clear up very gradually. Moreover the atmosphere will soon be warm and dry *everywhere* (which, however, raises fears of a water shortage); the intensity of the sun's action will be all the greater for its being strewn with large spots. So everywhere there will soon be the kind of weather I need.

As I am not sure how long I shall be staying here, I should like you to let me know at once from Paris *where* I can find you; it would be best if you *telegraphed* me here, for a telegram will give me sufficient information in 3 or 4 words.

Lots of kisses for the children.

Your
OLD Moor

First published, in Russian, in the magazine *Nachalo*, No. 5, St Petersburg, 1899

Printed according to the original

---

[a] See this volume, p. 250.

144

ENGELS TO EDUARD BERNSTEIN [113]

IN ZURICH

London, 10 May [313] 1882

Dear Mr Bernstein,

My afternoon having already been broken into, I shall employ it in writing to you. As regards the Virgin Mary-Isis, that was a point upon which I could not enlarge, if only for reasons of space. [314] Like all hagiolatry, the Marian cult belongs to a much later period than the one I am considering (a time when it was clerical policy to produce in the persons of the saints a new version of the polytheistic peasantry's numerous tutelary gods), and finally it would be necessary to provide historical *proof* of the derivation, which would demand specialised study. The same applies to the gloria and moonlight. In the imperial days of Rome, by the way, the cult of Isis was part of the state religion.

Bimetallism. [3] The main thing — particularly after many of the 'leaders' have been so frightfully cock-a-hoop about our party's superiority over the bourgeois in matters of economics, a superiority of which those gentlemen are totally innocent — the main thing is that we should beware of inviting censure in this field as is unblushingly done by the said gentlemen the moment they think it will serve to flatter a particular kind of worker, win an electoral victory or gain some other advantage. Thus, because silver is mined in Saxony, they think it in order to dabble in the bimetallist nonsense. So to catch a few more votes, our party is to go and make an immortal ass of itself in the very sphere which is *supposed* to be its forte!

But that's our literary gents all over! Just like the bourgeois literati, they think themselves entitled to the privilege of learning nothing and laying down the law about everything. They have, for our benefit, concocted a hotch-potch of literature which, for ignorance of economics, new-fangled utopianism and arrogance, has yet to find an equal, and Bismarck did us a tremendous favour by banning it.

When we speak of bimetallism today, it is not so much bimetallism generally as the specific case of bimetallism in which the ratio of gold to silver is, say, $15^1/_2 : 1$. A distinction must therefore be drawn here.

Bimetallism is becoming daily more impracticable in that the ratio

of the value of silver to that of gold which, at one time, was at least
fairly constant and changed only gradually, is now subject to daily
and violent fluctuations, the initial tendency being for the value of silver to fall as a result of the colossal increase in production, especially
in North America. The exhaustion of gold is an invention of the silver
barons. But whatever the cause of the change in value, it remains
a fact and that is what concerns us first of all. Silver is becoming daily
less capable of serving as a measure of value, whereas gold is not.
The ratio of the value of the two is now about $17^1/_2:1$. But the silver people want to reimpose upon the world the old ratio of $15^1/_2:1$,
and that is just as impossible as maintaining the price of mechanically
produced yarn and cloth everywhere and for all time at that of man-
ually produced yarn and cloth. The die does not determine the value
of the coin, it is merely a guarantee, for the recipient, of weight and
standard and can never confer on $15^1/_2$ lbs of silver the value of $17^1/_2$.
All this is dealt with so lucidly and exhaustively in *Capital*, chapter
on money (Chap. III, pp. 72-120) [315] that there's nothing more to
add. For material relating to more recent fluctuations, cf. Soetbeer:
Edelmetall — Produktion und Werthverhältnis etc. (Gotha, Perthes, 1879).
Soetbeer is the leading authority in this sphere, and the father of
German currency reform — even before 1840 he was advocating
a 'mark' equivalent to $^1/_3$ taler.
Hence, if silver is minted at $15^1/_2$ lbs = 1 lb. gold, it flows back into
the state treasuries, everyone wants to be rid of it. That's what the
United States discovered in the case of its silver dollar minted to the
old standard and worth only 90 c., as did Bismarck when he tried forcibly to put back into circulation the silver talers that had been withdrawn and replaced by gold.
Mr Dechend, the chairman of the Bank, imagines that bimetallism
will enable him to pay off Germany's external debts in bad silver instead of gold at full value, and thus avoid any kind of gold crisis,
something that would certainly be most convenient for the Reichsbank if only it were feasible. But all that is forthcoming is the proof
provided by Mr Dechend himself, that he is totally unfitted to preside
over a bank and would be more at home at a school desk than a
board-room table.
Your Prussian Junker, too, would certainly be happy if the mortgages he contracted in silver at $15^1/_2:1$ could be repaid or serviced in
silver at $17^1/_2:1$. And since this would necessarily occur inside the
country, it would be perfectly feasible for debtors to rook their credi-

tors by this means — provided only the aristocracy could find people to lend them silver at $17^1/_2 : 1$ in order that they might make repayments at $15^1/_2 : 1$. For their own means certainly do not permit them to make repayments. But they would, of course, be compelled to accept their silver at $15^1/_2$ and thus, so far as they were concerned, everything would remain as before.

As regards the German production of silver, its extraction from *German* ore dwindles yearly in importance as compared with (Rhenish) extraction from *South American* ore. Total production in Germany in 1876 amounted to about 280,000 lbs, of which 58,000 were from South American ore; since that time this figure has risen considerably.

That the debasing of silver to the status of a fractional currency must depress the value of silver still further is obvious; the use of silver for purposes other than money is minimal, nor is it likely to show a rapid increase because demonetisation throws more silver on to the market.

It is inconceivable that England should ever introduce bimetallism. No country that is on the gold standard could re-introduce bimetallism *now* and on a permanent basis. In any case, *universal* bimetallism does not admit of general application; if all men were to agree today that silver was once more to be worth $15^1/_2 : 1$, they could not alter the fact that it is worth only $17^1/_2 : 1$, and there's absolutely nothing to be done about it. One might just as well decide that twice two equals five.

During our early days of exile Bamberger did us many a good turn; he was a decent and obliging man, secretary to Karl of Brunswick. We subsequently lost sight of him.[316]

Kindest regards,

Yours,

F. E.

First published, in Russian, in *Marx-Engels Archives*, Book I, Moscow, 1924

Printed according to the original

Published in English in full for the first time

145

ENGELS TO AUGUST BEBEL

IN LEIPZIG

London, 16 May 1882

Dear Bebel,

I have been long meaning to write to you. Particularly since I don't know whether Marx has answered your last letter.[317] He several times promised me that he would, but you know how it is when one is ill. So today I have at last got round to it.

Marx first went to the Isle of Wight,[234] but the weather there was cold and wet. Then to Algiers via Paris. Caught cold again during the journey, encountering more wet, chilly weather in Algiers, later succeeded by rapid variations in temperature. Once again his cold assumed the form of pleurisy, less severe than his first attack here, but long drawn-out. Now he is thoroughly recovered and, since it has at last got really hot in Africa, has fled to Monte Carlo, the gaming establishment of the Prince of Monaco.[a] As soon as the summer has really begun, he will leave and join Madame Longuet and her children on the Normandy coast; is unlikely to be back before the beginning of July. All he has got to do now is shake off once and for all his obstinate cough, and in this he will probably succeed. He had his photograph taken in Algiers and is looking quite his old self again.

It is a great misfortune that you, of all people, should have suffered defeat in elections which otherwise went off so splendidly.[222] Your presence was doubly necessary in view of the many new, and in some cases unreliable, elements that have got in. Indeed it would seem that, at the start, a number of not very edifying blunders were perpetrated. Now things seem to be going rather better. I was therefore doubly delighted (and Marx no less so) by the courageous attitude of the *Sozialdemokrat*, which did not hesitate to come out unequivocally against the whining and pusillanimity of Breuel & Co., even when deputies such as Blos and Geiser came out in favour of it.[318] We, too, were appealed to, and Viereck wrote me a very pathetic letter about the paper whereat I informed him of my view in altogether amiable if no uncertain terms[284] and, since that time, have heard nothing more

---

[a] Charles III

of him. Hepner, too, has passed this way, 'sick at heart and poor of purse'[a] and terribly sorry for himself; he had written a very indifferent little pamphlet [262] from which I could see how greatly he had deteriorated morally. The chief plaint in both cases was that the *Sozialdemokrat* failed to take account of the laws presently in force in Germany, the contents of the paper being such that its distributors were had up by the German courts for *lèse majesté*, high treason, etc. Yet it is perfectly evident from the paper itself and the reports of the proceedings against our people that, whatever the circumstances, and no matter how the paper was written, those swine on the bench would find some pretext for committing them. To write a paper in such a way as to afford no handle to the said judges is an art that has yet to be discovered. And, what is more, these gentlemen forget that an organ as weak-kneed as they desire would drive our people pretty well *en masse* into Most's camp. However, I shall none the less advise Bernstein,[b] to whom we have otherwise lent our moral support whenever possible, to modulate the tone of moral indignation a bit by the use of irony and derision, for such a tone, if it is not to become boring, has to be so stepped up as ultimately to become ridiculous.

Singer came to see me the day before yesterday and from him I learned that the forwarding address is still all right, something I was not quite sure about since we haven't used it for so long. He has another drawback. He belongs to those who regard the nationalisation of anything as a semi-, or at all events pre-, socialist measure and are therefore secret devotees of protective tariffs, tobacco monopoly, nationalised railways, etc. These prevarications are the legacy of the unduly one-sided fight against Manchesterism [176] and, because they facilitate debate in a middle-class and 'eddicated' environment, enjoy a considerable following particularly among those bourgeois and academic elements who have come over to us. You in Berlin, he tells me, recently debated the point, he being luckily outvoted. We cannot, for the sake of such minor considerations, afford to discredit ourselves either politically or economically. I tried to make him see that in our view 1. protective tariffs are quite the wrong thing for Germany (not, however, for America), because our industry has expanded and become a viable exporter under free trade, but for it to be a viable exporter, competition from foreign semi-manufactures on the home market is absolutely essential; that the iron industry, which produces

---

[a] A paraphrase from Goethe's 'Der Schatzgräber'. - [b] See this volume, pp. 288-89.

4 times more than is required by the home market, uses the protective tariff only against the *home market* while selling *abroad*, as the facts go to show, at give-away prices; 2. that the tobacco monopoly is nationalisation on so minute a scale that it can't even do duty for an example in the debate nor, for that matter, do I give a damn whether or not Bismarck puts it into effect since either way it must eventually redound to our benefit; 3. that the nationalisation of railways is of benefit only to the shareholders who sell their shares above value, but of no benefit at all to us because we should be able to deal as summarily with one or two big companies as with the state, once we had the latter; that the joint-stock companies have already provided proof of the extent to which the bourgeois as such is redundant, in as much as the management is wholly in the hands of salaried officials, nor would nationalisation provide any further argument. However, he had got the thing too firmly fixed in his mind and agreed with me only to the extent of admitting that, from a political viewpoint, your dismissive attitude was the only correct one.

Time for the post. Kindest regards to yourself and Liebknecht.

Your
F. E.

First published, in Russian, in *Marx-Engels Archives*, Vol. I (VI), Moscow, 1932

Printed according to the original

Published in English for the first time

146

MARX TO ENGELS [72]

IN LONDON

Monte Carlo (Monaco), 20 May 1882
Hôtel de Russie

PRIVATELY

DEAR FRED,

It would be pointless to impart all this to the children, since it would alarm them unnecessarily. But I must tell SOMEBODY AT LEAST about what I have just gone through.

In my last letter (I don't know exactly whether I wrote to you direct, or to Tussy or to Laura), I said I would let you have further details after my encounter with Dr Kunemann.[a] This took place on 8th May; he is an Alsatian, a scientifically (medically) educated man; e. g. he told me about Dr Koch on the bacillus before I got your letter [284]; has a large practice; 52-54 years old at the very least, since he was a student at Strasbourg university in 1848; politically, he has found the paper *Le Temps* to be the organ that corresponds most closely to his temperament; science, he said, had convinced him that progress could only be 'slow'; no revolutionary upheaval — for otherwise, progress would, in consequence, be forced to 'double back' almost as far as it had come (as in the Echternach procession,[319] *p. e.*[b]); first prerequisite, education of the masses and 'non-masses', etc. IN ONE WORD, POLITICALLY, A REPUBLICAN PHILISTINE; I mention this merely to show why I didn't go into such matters with him aside from discussing the 'Machiavellian' politics of Charles III, absolute tyrant of Monaco. He regards me as an 1848 man and, apart from that date, I vouchsafed no further particulars as to the rest of my PUBLIC ACTIVITY. Now to the matter in hand. Originally he concluded from my *visiting card*, which has Dr on it and which I had had conveyed to him through his maid, that I was a Dr of Med., his view being further confirmed by *Dr Stephann's card* which I handed to him, ditto those of *my new medical acquaintance*[c] from Interlaken, and of Dr Donkin, whom I mentioned as the friend of my friend Prof. Ray Lankester, since he wished to know who had treated me in London, etc. Then I gave him Stephann's *consultation écrite*[d] to read.

Well, since he regarded me as a medical colleague, EITHER THEORETICALLY OR PRACTICALLY, he freely spoke his mind after having ausculated and percussed me. And to my horror, the *pleurisy had returned*, even if not in so severe a form, *being confined to one spot on the left of my back*; bronchitis, on the other hand, pretty well — *chronic*! He thought that 1 or 2 *vésicatoires*[e] might put paid to the thing (*pleurésie*); during *9 May (Mardi)*[f] first *vésicatoire*, on *13 May (Samedi)*[g] only my 2nd visit to Kunemann, second *vésicatoire* prescribed; could not be applied until 16 May (*Mardi*) after my skin had dried up; I visited him on *19 May* (Friday); ausculation and percussion; found an improvement, the

---

[a] See this volume, p. 254. - [b] *par exemple*, for example - [c] Delachaux - [d] written diagnosis - [e] vesicatories - [f] Tuesday - [g] Saturday

épanchement^a in particular being reduced to almost nothing; he suggested (these doctors are always afraid that their patient will grow restive, the whole of this week having been *plus ou moins*^b ruined and tormented) that to continue with *vésicatoires* was no longer essential; I need do no more than embrocate with TINCTURE OF iodine (prescribed by Stephann for bronchial trouble), this time the upper *as well as the lower* places on my left side, chest and back. I thereupon declared that, if the *épanchement* had not altogether disappeared, I would, on the contrary, prefer another *vésicatoire* (on 23 May, *Mardi*); I had, I said, been told by Dr Stephann that in cases of pleurisy tincture of iodine was an ineffectual, uncertain antidote which only served to prolong the trouble. My plumping for the heroic remedy was obviously far more agreeable to Dr Kunemann himself; I now hope that, on 26 or 27 May, he will [tell] me this 2nd *rechute*^c is the FINAL one (*pro nunc*^d).

Indeed, as regards [myself], 'fate' would seem on this occasion to have displayed an alarming consistency — almost, one might say, as in Dr Müllner's tragedies.[320] Why does Dr Kunemann declare my bronchial condition (and I already knew I would be told as much) to be thus 'chronic'? Because the weather throughout the Riviera has been so exceptionally bad, has taken such an abnormal turn; but he suggested that this might be normal to the extent that *from January to the beginning of May*, there had been too little rain — virtually none; the weather had been too warm and fine and a reaction to it must have set in. I explained this to him more simply by pointing out that all this must be blamed on my arrival from Algiers; I had brought rain with me to Marseilles on the 4th May and, with some reluctance, the weather in the place of my present abode had — *mutatis mutandis*^e — assumed the character of the 'bad weather' I had recently gone through in Algeria. Much patience is demanded, especially on the part of the recipients of my letters. Such repetitiveness is altogether too boring. A pointless, arid, not to say expensive, existence!

Tomorrow I shall write to Tussy,^f since her unanswered letter dates back furthest. Today it's awkward for me since the new skin formed after the *vésicatoire* still tends, when I stoop, to rub painfully against my coat or shirt. *Notabene*: What I write and tell the children

---

^a effusion - ^b more or less - ^c relapse - ^d for the time being - ^e allowing for different circumstances - ^f See next letter.

is the truth, but *not the whole truth.* What's the point of alarming them?

Your

Moor

Dr Kunemann's error about my being a '*medical*' *colleague* was cleared up when, at the end of my first visit, he refused payment; was all the more honeyed when I informed him that, as a *layman*, I should have to 'shell out'.

First published in *Der Briefwechsel zwischen F. Engels und K. Marx*, Bd. 4, Stuttgart, 1913

Printed according to the original

147

MARX TO ELEANOR MARX

IN LONDON

[Postcard]

Monte Carlo (Monaco), 21 May 1882
Hôtel de Russie

Dearest Child,

Your being my oldest creditor, I had in fact intended writing today (Sunday) a long letter, but *l'homme propose, mais le thermomètre dispose. Il y a aujourd'hui un jour parfaitement beau, mais* exceptionnel: *donc je veux l'exploiter en air libre, au lieu 'd'écrire', et de ne pas écrire le soir. C'est convenu avec mes conseillers de santé.*[a]

Before leaving *ami*[b] Fermé, I told him: On landing at the Southern coast of France, the weather at once will come out a turn-coat. And indeed — so 'fatal' a man I pride myself upon this my quality — the prophecy has been partially fulfilled. From the *beginning of January* the Riviera enjoyed a summer weather never so brilliant, some grumblers

---

[a] man proposes but the thermometer disposes. Today is a wonderfully fine day, but it's *exceptional.* Accordingly I intend to take advantage of it in the open air instead of 'writing', and to desist from writing in the evening. That has been agreed with my medical advisers. - [b] friend

only complaining of an absolute lack of rain almost. The moment I arrived on the 4th May at Marseille, there set in rain, lasting sometimes a whole, more generally a half day, and mostly during the nights; a general lowering of temperature; then and there cold winds; altogether changeable, variable weather; atmosphere, even if not often, too saturated with aqueous vapours. With all that, here *a relatively good warm weather*, only not so dry and more constant than I want just now for my lungs. But nowhere in Italy or elsewhere you will find it a better one now: Cannes, Monte Carlo and Mentone are the three most healthsome places, of the most *equable* and *on an average*—warmer temperature than Nizza, Rome and Naples.

Yours,
Old Nick

[On the side reserved for the address]

Miss Marx
41 Maitland Park Road
Maitland *Park*
London (N. W.) (*Angleterre*)

First published, in Russian, in the magazine *Voinstvuyushchiy materialist*, Book IV, Moscow, 1925

Reproduced from the original

Published in English for the first time

148

MARX TO JENNY LONGUET

IN ARGENTEUIL

[Postcard]

Monte Carlo, 26 May 1882
Hôtel de Russie

Dearest Child,

I am always happy to receive a letter from you, though regretting that your Old Nick steals some time of your night's rest.

My health is improving with the weather; possibly I shall perhaps at the beginning of June go to Cannes, and remain there for a week or so. Everything depends of medical advice, and the character of the summer opening in June.

[As to] Lafargue's (I mean the *man's of Cuba*) paper ª has committed great blunders, mostly from ignorance, and the childish aspiration 'to go as far as possible'.

As to the *Bataille*, I have seen till now not anything brilliant. In fact I do know it only to No. 4; but I will have always the time to see that!

My heart is with you and the children; I yearn for them. However, I shall, after a series of most disagreeable 'medical' experiments, precipitate nothing. With all that, I hope to be soon with them.

Your
Old Nick

[On the side reserved for the address]

Madame Charles Longuet
11, Boulevard Thiers, Argenteuil
près Paris

First published, in Russian, in the magazine *Nachalo*, No. 5, St Petersburg, 1899

Reproduced from the original

Published in English for the first time

149

MARX TO ELEANOR MARX [72]

IN LONDON

Monte Carlo, 28 May 1882
Hôtel de Russie

Dear Tussychen,

There was nothing from Bebel either in Engels' letter [321] or your letter which I got yesterday evening. It must have remained in London by mistake. AT ALL EVENTS, I WASH MY HANDS OF IT.

ª *L'Égalité*

Today 24 degrees in the shade, and summer temperatures have generally prevailed here ever since the date of my last postcard to you[a] (although the sky isn't as completely cloudless as the *cognoscenti* of this place demand). In such circumstances, my lengthy report has come to nothing for all my 'good intentions'; not that anything of much value is lost thereby.

As regards the sea-crossing from Algiers, nothing need be said save that it was made in unfavourable weather conditions; during the night of 4 to 5 May, in particular, there was a violent storm that turned my cabin (which, for good measure, I had to share with a philistine businessman from Lyons) into a veritable wind tunnel. It was cold and pouring with rain when we arrived off Marseilles in the early morning (5 May). The STEAMER didn't actually go right in, so the passengers and baggage had to be taken off by boat and, for their further delectation, spend several hours in a cold, draughty *douane-purgatorio*[b] until the time came for them to depart for Nice. Those chilling 'moments' *détraquaient plus ou moins de nouveau ma machine*[c] and, in Monte Carlo, once more precipitated me *entre les mains d'un Esculape*[d]; for I have no need of such when it's merely a question of treating the 'bronchial trouble' since all I have to do is follow Dr Stephann's instructions. In a few days' time (next Tuesday, 30 May, perhaps) I expect to be given a clean bill of health by Dr Kunemann. So whatever happens I shan't be leaving this den of thieves before the beginning of June. Whether I stay on or not is for Dr Kunemann to decide. The sensitivity of people suffering from disorders of the respiratory organs (who by the same token are also more liable to a relapse) is greater in what is normally a favourable climate. In the North, for instance, a sudden draught would not instantly evoke the spectre of pleurisy, bronchitis and the like, whereas in Algiers your French philistine must always [be] on his guard against them. A Madame Fleury, here in the Hôtel de Russie, was sent to Cannes from Paris because of her bronchitis. She recovered completely during March and April, enjoyed climbing the hills, etc. By way of an after-cure and distraction, she then left Cannes for Monte Carlo, a quite short 2-hour journey during which she caught cold while in Antibes station—and is now in worse case than previously in Paris. One hears of visitors to this place who haven't

---

[a] See this volume, pp. 264-65. - [b] customs purgatory - [c] again more or less threw my machine out of gear - [d] into the hands of an Aesculapius

come simply to gamble and enjoy themselves, and of whom 9 out of every 10 undoubtedly fall victim to '*rechutes*'.[a]

Goethe, when he applauds a man for 'sloughing' his old snake's skin,[b] does not in all likelihood see the sloughing of artificially produced '*fausses peaux*'[c] as part of the rejuvenation process.

Another time, when it isn't as 'sweltering' as it is today, I must really tell you something about this Principality of Gerolstein (not even Offenbach's music is wanting, or Mademoiselle Schneider,[322] or, indeed, the spruce and dapper *carabiniers*[d] — not 100 all told). Nature here magnificent and art has actually improved on it, — I refer to the gardens, conjured out of the barren rock, which cover the steep incline from top to bottom, often going right down to the exquisitely blue sea, like the terraces of the hanging gardens of Babylon. But the economic basis of Monaco-Gerolstein is the casino; if it were to close tomorrow it would be all up with Monaco-Gerolstein — the whole of it. I dislike visiting the gaming room; it reminds me that at the *table d'hôte*,[e] in the cafés, etc., almost the only topic that is talked or whispered about is the *tables de roulette et de trente et quarante*.[f] Every now and again something is won, as for instance 100 frs by a young Russian lady (wife of a Russian diplomat-cum-agent) (she is one of the guests at the Hôtel de Russie) who, in return, loses 6,000 frs, while someone else can't keep enough for the journey home; others gamble away the whole of large family fortunes; very few take away a share of the plunder — few of the gamblers, I mean, and those that do are almost without exception rich. There can be no question of intelligence or calculation here; no one can count with any probability on being favoured by 'chance' unless he can venture a considerable sum. But I can understand the attraction it holds out, particularly for *le beau sexe*[g]; *les mondaines*[h] not less than the *demi-mondaines*, SCHOOL-GIRLS and bourgeoises alike ALL PUSH ON, a fact to which this place can supply eye-witnesses and to spare. Apart from Monaco-Gerolstein, which would founder along with the casino, I don't believe that Nice — the rendez-vous in the winter months of the quality and of fortune-hunters alike — could continue to subsist as a fashionable centre without the casino at Monte Carlo. And withal, how childish is the casino by comparison with the Bourse!

---

[a] relapses - [b] From Goethe's *Zahme Xenien*, V. - [c] artificial skins - [d] carabineers - [e] Here: in the hotel dining-room. - [f] roulette and trente-et-quarante tables - [g] the fair sex - [h] society women

(This pen and this ink need replacing; they elicit from me the outburst that it requires real artistry to write with them!)

To the right of the casino (where the gambling goes on), almost cheek by jowl with it, is the Café de Paris and next to that a kiosk. This is daily adorned with a placard, not printed, but handwritten and signed with the initials of the quill-pusher; for 600 frs he will provide, in black and white, the secret of the science of winning a million francs with a 1,000 at the *tables de roulette et de trente-et-quarante.* Nor, or so it is said, is it by any means rare for people to fall victim to this confidence trick. Indeed, most of the gamblers, both male and female, believe there is a science in what are pure games of chance; the ladies and gentlemen sit outside the said Café de Paris, IN FRONT of, or on the seats in, the wonderful garden that belongs to the casino, heads bent over little (printed) tables, scribbling and doing sums, while one of them may earnestly expound to another 'what system' he prefers, whether one should play in 'series', etc., etc. It's like watching a bunch of lunatics. However, Grimaldi of Monaco[a] and his Principality of Gerolstein and the lessees of his casino are thriving and are, AFTER ALL, more 'interesting' in the Offenbachian sense than those whom they fleece.

Should I change my address, *I shall send it to you by telegraph.* At all events the return journey, initially to Paris, will be made in stages and 'with caution'.

Love to all,

OLD NICK

First published, in the language of the original (German), in *Annali*, an. I, Milano, 1958

Printed according to the original

---

[a] Charles III

270   150. Marx to Engels. 30 May 1882

150

MARX TO ENGELS [72]

IN LONDON

[Monte Carlo,] 30 May 1882

DEAR FRED,

After the application (the 3rd in Monte Carlo) of a *vésicatoire* [a] on 23 May I did in fact have another appointment with Dr Kunemann before today, but only in connection with my 'bronchial trouble'. *Quo-ad* [b] my *pleurésie*, however, he found today, after a lengthy final examination, that the *épanchement* [c] was '*gone*'; what remains is so-called *dry pleurésie*; there is no longer any moisture to retard matters; however the sound of one membrane rubbing against the other, to put it in popular if incorrect terms, still remains. He thought it would be beneficial to finish up with one more *vésicatoire* today and then move on to Cannes for *a day or two*, after which I would be able to take myself off to Paris.

He thought I had contracted pleurisy quite accidentally; considering my normal, robust physique I might just as well never have got it, or, by the same token, have done so — accidentally! — as much as 40 years ago. Getting rid of it is harder because of the danger of a relapse.

As I was made to parade my naked charms, front and back, he drew my attention to the fact that, previously, as a result of pleurisy, my left side had swollen by comparison with the right; now it was the other way round, for my left side (I refer to the affected spot) had contracted by contrast with the right, this being the result of my *traitement*. [d] So as to rid myself completely of the last mementoes, as it were, of pleurisy, I am to spend some time *later on* in the mountains where the air is more rarified. My lungs must be 'set to rights' again by gymnastics of this kind, gymnastics imposed upon them by the locality. It was all the more difficult for me to follow the details in that he sought to bring them (the details) home to me in French frequently interspersed with Alsatian German, but also with some

---

[a] vesicatory - [b] As to - [c] discharge - [d] treatment

YANKEE-English. However one thing was clear, and that was what Dr Stephann had told me on the first day: Your thorax is what it is, so if spurious tissue takes up some of the space that one lung should occupy, that lung must make do with less space. The said tissue disappears in proportion as the lung re-expands. I have only just left Dr Kunemann, i. e. it's now nearly 6 o'clock in the evening which (6 o'clock) is the latest posting time FOR TO-DAY. *Tomorrow* — because of the final *vésicatoire* to be applied tonight — writing will be OUT OF THE QUESTION; day after tomorrow I shall have to recuperate and so it's 'unlikely' that you'll get any further news before the 2nd or 3rd of June (as I shall also have to pack).

With best wishes.

OLD Moor

First published in *Der Briefwechsel zwischen F. Engels und K. Marx*, Bd. 4, Stuttgart, 1913

Printed according to the original

151

MARX TO JENNY LONGUET [72]

IN ARGENTEUIL

[Postcard]

Cannes, 4 *Juin*[a] 1882

Dearest Child,

I'll come at *some of the first days of the week beginning on the 6th June.* I cannot specify; it will depend on circumstance not to be exactly foreseen. Hence *you oblige me* greatly by not bothering about the exact day or hour of arrival. Till now, I have always found that *nothing has done me more harm than people, at the station, waiting for me.* Do not tell anybody else (*ci-inclus le Gascon, le Russe et le* Hirsch)[b] that I am expected that week. I'll want some absolute quietness *alone with your family, No. 11, Boulevard Thiers.*

Yours,

Old Nick

---

[a] June - [b] (this includes the *Gascon* [Lafargue], the Russian [Lavrov] and Hirsch)

By 'quietness' I mean the 'family life', 'the children's noise', that 'microscopic world' more interesting than the 'macroscopic'.

[On the side reserved for the address]
Madame Charles Longuet
11, Boulevard Thiers, Argenteuil
près Paris

First published, in Russian, in the magazine *Nachalo*, No. 5, St Petersburg, 1899

Reproduced from the original

152

MARX TO ENGELS [72]

IN LONDON

Cannes, 5 *Juin*[a] 1882

DEAR FRED,

ON 30TH MAY (*pro* Monte Carlo) my back last branded; on 31ST MAY post-operative treatment confined me to the house; on 3rd June I was set free by Kunemann and left the same day. He advised me to stay in Cannes for a couple of days, whatever the circumstances,[323] this being essential if only to allow the wounds inflicted on me to 'dry out'.

Thus I have spent an entire month vegetating in this *repaire*[b] of aristocratic idlers or ADVENTURERS. Nature superb, in other respects a dreary hole; it is 'monumental' because consisting solely of hotels; no plebeian 'masses' here, apart from the *garçons d'hotels, de café*, etc., and *domestiques*,[c] who belong to the *Lumpenproletariat*. The old robber's lair on its rocky promontory surrounded on 3 sides by the bay, i. e. *Monaco*, was at least an ancient, crumbling, medieval sort of Italian townlet; on the other hand, *Condamine*, built for the most part low down by the sea, between the 'town' of Monaco and the *maison de jeu*[d] (i. e. Monte Carlo), and growing fast. *Monaco* is, IN THE STRICT SENSE,

---

[a] June - [b] haunt - [c] waiters in hotels and cafés etc., and servants - [d] gaming establishment

the 'polity', the 'state', the 'government'; *Condamine* is common-or-garden 'petty-bourgeois' society; but Monte Carlo is 'THE PLEASURE', AND, THANKS TO THE *banque de jeu*,[a] THE FINANCIAL BASIS OF THE WHOLE TRINITY. Odd that these Grimaldis should have turned out to be what they have always been; formerly, they lived off piracy and one of them,[b] F. I.,[c] wrote to Lorenzo dei Medici saying their territory was very restricted and, moreover, barren; hence Nature had pointed the way to buccaneering; it would therefore be magnanimous on Lorenzo's part, since they did not 'venture' to hunt down Florentine vessels, if he were to guarantee them an annual 'gratuity'. CONSEQUENTLY Lorenzo paid them a small annual fee.— After the HOLY ALLIANCE'S [266] victory over Napoleon, Talleyrand, who, for his own diversion, had selected from amongst the émigrés that arch-blackguard, the ex-tyrant of Monaco,[d] to be one of the companions — Talleyrand, then, thought it amusing to 'restore' him, the father of 'Florestan',[e] '*au nom du principe de le légitimité*'.[f] The restoration of these 2 men, this COUPLE — him of Hesse-Cassel[g] and him of Monaco — is worthy of a place in a new edition of Plutarch[h]; at the same time, what a contrast between the German 'patriarch' and the Genoese (his main preoccupation, financial loot)!

A grievance nursed in private by our Dr Kunemann is that, when already functioning as physician in ordinary to His Most Serene Highness, the present Charles III (blind as a bat), he (Kunemann) became unacceptable as a result of his liberal principles and had to make way for an Englishman (Dr Pickering). THE SURVIVAL OF THE BEST — i. e. as a little duodecimo tyrant's physician in ordinary — *to a Britisher, of course, warranted by the nature of the beast! And that is the worst; this same Dr Pickering, before being called by natural selection, he had dangerously fallen ill at Monaco, was treated and cured by* Dr Kunemann. There are many such piteous dramas of destiny in this world of ours!

Oddly enough, this hot weather has made my bronchial cough worse rather than better. All the greater 'pretext', of course, for catching cold! Kunemann, by the by, (and the fellow's a first-rate doctor, familiar with English, German and French medical literature, a specialist in diseases of the chest and lungs) is not of your

---

[a] casino -[b] Lamberto Grimaldi -[c] for instance -[d] Honoré IV Grimaldi -[e] Florestan I -[f] in the name of the principle of legitimacy -[g] Elector William I -[h] Plutarch, *Vitae parallelae.*

opinion regarding my journey back to Paris. I ought not, he says, to make it by easy stages; the weather is now hot and not only during the day, the nights, too, being warm. The most likely place to catch cold now, he avers, is at railway stations and the more often I break the journey, the greater the probability of *rechutes*[a]; rather, I ought, while in Cannes, to equip myself for the journey with 2 bottles of good old claret. Like Dr Stephann, he bases his view on the grounds that, in the treatment of pleurisy like that of bronchitis, etc., the stomach should be treated as the *basis*; eat well and amply even if it goes against the grain, and 'accustom' oneself to so doing; 'drink' 'decent stuff' and go for drives, etc., to distract oneself, if not allowed to walk, climb, etc., much; think as little as possible, etc.

So, having followed these 'directions', I am well on the way to 'idiocy', and for all that have not rid myself of the bronchial catarrh.

A consoling thought for me is that it was bronchitis that sent old Garibaldi to his 'eternal rest'.[324] Of course, AT A CERTAIN AGE it becomes completely INDIFFERENT how one may be 'LAUNCHED INTO ETERNITY'.

I have been here since 3 June,[b] and shall be leaving this evening. In Nice and, on this occasion likewise in *Cannes*, where it is exceptional, a *strong (if warm) wind and eddies of dust*. Nature, too, can evince a certain philistine humour (after the manner, already humorously anticipated in the Old Testament, of the serpent feeding on dust, cf. the dusty diet of Darwin's worms [325]). Similarly, there is a vein of natural wit that runs all through the Riviera's local press. On 24 May, for instance, there was a terrible *orage*,[c] notably at *Menton*; lightning struck close *auprès de la gare*[d] (of Menton) and tore the sole off a passing philistine's shoe while leaving the rest of the philistine intact.

With love to all.

OLD MOOR

I shall not [let] friends know about my presence in Paris until I've been there a few days. It is still necessary for me to have as little 'intercourse with people' [326] as possible. I shall have a good doctor to consult in the person of Dr Dourlen.

First published in: Marx and Engels, *Works*, Second Russian Edition, Vol. 35, Moscow, 1964

Printed according to the original

---

[a] relapses - [b] May in the ms. - [c] storm - [d] beside the station

153

MARX TO ENGELS

IN LONDON

[Postcard]

Argenteuil, 9 June 1882
11 Boulevard Thiers

DEAR FRED,

As you know, everywhere I go I must, like TICKETS OF LEAVE, report to the doctor nearest to the place where I first take up my abode.[327] Yesterday, therefore, EXAMINATION by Dr Dourlen. *State of health exactly *the same* I left in which it was at Monte Carlo. As to the *bronchite*, I shall for a few weeks try the sulphurous waters of Enghien, about 15 minutes distance from Argenteuil; if this will not work, he wants to send me to the Pyrenées (Cauterets). (The same things had me already told by Dr Kunemann, who, in the last time, commenced to feed me with *pastilles de sulphure*.[a] A specialist[b] at Enghien is a special friend of Dr Dourlen to whom he will give me a letter. Generally Dr Dourlen found the tone and strength of my body much other than when I left; he was even astonished that I was in so good a condition after two* *rechutes et apres 14 vésicatoires.*[c]
*Compliments to all.

Old* Moor

*Longuet brings me every evening the *Standard*, so useless to him. I have not yet written to the Gascon[d328]; my cough warns me to be careful before seeing friends.*

[On the side reserved for the address]

Frederick Engels, Esq.
122 Regent's Park Road,
London, N. W., *Angleterre*

First published abridged in *Der Briefwechsel zwischen F. Engels und K. Marx*, Bd. 4, Stuttgart, 1913 and in full in *MEGA*, Abt. III, Bd. 4, Berlin, 1931

Printed according to the original

Published in English for the first time

---

[a] sulphur pills - [b] Dr Feugier - [c] relapses and after 14 vesicatories - [d] Paul Lafargue

154

MARX TO ENGELS

IN LONDON

[Postcard]

[Argenteuil,] 15 June 1882

DEAR FRED,

I thought I should be able to report progress over the past week or so. But the *temperature fell* as soon as I arrived, in fact *one day after my arrival*. The weather, therefore, according to what I've been told by Dr Dourlen, as also by his MEDICAL FRIEND[a] in Enghien, won't allow me to begin my sulphur treatment yet. In my former condition, during the happy time when I could smoke, I should have found the weather DELIGHTFUL. True, the sky is overcast more often than not, a bit of rain now and again, gusts of wind, not so much summer as late autumn, but nice weather for all that, if you're in good health!

Yesterday — as a result of a note to St Paul the Gascon[b] — he came to visit me.[328] I WAS GLAD TO SEE HIM. In compliance with my *avis*[c] he will keep silent — *until further orders* — about my presence here.

I go early to bed, get up late, spend a large part of the day with the children and Jennychen and take advantage of every favourable moment to go for a short stroll. All things considered I feel better than AT ANY TIME in Algiers, Monte Carlo or Cannes. It seems likely that the weather too will change for the better here. I shall write you a letter as soon as I've made my first trip to Enghien.

Best wishes to everyone.

Your

Moor

Tussychen has sent Jennychen an interesting eye-witness account of the Hyde Park meeting.[329]

[On the side reserved for the address]

Fr. Engels
122 Regent's Park Road,
London, N. W., *Angleterre*

First published in *Der Briefwechsel zwischen F. Engels und K. Marx*, Bd. 4, Stuttgart, 1913

Printed according to the original

Published in English for the first time

---

[a] Dr Feugier - [b] Paul Lafargue - [c] admonition

155

MARX TO LAURA LAFARGUE [72]

IN LONDON

[Postcard]

Argenteuil, 17 June 1882
11 Boulevard Thiers

PRIVATE AND CONFIDENTIAL

Dearest Child,

I had previously arranged with Engels — as I since explained verbally to Paul[a] — that, as soon as I was able to leave for Switzerland (probably in the latter half of July), *you should accompany me.* In fact I could hardly set forth on this hazardous journey ALONE. So, you see, it's *plus ou moins votre devoir d'accompagner le vieux de la montagne.*[b]

However, as I shall have to stay here for at least another 3 weeks on account of the sulphur treatment at Enghien, I trust that Helen[c] and Tussy will make a SHORT TRIP here during that time. *I have written to Helen and Tussy in that sense.*

Jennychen has invited Lafargue for tomorrow.
Adio.

OLD NICK

[On the side reserved for the address]

Madame Paul Lafargue
37 Tremlett Grove, Junction Road,
London, N., Angleterre

First published, in the language of the   Printed according to the original
original (German), in *Annali*, an. I,
Milano, 1958

---

[a] Lafargue - [b] more or less your duty to accompany the old man of the mountain -
[c] Demuth

156

ENGELS TO FRIEDRICH ADOLPH SORGE[330]

IN HOBOKEN

London, 20 June 1882

Dear Sorge,

I shall attend to your business affairs within the next few days.[331] I am sending the money for the *Égalité* to Lafargue, who is in Paris, and shall extract a receipt from him, however irregular the form it may take. As regards *The Labour Standard* you'll lose nothing if I only arrange for the subscription to run from 1 July; the paper gets more pitiful all the time.

Marx was in Algiers for approx. 2 months where, as I think I told you,[a] he had a relapse of PLEURISY; having been cured of it, he went to Monte Carlo in Monaco and had another but milder one. He left there for Paris approx. 3 weeks ago and is now staying with his daughter, Madame Longuet, in Argenteuil near Paris whence he travels daily to Enghien to avail himself of the local sulphur springs for his chronic bronchial catarrh and cough. His general state of health is very good; as to his further MOVEMENTS, that depends entirely upon the doctors.

The English translation of the *Manifesto* we have been sent is quite unpublishable without total revision. But you will realise that anything of the kind is inconceivable under present circumstances.

I have not seen or heard anything of Leo[b] for months. He's a peculiar cove who must be allowed to go his own way. I have not even got his address. Apropos, for some time I have been receiving communications for Leo from Dr Lilienthal in New York, which I can only deal with via Paris. Who is this Lilienthal?

The Lassalleans' thrustfulness after their arrival in America was inevitable. People who carried the one true gospel in their pack could hardly have behaved with less pretentiousness towards those Americans still languishing in spiritual darkness. Moreover it was for them to find new ground in America to replace that which was being in-

---

[a] See this volume, p. 237. - [b] Lev Hartmann

creasingly cut from under their feet in Germany. By way of return we are happily rid of them in Germany; in America, where everything proceeds ten times as quickly, they'll soon be bested. I trust your eyes will improve through being spared. I too had something of the sort once and know what a vile business it is. In Germany things are going splendidly on the whole. It is true that the literary gentlemen in the party have tried to bring about a change of front, at once reactionary, bourgeois, tame and cultured, but it has proved a resounding failure. The infamies to which socialist workers everywhere have been subjected have everywhere made them much more revolutionary than they were even 3 years ago. You will have seen the details in the *Sozialdemokrat*. Of the leaders, Bebel is the man who behaved best over the affair. Liebknecht shilly-shallied somewhat, for not only did he himself welcome every 'eddicated' semi-social democrat with open arms while failing to run a careful eye over him, but his son-in-law, that obese sluggard Bruno Geiser, is one of the biggest wailers.[332] Because it makes short work of their literary earnings, these people would like to get rid of the Anti-Socialist Law [16] at any cost and to do so ignominiously by means of moderation and meekness, tameness and toadyism. As soon as the law is repealed (not even the bourgeois believe that it will be renewed either by the present or some other eventual Reichstag, since it has proved totally ineffective), the split will probably be brought out into the open, whereupon your Vierecks, Höchbergs, Geisers, Bloses & Co. will form a separate right wing, in which case we shall be able to negotiate with them as occasion arises, until they eventually come to grief for good and all. We said as much[a] immediately after the promulgation of the Anti-Socialist Law when Höchberg and Schramm published in the *Jahrbuch* [333] what was, under the circumstances, a quite infamous assessment of the party's activities up till that date, and demanded that the party conduct itself in a more 'eddicated', decorous and presentable manner.[b]

---

[a] K. Marx and F. Engels, 'Circular Letter to August Bebel, Wilhelm Liebknecht, Wilhelm Bracke and Others'. - [b] [K. Höchberg, E. Bernstein and C. A. Schramm,] 'Rückblicke auf die sozialistische Bewegung in Deutschland. Kritische Aphorismen von*⁎*', *Jahrbuch für Sozialwissenschaft und Sozialpolitik*, 1. Jg., 1. Hälfte, Zurich-Oberstrass, 1879.

My regards to Adolph,[a] have had no sign of life from him.
Kindest regards.

Your
F. Engels

Tell Adolph that Pumps has had a little girl.[b]

First published abridged in *Briefe und
Auszüge aus Briefen von Joh. Phil. Becker,
Jos. Dietzgen, Friedrich Engels, Karl Marx
u. A. an F. A. Sorge und Andere*, Stuttgart,
1906 and in full in: Marx and Engels,
Works, First Russian Edition, Vol. XXVI,
Moscow, 1935

Printed according to the original

Published in English in full for the
first time

157

ENGELS TO AUGUST BEBEL

IN LEIPZIG

London, 21 June 1882

Dear Bebel,

I shall have to answer your letter from memory, having given it
to Tussy for forwarding to Marx[c] since when I have not seen it
again.

For the past 3 weeks or so Marx has been staying with his daughter[d]
at Argenteuil near Paris, is said to be looking very well, brown as a
real 'Moor' (this being his nickname, as you know), and in very good
humour, his only ailment now being a bronchial cough. In order to
get rid of this he has at last had to do Vogt the favour of becoming
a member of the Brimstone gang.[334] For he is undergoing a sulphur
cure at the neighbouring town of Enghien. What further peregrinations he makes is for the doctors to decide.

That there will ultimately be a show-down with the bourgeois-

---

[a] Adolph Sorge - [b] Lilian Rosher - [c] See this volume, p. 266. - [d] Jenny Longuet

minded elements in the party and a parting of the ways between right and left wings is something about which I have long harboured no illusions and, indeed, had already declared desirable in my handwritten commentary^a on the *Jahrbuch* article. That you should have come to take the same view can only be most welcome to us. If I did not expressly mention the point in my last letter,^b it was because I saw no immediate necessity for a split of this kind. Were the gentlemen to decide of their own free will to form a separate right wing, everything would soon be in order. But they are hardly likely to do so; they know they would be an army consisting solely of officers without soldiers, like the 'Robert Blum column' which came over to us in the 1849 campaign and insisted on fighting only 'under the command of that brave man Willich'.[335] Upon our asking how many effectives went to make up this heroic column, we were told — and you can imagine our mirth — one colonel, eleven officers, a bugler and two men. On top of which the colonel was at great pains to look like a stalwart Schinderhannes and had a horse he was unable to ride.— Every one of these gentry wants to be a leader, but they can't even *act the part* of leader except within our party, and so *they* will take good care not to provoke a schism. On the other hand they know that, subject as we are to the Anti-Socialist Law,[16] *we* too have reasons for avoiding internal splits which we cannot debate in an open forum. Hence we shall have to put up with epistolary and verbal cabalism and jeremiads from these people until we are again in a position to thrash out inside the country itself and before the workers those points on which we differ as to tactics and principles unless, of course, their antics are such that our hand is forced. Meanwhile the Anti-Socialist Law will, one way or another, shuffle off this mortal coil and, as soon as that's been got rid of, the position, or so it seems to me, must be fairly and squarely stated; what should be done next will automatically emerge from the attitude adopted by these gentry.

Once they have organised a separate right wing we shall be able, as and when occasion arises and in so far as it is admissible, to come to an agreement with them as to common action, or even enter into a compact with them, etc. Although this is unlikely to be necessary: the schism itself will lay bare their impotence. They have neither adherents amongst the masses, nor talent, nor knowledge — all

^a K. Marx and F. Engels, 'Circular Letter to August Bebel, Wilhelm Liebknecht, Wilhelm Bracke and Others'. -^b See this volume, pp. 259-61.

they have is pretensions, and those in plenty. However, we shall have to wait and see. Whatever happens, it will serve to elucidate the situation and we shall be rid of an element that in no way belongs to us. There is no need to fear that, in such a case, we shall no longer have any presentable candidates for the Reichstag. That is a pure figment. If a working man in the Reichstag now and then says I when he ought to say me, all we need ask is how long the Hohenzollerns, let alone field marshals, have been able to distinguish between I and me. Frederick William III and his adored Louise perpetrated more howlers in the matter of I and me than did even A. Kapell. And if Bismarck isn't afraid of appointing to his economics council workers who speak ungrammatically, but vote grammatically, can *we* afford to jib? But I know that to many it's an abomination. To us not in the least. And it would put an end to the utterly senseless practice of our deputies, which is supposed to be 'democratic' but isn't, whereby every man must speak in turn. How could any party possess as many good parliamentary speakers as that, and what is supposed to happen when there are, say, 200 of our men in the Reichstag?

But of one thing you may be sure: When it comes to a show-down with these gentry and the party's left wing declares itself, we shall go along with you whatever the circumstances, and do so actively and with our visors up. If I did not contribute to the *Sozialdemokrat* in my own name before,[336] this was due solely to the influence so long exerted upon the paper by these people and the prolonged absence of any guarantee that they would not regain it.

As you know, there's a split in the workers' party in Paris. The *Égalité* people (our best, Guesde, Deville, Lafargue, etc.) were unceremoniously thrown out by those on the *Prolétaire* (Malon, Brousse, etc.) at the recent congress of the Centre of France. The *Sozialdemokrat* rightly censured this procedure in a passage which the *Égalité* translated. Thereupon the *Prolétaire* replied, saying that its own point of view concerning this matter had been put to the German party leadership with whom it had since been in complete accord.[337] Do you know anything about this? The *Prolétaire* people are the most egregious liars; but on the other hand I recall all too many instances of stupendous blunders perpetrated in the Leipzig *Volksstaat* and *Vorwärts* in regard to French affairs and persons. Can you tell me anything about what actually happened? I shall try and let you have the cutting from the *Prolétaire*. Malon, Brousse & Co. are finding their labours as workers' candidates unduly tedious and are therefore consorting with sundry radical bourgeois and *literati*, and inviting others of that ilk to join forces with them; they imagine that they will thereby get themselves elected more quickly. They are fighting the *Égalité* with the same old infamous weapons used by the Bakuninists.

Your
F. E.

First published, in Russian, in *Marx-Engels Archives*, Vol. I (VI), Moscow, 1932

Printed according to the original

Published in English for the first time

158

MARX TO ENGELS

IN LONDON

[Argenteuil,] 22 June 1882

DEAR FRED,

Your letter [284] arrived no more than a minute or two before the post which goes damned early. Hence only a few words.

I have not been able to REPORT PROGRESS until today because the sulphur operations were suspended from Sunday[a] until yesterday inclusive on account of the rainy weather and did not begin again until today. AT PRESENT TIME it's devilish cold at Cauterets and the season there doesn't NORMALLY begin until the middle of JULY. So in the event Enghien has proved most opportune, although up till now the weather has not been good enough to permit UNINTERRUPTED use of the *institution thermale*. Other people, who need not be careful about a

---

[a] 11 June

'*résidu*',[a] wouldn't have to bother so much. Dr Dourlen says that the whole difficulty lies in avoiding anything that might cause a recurrence of pleurisy.

Let the chaps in New York go ahead with their own 'reprint', though they must take care that there are no unauthorised additions.[338]

We shall, then, expect Helen[b] on Sunday.

It is still too early — for I must fight shy of all lengthy conversations just now — to advise Lavrov of my presence. He's just the man to make me prattle on for hours.

Love to Jennychen.[c]

Your

K. M.

First published abridged in *Der Briefwechsel zwischen F. Engels und K. Marx*, Bd. 4, Stuttgart, 1913 and in full in *MEGA*, Abt. III, Bd. 4, Berlin, 1931

Printed according to the original

Published in English for the first time

159

MARX TO ENGELS

IN LONDON

[Postcard]

[Argenteuil,] 24 June 1882

DEAR FRED,

I got the REGISTERED LETTER yesterday; today I realised it in Paris. As a result of the present changeable weather I had an attack of muscular rheumatism in the region of my hips; as a result of this and other things a sleepless night from the 22nd to the 23rd on account of severe pain. No food the next day (though absolved my sulphur inhalation at Enghien yesterday); Dourlen called in the evening and helped by embrocating me with laudanum; ALL RIGHT now as regards this INCIDENT, except that slight twinges of muscular rheumatism still persist.

As regards Enghien the first question to be answered — for this depends upon the individual — is whether the local sulphur spring is

---

[a] residue - [b] Demuth - [c] A slip of the pen in the ms.: Marx probably means his daughter Eleanor.

strong enough. AT ALL EVENTS Reinhardt got rid of his bronchitis here, like Longuet before him. The latter was also at Cauterets *at an earlier time long before his marriage. Its height above the sea level 1200-1400 *mètres* about. I should be very glad if I should not want it for the bronchial catarrh; at all events Cauterets was out of the question for this time. Helen[a] will arrive at St Lazare *gare où*[b] Longuet there to receive her.*

Salut.

Your

Moor

[On the side reserved for the address]

F. Engels. Esq.
122 Regent's Park Road,
London, N. W.

First published abridged in *Der Briefwechsel zwischen F. Engels und K. Marx*, Bd. 4, Stuttgart, 1913 and in full in *MEGA*, Abt. III, Bd. 4, Berlin, 1931

Printed according to the original

Published in English for the first time

160

ENGELS TO EDUARD BERNSTEIN[339]

IN ZURICH

[London, 26 June 1882]

...In Ireland there are two tendencies within the movement, the first and earliest being the *agrarian*. Out of organised brigandage, backed by the farmers, on the part of the clan chiefs whom the English had dispossessed, and the big Catholic landowners (in the 17th century these brigands were called *Tories*, a name that has descended by direct line to the Tories of today), there gradually evolved an indigenous resistance, organised according to locality and province, on the part of the farmers against the interloping English landlords. The names — RIBBONMEN, WHITEBOYS, CAPTAIN ROCK, CAPTAIN MOONLIGHT,[340]

---

[a] Demuth - [b] Station where

etc.—have changed, the form the resistance has taken—the shooting, not only of hated LANDLORDS and agents (collectors in the LANDLORDS' service), but also of those farmers who take over a farm from others who have been forcibly evicted,—BOYCOTTING, threatening letters, nocturnal attacks with intimidation, etc.—all this has been going on for as long as the English have owned land in Ireland, i. e. at least since the end of the 17th century. This form of resistance is irrepressible, cannot be curbed by force and will disappear only with its causes. But by its nature it is *local* and *sporadic*, nor can it ever become a general form of *political* struggle.

The period immediately after the Union (1800) [109] saw the beginnings of the *liberal-national* opposition of the *urban bourgeoisie* who, as in every agrarian country with small towns in process of decay (e. g. Denmark), found their natural leaders in the *lawyers*. The latter also need the farmers; hence they have to invent slogans to attract the farmers. Thus *O'Connell* lit, first, upon *Catholic emancipation*,[341] and then upon the *Repeal of the Union*. Latterly supporters of this trend have been forced by the infamies of the landowners to adopt a different course. Whereas, in the *social* sphere, the *Land League* [139] pursues more revolutionary (and in this instance attainable) aims, namely the total elimination of the interloping LANDLORDS, its *political* posture is, if anything, rather tame since its only demand is HOMERULE, i. e. a local Irish parliament alongside and subject to the parliament of the Empire. This, too, is undoubtedly attainable by constitutional means. The frightened landlords are already clamouring for (and the Tories themselves proposing) the speediest possible redemption of farmland in order to save what can still be saved, while *Gladstone*, for his part, is declaring a greater measure of self-government for Ireland to be altogether admissible.

After the American Civil War these two tendencies were infiltrated by a third—*Fenianism*.[312] The hundreds of thousands of Irish soldiers and officers who fought in that war did so with the ulterior motive of building up an army for the liberation of Ireland. The dissension between England and America after the war became the Fenians' principal lever. Should war supervene, Ireland would, within a few months, be either a member of the United States or a republic under the latter's protection. The sum which England so willingly undertook to pay and did pay during the Alabama negotiations with the Geneva arbitrators [342] was the *price* at which *American intervention in Ireland was bought off*.

As from that moment, the principal danger was eliminated. The police were enough to keep the Fenians in order. In this they were helped by the betrayals inseparable from any conspiracy, and yet it was only the *leaders* who betrayed, going on to become downright spies and falsifiers of evidence. The leaders who got away to America indulged in émigré revolutionary politics there and, for the most part, went to seed like O'Donovan Rossa. All of this — if, of course, on an exaggerated American scale — will seem very familiar to anyone who witnessed the European emigration over here between 1849 and 1852.

There can be no doubt that many Fenians have now come home again and have revived the former armed organisation. They provide an important impulse within the movement and compel the liberals to adopt a more resolute posture. But otherwise they achieve nothing unless it be to frighten John Bull. True, the latter is growing perceptibly weaker on the periphery of his empire, but as close to home as this he is still in a position to suppress with ease any kind of Irish rebellion. For a start there is, in Ireland, a permanent 'CONSTABULARY' 14,000 strong, equipped with rifles and bayonets and having had a military training. Then some 30,000 line troops who could easily be reinforced by an equal number of line and English militia. In addition, the navy. And in suppressing rebellion, John Bull's brutality is without equal. *In the absence of a foreign war or the threat thereof, an Irish uprising has not the remotest prospect of success*; and here *only two* powers might constitute a threat — *France* and, to a far greater degree, the *United States*. France is out of the question. In America the parties are coquetting with the Irish vote; they make many promises but abide by none. Nor have they any intention of involving themselves in a war on Ireland's behalf. It even serves their interests that conditions in Ireland should be such as to encourage massive Irish emigration to America. And it is understandable that a country which, in 20 years' time, will be the most populous, wealthy and powerful in the world, should feel small inclination to rush headlong into adventures which could and would upset its gigantic internal development. In 20 years' time it will have completely changed its tune.

But should the danger of a war with America arise, England would give the Irish anything they asked, and with both hands — saving only complete independence which, in view of that country's geographical position, is not at all desirable.

Accordingly the only recourse remaining to the Irish is the constitutional method of gradual conquest, whereby one position is taken after another; and here the lurking presence of armed Fenian conspiracy can still furnish a most effective element. But these very Fenians are being increasingly impelled into a kind of Bakuninism; the only purpose to be served by the assassination of Burke and Cavendish was the frustration of the compromise between the Land League and Gladstone. In the circumstances, however, that compromise would have been the best thing for Ireland. Because of rent arrears the LAND-LORDS are evicting the tenants from house and home in their tens of thousands and are doing so under the protection of the military. To check this systematic depopulation of Ireland (those who are evicted either starve to death or have to go to America) is the prime necessity just now. Gladstone is prepared to table a Bill whereby arrears will be paid on lines similar to the redemption of feudal taxes in Austria in 1848 — one-third by the farmer, one-third by the state, one-third written off by the LANDLORDS. That is the Land League's own proposal. Thus the 'heroic deed' of Phoenix Park appears to be, if not [a] sheer folly, at all events a piece of pure Bakuninist, histrionic, senseless '*propagande par le fait*'.[b] If its consequences have not been the same as those of the similar follies perpetrated by Hödel and Nobiling,[120] this has been due solely to the fact that Ireland does not, as yet, lie within the purlieus of Prussia. Hence it must be left to the Bakuninists and Mostians to place such puerilities on a par with the execution of Alexander II, and to pose the threat of an 'Irish revolution' that never happens.

One more thing that should be noted about Ireland: never praise an Irishman — politician — unconditionally or give him your unqualified support, until he's dead. Celtic blood and the habitual exploitation of the farmers (after all, in Ireland this constitutes the sole livelihood of all the 'educated' classes, and of the lawyers in particular) make professional Irish politicians exceedingly prone to corruption. In return for his agitation, O'Connell got the farmers to pay him £30,000 a year no less. When England effected the Union at a cost of £1,000,000 in bribes, one of those who had been bribed was reproached with having sold his country. Says he: 'Aye, and damned glad I was to have a country I could sell.'

The infamies perpetrated against our people by the German governments, police and judges are gradually assuming a character that

---

[a] Up to here the letter is printed according to the ms. - [b] propaganda by deeds

makes even the strongest language employed in condemning them look insipid. But since language is not necessarily given added emphasis by forceful expressions, and the repeated use of the same expressions such as scoundrel, etc., detracts from the effect, so that one has to have recourse to ever more 'forceful' expressions and thus lapse into the style of Most-Schneidt,[343] it would be desirable to adopt a method whereby forcefulness of expression would be assured even in the absence of intemperate language. And that method exists; it consists primarily in the use of irony, derision, sarcasm, which have a more deadly effect on an opponent than the crudest expressions of indignation. I think the *Sozialdemokrat* would be well advised to adopt the old, predominantly *derisive* style whenever this is feasible, as indeed was done in the last number. An occasional application of the cudgel would then be all the more effective. Bebel is also in complete agreement with me here. And, besides, your present correspondents already attend pretty adequately to lurid descriptions of events.

In response to the *Égalité*'s translation of the passage in the *Sozialdemokrat* about the expulsion of their people from the Congrès du Centre, the *Prolétaire* published a pharisaical article about an *échange de lettres courtoises entre le* Comité extérieur *du parti ouvrier socialiste allemand et le Comité national français.*[a][344] Can you tell me anything about this? I was quite unaware of the existence of a *Comité extérieur*; might it perhaps be the much-celebrated *Communications Office*[345]?

The *Bataille* is on its last legs — *c'est une défaite, et méritée.*[b] Lissagaray has proved totally unfit to be a journalist and he, like his collaborators, Malon and Brousse, appeals to the Parisians' chauvinistic Germanophobia vis-à-vis Guesde, etc., *Marxistes, nébulosités allemandes,*[c] etc. None of which has deterred Lissagaray from informing the *Citoyen*'s proprietor[d] of his desire to join the editorial department! Needless to say the editorial department instantly turned him down (this *privatim*).

Marx is in Argenteuil with his daughter,[e] hiding away from Paris and availing himself of the sulphur springs in Enghien for his chronic bronchitis and cough; otherwise he is well and cheerful, but must still take great care of himself.

---

[a] exchange of polite letters between the *External Committee* of the German Socialist Workers' Party and the French National Committee - [b] it's a defeat and a deserved one - [c] German nebulosities - [d] Blommestein - [e] Jenny Longuet

Did Adolf Beust give you Mirabeau's *Secret History of the Court of Berlin* which I gave him to pass on to you? The book will be very useful to the *Sozialdemokrat*.

Yours,

F. E.

First published abridged in *Der Sozialdemokrat*, Nr. 29, 13 July 1882 and in full, in Russian, in *Marx-Engels Archives*, Book I, Moscow, 1924

Printed according to the newspaper and the extant part of the original

Published in English in full for the first time

161

MARX TO ENGELS [72]

IN LONDON

[Postcard, unsigned]

[Argenteuil,] 4 JULY 1882

DEAR FRED,

Summer did not actually begin until the 1ST of JULY (or RATHER THE SECOND ONLY). Up till now I've had 2 sulphur baths *with douches*, the 3rd will be tomorrow; never before have I encountered anything as magnificent as the shower-bath (alias douche); one climbs out of the bath on to a slightly raised board, and this *en 'nature'* [a]; the bath attendant then manipulates the spray (about the size of a fire extinguisher) like a virtuoso his instrument, dictates the movements of the *corpus* and bombards all PARTS of that *corpus* in turn (*SAVE THE HEAD*, (*the cranium*)) for 180 seconds (alias 3 MINUTES) now with greater, now with lesser force, even unto the legs and feet incl. in an ever mounting CRESCENDO.

As you will see, there is little inducement here for a man to write. I have to be at the RAILWAY by half past eight in the morning (i. e. THIS THE TIME OF LEAVING EXACTLY FOR Enghien), back to Argenteuil ABOUT 12 O'CLOCK, *déjeuner* [b] shortly afterwards; *après* [c] a great need for rest, as this sulphur is tiring in whatever form; then out and about, etc. The air in the inhalation room is murky with sulphurous vapours; 30-40 MINUTES'

---

[a] in a state of nature - [b] luncheon - [c] afterwards

spell here; every 5 minutes, at a special table, one inhales steam laden with specially pulverised sulphur (from one of the pipes (zinc) with stopcocks); each man encased in *caoutchouc*[a] from head to foot; after which they march in file round the table; innocent scene from Dante's inferno.

Regards to Schorlemmer. I still have a photograph of me for him, taken in Algiers.

Lafargue regards himself *as a gros*[b] *oracle* here. Paris is for him THE ONLY PLACE OF THE WORLD WORTH MANHOOD.

[On the side reserved for the address]

Fr. Engels
122 Regent's Park Road
London, N. W., Angleterre

First published abridged in *Der Briefwech-sel zwischen F. Engels und K. Marx*, Bd. 4, Stuttgart, 1913 and in full in *MEGA*, Abt. III, Bd. 4, Berlin, 1931

Printed according to the original

162

ENGELS TO EDUARD BERNSTEIN

IN ZURICH

London, 15 July 1882

Dear Mr Bernstein,

I am replying to your last letter straight away as there would otherwise be a 3 days' gap on account of the Sunday postal arrangements.

I was shown the Mehringiad[346] by an acquaintance here and at once recognised both author and prompter. Ever since the time his plans for the *Sozialdemokrat* went so completely awry because of the presence of yourself and Bebel, Hirsch[c] has been working himself up into a ludicrous rage against the 'Zurich people'. We have often

---

[a] rubber - [b] great - [c] Carl Hirsch

enough given him the broadest hints to the effect that we were not in accord with him in this respect; rather, anything he did, he did on his own responsibility, but this has helped only to the extent that he doesn't pester *us* with his lamentations. He has, by the way, been back in Paris (on sufferance) for some considerable time, and last Saturday (8 July) married a certain Miss Lina Haschert.

As for the actual contents of the thing, there is no reason for us to intervene. Mehring has treated the world to so many lies about us that, were we to deny just one of them, it would be tantamount to an admission that all the rest were true. For years we have let all this mendacious tittle-tattle pass unheeded, unless absolute necessity compelled us to reply. Our people have the *Volks-Zeitung* at their disposal, so all that is needed is a communication to the effect that an article of mine, signed by me, appeared in the *Sozialdemokrat* of ? June.[347] That is the best way to reply. You yourself can, of course, also refer to it in the *Sozialdemokrat* as you intended, and say that Marx and I always agree beforehand on any public move we make. I'm very glad that the article in the *Sozialdemokrat* appeared at this precise moment; it will knock all these inanities on the head.

On the other hand I think you would be well advised to leave Höchberg out of it. After all, he simply wants to appear as a private individual and hence will be able to conduct his own defence if he thinks it necessary. I don't know whether it would be doing him a service to rake up the old affair of the *Jahrbuch* article, etc.[a] — should there be doubts *within the party* about our position, we might be compelled to revert to it, though I for one think it quite unnecessary.

Since Marx leads a completely secluded existence in Argenteuil and keeps his presence there as secret as possible, he has seen nothing of Hirsch, at least so far as I know, nor is he in any way anxious to do so. Marx needs peace and quiet, and I shall not therefore bother him with all this business before it proves absolutely necessary, i. e. before Hirsch forms any further cabals.

Kautsky has written me one, indeed two, long letters[348] about everything under the sun. However, as I have already told you,[b] I no longer have the time for such lengthy correspondence and to be able to investigate and reply to this or that I should, what's more, actually have to embark on specialised studies. That is the whole reason for my silence.

---

[a] See this volume, p. 279. - [b] Ibid., p. 203.

I know absolutely nothing of value about Chartism.[159] If I could persuade our old friend Harney in Boston (ex-editor of *The Northern Star*) to write a history of Chartism, he would be the man. Kindest regards.

Yours,

F. Engels

I myself have been so much out of touch with Hirsch that I have no occasion whatever to give him my views on this business. If occasion arose, I should of course do so.

First published, in Russian, in *Marx-Engels Archives*, Book I, Moscow, 1924

Printed according to the original

Published in English for the first time

163

ENGELS TO ADOLF HEPNER [349]

IN NEW YORK

[Draft]

London, 25 July 1882

Dear Mr Hepner,

My delay in replying has been due to Marx's illness and frequent changes of abode. It was not until recently that I was able to correspond with him about business matters. Our views [a] on your projected undertaking [350] are as follows:

As you are fully entitled in law to reprint anything that appears in Europe, you would, in our opinion, do best to go ahead and exercise that right without asking anybody. If you wish to reprint the *Communist Manifesto* we can have no objection whatever, nor would it occur to us to protest against it, provided there were no changes or omissions — in any case inadmissible in an historical document — or unless compelled to do so by unwarranted notes. We cannot write a preface, not only because we are not together, but also, and still

---

[a] Ibid., p. 284.

more, because we should thereby be identifying ourselves to some extent with an undertaking which we are not in a position either to supervise or to control, nor, indeed, might we wish to do so. As it is, you will be entirely at liberty to reprint anything else you wish, without our ever having cause to complain of the company in which our works appear.

The same applies to my *Condition of the Working Class*. If you reprint it as it stands I can have no objection. Were I, however, to give you my special consent, I should be obliged to provide the addenda and notes needed to bring the book up to date, and that would be 6 months' work. Moreover I should require prior guarantees that the undertaking, once begun, would be brought to a conclusion.

I trust I have convinced you that it would be in your best interests to go ahead on your own. We shall certainly not place any obstacle in the way of the undertaking unless compelled to do so; rather the reverse.

As regards a new abridgement of *Capital*, Marx has had so many unpleasant experiences with this kind of thing that no further approaches should be made to him about the matter, especially not at the moment. However (*this in confidence*) Marx has purged the *second* edition of *Most*'s abridgement [351] of its grosser errors and made a few addenda, so that this edition is not without its merits and could be reprinted.

Otherwise there is little that I can recommend for reprinting. The literature produced by Leipzig consists largely in the socialism of the future and doctoral dissertations by parliamentary candidates. Jules Guesde's French stuff is good on the whole, but too closely geared to French conditions. Bracke's *Nieder mit den Sozialdemokraten!* is perhaps not suitable for America. Bebel's parliamentary speeches are by far the best thing that Germany has produced in our line, but they are, of course, made for the occasion. Lassalle teems with economic howlers and his whole viewpoint was superseded long ago. Bracke's *Lassalle'scher Vorschlag* is a pretty good piece of criticism, though not exhaustive.

Well, it's for you to choose. Wishing your undertaking the best of luck,

Yours,

F. E.

First published, in Russian, in *Marx-Engels Archives*, Vol. I (VI), Moscow, 1932   Printed according to the original

164

ENGELS TO PYOTR LAVROV

IN PARIS

[Postcard]

[London,] 31 July 1882

My dear Lavrov,

I should have thanked you long since for sending me the Russian *Manifesto*,[352] but I couldn't very well write to you without giving you news of Marx and he had expressly forbidden me to tell anyone in Paris, no matter whom, that he was in Argenteuil. Unfortunately the prohibition of the doctors, who have given him strict instructions to talk as little as possible, means he is still in *solitary confinement*.

Kovalevsky called while I was out. He only saw Miss Marx[a] and left no address. He must have departed a few days after his arrival, but I have absolutely no idea what route he took. It would seem that he intended to return to his own country. Miss Marx is at Argenteuil; if you wrote to Longuet, perhaps you might be able to learn more.

Yours ever,

F. E.

[On the side reserved for the address]

Monsieur P. Lavroff
328 rue St Jacques
Paris
France

First published in: Marx and Engels, *Works*, First Russian Edition, Vol. XXVII, Moscow, 1935

Printed according to the original

Translated from the French

Published in English for the first time

---

[a] Eleanor Marx

165

MARX TO ENGELS

IN LONDON

Argenteuil, *jeudi, 3 août* [a] 1882
11 Boulevard Thiers

DEAR FRED,

The difficulty over letter-writing is due to the following: at 7.30 a. m. I start off by washing and dressing myself, taking early morning coffee, etc.; at 8.30 a. m. departure for Enghien, not as a rule returning before noon, then *déjeuner en famille* [b] at Argenteuil; from 2-4 p. m., rest, then a walk and pottering about with the children with consequences more detrimental to one's faculties of sight and hearing (let alone thought) than were ever experienced even by the Hegel of the *Phänomenologie*; finally, at 8 p. m., evening SUPPER, thereby concluding the day's work. So when would one find time for correspondence?

Tussychen is being of enormous help to Jennychen, nor could her stay here really be considered as a rest cure if she were not so fond of the children [c] and of poor Jennychen and evincing in these particular circumstances qualities which lie dormant in London. Tussy and Laura have not seen one another yet and aren't exactly longing to do so. But for decency's sake they will have to meet at least once while I am here.

Now for a health bulletin. My cure began on 17 June. The weather up till now has been so far below the average for summer (French) that the season which starts in June in Enghien is regarded as a FAIL-URE by the *établissement thermal* [d] and something 'better' is looked for in August and September. Constant changes of temperature, the sky often heavily overcast, *particularly in the mornings* after rain and *orages*, [e] violent winds, moisture-laden atmosphere and hence often *une chaleur lourde*, [f] alias London's 'CLOSE' STATUS. The French have been at pains to stave off an alliance with England [353]; by contrast, the English climate (I MEAN specifically the London climate) would seem to be making itself increasingly at home here, in Paris and environs. Such is the case this year at any rate. In between times, of course, we

---

[a] Thursday, 3 August - [b] lunch en famille - [c] Jean, Henri, Edgar and Marcel Longuet - [d] thermal establishment - [e] storms - [f] oppressive heat

have an occasional fine day, or fragments thereof. In these circumstances my cure is having to contend with 'agreeable obstacles'. As Lenchen will recall, there was one particular day when Dr Feugier's examination, and the one undertaken a few hours later by Dr Dourlen, resulted in the same verdict: the *râlements*[a] had disappeared and this meant the 'bronchial' character of the catarrh had been eliminated. I didn't pass on 'such matters' to you; I suspected that the said bronchial catarrh had by no means croaked its last, and, indeed, during a brief spell of bad weather, it began to croak anew. That the cough hadn't 'disappeared' (though greatly alleviated, of course), I was aware, but didn't much mind about what remained of the cough once its character had changed.

Indeed, upon auscultating me last Monday (31 July), Dr Feugier found that the râle was still there, although grown fainter; the weather, he said, was especially malign and harmful in the case of these particular complaints. As a rule, patients only continue the sulphur cure for 3 weeks; indeed, many people cannot tolerate it for a longer period without the risk of feverish attacks, etc. In view of my otherwise strong constitution and since I am still troubled by a cough, especially of a morning, he thought it best to continue the cure *until the middle of August*, with INHALATION, BATHS, DOUCHES and the drinking of sulphurous waters; no purpose would be served by prolonging it beyond that date. I shall, of course, follow the doctor's advice. On the other hand, however, it will by then probably be *too late* for the Engadine plan [354]; both Feugier and Dourlen are afraid that I might otherwise expose myself to climatic ADVENTURES which a man, above all one in my condition, would do better not to invite unnecessarily.— I hope you will *in any case* come and spend a few days here (in which case the Lafargues would easily find you accommodation in Paris), not only so that we may confer about *que faire après*,[b] but more especially, you must understand, because I long to see you again after all these DAMNED *vésicatoires*[c] and one or two very close shaves!

Laurachen wrote and told me that *Deville* is leaving for his home town of Tarbes on the evening of 2 August. But since I had expressed a desire to see him, Mesa proposed we should come to *déjeuner*[d] with him on 2 August, when I should meet, besides the Lafargues, also Deville and Guesde. This was the first time that I had agreed to such a meeting. (It is always the livelier talk, and/or chatter which tells on

---

[a] râle - [b] what's to be done next - [c] vesicatories - [d] luncheon

me — after the event.) Went off well. The *Citoyen* people seem to me to be succeeding with their public MEETINGS on the Egyptian, etc., *affaires* [355]; however, as far as the performance of their paper is concerned, *ils laissent beaucoup à désirer*.[a] Incidentally, *and aside from the self-styled socialist journals*, a large and most influential part of the *Paris press* is incomparably more independent than that of London. Despite pressure from most of the PROFESSIONAL POLITICIANS, despite collusion between the *République Française*, the *Temps* and the *Journal des Débats*, working hand-in-glove under the immediate direction of Gambetta; despite, what is more, the attempts at bribery by the FINANCIERS (Rothschilds, etc.) who have an immediate interest in joining the English crusade against Egypt, the Paris press has quashed every attempt (even Freycinet's disguised ones [356]) at joint intervention with England or with a Quadruple Alliance [357]; without that press, Clemenceau would not have won his victory in parliament. But where in London is there even a modicum of an 'independent' press?

I cannot in fact remember where Loria's *grandes*[b] opus[c] is to be found in my library; nor would it seem to me worth your while taking the trouble to look for it. As you know, after reading the 'opus' (or RATHER the first half of the book, for I hadn't the patience to do more than skim through the 2nd half containing Mr Loria's fantasies about how his ideal norm, small landed property, i. e. smallholdings, could *adequately* be *constructed*), I was far from edified by the sickening covert flattery vis-à-vis myself and the overt assumption of 'superiority' not to mention falsification of certain of my views the better to refute them. Yet, though my first reaction was that I wanted to have no truck with him, I allowed myself to become further involved because he showed talent, because he had done a lot of swotting; because he was a poor devil who had written to me at length about his thirst for knowledge; because he was still very young and his admittedly far from youthful tendencies — they were, if anything, wise beyond his years — seemed understandable in view, partly of conditions in Italy, and partly of the school from which he derived; also because he sought to make his own, in so far as in him lay and not always without success, the methods of research he had found in *Capital*. I was 'amused' and pleased by his way of openly preening himself on having 'antiquated' *Capital* with his 'landed property'. For all that, I still harbour serious doubts about the young man's character.

---

[a] they were much disappointed - [b] great - [c] A. Loria, *La rendita fondiaria e la sua elisione naturale*, Milan, Naples, Pisa, 1880.

After I had read through these 2 pamphlets,[a] however, and a couple of days after Tussy's arrival here, I gave her my very categorical and final verdict—in words—I give you three guesses!—in *the exactly same terms* which *the said Tussychen was amazed to find again, word for word, in your letter of 31 July* which I showed her! Thus we, you and I, not only came to exactly the same conclusion, but *formulated* the same *in exactly the same way*! Such being the case, we can, in future, *only* adopt an attitude of *ironical aloofness* towards him, without in any way becoming further involved in the business! He is far worse than the Kauzkitten,[b] who at least has the best of intentions.

Apropos Hirsch. If he really has collaborated with Mehring,[346] the party will never forgive him. Should I see him, I shall ask him point-blank. Come to that, as regards the controversy over my *status*, it would have been better had nothing been said. What are the workers to believe, unless it be that I was, so to speak, shamming sick, and had squandered all that time and money without good reason?

Next week the Lafargues are moving into their proper quarters which are said to be very pleasant, and cheap as local *logements*[c] go. *Au revoir*, OLD BOY. My love also to Lenchen.

Your
Moor

First published abridged in *Der Briefwechsel zwischen F. Engels und K. Marx*, Bd. 4, Stuttgart, 1913 and in full in *MEGA*, Abt. III, Bd. 4, Berlin, 1931

Printed according to the original

Published in English for the first time

166

ENGELS TO JOHANN PHILIPP BECKER

IN GENEVA

London, 9 August 1882

Dear Old Man,

I had no opportunity yesterday of taking out a money order for you. But I did so first thing today and you will be paid £5 sterling

---

[a] A. Loria, *La legge di popolazione ed il sistema sociale*, Siena, 1882 and *La teoria del valore negli economisti italiani*, Bologna, 1882. - [b] Karl Kautsky - [c] lodgings

over there, which, according to the table, equals 126 frs. I was very glad to get another letter from you [358] and hear how you are getting on. I, too, would give I don't know how much if you, Marx and I could foregather once more, but this year it's unlikely I shall have any such luck. There might still be a chance of your seeing Marx this summer, but that depends on where the doctors send him. I shall have to postpone the rest of my reply for a day or two as it's nearly time for the post and I still have to write at some length to Bernstein about this and that.

In the meantime keep yourself hale and hearty as always. Kindest regards.

Your old friend
F. Engels

First published in: F. Engels, *Vergessene Briefe (Briefe Friedrich Engels' an Johann Philipp Becker)*, Berlin, 1920

Printed according to the original

Published in English for the first time

167

ENGELS TO EDUARD BERNSTEIN [359]

IN ZURICH

London, 9 August 1882

Dear Mr Bernstein,

Today just a few comments in great haste, as I shall be going to the seaside in a few days' time and my hands are absolutely full.

1. A *German* edition of *Socialisme utopique et socialisme scientifique* is something I have long had in mind, particularly now that I have seen what a regular revolution the thing has wrought in the minds of many of the better people in France.[360] I am glad that we see eye to eye here. The only thing is that the German text, because more concentrated, is appreciably more difficult than the French from which quite a lot is omitted. To popularise the work without prejudice to the substance, and in such a way as to make it fit for general use as a propaganda pamphlet is a difficult task; however, I shall do the best I can at the seaside. When shall you be able to start printing and how long will the impression take? I must, of course, be sent the proofs (in

duplicate, as in France, which has a number of advantages).

2. Naturally you would have thought that, in view of our old friendship, Liebknecht was really within his rights in asking you to hand over my letter[a] to him, and that you were under an obligation to put it at his disposal. I can find nothing to complain about in that. Nor could you know that, of the many differences I have had with Liebknecht, four-fifths were due to similar high-handed acts on his part, to the public misuse of private letters, to notes, etc., on my articles that were either silly or ran immediately counter to the sense of the passage. On this occasion, too, he has made unjustifiable use of my letter. That letter was written with specific reference to your article.[339] Liebknecht treated it as though it were 'my' account of the Irish question *as a whole*. Frightfully easy and all the more so if one trots out in refutation Davitt's speeches which *had not as yet been made at all* at the time the letter was written and, indeed, have no bearing at all on that letter, Davitt and his state ownership of land having hitherto been no more than a *straw in the wind*. But Liebknecht always takes this kind of easy way out when trying to come the 'top dog'. Now, I don't begrudge him his fun, but he ought not to misuse my letters for the purpose and in this way *he* has compelled me to request you in future (let me try to make this sound as formally diplomatic as possible) *de lui donner — tout au plus — lecture de mes lettres sans cependant lui abandonner l'original ni lui en laisser copie.*[b]

3. I have passed on to Marx, in as humorous a form as possible, the substance of the Hirsch-Mehringiad[346] and I fear that, should little Carl[c] see Marx, he will go through a not altogether agreeable quarter of an hour.

4. I should say that, in the Egyptian affair,[355] you take the so-called National Party rather too much under your wing.[361] We don't know much about Arabi, but I'd wager 10 to 1 that he is a run-of-the-mill Pasha who begrudges the financial chaps their tax revenue because he would, in good oriental fashion, sooner pocket it himself. Here we have the same old story as in all agrarian countries. From Ireland to Russia, from Asia Minor to Egypt, the peasant of an agrarian country is there to be exploited. It has been the same since the time of the Assyrian and Persian empires. The satrap, alias pasha, is the eastern prototype of the exploiter, as are the business men and

<hr/>

[a] See this volume, pp. 285-90. - [b] at most to permit him to read my letters, without, however, handing over the original to him or letting him keep a copy.- [c] Carl Hirsch

jurists in the west today. REPUDIATION of the Khedive's [362] debts may
be all right, but the question is, what then? And we West European
socialists ought not to allow ourselves to be so easily duped as the
Egyptian fellaheen [363] or as—all Latins. Strange. All Latin revolutionaries lament the fact that their revolutions invariably redound to
someone else's advantage—quite simply because they have always
been taken in by the word 'revolution'. And yet it's hardly possible
for a scrap to break out anywhere without revolutionary Latins rav-
ing about it with one voice—and quite uncritically. As I see it, we
can perfectly well enter the arena on behalf of the oppressed fellaheen
without sharing their current illusions (for a peasant population has
to be fleeced for centuries before it learns from experience), and
against the brutality of the English without, for all that, espousing the
cause of those who are currently their military opponents. The utmost caution should be observed in making use of the politically emotional French and Italian party papers in all questions of international politics; we Germans, however, now we have attained superiority where theory is concerned, are duty bound to preserve it in this
sphere also by the exercise of criticism.

But now, enough of criticism. Unfortunately I haven't got sufficient time left today to send you a contribution for the feuilleton.[364]
I am particularly keen to prove to our good little Carl in black and
white what tremendous piffle it was he fobbed off on Mehring about
my relations with the *Sozialdemokrat*. However, you will get it before
long and may then, if you like—it's all the same to me—make some
direct allusion to it in a note, without, of course, actually mentioning
our little Carl, who must surely by now be panting for cooling
streams.[a]

Well, my kindest regards. If at all possible, I shall also send you
a letter from the coast for *ce brave*[b] Kautsky whose address, or such as
I have, is of somewhat ancient date. The last one was that of some las-
sie with a French name—a genuine *accommodation* address, I trust.

Yours,

F. E.

First published in full, in Russian, in *Marx-*
Engels Archives, Book I, Moscow, 1924

Printed according to the original

Published in English in full for the
first time

---

[a] Hirsch = hart, hence 'as pants the hart for cooling streams'.- [b] the good

168

MARX TO ENGELS [72]

IN LONDON

[Argenteuil,] *jeudi*,[a] 10 August 1882

DEAR FRED,

Next Tuesday Dr Feugier will be letting me know whether I am to quit Enghien for good or carry on as I have been doing for another day or so.

Unfortunately I must first—supposing I (and Laura) go from here to Switzerland (Vevey or some such place is recommended)— have an additional MONETARY SUBSIDY. For I discovered *by chance* that Jenny is under severe pressure from her LANDLORD (and it's no laughing matter here) for the rent, and today I had the utmost difficulty in getting her to accept enough money to settle the business.

Furthermore, I am hoping that Johnny will go to London with Tussy (the *only opposition comes from Longuet,* who doesn't care a damn whether it's a respite for Jennychen or good for Johnny), in which case I shall have to give Tussy some extra money to take the lad for a couple of weeks to the seaside in England. Monsieur Longuet's main objection to letting us have Johnny for six months is that, for reasons of health, Johnny ought to go to the seaside in Normandy whither he would accordingly be accompanied by Longuet to stay with OLD Madame Longuet [b] at Caen.

In fact, Johnny is running wild here and has, in France, forgotten such rudiments of reading, writing, etc., as he had. He has grown naughty out of boredom (i. e. [for want of] occupation) and gives Jennychen more trouble than the 3 younger ones.[c] Monsieur Longuet does 'nothing' for the child, but his 'love' consists in not letting him out of his sight during the brief intervals when he himself is visible, for in Argenteuil he usually spends the morning in bed and leaves for Paris again at 5 in the afternoon.

In view of what lies ahead of Jennychen, [365] it will be absolutely impossible for him to restrain young Johnny. Tussy is AN EXCELLENT DIS-CIPLINARIAN and will bring him to heel again. So at least we can put

---

[a] Thursday - [b] Felicitas Longuet - [c] Henri, Edgar and Marcel Longuet

paid to Longuet's 'objection' that Johnny cannot go to England (where Tussy would also send him to school) because he must go 'to the seaside'; he is to go 'to the seaside', but do so in England. Aside from the aforementioned expenses, I shall not, after paying the doctor [a] and buying various necessities, have very much left for the trip from here to Switzerland. I hate squeezing you like this, but am forced to do so if I am not to come straight back to London. *Salut.*

Moor

The announcement in the French, i. e. Parisian, newspapers, starting with the *Temps*, that Liebknecht was on his way to Paris, 'to establish contact with the German workers and visit the socialist, Karl Marx, who is now living at Argenteuil after his return from Algiers', [b] this note, I say, and the way it was couched, smacked of the 'police' and was too indiscreet even for Liebknecht. If he should still find me here, I shall tell him exactly what I think of his 'indiscretion' (it's all due to his wanting to make himself look important).

First published abridged in *Der Briefwechsel zwischen F. Engels und K. Marx*, Bd. 4, Stuttgart, 1913 and in full in *MEGA*, Abt. III, Bd. 4, Berlin, 1931

Printed according to the original

169

ENGELS TO FRIEDRICH ADOLPH SORGE

IN HOBOKEN

London, 10 August 1882

Dear Sorge,

Herewith receipt from the *Égalité*; I haven't been able to obtain a better one for you from that remarkably businesslike office. Since Laura Lafargue moved to Paris, we over here no longer see or hear anything of that paper. The amount paid was 14/-.

---

[a] Dr Feugier - [b] 'Allemagne', *Le Temps*, No. 7773, 6 August 1882.

The Labour Standard, 1 July-5 August, goes off today in 2 parcels. It would be madness for you to take out a separate subscription to the thing. I shall simply send you my copy instead of throwing it into the waste-paper basket. Marx still at Argenteuil,[327] undergoing a sulphur cure in Enghien for chronic bronchitis. He still has to take considerable precautions against a recurrence of pleurisy. As for the rest, only the doctors know, or again they may not.

In great haste.

Your

F. E.

First published abridged in *Briefe und Auszüge aus Briefen von Joh. Phil. Becker, Jos. Dietzgen, Friedrich Engels, Karl Marx u. A. an F. A. Sorge und Andere*, Stuttgart, 1906 and in full in: Marx and Engels, *Works*, First Russian Edition, Vol. XXVII, Moscow, 1935

Printed according to the original

Published in English for the first time

170

ENGELS TO MARX

IN ARGENTEUIL

Great Yarmouth,[366] 20 August 1882
10 Columbia Terrace

Dear Moor,

The money has been paid in so I went straight to the bank today and requested a draft for 1,200 frs. I hope to have it on Tuesday. How did last Tuesday's[a] great medical examination go[b]? Not a word about it so far.

If there is any difficulty about the CHEQUE, just send it back and I shall then send you a draft on Paris instead. It was simply a make-shift arrangement.

---

[a] 15 August - [b] See this volume, pp. 303, 308.

Pumps and BABY[a] are very lively; the little thing has already got two teeth. Schorlemmer leaves for Germany tomorrow week. The table is being laid so I've got to stop.

Your

F. E.

First published in *Der Briefwechsel zwischen F. Engels und K. Marx*, Bd. 4, Stuttgart, 1913

Printed according to the original

Published in English for the first time

171

ENGELS TO EMIL ENGELS Jun.

IN ENGELSKIRCHEN

Great Yarmouth, 20 August 1882

10 Columbia Terrace

Dear Emil,

We have been here for the past 10 days,[366] Schorlemmer, Pumps, BABY[a] and I, and the fact that I haven't got round to replying to you until today can be blamed on the sweet indolence of a seaside resort.

First of all, I have written direct to Sam Moore recommending you to him and asking him to send you the address of his office in town (in the case of BARRISTERS these are called CHAMBERS), for I haven't got it here and during the daytime it is, of course, the only place where he can be found. You will find him an exemplary Englishman, possessing all the good qualities of his nation and none of the bad. Needless to say he is also a Social Democrat and also speaks German though it's a bit rusty. He will be happy to oblige you in any way, provided it is in his power to do so, and will be of more use to you than I could be. When one has been out of touch with the business world for nearly 13 years and with Manchester for 12,[367] one no longer has much influence over people for whom it is axiomatic that one hand washes the other. Moore, on the other hand, has only been out of

_____
[a] Lilian Rosher

touch with it for 3-4 years and still lives in their midst, so in his case it's more likely that something can be arranged. I, for example, don't even know whether the people I used to be connected with are still alive, whether they still own the same business, or whether they may not have sold up entirely. To introduce you to Ermen & Roby would be far more likely to do harm than good; those chaps certainly wouldn't show you their mill and would end up by telling all their other spinning and manufacturing acquaintances on the Exchange to be on their guard against you.

You won't get inside any mills making knitting or sewing yarns, because to my knowledge there are none in Manchester apart from Ermen & Roby. There is a variety of DOUBLERS of SEWINGS where all you will see are the old doubling machines; they sell the yarn untreated. How best to get inside a mill depends upon each particular case; on the whole I have always found that it works best if you make a clean breast of things to the people you've been otherwise recommended to and tell them who you are. To try and get what you want by trickery, as many German spinners have done, nearly always leads to your being found out and denounced to the others on the Exchange, after which you never get to see anything at all. People here compete with one another on a much grander scale than in Germany and the little dodges that are often appropriate enough over there, don't go down at all over here.

Schorlemmer will also be back there at the beginning of October and he, too, will be able to help you. *More* useful to you than anything would be a letter of recommendation from Ermen & Engels to a big German commission house who will surely be able to give you further help and also tell you in which particular instances it might be advisable to keep quiet about what you yourself are.

Well, that's enough for today. The table is about to be laid. Otherwise things are going very well here; the fine weather, Pilsener beer, sea air and sea-bathing have quite driven away the gastric catarrh I had on the Monday of your departure. Pumps and Schorlemmer send you their best wishes.

Your
F. Engels

First published in the magazine *Deutsche Revue*, Jg. 46, Bd. 3, 1921

Printed according to the original

Published in English for the first time

172

MARX TO ENGELS

IN GREAT YARMOUTH

Argenteuil, Monday, 21 August 1882
11 Boulevard Thiers

Dear Fred,

The 'conversion into silver'[a] took place the day before yester-day.

The week beginning last Monday[b] distinguished itself by abominable weather: rain (at times cold), storms, sultriness; above all wet, while a 'water shortage' was 'officially' announced in Paris. Not even the Flood would have deterred the bureaucrats here from contriving an 'official drought' in respect of water for drinking, washing, domestic and industrial purposes, etc.

Yesterday, my last perambulation in the *salle d'inhalation*[c] and the pleasure of a bath and douche at Enghien, where I was also given my valedictory examination by Dr Feugier; result:

1. The bronchial râle much reduced; would have gone completely but for my ill-luck with the weather.

2. The pleuritic *frottement*[d] noise remains in *status quo*; an altogether predictable circumstance. At best, and this is by no means frequent, the after-effects of *pleurésie* may last for years. They are sending me to Lake Geneva, whence the weather reports have so far been favourable, since both *doctores*[e] are of the opinion that the last traces of my bronchial catarrh might well depart of their own accord there. *Qui vivra verra.*[f] The season, they say, is too far advanced for respiratory gymnastics in the mountains, and I must, above all, avoid the cold.

On this occasion I have been ordered to travel to Switzerland only by day and shall therefore have to stay overnight in Dijon and not betake myself to my destination until the morrow. They are absolutely determined, of course, to obviate any pretext for a *'rechute'*.[g]

Tussychen left last Wednesday with Johnny; we have had a letter

---

[a] A jocular hint at the receipt of money from Engels. - [b] 14 August - [c] inhalation room - [d] rubbing - [e] Dourlen and Feugier - [f] We shall see. - [g] relapse

from her; all went well. She intended to go to Eastbourne with Johnny on 19 August (Saturday). Because her pedagogic purposes demand above all that to begin with THE YOUNG MAN should be solely under her supervision, Tussy has chosen a seaside resort where he won't find any 'friends'.

Jennychen is, alas, poorly. What is more, present 'circumstances'[365] make rest and recuperation completely impossible for her.

Laura IS ALL RIGHT, leaves with me *tomorrow*.

Lissagaray's row with the Brousse gang[368] has had one good result in that the latter no longer has a daily paper at its disposal. That diplomat Malon is keeping neutral vis-à-vis Brousse in this affair, since he (Malon) could not permit himself, vis-à-vis Rochefort, his editor-*en-chef*, to express sympathy for Brousse *et cie* in the *Intransigeant* (nor does he 'wish' he 'could').

Guesde and his party are gaining the upper hand.

Best wishes to Jollymeyer[a] and Pumps.

Salut.

'Moor'

Mr Longuet, with his usual tact, is fetching *Roy* to meet me at *déjeuner*[b]; in the course of 3 months the only day he could hit on for the purpose was today, when I have to pack, etc., etc.; in addition, I must pay a farewell visit to Dr Dourlen and, finally, would like to be on my own with Jennychen.

First published abridged in *Der Briefwechsel zwischen F. Engels und K. Marx*, Bd. 4, Stuttgart, 1913 and in full in *MEGA*, Abt. III, Bd. 4, Berlin, 1931

Printed according to the original

Published in English for the first time

---

[a] See this volume, p. 229. - [b] luncheon

173

MARX TO ENGELS

IN GREAT YARMOUTH

Lausanne, 24.August 1882
Hôtel du Nord

Dᴇᴀʀ [Fred],ᵃ

Yesterday, on from Dijon to Lausanne,³⁶⁹ wet and relatively cold. Nine o'clock at night arrived at Lausanne in the rain. First question I asked the waiter: 'How long has it been raining here?' Reply: 'Only been wet for 2 days' (i.e. since the day I left Paris). *C'est drôle!* ᵇ

Today we shall look round in Vevey, Montreux, etc., for somewhere to stay. *In the meantime* write to Lausanne, *poste restante.* I should like to have a timely supply of extra ᴍᴜɴɪᴛɪᴏɴ so that some may always be available against any and every eventuality. Address letters tᴏ Dr Charles Marx, not Karl Marx.

Longuet remained true to his own self till the day of my departure. For during both my previous visits to Argenteuil,³⁷⁰ Longuet kept promising the translator of *Capital,* that poor devil Roy, to arrange a meeting with me; on neither occasion was Longuet able to find a suitable time. And on this occasion, when Longuet again started to maunder on about my meeting Roy, I told him he might arrange it at any time during the last 4 weeks. *Eh bien!* ᶜ *Not until the day of my departure* when I had to pack, pay a farewell call on Dr Dourlen and still had a great deal to discuss with Jennychen, etc., does Longuet go off to Paris without my prior knowledge, pick up Roy and bring him back to *déjeuner* ᵈ (1 o'clock) in Argenteuil. There was a chilly northeast wind and, as a result of my obligatory ᴄᴏɴᴠᴇʀsᴀᴛɪᴏɴ with ᴘᴏᴏʀ Roy in the garden, I caught cold. Tʜᴀɴᴋs ᴛᴏ Longuet!

Apropos. A German who is Paris correspondent to a lot of bourgeois German newspapers wrote to me as my most humble and obedient servant, saying that, while honesty demanded I should know that he was not a Social Democrat, still less correspondent to newspapers of that complexion, people in all circles of German 'society' were

---

ᵃ illegible - ᵇ Funny! - ᶜ Well! - ᵈ luncheon

anxious to have official news of my health; therefore requested TO INTERVIEW me at Argenteuil, etc.

OF COURSE, I DID NOT REPLY TO THAT SOFTSAWDER PENMAN.

Love to all.

Moor

I shall go and see OLD Becker^a and Wróblewski in Geneva as soon as my cough has eased up again.

First published in *MEGA*, Abt. III, Bd. 4, Berlin, 1931

Printed according to the original

Published in English for the first time

174

ENGELS TO MARX

IN LAUSANNE

Great Yarmouth, 25 August 1882
10 Columbia Terrace

Dear Moor,

Telegram just received [284]; a line or two on business in the utmost haste.

Your letter arrived on Monday evening,^b but by then I had sent off to Argenteuil the money order received from A. Kayser & Co. on Hirsch *fils aîné*,^c Paris, 1,200 frs *à présentation*.^d The very next day I wrote to Jenny,[284] telling her what was in the letter, and asked her to make sure it was forwarded. Paying it in from where you are will present little difficulty.

We shall be staying here for another fortnight — it suits everyone marvellously, save for Jollymeyer who sometimes gets rheumatism as a result of the weather we're having. On Monday^e he's off to Ger-

---

^a Johann Philipp Becker - ^b Presumably a slip of the pen in the original. Engels may have received Marx's letter of Monday, 21 August (see this volume, pp. 308-09) either on Tuesday 22 August or Wednesday 23 August.- ^c elder son - ^d at sight - ^e 28 August

many. I shall accompany him to London and hope to bring Tussy and Johnny back here with me.

I wish you better weather than we have been having for the past 4 days, but as much benefit as we are deriving from sea air. The infant[a] is developing a ravenous appetite and visibly gaining weight. Warmest regards from all to you and Laura.

Your
F. E.

What do you think of De Paepe's firing his revolver at Duverger[371]? O GREEN EYED MONSTER![b]

First published abridged in *Der Briefwechsel zwischen F. Engels und K. Marx*, Bd. 4, Stuttgart, 1913 and in full in *MEGA*, Abt. III, Bd. 4, Berlin, 1931

Printed according to the original

Published in English for the first time

175

ENGELS TO MARX

IN LAUSANNE

Great Yarmouth, 26 August 1882
10 Columbia Terrace

Dear Moor,

Your[c] and Laura's letter arrived from Lausanne this morning, and I am using the lull momentarily prevailing in this room to write to you. This time it wasn't you who brought on the bad weather, but *The New York Herald* with its forecast of a depression. Whereas Tussy was able to attribute the previous bout of wet weather here to your undue proximity in Paris, we cannot but observe now that the latest change for the worse coincides precisely with your removal farther afield, and that on Wednesday evening[d] we here were subjected to the same violent downpour as were you in Lausanne. This morning,

---

[a] Lilian Rosher - [b] Shakespeare, *Othello*, Act III, Scene 3. - [c] See this volume, pp. 310-11. - [d] 23 August

too, there has been one shower after another, and there's still no sign of the 'FINER LATER ON' that was predicted. An anathema upon Longuet and his tactlessness. But then, was it absolutely necessary, in a cold north-easter, to entertain Roy in the *garden* of all places? The Egyptian campaign [355] is off to a good start. The *Kölnische Zeitung* goes so far as to maintain that the FORTS of Alexandria were silenced in $2^1/_2$ hours and that the English had continued the bombardment for the remaining 5 hours simply with a view to destroying the city.— The rapid occupation of the Canal was nicely done, but as soon as I saw that upon embarking Wolseley had ostentatiously proclaimed the bombardment of Abukir to be his intention, the whole thing became clear to me and I was able to give Schorlemmer an exposé of the whole plan of campaign as presently being carried out. Since then I have seen from back numbers of the *Kölnische Zeitung* that the plan to march on Cairo via Ismailia had already been common knowledge in London 10 or 12 days beforehand,[a] so well had the secret been kept! The plan itself is still the most rational that could have been devised in the circumstances. However its execution won't be particularly rapid. Admittedly the clever English have sent field guns there, but not horses or mules for the teams. They are presently buying up mules in southern Europe and Africa. *Ballons captifs*,[b] essential for reconnaissance in a flat, treeless country, were rejected, but are now being sent out *belatedly*. Reconnaissances in force were carried out against the fortified Egyptian position before Alexandria—senseless since no one is so stupid as to deploy in strength *before* a fortified position. The heroism at Shafuir is ludicrous—a five-hour engagement and 2 English wounded! Wolseley, who already has 30,000 men, is now calling for his third division, but this is still in process of mobilisation. And when it does arrive he will have barely enough in hand, once he has occupied Cairo and Alexandria, to clear the Delta and occupy the coastal towns. If Arabi is clever enough to parry each main blow and withdraw to Central and/or Upper Egypt, the affair could become extremely protracted. Apart from the fact that, given a somewhat early rise in the level of the Nile, a breaching of the dams can turn everything to water for the

---

[a] 'Paris, 12. Juli', 'Das Bombardement von Alexandrien', *Kölnische Zeitung*, No. 192, 13 July 1882, second edition. - [b] captive balloons

English. However, it is more than probable that the affair will be brought to a conclusion, not by military action, but by diplomatic collusion behind the scenes.

A nice little item: the merits of RED TAPE have been brought to light by C. W. Siemens in his capacity as president of the BRITISH ASSOCIATION.[372] The metric system was, after all, legalised in England alongside the existing one some years ago. Moreover authentic copies of the original metre and original kilogram were sent for from Paris. But if anyone wants to obtain an authentic, standard copy of these units from the appropriate authority, the latter informs him that the relevant Act of Parliament neither entitles nor obliges it to provide one. If, however, you sell by metres or kgs that have *not* been authorised by the aforementioned authority, that is FRAUDULENT and criminal. So this prudent little omission nullifies the whole Act and *basta*, you're back where you started. Moreover, Siemens maintains that, since the introduction of the metric system on the Continent generally, the damage done to English industry by its adherence to the old system has been enormous; a great deal of machinery, etc., he says, is no longer exportable, because built in conformity with units other than metres and kgs.

I hope that your cough has abated and that you, too, may get some better weather at last. Watch out when travelling by steamer. In the evenings it is often cold and misty on the water. You'll probably have to continue to take care of yourself until the spring and then, when you have finally got rid of your bronchitis, some respiratory gymnastics in the mountains will see us round the corner.

In Vaud there is a splendid wine called Ivorne which I highly recommend, especially when it's *old*. Then they drink Cortaillod, a red from Neuchâtel, which has a slight sparkle; the froth forms a star in the centre of the glass; also pretty good. Lastly Veltliner (Valtellina), the best wine in Switzerland. Besides these the *petit*[a] Burgundy, Macon and Beaujolais were pretty good in my day[373] and not dear. Take heroic draughts of all these varieties and, when bored for long spells by your peregrinations, reflect that this is, after all, the only way to restore your former verve; though it may lie dormant for a little while, the day will come when it will be only too necessary to us. My regards to Becker[b] and Wróblewski if you see them.

---

[a] little - [b] Johann Philipp Becker

Warmest regards from everyone here to you and Laura, who will
be the recipient of my *next* letter.[284]

Your

F. E.

First published abridged in *Der Briefwechsel
zwischen F. Engels und K. Marx*, Bd. 4,
Stuttgart, 1913 and in full in *MEGA*,
Abt. III, Bd. 4, Berlin, 1931

Printed according to the original

Published in English for the first
time

176

ENGELS TO JENNY LONGUET

IN ARGENTEUIL

Great Yarmouth, 27 August 1882
10 Columbia Terrace

My dear Jenny,

Many thanks for your letter. I should have been satisfied with
a postcard. I am glad you opened my letter to Mohr and so took care
of the contents.[a]

I had a letter from Lausanne [b] and a telegram from Vevey [374] with
their [c] new address, Hôtel du Léman, where they seem to be inclined
to settle down. As to Mohr's health I was really glad to have a cool
and impartial report from you, Laura who saw him only a few hours,
reported rather over favorably and Tussy on the other hand, on seeing him again at Argenteuil, was rather disappointed that no more
progress had been made. I am quite of your opinion that we have
every reason to be content with what progress he *has* made under the
very unfavorable weather that has persecuted him so tenaciously, and
after three pleurisies, two of which were so severe. I never expected
that he would be able to pass next winter in England, and said so before he went to Algiers to Helen [d] and other discreet people. So that is
no surprise to me; I am only disappointed that he will scarcely be able
to come over before for a few weeks. Anyhow I am glad that the doc-

---

[a] See this volume, p. 311. - [b] Ibid., pp. 310-11. - [c] Marx and Laura Lafargue -
[d] Demuth

tors are so unanimous upon this point, that will make him submit all the easier. A little more Enghien or Cauterets for his remnant of bronchitis and then a climatic cure on high ground in the Alps or Pyrenees will then set him completely up again ready for work. But as you say, all this would be upset by a relapse, which, however, is now unlikely especially with the experience he has gained.

My dear Jenny, I know all the fearful troubles you have had to go through and are going through even now. My thoughts have been often with you and I was sorry I could not find any way in which to make myself useful to you. You and Mohr were almost the constant subjects of our almost daily conversation when I called in the morning at Nim's[a] for my Pilsener beer. But I know my brave Jenny will not lose heart and when you are over the next trial,[b] I hope and expect you will be able to arrange your household in a way that will give you some rest and peace.

You have no idea what a change has come over Pumps since she is here. She occupies herself with nothing but her baby,[c] dress, amusements, pleasure trips, everything seems to have gone out of her head. And she treats the little one well, with excellent temper and patience, but then it is really a very good child, and even now while cutting two teeth, almost always laughing. Let us hope mother and child will continue in the same way.

Schorlemmer who sends his kindest regards leaves tomorrow for Germany, and I shall go to London with him for a day or two to look after business. We shall stay here for another fortnight unless driven away by the weather which has been exceedingly changeable since last Tuesday.[d] Poor Percy[e] who came last Wednesday seems to be destined to have a wet holiday, a bad lookout for a rheumatic subject. As for myself the sea air and bathing is bracing me up famously and I expect this winter I shall do some real work. .

Kind regards from all to Longuet and yourself and children[f] and best love from your affectionately

F. Engels

First published in: Marx and Engels, *Works*, Second Russian Edition, Vol. 35, Moscow, 1964

Reproduced from the original

Published in English for the first time

---

[a] Helene Demuth - [b] birth of a child - [c] Lilian - [d] 22 August - [e] Rosher - [f] Jean, Henri, Edgar and Marcel Longuet

177

MARX TO ENGELS [72]

IN LONDON

[Postcard, unsigned]

Vevey, 4 September 1882
Hôtel du Léman

DEAR FRED,

Laura will be writing to you at length about events, or rather the uneventfulness here, since we are living in the Land of Cockaigne. [374] Like others, we have been for TRIPS on the LAKE.

On 31ST August I got Jennychen's letter enclosing your letter [284] and the CHEQUE which last I handed in at the local bank of Genton et Co. for *encaissement* [a] in Paris.

On 31 August, 1ST, 2ND and 3RD SEPTEMBER marvellous weather (too hot yesterday). Today wet and stormy; hope it won't degenerate into general rain. Odd that I should still be coughing; I think I'm the only person in Vevey who coughs; at all events I haven't met anyone else who does. My GENERAL STATE, however, is most satisfactory; with Laura I climbed not only to the top of the local vineyard, but also to the top of the much higher vineyard at Montreux, without feeling the slightest discomfort.

I was called on at our hotel by a MR Songeon, *président du conseil municipal de Paris* [b]; is one of the *réfugiés* [c] whom I knew in London in 1849-1850. He presented me with the official report made to the *conseil municipal* of Paris by the deputation (amongst whom Mr Songeon) it had sent to Rome for Garibaldi's apotheosis [375]; the thing is mainly concerned with 'Songeon's' own apotheosis, since he always acted as spokesman for the other French delegates. Also showed me a copy of *Capital* which is to accompany him to the sylvan retreat not far removed from here, whither he was wending his way.

So far the English haven't made such rapid progress in Egypt [355] as Wolseley 'prognosticated'.

Mr Virchow, or so I see from the *supplément* to yesterday's *Journal de Genève*, has again demonstrated that he is far and away above

---

[a] collection - [b] Chairman of the Municipal Council of Paris - [c] refugees

Darwin, he alone, in fact, being scientific and hence also 'contemptuous' of organic chemistry.

[On the side reserved for the address]

Fr. Engels, Esq.
122 Regent's Park Road,
London, N. W., *Angleterre*

First published in *Der Briefwechsel zwischen F. Engels und K. Marx*, Bd. 4, Stuttgart, 1913

Printed according to the original

178

ENGELS TO MARX

IN VEVEY

London, 12 September 1882

Dear Moor,

Postcard[a] and Laura's letter received. Am glad to hear you are having good weather at last and hope it will continue. We have been back here since Saturday; Tussy and Johnny spent a week at Yarmouth with us.

I remember Songeon very well; I often used to wonder what destiny might lie in store for that patronising, bonhomous countenance, until I eventually found it in the paper — chairman of the municipal council! That, in fact, was what was already written all over his face in 1850.

Many a bill on London from Genton & Co. has passed through my hands!

If you are planning to see something more of Switzerland, you could hardly take a better or more convenient route than that from Geneva via Berne to Interlaken and Brienz, thence over the Brünig Pass (only 3,150 feet up) to Lake Lucerne and, if you feel like it, from there to Zurich. It's an easy trip for a convalescent and would take

---

[a] See previous letter.

you to some of the loveliest spots in Switzerland. You could make a longish halt at Interlaken and Lucerne or some other place on the shores of that lake. Morges, on Lake Geneva, is also a pretty spot and from it you get the finest view of Mont Blanc.

It is becoming increasingly evident that the Egyptian affair [355] was contrived by Russian diplomacy. Now that Gladstone has been sufficiently soft-sawdered by sweet Olga,[a] he is to be entrusted to a wilier mentor for treatment of a more drastic kind. England has got to occupy Egypt in the midst of peace so that, in self-defence, poor old Russia may thereby be compelled to occupy Armenia, likewise in the midst of peace. The Caucasian army has already moved up to the border, and there are 48 battalions at Kars alone — a constantly mobile army, this. And in order to prove that Gladstone assents to the liberation of yet another 'Christian' country from the yoke of the UNSPEAK-ABLE TURK, this particular moment has been chosen for the ostentatious recall of the English commissions despatched to Asia Minor after the Congress of Berlin [376] to supervise the reforms, and for the publication of their reports which show that they have been fooled by the Turks and that everything remains as before, official corruption being ineradicable. *Palmerston est mort, vive Gladstone! Vive Gambetta,*[b] who would also have gladly put his seal to the Russian alliance in Egypt. Alas, the good old times are a thing of the past, and Russia no longer *backs* Russian diplomacy, but confronts it.

I'd be damned glad if I could come over and see you, but were anything to happen to me, even temporarily, all our financial arrangements would be thrown out of gear. There's not a soul here to whom I could give power of attorney or entrust what are really rather complicated cash transactions. Sam Moore would have been the only possible man, but he is away and these matters can only be attended to on the spot. Besides I had been hoping that you might come over, at any rate this summer, if only for a brief spell. It was obvious to me even before you left England and suffered your relapses that you wouldn't be able to spend next winter here, and I said as much to Lenchen. Now, having had relapses, it is absolutely essential for you to spend a winter that takes the form of spring, and I was glad when I heard that Dourlen and Feugier had said so unequivocally, and with one voice. Lonely though it is here without you, there's nowt as we can do about it, and everything must be subordinated to your

---

[a] Olga Novikova - [b] Palmerston is dead, long live Gladstone! Long live Gambetta

making a complete recovery. But this also demands that finances be kept on an even keel, and I therefore consider it my bounden duty not to run any risks so long as this remains the case.

Hartmann[a] has invented and patented an electric lamp and has sold it for £3,000 to a stingy fellow under a no less stingy contract, so that it is exceedingly doubtful when and whether he will get his money. Meanwhile he has got himself another post — but for how long? It's difficult to make head or tail of his perpetual UPS AND DOWNS.

Best thanks for the Algerian presents brought back by Tussy. The dagger is genuinely oriental — no grass will grow where it's stuck into the ground. I shall have to obtain a stem for the pipe before I can try it out. Pumps is very proud of her Arabian bracelets. She is busy furnishing her new house which will probably take her another week. Her little girl[b] came on remarkably at Yarmouth. Johnny has been going to infant school since yesterday (in Grafton Terrace, opposite your old home).

Love from all to yourself and Laura.

Your
F. E.

First published in *Der Briefwechsel zwischen F. Engels und K. Marx*, Bd. 4, Stuttgart, 1913

Printed according to the original

Published in English for the first time

179

ENGELS TO KARL KAUTSKY [7]

IN VIENNA

London, 12 September 1882

Dear Mr Kautsky,

You really must forgive me for having kept you waiting so long for an answer. I have had so many interruptions of every kind that finally, in order to get any work done at all, I had to give short shrift to

---

[a] Lev Hartmann - [b] Lilian Rosher

everything of lesser importance and put aside all such correspondence as was not absolutely necessary. And since, with your colonial question,[377] you had set me a task that was by no means easy to tackle, your letters met with the same fate, and in the process the good Walter got overlooked.

Should Walter and Dr Braun come over here, I shall be glad to see them and whatever can be done for them I will gladly do. As for the rest, it will no doubt turn out all right. But *what* is Walter actually expected to study over here? That's what needs clearing up first of all. Socialism as such? No need for him to come over here for that, since it's to be had everywhere save in Austria and Germany; moreover, he will quickly exhaust that field, i. e. such literature as is worth reading. Economics? History? Of these he will find an *embarras de richesses* ᵃ at the British Museum — so much so, indeed, that a newcomer runs the risk of instantly losing his bearings. Natural science? That would mean lectures which are wildly expensive here. It seems to me that, before the chap is sent over here, a definite curriculum should be laid down for his studies — at least in outline — and if this were sent to me, it would be easier to judge whether it could best be carried out in this country or somewhere else. Without at least *some* knowledge of English, he would be completely at a loss here. It would, I think, be a good idea to get him to study French and English for 6 months beforehand, so that he could at least read a modicum of both before he went abroad. He should, besides, have some previous knowledge of history, geography and, if possible, also mathematics and natural science if he wants to study profitably. What the situation is in this respect I cannot know; but if it's at all unsatisfactory, it would certainly be better if you first got him to come to Vienna, so that he might acquire these things under the guidance of his friends and generally learn exactly *how* one sets about learning something thoroughly off one's own bat. Otherwise, here in London, it would, for the most part, be money down the drain. These are simply thoughts that have passed through my mind when pondering on the case and which may be completely irrelevant, but after all I know little or nothing about the young man's level of education, and that is why I considered it necessary to raise these points. If you let me know more about this, you will not be kept waiting for an answer. All things being equal I am, as you know, always in favour of getting ambitious young peo-

---

ᵃ too great a profusion

ple to come abroad so that they may extend their horizons and rid themselves of the parochial prejudices which they must needs acquire at home.

You should not, by the way, count too much on Marx so far as Walter is concerned. He is unlikely to come home before next May, and even then he will probably have to take great care of himself if he is to get his work completed. In particular he is now strictly forbidden to talk overmuch, on top of which he has to spend his evenings quietly if he is not to have bad nights. In the daytime, however, he will, of course, be working. If one is trying to get rid of chronic bronchitis of many years' standing and ensure, after three serious bouts of pleurisy, not only that it disappears without trace, but also that it doesn't recur, and to do all this in one's sixty-fifth year, one has enough to contend with on that account alone.

You ask me what the English workers think of colonial policy. Well, exactly what they think of any policy — the same as what the middle classes think. There is, after all, no labour party here, only conservatives and liberal radicals, and the workers cheerfully go snacks in England's monopoly of the world market and colonies. As I see it, the actual colonies, i. e. the countries occupied by European settlers, such as Canada, the Cape, Australia, will all become independent; on the other hand, countries that are merely ruled and are inhabited by natives, such as India, Algeria and the Dutch, Portuguese and Spanish possessions, will have to be temporarily taken over by the proletariat and guided as rapidly as possible towards independence. How this process will develop is difficult to say. India may, indeed very probably will, start a revolution and, since a proletariat that is effecting its own emancipation cannot wage a colonial war, it would have to be given its head, which would obviously entail a great deal of destruction, but after all that sort of thing is inseparable from any revolution. The same thing could also happen elsewhere, say in Algeria or Egypt, and would certainly suit *us* best. We shall have enough on our hands at home. Once Europe has been reorganised, and North America, the resulting power will be so colossal and the example set will be such that the semi-civilised countries will follow suit quite of their own accord; their economic needs alone will see to that. What social and political phases those countries will then have to traverse before they likewise acquire a socialist organisation is something about which I do not believe we can profitably speculate at present. Only one thing is certain, namely that a victorious proletariat cannot forcibly confer any boon whatever on another country without undermining its own victory in the process. Which does not, of course, in any way preclude defensive wars of various kinds. This business in Egypt [355] has been contrived by Russian diplomacy. Gladstone is to take Egypt (which he is far from having or from holding, even if he had it), so that Russia may take Armenia; which would, according to Gladstone, be the liberation of another Christian country from the Mohammedan yoke. Everything else to do with the affair is pretence, humbug, prevarication. Whether the little scheme will succeed will soon become apparent.

With kindest regards.

Yours,

F. E.

Dr Sax has just sent me his book on Thuringia.[a] Would you thank him for it on my behalf and tell him I shall reply as soon as I have read it.

My forwarding address is: Mrs P. W. Rosher, 122 Regent's Park Road; *no* inner envelope. It's Pumps who, incidentally, has already got a baby girl.[b] She doesn't actually live with me any more, but that doesn't matter.

First published in full, in Russian, in *Marx-Engels Archives*, Vol. I (VI), Moscow, 1932

Printed according to the original

Published in English in full for the first time

180

ENGELS TO EDUARD BERNSTEIN

IN ZURICH

London, 13 September 1882

Dear Mr Bernstein,

Nothing came of working at the seaside resort of Yarmouth —

---

[a] E. Sax, *Die Hausindustrie in Thüringen*. - [b] Lilian Rosher

5 people in one room, including my niece[a] and her 4-month-old baby,[b] made it impossible to do anything, and work was dissipated in pleasure and the consumption of excellent Pilsener beer. But tomorrow I go into action, and there'll be no respite until the pamphlet is finished.[378]

Your suggestion *re* a preface on Bismarckian socialism is quite all right so far as it goes, and up to a point accords with what I myself want. But this stuff could not be dealt with in a preface; it would make it far too long. Besides, I could do with more material on accident insurance, etc., especially the proposed legislation, without which I cannot manage.

I have been turning the matter over in my mind for a long time, and I can well see that something ought to be written about it. I now propose to write (for the *Sozialdemokrat*) a series of articles (each of which would constitute an independent whole) on the kind of bogus socialism now proliferating in Germany — a series which could subsequently be published in pamphlet form.[379] First part: Bismarckian socialism. 1. Protective tariffs. 2. Nationalisation of railways. 3. Tobacco monopoly. 4. Workmen's insurance. But for this I should have to have:

ad[c] 2, a stock-exchange list giving the prices of the recently nationalised railways (Berg. Märk., Berlin-Görlitz, Berlin-Stettin, Märkisch-Posen) shortly *before* nationalisation and, wherever possible, the price paid by the state for these railways;

ad 4, the Bill as submitted to the Reichstag by Bismarck.

If you can procure these things for me, I shall have sufficient material.

To this, I would, however, append a second part in which I would criticise a number of woolly ideas enfranchised by Lassalle and still echoed now and again by our people — e. g. the 'iron law of wages',[289] 'the full return to the *labourer*' (not *labourers*) 'for work performed',[380] etc. To make a clean sweep here is even more necessary than it would be in respect of the first part, and if this annoys some of those Lassallean 'leaders' who have unfortunately come to be accepted,[381] so much the better. Hence I do in fact regard the second part as the more important one.

On the other hand, there's no knowing whether it mightn't just suit

---

[a] Mary Ellen Rosher (Pumps) - [b] Lilian Rosher - [c] as regards

the book of certain persons if St Ferdinand[a] were to be subjected to this kind of unbiassed criticism. It might be said, should anything of the sort appear in the party organ, that it was an attempt to provoke a split in the party and a breach of the long-standing compact with the Lassalleans. In which case the whole thing might be brought out in pamphlet form as soon as it was finished, without prior publication in the *Sozialdemokrat*.

So either the *whole thing* appears in the *Sozialdemokrat*, and subsequently as a pamphlet,

or it appears straight away as a pamphlet,

or, for the time being, does not get written at all.

Voilà mon cas.[b] Well, you choose what you would prefer and, if necessary, consult one or two others. But once something has been settled, there must be no going back on it. I cannot expose myself to another dose of the unpleasantness occasioned by Most's protests against the *Dühring*.[382]

Incidentally, some very nice preparatory work relating to Bismarckery and attendant phenomena has already been done in two articles in the *Sozialdemokrat* on the possible repeal of the Anti-Socialist Law.[383] I assume they are by Bebel; if not, the party can congratulate itself upon possessing another chap who is so splendidly capable of getting to the root of the matter and disregarding all considerations of a secondary nature, and this in a style at once so straightforward and lucid. The articles are first-rate.

What you say by way of an excuse for the flabbiness of various people in Germany is something I have already told myself on more than one occasion. Yet again and again we find the same old German want of character and backbone, coupled with the urge to play the role — vis-à-vis the philistine, not the worker — of a worthy, respectable citizen who is a very far cry from the dangerous ogre he is made out to be. These always turn out to be people who consider their modicum of education absolutely essential if the worker is not to emancipate himself but rather be liberated by them. In their eyes, the emancipation of the working class is attainable only through your eddicated mediocrity; how could the poor, helpless, uneddicated workers hope to achieve it on their own account?

I wrote to Kautsky yesterday.[c] He tells me he has found some quite

---

[a] Ferdinand Lassalle - [b] That's my position. - [c] See previous letter.

passable *doctores philosophiae*ᵃ there. If they *really* are passable, they would be most welcome.

Adolf Beust will be able to sing you the tune of 'The Vicar of Bray'.³⁸⁴

Kindest regards.

Yours,

F. E.

First published, in Russian, in *Marx-Engels Archives*, Book I, Moscow, 1924

Printed according to the original

Published in English for the first time

181

MARX TO ENGELS

IN LONDON

Vevey, 16 September 1882
Hôtel du Léman

DEAR FRED,

Just as I was about to write to you, the *garçon*ᵇ brought me the *Journal de Genève* with the news of Bebel's death.ᶜ It's frightful — the greatest misfortune for our party! He was a unique phenomenon in the German (one might say in the 'European') working class.

Your altruistic concern for me is unbelievable, and I am often secretly ashamed — but I won't pursue this theme any further for the present.

My plan, before I left Paris, was AT ALL EVENTS to spend at least October in London and to be together with you. Feugier and Dourlen also thought there could be no objection to this, should October prove passable. It might yet be so, despite September being wet. The barometer rose here on the 8th, reached the top of the scale on the 9th,

---

ᵃ doctors of philosophy - ᵇ waiter - ᶜ The news turned out to be false (see this volume, pp. 328, 330).

gradually fell right down to the bottom on the 12th, rose again on the 13th (having reached about the same level as on the 11th), then fell and has, since last night, been slowly rising again. Although GENERALLY throughout Switzerland there has been heavy rain and storms (many landslides and 'ACCIDENTS' resulting therefrom), the weather round about Vevey in particular has been relatively good (cold only by way of an exception in the mornings and early hours of the evening). This is why we have continued to stay here. The air is invigorating. Despite perpetual changes of temperature and humidity in the course of the same day, my sense of well-being is steadily mounting. My catarrh is, I think, no longer bronchial but has turned into the ordinary kind; but I shall not know this for certain until I get to Geneva where I shall consult a good German doctor, i. e. get him to auscultate me. But the trip you suggest,[a] delightful though it would be, is unlikely to be feasible in present Swiss weather conditions. This year's vintage would seem to be a 'flop'. Indeed, snow can already be seen to be falling — earlier than usual — on the *montagnes de la*[b] Dent du Midi; it's 'REGULAR' on the Jura.

The Bernese *Bund* has declared that as a military commander Wolseley almost surpasses the old Napoleon.

There's one snag about the goings-on with the Russians[c]; it's quite possible that Bismarck would allow them — the last-mentioned — to commit themselves, but what we should see next would be 'consolation prizes' for Austria and COMPENSATION for the Prussian imperium. Thus Russian intervention in Armenia might lead to general war, and that is probably what Bismarck wants.

Apropos! The dagger, as you can no doubt see from the crudeness of the workmanship, is of Kabyle [385] origin. As regards the stem for the pipe, I brought 3 such — bamboo stems — with me (at the *jardin d'acclimatation*[d] the pipes were provided with only one); I didn't want to burden Helen[e] and Tussy with these stems which were too long for their *malles*,[f] but was planning to bring them to London myself.

From Jennychen's letter — just received by Laura — I see that *Longuet* has gone to Aubin *with Wolf*[g] *and Harry*. Unfortunately Jennychen's health gives cause for concern, as I had already been told by the doctors (Feugier and Dourlen) in Paris. Jennychen anxiously awaits news of Johnny from London; she has had NO NEWS since Tus-

---

[a] See this volume, pp. 318-19. - [b] mountains of the - [c] See this volume, p. 319. - [d] Botanical Gardens - [e] Demuth - [f] trunks - [g] Edgar Longuet

sychen's trip to Yarmouth with Johnny. Indeed Laurachen is writing to Jennychen today and telling her that John is ALL RIGHT and has already started going to infant school, as we saw from your letter. [a]

Love to Tussychen, Lenchen and Pumps, AND NOT TO FORGET, MY GRANDSON. [b]

We shall in any case write and tell you if we leave Vevey.

Your
Moor

Have not the Prussian scoundrels, by imprisonment, etc., been party to Bebel's death?

First published abridged in *Der Briefwechsel zwischen F. Engels und K. Marx*, Bd. 4, Stuttgart, 1913 and in full in *MEGA*, Abt. III, Bd. 4, Berlin, 1931

Printed according to the original

Published in English for the first time

182

ENGELS TO MARX

IN VEVEY

London, 18 September 1882

Dear Moor,

Your [c] and Laura's letter arrived at 9 o'clock in the evening; I at once went to impart what was necessary to Tussy and Lenchen.

We over here were also exceedingly perturbed by the false news of Bebel's death. [386] Since Saturday night there had been many indications that it was false, and in the *Justice*, just received, there's a telegram from Liebknecht saying that, while Bebel had been dangerously ill, he was now on the mend.

At the same time I turned up most opportunely, the news having

---

[a] See this volume, pp. 318-20. - [b] Jean Longuet - [c] See previous letter.

just been received that Jenny had had a baby girl [365] and that everything was going as well as could be expected.

When you go away from Vevey, leave an address (poste restante or
something of the sort) for letters. Will write at greater length tomorrow or the day after.

Your

F. E.

Love to Laura.

First published in *Der Briefwechsel zwischen
F. Engels und K. Marx*, Bd. 4, Stuttgart,
1913

Printed according to the original

Published in English for the first
time

183

ENGELS TO LAURA LAFARGUE

IN VEVEY

London, 20 September 1882

My dear Laura,

I hope Mohr got my short note of the 18th.[a] Today, though under
difficulties, I must fulfil my word to you. Have worked all day till six,
then dined, now it's just nine, and so I am still a little under the influence of digestion, and besides Percy[b] is sitting in the room but fortunately has got hold of *Joseph Andrews*.[c]

Do I know Vevey? Why I was quartered there in September
1849 [373] for about a fortnight and know all the Swiss shore of the lake
from Villeneuve to Geneva, the Dent du Midi and the Mont Blanc
and all the rest. If I am not much mistaken we officers were quartered
in your Hotel on the Quay. On the square under the trees, facing the
lake, Willich used to exercise his two horses.

I am only sorry you cannot even partially follow the route I made

---

[a] See previous letter. - [b] Rosher - [c] H. Fielding, *The History of the Adventures of Joseph
Andrews and His Friend Mr. Abraham Adams.*

out for you, [a] the Bernese Oberland in many respects beats the lake of Geneva hollow. But if Mohr is to try for a visit to England in October, it will soon be time for you to leave the Alps. I do hope there will be no risk to him in trying to come. Otherwise it would be folly. But let the doctors decide, as also about his winter-resort. Only if he is to come he ought not to drive it too late. We have had fine but rather cold weather, especially night and morning; yesterday rain all day, today dry but mostly dull. By the way, Mohr's statistics of the barometer [b] tally exactly with our experiences at the time at Yarmouth, only that we had a very wet day with the highest barometer, Tussy praying all the time for the stupid thing to fall again!

As to the star-foaming wine, that quality is the exclusive property of *Cortaillod* — the other Neuchâtel wines do not possess it as far as I know, nor are they so good.

I wonder who got up that foolish story about Bebel. [c] The Cologne Gazette [d] up to Friday last week [c] (date of the Paris papers that reported it) knows or at least tells nothing about it. The thing looks as if it was a canard concocted by Mehring and worked at Paris by Hirsch. I may be on the wrong scent, but I should not be at all astonished if it was so. Who else should have so quickly put in the *Bataille* and in the *Citoyen* a necrology, in which (in the *Bataille* at least) an *o l d* speech of Bebel's was quoted that he was for lawful means exclusively? The fright we got was something awful. On Friday night two members of the Working Men's Society Tottenham St. [297] came and asked me, was it true? That was the first I heard. Tussy had the *Bataille* with the article mentioned above same night; the silence of the *Justice* might be explained by Longuet's absence. Hunting up German papers in the cafés was useless; the nos that could contain anything would no longer lie on the tables on Saturday. At last, Tussy (not I) got her *Sozialdemokrat* on Saturday night, and that was not only silent, but stated that Bebel was fit to go out again. To lose Bebel would have been irreparable. Where to find such another head not only in Germany but anywhere else? Where such theoretical clearness, such practical tact, such quiet determination among the younger generation? Well, it's not true and the relief I felt when all doubt had disappeared, I cannot describe.

I am also extremely glad that Jenny has got over her crisis and that

---

[a] See this volume, pp. 318-19. - [b] Ibid., pp. 326-27.- [c] A reference to the false news of Bebel's death. - [d] *Kölnische Zeitung* - [e] 15 September

the result is the fulfilment of a wish long felt by many.[365] I believe she had a very hard time of it. No doubt Dourlen has provided her with someone to look after her, the people at 41 Maitland Park[a] make no doubt he has, and in that case the absence of the 'creator'[b] might perhaps be a blessing.

Little Pumpsia[c] has the chicken-pox and is very restless and takes at last to crying. The whole affair will be over in a few days and would not upset her so but for two pimples having come out on her tongue which, together with the coming of two teeth, make her mouth feel rather painful. Otherwise everything all well.

Love from all to yourself and Mohr and from yours affectionately,

F. Engels

Bernstein writes that 'The Vicar of Bray'[384] has created a tremendous sensation.

Tussy had written *three times* to Jenny, since her return here, up to *last Sunday*!

First published, in the language of the original (English), in: F. Engels, P. et L. Lafargue, *Correspondance*, t. I, Paris, 1956

Reproduced from the original

184

ENGELS TO EDUARD BERNSTEIN

IN ZURICH

London, 22 September 1882

Dear Mr Bernstein,

Herewith preface, chapters I and II. No. III has also been completed, as has a concluding note of some 7 pages on early German common ownership of land ('The Mark').[378] But I want to revise it thoroughly once again and shall keep it here for a while.

The puff at the beginning is something I cannot allow. Because

---

[a] Eleanor Marx and Helene Demuth - [b] Charles Longuet - [c] Lilian Rosher

Lafargue was the editor of the French edition and Malon sent in a highly inadequate affair, Marx wrote this introduction [20] with Lafargue, which may have been suitable on that occasion. In a German edition edited by myself, that sort of thing simply wouldn't do. However, once Marx is back here I might at some time write a little pamphlet for you on the theme of German socialism from 1840 to '52. [387] It's got to be done some day. But Marx has got more than half the material, and God knows where he's tucked it away.

I would, of course, have to have *both* drafts of the Accident Insurance Act, ditto all the new bills of a social nature submitted to the Reichstag in the autumn.

The wholesale condemnation of indirect taxation had been mooted by us as far back as 1849 and '50, [388] and that's where Lassalle got it from. I have noted the other things you say about Lassalle. Certain points are open to objection, but that's neither here nor there. Lassalle as a *person* simply doesn't come into it, but I cannot do otherwise than demolish the illusion that Lassalle was an original thinker in the economic (or indeed any other) field. [a]

I am glad to hear that the articles were written by Vollmar [383]; it shows how much he has come on. I quite agree with what you say about the Anti-Socialist Law. [16] We shall benefit only if the law is *purement et simplement* [b] abrogated. And that will happen only if new life can somehow be injected into the German political puppet-show, and if something should happen immediately conducive to a revolution, a new era, [277] Russian constitution or something of the sort. In which case there can be no doubt that we shall obtain majorities everywhere where there are now strong minorities and, besides Saxony, win over all the larger towns.

As for the French, your plaint is the eternal one which everybody voices. They are governed by the moment, and by personalities. I don't read the *Citoyen* and do not get the *Égalité* at all regularly, nor do I know whether it still exists, so cannot have any real idea of what the chaps have been up to of late. But of one thing you may be sure — there can be no peace with Brousse. The latter is, and will remain, a consummate anarchist, his only concession being the admissibility of participating in elections; moreover *he* and Malon, by throwing the others out of the Fédération du Centre, [265] have intensified the struggle in the conduct of which Brousse is employing wholly Bakuninist

---

[a] See this volume, pp. 324-25. - [b] purely and simply

tactics—slander, lies and every imaginable dirty trick. The tactics the others employ may on occasion be silly and childish, may fail in their objective and make it impossible for us foreigners to intervene on their behalf (as, indeed, we have regularly refused to do), but the fact remains that it has become impossible, once and for all, to do anything whatever in concert with Brousse. He will not rest content until his clique, 'Alliance'-fashion, [67] has gained control of the entire movement. Come to that, the whole of the 'workers' party', both factions included, constitutes only a small and dwindling portion of the Parisian working-class masses. The latter still continue to follow men like Clemenceau, against whom Guesde has conducted his polemic in a way that is far too personal and also quite wrong in other respects. Besides, Clemenceau is perfectly capable of development and might, given the chance, go much further than at present, especially once he has realised that what is entailed is a *class struggle*; true, he won't realise this until he *has to*. Now, Guesde has got it firmly into his head that Gambetta's *république athénienne* [a] is far less of a threat to socialists than Clemenceau's *république spartiate*, [b] and hence wishes to prevent the latter, as though we or any party in the world could prevent a country from passing through its historically necessary stages of development; nor has he stopped to think that it would be difficult to attain socialism in the France of a republic *à la* Gambetta without having first passed through a republic *à la* Clemenceau. But in the absence of such an insight into the necessary historical context of things and hence into the probable course of their development, party politics cannot be pursued with success. However, I have thrown up the sponge and am leaving the chaps to their own devices. Nor will the Belgians get anywhere with their admonitions.

John Stuart Mill's niece and adoptive daughter, who contributed to the election fund, is called *Helen* Taylor and is not therefore the same as Ellen M. Taylor. Although both these Christian names mean Helena, they are two quite distinct persons.

I know absolutely nothing about Garcia. [c] From time to time someone from the club [8] comes to see me, and I shall ask about him when the occasion arises.

Apropos. How did the rumour about Bebel's death get into the *Citoyen* and the *Bataille?* It came as a tremendous shock to us over

---

[a] Athenian republic - [b] Spartan republic - [c] See this volume, pp. 347-48.

here—as it did to Marx in Vevey, where he spent 3 weeks, [374] and we had no means of verifying it until we got the *Justice* on Monday evening, containing a telegram with Liebknecht's *démenti*; for the information, or lack of it, in the *Sozialdemokrat* could not reassure us completely because of its having been published on the Thursday.—By now Marx will probably be on his way back to Argenteuil, though he might spend a few days in Geneva. He is better but the poor summer has undone most of the good work effected by the cure.

I would ask you to briefly acknowledge receipt of the ms., and also to send me the ms. *with* the proofs,—in a wrapper, of course. How long can I keep the remainder [a] here without causing inconvenience?

Kindest regards,

Yours,

F. E.

First published, in Russian, in *Marx-Engels Archives*, Book I, Moscow, 1924

Printed according to the original

Published in English for the first time

185

ENGELS TO AUGUST BEBEL

IN LEIPZIG

London, 23 September 1882

Dear Bebel,

We have had a fine old fright on your account. A week ago yesterday, on Friday the 15th [b] inst., 2 people from the Society [8] came to see me at 10 o'clock at night in order to ascertain the truth of the report, which had already appeared (with obituary) in 2 issues of the *Citoyen*, that you were dead. I told them that it was highly unlikely but could

---

[a] A reference to Chapter III of the German translation of Engels' *Socialism: Utopian and Scientific* and the article 'The Mark' appended to it (see this volume, pp. 331-32). -
[b] 16th in the ms.

say nothing definite. As I had a boring visitor sitting with me, who wouldn't go although I had ceased to utter a word, it was not until after 11 that I was able to hurry round to Tussy Marx and found her still up. She had the *Bataille*, likewise with an obituary, but with no details as to the source of the news which was, however, considered to be beyond doubt. Hence general consternation. The greatest misfortune that could befall the German party was at least a strong probability. That there should have been no mention of it in the English papers, exulting as they were over Egypt,[355] was only too understandable. Well, on Saturday evening my *Sozialdemokrat* failed to arrive, which sometimes happens, but on Sunday morning I was lucky enough to discover that Tussy had got hers and, to judge by its contents, the news seemed highly improbable. To have consulted German newspapers in cafés would have been hopeless from the start, since they replace them each day. And so we remained in a state of the most excruciating uncertainty until finally, on Monday evening, the *Justice* arrived with an official denial.

Marx had just the same experience. He was at Vevey on Lake Geneva[374] and read the story in the reactionary *Journal de Genève* which naturally retailed it as being beyond doubt. He wrote to me the same day absolutely aghast.[a] His letter arrived that same Monday evening and so I was able to convey to him by the early post the happy news that the whole thing was an invention.[b]

No, old fellow, you won't be allowed to peg out on us at such a tender age. You're 20 years younger than I am, we have many a jolly battle ahead of us and, when we have fought them side by side, it will be your duty to stay in the firing line, even though I may have cut my last caper. And, since people alleged to be dead are supposed to live longest, you, like Marx,[389] have now doubtless been condemned to a good long life.

But who in heaven's name brought this nonsense up—is that liar Mehring at the back of it again[390]?

Did you get my last letter—written some 2-3 months ago? The one in which I replied about the tamer elements in the party?[c]

Meanwhile you will have seen that your wish that I should contribute openly to the *Sozialdemokrat* has been met on several occasions. Moreover I yesterday sent off to Bernstein the first two of the three

---

[a] See this volume, p. 326. - [b] Ibid., p. 328. - [c] Ibid., pp. 280-83.

Dühring chapters which are to come out in German after the French edition [360] and which I have extensively revised and popularised. The rest is finished but I shall keep it here, provided it does not upset the printing arrangements, so that this, the most difficult section, can be thoroughly gone over again. An appendix will follow in the shape of a lengthy note on early German common ownership of land. When you go to quod I would advise you to procure from one library or another:

G. L. v. Maurer, *Einleitung in die Geschichte der Marken-, Hof-, Dorf- und Städteverfassung in Deutschland,*
also his *Geschichte der Markenverfassung in Deutschland.*

It is very necessary that someone in Germany should familiarise himself to some extent with the subject — a person capable of reading these things with an open mind and without ready-made 'cultivated' preconceptions. These are the chief works and a knowledge of them would mean that you would have extremely solid foundations to go on in any debate about landownership or agrarian questions.

Judging by the few articles he has written in the *Sozialdemokrat* (on the possible repeal of the Anti-Socialist Law), [383] Vollmar would appear to have turned out very well. I should be glad if this also proved to be the case elsewhere; we could damned well do with some efficient chaps.

Marx is slowly recovering from his three attacks of pleurisy. For his long-standing, highly troublesome, sleep-inhibiting bronchial cough he had recourse while in Argenteuil to the nearby sulphur springs at Enghien, but in view of the bad weather did not, out of consideration for his general condition, effect the complete recovery that would otherwise have been virtually certain. After that he went to Vevey for three weeks with Madame Lafargue, intending to leave there the day before yesterday, first for Geneva, then Paris and then, given passable weather, to come over here for a few weeks in October. Under no circumstances ought he to spend the winter in London, but whether in the south of England or elsewhere is for the doctors to decide. However I can tell from his letters that there has been a steady improvement, albeit hampered by the bad summer.

Where exactly are you chaps at this moment? It seems as though you have all been turned by the 'Lesser' [198] into a lot of Flying Dutchmen, just as Marx has been by his illness.

Give Liebknecht my kindest regards when you see him.

The whole Egyptian affair is an act of vengeance by the Jews (Rothschild, Erlanger, etc.) for their erstwhile expulsion from Egypt under Pharaoh. [391]

Your

F. E.

First published abridged in the newspaper *Vorwärts*, Nr. 44, 22 February 1910 and in full, in Russian, in *Marx-Engels Archives*, Vol. I (VI), Moscow, 1932

Printed according to the original

Published in English for the first time

186

MARX TO ENGELS

IN LONDON

Paris, [392] 28 September 1882

DEAR FRED,

A letter from Laura in which I had enclosed a note [284] was accidentally left lying on the writing-desk at Laura's and so cannot be sent off before the post goes. [393] But in order that no time may be lost, I would again ask you to send me some bank notes from London as soon as possible (*address* as before to Argenteuil), in case Dr Dourlen, as I hope, allows me TO CROSS THE CHANNEL.

Today rain is pelting down from the so-called heavens, despite the fact that Alphand continues to fear a *famine d'eau*. [a]

At the same time, drop me a couple of LINES AS TO THE state of the weather in London.

Moor

First published in *Der Briefwechsel zwischen F. Engels und K. Marx*, Bd. 4, Stuttgart, 1913

Printed according to the original

Published in English for the first time

---

[a] water shortage

187

MARX TO ENGELS [72]

IN LONDON

Paris, 30 September 1882

Dear FRED,

Just as I was on the point of leaving Argenteuil for here (i. e. *la Gare* [a] St Lazare), to wait for Laura, dine with her in Paris and return with her to Argenteuil, I was caught by the *facteur* [b] with your letter [284] and enclosure. Laura will be arriving in ABOUT A quarter of an hour, PROBABLY with your letter to her.

Today I was examined by Dr Dourlen in Jennychen's PRESENCE. The *r â l e m e n t m u q u e u x* [c] *has disappeared*; SOME *whistling* remains but I am well on the way to ridding myself of this persistent catarrh, the character of which has already changed considerably. My GENERAL *habitus* [d] has, it appears, improved enormously in addition to which I have grown 'fatter'.

Under no circumstances does he wish me to spend more than a fortnight — 3 weeks if the weather is really fine — in London. He is less afraid of moderate cold than of a moist atmosphere. Nor, under any circumstances, am I to travel via Calais by the special night train, but go to Calais by day and not leave there till the day after, by the morning STEAMER.

For the rest, *la campagne de l'hiver,* [e] as he called it, should start early, in the Isle of Wight, Jersey, Morlaix (Brittany) or Pau. Otherwise he would sooner I *didn't stay anywhere too far south* except IN CASE OF NEED, which is also why he had considered Vevey a better place for me than Montreux which is warmer. He assumes that normal temperatures, etc., will not suddenly rebel again in consequence of my arrival. Finally, he will *not* give me *definite* 'permission' to leave for London *until* his mind has been set at rest by the meteorological bulletins for the next few days. (French doctors are strongly prejudiced against the London climate.) He is now certain the cure will be complete, provided no mistakes are made. Hence I shall not get away before Tuesday [f] at the earliest.

---

[a] the station - [b] postman - [c] *mucous râle* - [d] condition - [e] winter campaign - [f] 3 October

If the French government — AS REPRESENTED BY THE SWINDLING FINANCIER Duclerc — knew of my presence here (particularly in view of the absence of the Chamber), it might, even without Dr Dourlen's permission, send me packing, the *'Marxistes'* and *'Anti-Marxistes'* having, at their respective socialist congresses at Roanne and St-Étienne, [394] both done their damnedest to ruin my stay in France. Nevertheless, I regard it as some compensation that the selfsame Alliance gang — the Malons, Brousses, etc. — should have seen their hopes so sadly dashed *in as much as* (to use our Bruno's [a] favourite turn of speech) the 'unspoken' innuendo, 'Marx is a "German", alias "Prussian", hence French *"Marxistes"* too are traitors', could no longer cut any ice with anyone, nor yet dare make itself 'heard', even for a moment. *C'est un progrès.* [b]

Clemenceau has been seriously ill and has not quite recovered yet. He, too, took *Capital* with him from Paris to read while he was ill. It would now seem to be the fashion for FRENCH REAL OR WOULD BE 'ADVANCED' LEADERS — IF 'THE DEVIL BE SICK'. [395]

Love to all, not forgetting Jollymeyer.

Moor

I shall write or telegraph before I leave France.

First published abridged in *Der Briefwechsel zwischen F. Engels und K. Marx*, Bd. 4, Stuttgart, 1913 and in full in *MEGA*, Abt. III, Bd. 4, Berlin, 1931

Printed according to the original

188

MARX TO LAURA LAFARGUE [72]

IN PARIS

[London,] 9 October 1882
41 Maitland Park Road, N. W.

Dear Cacadou,

The weather over here isn't bad, i. e. there are a few reasonably fine hours when the sun is shining brightly; for the rest a cloudy sky

_____
[a] Bauer - [b] It's a step forward.

and occasional showers of rain; not cold generally speaking and the old, familiar fog only in the mornings and evenings.

Schorlemmer came up to London on Saturday, [a] just for a friendly reunion; he has got to return to Manchester this evening, since he has to 'perpetrate' a lecture there tomorrow. He sends you his kindest regards.

Engels is most annoyed at not having been sent the *Égalité* for many months past, nor is my copy of that paper now being despatched to London. How much is the subscription to the *Citoyen*, incl. postage to London? I forgot about it when I left Paris and shall send a MONEY ORDER immediately on hearing from you.

Yesterday we dined with Engels; Pumps was there too, OF COURSE, with her BABY [b] and Percy. [c] The BABY is very cheerful and her conversation livelier than that of her *maman* — at all events.

Yesterday evening Donkin came to see me, but won't be giving me a medical examination until later this week; he thought I was looking better. He considers the ISLE OF Wight to be the best place for me to stay during the approaching FOG TIME OF England.

Johnny is cheerful and, on the whole, 'HAPPY', although it's touching how often he speaks of his *maman* [d] and Harry. Under Tussy's guidance he has once again acquired the habit of washing himself from head to foot in 'cold water' every morning. His 'well-being' leaves nothing to be desired; going to bed regularly at an early hour (8 p. m.) also suits him. His learning has progressed as far as 'capital letters', likewise to deciphering the large Roman numerals on clocks.

I am most anxious that you should send me news of Jenny's STATE, personal and domestic. Is the Longuet FAMILY [e] back yet?

The great agitator, St Paul, [f] will, OF COURSE, again be enthroned on the heights of the Boulevard de Port-Royal. [g] Write and tell me about his ADVENTURES, but above all about yourself — how you are and how things are going.

My cough is still tiresome, but more as a *MEMENTO* that I have got to throw it off completely if I am to become ALTOGETHER fit for action again.

Lenchen and Johnny send their love.

---

[a] 7 October - [b] Lilian Rosher - [c] Percy Rosher - [d] Jenny Longuet - [e] Charles Longuet and his sons Henri, Edgar and Marcel - [f] Paul Lafargue - [g] Paris address of the Lafargues

Farewell, Cacadou, my trusty and beloved travelling companion,

OLD NICK

First published, in the language of the original (German), in *Annali*, an. I, Milano, 1958

Printed according to the original

189

ENGELS TO EDUARD BERNSTEIN [113]

IN ZURICH

London, 20 October 1882

Dear Mr Bernstein,

I have long been intending to write to you about French affairs, but have only just got round to it. Just as well, since it means that I can kill two birds with one stone.

1. *St-Étienne.*— Despite the well-meant advice of the Belgians, the inevitable has happened; the incompatible elements have taken themselves off. [394] And that is a good thing. In the beginning, when the *parti ouvrier* [a] was formed, it was necessary to admit all elements who accepted the programme; if they did so with mental reservations this would be bound to emerge later on. We over here have never been under any illusion about Malon and Brousse. Both were educated in the Bakuninist school of intrigue; Malon was actually one of those responsible for the foundation of Bakunin's secret 'Alliance' [67] (one of the 17 founders). But *enfin*, [b] they had to be given a chance to show whether, along with Bakunin's theory, they had also sloughed off his practice. Developments have shown that, if they accepted the programme (and adulterated it, Malon having introduced sundry changes for the worse), it was with the mental reservation that they would subvert it. What was begun at Rheims [223] and Paris [337] has been completed at St-Étienne. The programme's proletarian class

_____
[a] workers' party - [b] after all

character has been eliminated. The communist *considérants* ª of 1880 ⁶ ⁸ have now been replaced with the Rules of the International of 1866 ᵇ which had to be couched in such elastic terms precisely because the French Proudhonists had lagged so far behind, yet could not be left out. The positive demands of the programme have been neutralised in that every locality may, whenever it wishes, formulate an individual programme for each individual occasion. Not only is the so-called party of St-Étienne not a workers' party — it isn't a party at all because it hasn't in fact got a programme: at most it is a Malon-Brousse party. The worst these two can reproach the old programme with is that it repelled more people than it attracted. That has now been put right: neither Proudhonists nor Radicals ³ ⁹ ⁶ can now have any grounds for remaining aloof and, if Malon and Co. were to have their way, the 'revolutionary pap' of which Vollmar complains ³ ⁹ ⁷ would be the official expression of the French proletariat.

In all Latin countries (and elsewhere too, perhaps), the practice as regards congressional mandates has always been exceedingly lax. Many of these could not stand close scrutiny. So long as it wasn't taken too far, and so long as only matters of little consequence were involved, small harm was done. But the Bakuninists were the first to introduce this (initially in the Jura) as a regular thing, going in for expert mandate-rigging and attempting by this means to make their way to the top. Similarly now at St-Étienne. The preliminaries to the congress have been generally dominated by all the old Bakuninist tactics which stop at nothing — lies, slander, covert cliquism. That's the only thing Brousse is master of. These chaps forget that subterfuges and the like, which may succeed in the case of small sections and in a small territory such as the Jura, will necessarily bring about the downfall of those who try them on in the case of a genuine workers' party in a large country. The apparent victory scored at St-Étienne will not be a lasting one and Malon-Brousse will soon be done for once and for all.

It would seem that *any* workers' party in a large country can develop only through internal struggle, as indeed has been generally established in the dialectical laws of development. The German party has come to be what it is through the struggle between the Eisenachers and Lassalleans, ² ⁶ ⁹ in which, after all, the actual scuffles played

---

ª preambles (see present edition, Vol. 24, p. 340) - ᵇ *Association Internationale des Travailleurs. Statuts et règlements,* London, 1866.

a leading role. Unification only became possible when the gang of scoundrels deliberately cultivated as a tool by Lassalle had lost its efficacity and even then we were in far too great a hurry to effect that unification. [381] In France, those people who have admittedly relinquished Bakuninist theory but continue to make use of Bakuninist weapons and at the same time seek to sacrifice the class character of the movement to their own particular ends, will likewise have to lose their efficacity before unification again becomes feasible. Such being the case, it would be sheer folly to advocate unification. Moral homilies are of no avail against teething troubles which, circumstances being what they are today, are something that has got to be gone through.

Come to that, the Roanne people stand in great need of constant and searching criticism. Revolutionary hot air and futile impetuosity are things they are all too often prepared to tolerate.

2. *Citoyen-Bataille*. As long ago as last summer, at a time when things were going badly for the *Bataille*, when its funds had been frittered away on advertising, etc., the capitalists had pulled out and Lissagaray had broken with Malon-Brousse, Lissagaray proposed to Guesde that the two papers be amalgamated, that they should both be editors-in-chief and each have the right to sling out three of the *other* paper's editors. Thus did Lissagaray think to rid himself of the hated Lafargue. This was unanimously rejected by the editors of the *Citoyen*. The *Bataille* continued to founder. Thereupon Lissagaray approached the proprietor (a Dutch FINANCIER [a]) of the *Citoyen*, and negotiated the amalgamation *behind its editors' backs* in the hope that this coup de main would place them at his mercy. The reverse happened. The editors of the *Citoyen* continued to publish the paper without a day's interruption, and sued the proprietor for breach of contract. Lissagaray's coup was thereby foiled and he himself utterly put to shame, as he has himself admitted by having recourse to the extreme measure of challenging the '*lâche* [b] Lafargue', as he describes him in the *Bataille*, to a duel which, it is to be hoped, the latter will not accept under any circumstances.— That Lissagaray has ruined himself for good and all by this Bonapartist coup can be pretty well assumed. To go and risk the very existence of a paper at a moment when it is more necessary than ever to the party in their struggle against the St-Étienne faction and to do so in order to save one's own paper from

---

[a] Blommestein - [b] cowardly

foundering, to change (had this coup succeeded) the character of that paper, no matter what the cost, and to change it, what's more, in alliance with the bourgeois proprietor and in the teeth of the editors, the representatives of the party,—that really is a bit too thick!

Should the enclosed be unduly strong, you must tone it down. [398] What's the position as regards printing the pamphlet? [378] Marx is here (but secretly!) and will, I hope, be able to spend the winter on the English coast.

Yours,
F. E.

Since this letter is being sent off at 5 p. m. on 20 October, it should be in your hands by tomorrow evening or Sunday[a] morning.

First published, in Russian, in *Marx-Engels Archives*, Book I, Moscow, 1924

Printed according to the original

Published in English in full for the first time

190

ENGELS TO LAURA LAFARGUE

IN PARIS

London, 21 October 1882

My dear Laura,

The day before yesterday we received from Paul[b] the two first nos of the transplanted *Citoyen*.[c] From the *Justice* we had already seen what a Coup de Jarnac [399] the noble-hearted *Prospère*[d] had tried to give the Parti ouvrier[e]; from the above two *Citoyens* we saw that *le coup avait manqué et*[f] from the stupid shot in the *Citoyen et Bataille* against '*le lâche*[g] Paul Lafargue' we saw that Prospère *le sa-*

---

[a] Saturday in the ms. -[b] Lafargue -[c] See this volume, pp. 346-47 and 370. -[d] Lissagaray -[e] Workers' Party -[f] the coup had failed and -[g] the cowardly

vait parfaitment,[a] and was reduced to unmask himself as what he really is, a Cassagnacquian spadassin. [400] Of course Paul will not have been such a fool as to *donner dans ce panneau.*[b]

Now for two days there have not arrived either *Citoyen,* or *Citoyen et Bataille,* and today even *La Justice* is not to hand. We are therefore quite at sea. Has the *Citoyen* been stopped for want of funds after two nos, or has it merely been owing to the *génie éminemment organisateur des français*[c] that we have not received it? You know, in a crisis like this we ought to be regularly supplied with that information which we cannot obtain here. I have written a long letter to Bernstein yesterday[d] about both Malon-Brousse and this last affair; but every day something may happen in Paris about which it would be important to communicate at once to Bernstein the correct version. How can I do so without materials? Is it really impossible for the Parisian friends to do those things which are the most important to their own interests?

I heard from Mohr today that you have written to him and that Jenny is better. Mohr is very well on the whole, Donkin who examined him was almost surprised at the great improvement he found (barring the unavoidable remnants of the two later pleurisies); he thinks he can pass the winter on the English South Coast. He will have to go soon, we have a perfectly beastly wet day to-day — but warm — and when other people have fine weather we begin to have fogs.

I wish you could first pop in some Sunday evening and see the change. Mohr of course cannot go out at nights, so there is nobody but the Pumpses and now and then Helen.[e] The 'crimm' has entirely disappeared. The other day the great Loria called again. That evening Jollymeier happened to be here, and as we were all a little bit on, poor Loria had to undergo some chaffing, he asked Helen had she *also studied political economy* and told us he had tasted Moselle wine in Berlin but it tasted like *sugar and water.* Well, you can imagine the explosions. I appreciate, the poor pedant has enough of our 'sarcastic' company. Imagine he would not believe that you and Tussy were sisters and stared when he heard who your father was.

Today Signor Alessandro Oldrini called at Mohr's while I was there, but with a consistency of which I was very glad, he was not

---

[a] was perfectly informed - [b] get into this trap - [c] Frenchmen's exceptional gift for organising - [d] See previous letter. - [e] Demuth

received. If Mohr had seen him, God knows how many Zanardellis would have followed.

The Pumpses are getting on very well, they have been a fortnight or so in their new house, but it is not yet quite furnished — for want of *cash*. The baby[a] has had an abscess on the chest but is getting better. Charley[b] and Miss Bevan have been married three weeks, I have not yet seen them since the happy despatch.

Now it is getting on fast for post-time and as I want you to have this letter tomorrow morning I must conclude. Kind regards to Paul and if you see them, Guesde and Mesa.

Yours affectionately,

F. E.

First published in: Marx and Engels, *Works*, Second Russian Edition, Vol. 35, Moscow, 1964

Reproduced from the original

Published in English for the first time

191

ENGELS TO EDUARD BERNSTEIN [401]

IN ZURICH

London, 27 October 1882

Dear Mr Bernstein,

In great haste the finale of the Paris affair,[c] for I can hardly suppose the Parisians send you these things — even we over here have to extract them from the chaps by force.

Well, the *Citoyen* continued to appear under its old editors, while Lissagaray edited *Le Citoyen et la Bataille* with the aid of two anarchists, Mals and Crié. On Friday evening *Citoyen et Bataille* made an attempt to have the *Citoyen* confiscated (by the police) on account of a Wanda Kryloff feuilleton, whereupon the proprietor of the old *Citoyen*, Blommestein, a Dutch financier and now Lissagaray's *associé*,[d] asserted his proprietorial rights. Having been warned in

---

[a] Lilian Rosher - [b] Presumably Roesgen - [c] See this volume, pp. 343-44, 344-45. - [d] partner

good time, they removed the feuilleton, and the police inspector who came to confiscate it had to go away discomfited. On Sunday, the editors of the *Citoyen et Bataille* declared that, should further attempts be made to confiscate the *Citoyen*, they would resign *en masse* (all 3 of them). That same evening, Sunday, the *Citoyen des deux mondes*, as it had been called on legal advice, was confiscated for bearing an unauthorised title, again at Blommestein's behest. On Monday, i. e. Tuesday morning, it reappeared as the *Citoyen international* and called upon the editors of the *Citoyen et Bataille* to stand by their word and resign. Not them! Mals and Crié declared secretly that *they* at any rate would resign, but did not; Crié was arrested for alleged complicity at Montceau-les-Mines [402] and is now in quod.

In the meantime, since the editors of the *Citoyen* would have gone in daily fear of its being confiscated unless they changed its name, the paper has, for the past 4 days, been calling itself *L'Égalité*, alongside which the weekly *Égalité* is to continue appearing. Where they are getting the money from I don't know; it's 3 weeks since we had any news of the chaps. Nor did we get an *Égalité* today. But since your Frenchman's *génie éminemment organisateur* [a] manifests itself, especially in our friends' case, in organising the most tremendous disorder, one cannot draw any conclusions from that.

The attempt to kill the *Citoyen* with the help of the judiciary and police has stripped Lissagaray of the last remnants of his disguise. He has combined stupidity and baseness in rare measure.

Marx asks whether you could procure for him a copy of the Swiss Factory Act. [403] We should be greatly obliged if you could let us know in which year the Factory Act now in force in Germany was passed and whether it is a separate Act or part of the Imperial Trade Regulations. We should then be able to get hold of it. Marx needs it for the 3rd edition of Volume I [b] and promises in return to send you something every now and again for the *Sozialdemokrat*. In a few days he will be leaving for the Isle of Wight where, provided nothing untoward happens, he will spend the whole winter (5 or 6 hours' journey from here).

Your MISTER Garcia is one of the many little democrats who scurry about London, and have a finger in every association. Their new central boss — or, as Stieber puts it, ringleader, [404] is a BARRISTER called

---

[a] exceptional gift for organising - [b] of *Capital*

Hyndman, a strongly democratic and ambitious man who unsuccessfully stood for parliament in the recent elections. All these little folk have no one behind them but each other. They split up into all manner of sects and into a befuddled non-sectarian tail consisting of those who hail democracy in whatever guise. They are intent on impressing the world with their own importance. Hence the catalogues of unknown celebrities in Garcia's articles. In most of them there are good intentions and to spare, but likewise the intention to cut a figure. Hence I would advise you to treat the chap's letters with *considerable reserve*; after all, his principal aim is to elevate to the position of an important party a small clique which has, for twenty years, remained one and the same nonentity, if under various names and in a variety of guises. But, or so it seems to me, the *Sozialdemokrat* is not there in order to create a continental reputation for these busy nobodies. Herewith the card of one of the little associations of which Garcia is secretary and to which he recently invited me to lecture; I, of course, refused.

I anxiously await the material on Bismarck.[a] If Marx goes away now, I shall set to work in earnest and, should I become engrossed in a lengthier piece of work[b] which ought to have been finished long ago, I shall *not be able to extricate myself at all quickly*, and I should warn you in advance that in that case you will have to wait. If I had got the stuff here, I could start in on it straight away and polish off this business *first of all*. Bebel promised but didn't send anything and now is actually bound for prison where Liebknecht already is,[405] and there's absolutely no hope of getting anything from the others.

Encl. for Kautsky.

Kindest regards,

Yours,

F. E.

First published, in Russian, in *Marx-Engels Archives*, Book I, Moscow, 1924

Printed according to the original

Published in English in full for the first time

---

[a] See this volume, p. 324. - [b] A reference to *Dialectics of Nature*.

192

ENGELS TO AUGUST BEBEL [7]

IN LEIPZIG

London, 28 October 1882

Dear Bebel,

I have at last got round to writing — Marx has been back here for about 3 weeks and leaves the day after tomorrow for the Isle of Wight, so I have had no respite in which to do anything.

As regards Vollmar's articles, [383] I was particularly taken with the first one on account of its rightful dismissal of the wails emitted by those 'right wing' gentlemen who are clamouring for the repeal of the Anti-Socialist Law, [16] even upon conditions that would be worse for the party than the Anti-Socialist Law itself, provided this would enable them to go back to founding newspapers *à la Gerichts-Zeitung* and hence to the old literary fleshpots of Egypt. [406] In my view it would be perfectly in order to point out to these people — and it was exclusively against them that the article was levelled — that a *voluntary* repeal of the Anti-Socialist Law might very easily be accompanied by conditions that aggravated the position of the *party*; to emphasise that the last way we shall rid ourselves of the Anti-Socialist Law is by begging and cringing.

Otherwise the question is an academic one so far as I am concerned. I believe that the Law will receive its quietus from the events which will usher in the revolution and which cannot be long in coming.

I read the second article pretty cursorily as there were 2 or 3 people with me who kept chatting all the time. Otherwise I should have detected, from the way he visualises revolution, the French influence and hence also, no doubt, my Vollmar. Your handling of this aspect has been absolutely right. [407] It is the longed-for, ultimate realisation of the phrase 'single reactionary mass'. [408] *Here* all the official parties combined in a lump, *there* we socialists in column; a great decisive battle, victory at one stroke all along the line. Things aren't that easy in reality. In reality, as you indeed point out, a revolution begins the other way round, in that the great majority of the people, as also of the official parties, band together *against* the government thus isolated and overthrow it and only after such of the official parties as still remain viable have reciprocally, collectively and successively brought about their own ruin, only then will Vollmar's great parting of the ways come about and with it our opportunity to rule. If, like Vollmar, we were to try and begin the revolution straight off with the *last act*, we should have a pretty rotten time of it.

I paid little attention at the time to the final passage on the new tactics—there's certainly a great deal of indictable stuff there if looked at in conjunction with the Penal Code. However no great harm can be done if someone occasionally goes a bit too far in this direction; as it is, they err all too often in the other. So if I have made too light of this passage you, or so it seems to me, have taken it too seriously; you will have seen from Viereck's jubilations in the *Süddeutsche Post* how the right wing is seeking to make capital out of your reply. [409] I don't believe our people in Germany would have accepted Vollmar's way of talking simply on the strength of his articles, though the proclamation he has called for, 'We are organising *in secret*', certainly deserves to be rejected.

I am eagerly awaiting the material on Bismarck, [a] but as you're both in jug, [405] no doubt I shall now have to wait some time. But if by then I have got my teeth into a different, longer work, which has also long been pending, [b] I shan't be able to break off, and Bismarck will have to wait.

In France the long-expected split has occurred. [394] The original association of Guesde and Lafargue with Malon and Brousse was probably inevitable when the party was founded, but Marx and I were never under any illusion that it could last. The point at issue is purely one of principle: ought the struggle of the proletariat against the bourgeoisie to be waged as a *class struggle*, or ought it to be conceded that, in good opportunist (or Possibilist, as the socialist translation has it) fashion, the programme and the movement's class character be dropped wherever this would enable more votes or more 'supporters' to be won? Malon and Brousse have come out in favour of the latter, thereby sacrificing the proletarian class character of the movement and making a division inevitable. Well and good. The development of the proletariat takes place everywhere to the accompaniment of internal struggles, and France, which is presently forming a work-

---

[a] See this volume, p. 324. - [b] Engels means *Dialectics of Nature* (see present edition, Vol. 25).

ers' party for the first time, is no exception. We in Germany have passed beyond the first phase of the internal struggle (with the Lassalleans) and others still lie ahead of us. Unification is perfectly all right provided it works, but there are things which take precedence over unification. And when, like Marx and me, one has spent a lifetime fighting harder against the self-styled socialists than against anyone else (for we regarded the bourgeoisie simply as a *class* and hardly ever took issue with individual bourgeois), one cannot feel unduly perturbed just because the inevitable struggle has broken out.

I hope this will reach you before you go to quod. Marx and Tussy send their love. Marx is recuperating in fine style and, if there's no recurrence of his pleurisy, he'll be stronger next autumn than he has been for years. When you see Liebknecht in the '*Käfigturm*',ᵃ as they call it in Berne, give him regards from us all.

Your
F. E.

First published, in Russian, in *Marx-Engels Archives*, Vol. I (VI), Moscow, 1932

Printed according to the original

Published in English in full for the first time

193

ENGELS TO PAUL LAFARGUE[19]

IN PARIS

London, 30 October 1882

My dear Lafargue,

I should be glad if you would send the daily *Égalité* r e g u l a r l y to the

Editors of the *Sozialdemokrat*
Zurich, Switzerland.

In return, they will send you the *Sozialdemokrat*. The exchange — a daily for a weekly paper — may not be fair, but all the same it is you

---

ᵃ prison (literally: cage tower)

who will benefit. The idea is to keep the editors of the *Sozialdemokrat* in touch with what is going on in Paris and, as you yourself will realise, it is impossible for a ± proletarian editorial board to subscribe to all the sheets that keep springing up and disappearing in Paris.

Up till now, the *Sozialdemokrat*'s chief source of Parisian news has been Vollmar, a German Reichstag deputy and ex-officer who was paralysed as a result of a wound. He is a friend of Malon's, so you can imagine the extent to which the latter has turned him against your party. To that end he has not only made use of the many mistakes with which you have unfailingly supplied him (an example being Léon Picard's absurd article about the Germans in Paris last September [410]) but, as is his wont, has also told him one lie after another.

For all that, Vollmar is a good chap; in Germany he issued a pamphlet so impossibilist [383] that he will no longer be able to remain a Possibilist in France. It would be worth finding an opportunity to talk to him and get him to see the other side of the coin. I haven't got his Paris address, but it shouldn't be difficult to find.

In Zurich I am bringing out a German edition of *Socialism: Utopian and Scientific* with a great many addenda. [378] I shall send you some copies as soon as they arrive. The thing will be about twice as long as your translation. [20] Would there be any chance of publishing a new French edition based on this German one?

Again I repeat that, for you, it is of the utmost importance to keep the *Sozialdemokrat* informed; Bernstein could not be more willing, but from over here we cannot keep him in touch with things of which we ourselves are so often left in ignorance. You would do well to seek occasion to write to him, asking for information of some sort, etc. It is by such *innocent* means that Malon succeeds in ingratiating himself with others, means which you persist in ignoring. You should remember from time to time that Paris is no longer the capital of the world (which no longer has a capital) and less still the world itself.

Love to Laura.

Yesterday Marx dined with me and in the evening we all had supper at his house, after which we sat together drinking rum until one o'clock, and today he has left for Ventnor.

Yours ever,
F. E.

First published in: F. Engels, P. et L. Lafargue, *Correspondance*, t. I, Paris, 1956

Printed according to the original

Translated from the French

194

ENGELS TO MARX

IN VENTNOR

[Postcard]

[London, 1 November 1882]

Dear Moor,

I trust all has gone well with you so far.[411] Two *Égalités* have gone off and 2 old *Kölnische Zeitungs* yesterday. This evening it's raining and blowing like fun here. Yesterday's brief debate about Maceo's extradition from Gibraltar discreditable to Gladstone & Co.[412] Johnny had 2 teeth pulled out today with a totally unexpected heroism that surprised even Dr Shyman. No other news.

Wednesday evening.

Your
F. E.

First published in *MEGA*, Abt. III, Bd. 4, Berlin, 1931

Printed according to the original

Published in English for the first time

195

ENGELS TO EDUARD BERNSTEIN [413]

IN ZURICH

London, 2-3 November 1882

Dear Mr Bernstein,

Have still received no proofs [378] (*just arrived* 3/11). On the other hand, have had from Bebel the Accident and Health Insurance Bill of *1882*, but not the earlier one [144] which represents *genuine* Bismarckian socialism, unclouded by parliamentary divisions. This I would much like to have, along, perhaps, with other matter relating to the Accident Insurance *Bank*; without it I can do nothing.[414]

Many thanks for Marquis Posener. [a] I do not need all the details in respect of the remaining railways. The *early or mid-1879 prices* (before anything was known about nationalisation) would suffice. The difference between then and now would be proof enough of the way the state has bought up the bourgeoisie.

In many respects Lassalle was a good jurist and, moreover, had studied his Roman law of inheritance sufficiently to impress jurists by the extent of his knowledge. (Impress was a favourite expression of his; while contemplating the Rosetta Stone [415] in the British Museum, he said to Marx: 'Should I, do you think, set aside six months in order that I may impress the Egyptologists?') In Germany all one has to do is elaborate some point in accordance with a particular theory, and the jurists of today have forgotten that the theory elaborated by Lassalle was *lifted word for word from Hegel's Philosophy of Law and History* [b] and, moreover, does not hold water if applied to the Roman law of inheritance; this did not evolve out of what Hegel called 'the *will*'; rather, it evolved out of the history of the Roman *gens*, the tribal kinship group about which, indeed, few jurists know very much. I only said, by the way, that I should be obliged to demolish the legend of Lassalle as an *original thinker*, [c] and that is absolutely essential.

I had not seen Lafargue's letter in the *Prolétaire* [d] and shall certainly ask for it to be sent me from Paris, though I am unlikely to get it. If you still have it, I should be glad if you could send it me; you shall have it back. Incidentally, Malon had better be on his guard; Lafargue has a whole pile of compromising letters from him.

Picard's absurd article [410] has *certainly been disclaimed* in the *Citoyen*, as Marx saw with his own eyes. Come to that, the man who sent it to you, marked in blue, does not know French; he *has underlined as a chauvinistic remark of the* Citoyen's *a passage* which Picard *attributes to the exploiteurs bourgeois ... ligue des patriotes ... dont Gambetta est la tête* [e]! I have marked it in red. Picard enjoys pitting himself against Guesde and, by way of playing a nasty prank on the latter, smuggled the article into the paper; if a proper editorial

[a] Stock Exchange nickname for the Märkisch-Posener Railway Company - [b] G. W. F. Hegel, *Grundlinien der Philosophie des Rechts oder Naturrecht und Staatswissenschaft im Grundrisse* and *Vorlesungen über die Philosophie der Geschichte.* - [c] See this volume, p. 332. - [d] Ibid., pp. 363-64. - [e] *bourgeois exploiters ... patriotic league ... of which Gambetta is the chief*

department were a possibility over there, this nonsense wouldn't have occurred.

Now for the 'nothing short of creditable performance put up by the editors of the *Citoyen* in the *affaire* Godard'. [416] We happen to know all about this, Marx having often heard the tale when in Paris, both from those who had taken part and those who had had nothing whatever to do with it. Following an incident at a meeting Godard went to the editorial office of the *Citoyen* where he was accorded an amiable reception by Guesde who still has something of a soft spot—of a *personal* nature—for his erstwhile anarchist brothers. In the middle of a quiet conversation Godard, with no excuse whatsoever, suddenly dealt Guesde a violent blow in the face. The others sprang to their feet, whereupon Godard, like the cowardly anarchist he is, took refuge in a corner—surely they would not ill-treat him, a *prisonnier*[a]? And, instead of beating him into pulp, the childlike *Citoyen* chaps conferred together and decided *qu'en effet il fallait le lâcher parce qu'il—était prisonnier*[b]!! Godard left in a hurry, sad to say, unchastised. But the following evening, when most of the editors were known to be absent, a dozen armed (with cudgels, etc.) anarchists forced their way into the office and, with threats, demanded satisfaction of some kind or other. Massard, however, stood firm, and they had to retire empty-handed. But now the *fédération du centre* [265] was informed; for several evenings they placed working men on guard, and *messieurs les anarchistes* did not return.

But now I would ask you to give me some idea of the sort of thing the 'nothing short of creditable', etc., is supposed to have consisted in.

The whole gist of your letter points to the conclusion that you are not getting the *Citoyen* regularly and hence, apart from the *Égalité* and the *Prolétaire*, have to depend on the accounts provided by comrades in Paris who, in turn, exclusively rely on the services of Malon and Co., in regard to whom their credulity would seem to have assumed no mean proportions. In my view, however, the party organ ought in no circumstances to allow its judgment of a workers' movement in a foreign country to be unduly influenced by comrades in that country's capital who are, after all, a shifting population. German associations abroad are unquestionably the worst sources of information on the movement abroad; they seldom command a bird's eye view and generally have their own particular connections to the

---

[a] prisoner - [b] that in fact he ought to be let go because he—was a prisoner!

exclusion of any others, which means that they are unable to participate in the daily life and development of the movement around them;
finally, they persist in the belief that, even today, they are still of more
than passing significance to the masses actually inside Germany.
What would have become of our freedom to form an opinion of the
English movement or non-movement, had we paid the slightest heed
to the changing majority in the London Society [8]? And are not the
German associations in New York equally uncritical in their attitude
towards the American labour movement? Every association desires
above all else to be thought important, and will therefore — in the
absence of a very energetic and intelligent leadership — fall an easy
prey to any foreigner who knows the ropes.

Nor have you any other source, i. e. other than *Malon at second
hand*, for your reiterated assertion that in France 'Marxism' suffers
from a marked lack of esteem. Now what is known as 'Marxism' in
France is, indeed, an altogether peculiar product — so much so that
Marx once said to Lafargue: *'Ce qu'il y a de certain c'est que moi, je ne
suis pas Marxiste.'* [a] But if, last summer, the *Citoyen* was able to sell
25,000 copies and attain a standing such that Lissagaray hazarded
his reputation in order to gain control of it,[b] would not this seem somewhat incompatible with the lack of esteem you insist upon? Even
more incompatible, however, is the fact that the said lack of esteem
does not prevent these chaps from enjoying an esteem so great as to
enable them, after being chucked out of the *Citoyen*, to start up an important new daily paper *the selfsame day* [c] and, supported *almost exclusively* by *workers and petty bourgeois* (*ouvriers et petits industriels* [d] as
Lafargue puts it), to keep it going for almost a fortnight despite harassment by the proprietor [e] of the old *Citoyen*, and find a capitalist
with whom they will be negotiating the paper's [f] fate — *oui ou non* [g] —
tomorrow. The facts speak so clearly for themselves that Malon will
doubtless have to swallow his 'lack of esteem'. However, so great is
the 'esteem' in which Mr Malon himself is held that, upon his apply-
ing to Rochefort for an increase in the fee he is paid for his *Intransigeant* articles, he received the reply: *'Je vous paierai plus s i v o u s é c r i-
v e z m o i n s.'* [h] One of these days Malon ought to have a go at founding a daily paper in Paris without so much as a farthing in his

---

[a] 'If anything is certain, it is that I myself am not a Marxist.' - [b] See this volume,
pp. 343-44 and 346-47. - [c] Ibid., pp. 344-45. - [d] workmen and small industrialists -
[e] Blommestein - [f] *L'Égalité* (daily edition) - [g] yes or no - [h] 'I shall pay you more *if you
write less.*'

pocket, and then he could show us just what the esteem he enjoys is capable of doing.

But enough. I have asked Lafargue to send the *Égalité* to the *Sozialdemokrat* by way of exchange,[a] and today he writes to say he will do so, in return for which kindly send the *Sozialdemokrat* to the *Égalité*. Should the *Égalité* not arrive regularly, you need only drop a line on a postcard to P. Lafargue, 66 boulevard de Port-Royal, Paris.

As regards Vollmar's articles,[383] the first in particular, levelled as it was directly against those people who, cost *what it may*, are clamouring for the repeal of the Anti-Socialist Law,[16] was very good and hit the nail on the head. The second I read rather cursorily before a journey, with 3 or 4 people chattering around me. Otherwise I would not have taken the lenient view I in fact did of the excessively fervent language which, in conclusion, he advocates for use by the party. Bebel is right about this point[407] which, however, I think he takes rather too seriously. The real weakness of the 2nd article (which I did note, but attached little importance to) lies in its childish idea of the coming revolution which is to *begin* by the whole world splitting itself 'À Guelph! À Waibling!',[417] into 2 armies — on one side ourselves, on the other the whole of the 'single reactionary mass'.[408] I. e. the revolution is to start with the *fifth act*, not with the first, in which the masses of the opposition parties stand shoulder to shoulder against the government and its blunders and thus win through, whereupon one after the other of the individual parties amongst the victors loses its efficacity and puts itself out of the running, until finally the mass of the people are thereby forced onto our side, at which juncture the decisive battle so much vaunted by Vollmar can take place. However, in this context the point was a subsidiary one; what mattered was the demonstration that, if the gentlemen of the 'right wing' were to have their way, we should indeed be able to rid ourselves of the Anti-Socialist Law on conditions which, while more detrimental to the party than the Anti-Socialist Law itself, would permit these gentlemen to publish sheets like the Hamburg *Gerichts-Zeitung*, etc., and pass them off as party organs. In this I agree entirely with Vollmar and have, indeed, written and told Bebel as much.[b]

Yesterday I took out in your name, 137 alte Landstrasse, Riesbach,

---

[a] See this volume, pp. 351-52.- [b] Ibid., p. 349.

a money order for 12/- = 15.10 frs in payment of Marx's and my subscription. Kindly remind me when this again falls due.

Congratulations on entering your seventh thousand.[a]

Yours,

F. E.

In view of your amendment in the preface,[b] there is no longer any
call for an allusion to the Wyden Conference,[418] and I shall therefore
delete it. Kindly send me 2 fair proofs.[378] Proof will go off today or tomorrow.

First published in full, in Russian, in *Marx-
Engels Archives*, Book I, Moscow, 1924

Printed according to the original

Published in English in full for the
first time

196

ENGELS TO MARX

IN VENTNOR

[London,] 3 November [1882]

Dear Moor,

Postcard received[284] — we were somewhat anxious, not having
heard how you felt on the day after your journey.— ALL RIGHT! Encl.
letter from Lafargue — so Brissac, Picard and Bouis did after all
waver for a moment![419]

You will have seen that Andrea Costa has been elected in Ravenna
and that there was a republican majority in Norway.[420]

Herewith the *Égalité* and the latest DOINGS of two 'locals' in whom
you have always taken an interest.

Your

F. E.

First published in *MEGA*, Abt. III, Bd. 4,
Berlin, 1931

Printed according to the original

Published in English for the first
time

---

[a] of *Der Sozialdemokrat* - [b] F. Engels, 'Preface to the First German Edition of *Socialism:
Utopian and Scientific*' (see present edition, Vol. 24, pp. 457-59).

197

ENGELS TO EDUARD BERNSTEIN

IN ZURICH

London, 4 November 1882

Dear Mr Bernstein,

'I beg to confirm mine of yesterday's date. I also have pleasure in acknowledging receipt of your favour of the 1st inst. and make haste to reply to same.' As you can see, the old counting-house style is not yet quite defunct.— In fact I am writing straight away in order to save you a great deal of unnecessary trouble. It is most kind of you to hunt out and send all those books for us but 'as of now we have no real use for them'. For in the 3rd edition[a] Marx merely intends to bring the state of factory legislation up to date by making emendations and additions; to that end he needs *the text of the original Acts and nothing more.* Secondary matters such as the protection of labour, liability, etc., are not of importance for *this* purpose. And I wrote and told you yesterday what I still need for Bismarck[414]: the early or mid-1879 stock market prices of the last 6 railways to be nationalised, and the *first* reading of Bismarck's Accident, etc., Insurance Bills. If I need the latest edition of Saling[b] due to come out in the meantime (it was kind of you to advise me of this), I can get hold of it within 4-5 days.

I was quite glad to have your information about Garcia; after all, one never knows when one may not run into the man. What he says about agitation on the part of certain TRADES UNION chiefs in regard to the channel tunnel is quite true. They are the very ones who were always open to purchase by the radical bourgeois (under Morley) and on this occasion they have been joined by G. Shipton, the editor of *The Labour Standard.* There is absolutely no doubt that these people are in the pay of the Channel Company; they are not running up travelling expenses, etc., out of sheer enthusiasm. Admittedly it is a pretty innocuous business at present, but Shipton himself has now had a taste of bourgeois money, of course, and in view of his utter spinelessness and unbounded craving for popularity, this may lead to

---

[a] 3rd German edition of Vol. I of *Capital* - [b] *Saling's Börsen-Papiere*

something more. He has lost his virginity and the other 'REPRESENTA-
TIVE WORKING MEN', those who have grown grey in the hurly-burly, will
doubtless take him completely in tow before long.

That you are being bombarded from Paris with pro-Malon anti-
Guesde letters I willingly believe. But after all, the correspondent you
cite pronounces himself an incompetent judge in as much as he admits writing under the impression of the current anti-German campaign and reproaches you for doing your duty as editor of the party
organ, namely 'taking a bird's eye view', critical and all-embracing,
of the affair and, unlike himself, refusing to be swayed by transitory
and local events. And if, 2 months later, the man is still harping on
this one unfortunate article [410] and permits his view of a significant
faction of the workers to be determined by this one incident alone,
does that mean that the party organ ought to proceed in an equally
blinkered fashion? If there exists in Paris a whole lot of non-socialist
and semi-socialist workers who vent their chauvinism on the hated
Germans, is the *Citoyen* at fault? Certainly no more at fault than the
German socialists in Paris if, when things come to a head, a whole lot
of non-socialist German workers in Paris, London, New York or any
other big American city accept a lower wage, thereby depressing the
wages of the natives (in America even those of the Irish!) and bringing the German workers *en masse* into not altogether undeserved disre-
pute? And, finally, if he found the article so hard to stomach, why
didn't he *object*? A disclaimer *did* appear and admittedly it made
pretty light of the matter, but Marx tells me that, according to the ten-
ets of the Paris press, it was as adequate as any that is customarily issued in respect of an editor who has blundered, always assuming that
no pressure has been brought to bear on the paper. But such pressure
could have been brought to bear, and very simply at that. Had a letter of protest been drawn up and delivered to the office either by
a single individual or a deputation, the editors would have had to
take the matter seriously. Had the editor in attendance (it might even
have been Picard himself) made difficulties, all that would have been
required was the threat, that, if the letter failed to appear in the *Citoyen* on the following day, it would be sent forthwith to the *Sozialdemokrat*, in Zurich. If your correspondent did not know enough French,
Vollmar was there; had the latter been absent, Hirsch [a] would have
gladly taken the thing on. If the chaps had acted in this way they

---

[a] Carl Hirsch

would have earned themselves respect, taught the *Citoyen* a useful lesson and I should have been heartily glad. But to submit to it all like so many sheep and then give vent to cries of woe is typically German and has earned the Germans the contempt they deserve. If *we* had put up with that sort of thing from the French and English, if our people had behaved so spinelessly in Germany, where should we be today? Before the German socialists in Paris demand it is their view of the French movement that should prevail in the party organ, they must demonstrate, firstly, that they are at all capable of free and impartial criticism and, secondly, that they are able to *stand their ground* vis-à-vis the French. Neither of these things has happened.

As to the undesirability of a daily paper in Paris, I am unable to share your view. In *Paris* the influence of a weekly is confined to small circles; if one wants to influence the masses one must have a daily. We too were opposed to a daily when there was no prospect of getting hold of one and the childish emigration to Lyons took place in connection with the *Émancipation*.[208] Things are different now. The *Citoyen* and its editors have made a name for themselves in Paris, bourgeois papers of all complexions have been compelled to engage in disputations with it and been triumphantly dismasted and, were we now to lose the daily, it would be a signal defeat. The fact that it cannot be an ideal, perfect paper, that a spuriously democratic system of editing by *comité* often ends up with there being no editing at all, as in the case of Picard's article, in no way alters the case. Not long ago, however, Lafargue sent me the issues, some 20 of them, dealing with the split,[394] and it seemed to me that the paper was by no means so bad — apart from those aspects we have long criticised and which would be no different in a weekly. But in the view of anyone familiar with conditions in the Paris press a paper appearing twice weekly would be impracticable from the start; it would come *stillborn* into the world. Either a weekly or a daily. And with the latter the former editors of the *Citoyen* undoubtedly now have a very considerable chance of succeeding, as is evident from their rapid transition to the daily *Égalité* which is already selling more than 5,000 copies in Paris.

Now for the Clemenceau MEETING. To assess this, like other things in Paris, by German standards, is quite impossible. When Gambetta was unable to make himself heard in his own constituency,[179] there were shouts of triumph from the entire radical and socialist press. The

same thing has now happened to Clemenceau.⁴²¹ Clemenceau is
a cool, calculating man, quite prepared to go further, when he sees
the need for it, and even become a communist, provided he can be
convinced: *convainquez-moi donc!* ª And the workers in his constituency
are employing a highly effective means of persuasion by demonstrating to him that his seat is in danger. That may give a shove to his
somewhat slothful study of socialism.

But who were the people who did it? Guesde & Co. on their own
perhaps? No, the chairman was in fact Joffrin, Malon's friend and
Clemenceau's future rival candidate in Montmartre! So our people
were decent enough, as always hitherto in the struggle against the
bourgeoisie, to vote for Malon's chairman and side with Malon's
people. If we are to censure the attitude of the workers, Malon's
people are far more deserving of censure than Guesde's.

The passage in the *Citoyen* simply says that these tactics should continue to be employed against Clemenceau; if they have been successful once, why not again? It remains to be seen whether the *Prolétaire*
would be able to pay the *Égalité* in the same coin at meetings. Nothing I have witnessed so far has given me cause to believe that this
would be so. But even were it momentarily to be the case, it wouldn't
matter, and would be unlikely to continue for long.

And now a quick word or two before the post goes — otherwise this
letter won't leave until Monday morning — on the campaign you
have in mind with regard to the programme.⁴²² I consider it most
untimely. The programme is a bad one, but no one discusses it any
more. An amended programme requires that it should not be open
to dispute. So long as delegates are not elected in public, therefore,
so long as *every* mandate can be disputed, it would be better not
to interfere with the programme unless absolutely necessary. An
amended programme would give the right wing an excuse to set
themselves up as the true faithful who have complete confidence in
the old well-tried programme, etc. So think twice about it before
sowing these seeds of discord among a party that is bound hand
and foot.

The greatest danger to any political émigrés lies in the urge to be
up and doing; something has really got to happen; something has
really got to be done! And so things happen whose import one fails to
appreciate and which, as one later realises oneself, had far better

---

ª Go on. Convince me!

never happened at all. Might you and Vollmar be suffering from the urge to be up and doing? If so beware — of yourselves. With kindest regards.

Yours,

F. E.

Marx is in Ventnor, ISLE OF Wight[411]; getting on well.

First published, in Russian, in *Marx-Engels Archives*, Book I, Moscow, 1924

Printed according to the original

Published in English for the first time

198

ENGELS TO MARX

IN VENTNOR

London, 6 November 1882

Dear Moor,

Today I got a note from Laura in which she tells me that the fate of the *Égalité* will not be decided until tomorrow[423]; prospects, however, are most favourable.

Have you seen today's *Standard*? Telegram from Frankfurt[a] to the effect that, since Ignatiev's arrival in Paris, there have been renewed attempts — initially, it would seem, of a fairly lukewarm kind — at a Russo-French compromise: if France were to do something more about the extradition of dynamiters,[424] Russia for its part would vigorously back up France in Tunis, Egypt, etc. So that explains the police campaign in France! We shall see if anything of a relevant nature is submitted to the Chambers.

Lafargue has sent me the *Prolétaire* containing the indictment of himself, Guesde, etc., which was read out at St-Étienne.[425] A truly Bakuninist concoction, but otherwise weak: its strongest props are mutually contradictory *letters*, written on the spur of the moment by *Lafargue to Malon*, and calmly reproduced by the latter without, it would seem, any fear of the same being done to *his* letters by

---

[a] 'Russia and France. Frankfort, Sunday Night', *The Standard*, No. 18191, 6 November 1882.

Lafargue. Nor is he wrong; these gentlemen have made opportune use of their material and were Lafargue then to come out with Malon's letters, it would be *moutarde après diner*.[a] I shall send you the thing tomorrow. But you must let me have it back for the sake of Bernstein, against whom I may well make use of it. In place of what I asked for, or along with it, the latter has proposed to send a small library of books *about* factory legislation, something which I can only hope I have nipped in the bud in good time [b]; I expect to get the Swiss Factory Act[403] any day now and shall order for you the latest German trade regulations which contain the provisions for factories.

No other news here.

Your

F. E.

First published in *Der Briefwechsel zwischen F. Engels und K. Marx*, Bd. 4, Stuttgart, 1913

Printed according to the original

Published in English for the first time

199

MARX TO ENGELS[72]

IN LONDON

[Ventnor,] 8 November 1882

DEAR FRED,

What do you think of Deprez' experiment at the Munich Electricity Exhibition?[426] It was almost a year ago that Longuet promised to procure Deprez' works for me (notably his demonstration that electricity makes it possible to convey energy over considerable distances by means of a simple telegraph wire).[427] For a close friend of Deprez', Dr D'Arsonval, is a contributor to the *Justice* and has published this and that about Deprez' investigations. Longuet, as is his wont, is always forgetting.

I greatly enjoyed looking at the 'PAPER' you sent in which Sher-

---

[a] Mustard after dinner, i.e. shutting the stable door after the horse has bolted. -
[b] See this volume, p. 359.

brooke and Rivers Wilson parade as 'TRUSTEES IN LONDON FOR THE BOND-
HOLDERS'.[428] In yesterday's *Standard, HOUSE OF COMMONS* DEBATES, Glad-
stone was severely rapped over the knuckles on account of the said
TRUSTEES,[a] since the above-named Rivers Wilson also occupies a senior
(i. e. well-paid) position in the English PUBLIC DEBTS administration.
Gladstone, clearly much embarrassed, at first attempted TO POOH-POOH
[the matter] but, upon notice being given of a MOTION of censure over
Rivers Wilson, Gladstone mendaciously denied all knowledge of the
Galveston and Eagle etc. Railway Co. OUR SAINTLY GRAND OLD MAN[b] is
playing a role no less glorious over the 'extradition' from Gibraltar.[412] It was not for nothing, one recalls, that this same Gladstone,
together with one Graham, etc., underwent his apprenticeship in the
captious official oligarchy under Sir Robert Peel.

No one could be better suited for the clumsy, lying, stupid equivo-
cation and lame excuses that characterise the Egyptian affair than Sir
Charles Dilke.[429] He has neither the pietistic casuistry of Gladstone,
nor the quizzical levity of the *quondam*[c] Palmerston. Dilke is simply an
ill-mannered parvenu who imagines himself great by reason of his
boorishness.

Since I take *The Standard* here, I too discovered therein the telegram from Frankfurt to which you allude.[d]

Apropos. I should be glad if Bernstein could send me the *Jahrbuch*
containing the *article* by *Oldenburg* (at least I think that's what the
author is called) on my theory of value.[e] Although I don't actually
need it, it would nevertheless be better if I had before my eyes what
was argued at the time. When I wrote to the little Dutch parson[f] the
whole thing was quite fresh in my mind. Since then there has been all
the business of my illness and also the loss of my wife — a long period
of intellectual twilight.

A violent wind rages ceaselessly here, particularly of an evening
and at night; first thing in the morning it's usually wet, or at any rate
GLOOMY; during the day there are always fine intervals which have to
be snatched; at the same time the weather is unsettled, capricious.
Last Sunday,[g] for instance, at 4 o'clock, I went up onto the Downs
where I walked along the cart-track past Bonchurch, the topmost of

---

[a] 'Imperial Parliament. House of Commons. Sir C. Rivers Wilson', *The Standard*,
No. 18192, 7 November 1882. - [b] Gladstone - [c] erstwhile; here: late - [d] See this vol-
ume, p. 363. - [e] H. O[ldenburg], 'Die Grundlage des wissenschaftlichen Sozialismus',
Jahrbuch für Sozialwissenschaft und Sozialpolitik, Jahrg. I., Zweite Hälfte, Zurich-
Oberstrass, 1880. - [f] Ferdinand Domela Nieuwenhuis (see this volume, pp. 65-67). -
[g] 5 November

whose houses, ascending in terraces, are almost on a level with the track (the lowest are right down by the sea); the track goes meandering on, sometimes up, sometimes down, between the hilly part of the Downs and where they dip down to the sea. (When I was here last time with Tussy [234] I didn't venture up as far as the track.) Here one can spend hours sauntering along, enjoying hill and sea air at one and the same time. It was as warm as summer; the sky pure blue, with only small, translucent white clouds; all at once a *cold shower*, SKY SUDDENLY OVERCAST. To this, no doubt, I owe the muscular rheumatism (afflicting the left side of my chest, close to the old *corpus delicti* [a]) which on Monday night became so severe that on Tuesday, overcoming my reluctance, I sent for a doctor. In reply to my questions, my OLD SPINSTER MacLean told me that there were 2 doctors who called at her house. *The greatest, the most fashionable man was 'J. G. Sinclair Coghill, Physician to the Royal Hospital for Consumption'.* I asked * whether he be the old fogey whose coach I had had the displeasure of meeting almost daily before the door of her house. Indeed,* he was the man. For he comes to see a permanent lodger here, an * old lady 'with whom nothing serious it was the matter', but 'she liked to see the doctor at least 3 times in the course of a week'.* This johnny I declined. However, the 2nd doctor who was consulted by her other lodgers was, she said, a young man called Dr James M. Williamson. It was him I called in; *indeed he is a nice young fellow, nothing priestly about him.* In fact, he could prescribe nothing save a LINIMENT for me to rub in. (So long as this muscular rheumatism persists it will hamper me, inducing as it does a feeling of discomfort, especially when I cough.) For the rest, he is apologetic about the bad weather. As regards the cough which has, particularly of late and also while I was in London, assumed an increasingly irksome, spasmodic character, I am my own health officer and hope I shall soon rid myself of it without the aid of a DOCTOR of medicine.

In order not to be too dependent on capricious variations in wind and temperature when loitering out of doors, I am again forced to carry a RESPIRATOR with me, in CASE OF NEED.

A great commotion has been caused here by a letter that appeared in *The Standard* [b] and the *Globe* TO THAT EFFECT that Ventnor is a CENTRAL HEAD OF TYPHOID FEVER and that a number of persons have fallen victim

---

[a] Here: seat of the trouble. - [b] 'Typhoid at Ventnor', *The Standard*, No. 18191, 6 November 1882.

to it of late. Official and unofficial replies to this 'LIBEL' have now appeared in the local press. But the funniest thing of all is that the Ventnor municipal panjandrum wants to start a LIBEL-CASE against the writer of the letter!

Salut.

Moor

First published abridged in *Der Briefwech-sel zwischen F. Engels und K. Marx*, Bd. 4, Stuttgart, 1913 and in full in *MEGA*, Abt. III, Bd. 4, Berlin, 1931

Printed according to the original

200

MARX TO PHILIP STEPHEN KING [33]

IN LONDON

Ventnor (Isle of Wight)
9 November 1882
1 St Boniface Gardens

Dear Sir,

I enclose Post Office Order for £ 4,10,10 (cf. your Fol. L. 83), your note having been sent over to me after my return from the continent. Please forward me the Reports etc. (see the other page) to my present residence at Ventnor. Please also send to the same address your monthly parliam. lists until my return to London. I do not know the title, nor the time of the publication, of a recent *Report on the London Bakehouses* the which, at all events, has been published in the spring or the summer of this year. You would oblige me by getting it for me.

Yours truly,
Karl Marx

P. S. King, Esq.

1) *Reports of the Inspectors of Factories for the years* 1877-1882.
2) *Agricultural Returns of Great Britain etc.* for 1881 and 1882.
3) *Agricultural Statistics*, Ireland, General abstracts for the *year 1880-1881* and the year *1881-1882*.

4) *Statistical Abstract for the United Kingdom.* The numbers: 28 and 29.
5) *Reports of the Commissioners of Her M's Inland Revenue* for the years *1874-1882.*
6) The last edition of:
   Alexander Redgrave: Factory and Workshop Act, 1878, with Introduction etc. (published by Shaw and Sons). [430]

First published, in the language of the orig-   Reproduced from the magazine
inal (English), in *Marx-Engels-Jahrbuch,*
Nr. 8, Berlin, 1985

201

ENGELS TO FRIEDRICH ADOLPH SORGE

IN HOBOKEN

London, 9 November 1882

Dear Sorge,

I have paid for *The Labour Standard* up till 3 December, 4/5d., and advised Shipton to send all future accounts to me.[431] Should you wish to cancel the subscription, perhaps you would let me have prompt notification.

Marx was here for 3 weeks, very much better; all he needs now is decent air and careful treatment. His minor ailments have been vanquished to the extent that he will certainly be rid of them next summer. The main thing is to get him through the winter without a recurrence of PLEURISY, and for that reason he has gone to Ventnor in the ISLE OF Wight [411] whence I have just received a line or two from him.[a] So far as circumstances permit, the 3rd edition [b] will now be taken vigorously in hand there and won't, I trust, occupy too much time. For the rest he was very cheerful and sprightly and, if all goes well until next autumn, he will be stronger than he has been for years.

My thanks with regard to Lilienthal. I now know the man as well as if we had been at school together.

I'm glad to hear that your Adolph [c] is getting on well; I trust he will

---

[a] See this volume, pp. 364-67. - [b] 3rd German edition of Vol. I of *Capital* - [c] Adolph Sorge jun.

soon find a LINE that will give him the opportunity he wants of getting on quickly. His letters have arrived but, like many others, unfortunately still remain unanswered.

Hepner is a proper Schlemihl [432]; moreover his campaigns, like the one he is waging against Schewitsch, are too much concerned with hair-splitting. Who, after all, is going to wax so enthusiastic about 'German culture'! He really ought to familiarise himself with American culture first. But that is typically German. Here we have someone arriving from a small town in the depths of Germany who cannot wait to enlighten America. However America will BREAK him IN all right and, since he has talent, and at one time also possessed a great deal of gumption, he may yet prove very useful.

16 November

That shows you what things are like here. Having had to break off a week ago I have only today got round to continuing this and, I trust, finishing it off.

Lafargue has been in Paris ever since the spring; his wife [a] followed later, during the summer; she spent a month with Marx in Vevey. [374] For Marx had first been in Algiers, [278] then in Monte Carlo (Monaco) [310] and in both places had suffered a recurrence of PLEURISY. After that he stayed with the Longuets in Argenteuil [327] where he availed himself of the sulphur springs at nearby Enghien for his chronic bronchitis. Then to Vevey and finally back here.

You might like to know that Lafargue (with a great deal of assistance from me, since he had absolutely no intention of learning German from his wife) has published in French 3 chapters from my *Anti-Dühring* (introduction and the two first chapters of Part III 'Socialism') under the title *Socialisme utopique et socialisme scientifique*. [20] It made a tremendous impression in France. Most people are too lazy to read stout tomes such as *Capital* and hence a slim little pamphlet like this has a much more rapid effect. I shall now publish the thing in German — with insertions calculated to give it a strong popular appeal; the ms. is already in Zurich and the first sheet has been printed. [378] I shall send it to you as soon as it is ready. Meanwhile you have, of course, in Dr Stiebeling a purveyor of popular knowledge to

---

[a] Laura Lafargue

America *in utraque lingua*.ᵃ He is a well-meaning man but no theorist and accordingly he is somewhat muddle-headed. The *Égalité* is now appearing daily *and* weekly. Whether the daily edition (in place of the *Citoyen* which our people were chucked out of thanks to a financial *coup* ᵇ) can keep going depends upon negotiations with a man of means. The *Sozialdemokrat* is being much too weak-kneed in regard to the split between our people and Malon, but the smooth, cunning, rascally Malon (one of the 17 founders of Bakunin's secret 'Alliance' ⁶⁷) has so ingratiated himself with the Germans in Paris and our people have made a number of such colossal blunders that the Paris people are doing their utmost to bring pressure to bear on Zurich. What's more, Liebknecht also intrigued with Malon when passing through Paris on his way home from here. If, however, Lafargue and Guesde commit some altogether too extravagant follies, I shall talk the *Sozialdemokrat* round, never fear.

Your
F. E.

Regards to Adolph.

First published abridged in *Briefe und Auszüge aus Briefen von Joh. Phil. Becker, Jos. Dietzgen, Friedrich Engels, Karl Marx u. A. an F. A. Sorge und Andere*, Stuttgart, 1906 and in full in: Marx and Engels, *Works*, First Russian Edition, Vol. XXVII, Moscow, 1935

Printed according to the original

Published in English for the first time

ᵃ Here: in two tongues (German and English).-ᵇ See this volume, pp. 343-44 and 346-47.

202

MARX TO ELEANOR MARX [72]

IN LONDON

[Ventnor,] 10 November[a] 1882
1 St Boniface Gardens

*My dear Tussychen,

On the whole, I cannot at all complain of Ventnor. The weather was unsettled, tempestuous, alternately rainy, dry, sunny, chilly, etc., but with all that very seldom foggy, a good deal of pure air and, except [for] a few days, generally always a few hours fit for longer promenades. Yesterday and today the air rather cold, but from 11 to 2 o'clock on the sea shore (where children are playing, and reminding me of poor Harry[b]) and on our Undercliff walk,[234] and up to the railway station, and even to the down, no want of sunshine!*

You should not forget, dear child, that I was by no means quite ALL RIGHT when I arrived here. On the contrary: a spasmodic cough pretty well all the time, a great deal of sputum, increasingly unsatisfactory nights during the previous 2 weeks, no sense of well-being whatever. That couldn't change all in one day; rather a progressive change for the better.

Au fond[c] I was in fact glad to have had recourse to Dr Williamson for my muscular rheumatism before Donkin's PRESCRIPTION arrived from London (today). The rheumatism is really very close to the former seat of my ITERATED PLEURISY, but Dr Williamson was able to convince me by percussion and auscultation that ALL WAS STILL RIGHT — and had been since Donkin's last examination. The cough has abated, but when he called today (his second visit) Williamson persuaded me to take yet another medicine; it would, he said, shorten the transitional period leading to the stage at which all I shall need to complete my recovery will be fresh air and plenty of outdoor exercise.

Under the circumstances I have not yet got down to any real work, though I have been occupying myself with one thing and another by way of preparation.

Do you have William Langland's *Complaint of Piers the Ploughman*?

---

[a] February in the ms. - [b] Henri Longuet - [c] At bottom

If not, you may be able to borrow it from Furnivall for me, or alternatively, as it isn't dear, I could also buy it in the EARLY etc. series.[433]

Also would you see if you could find among the (old-style) *Égalités* (I mean the old weekly *Égalité*) on the table by my bed an article, or rather a report, on the encomiums of *official economists in Paris* with regard to cheap Chinese labour in Europe? I don't know whether this same matter of the Chinese was discussed in the copy of Malon's former *Revue*[434] (the copy is behind the sofa on one of the shelves of my book-case). If so you might send it to me if you cannot lay your hands on the *Égalité*.

How is my Johnny faring? Cough gone? My love to him and Lenchen. And how is your health?

Finally, I must write to poor Jennychen. It distresses me; I fear that this burden is more than she can bear.[365]

Salut.

OLD NICK

First published, in the languages of the original (German and English), in *Annali*, an. I, Milano, 1958

Printed according to the original

203

ENGELS TO MARX

IN VENTNOR

London, 11 November 1882

Dear Moor,

I was able to show Tussy your letter[a] on the evening it arrived, for in the morning Lenchen and Johnny had gone to Percy's[b] OFFICE to watch the LORD MAYOR'S SHOW and in the evening we all foregathered at Pumps's for DINNER. Johnny was very charming and Pumps's gosling very well-behaved.

I am very glad you should have found a pleasant doctor[c]; it is always better if a convalescent has someone like that at hand, and what

---

[a] See this volume, pp. 364-67. - [b] Rosher - [c] James M. Williamson

good can it do if every trifle must first be referred back here? I trust the rheumatism and cough are now on the mend.

Today I am sending you 2 *Égalités* and one weekly ditto. The manifesto of the (Lyons) Conseil national [435] will convince you that the Lyonnais are still the typical louts they have always been. No further news about the progress of the negotiations with the Parisian capitalist,[423] so nothing would appear to have been settled yet.

The rudeness with which Dilke replies to awkward questions [436] is indeed striking, but seems very much to the taste of the bunch of liberal parvenus who sit behind him. Well, they'll feel the *clôture*[a] [437] soon enough. The business in Gibraltar [412] stinks more every day; the extradition was ordered, not only by the police, but also by a magistrate, i. e. a *judge*, and the Governor reads about it in the paper and doesn't lift a finger! Meanwhile the Russians are encroaching more and more on Persia and Afghanistan and building roads to Meshed in Persia and from Samarkand via Bukhara to Balkh (the Bactria of the Ancients) in Afghanistan, while their intrigues in Turkey are such that not even Aleko Pasha, their protégé in East Rumelia, can swallow them. But neither big Gladstone nor little Dilke have any eyes for this. The Russians certainly have something in mind for next spring. But the kind of credit they enjoy will be evident to you from the announcement of the Poti-Baku Railway's Preference Loan. They have to use a company as a cloak and, moreover, on what terms!

Vollmar has opened his pro-Malon campaign in the *Sozialdemokrat*—Malon's promptings being instantly recognisable in the saccharine tone of the apologia with which the article concludes.[438] But what do you think of Wilhelm's[b] panegyric of Bennigsen in the *Justice*? It's really laid on a bit thick, even for the worthy Wilhelm.

The Swiss Factory Act [403] also goes off in today's parcel. I shall ask Bernstein for Oldenburg's article[c] at the earliest opportunity. Bernstein will probably think twice before writing to me; I made such good use of his own arguments to refute his conclusions concerning the French business that he is unlikely to find very much more to say.[d]

Now, with the closure of the debate, the House of Commons has sunk wholly to the level of a continental Chamber which, in view of its present composition, is the position best suited to it.

----

[a] closure - [b] Presumably Wilhelm Liebknecht. - [c] See this volume, p. 365. - [d] Ibid., pp. 354-57, 360-62.

I am very curious to hear more about the experiment made by Deprez at Munich.[426] However, I completely fail to understand how, in that case, laws for estimating resistance in wires hitherto regarded as valid and still applied in practice by engineers (in their calculations) can continue in force. Hitherto it has been calculated that, given the same conductive material, resistance *increases* in proportion as the diameter of the conducting wire *decreases*. I wish Longuet could be induced to cough up those things. For this means that the vast and hitherto untapped sources of hydraulic power have suddenly become exploitable.

But now I must pack up the papers. All well here.

Your
F. E.

First published abridged in *Der Briefwechsel zwischen F. Engels und K. Marx*, Bd. 4, Stuttgart, 1913 and in full in *MEGA*, Abt. III, Bd. 4, Berlin, 1931

Printed according to the original

Published in English for the first time

204

MARX TO ENGELS[166]

IN LONDON

[Ventnor,] 11 November 1882

DEAR FRED,

I return the *Prolétaire*.[a] Difficult to say who is the greater — Lafargue, who pours out his oracular inspiration upon the bosoms of Malon and Brousse, or these two heroes, heavenly twins who not only tell deliberate lies, but deceive themselves into thinking that the outside world has nothing better to do than to 'intrigue' against them and, indeed, that everyone has the same cranial structure as the magnanimous twain.

Lafargue has the blemish customarily found in the negro tribe — *no sense of shame*, by which I mean shame about making a fool of oneself.

But it is time, if the journal[b] is not to be wilfully ruined and if they

---

[a] See this volume, pp. 363-64. - [b] *L'Égalité*

do not *intend* (which I can't believe) to *let* it go under as a result of proceedings taken by the government — it is time, I say, for Lafargue to put a stop to his childish bragging about the grisly deeds of his revolution of the future. But on this occasion he has been properly hoist with his own petard. Naturally alarmed because some denunciatory sheet or other, in defiance of police regulations, has reprinted hair-raising anarchist excerpts from the suppressed *Étendard*, thus making the latter seem 'more progressive' than Paul Lafargue, the licensed oracle of *socialisme scientifique* — alarmed at such revolutionary competition, Lafargue quotes himself (and he has, of late, acquired a pretty habit, not only of unloosing his oracles on the world, but of 'perpetuating' them by self-quotation) as proof that the *Étendard*, i. e. that *anarchism*, has merely aped the wisdom of Lafargue and Co., though merely with the intention of realising it prematurely, before the time is ripe. That's what sometimes happens to oracles; what they believe to be their own inspiration is, on the contrary and more often than not, merely a recollection that has remained stuck in their minds. And what Lafargue has written and 'quoted' from himself is, in fact, no more than the recollection of a Bakunian precept. Lafargue is, indeed, the last remaining disciple of Bakunin seriously to believe in him. He should reread the pamphlet he and you wrote about the 'Alliance',[a] and then he would realise whence he has derived this, his most recent ammunition. Indeed, much time has had to pass before he HAD UNDERSTOOD Bakunin AND, INTO THE BARGAIN, HAS MISUNDERSTOOD HIM.

Longuet as the last Proudhonist and Lafargue as the last Bakuninist! *Que le diable les emporte!* [b]

It's a fine day today, and I must go out of doors (it's only half past ten in the morning).

In my last letter, I told you I intended to get rid of my cough without the help of MEDICAL MEN. But Dr Williamson gave me to understand *d'une manière autoritaire* [c] that I must for all that be so good as to swallow my medicine. In fact, the brew has done me good; its main ingredient is quinine disulphuricum; the others — morphia, chloroform, etc., have invariably formed part of the brews I have previously had to swallow.

---

[a] K. Marx and F. Engels, *The Alliance of Socialist Democracy and the International Working Men's Association* (written in collaboration with Paul Lafargue). - [b] May the devil take them! - [c] in authoritative manner

What's the position in regard to Hartmann's pangs *qua* inventor [a]?
Salut.

Moor

You'll have seen from the PARLIAMENTARY DEBATES in yesterday's *Standard* [b] that the 'worthy' *Rivers Wilson* has obliged to the extent of sorrowfully offering up on the altar of country his project, the TRUSTEE-SHIP he assumed in company with the magnanimous Lowe alias Sherbrooke. [428] A bitter pill for Rivers Wilson.

First published abridged in *Der Briefwech-sel zwischen F. Engels und K. Marx*, Bd. 4, Stuttgart, 1913 and in full in *MEGA*, Abt. III, Bd. 4, Berlin, 1931

Printed according to the original

Published in English in full for the first time

205

ENGELS TO KARL KAUTSKY

IN VIENNA

London, 15 November 1882

Dear Mr Kautsky,

I got your telegram at 3 p. m. today and at once replied by telegraph: 'Impossible'. Not having your home address to hand and necessarily assuming from the 'Reply paid' that the office of origin would know *where* to send the reply, I addressed the telegram simply 'Kautsky, Vienna'. Well, I have this moment, 9.30 p. m., received the enclosed slip. There is no possibility of tracing the letter with your home address, so all I can do is write to you at once in order not to miss the morning post.

If I am not to dissipate every bit of my energy again, and I have been doing this for years, I shall have to draw a very strict line so far as my journalistic activity is concerned — confining myself to the *Sozialdemokrat* and even then writing only when practical need arises

---

[a] See this volume, p. 320. - [b] 'Imperial Parliament. House of Commons. The Obligations of Civil Servants', *The Standard*, No. 18195, 10 November 1882.

or when, as in the recent case of Mehring's inanities,[346] it has to be shown that there is no hostility between the *Sozialdemokrat* and us over here. As a result of Marx's absence and illness, party correspondence with diverse countries has devolved exclusively upon myself, and that is a heavy enough burden anyway. So if I am to devote my advancing years to the completion of my more weighty works,[439] it will be utterly impossible for me to contribute to your periodical,[a] though I wish it every success.

The Darwin article in particular is an impossibility just now. I wrote to Bernstein saying he should have it as soon as I lit upon this subject in the course of my studies, and that might be months ahead; not that he is entirely blameless for he has encouraged me to work in a quite different field — one that I, too, consider to be more necessary.[b] So until I have slogged my way through that, returned to natural science and then progressed to zoology, there can be no question of it. To dash off a few commonplaces on Darwin would serve neither you nor me. For the rest I must confine myself, in view of the late hour, to thanking you for the various interesting reports on the situation over there and in conclusion sending you my heartiest congratulations on your engagement.[c]

Yours very sincerely,

F. E.

First published, in Russian, in *Marx-Engels Archives*, Vol. I (VI), Moscow, 1932

Printed according to the original

Published in English for the first time

206

MARX TO ENGELS

IN LONDON

[Ventnor,] 20 November 1882

DEAR FRED,

By the end of this week (i. e. next Monday, *27 November*) I shall be on my uppers. As I am supposed to advise you a week beforehand,

---

[a] *Die Neue Zeit* - [b] See this volume, pp. 324-25. - [c] to Louise Strasser

I am now doing so. Before leaving London I paid ABOUT £5 to the PARLIAMENTARY BOOKSELLER St. King and ABOUT £2 to Kolkmann (bookseller), but also spent £3 on sundry items.

Tussy and Johnny left me at ABOUT 3 O'CLOCK today in passable weather.

I am perturbed over the news from Paris; it's unpardonable that Lafargue, Guesde, etc., should permit themselves to be caught up in legal proceedings [440]; it could have been foreseen; the whole thing was simply occasioned by 'anxiety' over competition from the 'anarchists'! Puerile!

Salut.

Your
K. M.

First published in *Der Briefwechsel zwischen F. Engels und K. Marx*, Bd. 4, Stuttgart, 1913

Printed according to the original

Published in English for the first time

207

ENGELS TO MARX

IN VENTNOR

London, 21 November 1882

Dear Moor,

I was on the point of asking you how your reserves stood when your letter[a] arrived today. Encl. CHEQUE for £30 which you will be able to cash in the usual way. That being so, you will get the money on Monday, possibly even on Saturday or, if you're prepared to lay out 1/- on a telegram, as early as Friday.

Encl. 1. a mathematical experiment by Moore.[441] His conclusion, namely that THE ALGEBRAIC METHOD IS ONLY THE DIFFERENTIAL METHOD DISGUISED, relates, of course, solely to his own method of geometrical construction and to that extent is fairly correct. I have written to tell

_____

[a] See previous letter.

him [284] that you attach no importance whatever to the way in which one symbolises things in a geometrical construction, the application of the curves to the equations being, after all, sufficient. What's more, I went on, the basic difference between your method and the old one consists in your transforming x into x′, i. e., making it a *true variable*, whereas the others proceed from x + h which simply represents the sum of two quantities but never the variation of a quantity. Which is why your x, even though it has passed through x′ and reverted to the first x, is nevertheless different from what it was before, whereas if one simply adds h to x and then subtracts it again, x remains constant throughout. But then any graphic depiction of variations must necessarily be the depiction of a *past* process, of the *result*, i. e. of a quantity that has become constant; the line x, the portion added to that constant, is depicted as x + h, two portions of one line. From this it clearly follows that a graphic depiction of how x becomes x′ and then x again is impossible.

Further, 2., a letter from Bernstein which has just arrived and which I should like to have back.[442]

(I was interrupted by Pumps and the baby[a] so shall have to get a move on with this letter as I have persuaded myself that it must go off at 5.30.)

I don't know whether I ought not to fire a broadside or two at Vollmar for his doctoring of history *à la* Malon.[438] His suppression of the Marseilles Congress[443] is carrying the falsification of history a bit too far. If Bernstein fails to raise this in the notes on the final article, it will have to be put right.

I shall send you the *Égalité* as soon as I have read it. As usual, a letter Lafargue promised to write has not yet arrived. His public reply to the examining magistrate, in which he came the professor, was a childish affair.[444] These people are acting as though they were absolutely intent on being arrested. Fortunately the government is pretty rocky, so it's possible that they will still get away with it.

Tussy and Johnny arrived ALL RIGHT yesterday.

Your

F. E.

First published abridged in *Der Briefwechsel zwischen F. Engels und K. Marx*, Bd. 4, Stuttgart, 1913 and in full in *MEGA*, Abt. III, Bd. 4, Berlin, 1931

Printed according to the original

Published in English for the first time

---

[a] Lilian Rosher

208

MARX TO ENGELS

IN LONDON

Ventnor, 22 November 1882
1 St Boniface Gardens

DEAR FRED,

CHEQUE most gratefully received.

Sam,[a] as you, too, immediately saw, criticises the analytic method as applied by me [441] in as much as he quietly sets it aside and instead turns his attention to the geometrical application, about which I said nothing at all.

I might similarly dismiss the development of the actual differential method as it is called — beginning with the mystical method of Newton and Leibniz, then going on to the rationalist method of d'Alembert and Euler and concluding with Lagrange's strictly algebraic method (still, however, emanating from the selfsame original premises of Newton and Leibniz) — I might dismiss the whole of this historical development of analysis by saying that, *in practice*, no essential change has been brought about in the geometrical application of differential calculus, i. e. in geometrical symbolisation.

Since the sun is just coming out and this, therefore, is the moment to go for a walk, I shall not, *pro nunc*,[b] enlarge further on the subject of mathematics but shall, on some later occasion, return to a detailed discussion of the various methods.

Bernstein's information about the 'nationalisation' of the railways in Prussia is interesting.[442]

I do not share his views about the great size of Malon's and Brousse's organisation [445]; the analysis provided at the time by Guesde of the 'numerous' (!) delegation attending the congress of St-Étienne has not been refuted, but this would be straining at gnats.[c] The first decision to organise a genuine workers' party in France dates back to the Marseilles Congress [443]; at the time Malon was in Switzerland; Brousse WAS NOWHERE, and the *Prolétaire* — along with its trade unions — held aloof.

---

[a] Samuel Moore - [b] for the time being - [c] Matthew 23:24

That jackass Amos—the mouthpiece of English officialdom in Egypt—has enormously impaired his clients' case by affording Keay, author of the pamphlet *Spoiling the Egyptians*, the opportunity for 'A Rejoinder' in *The Contemporary Review*.[446] Prominent among those whom Keay has ground ever more deeply into the MUD are Rivers Wilson, Rowsell and Goschen, and with them the British Ministry.

Salut.

Moor

First published in *Der Briefwechsel zwischen F. Engels und K. Marx*, Bd. 4, Stuttgart, 1913

Printed according to the original

Published in English for the first time

209

ENGELS TO MARX[447]

IN VENTNOR

London, 22 November 1882

Dear Moor,

You will have received my letter of yesterday's date, with CHEQUE for £30.

Hartmann[a] was here on Sunday evening in a state of intense inventor's euphoria. His cell has been in action since Friday, operating a galvanometer with high resistance which at first registered more than 50° and is now steady at 46°. It would, he said, continue to run smoothly without further attention not just for three, but actually for six months or even a year. However, he had no intention of showing it to buyers because of as yet unpatented improvements. So my intervention was again required. I firmly refused and arranged for the matter — a perfectly simple one that presents no real difficulty — to be settled by Percy[b] (which it has), advising him [Hartmann] in future to supply his

---

[a] Lev Hartmann - [b] Rosher

English buyers with the article he had sold them and not something else, either better or worse. Whether it will do any good is another question. The chap's a fanatical worker; work and fanaticism are wearing him out; the only sleep he gets is between 3 and 5 in the morning, and he looks ghastly but is correspondingly well turned out and every time he comes here he is wearing a different suit. One of his new patent improvements is as follows: To protect the cell's caustic potash, KOH, against the carbonic acid in the air, and to prevent it turning into potassium carbonate, he poured *oil* onto the solution and, according to Percy, simply couldn't understand why this failed to do the trick, the combination of fat and alkali forming instead something that looked like soap and, indeed, *was* soap!

I have recently obtained SECOND HAND what I have long been looking for—a complete bound edition of *Geschichtschreiber der deutschen Vorzeit*, and guess from the sale of whose library it had come?—*Dr Strousberg's!* I found therein a passage in Plutarch's *Marius* which, seen in conjunction with Caesar and Tacitus,[a] explains the entire agrarian structure.

> The Cimbri 'had migrated, but not, as it were, all at one go, or in a regular stream; rather, they had always pushed on, year after year, during the good season and in this way had, over a long period, fought and battled their way across the Continent'.[b]

This passage, seen in conjunction with the Suebi's annual move to new lands, as described 70 years later by Caesar, reveals the manner in which the Germanic migrations took place. Where they spent the winter, there they would sow in the spring and, having reaped, would move on until winter brought them to a halt again. That they *regularly* tilled the land in summer (if they did not engage in rapine instead) can be assumed with some certainty in the case of peoples who had brought agriculture with them from Asia. In the case of the Cimbri, the process of migration is still in evidence; in Caesar it comes to an end, the Rhine forming an impassable frontier. Together, these two manifestations explain why, in Caesar, '*privati ac separati agri apud eos nihil est*'[c]: migration means that collective cultivation was only possible by kinship community, and to pace out individual fields

---

[a] Caesar, *Commentarii de bello Gallico* and Tacitus, *Germania*, both in the above-mentioned edition. - [b] Quated from Plutarch's *Life of Marius* according to *Die Geschichtschreiber der deutschen Vorzeit...*, Vol. 1, 'Die Urzeit', p. 61. - [c] amongst them there are no private or separate fields

would have been absurd. In Tacitus, the step forward — or, perhaps, back — to individual cultivation within the framework of common ownership has been made.

Tussy has sent me by hand various newspapers for onward transmission to you; with them, I enclose an *Égalité*. The *Égalité*'s impertinence would really seem to have made an impression on the *Parquet*ᵃ; the addresses are still written in Lafargue's hand.

Kindest regards.

Your
F. E.

First published abridged in *Der Briefwechsel zwischen F. Engels und K. Marx*, Bd. 4, Stuttgart, 1913 and in full in *MEGA*, Abt. III, Bd. 4, Berlin, 1931

Printed according to the original

Published in English in full for the first time

210

ENGELS TO MARX

IN VENTNOR

London, 23 November 1882

Dear Moor,

Encl. letter from Lafargue which you might let me have back as I only got it this morning. So he will doubtless have to wend his way to the *cachot*ᵇ within the next few days. What incurable fools they are. If Guesde and Lafargue are locked up in Montluçon, the paperᶜ will be pretty well done for. The government dare not bring them before a court in Paris, but may well take the liberty of quietly neutralising one after the other in the provinces. Until the paper had been firmly established, they ought not to have provided any pretexts for intervention; instead of that we have these Bakuninist antics.

I had asked Lafargue for information about the relative strength of the two parties and also about the Maret-Godard affair.[416] You see

---

ᵃ Public Prosecutor's Department - ᵇ prison - ᶜ *L'Égalité*

what he says. Obviously it was to please the *Chambres Syndicales* [a] and none other than Malon & Co. sacrificed the programme and the movement's entire past since the time of the Marseilles Congress.[448] His apparent strength is his real weakness. If you debase your programme to the level of the most ordinary TRADES UNIONS, you will clearly have no difficulty in obtaining a 'large public'.

Electricity has enabled me to score a minor triumph. You may perhaps remember my discussing the Cartesian-Leibnizian point of dispute in regard to mv and mv^2 as measures of motion.[449] What it boils down to is that mv is the measure of mechanical motion when transmitted by mechanical motion *as such*, whereas $\dfrac{mv^2}{2}$ is the measure of motion when it changes its form, i. e. the measure in conformity with which it turns into heat, electricity, etc. Now, so long as the chaps in the physical laboratories had the sole say in electrical matters, the measure of electromotive force, the force regarded as representative of electrical energy, was the volt (E), the product of the intensity of the current (ampère, C) and resistance (ohm, R).

$$E = C \times R.$$

And that is correct so long as electrical energy does not change on transmission into another form of motion. Now, however, in his presidential address at the last meeting of the British Association,[372] we have Siemens proposing an additional unit, the watt (hereafter W) which is intended to express the true energy of an electric current (i. e. as distinct from other forms of motion, *vulgo* energy) and whose value is volt × ampère, W = E × C.

But $W = E \times C = C \times R \times C = C^2R$.

Resistance in electricity represents the same as *mass* in mechanical motion. Hence it would appear that in electrical as in mechanical motion the quantitatively measurable manifestation of this motion — on the one hand velocity, on the other intensity of current — functions, in the case of simple transmission *without* change of form, as a simple factor of the first power, while in the case of transmission *with* change of form, as a factor *squared*. Thus what I have formulated for the first time is a universal natural law of motion. Now, however, I must really go ahead and finish my dialectics of nature.

---

[a] Syndicalist Chambers (more on these trade union organisations see on pp. 388-89)

All is well at your house, but the beer everywhere is rotten; only the German stuff in the West End is any good.

Your
F. E.

First published abridged in *Der Briefwech-sel zwischen F. Engels und K. Marx*, Bd. 4, Stuttgart, 1913 and in full in *MEGA*, Abt. III, Bd. 4, Berlin, 1931

Printed according to the original

Published in English for the first time

211

MARX TO ENGELS

IN LONDON

[Ventnor,] 27 November 1882

DEAR FRED,

Enclosed Lafargue's letter. In my note to you[a] I had already given vent in advance to my vexation over Lafargue's and Guesde's foolishness, and thus discounted it. Inconceivable that anyone at the head of a movement could place everything at risk in so frivolous, to put it bluntly, in *so inane* a way—*pour le roi de Prusse*[b]! Lafargue's article on the spellbound Ministry of Finance was very well done.[450]

As regards the Paris 'syndicates', I know from impartial reports I received from Paris (while staying at Argenteuil[451]) that the said syndicates are a great deal worse, if such a thing be possible, than the London TRADES UNIONS.

Your verification of the role of the *second power* when energy is transmitted with change of form is very pretty and I congratulate you on it.[c]

Salut.

Moor

First published in *Der Briefwechsel zwischen F. Engels und K. Marx*, Bd. 4, Stuttgart, 1913

Printed according to the original

Published in English for the first time

---

[a] See this volume, pp. 374-76. - [b] for the King of Prussia, i. e. for nothing - [c] See this volume, p. 384.

212

ENGELS TO EDUARD BERNSTEIN

IN ZURICH

London, 28 November 1882

Dear Mr Bernstein,

To begin with, my best thanks for the information about the nationalised railways. It is amply sufficient.[452] I have received from Bebel the Accident and Health Insurance Bills of *1882*, but must, of course, also have those of 1881, the original wording [144] being precisely the one in which Bismarck's soul, filled with ardour for the poor, has ample space to flap its wings; in the second wording, in which the said wings have already been substantially clipped as a result of bourgeois divisions, we no longer find Bismarck in his entirety.

Marx used to get the *Arbeiterstimme*, but as he has probably failed to renew his subscription it no longer arrives.

Aside from a few minor points, Vollmar's article [438] is pure Malon at one remove. In it the history of the French workers' movement since 1871 is *completely falsified*, and that sort of thing simply should not happen. For instance, in the 2nd article Guesde is blamed for not having joined up with the few small cliques (later the progenitors of the *Prolétaire* or, in other words, the out and out *coopérateurs* against whom he was just then conducting a campaign)! As though the chaps who were subsequently to bring out the *Prolétaire* would have even considered admitting a 'non-worker'! But more falsified than anything else is what Deville has correctly depicted in the *Égalité* of 19 November ('*Il y a cinq ans*',[a] history of the *Égalité*), namely, the fight for the 'collectivist' programme [68] at the congresses and *the victory of that programme in 1879 at the Marseilles Congress*.[443] This is completely suppressed in Vollmar's article. I cannot assume that Vollmar deliberately perpetrated this falsification, but nor is it any easier to explain his ignorance of the subject and the fact that he appears to know nothing at all about the French workers' movement save what Malon thought fit to tell him.

Hence, by omitting the Marseilles Congress, he suppresses the vital fact that the French workers' party had accepted the collectivist

---

[a] 'Five Years Ago'.

programme 3 years ago, so that Malon's abandonment of it was a *definitely retrograde step*. Since it is now essential that our people in Germany should be told the story of the French movement, not as it ought to have happened to fit in with Malon's present requirements, but as it really did happen, this is something which must unquestionably be put right. In my view, the simplest way of doing so would be to relate it to the above-mentioned article by Deville, precisely because this is so utterly unpolemical. Should you no longer have it, I can send it you forthwith on a postcard.

Malon, by the way, had better watch out. Should we at any time wish to portray his *faits et gestes*[a] more accurately if as minutely as he got Vollmar to depict those of Guesde, he would have a rough time of it. We still have all the documents in which, on 18 March '71, he *disavowed the rising*, only to join it after the event, when things were doing better than he had expected.

Now as regards the strength of the two factions, I have obtained a report on the subject from Lafargue.[453] In Paris the Roanne people have 15 groups with whose help they have kept the *Égalité* going for a whole month now, which does at any rate say something for the quality of these chaps. In the provinces they are, so Lafargue says, very strong. The Fédération du Nord[454] is, in essence, on their side; they do not wish to *prendre part aux querelles des Parisiens*[b] but they uphold the old collectivist programme which also features prominently in their *Forçat*; the Roanne people are holding their next congress at Roubaix, to which *all* the delegates of the North will be going, and are constantly in the closest touch with the Fédération du Nord. The other provincial workers' paper, *L'Exploité de Nantes*, has similarly printed the old programme together with the *considérants*[c][455] in a prominent position. It reprints articles from the *Égalité*, and Deville is a contributor. This means that *the only* two workers' organs in the provinces are *both* on their side. '*En province*',[d] aside from the North, '*partout où il y a un groupement ouvrier, à Reims, Epinay, Lyon, dans tout le bassin houillier de l'Allier, à Bordeaux, Angoulême, Rochefort, nous battons les Possibilistes qui n'ont de force qu'en Bretagne at à Marseille — et encore.*'[e]

---

[a] goings-on -[b] take part in the squabbles of the Parisians -[c] preambles -[d] 'In the provinces' -[e] 'wherever there is a concentration of workers, at Rheims, Epinay, Lyons, throughout the Allier mining district, at Bordeaux, Angoulême, and Rochefort, we are vanquishing the Possibilists who are strong only in Brittany and in Marseilles — if strong is the right word.'

That Malon should obtain a wide hearing for the empty verbiage of his *considérants* without a programme is not surprising. But if one founds a party without a programme in which everyone can have a say, it cannot properly be called a party. The impotence of the old sectarians, for whom Malon and Vollmar show such tender regard, has been in evidence for years and it would be best to let them wither quietly away. As for the *Chambres Syndicales* [a] — well, if one is going to account a member of the workers' party every STRIKE association which, like the English TRADES UNIONS, fights solely for high wages and short working hours but doesn't otherwise give a damn for the movement,— then the only party one will actually form is one for the *preservation* of wage labour rather than its abolition. And, or so Marx tells me,[b] these Parisian *Chambres Syndicales* are for the most part even more colourless than the English TRADES UNIONS. To abolish a party programme just to please these people is no way to spur them on. And has the like ever been seen before— a party without a programme, a party whose wishy-washy *considérants* (written wholly in the spirit of the communist Miquel, who likewise believed communism to be feasible in 500 years' time [456]) lead up to the conclusion that each group should concoct its own private programme?

Well, now, what benefit does Malon derive from the *Chambres Syndicales*? They pay no contributions, they send no delegates to the Federal Council, they were nominal members of the Union fédérative [265] before the split and have nominally remained so— they are, as Lafargue puts it, '*complétement platoniques*'. They are there for show. As for Malon's other groups, Lafargue writes:

'*Dans le XVII arrondissement nos amis ont organisé, après le congrès, un groupe qui immédiatement s'est trouvé composé de 29 membres. Pour nous faire pièce, les possibilistes ont s u b d i v i s é leur groupe qui, à ce que l'on me dit, ne se composait que d'une vingtaine de membres, e n c i n q s o u s - g r o u p e s réunis par un comité fédéral du quartier. Le tour est joli, mais ne trompe que les indifférents et ceux qui sont éloignés.*' [c]

That's just what the Bakuninists used to do. On the other hand, so Lafargue says, the Possibilists are really strong only in Montmartre, where they are also well-organised.

---

[a] Syndicalist Chambers - [b] See this volume, p. 385. - [c] 'In the XVII arrondissement our friends organised, after the Congress, a group of which the immediate composition was 29 members. To play a trick on us the Possibilists *subdivided* their group, which by all accounts consisted of some twenty members only, *into five sub-groups* convened by a federal committee in the quarter. It's a pretty trick, but one that can deceive only those who are indifferent or far away.'

To be momentarily in the minority — *quoad*[a] organisation — and
have the right programme is at least better than having no programme and a large, though almost entirely nominal and bogus, following. We have been in the minority all our lives and have thrived
on it. And the comparative weakness (supposing it exists, which I am
very much inclined to doubt — the Possibilists did not dare attend the
Roanne people's *conférence contradictoire*[b] on the two congresses [457]);
the comparative weakness where organisations in Paris are concerned would be outweighed two or three times over by journalistic
influence.

So how your Paris correspondents are able to regard the St-Étienne
folk as the 'genuine workers' party' is beyond me. In the first place
they are not a party at all, let alone a *workers'* party, any more than
are the workers over here. But they are in embryo what those over
here have become in full maturity, namely the *tail of the radical
bourgeois party*. The only thing that keeps them together is bourgeois
radicalism, for they have no labour programme. And as for those
labour leaders who descend to manufacturing a docile labour vote for
the radicals, they are, in my view, *downright traitors*.

Your remarks also led me, just for fun, to ask about Godard.[416]
The said Godard, *'qui se dit anarchiste comme son maître Maret, écrit
dans un journal opportuniste de Toulouse'.*[c] To refuse
a chap of this kind what is known as a rectification is quite in keeping
with the customs of the Paris, as of any other, press.

On the other hand our friends have again perpetrated a really colossal bloomer in as much as they have, by their rrrevolutionary bragging, exposed themselves to prosecution before the paper[d] had found
its feet. Guesde has been arrested, as you know, and Lafargue will
probably soon follow in his wake. When both are in jug, the most active — not only writing, but fighting — men will have been got out of
the way. Deville is lazy, Massard quite good for his post of *secrétaire de
la rédaction,*[e] but they are hardly the people to keep a paper going in
difficult circumstances. I won't mention the other 3 — Brissac and
Bouis, old Communards, are so much ballast, and Picard is a common-or-garden journalist.

Whatever you do, by the way, don't allow anyone to persuade you
that Guesde and Lafargue intended, 'by hook or by crook, to make

---

[a] as to - [b] public debate - [c] 'who professes to be an anarchist like his master Maret,
writes for an opportunist Toulouse journal' - [d] *L'Égalité* - [e] secretary to the editors

all organisations subject to their own directives'. It is a constantly recurring catchword in Bakuninist tactics, and in other contexts in
France it may always be resorted to in lieu of other arguments.

Treatment of other countries in the *Égalité*! If only you knew what
disorder reigns and what the standard of German is like in *that* office!
Should Lafargue remain at large, you would do best always to address yourself to him; he does at least forward the things. Otherwise
I have no advice to offer.

If you want to use the resumé of the pamphlet, [378] I am quite
agreeable. The concluding note will follow shortly. The *affaire*
Schmidt [458] is very nice. *Pollaky* has been running a private detec-
tive's office in London for some time. In the directory, under the heading INQUIRY OFFICER (of whom 18 are listed), there is an entry:
'Pollaky, Ignatius Paul, 13 Paddington Green, W. (not at all far from
where I live), Correspondent to the *Foreign Police Gazette*.'

I trust my congratulations on your attaining your 7th thousand [a]
will again prove outdated. I, for my part, am 62 years old today.
Kindest regards.

Yours,

F. E.

First published, in Russian, in *Marx-
Engels Archives*, Book I, Moscow, 1924

Printed according to the original

Published in English for the first
time

213

ENGELS TO MARX

IN VENTNOR

London, 30 November 1882

Dear Moor,

Encl. a letter from Bebel [459] received today. The 'mystery' which
he is unable to understand all of a sudden and which may release
them from the Anti-Socialist Law, [16] is, of course, the outbreak of the
crisis in Russia. [b] Curious that none of these people can get used to the

---

[a] of *Der Sozialdemokrat* - [b] See this volume, pp. 414-15.

idea that the impulse might come from that quarter. And it is not as though I haven't explained this to him more than once. I regard his hopes for a new *major* crisis as premature — there could be an interim crisis as in 1842, and Germany, the most backward country industrially, which must content itself with the crumbs that fall to it from the demand of the world market, would certainly suffer worse than any other.

Guesde was released in Montluçon immediately after the first hearing, and neither Bazin nor Lafargue was arrested; on the contrary, Bazin published in the *Égalité* a letter to the chief of police of his *arrondissement*, objecting to the *mouchards*[a] that sniffed round his house and advising him of the times at which he could be arrested at home.[b] Those chaps have more luck than sense. I shan't be able to read the *Égalité* until after the 5.30 post has gone; so it will reach you tomorrow by the 2nd post (2 nos).

I have obtained, second-hand, *Vom Entstehen und Untergange der polnischen Konstitution vom 3. Mai 1791*, 1793, place of publication not given. This is the book you have mentioned so often[460] in which the infamies perpetrated upon Poland by Frederick William II are described at length. Cost one whole mark!

Hartmann's battery for lighting 6 Swan incandescent lamps is expected to be ready tomorrow. If the thing proves a success, i. e. provides a steady light over an extended period, hence actual proof of the constant intensity of the current, it will at once be exhibited in public and a company 'founded' to exploit it. Hartmann will also be showing sundry items at the Crystal Palace[461] where a new electrical exhibition is shortly to be held. He and his backer, whom Percy[c] found for him, are highly enthusiastic about the invention.

All well here.

Your
F. E.

First published abridged in *Der Briefwechsel zwischen F. Engels und K. Marx*, Bd. 4, Stuttgart, 1913 and in full in *MEGA*, Abt. III, Bd. 4, Berlin, 1931

Printed according to the original

Published in English for the first time

---

[a] informers - [b] G. Bazin, 'À Monsieur le commissaire de police', *L'Égalité*, 4th series, No. 38, 30 November 1882. - [c] Rosher

214

MARX TO ENGELS [72]

IN LONDON

[Ventnor,] 4 December 1882

DEAR FRED,

Herewith Bebel's letter [459] which I found most interesting. I do not believe an industrial crisis will supervene as soon as all that.

The weather in November was good on the whole, though very changeable. The first days of December alternated between bitter cold and a nasty, damp mugginess. Today it is fine, but I am nevertheless condemned to remain in my room. In the last few days I have suffered from hoarseness (certainly not due to talking) and an unpleasant sensation in my gullet; I have also been coughing more and not sleeping very well, despite my long, regular and constant walks. Hence I have again called in the doctor.[a] These gentlemen cannot be shaken off so easily! It is only a tracheal catarrh, but all the same he thought I ought to keep within doors until the inflammation has gone. Besides giving me some soothing medicine to take, he has ordered me to inhale vapour of benzoin (with something else added— seems to me something like chloroform). Today he again auscultated and percussed me—for the 3rd time since my arrival—and found that everything was otherwise in order. He will drop in again in a few days' time to see if I can be released from my confinement.

What is remarkable about the stuff in the *Plebe* concerning my theory of value is the rubbish talked by all 3, Laveleye, Cafiero and Candelari, [462] in mutual opposition *l'un contre l'autre*.[b] In the quotation concerning my aforementioned theory of value which Candelari adduced from *Malon's Histoire critique de l'économie politique*, Malon's superficiality is such that it actually surpasses that of all 3 smatterers.

*I hope *that all right in 41*, Maitland Park Road.*[c] I was ex-

---

[a] James M. Williamson - [b] one against the other - [c] Marx's address in London

pecting a line or two from there, but I know that POOR Tussy OVER-
WORKED.

Salut.

Moor

First published in *Der Briefwechsel zwischen*
F. Engels und K. Marx, Bd. 4, Stuttgart,
1913

Printed according to the original

215

MARX TO ENGELS

IN LONDON

[Postcard]

[Postmarked Ventnor, 8 December 1882]

Returned herewith *Prolétaire* received today, containing account
of Shipton & Co.[463] (whom, incidentally, Lafargue praised to
the skies in the selfsame *Égalité* because of a collection made for
a FRENCH 'STRIKE'. That's what happens when every momentary STIMU-
LUS immediately causes him to turn in some 'predestined' direction).

In your last postcard [284] delivered today, on the other hand, you
mention a *Prolétaire*, sent me by mistake and to be returned to you,
which never arrived here.[a] It should have come yesterday or today, or
at least within the past week, but *quod non* [b] — *perhaps it has got lost in*
the post?

The *Sozialdemokrat* ought to procure some *material* (*detailed*) on the
treatment of workers in Prussian state mines, etc., to help define
the nature of Wagener-Bismarckian state socialism.

Salut.

Moor

---

[a] See this volume, p. 394. - [b] not so

[On the side reserved for the address]

Ḟ. Engels, Esq.
122 Regent's Park Road,
London, N. W.

First published in *Der Briefwechsel zwischen F. Engels und K. Marx*, Bd. 4, Stuttgart, 1913

Printed according to the original

Published in English for the first time

216

ENGELS TO MARX [7]

IN VENTNOR

London, 8 December 1882

Dear Moor,

What happened about the *Prolétaire* was this: when I recently sent you a parcel of *Égalités* and *Kölnische Zeitungs*, I also meant to send you the TRADES UNION *Prolétaire* [463] and supposed I had included it. Somebody was in the room while I was packing up the parcel and I did this rather hurriedly. Finding next day that the TRADES UNION *Prolétaire* was still here, but not the other containing the Saint-Étienne skulduggery, [425] I thought I must have sent it you twice over. Now, looking around by the light of day, I have found it — still in the original wrapper in which you returned it, this being undoubtedly the reason why I couldn't find the same.

From your postcard to Tussy, [284] I see that you are still confined to the house — which is all to the good considering the snow we're getting and the wet slush on the ground; but no doubt we shall soon have better weather (not the very best, but better than at present). During your first winter in the north since your attack of pleurisy you will have to resign yourself to tracheal affections of a milder kind; only next summer's cure will be able to scotch those.

In order to get the parallel between Tacitus' Germans [a] and the American Redskins sorted out at last, I have gently been making excerpts from the first volume of your Bancroft. [b] The similarity is,

---

[a] Tacitus, *Germania*. - [b] H. H. Bancroft, *The Native Races of the Pacific States of North America*, Vol. I, New York, 1875.

I must say, all the more surprising in that the modes of production are so utterly different — on the one hand fishermen and hunters and no stock-breeding or crop farming, on the other migratory stock-breeding overlapping with crop farming. It just goes to show how, at this stage, the method of production is less crucial than is the degree to which old blood ties and the ancient mutual community of the sexes within the tribe are being dissolved. Otherwise the Tlingits in what was once Russian America could not be the exact counterpart of the Germans — probably even to a greater extent than your Iroquois.[464] Another puzzle which is solved here is how placing the main burden of work on women is perfectly compatible with great respect for those women. In addition, I have found confirmation of my assumption that the *jus primae noctis*,[a] originally found in Europe among the Celts and Slavs, is a survival of the ancient sexual community: in two tribes, widely separated and not of the same race, it is still exercised by the shamans as representatives of the tribe. I have learned a great deal from the book — enough for the present as regards the Germans. I shall have to save up Mexico and Peru until later. For I have returned the Bancroft and, in exchange, taken the remaining things by Maurer,[465] *all* of which are therefore now at my house. I had to look through them because of my concluding note on the Mark,[378] which is growing rather long and is still not to my liking although I have rewritten it 2 or 3 times. But to sum up in 8 to 10 pages what happened after rise, flowering and decline is no joke. If I have the time, I shall send it you so that you can give me your opinion. As for myself, I should be glad to be quit of the stuff and to have another go at the natural sciences.[449]

It's odd, the way one can see how the concept of *holiness* arose among the so-called aboriginal peoples. What was holy, originally, is what we took over from the animal kingdom — the *bestial*; as compared with that, 'human institutions' were as much of an abomination as they are in the gospels by comparison with divine law.

Hartmann's installation of his battery for lighting 6 Swan lamps (incandescent bulbs à 6 candle-power) was supposed to have been ready yesterday, but I don't know whether it succeeded or not.[b]

I shall draw Bernstein's attention to Saarbrücken, as I have already done before. But the Anti-Socialist Law[16] will make material

---

[a] the right of the first night. -[b] See this volume, pp. 381-82, 391.

hard to come by there. Even prior to that, every effort was made to keep this area *undefiled*.

Égalité by the second post. Lafargue is still at liberty since it was he who addressed it to me.

Apropos TRADES UNION DEPUTATION [463]: When, at the meeting of the Possibilists, the French had sung the *Marseillaise* in their honour, the virtuous Shipton and his mates thought fit to retort by singing in unison '*GOD SAVE THE QUEEN!*' This according to the *Kölnische Zeitung* which I sent to Laura.

Well, I wish your throat, no less than the weather, a good recovery.

Your

F. E.

First published abridged in *Der Briefwechsel zwischen F. Engels und K. Marx*, Bd. 4, Stuttgart, 1913 and in full in *MEGA*, Abt. III, Bd. 4, Berlin, 1931

Printed according to the original

Published in English in full for the first time

217

ENGELS TO MARX [466]

IN VENTNOR

[London, 13 December 1882]

Just received this, 9.20 p. m. After appearing at Montluçon Paul[a] will, of course, be released at once. In the meantime I shall send Laura THE NEEDFUL tomorrow without fail. At 41 Maitland Park[b] ALL RIGHT.

First published, in the language of the original (German), in: F. Engels, P. et L. Lafargue, *Correspondance*, t. I, Paris, 1956

Printed according to the original

Published in English for the first time

---

[a] Lafargue - [b] Marx's address in London

218

ENGELS TO LAURA LAFARGUE

IN PARIS

London, 14 December 1882

My dear Laura,

I received your letter last night at half past nine, too late even to send a line by this morning's post, as foreign letters posted up here after nine are not forwarded until next evening.

I had scarcely any money in the house, and had given Percy[a] a cheque to cash for me today in town. But he will not be here before six at best, also too late to send you a banknote by 5.30 mail. However as soon as I get the money I shall forward one so as to help you over the first few days. No doubt Paul[b] will fare as Guesde and Bazin did and be at liberty if not to-day, at least to-morrow, as soon as the comedy of an examination before the austere Piquand shall have been gone through.[440] I forwarded both Paul's and your letter to Mohr, and told Nim[c] about the affair this morning.

More anon, when I shall be able to send substantial comfort.

Yours affectionately,

F. Engels

First published, in the language of the original (English), in: F. Engels, P. et L. Lafargue, *Correspondance*, t. I, Paris, 1956

Reproduced from the original

---

[a] Rosher - [b] Lafargue - [c] Helene Demuth

219

MARX TO LAURA LAFARGUE[72]

IN PARIS

Ventnor, Isle of Wight,
14 December 1882
1 St Boniface Gardens

Darling Cacadou,

All your letters have arrived on time and yet, miserable sinner
that I am, it is only now that I write to you, having learned from the
General's letter[a] just received that Paul[b] has been arrested. The
General enclosed Paul's letter and yours, so that I am *au fait*. No
doubt Paul will be released within a few days.

Why haven't I written before? Because I had nothing particularly
cheerful to report, for you will anyhow have learned from your correspondence with the General that I myself am not *at all* in bad
shape and have only been confined to the house for the past fortnight
because of a TRACHEAL CATARRH, nor have I again succumbed either to
pleurisy or to bronchitis. This, then, is most encouraging, CONSIDERING
THAT MOST OF MY CONTEMPORARIES, I MEAN FELLOWS OF THE SAME AGE, JUST NOW KICK
THE BUCKET in gratifying numbers. There are too many young donkeys
for the old ones to be kept alive.

Paul has *latterly* been writing his best *stuff*[c] with humour, impudence, and solidity combined with verve, whereas *before* that I had
been troubled by certain ultra-revolutionary turns of phrase, having
always regarded these as 'hot air' — a speciality our people would be
well-advised to leave to the so-called anarchists who are, in fact,
props of the existing order, not creators of disorder, and are, by their
nature, poor, childish creatures — *ce n'est pas leur faute, le chaos.*[d] Just
now they have, as *'péril social'*,[e] come to the aid of the *'affaires véreuses cabinet'*.[467] The worst of it is that, even if there were in existence
a purely impartial 'examining magistrate', he would be compelled
publicly to pronounce them wholly and utterly 'innocuous'! One
could forgive these anarchists anything if only they weren't too 'inno-

---

[a] 'General' was the Marx family's nickname for Engels. See this volume, p. 396. -
[b] Lafargue - [c] See this volume, pp. 385, 402. - [d] it is not their fault if there's chaos -
[e] 'social menace'

cent' for words! Not that that means they are 'saints'. A good joke was
made by a Pope[a] upon his being asked by Henry VII (Richard III's
victorious antagonist) to translate Henry VI to the community of
saints; the Pope replied that an *'innocens'*[b] (alias 'IDIOT') was not, as
such, eligible to be nominated a *'sanctus'*.[c] [468]

Here, my child, you would at any rate find better weather than in
most other districts including, I need hardly say, France and Italy.
I live the life of a hermit here, consorting with no one, SAVE when Dr
Williamson's visits, costing SUCH PER MINUTE,[d] bring me in contact with
the latter.

Well, child, as soon as your *devoirs*[e] permit (for Paul's GALLANT FIGHT
WITH THE POWERS THAT BE MAKE THE MAN SYMPATHIC [SIC], TO USE THIS, A FRENCH
PENNY-A-LINER'S PHRASE) *come over here and stay with me!*

*Some *recent Russian publications*, printed in Holy Russia, not
abroad, show the great run of my theories in that country.[469] Nowhere
my success is to me more delightful; it gives me the satisfaction that
I damage a power, which, besides England, is the true bulwark of the
old society.

Yours,

Nick *

First published, in the languages of the   Printed according to the original
original (German and English), in *Annali*,
an. I, Milano, 1958

220

ENGELS TO MARX [470]

IN VENTNOR

London, 15 December 1882

Dear Moor,

Herewith the appendix on the Mark.[f] Be so kind as to return it on
Sunday so that I can revise it on Monday — I didn't get the final revision done today.

---

[a] Julius II - [b] an innocent - [c] a saint - [d] Should read 'so much per minute'. -
[e] duties - [f] F. Engels, 'The Mark'.

I consider that the view here put forward concerning rural conditions in the Middle Ages and the *second* phase of serfdom from the
middle of the 15th century onwards is, on the whole, incontrovertible.
I have read all the passages in Maurer [465] that relate to this, finding
therein almost all my propositions — and, *what's more, substantiated*;
also, precisely the opposite, but either unsubstantiated or drawn
from a period which happens *not* to be the one under discussion. This
applies in particular to *Fronhöfe*, Vol. 4, conclusion. These contradictions are due in Maurer's case 1. to the habit of adducing, indiscrimi-
nately and side by side, documentary proof and examples from any
and every period, 2. to a residue of legalistic prejudice which invariably trips him up when it comes to understanding a *process of development*, 3. to his gross underestimation of *force* and the role it plays, 4. to
the enlightened presupposition that, since the dark Middle Ages,
things *must* have changed steadily for the better; this prevents him
from perceiving, not only the antagonistic nature of true progress, but
likewise individual setbacks.

As you will see, the thing isn't all of one piece, but is a proper
paste-and-scissors job. The first draft was all of one piece, but unfortunately it was wrong. Only by slow degrees have I mastered the
material, which is why there's so much patchwork.

Incidentally, the general reintroduction of serfdom is *one* of the reasons why no kind of industry could develop in Germany in the 17th
and 18th centuries. First, there was the division of labour in the
guilds which was the *reverse* of that in manufacturing; instead of
being divided within the workshop, labour is divided *among the
guilds*. Here in England, there was migration to those parts of the
country where there were no guilds. This was prevented in Germany
by the transformation of country folk and the inhabitants of
agricultural market towns into serfs. But it was also this which eventually proved the undoing of the guilds the moment they encountered
competition from foreign manufactures. I shall not mention here the
other reasons that contributed to the suppression of German manufactures.

Today has again been all fog and gaslight. Hartmann's battery
probably a FAILURE where lighting is concerned, being useful at most
for telegraphy, etc.[a] More about this as soon as anything definite has
been established.

---

[a] See this volume, pp. 381-82, 391.

Look after yourself, and let's hope the weather will soon be such that you will be allowed out.

Your

F. E.

First published in *Der Briefwechsel zwischen F. Engels und K. Marx*, Bd. 4, Stuttgart, 1913

Printed according to the original

221

ENGELS TO LAURA LAFARGUE

IN PARIS

London, 15 December 1882

My dear Laura,

Only after 7 last night Percy[a] came with the needful so there was nothing to be done before today, so now I enclose a five-pound Bank of England note the number of which I have kept here, and will run the risk to send it *whole* for once.

No doubt you will by this time be quite assured about Paul's[b] fate, at least for the present. [440] I have no doubt he is free again now, if not already back in Paris. But I am afraid the Bonapartist and other conservative judges of Montluçon will give them[c] a couple of months each of retired life. The government evidently wishes to create a few precedents in the provinces before it dares to try repression in Paris. And thus the *parquet*[d] at Montluçon engaged the business, which, once engaged, must be carried out by the judges to the desired end, were it only to save the credit of the magistrature. And as the case will no doubt come before the *police correctionnelle*,[e] there can be not even that shadow of a doubt which a jury might still have rendered possible.

The change to a short prison life would not in itself have anything very dreadful, indeed I think it would do Paul more good than harm.

___

[a] Rosher - [b] Lafargue - [c] Lafargue and Guesde - [d] prosecutor's office - [e] disciplinary court

But very likely their time will come at a moment when they, Paul and Guesde, are both most wanted for the *Égalité*. And the paper had so much improved lately. Whether it is the cumulative effect of Parisian life and journalistic activity, Paul's articles lately have been very much better, since he dropped the dogmatism of the scientific oracle and took up the *ligne spirituelle*.[a] That on the candidature [of] Bontoux was charming,[471] but I think I discover a little female hand in that here and there. So was that on the *behexte ministerium*[b][450] (I forgot the French title) which also pleased Mohr specially.[c] Now if Paul and Guesde are locked up, the soul of the paper is gone. Deville is witty and amusing only at intervals, generally he is clear but dull and doctrinaire, Massard is the reverse of a good Christian, for that with him the flesh is willing but the spirit (*esprit*) is weak. And I must conclude, from what information I possess, that Paul and Guesde are also the two who will be most wanted in a financially critical moment. Thus it will be a great pity that just at this time dynamitic brag and competition with the rrrrevolutionarism of the anarchists should have brought them in this predicament.

Anyhow I hope you look down upon these *petites misères du haut de votre troisième*[d] with the same calmness as the *quarante siècles*[e] of General Bonaparte *du haut de leurs pyramides*[f] on the French army and Bonaparte himself.

How is Jenny[g] getting on? is she better? I do not hear much about her at Maitland Park,[h] indeed they[i] do not know much themselves.

Very affectionately yours,

F. E.

First published in: Marx and Engels, *Works*, Second Russian Edition, Vol. 35, Moscow, 1964

Reproduced from the original

Published in English for the first time

---

[a] line of wit - [b] spellbound ministry - [c] See this volume, p. 385. - [d] petty miseries from the height of your third floor - [e] forty centuries - [f] from the height of their pyramids - [g] Longuet - [h] the Marx family's address in London - [i] Eleanor Marx and Helene Demuth

222

ENGELS TO MARX [7]

IN VENTNOR

London, 16 December 1882

Dear Moor,

Having been interrupted yesterday,[a] I shall continue today. You will have noticed how hurriedly my letter was dashed off—I was being perpetually disturbed by Pumps and BABY,[b] first while revising the ms.,[c] then while writing the letter. The point by which I set most store—because of the dissentient view you once expressed—is the almost total recession—*de jure* or *de facto*—of serfdom in the 13th and 14th centuries. So far as the country east of the Elbe is concerned, the freedom of *German* peasants is an established fact by reason of colonisation; as regards Schleswig-Holstein, Maurer admits[d] that at the time (somewhat later, perhaps, than the 14th century) 'all' peasants had regained their freedom. Again, as regards the South of Germany, he admits that it was in this particular period that the bondsmen were treated best. The same thing applies to a greater or lesser extent in Lower Saxony (e. g. the new 'tenant farmers', virtually copyholders). He does not, however, share Kindlinger's view[c] that serfdom did not *come into being* until the 16th century. That it subsequently reappeared, however, in a 2nd refurbished edition, seems to me indubitable. Meitzen[f] specifies the years in which allusions to serfs first recur in East Prussia, Brandenburg and Silesia: mid-16th century, ditto Hanssen in respect of Schleswig-Holstein.[g] When Maurer calls this a *mitigated* form of serfdom he is right, if one compares it with the period between the 9th and 11th centuries which, in fact, saw the continuation of ancient Germanic slavery; right, too, if one compares it with the legal rights still exercised, as the statute books of the 13th century

---

[a] See this volume, p. 400. - [b] Lilian Rosher - [c] F. Engels, 'The Mark'. - [d] G. L. von Maurer, *Geschichte der Fronhöfe, der Bauernhöfe und der Hofverfassung in Deutschland.* - [e] N. Kindlinger, *Geschichte der Deutschen Hörigkeit insbesondere der sogenannten Leibeigenschaft.* - [f] A. Meitzen, *Der Boden und die landwirthschaftlichen Verhältnisse des Preussischen Staates...* - [g] G. Hanssen, *Die Aufhebung der Leibeigenschaft und die Umgestaltung der gutsherrlich-bäuerlichen Verhältnisse überhaupt in den Herzogthümern Schleswig und Holstein.*

confirm, both then and later, by the lord over his serfs. But as compared with the *de facto* position of the peasants in the 13th and 14th — and in North Germany also the 15th — centuries, the new serfdom was ANYTHING BUT a mitigation. Let alone after the Thirty Years' War [472]! It is also significant that, whereas in the Middle Ages there were innumerable degrees of bondage and serfdom, so that the *Sachsenspiegel* [473] gives up the attempt to 'make a tally', this becomes remarkably easy after the Thirty Years' War. *Enfin,* [a] I look forward to hearing your opinion.

It was also Pumps' fault if, at the place where I mention Russian common ownership, I failed to paste on a note saying that this information came from you.

The enclosed is from old Becker [474]; luckily I was able to respond to his gentle nudging straight away and send him £5, as I had just sold some SHARES and the money had been paid on the same day.

Herewith 2 *Égalités* — hope they'll be delivered tomorrow — from which you will see that Lafargue was immediately released [b] and was expected back in Paris yesterday evening. [440]

Hartmann's battery [c]: so long as he only plugged in the galvanometer, in which the resistance is represented by a very long wire so that there is only a gradual consumption of electro-mechanical power, all went well. But as soon as he plugged in the lamp in which the resistance is concentrated at one point, namely the thin, short, incandescent wire, that was that; the hydrogen immediately polarised the silver electrode, and the weak current produced only a faint red glow in the wire. Now his head is again full of all manner of innovations, each of which proves that he is looking for the difficulty in the wrong place. But whether the gents who are advancing the money will agree to any further experiments is a moot point.

Do you think you might be able to book a couple of beds down there for Schorlemmer and myself in the first week of January? We would not be at all averse to nipping down for a day or two, if nothing intervenes. But that something will intervene is all too probable in view of Schorlemmer's rheumatism, etc. However, if we knew that you could arrange for us to stay either with you or close by, and

---

[a] Well - [b] See 'L'Arrestation de Lafargue' and 'L'Affaire de Montluçon', *L'Égalité*, 4th series, Nos. 53 and 54, 15 and 16 December 1882. - [c] See this volume, pp. 381-82, 391.

exactly how much notice we should have to give you, we could make our arrangements accordingly.

Your

F. E.

First published in *Der Briefwechsel zwischen F. Engels und K. Marx*, Bd. 4, Stuttgart, 1913

Printed according to the original

Published in English in full for the first time

223

ENGELS TO JOHANN PHILIPP BECKER

IN GENEVA

London, 16 December 1882

Dear Old Man,

I have been waiting for some time for some money to come in so that I could send you another fiver. It eventually came in yesterday, followed that very evening by your postcard.[a] I therefore immediately took out a money order for the said fiver = 126 frs, and hope the money will reach you without delay.

I was very glad to hear that you have extricated yourself from the cantonal and communal mire; it's a sheer waste of time and productive of nothing but tittle-tattle and pointless vexation. Incidentally, that jackass Solari is still sending me 2 copies of the *Précurseur*. It must be a fine despatch department!

Every year the anarchists commit suicide and every year rise anew from their ashes, and so it will go on until such time as anarchism is subjected to serious persecution. It is the only socialist sect that really can be destroyed by means of persecution. For its perpetual rebirth depends on a steady supply of would-be bigwigs who wish to play a role on the cheap. Anarchism is as if tailor-made for that. But run a risk? Not on your life! Hence the present harassment of anarchists in

---

[a] See this volume, p. 404.

France will damage that gang only if it isn't sheer make-believe or hanky-panky on the part of the police. But either way its victims will be those poor devils, the miners of Montceau. [402] Incidentally, I have grown so used to the anarchist buffoons that it seems to me quite natural to have that clownish caricature tagging along like this beside the movement proper. They are dangerous only in such countries as Austria and Spain, and then only for the time being. Again the Jura, where watch-making is carried on in houses scattered all over the place, would seem a foreordained hotbed of this ballyhoo, and here your blows could prove quite beneficial.

Marx has been given permission by the doctors to spend the winter on the south coast of England and has been in the Isle of Wight for 6 weeks or so. [411] Hitherto, all has been well as regards the two main counts: no sign of any recurrence of pleurisy or bronchitis. The rotten weather we have been having here (for a week the fog has scarcely lifted at all) means that convalescents are inevitably subject to colds of all sorts and, for one in Marx's condition, these are lingering and troublesome. But if it remains at that, no matter. However, he might well be sent out to Switzerland again next summer, in which case you will certainly see one another.

Madame Lafargue's address is 66 Boulevard de Port-Royal, Paris. Not long ago her husband was arrested, but has already been set free. The point at issue was certain speeches he had made in the provinces and, upon their being summoned by the examining magistrate of Montluçon, he and Guesde, instead of obeying, poured vile scorn upon him in the *Égalité*. Whereupon he naturally issued a warrant for their arrest but, although Lafargue went daily to the newspaper office and was at so little pains to conceal his whereabouts that he actually announced he was going to speak, and did speak, at meetings, it took the clever Parisian police three weeks to seek him out. Like Guesde before him, he was immediately released after the first hearing at Montluçon. They might still get a couple of months apiece. [440]

As you know, the workers' party in France has split. [394] Malon and Brousse can hardly wait for the day when they become deputies, which means that a herd of voters has to be quickly rounded up. In other words a party created *without a programme* (literally — for a long series of '*considérants*' [a] is followed by the conclusion that every local-

---

[a] preambles

ity must draw up its own programme), in which every Tom, Dick and Harry is welcome and, to carry this through, people are being admitted into the party before the congress who accept the old programme with the reservation that, come the congress, they will subvert it. Guesde, Lafargue, etc., were outvoted and those who stood by the programme went to Roanne. Our people are no tacticians and have committed hopeless blunders, but nevertheless they will win through and the 'Possibilists' won't have it all their own way for long. Our chaps have a very considerable lever in the shape of the daily *Égalité* and, moreover, are all of them devoted to the *cause*, something which cannot be said of those intriguers, Malon and Brousse.

Well, good-bye, old man, and keep your pecker up. You're unlikely to decline as fast as all that and, as you know, we're all heading the same way!

Your
F. E.

First published in: F. Engels, *Vergessene Briefe (Briefe Friedrich Engels' an Johann Philipp Becker)*, Berlin, 1920

Printed according to the original

Published in English for the first time

224

ENGELS TO EDUARD BERNSTEIN

IN ZURICH

London, 16 December 1882

Dear Mr Bernstein,

Schorlemmer complains that he has not received the *Sozialdemokrat* for some little while; his subscription expired and he sent me the encl. CHEQUE (which I forgot about) no less than a month ago with the request that his *annual* subscription be renewed and 'the balance be used for party purposes'.

The ms. of the Mark has had to be completely rewritten 3 times; on top of that I again had to go through about 5 or 6 of Maurer's 10 fat volumes,[465] besides which there were other sources to compare. I have now sent it to Marx who has slogged away at the subject much more thoroughly and for much longer than I have[475]; I expect it back on Monday.

Malon *se moque de*[a] Vollmar. Otherwise he would certainly have corrected the latter's howler to the effect that the 'Alliancists' attacked by the *Égalité* were understood in the sense of the Bakuninist Alliance.[67] Far from it. The Possibilists were thus described because they are now wholly indistinguishable from the people in the Alliance socialiste[476] which was founded some 4 years ago by Jourde, the ex-Communard for finance, with the help of past and present Proudhonists (e. g. Longuet) and which constitutes La *Justice*'s socialist reserve. You must certainly have seen this Alliance mentioned in connection with elections; it put up candidates for the recent general election to the Chamber and obtained nearly as many votes—in some *arrondissements* at any rate—as the Parti ouvrier.[b] If Vollmar knew nothing of this, despite his year and a half in Paris, it was because Malon deliberately kept it from him like much else. That's what happens when you give a gang your uncritical support.

I have to chuckle when Vollmar praises Malon as the party disciplinarian and accuses the others of a breach of discipline.[438] Who, I ask, is guilty of indiscipline—he who carries the old flag high or he who recruits people with the express aim of deserting the colours and exchanging the old flag for a new one? Where, I ask, would Malon have got his majority at St-Étienne from[394] if he hadn't first recruited people whose intention from the start, and this was precisely why they had been recruited, was to subvert the old programme?

That was a choice row between Malon and his Clovis Hugues over Louis Blanc. And they call themselves a party!

You will have seen that the Fédération du Nord[454] has declared outright for Roanne.

Some of Lafargue's articles in the more recent issues of the *Égalité* have been truly delightful, e. g. on Bontoux's candidature.[471] Witticisms are better suited to them than doctrinaire pontifications.

---

[a] is making fun of-[b] Workers' Party

Would you please be good enough to see that the issues are sent on to Schorlemmer.

Yours very sincerely,

F. E.

First published, in Russian, in *Marx-Engels Archives*, Book I, Moscow, 1924

Printed according to the original

Published in English for the first time

225

MARX TO ENGELS [72]

IN LONDON

[Ventnor,] 18 December 1882

DEAR FRED,

I return the ms.[a]; *very good!*

The doctor[b] has just left; I can't say that I notice any PROGRESS, rather the reverse. Though not cold out of doors, it is damp and rainy and the doctor says he cannot allow me to go out until the next fine day; otherwise he wouldn't accept the responsibility.

Au diable! il faut patienter! [c]

Salut.

Moor

First published in *Der Briefwechsel zwischen F. Engels und K. Marx*, Bd. 4, Stuttgart, 1913

Printed according to the original

---

[a] F. Engels, 'The Mark'. - [b] James M. Williamson - [c] Drat it! One must be patient!

226

ENGELS TO MARX [7]

IN VENTNOR

London, 19 December 1882

Dear Moor,

Your letter arrived at 5 o'clock yesterday afternoon and this morning I got back the ms.[a] Your opinion is most flattering though it is one I cannot share, at any rate so far as form is concerned. As it was fine and warm at midday you will doubtless be released at last for an hour or two from your confinement indoors. Here, though, the fog has grown worse again since 1 o'clock and at times it is like night.

This is how I see the Podolinski business.[477] His real discovery is that human labour is capable of retaining solar energy on the earth's surface and harnessing it for a longer period than would otherwise have been the case. All the economic conclusions he draws from this are wrong. I have not got the thing to hand but read it in Italian not long ago in the *Plebe*. The point in question, namely how the amount of energy contained in a specific amount of foodstuffs can, through labour, yield a greater amount of energy than itself, I resolve as follows: Let us assume that the amount of food a person needs each day represents an amount of energy expressed as 10,000 cal (units of heat). These 10,000 cal will, *ad infinitum*, = 10,000 cal and are known in practice to lose on conversion into other forms of energy as a result of friction, etc., a portion that cannot be put to use. Significantly so in the case of the human body. Hence the *physical* labour performed in economic labour can never = 10,000 cal; it is invariably less.

But this is by no means to imply that physical labour is *economic* labour. The economic labour performed by 10,000 cal in no way consists in the *reproduction*, complete or partial, of these same 10,000 cal in any form whatever. On the contrary, they are for the most part lost in the increased heat given off by the body, etc., and such useful residue as remains lies in the fertilising property of excretions. The economic labour performed by an individual through the expenditure of these 10,000 cal consists rather in the stabilisation over a longer or shorter

---
[a] F. Engels, 'The Mark'.

period of the *fresh* cal he absorbs from the radiation of the sun, and this is the only connection the latter have, so far as labour is concerned, with the first 10,000 cal. Now whether the *fresh* cal stabilised by the expenditure of 10,000 cal of daily nourishment amount to 5,000, 10,000, 20,000 or a million is dependent solely upon the level of development of the means of production.

To demonstrate this in the form of calculations is possible only in the case of the most primitive branches of production: hunting, fishing, stock farming, agriculture. In hunting and fishing fresh solar energy is not even stabilised; rather, use is simply made of what has been stabilised already. At the same time it is clear that, assuming the individual concerned takes normal nourishment, the amount of protein and fat he obtains by hunting or fishing is independent of the amount of these substances he consumes.

In stock farming energy is stabilised in as much as the vegetation, that would otherwise rapidly wither, die and decompose, is systematically converted into animal protein, fat, skin, bone, etc., hence stabilised over a longer period. Here calculations already become complicated.

Even more so in agriculture where the energy value of auxiliary materials, fertilisers, etc., must also be taken into consideration.

In industry all calculations come to a full stop; for the most part the labour added to a product simply does not permit of being expressed in terms of cal. This might be done at a pinch in the case of a pound of yarn by laboriously reproducing its durability and tensile strength in yet another mechanical formula, but even then it would smack of quite useless pedantry and, in the case of a piece of grey cloth, let alone one that has been bleached, dyed or printed, would actually become absurd. The energy value conforming to the production costs of a hammer, a screw, a sewing needle, is an impossible quantity.

To express economic conditions in terms of physical measures is, in my view, a sheer impossibility.

What Podolinski has completely forgotten is that the working individual is not only a stabiliser of *present* but also, and to a far greater extent, a squanderer of *past*, solar heat. As to what we have done in the way of squandering our reserves of energy, our coal, ore, forests, etc., you are better informed than I am. From this point of view, hunting and fishing may also be seen not as stabilisers of fresh solar heat but as exhausters and even incipient squanderers of the solar energy that has accumulated from the past.

Further: Man, by his labour, does deliberately what plants do unconsciously. Plants — and there is nothing new in this of course — are the great absorbers and repositories of solar heat in modified form. Thus man, by his labour, in so far as it stabilises solar energy (which in industry and elsewhere is by no means always the case), succeeds in combining the natural functions of the energy-consuming animal with those of the energy-gathering plant.

Podolinski went astray after his very valuable discovery, because he sought to find in the field of natural science fresh evidence of the rightness of socialism and hence has confused the physical with the economic.

Encl. CHEQUE for £40 so that you can cash it when you want and will have something to fall back on.

As regards Tussy's coming, I shall speak to her this evening. So far as we ourselves are concerned Jollymeier at once agreed, of course; the details can only be arranged if he does come.[a] More tomorrow.

Your
F. E.

First published in *Der Briefwechsel zwischen F. Engels und K. Marx*, Bd. 4, Stuttgart, 1913

Printed according to the original

Published in English in full for the first time

227

ENGELS TO MARX [7]

IN VENTNOR

London, 22 December 1882

Dear Moor,

To come back to Podolinski again,[b] I stand corrected: storage of energy by means of labour takes place strictly speaking only in *arable*

---

[a] See this volume, pp. 404-05. - [b] See previous letter.

227. Engels to Marx. 22 December 1882

farming. In stock farming the energy stored in plants is, in general, merely transferred to the animal, hence we can only speak of storage in so far as nutritive plants are put to use which would, in the absence of stock farming, go to waste. In all branches of industry, on the other hand, energy is merely *expended*. The most one can say is that vegetable products such as wood, straw, flax, etc., and animal products in which plant energy is stored, are made available by processing, i. e. are *preserved for a longer space of time* than if they had been allowed to decay naturally. Hence the time-honoured economic fact that all industrial producers are dependent for their subsistence on the products of agriculture, stock farming, hunting and fishing can, if desired, also be translated into physical terms, though this is not particularly rewarding.

Herewith letter from Laura[478]; Jenny's case would not, in fact, appear to be too bad, always providing she obtains proper and regular treatment — this being necessary not because of any immediate danger, but because of the extremely unpleasant consequences that might result from neglect.

Hartmann has thrown up the sponge here and tomorrow is crossing the ocean again. It's just as well. His contracts over here have involved him in such a mass of legal obligations (some of them unfulfilled) that he himself no longer knows where he stands. I shall tell you all about it when I see you and am glad he is going away. It has now transpired that, all the while he was touching me for loans, he was pocketing anything from five to six pounds a week.

You are right when you say that Bernstein doesn't always allow himself adequate time for reflection. But he's not alone in that. Take a look at Lafargue's recent discoveries in '*Prêtres et commerçants*' (*Égalité*, 20 December) and, ibid., Deville's latest reconstruction[a] of Weitlingianism[479]— by no means an improvement.

I am glad that 'we concur', as they say in business, on the subject of serfdom.[b] Certainly, serfdom and bondage are not a form peculiar to the Middle Ages and feudalism; we find them everywhere, or almost everywhere where conquerors have the land tilled for them by the original inhabitants — e. g. at a very early date in Thessaly. Indeed, this fact has clouded my view, like that of many others, of medieval servitude; we were all too eager to see it as being simply based upon

---

[a] G. Deville, 'Le travail', *L'Égalité*, 4th series, Nos. 57 and 58, 19 and 20 December 1882. - [b] See this volume, pp. 400, 403-04.

conquest; it rounded things off so neatly and tidily. Cf. Thierry, among others.[a]

Again, the position of the Christians in Turkey during the heyday of ancient Turkish semi-feudalism was not dissimilar.

But here is Pumps arriving for dinner, it being now 5 o'clock, and thus I am the victim of *force majeure*.[b] I hope that this glorious weather has pulled you round again.

Your
Fred

First published abridged in *Der Briefwech-sel zwischen F. Engels und K. Marx*, Bd. 4, Stuttgart, 1913 and in full in *MEGA*, Abt. III, Bd. 4, Berlin, 1931

Printed according to the original

Published in English in full for the first time

228

ENGELS TO AUGUST BEBEL

IN LEIPZIG

London, 22 December 1882

Dear Bebel,

I hope you will be set free the day after tomorrow for 24 hours[480] and thus have no difficulty in getting hold of this note.

All that was meant by the bit you found mystifying in my last letter[c] was that I expected the repeal of the Exceptional Law[16] to be brought about by events either of a revolutionary nature themselves (e. g. a fresh coup or the convocation of a national assembly in Russia, whose repercussions on Germany would at once become apparent), or those which at any rate would give impetus to the movement and pave the way for revolution (change of monarch in

---

[a] A. Thierry, *Histoire de la conquête de l'Angleterre par les Normands, de ses causes, et de ses suites jusqu'à nos jours, en Angleterre, en Écosse, en Irlande et sur le continent*, vols I-III, Paris, 1825. - [b] superior strength - [c] See this volume, p. 349.

Berlin, death or resignation of Bismarck), either of which would almost inevitably usher in a 'new era'.[277]

The crisis in America would seem to me, like the one over here and
like the pressure on German industry that has not yet lifted everywhere, to be not a crisis proper, but the after-effect of overproduction
dating back to the previous crisis. On the last occasion the crash in
Germany came prematurely because of the milliard racket, whereas
here and in America it came at the proper time, in 1877. But never,
during a period of prosperity, had the productive forces been so expanded as in the years between 1871 and 1877, hence, as in 1837-42,
the chronic pressure here[a] and in Germany on the main branches of
industry, especially cotton and iron; the markets are still not able to
absorb all those products. Since American industry is, in the main,
still working for the protected home market, a local interim crisis may
very easily arise there, in consequence of the rapid increase in production, but ultimately it will only serve to hasten the time when America becomes capable of exporting and of entering the world market
as England's most dangerous competitor. Hence I do not believe —
and Marx shares my view[b] — that the real crisis will come very much
before it is due.

I would consider a European war to be a disaster; this time it
would prove frightfully serious and inflame chauvinism everywhere
for years to come, since all peoples would be fighting for their own
existence. All the work done by the Russian revolutionaries, who are
on the eve of victory, would be ruined and set at nought; our party in
Germany, temporarily overwhelmed by the tide of chauvinism,
would be dispersed, while exactly the same would happen in France.
The only good thing that might come of it would be the setting-up of
a Little Poland — which would also and automatically ensue from
revolution; a Russian constitution resulting from a disastrous war
would have an import, probably of a conservative nature, quite different from one forcibly imposed by revolutionary means. Such a war
would, I believe, retard the revolution by 10 years, at the end of
which, however, the upheaval would doubtless be all the more drastic. Incidentally, there has again been a prospect of war. Bismarck
has been flaunting the Austrian alliance just as he did the South
German alliances at the time of the Luxembourg affair in 1867.[481]
Whether anything will come of this in the spring remains to be seen.

---

[a] in England - [b] See this volume, p. 392.

We found your reports on the state of German industry most inter-esting, in particular the express confirmation that the cartel agree-ment between the ironmasters had collapsed. It could not possibly last, least of all between German industrialists for whom the pettiest fraudulence is the very breath of life.

We haven't as yet seen the things by Meyer [482] and what you say is therefore news to us. That Marx would figure alongside his cardinals was only to be expected; Meyer always derived quite exceptional pleasure from proceeding direct from Cardinal Manning to Marx, nor did he ever fail to mention the fact.

In his *Sociale Briefe* Rodbertus was hot on the scent of surplus value, but that was as close as he got. Otherwise it would have put paid to his thoughts and endeavours as to how best to help the debt-ridden country Junkers, something the good man surely could not have wished. But as you say, he is worth infinitely more than the majority of German vulgar economists, including the armchair social-ists [82] who after all live solely off our leavings.

The story of Carlchen's [a] wooing was also new to us. The wedding, or so I have been told by eye-witnesses, was a most mournful affair, so much so that someone who was present at the civil ceremony ex-claimed: '*C'est l'enterrement de A!*' [b]

Yesterday I sent off to Zurich the final ms. for the pamphlet, namely an appendix on the constitution of the Mark and a short history of the German peasantry generally. [378] Since Maurer [465] writes very badly and confuses many things, it is difficult to track down what you want at the first reading. As soon as I get the proofs I shall send you the thing, which contains, not simply abstracts from Maurer, but indirect criticism of him, as also much else that is new. These are the first-fruits of long years of study devoted to German history, and I am delighted at being able to present it first of all to the workers rather than to schoolmasters and other 'eddicated' gents.

Now I must stop, for otherwise I shall not be able to register the let-ter in time to catch the evening post. The Prussians would not as yet seem to have reached the stage of Stiebering [c] registered letters, all of which have so far arrived in proper condition. I have by long practice acquired a pretty shrewd eye for such things.

---

[a] Carl Hirsch - [b] It's a rattling good funeral! - [c] from Stieber, chief of the Prussian police

I should be glad if your wife ᵃ would kindly accept the enclosed Christmas card and the compliments of the season.

Your
F. E.

First published abridged in: A. Bebel, *Aus meinem Leben*, Teil III, Stuttgart, 1914 and in full, in Russian, in *Marx-Engels Archives*, Vol. I (VI), Moscow, 1932

Printed according to the original

Published in English for the first time

229

MARX TO ELEANOR MARX [72]

IN LONDON

[Postcard, unsigned]

[Ventnor, 23 December 1882]

Dear Child,

From Laura's letter (which Engels sent me for information today ᵇ) I see that Jennychen is again afflicted by that beastly inflammation.[478] Should it be neglected, I can only fear the worst. We must really consider (and you should talk this over with Lenchen before coming to join me here) whether we ought not to relieve Jennychen at any rate of Harry, even if it should necessitate his coming here. How can Jennychen find time for the treatment of her illness WITH ALL THESE BABIES TOGETHER? And again, how neglected (as regards health) our Johnny will be should one of the others not be displaced in his stead?

Harry makes a difficult position doubly difficult for poor Jennychen.

All I want you to bring is *Physiologie* by *Rank* (or *Ranke* — I'm not sure). Also *Freeman's* rotten *little book* (*History of Europe*), since it

ᵃ Julie Bebel - ᵇ See this volume, p. 413.

serves me in lieu of a chronological table; it is in my bedroom on the shelves where the newspapers, etc., are.

[On the side reserved for the address]

Miss Marx
41 Maitland Park Road, Maitland Park,
London, N. W.

First published in: Marx and Engels, *Works*, Second Russian Edition, Vol. 35, Moscow, 1964

Printed according to the original

1883

230

MARX TO JAMES M. WILLIAMSON

IN VENTNOR [411]

Ventnor, 6 January 1883
1 St Boniface Gardens

Dear Dr Williamson,

I return with best thanks the enclosed letter.[483] My intended promenade was yesterday stopped by the rain. When rising this morning about a quarter past 9 o'clock, I got suddenly into a spasmodic cough, gasping, wrestling as if it were with suffocation. Unfortunately, I had used up the morphia, nor had I any of the 'lozenges' prescribed by you, but I took a table-spoon-(rather somewhat more)-ful of the tonic. What in point of fact surprised me was, that during the course of yesterday my cough was much less troublesome than it had been for the last weeks. Nor was my night specially disturbed. Mere moral agencies, I suppose, do not touch the movements of the mucus.

Yesterday afternoon I had received from Paris a letter with bad news as to the health of Madame Longuet, my oldest daughter. I knew of course that her illness was serious, but I was not prepared to hear that it passes now through a critical phasis.

Yours very truly,
Karl Marx

First published as a facsimile and in German translation in *Neues Deutschland*, 12./13. März 1983

231

MARX TO ELEANOR MARX [72]

IN LONDON

Ventnor, 8 January 1883
1 St Boniface Gardens

Dear Tussychen,

I received a short note on Saturday from Dr Williamson enclosing a letter to Williamson from Dr F. Bayshawe dated 4 January '83, 5 Warrior Square, St Leonards on Sea, in which he says amongst other things:

* 'We had a week of almost continuous rain or moist air, which gave place on the 2nd to *dry weather*, of varying direction. Since that we have had sunshine each afternoon, tho' not much of it. I will endeavour to send you some further statistics tomorrow. I believe we may say generally that the climate of Hastings is dryer than much of the South Coast, tho' this may be at the expense of some warmth etc.' *

On Saturday (6 January) the weather here was fine round about midday; yesterday, too, it was dry, but colder; it is always sunniest on the esplanade. I went for a stroll yesterday and the day before, and today it promises to remain fine. It is generally coolish unless one is actually in the sun. At all events, a steady rise in temperature has now been predicted.

There's always Hastings to move to if prospects here prove deceptive; besides which, there comes a moment when a change of place is of itself beneficial. This much at least we know — there is SOME SENSE in exchanging Ventnor for Hastings, but not for places on the South Coast that are closer to Ventnor and in which conditions are almost exactly the same as in the ISLE OF Wight.

Every now and again I still have to tussle furiously with the accumulation of MUCUS; after getting up on Saturday morning I EVEN had a spasmodic attack [of coughing] so that for several seconds I vainly struggled for breath. I believe it was due to nervous irritation — my anxiety over Jennychen! Upon that I need not enlarge. I would have hastened to Argenteuil *at once*, but for the possibility of saddling the child with the extra burden of a sick visitor! For no one can guarantee

that the journey WOULD [not] HAVE PUNISHED ME WITH A RELAPSE such as
I have so far fortunately escaped. All the same, it's hard not being
able to go and see her.

Love from
OLD NICK

First published, in the languages of the orig-   Printed according to the original
inal (German and English), in *Annali*,
an. I, Milano, 1958

232

ENGELS TO MARX

IN VENTNOR

London, 9 January 1883

Dear Moor,

In great haste I am sending you the following enclosures:
1. Lafargue, 2. Bebel, 3. Hepner,[484] of which I should like to have
2. and 3. back.

So at last there has been a report on Jenny's condition from which
one can tell how matters really stand. In my opinion the case isn't as
bad as it looks; the poor child has allowed herself to grow unduly
weak as a result of over-exertion and her distaste for medical treatment, but she will soon pick up again under Laura's management.
I at once sent Laura £15, the last five being intended to give Laura
a somewhat freer hand when she visits Jenny and buys things for her.
Until Jenny is able to run her house again, Johnny ought certainly
to remain over here.

Bebel's information on German industry is interesting, though it
strikes me that one ought to take it *cum grano salis*.ᵃ What are ex-
panding are for the most part the luxury industries and possibly
mechanical weaving — though in the latter case export opportunities
are restricted by the tariffs on yarn. Since the annexation of Alsace

---

ᵃ with a grain of salt

they have had more spindles than they need as also, since 1870, iron-
works, so how can *big* industry as such expand to any great extent?
Moreover the fact that beet sugar has made such an impression on
him suggests a narrow view. The circumstance that the state pays for
the profits of the sugar-manufacturing Junkers has already been
debated in the Landtag.

Hepner. What do you make of the little Jew's proposal (obviously
at the insistence of his *associé*ᵃ Jonas) to hold a pistol to our heads as
regards a preface to the *Manifesto*? In my view, either one completely
ignores insolent letters like these or at most refers him to the preface of
the Leipzig edition ᵇ; if that isn't good enough for him he ought to
leave the *Manifesto* unprinted.

If you write to Sorge about Hartmann ᶜ (supposing that you have
not already done so) you might slip in a line or two about little
Hepner.

Time for the post — I had to go into town to see to the money and
then get it off, have therefore been delayed.

Your

F. E.

First published abridged in *Der Briefwech-
sel zwischen F. Engels und K. Marx*, Bd. 4,
Stuttgart, 1913 and in full in *MEGA*,
Abt. III, Bd. 4, Berlin, 1931

Printed according to the original

Published in English for the first
time

233

MARX TO ELEANOR MARX [166]

IN LONDON

[Ventnor,] 9 January 1883

My Dear Good Child,

How kind of you to write to me so often and at such length; however I do not wish TO ENCROACH ON THE VERY LITTLE 'FREE' TIME YOU HAVE TO

ᵃ partner - ᵇ K. Marx and F. Engels, 'Preface to the 1872 German Edition of the
Manifesto of the Communist Party'. - ᶜ Lev Hartmann

DISPOSE OF. I got your letter after I had sent off mine,ᵃ after my return from an excursion by the sea. I have had no further news from Paris.

Today I was on the point of 'setting forth on foot' again — DESPITE THE NOISE OF THE WIND — when my doctor ᵇ arrived; he told me I was to stay at home as it was very cold outdoors. He examined me again. All as before, in as much as the catarrh is *chronic* (hence, too, the persistent hoarseness), though from a 'higher' viewpoint my condition has improved in as much as the critical spots have not been affected in any way. This semi-permanent cough would be tiresome enough, but with the daily *vomissements* ᶜ it becomes loathsome. This frequently makes work impossible, though the doctor believes — he still believes AND THAT IS SOMETHING! — he can rid me of this torment (with the help of a little remedy he has just prescribed). *Qui vivra, verra.*ᵈ

Apropos. SOMEWHERE in my bedroom or my desk there must still be COPIES of my photograph from Algiers in a writing case or some LITTLE BOX or other. * If you could find them, you might send me two photogramms. One of them I have promised to forward to Madame Williamson.* ⁴⁸⁵

Yesterday Mr Meissner sent me his account for 1881; it shows a very slight drop, so there is bound to be a corresponding increase for 1882 as he also wrote saying that he is rapidly running out of copies of *Capital*.⁴⁸⁶ Naturally he is getting impatient about the revised sheets.ᵉ It is an unconscionable time since he heard from me on the subject. Now he will get some definite news.

Cowen's SPEECH *quoad* ᶠ '*EGYPT*' ⁴⁸⁷ is on the same lines as Hyndman's political music of the future, English style. These groaning bourgeois (and even Cowen is a bourgeois in this respect), these poor British bourgeois, who groan as they assume more and more 'RESPONSABILITIES' ᵍ in the service of their historic mission, while vainly protesting against it — and can even Cowen himself help smirking over the entrancing little prospect of all those fortified offensive positions between the Atlantic and the Indian Ocean and, INTO THE BARGAIN, an 'African-British Empire' from the Delta to the Cape? Very naice! In fact there could be no more blatant example of Christian hypocrisy than the 'conquest' of Egypt — conquest in the midst of peace! Even Cowen, and he is certainly the best of the English *parlementaires*,ʰ secretly admires

---

ᵃ See this volume, pp. 420-21. - ᵇ James M. Williamson - ᶜ vomiting - ᵈ We shall see. - ᵉ of the first volume of *Capital*, 3rd German edition - ᶠ as to - ᵍ sic - ʰ parliamentarians

this 'heroic exploit'; 'THE DAZZLE OF OUR MILITARY PARADE'. POOR Cowen! He is a typical British 'BOURGEOIS' (on this point); he believes he has done a splendid 'deal', and very cheaply at that; he doesn't even see that the English 'OLD GRAND MAN'^a is simply the tool of other, non-British smart Alecs in so far as 'policy' plays a part in this event; however Goschen & Co. coolly assumed 'RESPONSABILITY' for the 'HOME' INTEREST.

Cowen has actually become such a prey to superstition that he regards Lord Dufferin as INDEED AN OVERWHELMING DIPLOMATIC GENIUS. But drat the British!

*Kiss my grandson ^b for me.

Farewell,

Old Nick *

First published, in the language of the original (German), in *Annali*, an. I, Milano, 1958

Printed according to the original

Published in English in full for the first time

234

MARX TO ENGELS [72]

IN LONDON

[Ventnor,] 10 January 1883

Dear FRED,

It was very good of you to forward me Lafargue's letter so promptly.[484] It reassured me very much, the more so since, by the same post today, I heard direct from Lafargue, according to whom a turn for the better would seem to be assured. I entirely share your view that Johnny ought *under no circumstances* to leave just now. There can be no question of that until Jenny has completely recovered. It would be unpardonable to add to the difficulty of the child's position. I shall write to Longuet direct this very day. I should be glad if you could drop Jennychen a few lines to the same effect. After all, it's not as though Johnny is going to be lost *pour l'armée territoriale.*^c

---

^a W. E. Gladstone - ^b Jean Longuet - ^c for the territorial army, meaning here his relations in Paris

It is curious how, nowadays, any sort of nervous excitement immediately grips me by the throat, as red Wolff did his brother, the corn profiteer.[488] *Alias*,[a] the initial shock of the bad news from Paris a few days ago induced a fit of spasmodic coughing during which I thought I was going to choke. Poor Jennychen must often have suffered from this highly DISTRESSING FEELING during the course of her asthma.

As for 'little Hepner', I suggest we treat him in a 'businesslike' way, telling him that he is at liberty to reprint our preface to the Leipzig edition[b] and also pointing out that the Russians published a new translation last year.[c] If he doesn't consider it worth while to reprint the *Manifesto without our writing another special preface*, he can take it or leave it, as he thinks fit in the circumstances. 'Holding a pistol to one's head' comes as second nature to 'our people' and, where little Hepner is concerned, it's something we have to accept as a matter of course.

POOR Meissner has sent me a statement of accounts *for 1881*,[486] saying it had been a poor year; not that this really signifies for, by his own account, he was getting 'short' of copies in 1882; so the fewer he sold in 1881, the more he must have sold in 1882. My prolonged silence must have bamboozled him. At last Mahomet will be going to him, though not, alas, what he would greatly prefer—a bundle of revised sheets.[d] Since my long—and only seldom interrupted—confinement to the house first began, but especially as a result of constant nausea or, to use the more *aesthetic South German* expression *à la* Madame Karl Blind, née Cohen,[e] as a result of daily '*puking*' (caused by my cough), I have up till now been scarcely capable of pressing on with the revision. But I believe that, given patience and rigorous self-discipline, I shall soon get back onto the rails again.

Moor

First published abridged in *Der Briefwechsel zwischen F. Engels und K. Marx*, Bd. 4, Stuttgart, 1913 and in full in *MEGA*, Abt. III, Bd. 4, Berlin, 1931

Printed according to the original

---

[a] Here: latterly - [b] See this volume, p. 422. - [c] K. Marx and F. Engels, 'Preface to the Second Russian Edition of the *Manifesto of the Communist Party*'. - [d] of the first volume of *Capital*, 3rd German edition - [e] The reference is to Mathilde Blind.

235

MARX TO ELEANOR MARX [72]

IN LONDON

[Ventnor,] 10 January 1883

Dear Child,

The enclosed letter from Lafargue (be so kind as to send it back sometime) reassured me greatly on Jennychen's account, although Lafargue may have painted too rosy a picture out of consideration for me; but it does seem as though the immediate danger is over.

Charming, the accounts of Wolf and Pa [a] (who is now an IDOLATER OF Wolf's), etc.

As things are at present (and Engels agrees with me over this) it would be a most unfavourable moment to send Johnny off to Argenteuil. He *cannot go back* until Jenny is again in a condition to look after her household. All one must concentrate on is the main issue, not lesser considerations, and it was those that were very nearly the death of Jenny. What difference would a few months here or there make, quite apart from the fact that the poor boy would, from the start, be precipitated into chaos.

I hope, Tussychen, that you will at once write to Jennychen telling her what I have said. I shall today drop Longuet a line on this subject, addressed to the *Justice*.

You must let Johnnychen have news of his brothers and sister; you will, OF COURSE, also give Lenchen the main gist of Lafargue's letter.

Yesterday the weather was horrible; today, too, it looks damp and far from 'glorious'. But I shall, I think, [take] my 'CONSTITUTIONAL' today [...] [b]

First published, in the language of the original (German), in *Annali*, an. I, Milano, 1958

Printed according to the original

---

[a] Edgar and Marcel Longuet - [b] The end of the letter is missing.

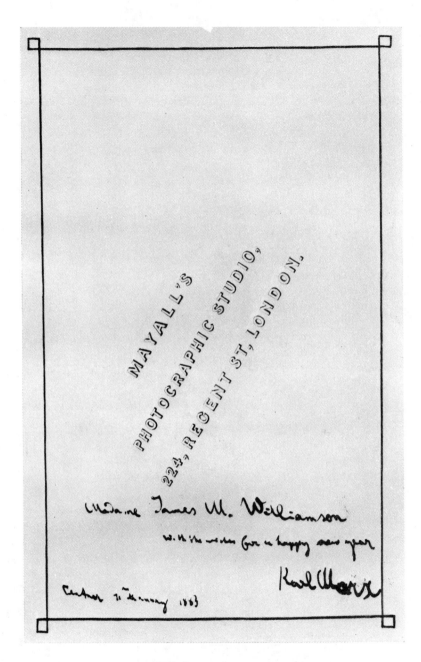

Marx's congratulation to Mrs James M. Williamson
on the reverse of his photograph of 1875

236

MARX TO Mrs JAMES M. WILLIAMSON [489]

IN VENTNOR

Ventnor, 11 January 1883

Madame James M. Williamson with the wishes for a happy New Year.

Karl Marx

Published for the first time   Reproduced from a photocopy of
                                                the original

237

MARX TO JAMES M. WILLIAMSON

IN VENTNOR

Ventnor, 13 January 1883
1 St Boniface Gardens

Dear Dr Williamson,

The fatal news of the death of my oldest daughter [490] forced me to at once return to London. [411]

Please, dear Doctor, send your bill to 41 Maitland Park, London, N. W. I regret that I had not the time of taking leave from you. — Indeed I find some relief in a grim headache. Physical pain is the only 'stunner' of mental pain.

Yours very truly,

Karl Marx

First published as a facsimile and in Ger-   Reproduced from the copy of the
man translation in *Neues Deutschland*,   original
12./13. März, 1983

238

ENGELS TO EDUARD BERNSTEIN [113]

IN ZURICH

London, 18 January 1883

Dear Mr Bernstein,

Days of festivity, followed by days of mourning, [490] constant obstructions. At present I have scarcely a moment to call my own, as you will understand when I tell you that Marx is back here from Ventnor, [411] confined to the house with bronchitis — so far, luckily, only a mild attack — and forbidden to talk much, while all the family business devolves on me. (But not a word of all this in the paper [a]; Marx would be furious if he were to see the worthy Viereck's indiscreet and, what's more, not altogether veracious comments in today's *Süddeutsche Post*.)

Enfin, [b] I still have an hour or so to spare for you. As for Gumbel, returned herewith, he resembles Heine's Gumpelino [c] in as much as he too is interested in stocks and shares. For that matter, he's an outstanding example of the German socialist abroad, having obviously been in Paris. Because we have provided these chaps with a theory of which they are entirely innocent, seldom bothering, moreover, to acquire a rudimentary — if indeed any — understanding of it, every provincial nincompoop among them considers himself superior to all other foreigners. Arriving from Heilbronn, or whatever the potty little place may be called, in London or Paris, he is appalled when he finds that his particular brand of provincialism does not hold good there. Instead of broadening his horizons and learning something, he deliberately makes himself more blinkered than before, for this serves to render all the more glaring the contrast between himself and the bad, stupid foreigners — i. e. his supposed superiority over them. Yet this is the kind of person who predominates in German associations abroad, and if you are now under pressure from them, just ask yourself who it was, after the promulgation of the Anti-Socialist Law, [16] that sought to give undeserved prominence to these associations by means of centralisation, etc. If you had known the chaps then as well

---

[a] *Der Sozialdemokrat* - [b] Well - [c] See Heine's *Reisebilder*, 2nd part.

as you do now, you would have been unlikely to go to so much trouble.

'The party with clean hands' — meaning what? The hands, perhaps, of Hasselmann or Fritzsche and of so many others, about whom everyone arriving here as an exile or something of the kind had a tale to tell?

Gumpelino is at his best when he comes to his stocks and shares. When some such provincial champion of moral virtue tilts thus pharisaically at practices, unpleasant enough in themselves, but from which the party none the less derives a real advantage that far outweighs any possible damage, there must be a catch somewhere. The workers do not have stocks and shares, nor do they give a damn for the financial page. Hence — the little bourgeois, who also wants to dabble in stocks and shares, proceeds to demand that his party paper carry a benevolent, honest, moral, financial page. In the first place, it is not the business of a socialist paper to indicate how best the workers can be exploited — income from stocks and shares is, however, also the product of unpaid labour. If, then, in the second place Gumpelino nevertheless demands that the socialist press should do this, it says little for his socialism and even less for his flair as a businessman. I, too, have stocks and shares, buying and selling from time to time. But I am not so simple as to look to the *socialist* press for advice on these operations. Anyone who does so will burn his fingers, and serve him right! Get yourself baptised, Abraham Gumpelino!

We were delighted by the way Grillenberger and the *Sozialdemokrat* replied to Puttkamer's piece of hypocrisy. [491] That's the way to do it. Not to twist and turn beneath the opponent's blows, or whine and whimper and stammer out excuses about no harm's being meant, as is still done by so many. Hit back — that's what one should do — for every blow dealt by the enemy, pay him back two or three. These have always been our tactics and up till now we have, I believe, always pretty well got the better of our opponents. 'Moreover, the genius of our soldiers lies in attacking, as is perfectly right,' says old Fritz in his orders to his generals [492] and that, indeed, is what our workers do in Germany. But when, in the debate on exceptional laws generally, — given that ☐'s[a] abstract is right — Kayser, for instance, retracts whining that we are revolutionaries only in the Pickwick-

---

[a] Louis Viereck (square in German = Viereck).

ian sense,^a what then? What he should have said was that neither the entire Reichstag nor the Federal Council would be sitting had it not been for a revolution; that old William, when he gobbled up three crowns and a free city,[493] was likewise a revolutionary; that legitimacy itself, and the very foundations of the so-called constitution, are no more than the product of innumerable revolutions effected against the will of the people and directed against the people. Oh, this damned German slackness of thought and will, introduced at such pains into the party with the 'eddicated' men,—if only we could rid ourselves of it again!

Time for the post. I shall reply as soon as possible to whatever points in your letter I may have overlooked. Thanks for the photograph. Proofs ^b when?

Regards, yours,

F. E.

First published, in Russian, in *Marx-Engels Archives*, Book I, Moscow, 1924

Printed according to the original

Published in English in full for the first time

239

ENGELS TO EDUARD BERNSTEIN [24]

IN ZURICH

London, 8 February 1883

Dear Mr Bernstein,

1. I trust you have received the final ms. (*The Mark*) which was sent off from here registered on 20 December. But the printing delays are now getting really too outrageous. If it goes on like this you had better reset the title and put 1884 on it. When, exactly, will there be another sheet?

---

^a A reference to Max Kayser's speech in the Reichstag on 11 January 1883. - ^b of Engels' *Socialism: Utopian and Scientific*, German edition

2. I have received — *neither* the first Accident Bill, *nor* Bebel's speech on the subject. Meanwhile it has struck me that a specific attack on Bismarckian socialism has become outdated. [a] Viereck's little paper [b] has lost all inclination for it. Singer, who had been suffering badly from nationalisation mania on the last occasion but one, was, on the last occasion, completely free of it and genuinely revolutionary, [494] while as for those weaklings in the Reichstag, Blos, Geiser & Co., their courage, if not their enthusiasm, would appear to have evaporated. So why crack a nut with a sledgehammer? I think we should let Bismarckian socialism dig its own grave. After which all that remains is a criticism of the rotten Lassallean remnants. But if the pamphlet [378] is printed so slowly, this attack, too, may have ceased to be topical by the time the thing comes out.

3. You are mistaken about Malon. The man is not as stupid, or rather as naive, as he makes himself out to be. *C'est un faux bonhomme* [c] who has learnt from the Bakuninists how to manipulate people on the sly while making out that it is he himself who is being manipulated. One of these days you will see that I am right.

4. Stock exchange tax. Has long existed here in England in the form of a simple, everyday stamp on the transfer document — $1/2\%$ of the amount paid and 5/- transfer fee (securities *au porteur* [d] are rare over here; they are free). The only consequence is that the *real* speculation on the stock exchange is in margin dealings where no actual transfer takes place. Hence only affects the so-called 'solid capital investment'. Nor has anything ever been devised that the stock market speculators cannot circumvent.

I am against it, 1. because we, after all, demand only *direct* taxation, rejecting *any* that is indirect, so that the people may know and sense what they are paying, and also so that capital can be got at in this way, 2. because we certainly cannot vote one penny to *this* government.

You are right in describing the outcry against the stock exchange as petty-bourgeois. The stock exchange simply adjusts the *distribution* of the surplus value *already stolen* from the workers, and how that is done may at first be a matter of indifference to the workers as such. However the stock exchange adjusts this distribution in the direction

---

[a] See this volume, pp. 324-25.- [b] *Süddeutsche Post* - [c] Shifty customer - [d] to bearer

of centralisation, vastly accelerates the concentration of capitals and is therefore as revolutionary as the steam engine.

Equally petty-bourgeois, though perhaps just excusable, are taxes with a moral purpose — beer, spirits. In this context they are quite ludicrous and altogether reactionary. Had the stock exchange in America not created colossal fortunes, how would large-scale industry and a social movement have been possible in that land of farmers?

It would be quite a good idea if you were to lash out here. But with circumspection. There must be no gap in one's defences where your Stoeckers are concerned.

5. 3rd edition of *Capital*. [227] Will doubtless take some time yet as Marx is still ailing. His stay in Ventnor, where it rained continuously, did him no good. On top of that there has been the loss of his daughter. [490] He has been back here for the past 3 weeks and is so hoarse that he can barely speak, so not much could be discussed (only don't mention this in the paper, [a] of course).

6. We should be grateful for the Rodbertus-Meyer book. [b] At one time the man was almost on the point of discovering surplus value, but his estate in Pomerania prevented him from doing so.

Very many thanks for the photograph.

Kautsky has sent me his pamphlet on American grain. Choice irony: 3 years ago the population was to be reduced because it would otherwise have nothing to eat; now the population does not even suffice to eat what America produces! [495] That's what happens when you study so-called 'questions' one by one without linking them together. In so doing you naturally fall victim to that dialectic which 'is objectively present', Dühring notwithstanding, 'in things themselves'. [496]

I am delighted to hear that the Hohenzollern family again boasts a professing pederast. It would not be complete without one. Admittedly Prince Karl, like Frederick William II, also 'operated' in that line, but he also included women. That reminds me, did Adolf Beust give you Mirabeau's *Secret History of the Court of Berlin* [c] which I gave him to pass on to you? If not, get hold of it. The book is inimitable on

---

[a] *Der Sozialdemokrat* - [b] [J. K.] Rodbertus-Jagetzow, *Briefe und Socialpolitische Aufsätze*, Berlin [1882], edited and with a preface by R. Meyer. - [c] H. G. Mirabeau, *Histoire secrète de la cour de Berlin...*

the subject of Frederick William II; the best bits have been dog's-eared.
Kindest regards.

Yours,

F. E.

First published, in Russian, in *Marx-Engels Archives*, Book I, Moscow, 1924

Printed according to the original

Published in English in full for the first time

240

ENGELS TO EDUARD BERNSTEIN [24]

IN ZURICH

London, 10 February 1883

Dear Mr Bernstein,

I respectfully confirm mine of yesterday's date[a] and herewith enclose a letter for Kautsky[b] whose old address may no longer be any good.

To come back to the stock exchange tax, there is absolutely no need for us to deny the 'immorality' and rascality of that exchange; we can even paint a really lurid picture of it as the spearhead of capitalist gain where ownership becomes directly synonymous with theft, but then go on to conclude that it is by no means in the interests of the proletariat to destroy this immaculate spearhead of the present economy; rather it should be allowed to deploy perfectly freely, so that even the most stupid can see where the present economy is taking them. We shall leave moral indignation to those who are avaricious enough to have recourse to the stock exchange without themselves being stock exchange men and who, as is only right, are cleaned out. And then if the stock exchange and 'solid business' come to blows and if the country Junkers, who also seek to dabble in securities and are inevitably fleeced, make a third in the three-sided battle between the

---

[a] See previous letter.- [b] See next letter.

main elements of the exploiting class, then we, the fourth, shall be the ones to laugh.

The request for an exact address with number and street applies to you as well. Otherwise I cannot send any money, which I must certainly do, inter alia, for 6 copies of the Schmidt pamphlet [458] which Schorlemmer and I wish to send to Germany and which I ask for.

But now I must close.

Yours,

F. E.

First published, in Russian, in *Marx-Engels Archives*, Book I, Moscow, 1924

Printed according to the original

Published in English in full for the first time

241

ENGELS TO KARL KAUTSKY

IN VIENNA

London, 10 February 1883

Dear Mr Kautsky,

At long last I can get round to answering you and thanking you for the various things you have sent. You have no idea of the way impediments of all kinds have prevented me, not only from working, but also from attending to the most urgent correspondence. Since Marx has been ill the burden has fallen upon myself alone and, on top of that, the number of inquiries, etc., has doubled. Moreover, I cannot very well write in the evenings because it tires my eyes and interferes with my sleep. Thus all written work is dependent on the few — in wintertime here, all too short — hours of daylight and, in view of the distances one has to cover here, a single trip into town will, as often as not, disrupt one's entire working day. And some fine to-ing and fro-ing I have had to do of late!

Enough of that. I have not yet seen *Die Neue Zeit*. But I shall write to Dietz today. I must have *street and house number* if I am to send the subscription per money order; that's the rule here.

Your treatise on American food production is most timely. The fact that you make such use of the information supplied by Mr Meyer must have made him very proud. [497] Is he still in Vienna, and do you still see him from time to time?

But what irony of history! 3 or 4 years ago you, a *neonato* [a] Malthusian, were advocating the necessity of restricting the population by artificial means, because otherwise the time would soon come when we should none of us have enough to eat. And now you prove that the population is not even large enough to consume America's surplus food production as well as what Europe herself produces. Solve, I pray, Count Oerindur, this conundrum posed by nature! [b] Presumably, then, it won't be rations that are withheld, but rather that much-vaunted little sponge! Which is not to say, of course, that this same or some other method might not be of great practical use in middle-class families to keep the number of children proportionate to income, and prevent the wife's health being ruined by too frequent confinements, etc. But I still maintain that this is a private matter between husband and wife, or at most the family doctor (in one such case I myself recommended what you call the 'Raciborski method'), and that our proletarians will continue as before to live up to their name by producing numerous *proles*. [c]

It will not surprise you to learn that my standpoint in regard to your article on hetaerism [498] still remains the same, namely that community of wives (and of men for women) was the basis for sexual relations within the tribe. The psychological argument against this, deriving from jealousy, interpolates more recent views, and is disproved by countless facts (some of which below). Darwin is no more of an authority in this field than in that of political economy, whence he imported his Malthusianism. We know practically nothing about apes in this respect, since observations in a menagerie prove nothing and are difficult to make in the case of a troop of wild apes, while such as are alleged to have been made cannot claim to be accurate, conclusive or even universally valid. Gorillas and orang-outangs must in any case be excluded, since they do not live in troops. Those primitive tribes you adduce, with a loose form of monogamy, are, in my view,

---

[a] new born - [b] A. Müllner, *Die Schuld*, Act 2, Scene 5. - [c] progeny

degenerate, as Bancroft has shown of the Californians of the peninsula. [a] Proof of primitivity is provided, not by barbarism, but by the degree of integrity of ancient tribal blood ties. These, therefore, must first be established in each individual instance before conclusions can be drawn from individual manifestations in this tribe or that. For instance, in the case of the peninsular Californians, these ancient ties have become very much looser, nor has any other organisation come to take their place; a sure sign of degeneracy. But even these argue *against you*. For amongst them, too, the women periodically revert to concubinage. And this is a crucial point though you do not so much as mention it. Just as it may be confidently inferred that, wherever,— e. g. with the *Hutzwang* [499] — the land periodically reverts to common ownership, there will once have been complete common ownership of land, so too, I believe, one may confidently conclude that there has originally been community of wives wherever women— symbolically or in reality—periodically revert to concubinage. And this happens, not only amongst your peninsular Californians, but also amongst many other Indian tribes, not to mention the Phoenicians, Babylonians, Indians, Slavs and Celts, either symbolically or in reality; hence it is very ancient and widespread and entirely refutes the psychological argument based on jealousy. I am curious to see how, in due course, you will contrive to overcome this obstacle, for you cannot after all omit all mention of it.

Here comes Pumps with her husband and child [b] and that means no more writing. This is always happening.

With kindest regards,

Yours,

F. E.

First published, in Russian, in *Marx-Engels Archives*, Vol. I (VI), Moscow, 1932

Printed according to the original

Published in English for the first time

---

[a] H. H. Bancroft, *The Native Races of the Pacific States of North America*, Vol. I, New York, 1875. - [b] Percy and Lilian Rosher

242

ENGELS TO LAURA LAFARGUE

IN PARIS

London, 16th February 1883

My dear Laura,

I begin this letter — 4 p. m.— uncertain when I may be able to finish it, the constant interruptions I have lately been subjected to leave me no quiet time except at night and then I dare not write much, as that affects my eyes.

Your *Salas y Gomez*[a] is on the whole a masterpiece. There is the same roughness of language as in the original — roughness as we like it in young good red wine, *gesunde Herbigkeit,*[b] and which makes Chamisso's terzine come nearer to Dante's than those of any other poet. I compared it with the original line for line and am astonished at the fidelity of the reproduction. Still I would wish you to try and alter a few passages so as to make it perfect. The end, you say yourself, is hurried and so indeed it is. But for details.

Introduction. Terz. 3. Thus towered it — it could not 'tower' while it could only be descried from the mast-head.— *From* the *Ruric*: impossible, because Chamisso himself was on board the *Ruric*.

Terz. 5. I think wants re-moulding. *Den Versuch zu w a g e n*[c] applies merely to the risk of getting the boats safely through the breakers caused by coral reefs which encircle all islands in those latitudes.

Terz. 7, 3. One syllable short, *our* cannot be used bisyllabic.

Terz. 15. The translation: *albeit* ... that *might* obliterate, is open to misleading. The original says clearly that it is the men's own steps that have obliterated the writing.

Terz. 31, 1. This *cold* rock will never do while it burns his feet through his soles.

1st Tablet. Terz. 1. *Ich sah bereits im Geiste*[d] — that cannot be suppressed in the beginning. The reader, from the translation, must believe that the man was already *in full possession* of all these fancied

---

[a] A reference to Laura Lafargue's English translation of Adelbert von Chamisso's narrative poem *Salas y Gomez* (written in 1829).- [b] healthy roughness - [c] *to venture* an attempt - [d] I already saw in my mind's eye

treasures, and only at the end, Terz. 8, there is an indication, and that, after the previous omission, not strong enough, that all this was a mere fancy-dream. The character of the adventurous seafarer in quest of wealth forms the basis of the whole piece, and ought therefore to come out strong from the beginning of the story.

Terz. 4, 1: and for myself too were content and gain, is not to be understood without reference to the original.[a]

Terz. 9, 3: the *cabins* gives a syllable too much in the verse, and is not literal. *Der untre Raum* is in ship's language the *hold*, and moreover monosyllabic.

2nd Tablet. Not a fault to find except one and that is one in copying. Terz. 16, 1: For they (have) sighted me, the *have* is omitted.

3rd Tablet. Terz. 7. 'Worser far' I prefer, but will the philistine public? And will you turn philistine enough to say 'worse by far'?

Terz. 15-20: your own variations indicate that you are not quite satisfied with your work. I do believe that here a fresh attempt might be made with advantage. The conclusion again is very good.

As usual the beginning, when one is not yet *recht im Zug*,[b] and the end when one gets tired a little, are the weak points, but I think after you have had it laid aside for a time, you will be able to go at it again with fresh vigour and make it what indeed you *can* make it.

Mohr wants to read it too, but not yet. Latterly he has had very bad sleepless nights which have broken down his intellectual appetite, so that he began to read, instead of novels, publisher's catalogues. However the night before last was good and he was quite another man yesterday; another good symptom: his feet, previously ice-cold in the evening and only to be warmed by hot mustard-baths, for the last two nights were quite warm and no baths required. The chronic inflammation of the larynx and bronchiae is slowly becoming subdued, but swallowing still painful and the voice very hoarse. I shall continue to-night after I have seen him. His appetite was very good yesterday, Nim[c] surpasses herself in inventing new dishes for his case.

17th February. It was 1 o'clock when I came back last night from Maitland Park,[d] so I could not finish this letter. Mohr was going on

---

[a] Chamisso has: 'und selber hat ich Ruhe nicht gewonnen' - [b] quite in full swing -
[c] Helene Demuth - [d] the Marx family's address in London

pretty much as usual, but he had given up the catalogues and returned to Frédéric Soulié, anyhow a good sign. What do you say to this, that he drinks a *pint of milk* a day, he who could not bear milk to be on the table! Anyhow it does him good. Besides rum now and then (in the milk especially) he takes a bottle of brandy about every four days. The worst is that his case is so complicated that while the most pressing things, the breathing organs, have to be attended to, and now and then a sleeping draft is to be given, other things have to be neglected, for instance the stomach which is as you know none of the most perfect organs of digestion. But still his appetite keeps up pretty well, and we do our best to supply him such food chiefly as contains much nourishment in a small compass.

I think our friends have been in too great a hurry with the new *Égalité*. What is to become of the paper if Paul [a] and Guesde get 'time to serve' at Moulins, and that is after all not quite impossible? [440] Guesde's opening article [b] is not at all what it should be. What he says of judges elected by universal suffrage, is quite as applicable to universal suffrage itself, to the Republic, to any political institution. If *Messieurs les français* do not know how to use this universal suffrage *tant pis pour eux*. [c] Give our people in Germany the right to elect the judges and they will carry the election in all large towns and make Berlin too hot a shop for old William and Bismarck, unless they have recourse to a coup d'état. But to say: *white* because my adversary says: *black*, is simply *subir la loi de son adversaire, et une politique de bébés*. [d] I am afraid Guesde's old anarchist rodomontades are cropping up again rather fast, and in that case he will lose himself. Paul's *deux embêtés* [e] [500] are charming. That is just his line. [f]

First published in: Marx and Engels, *Works*, Second Russian Edition, Vol. 35, Moscow, 1964

Reproduced from the original

Published in English for the first time

---

[a] Lafargue - [b] J. Guesde, 'Rentrée en ligne', *L'Égalité*, 5th series, No. 1, 16 February 1883. - [c] so much the worse for them - [d] to adopt the ways of one's adversary, which is a puerile policy - [e] two bored ones - [f] The end of the letter is missing.

243

ENGELS TO EDUARD BERNSTEIN [501]

IN ZURICH

London, 27 February 1883

Dear Mr Bernstein,

I recently had a little dispute with Viereck which has forced me to break with him. As he might possibly come to Zurich for the congress [502] and make use of the occasion to mention the matter in *private* conversation, I am concerned lest in that event *his* version be the only one to go the rounds. I therefore authorise you to read this letter to anyone Viereck may discuss the matter with, but at all events to Bebel and Liebknecht.

Some little while before Christmas Viereck, or rather his wife, [a] sent me the visiting card of one Deinhardt, a Munich engineer, with three questions of a chemico-physico-industrial nature and asked me to get hold of the information if possible. I sent the card to Schorlemmer in Manchester who rightly suspected from the questions a pushful and importunate inventor and for good measure appended a 'motto' to his extremely terse reply. Here is the card as returned to Viereck:

'1. Has ozone come into use alongside chlorine and chloride of lime for bleaching rags in English paper mills? — *No.*

'2. Compared with other bleaching agents, does ozone offer a manufacturing concern any noteworthy advantages in a technical or financial sense? — *No.*

'3. Is the production and use of ozone in an industrial concern attended by considerable difficulties? — *Yes.*

'C. Deinhardt, Engineer (printed on card).

'Motto: *Apage inventor!*' [b]

In this form the card went back. So if Viereck did not wish to show Deinhardt the motto, all he had to do was copy questions and answers onto a sheet of paper or a postcard, and that would have been that.

Next I received No. 7 (17 January) of the *Süddeutsche Post* (which Viereck sent me in exchange for *The Labour Standard*) and, in the 'Letter Box', saw the following:

'To Mr Deinhardt, engineer of this city. The author of the 'electrotechnical revolution' writes to tell us that, *despite information to the contrary supplied by Prof. Schorlemmer,*

---

[a] Laura Viereck - [b] Be off with you, inventor!

of Manchester, he must stand by his contention *that the production of ozone would be effected by means of a dynamo, etc.'*

What was the meaning of this? How was it that this purely private piece of information found its way into the paper rather than into a proper letter box? And how could Viereck have had the impudence to make public use in his paper of private information supplied by Schorlemmer for Deinhardt — on Viereck's own evidence an extremely importunate man — purely to oblige Viereck? Either Viereck didn't know what he was doing or he did it out of revenge for the 'motto'.

But there is nothing whatever in the 3 questions and answers that turns on whether the production of ozone is effected by means of a dynamo; a dynamo is not mentioned at all. Thus, by indirectly attributing to Schorlemmer a statement actually denying that the production of ozone is effected with a dynamo, Viereck is guilty of outright *falsification*; he is attributing to Schorlemmer things he has never said. But obviously it cannot be a matter of indifference to a chemist whose reputation extends beyond Europe if someone attributes to him things about chemico-physical questions he has never said, and does so publicly in the university city of Munich where, after all, there are also chemists and physicists who might possibly read it.

So I sent the paper, as was only my duty, to Schorlemmer who sent me the following letter for Viereck:

'If anyone' (I am quoting from memory) 'publishes a private communication without permission, then it is improper. But if in addition he goes on to distort the said communication, then it is barely ethical.'

Accordingly Schorlemmer called for the publication of the card as it stood, with questions, answers and motto, in order that the matter might be clarified.

Whereupon a long letter arrived from Viereck addressed to me. Deinhardt, he said, had bombarded him with three letters on the subject of ozone (so the *Apage inventor* was *wholly appropriate!*). By sending him [Viereck] the above-mentioned letter I was now holding a *pistol to his head* (*which is untrue*, let him show it to you; all I did was demand in polite terms full satisfaction for Schorlemmer), while Schorlemmer's letter and the demands made therein were even more intemperate. He could not, he added, publish the motto (needless to say this request was not intended seriously) and the remainder only if Schorlemmer *withdrew* the insulting expressions contained in his letter; for the time being he could not admit having made a mistake, but

must refuse to accede to our peremptory demands in 'this entirely un-
qualifiable form'.

'*I did not even know*,' his letter goes on, 'that Prof. Schorlemmer read the *Süddeutsche Post* and surely cannot in any circumstances assume that you had sent him this issue *ad hoc*[a]! For I regard it ... as out of the question that you *could inform against me* and I should have been only too pleased had you suggested what steps ought to have been taken to pacify the much agitated professor.' ... $^{11}/_{12}$ of his readers consisted of party members ... nothing ought to be imputed to him that was 'inconsistent with the conduct of a man of honour', etc.

So they make improper use of Schorlemmer's name and, *on their own admission*, distort what he says because they hope *he won't find out*. And when I, the sole cause of his involvement in the affair, tell him about it, then I am '*informing*' against Viereck. Not Schorlemmer but Viereck is the injured party, because Schorlemmer characterises Viereck's conduct, and with great restraint at that. Not a word about the *falsification* of which Schorlemmer was the victim.

Well, Viereck may read our reply to anyone he chooses. We sent him a statement, addressed not to him but to the editorial board, i. e. a statement intended for publication, together with a request that at the same time they print questions and answers. What does Viereck do? First, a polite apology in the 'Letter Box', to wit:

'We profoundly regret this tiresome misunderstanding' and promise to put the matter right.

And then? In No. 17, 9 February:

'*In regard to the electrotechnical revolution*. On being consulted, Prof. Schorlemmer of Manchester supplied the following information which we herewith print in order to clear up a (!) misunderstanding (!)': (the questions and answers follow).

The clarification of this 'misunderstanding' is tantamount to the total obfuscation of the affair, as is satisfaction for Schorlemmer to attempted mockery and to further misuse of his name. Thereafter I returned the *Süddeutsche Post* unopened. Yet another postcard from Viereck, asking what he had done to deserve being rebuffed in this *insulting* (everything is insulting!) way, etc. What I said in my reply — also per postcard — he can read to you himself if he likes. 'One must

---
[a] for this purpose

make a complete break with a swine like that,' Schorlemmer writes to me. And that has been done.

Yours,

F. Engels

First published in *Die Briefe von Friedrich Engels an Eduard Bernstein*, Berlin, 1925

Printed according to the original

Published in English for the first time

244

ENGELS TO EDUARD BERNSTEIN [7]

IN ZURICH

London, 27 February 1883

Dear Mr Bernstein,

Your letter received yesterday evening. [503] The *Égalité* has gone phut again and I would ask you to publish the following facts (see enclosed slip of paper) in the *Sozialdemokrat*. [504] Let us hope that the chaps will finally learn some sense and not go founding daily papers on the strength of contracts of this kind. Taking legal action is a mug's game and costs money, and any French court of law would revel in non-suiting socialists and losing them their case, while the paper would still remain defunct.

Guesde and Lafargue, amongst others, were arraigned [440] under Article 91 of the *Code pénal* [167] — conspiracy and incitement to civil war — death penalty. What a farce!

At any rate, it's a good thing that they can no longer publicly declare their solidarity with the anarchists, the latter being now *behind bars* — mere children who play with fire and, when given a hiding, try and make out they're the most innocent fellows in the world. And now some fool in Brussels sets off a bomb in his own trousers pocket! In due course dynamite will come to seem plain ridiculous.

Now for a different tableau. Because of a dirty trick Viereck played on Schorlemmer in the *Süddeutsche Post*, I have broken with him. Further details are contained in a letter I have sent to Schorlemmer[a]

[a] See previous letter.

and which he, if he is agreeable, will send on to you tomorrow direct from Manchester (I have got it here, returned because I had forgotten to sign it).[a] I need hardly tell you that, when Viereck and Fritzsche were over here, they would have been given a very cool reception by us had they not come as the official emissaries of the party. As it was, however, and since Marx was exempted by his indisposition, I had to some extent to do them the honours.[505] Moreover, a certain intimacy grew up between his (Viereck's) present wife[b] and my niece[c] (both of whom were then secretly engaged), etc., etc. At the same time I told him pretty plainly what I thought of his proclivity for vulgar democracy. In short, I became involved with him, but now it is all over.

The veriest boot-black could not have tolerated the treatment meted out to Schorlemmer by Viereck. Yet Schorlemmer is, after Marx, undoubtedly the most eminent man in the European socialist party. When I got to know him 20 years ago he was already a communist. At that time an impoverished private assistant to English professors, he is now a member of the ROYAL SOCIETY (the equivalent over here of the *Akademie der Wissenschaften*), and the world's leading authority in his own speciality, the chemistry of the simpler hydrocarbons (paraffin and its derivatives). His great *Treatise on Chemistry*, brought out jointly with Roscoe,[d] but written almost entirely by Schorlemmer (as all chemists know), is now without a rival in England and Germany. And this position he has carved out for himself abroad, in competition with men who exploited him for as long as they could, and he has done so entirely on the strength of genuinely scientific work, without ever making any concession to humbug. Moreover, he never hesitates to proclaim himself a socialist as, for instance, when he reads jokes aloud from the *Sozialdemokrat* for the benefit of the other lecturers with whom he is lunching; but he also demands, and justly so, that he should not have unwanted publicity, in whatever guise, thrust upon him, as was done by Viereck. But now, good-bye until tomorrow. It is almost midnight and I have broken my rule of not writing at night.

28 February. There is, however, one favour I would ask of you, and that is not to keep chucking the word 'comrade' at me in the paper.[e]

---

[a] Words in brackets were added by Engels at the bottom of the page.- [b] Laura Viereck - [c] Mary Ellen Rosher - [d] H. E. Roscoe, C. Schorlemmer, *Ausführliches Lehrbuch der Chemie*, vols I-III, Brunswick, 1877-82. - [e] *Der Sozialdemokrat*

To begin with, I detest anything that smacks of title-mongering and since, in all the German literature that counts for anything, people are called simply by their names and are not given titles unless under attack, we too should conform to this unless the designation 'comrade' is *really* intended to *inform* the reader that the person concerned belongs to the party. What is in place and normal on the platform and in verbal debate can look pretty awful in print. And then again, we here are not in fact 'comrades' in the narrower sense of the term. We can hardly be said to belong to the German party any more than to the French, American or Russian, nor can we regard ourselves as any more bound by the German programme [506] than by the minimum programme. [68] We set no little store by this, our special position as representatives of *international* socialism. But it also precludes us from belonging to one particular national party — so long, that is, as we are unable to return to Germany and participate immediately in the struggle there. Just now it would be pointless.

What you say about Liebknecht's complicity in importing philistine elements has long been our view. For all his excellent qualities, Liebknecht has one fault, namely the desire to attract 'educated' elements to the party by hook or by crook, and to him, a former teacher, the worst thing that can happen is for a working man in the Reichstag to say '*me*' for '*I*'. A man like Viereck ought never to have been put up as a candidate. He would have exposed us in the Reichstag to far more deadly ridicule than would a hundred wrong '*mes*' of which, after all, the Hohenzollerns and field marshals are likewise guilty. Unless the newcomers — the educated ones and those from bourgeois circles generally — adopt the proletarian standpoint *unreservedly*, they can do nothing but harm. But if they have genuinely adopted that standpoint, then they are exceedingly useful and welcome. Another of Liebknecht's characteristics is that, for the sake of a momentary success, he will unhesitatingly sacrifice subsequent, more important successes. Thus Viereck and Fritzsche's highly dubious mission to America. [119] It went off reasonably well, but is there any knowing to what ridicule Fritzsche may not expose us later on in America? And then people will say: 'And there you have the representative of German Social Democracy in America, sent over officially!' And the caution one has to observe vis-à-vis this type of person when it comes to candidatures is evident from the Oppenheimer case. [507]

Yet another interruption!

1 March. We have always done our utmost to combat the narrow, petty-bourgeois philistine mentality within the party because, having developed since the Thirty Years' War, [472] it has infected *all* classes in Germany, and has become a German hereditary ill, sister to servility and humble submissiveness and every German hereditary vice! This it is that has made us ridiculous and contemptible abroad. It is the chief cause of the slackness and weakness of character so prevalent in our midst. It prevails on the throne no less frequently than in a cobbler's lodging. Only since the time a *modern* proletariat took shape in Germany, only since then has a class developed there that is virtually untainted by this hereditary German scourge, a class which has given proof of clear-sightedness, energy, humour and tenacity in the fray. And can we be expected not to combat every attempt at artificially inoculating that healthy — in Germany, the only healthy — class with the old hereditary germ of philistine narrow-mindedness and philistine slackness? But during the first period of shock after the assassination attempts [120] and the Anti-Socialist Law, [16] the leaders fell prey to an anxiety which in itself is proof of their having lived far too much amongst philistines and been subject to pressure from philistine opinion. The idea at the time was that the party should, if not actually *become* philistine, at any rate *appear* to be so. That, I am glad to say, has now been overcome, but the philistine elements — these being particularly prevalent among university men, most of them incapable of passing their examinations — introduced in pre-Anti-Socialist Law days are still there, and a close watch must be kept upon them. We are glad to have your assistance here and, being on the *Sozialdemokrat*, you are in a key position.

But for goodness sake don't go raking up that wretched *Jahrbuch* article. [a] It was an apologia for the stock exchange men. But one can perfectly well be at one and the same time a stock exchange man and a socialist and therefore detest and despise the *class* of stock exchange men. Would it ever occur to me to apologise for the fact that I myself was once a partner in a firm of manufacturers? There's a fine reception waiting for anyone who tries to throw that in my teeth! And if I could be certain of making a million on the stock exchange tomorrow, and thus put an ample supply of funds at the disposal

---

[a] [K. Höchberg, E. Bernstein, C. A. Schramm,] 'Rückblicke auf die sozialistische Bewegung in Deutschland. Kritische Aphorismen', *Jahrbuch für Sozialwissenschaft und Sozialpolitik*, 1. Jg., 1. Hälfte, Zürich-Oberstrass, 1879.

of the party in Europe and America, to the stock exchange I should promptly go.

What you say about courting the enemy's praise is perfectly right. We have often been infuriated by the glee with which the slightest sign, be it only a fart, of recognition from the armchair socialists [82] was recorded in the *Volksstaat* and the *Vorwärts*. It was the phrase, 'We must exact recognition from the bourgeoisie in every sphere', that marked the beginning of Miquel's betrayal. [456] And however much Rudolf Meyer may butter us up, [482] all the recognition he is likely to get in return is for his really meritorious *Politische Gründer*. [a] We never, of course, discussed serious topics with him, but confined ourselves almost entirely to Bismarck and the like. But Meyer is at least a decent fellow and one who is also quite capable of defying the aristos, nor is he ambitious like all the rest of the armchair socialists, who are now also flourishing in Italy; one specimen, Achille Loria, was over here recently but two calls on me were enough for him.

In the case of Viereck, who knows absolutely nothing about the matter, the to-do over the electrotechnical revolution is merely an advertisement for the pamphlet he has published. [b] In fact, however, it's a tremendously revolutionary affair. The steam engine taught us to transform heat into mechanical motion, but the exploitation of electricity has opened up the way to transforming *all* forms of energy — heat, mechanical motion, electricity, magnetism, light — one into the other and back again, and to their industrial exploitation. The circle is complete. And Deprez's latest discovery, namely that electric currents of very high voltage can, with a comparatively small loss of energy, be conveyed by simple telegraph wire over hitherto undreamed-of distances and be harnessed at the place of destination [426] — the thing is still in embryo — this discovery frees industry for good from virtually all local limitations, makes possible the harnessing of even the most remote hydraulic power and, though it may benefit the *towns* at the outset, will in the end inevitably prove the most powerful of levers in eliminating the antithesis between town and country. Again, it is obvious that the productive forces will thereby acquire a range such that they will, with increasing rapidity, outstrip the control of the bourgeoisie. All Viereck sees in it, short-sighted as he is, is

---

[a] R. Meyer, *Politische Gründer und die Corruption in Deutschland*, Leipzig, 1877. - [b] See previous letter.

a fresh argument in favour of his beloved nationalisation. What the bourgeoisie cannot do must be done by Bismarck.

I'm sorry about the Schumacher business. Let's hope it's just a passing phase; he used to be such a lively, resolute chap. But, as you say, it's that damned German imperial atmosphere! [508]

There are a great many reasons why I should not consider coming to the congress. [502] Things being what they are just now on the Continent, I would sooner remain here.

Kautsky has sent me his second piece on marriage [498] in which he again tries to sneak in community of wives as a secondary manifestation. But that won't do. Indeed, I shall write to him about it [a] and enclose the letter in one to you. It is Kautsky's misfortune that, in his hands, complex questions do not resolve themselves into simple ones—rather, simple questions become complex. And then, it's impossible to achieve anything if one is so prolific. He ought to write popular stuff for the sake of the fee, and take his time over scientific matters, thus dealing with them in a considered and exhaustive way, which alone can be rewarding.

The pederast, who made us laugh a great deal, has already been posted on to Manchester where he will be widely disseminated.

Marx is still incapable of work, keeps to his room (he returned here immediately after his daughter's death [490]), and reads French novels. His case seems to be a very complicated one. My hopes are high, now that a better season is on its way.

Yours,

F. Engels

Whatever you do, don't put anything about Marx's state of health into the paper [b]; Viereck shamefully exploited in the *Süddeutsche Post* the information I sent his wife [c] from time to time (he hardly ever wrote to me himself!), but naturally I was able to keep this from Marx, otherwise he would have hauled me over the coals. Here again Viereck had failed to ask my permission.

First published, in Russian, in *Marx-Engels Archives*, Book I, Moscow, 1924

Printed according to the original

Published in English in full for the first time

---

[a] See next letter. - [b] *Der Sozialdemokrat* - [c] Laura Viereck

245

ENGELS TO KARL KAUTSKY

IN VIENNA

London, 2 March 1883

Dear Mr Kautsky,

I have received your second article on marriage [498] and, since this contains your answer to my criticism of the first one, [a] I shall continue where I left off; I happen to have an hour to spare which will not be the case tomorrow.

To begin with I consider it absolutely inadmissible that, having contested community of wives as a primary manifestation, you should seek to reintroduce it as a secondary one. Wherever common ownership exists, be it of land, women or anything else, it will necessarily be primitive, a legacy of the animal kingdom. The subsequent process of development consists entirely in the gradual *dissolution* of this primeval common ownership; in no case do we find an instance of secondary common ownership evolving out of primitive private ownership. So irrefutable and universally valid do I consider this proposition to be that, even were you to produce what appeared to be exceptions — and however striking these might be at first sight — I would not regard them as an argument to the contrary, but only as a question yet to be solved.

Moreover, having made jealousy the one decisive factor in the first article, you ought not to discard it entirely in the second. Article I presupposes a loose form of monogamy, and this very largely on the strength of jealousy for, as I have said, your other reasons carry very little weight with me. But if jealousy is able to overcome natural community of sexes — and you do *after all* indirectly concede the existence of the latter when you say: 'Within the tribe *complete sexual licence* prevailed' — if jealousy can relegate that natural licence to the confines of temporary monogamy, how much more easily must it be able to overcome lesser obstacles. The tribe's common ownership of captives is, however, an obstacle of much less magnitude. A woman remains a woman, whether she is free or a slave; true, in the case of

---

[a] See this volume, pp. 437-38.

female slaves, a man's jealousy is able to impose sole possession much more easily than in the case of free women who have a *right* to adultery! But the moment there is any question of marriage with captives, the jealousy of the husbands suddenly evaporates; the community of sexes which so appalled them in the primitive state, becomes acceptable and pleasing and, even after monogamy or polygamy has already been introduced, even in the case of Semitic peoples where harems are the rule, husbands do not object to their wives coupling with every Tom, Dick and Harry, either in the temple or at special seasons. No, my dear fellow, you can't dismiss the thing as easily as all that. For you are duty-bound to stick to the point even when it becomes awkward for you to do so. If *primary* community of sexes was inhibited by jealousy, then community of sexes is excluded once and for all, right down to and including capitalist society. Either your second article refutes the first or vice versa.

Incidentally, I would contest your statement that the freedom of women, at your first stage, contributed to monogamy because there could be no question of repression. The argument that community of sexes is dependent on repression is itself false and a modern distortion arising out of the idea that common ownership in the sexual sphere was only *of* women *by* men and at the *latter's pleasure*. This is totally foreign to the primitive state. Common ownership in this sphere was available to *both* sexes. To refute the false assumption, however, is not the same thing as refuting the correct facts on which the distortion is based.

Again, by reducing all community of sexes and traces thereof to marriage by rapine with foreign women, you attribute to that form of marriage, *qua* predominant form, a really vast range. Yet you adduce not the slightest proof of this.

What follows is lost in a welter of hypotheses [among them much] [a] that is undoubtedly correct [in regard to specific times and] [a] places. But you generalise at the speed of an express train, whereas questions of this kind do not lend themselves to such rapid despatch. And while the Celtic clan, the Roman *gens* and the German *Geschlecht* are, it is true, all sub-divisions of the tribe, they all have very marked differences and also, surely, different origins. As do the various kinds of clan amongst non-Celtic peoples.

I am convinced that, should you pursue these studies or resume

---

[a] Ms. damaged.

them after a lapse of time, you will arrive at quite different conclusions and, perhaps, regret your premature endeavours in this difficult field. You have done some hard slogging, but you have leapt too rapidly to conclusions, at the same time laying too much weight on the opinions of self-styled anthropologists, all of whom have what I might call a certain obliquity reminiscent of your armchair socialist.[82] While you may refute Bachofen's deification and mystification of community of sexes,[a] this is not to say that community of sexes does not and will not continue to exist.

Well, the dinner-bell is being rung—no offence meant, and so I still remain,

Your old friend,
F. Engels

First published, in Russian, in *Marx-Engels Archives*, Vol. I (VI), Moscow, 1932

Printed according to the original

Published in English for the first time

246

ENGELS TO AUGUST BEBEL

IN LEIPZIG

London, 7 March 1883

Dear Bebel,

I shall have to reply to you from memory today as I must have left your letter with Marx, but first of all I should like to congratulate you on your release the day after tomorrow.[405]

The rapid advances in German industry you have described please me enormously. What we are now experiencing is the second Bonapartist empire in all its aspects: the stock exchange is mobilising all capitals that are still wholly or partially idle by attracting them and

---

[a] J. J. Bachofen, *Das Mutterrecht. Eine Untersuchung über die Gynaikokratie der alten Welt nach ihrer religiösen und rechtlichen Natur*, Stuttgart, 1861.

rapidly concentrating them in a few hands; the capitals thus made available to industry are ushering in an industrial boom (which is by no means necessarily the same thing as a high level of business activity) and, once the affair gets going, it will continue to accelerate. Only two things distinguish the era of Bismarck from the era of Bonaparte III: The latter owed its prosperity to what was relatively free trade; the former is making headway despite protective tariffs that are wholly uncalled for, particularly in Germany. And, secondly, the Bismarckian era is putting far more people out of work. This is partly because the increase in population is much greater in our case than in that of France where two children are the rule, partly because Bonaparte, thanks to his building operations in Paris, generated an artificial demand for labour, whereas in our case the milliard era [169] came to an early end; but again it must partly be due to other causes about which I am not clear. At all events philistine Germany is at last becoming a modern country, and that is absolutely vital if we are to make rapid progress.

When one reads the German bourgeois papers and the speeches in the Chamber one might imagine that one was living in the England of Henry VII and VIII; the same complaints about danger from vagrants, the same outcry for the forcible suppression of vagrancy — the *cachot*[a] and the lash. Here is the best proof of how rapidly the producers are losing touch with their means of production, of how rapidly the smaller enterprises are being supplanted by the machine and the perfecting of the machine. But what could be more ludicrous and despicable than those bourgeois who hope that moral sermons and penal methods sermons will enable them to do away with the inevitable consequences of their own actions. It is a crying shame that you are not in the Reichstag [222]; this is a theme that would be right up your street.

The precedent you set in the Saxon Landtag by calmly taking the oath [509] has had its imitators. The Italians have unanimously declared that the oath need not be a stumbling-block and Costa took the oath without demur.[420] And, after all, these are people who declare themselves to be 'anarchists', even though they vote and are elected by vote!

There has been a scandalous delay over my pamphlet [378] in Zurich, but the printing ought to be done by now; whether the binding will

---

[a] prison

take as long in tin-pot Zurich, I don't know. At all events I am still awaiting copies, having as yet had none. The part on the 'Mark' will clarify much of Maurer for you; the man's writing is atrociously slipshod but the content is excellent. I have read the book 5 or 6 times and shall reread it next week after I have again been through the relevant material in the remainder of his collected works.[465]

We were most delighted at the way the virtuously religious Puttkamer was dealt with, first by Grillenberger in the Reichstag and then several times in the *Sozialdemokrat*.[491] He will be on his guard now!

Little Hepner has reprinted *Unsere Ziele*[510] in New York, allegedly improved and with a little picture that is said to represent your portrait but in fact represents an honest to God Yankee. As I only have the 1st edition, I can't say whether or what changes have been made by him for the worse/better. If you haven't got his edition I can send you one; after all, you had better see what the Americans think you ought to look like.

Now I must close, for I must go and see Marx whose health is still not really making the progress it should. If it were two months from now, the warmth and air would do their work but as it is there's a north-east wind, a storm almost, with flurries of snow, so how can a man expect to cure himself of a long-standing case of bronchitis!

Regards to Liebknecht.

Your
F. E.

First published abridged in: A. Bebel, *Aus meinem Leben*, Teil III, Stuttgart, 1914 and in full, in Russian, in *Marx-Engels Archives*, Vol. I (VI), Moscow, 1932

Printed according to the original

Published in English for the first time

247

ENGELS TO LAURA LAFARGUE

IN PARIS

London, 10 March 1883

My dear Laura,

Not having received a letter from Paul[a] this morning, I conclude that in this frosty and snowy weather with east wind, you will not be in too great a hurry to come to London. Anyhow, if you should make up your mind to come, everything is prepared for you.

Donkin saw Mohr yesterday evening and I am glad to say gave a far more favorable account of his health than a fortnight ago. He said Mohr was decidedly not worse, but better, if anything, than then; and if we could keep him up for the next two months, there would be a good chance of bringing him round again. Of course he is still getting weaker, on account of the difficulty of swallowing, but we *must* force him to eat and drink. This is what Tussy wrote me on a post-card last night and what Nim[b] told me today; I shall see Tussy to-night and if any more details are to be had shall write again at once. The abscess in the lungs he considers to be going on very favorably at present. The nocturnal sweats have now ceased the last 4 nights (or 5) but instead of that there is a certain feverishness in the day-time which of course is also weakening.

He gave me the *Prolétaire* and the reply of Guesde's Committee, as well as the '*vil*'[c] number of the *Citoyen and Bataille* which I am to keep for him. The copy sent by Paul can therefore with the rest be used for Zurich.[d] So this time the business part of the affair can be attended to, fortunately, but with Mohr's present state of health, that cannot always be reckoned upon if he be in exclusive possession of the materials.

These ex-Bakounists Malon and Brousse are a beastly dirty lot. Such barefaced forgery would be enough, anywhere out of Paris, to kill them for ever. But with the immense hold of *la phrase* upon the Parisians, who knows how many thousand votes the '*ouvrier manuel*'[e] will not concentrate upon himself? *Enfin espérons le mieux.*[f]

---

[a] Lafargue - [b] Helene Demuth - [c] base - [d] *Der Sozialdemokrat* - [e] manual labourer -
[f] Finally, let's hope for the best.

Kind regards to Paul.

Very affectionately yours,
F. Engels

First published, in the language of the original (English), in: F. Engels, P. et L. Lafargue, *Correspondance*, t. I, Paris, 1956

Reproduced from the original

248

ENGELS TO CHARLES LONGUET

IN ARGENTEUIL

[Telegram]

London, 14 March, 4:32 afternoon [1883]

Marx expired suddenly at three this afternoon letter follows

Engels London

First published in: Marx and Engels, *Works*, Second Russian Edition, Vol. 35, Moscow, 1964

Reproduced from the original

Published in English for the first time

249

ENGELS TO FRIEDRICH ADOLPH SORGE [511]

IN HOBOKEN

[Telegram]

London, 14 March 1883

Marx died today

Engels London

First published, in the language of the original (English), in *New Yorker Volkszeitung*, No. 64, 15 March 1883

Reproduced from the original

250

ENGELS TO WILHELM LIEBKNECHT [512]

IN LEIPZIG

London, 14 March 1883

Dear Liebknecht,

You will all have learned from my telegram to Mrs Bebel [284] — the only address I have got — of the terrible loss suffered by the European socialist revolutionary party. Only last Friday the doctor [a] — one of the leading medical men in London — had told us that there was every prospect of getting him as well as he had ever been, provided only he sustained his strength by taking food. And from that very moment he began eating with a better appetite again. Then, just after two o'clock this afternoon, I found the household in tears and was told he was terribly weak; Lenchen called out to me to come upstairs, saying he was half asleep, and, when I got there — she had been out of the room for barely two minutes — he was sound asleep, but it was for ever. The greatest intellect of the second half of this century had ceased to think. What the immediate cause of death was, I would not venture to guess without medical advice, the whole case being so complex as to require pages if it were to be described adequately, even by a doctor. And, indeed, it is no longer of any real importance. I have suffered anxiety enough over the past six weeks, and all I can say is that, in my opinion, the death, first of his wife, [513] and then, in a most critical period, of Jenny, [490] helped to bring on the final crisis.

Although I have seen him this evening laid out on his bed, his features rigid in death, I simply cannot conceive that this man of genius has ceased to fructify the proletarian movement of both worlds with his stupendous ideas. We all of us are what we are because of him; and the movement is what it is today because of his theoretical and practical activities; but for him we should still be in a welter of confusion.

Your
F. Engels

First published, as a facsimile, in: W. Liebknecht, *Karl Marx zum Gedächtnis*, Nürnberg, 1896

Printed according to the facsimile in the book

[a] Donkin

251

ENGELS TO EDUARD BERNSTEIN [512]

IN ZURICH

London, 14 March 1883

Dear Bernstein,

You will have got my telegram. [284] The thing happened frightfully quickly. Our hopes were at their highest when, this morning, his strength suddenly failed him, after which he simply fell asleep. Within two minutes this intellect of genius had ceased to think, and at precisely the moment when we had been encouraged by the doctors to entertain the highest hopes. Only someone who constantly kept company with him could have any idea of how valuable this man was to us in regard to theory and also, at every critical moment, in regard to practice. Along with him, his great breadth of vision will also disappear from the stage for years to come. These are things we others are not equal to. The movement will continue on its way but it will miss the calm, timely, considered interventions which have hitherto saved it many a weary digression.

More shortly. It is now midnight and I have had to spend the entire afternoon and evening writing letters and seeing to all manner of things.

Yours,
F. E.

First published in the magazine *Der Wahre Jacob*, Nr. 565 (6), 17. März 1908   Printed according to the original

252

ENGELS TO JOHANN PHILIPP BECKER [512]

IN GENEVA

London, 15 March 1883

Dear Old Man,

Rejoice that you saw Marx once more last autumn, [514] you will never see him again. Yesterday afternoon, at 2.45, when he had been left on his own for barely two minutes, we found him peacefully asleep in his chair. The most powerful intellect our party possessed had ceased to think, the stoutest heart I have ever known was beating no more. An internal haemorrhage would seem to be indicated.

We two are now pretty well all that is left of the old guard of the days before '48. Well, we shall continue to man the breach. Though bullets may whistle and friends fall, it won't be the first time we two have seen that happen. And if one of us is hit by a bullet — well and good, provided only it is properly lodged so that one isn't left writhing for too long.

Your old comrade in arms,

F. Engels

First published in: F. Engels, *Vergessene Briefe (Briefe Friedrich Engels' an Johann Philipp Becker)*, Berlin, 1920

Printed according to the original

253

ENGELS TO FRIEDRICH ADOLPH SORGE [512]

IN HOBOKEN

London, 15 March 1883
11.45 p.m.

Dear Sorge,

Your telegram arrived this evening. Many thanks.

To keep you regularly informed about Marx's state of health was impossible because of his perpetual ups and downs. But here, briefly, are the main facts.

In October '81, shortly before the death of his wife, [513] he went down with PLEURISY. Having recovered from that, he was sent to Algiers in February '82 and, the weather during the journey being wet and cold, arrived there suffering from another bout of PLEURISY. The execrable weather persisted; he had only just recovered when, because of the approach of hot summer weather, he was sent to Monte Carlo (Monaco). Arrived there suffering from another, though milder, bout of PLEURISY. Further execrable weather. Cured again at last, he went to Argenteuil near Paris, to stay with his daughter, Madame Longuet. There he availed himself of the nearby sulphur springs at Enghien for the treatment of his long-standing bronchitis. And there, too, the weather continued to be really appalling, but the cure did some good. Next, 6 weeks in Vevey, whence he came back here in September, apparently almost restored to health. He had been authorised to spend the winter on the south coast of England. And he himself was so sick of a wandering and idle life that renewed exile in southern Europe would probably have damaged his morale as much as it would have benefited his physique. With the onset of London's foggy season he was sent to the Isle of Wight where it rained continuously and he again caught cold. Schorlemmer and I had intended to visit him early in the New Year, but then reports reached us which necessitated Tussy's going there at once. Immediately afterwards came the news of Jenny's death [490] — whereupon he came back here, again suffering from bronchitis. After all that had happened and at his age this spelt danger. On top of that there was a host of complications, in particular an abcess of the lung and a tremendously rapid loss of strength. Nevertheless, the illness as a whole was taking a favourable course, and only last Friday the doctor *en chef*[a] in whose hands he was — one of the leading younger doctors in London who had been specially recommended to him by Ray Lankester — held out the rosiest hopes. But anyone who has ever examined lung tissue under a microscope knows how great is the danger, when a lung is festering, of the wall of a blood vessel becoming perforated. And that is why, every morning for the past 6 weeks, as I turned the corner, I was mortally afraid that the blinds might have been lowered. Yesterday, at half past two in the afternoon, his best time for receiving visitors, I arrived to find

---

[a] Donkin

the household in tears; it seemed as if he was nearing his end. I asked for news, tried to get to the bottom of the matter and to offer consolation. There had been a slight haemorrhage, followed, however, by a sudden collapse. Our good, old Lenchen, [a] who has looked after him better than a mother would after her child, went upstairs, came down again: he was half asleep, she said, and invited me to come up with her. When we went in, he lay there sleeping, never to wake again. His pulse and breathing had stopped. In the space of two minutes he had passed away painlessly and peacefully.

All events, however terrible they may be, that come about with natural inevitability, bear within them their own consolation. So it was here. The art of medicine might, perhaps, have been able to secure for him a few years of vegetable-like existence, the life of a helpless creature, not dying suddenly but inch by inch, a triumphant testimony to the skill of the doctors. But that is something our Marx could never have stood. To live with so many uncompleted works before him, with the tantalising desire to complete them and the impossibility of doing so — that would have been a thousand times more bitter for him than the gentle death that overtook him. 'Death is not a misfortune for the one that dies but for the one that survives', [b] as he used to say with Epicurus. And to see this powerful man of genius continue to vegetate, a total wreck, for the greater glory of medicine and as a laughing-stock for the philistines whom, at the height of his powers, he had so often felled to the ground — no! A thousand times better that it should be as it is, a thousand times better that we should bear him the day after tomorrow to the grave in which his wife lies sleeping.

And after all that had gone before, with which not even the doctors are as familiar as I am, there could, in my view, have been only one choice.

Be that as it may. Mankind is the poorer for the loss of this intellect — the most important intellect, indeed, which it could boast today. The movement of the proletariat will continue on its course but it has lost its focal point, the point to which Frenchmen, Russians, Americans and Germans would automatically turn at moments of crisis, on every occasion receiving clear, indisputable advice such as only genius and consummate expertise can give. Local bigwigs and lesser luminaries, if not imposters, will be given a free hand. Ultimate

---

[a] Helene Demuth - [b] Epicurus to Menoeceus

victory remains assured, but the digressions, the temporary and local aberrations — already so inevitable — will now proliferate as never before. Well, we have got to see it through — what else are we here for? But we're not going to lose heart, for all that — not by a long chalk.

Your
F. Engels

First published in full in *Briefe und Auszüge aus Briefen von Joh. Phil. Becker, Jos. Dietzgen, Friedrich Engels, Karl Marx u. A. an F. A. Sorge und Andere*, Stuttgart, 1906

Printed according to the original

254

ENGELS TO FRIEDRICH LESSNER [515]

IN LONDON

London, 15 March 1883

Dear Lessner,

At three o'clock yesterday our old friend Marx went gently and peacefully to his eternal rest; the immediate cause of death was, or so we presume, an internal haemorrhage.

The funeral will take place on Saturday[a] at 12 noon, and Tussy asks you to attend.

In great haste,

Your
F. Engels

First published in *Deutsche Worte*, Jg. XVIII, Nr. 5, Wien, 1898

Printed according to the original

---

[a] 17 March

255

ENGELS TO PYOTR LAVROV

IN PARIS

London, 24 March 1883

My dear Lavrov,

I have received a long telegram from Moscow asking me to lay a wreath on Marx's grave on behalf of the students of the Petrovsky Academy of Agriculture [516]; not having my address, they telegraphed the editorial department of *The Daily News*. Now they are asking me to let them know the price of the wreath and my address. But it is not signed with a name — merely: Students of the Petrovsky Academy in Moscow.

To whom should I reply? Perhaps you could advise me. As the telegram arrived after the burial, and the grave has today been reopened for the burial of Longuet's little boy[a] who died last Tuesday,[b] I shall not be able to lay the wreath on it till next week. But then I should like to let the worthy young men know that I have received their telegram and carried out the task they entrusted to me.

Yours ever, in haste,

F. Engels

First published in: Marx and Engels, *Works*, First Russian Edition, Vol. XXVII, Moscow, 1935

Printed according to the original

Translated from the French

Published in English for the first time

---

[a] Henri Longuet - [b] 20 March

256

ENGELS TO LAURA LAFARGUE

IN PARIS

London, 25 March 1883

My dear Laura,

Enclosed a letter from Meyer which was directed to Maitland Park[a] — Tussy opened it without looking at the address, but when she saw from whom it was, she gave it at once to Nim[b] who handed it to me.

To-day Nim found among Mohr's manuscripts a large parcel containing the best part if not the whole of the second volume of the *Capital*[227] — above 500 pages in folio. As we do not yet know in what state of preparation for the press it is, nor either what else we may find, it will be better to keep this piece of good news out of the press for the present.

Pumps is expecting No. 2 daily and nightly if indeed it has not arrived to-day — since Friday no news from her. No. 1[c] is a year old to-day. Jollymeier sends his love to you. Kind regards from both of us to Paul.[d] Tell him that the last No. of the *Sozialdemokrat* contains but the report of the funeral[e] — the same essentially which was in the *Justice*.[f]

The English and German press have been inexact and badly informed but upon the whole decent. Even Malon was not so bad.

Latest news. In walks Pumps and Percy[g]! So there the full 12 months is happily passed.

Most affectionately yours,

F. Engels

First published, in the language of the original (English), in F. Engels, P. et L. Lafargue, *Correspondance*, t. I, Paris, 1956

Reproduced from the original

---

[a] London address of the Marx family - [b] Helene Demuth - [c] Lilian Rosher - [d] Lafargue - [e] F. Engels, 'Karl Marx's Funeral'. - [f] 'Discours de Frédéric Engels', *La Justice*, No. 27, 20 March 1883. - [g] Mary Ellen and Percy Rosher

257

ENGELS TO FRIEDRICH THEODOR CUNO [349]

IN NEW YORK

London, 29 March 1883

Dear Cuno,

Your letter evoked roars of laughter over here. [517] Anyone who knew Moor as he was at home and within his intimate circle, is aware that he was never called Marx there, or even Karl, but only Moor, just as each of us had his own nickname; indeed, at the point where nicknames ceased so too did the closest intimacy. Moor had been his nickname since his university days and on the *Neue Rheinische Zeitung* he was always called Moor. If I had addressed him in any other way he would have thought something was amiss that needed putting right.

Your

F. Engels

First published in the journal *Die Gesell-schaft*, Jg. 11, Nr. 11, Berlin, 1925   Printed according to the original

APPENDICES

1

JENNY LONGUET TO CHARLES LONGUET

IN PARIS

[London,] 1 October 1880

My dear Charles,

I was well rewarded yesterday for spending without murmuring a most dreary evening — the evenings are getting so long and chill — by the arrival of your article. It gave me much pleasure for it is wittily written, and I rejoice to think that it will give much satisfaction to Liebknecht. Liebknecht is a great enthusiast with regard to revolutionary France — so great an optimist indeed in this respect, that during the Franco-Prussian war etc. he even lost all discrimination in judging of Trouchu and Co.— therefore your praise of him in the *Justice* will sound like sweetest music to his ear and make him forget for a moment the troubles that lie so heavily upon him. He seems to me to be quite broken down by the last two years. With tears in his eyes he spoke to me of the struggles he and his family had passed through and which were yet in store for them. From all his sons he must part if he does not wish them to be shot or crippled, they must emigrate to America. 'My happiest time,' he said, 'was that spent in England' — and yet heaven knows, he did not lie on a bed of roses here! 'I often think of it with regret. But there was a fate that drove me to Germany, that has driven me on ever since and will shape my destiny to the end.— When I heard of the Amnesty, [518] my first thoughts were with you all — I already saw you hopelessly restlessly tossed on a small skiff on the wild ocean of Paris. But what must be must be.' To which I said Amen. There is a Providence (or rather a fate) that shapes our ends, rough-hew them as we will! — I quite agree with you in thinking that the men of the Commune should never forget how boldly the German socialists fought for the cause of the vanquished, and that therefore by writing your article you have paid a debt of gratitude, and I think *now* that if Bebel and Liebknecht have evinced less sympathy for the Nihilists [242] of Russia, it is because they have had altogether false notions on the subject and have had the misfortune of meeting with a quantity of Russian humbugs calling themselves Nihilists, with which the Continent swarms.

Fortunately for Liebknecht he has had his eyes opened now by Papa and Hartmann, who has interested him deeply and has shown him the importance of the Russian movement and the unparalleled grandeur of the true Nihilist heroes. The *soi-disant*[a] Nihilists that infest the Continent, Hartmann said, are nearly always fellows whose only reason for leaving Russia is that they will not work, and that they can find ways and means to live without working elsewhere — numbers of them are not refugees.

Pardon this endless letter in which I have not yet found time to mention that which lies nearest your heart. My object is to make it last until I shall hear the welcome sound of the postman's knock — shall get a letter from you, or read an article written by you. It is only since you are gone, my dear Charles, that I feel how dear you are to me and how lonely life would be without you! I was not quite well this morning and yesterday, having horrid fits of sickness — but when they are over I am all right again — my misgivings will come but too true!!! The children are blooming like roses and I can see that Harry[b] is daily gaining strength. He begins to grow wonderfully fond of and interested in all that the Wolf[c] does, and follows him about from room to room, calling for him when away. Little Edgar is a very sunbeam of brightness, in his delightful joyousness he constantly reminds me of our poor little Caro[d] and I tremble lest anything should happen to this lovely child — you alarmed me by telling me of your neuralgia — I hope Tussy's cordial has spelled it away.

Your
Jenny

How is it I only receive one copy of the *Justice* when your articles are in it? Do not forget to send two.

First published in: Marx and Engels, *Works*, Second Russian Edition, Vol. 34, Moscow, 1964

Reproduced from the original

Published in English for the first time

---

[a] so-called - [b] Henri, Jenny Longuet's second son - [c] nickname of Edgar, Jenny's third son - [d] Jenny's first-born son, who died eleven months old.

2

From JENNY LONGUET'S LETTER
TO CHARLES LONGUET

IN PARIS

[London,] 27 October 1880

... I was very glad to see that the notes on Eastern affairs are bearing such good fruit. Pelletan of late has written the most childish trash on the subject, every line giving evidence of the darkest ignorance. Your article is written in the simple, clear, elegant style for which French prose is famous, and which makes the stuff of treaties go down quite pleasantly. But how is it you are so stingy? Why not send me *four* copies of your own articles always—or at least *three*. Now again, I have no number to send my correspondent Collet, who would send more matter, if he saw that some use was made of the information given. From Papa it is impossible to get a paper returned, besides if returned, I could not send it to anyone, as it would be marked all over with blue pencil marks. That is the reason why I could not at once send your last article to Parnell. If he were to take an interest in the *Justice*—a great end would be gained. Notes direct from him would be invaluable at this crisis. [519] Your article on the Treaty of Berlin, [376] Papa has not seen yet, therefore I cannot give you his opinion. He told me last Sunday, shocked at the ignorance displayed by Pelletan on Eastern affairs, that he would order the 'blue books' [89] and write to you himself on the subject. Good-bye.

Your loving
Jenny

First published in: Marx and Engels, *Works*, Second Russian Edition, Vol. 34, Moscow, 1964

Reproduced from the original

Published in English for the first time

3

From JENNY LONGUET'S LETTER
TO CHARLES LONGUET

IN PARIS

[London,] 31 October 1880

... I had the *Justice* with your two articles in it last night, and feel quite elated to see what excellent use you have made of the matter I sent you. Your article on the frontier must create a sensation, what you disclose is quite new in France, and even little known in England, because intentionally suppressed. And then the form you give to heavy stuff is so amusing and sarcastic, that even the French reader will not consider the matter too dry. The pity is, that you always send me one copy, and that I am not able to send a paper to Collet, which would keep my correspondence with that short-armed but long-sighted individual alive and procure for you an abstract of the intrigues now going on, and save you the trouble of reading blue books [89] yourself: I also want the first article[a] on the Berlin Treaty [376] for Collet. Papa was greatly pleased with your article—he had often grumbled at childish notes in the *Justice* on the delays caused by the Turks etc.—delays in reality skilfully brought about by the Russians! Papa also liked your article on Girardin and relished the quotation *sur le mâle et l'âne*[b] from Proudhon.—But I am sure *you* relished still more the pleasure of quoting the name of your master than the quotation itself!!! Am I right?

I am sorry to think you should have taken the trouble to translate what I sent you on Ireland. I never intended you to do that, fancying that you would take parts here and there and scribble down in an hour at most some sort of correspondence. As you make such a serious matter of it, I shall not send any more of my productions. They would only waste your time. My intention had been to save your time by reading much matter referring to Ireland for you. It is so long ago since I sent you my letter, that I do not remember what I wrote, but fancy the news will be too stale now.

I have not read Roy's articles. Papa considers the second one to

----

[a] See previous letter.- [b] about a man and an ass

be superior to anything that has hitherto been published on Littré.
Love and kisses from all.

Your

Jenny

First published in: Marx and Engels, *Works*, Second Russian Edition, Vol. 34, Moscow, 1964

Reproduced from the original

Published in English for the first time

4

JENNY LONGUET TO CHARLES LONGUET

IN PARIS

[London,] 23 November 1880

My dear Charles,

I was just going to write to Papa to ask him to send you a copy of the *Capital*, when I heard from Mama that a volume had already been sent you.[a] To-day, being Sunday, Johnny and I paid our usual visit at Maitland Park[b] (I have only time to go there once a week) and so I had at length an opportunity of asking Papa's opinion of your latest productions. He seemed very pleased at the publication of Bright's opinion on the Irish question, considering it most opportune and wondering how you had got hold of that interesting document. Liebknecht's letter he thinks will do really good service. You have made Liebknecht's style sound quite elegant, which is not its general characteristic. As to your own article in answer to Massard, Papa also much approved of it, though I must add that his praise is rather more qualified than was mine.— First, he does not agree with you as to the greatness of the fact of the 4 *août*,[520] declaring that a careful study of the history of that event diminishes it wonderfully in importance and shows that only minor points were conceded. As to the revolutionary side of the struggle for the limitation of the working day, he thinks

---

[a] French edition of the first volume of *Capital* - [b] London address of the Marx family

you have passed it over without notice in your answer to those revolutionists of the fire and sword.— From the *Capital* you will see that the fight of the English working class assumed more than once the character of a revolution, and that the governing classes only granted what they dared not refuse. If Massard and Co. thirst for fight, they will derive much satisfaction by a perusal of the history in England of the limitation of the working day! Apropos, as to the question of the fixation of a minimum salary, it may perhaps interest you to know that Papa did all he could to persuade Guesde to omit it from their programme,[68] explaining to him that such a measure, if adopted, would, according to economical laws, produce the result of making of this fixed minimum *a maximum*. But Guesde stuck to it, on the plea that it would give them a hold on the working classes if it did nothing else. Guesde, you see, is opportunist like the rest of them.[a]

Papa is much surprised to see the want of judgment the French radical press is evincing in its treatment of General Farre who, he considers, acts like a man who knows that judged by his *compères*,[b] Cissey would be saved, *qu'ils s'entendraient comme larrons en foire*.[c] If the Press by its foolish noise gets Farre revoked, Papa thinks they will have lost the best man in the Gambettist camp.

I have not yet received the promised series of your articles. As I suppose I shall have to wait for some time before you carry out that good intention of yours, will you in the meantime, nay by *return of post*, send me your last article containing Bright's letter, ...[d]

First published in: Marx and Engels, *Works*, Second Russian Edition, Vol. 34, Moscow, 1964

Reproduced from the original

Published in English for the first time

---

[a] See this volume, pp. 43-44. - [b] accomplices - [c] that birds of a feather flock together - [d] The end of the letter is missing.

5

JENNY MARX TO JENNY LONGUET

IN ARGENTEUIL

London, 20 August 1881
41 Maitland Park Road, N. W.

My darling little Jenny,

Our trip went off wonderfully well, thanks to Helen's [a] energy and circumspection. I still don't know how she managed to drag all the BAGS AND BAGGAGES about or to cart this old bundle of bones from place to place. At Folkestone she actually contrived to get hold of a SLEEPING COUPÉ in which we lay and slept like in our own beds. At Boulogne I sent you and Moor a telegram. Moor never got his. What is more, the ship only sailed at 6 o'clock so we didn't arrive here until 11. I came upon Moor and Tussy COSY in the PARLOUR. Tussy propped up with cushions on the sofa. Her crazy mode of life has left her in such a weak and feverish state that she can walk no better than I do. Radford has proved a faithful friend. He brought her JELLIES and DAINTIES every day, took her out in CABS, rushed in despair to Mrs Anderson who, in her stead, sent another lady WHO DID HER NOT MUCH GOOD. I trust the modern young Aesculapus [sic] will make an impression on her. Although I never ceased grieving for one moment at Argenteuil and left you IN TEARS AND SORROWS, the memory of you and your love and kindness remains nevertheless as the richest treasure of my heart, on which and I shall feed like a MISER. No more, *as I am poor even in thanks.

Poor Longuet! He frightened me quite. He looked so ill and stared at me with such big eyes.

The darling Harry and my poor Johnny. He will not much regret old granny.* I was so unjust to the dear child when he rushed about screeching—a peculiarity of childhood and part of its happiness.

Adio.

---

[a] Demuth

Apropos: I only gave you 110 frs and the TICKETS are marked 70 per TICKET, so you had to make up the amount. THANKS AND KISSES TO ALL OF YOU FROM OLD GRANNY.

First published in: Marx and Engels, *Works*, Second Russian Edition, Vol. 50, Moscow, 1981

Printed according to the original

Published in English for the first time

NOTES
AND
INDEXES

NOTES

[1] On 18 August 1879, in Ramsgate, Marx's daughter Jenny Longuet gave birth to a son, Edgar.— 3

[2] The reference is to two trade unionists, Alexander Macdonald and Thomas Burt, who were elected to the House of Commons in 1874.— 3

[3] *Bimetallism*, the practice of using both gold and silver as a monetary standard by specifying that both constitute legal tender at a fixed ratio to each other.

This practice existed in a number of countries in the 18th and 19th centuries but did not meet the needs of developed commodity economy and went against the very nature of money as the only commodity which was to be a universal equivalent.

Liebknecht quoted from this letter by Engels in his speech in the Saxon Landtag on 16 January 1880, opposing a return to bimetallism.

Engels analysed the issue of bimetallism in some detail also in his letter to Eduard Bernstein of 10 May 1882 (see this volume, pp. 256-58).— 3, 256

[4] A reference to Bismarck's visit to Austria in September 1879 and the Austro-German alliance concluded in Vienna on 7 October of that year. Art. 1 of the treaty stipulated that, should one of the contracting parties be attacked by Russia, the other was obliged to come to its aid. Art. 2 stated that, should one of the signatories be attacked by any other country, the other was to maintain benevolent neutrality. Should the aggressor have Russian support, Art. 1 was to apply. Concluded for a term of five years and later repeatedly extended, this treaty was the first in a series of agreements that ultimately led to the establishment of a military bloc headed by Germany and to a division of the European countries into two hostile camps that subsequently clashed in the First World War.— 4

[5] The originals of this letter and that of 13 December 1879 (present edition, Vol. 45, p. 427) are kept in the family archive of Lord Walstone, who presented photocopies of them to the Institute of Marxism-Leninism in 1968. The addressee was Lord

Walstone's father, the English archaeologist Charles Walstone, who held his father's surname, Waldstein, at the time.— 5

⁶ This letter is printed according to a handwritten copy made by an unknown person. Failing to decipher Marx's handwriting, he put 'Kranz?' in square brackets after the addressee's name, Kraus. Also in square brackets and with a question mark is the word 'proceeded'. The copy contains further notes made by the same person.— 6

⁷ Part of this letter was published in English for the first time in: Karl Marx and Friedrich Engels, *Correspondence. 1846-1895.* A Selection with Commentary and Notes, Martin Lawrence Ltd., London [1934].— 7, 60, 320, 349, 394, 403, 410, 412, 445

⁸ A reference to the *German Workers' Educational Society* in London, which was founded in February 1840 by Karl Schapper, Joseph Moll and other leaders of the League of the Just. In 1847 and 1849-50 Marx and Engels took an active part in the Society's work, but on 17 September 1850 they and a number of their followers withdrew from it because the Willich-Schapper sectarian and adventurist faction had temporarily increased its influence in the Society. The subsequent weakening of the sectarians' influence made it possible for Marx and Engels to resume their work in the Educational Society late in 1850. When the International Working Men's Association was set up, the Society, with Friedrich Lessner as one of its leaders, became the German Section of the International in London.

This letter deals with the differences of opinion associated with the need to work out a new tactics for the German Social-Democrats after the introduction of the Anti-Socialist Law in October 1878 (see Note 16).— 7, 72, 252, 333, 334, 356

⁹ At the Reichstag elections on 30 July 1878, shortly before the promulgation of the Anti-Socialist Law (see Note 16), the Social-Democrats won 437,158 votes.— 8

¹⁰ Despite the Anti-Socialist Law, most of the primary organisations continued to function, using every available legal opportunity to make known the proletariat's feelings and sentiments (e. g., a meeting held at the funeral of Wilhelm Bracke, one of the party leaders). The obstacles put up by the authorities, failed to stop the socialists from carrying out a major campaign to collect funds for the persons deported from Berlin, renewing the contacts lost in the initial confusion, and setting up illegal organisations.— 9

¹¹ On behalf of the German Workers' Educational Society in London (see Note 8), H. Meyer invited Engels to its meeting of 27 March 1880, which was to discuss the Society's reorganisation.— 9

¹² The real date of the letter, erroneously indicated by Bebel as 27 March 1880 in his letter to Engels of 22 September 1880, has been ascertained by the event mentioned in it, the Hamburg Reichstag elections on 27 April. In the second Russian edition of Marx's and Engels' *Works* and in *Werke*, the letter is dated early May 1880.— 10

¹³ In March-May 1880, the Reichstag debated the extension of the Anti-Socialist Law (see Note 16) until 1886. At the third reading of the Bill on 4 May, an ultra-'revolutionary' speech was made by the Social-Democratic deputy and former Lassallean Wilhelm Hasselmann, who sided with the Russian terrorists and the French anarchists and openly opposed the Social-Democrats' line. *Der Sozialdemokrat* (No.

20, 16 May 1880) declared that Hasselmann had placed himself outside the party. By Bebel's 'speech on the persecutions', Engels means the latter's speech in the Reichstag on 6 March, which was carried, in a slightly abridged form, by *Der Sozialdemokrat*, No. 11, 14 March 1880, under the heading 'Polizei-Orgien in Berlin unter dem Belagerungszustand'.— 10

[14] Engels is referring to the victory of the Social-Democratic candidate Georg Wilhelm Hartmann at the Reichstag elections in Hamburg on 27 April 1880. He obtained 13,155 votes out of the 23,231 cast.— 11

[15] The *National Liberals* (die Nationalliberale Partei) was the party of the German, mostly Prussian, bourgeoisie, which emerged in the autumn of 1866 as a result of the split in the Party of Progress (see Note 256). The policy of National Liberals showed that a considerable section of the liberal bourgeoisie renounced claims to broader political rights and capitulated before Bismarck's Junker government. After the unification of Germany, the National Liberal Party acquired its final shape as a party of the big bourgeoisie, notably the industrial tycoons.— 11

[16] The *Exceptional Law against the Socialists* (Gesetz gegen die gemeingefährlichen Bestrebungen der Sozialdemokratie — the Law against the Harmful and Dangerous Aspirations of Social-Democracy) was introduced by the Bismarck government, supported by the majority in the Reichstag, on 21 October 1878 to counter the socialist and workers' movement. Better known as the Anti-Socialist Law, it made the Social-Democratic Party of Germany illegal, banned all party and mass workers' organisations and suppressed the socialist and workers' press. Socialist literature was confiscated and the Social-Democrats subjected to reprisals. However, during its operation, the Social-Democratic Party assisted by Marx and Engels uprooted both opportunist and 'ultra-Left' elements and substantially strengthened its influence among the people. Under pressure from the mass workers' movement, the Anti-Socialist Law was abrogated on 1 October 1890. For Engels' assessment of the Law, see his article 'Bismarck and the German Working Men's Party' (present edition, Vol. 24, pp. 407-09).— 11, 38, 40, 50, 127, 152, 153; 192, 209, 279, 281, 332, 349, 390, 395, 414, 430, 448

[17] The British general elections, held between late March and mid-April 1880, produced a victory for the Liberals. They obtained 349 seats in the new Parliament as against 243 received by the Conservatives. Leadership of the Cabinet was assumed by Gladstone, who opposed the policy of rapprochement with Germany.— 11

[18] Engels is referring to the events of the Danish War of 1864, in which Prussia and Austria were allies. After their victory over Denmark, Austria established its government in Holstein, and Prussia in Schleswig. But as a result of its defeat in the Austro-Prussian War which Bismarck unleashed in 1866 and the establishment of the North German Confederation, Austria lost all rights to Holstein, and Schleswig-Holstein became a Prussian province.— 12

[19] This letter was published in English for the first time in: Frederick Engels, Paul and Laura Lafargue, *Correspondence*, Vol. I: 1868-1886, Foreign Languages Publishing House, Moscow, 1959.— 12, 27, 351

[20] A reference to the introduction to the French edition of Engels' work *Socialism: Utopian and Scientific*, which appeared in Paris in 1880 in Paul Lafargue's translation under the title *Socialisme utopique et socialisme scientifique*. Engels produced the pam-

phlet at Lafargue's request, having rewritten three chapters of *Anti-Dühring* (Chapter I of the Introduction and chapters I and II of Part III) to form a popular work in its own right. It was first printed by the French socialist magazine *La Revue socialiste*, Nos. 3, 4 and 5, 1880, and then published, also in 1880, as a pamphlet. The French socialist Benoît Malon embarked on an introduction to it, but his effort was deemed unacceptable, and the introduction as it appeared was written by Marx, who had first consulted Engels (see present edition, Vol. 24, pp. 335-39). In the pamphlet, the introduction carried the signature of Lafargue, whom Marx requested to 'polish the phrases, leaving the gist intact' (see this volume, p. 16).— 12, 332, 352, 369

[21] Lassalle was Countess Sophie von Hatzfeldt's lawyer in her divorce case in 1846-54.— 15

[22] On the reasons for Marx's and Engels' refusal in January 1861 to collaborate with Lassalle in the publication of a newspaper, see present edition, Vol. 41, pp. 252, 261 and 281-82.— 15

[23] Marx wrote this on the last page of his introduction to the French edition of Engels' pamphlet (see Note 20).— 15

[24] Part of this letter was published in English for the first time in: Karl Marx and Frederick Engels, *Letters on 'Capital'*, New Park Publications, London, 1983.— 16, 203, 432, 435

[25] In a letter of 19 June 1880, the Dutch socialist Ferdinand Domela Nieuwenhuis requested Marx to look through a popular outline of Volume One of *Capital* he had written in Dutch. Nieuwenhuis' work, entitled *Karl Marx. Kapitaal en Arbeid*, appeared in The Hague in 1881.— 16

[26] The book review column of the *Jahrbuch für Sozialwissenschaft und Sozialpolitik* (Erster Jahrgang. Zweite Hälfte, Zürich-Oberstrass, 1880) featured two reviews by Nieuwenhuis, one of Eduard von Hartmann's *Die Phänomenologie des sittlichen Bewusstseins* (Berlin, 1879), and the other, of Dr J. A. Levy's *Engelsch Kathedersocialisme* (Belinfanto, s' Gravenhage, 1879).— 16

[27] The reference is to one of the notes to Chapter V of Volume One of *Capital* (see present edition, Vol. 35). In it, Marx replaced the term 'price of production' with its synonym, 'average price'.— 16

[28] As Marx's principal economic work advanced, the plan and structure of *Capital* repeatedly changed. As of 1867, when Volume One appeared in print, Marx proposed to publish the work in three volumes of four books, with the second and third books making up the second volume (see present edition, Vol. 35). After Marx's death, Engels prepared for the press and published the manuscripts of the second and third books as volumes Two and Three. He died before he was able to publish the fourth and last book, *Theories of Surplus Value* (Volume Four of *Capital*).— 16

[29] The reference is to Minna Gorbunova's letter to Engels written in the first half of July 1880. She said she wanted to use in Russia the already available experience, and asked Engels to recommend her books on vocational training in England.— 17

[30] Between mid-August and 18 September 1880, Engels was on holiday in Ramsgate and Bridlington Quay.— 17, 23, 34, 35, 39

[31] The reference is to the World Exhibition of 1878 in Paris.— 17

32 Rue de Richelieu in Paris is the address of Bibliothèque nationale.— 17

33 The London-based book trading firm of Philip Stephen King specialised in the sale
of government and parliamentary publications, statistical material, etc. Marx used
its services between 1867 and 1882. He probably needed the book ordered in this
letter for his work on Volume Two of *Capital*.— 19, 367

34 This letter was published in English for the first time in: Karl Marx and Frederick
Engels, *Selected Correspondence*, Foreign Languages Publishing House, Moscow,
1955.— 20

35 In her letter to Engels of 25 July 1880, Minna Gorbunova mentioned the Acts of
Parliament on primary education of 1870, 1873 and 1876, as well as the *Report of the
Committee of the Council on Education 1878-1879*.— 20

36 In her letter of 25 July 1880, Gorbunova wrote that she was shortly to return to
Moscow and gave Engels her address: Toporov's House, Bolshaya Molchanovka
St., Moscow.— 20

37 *Zemstvos*—local self-government bodies set up in a number of gubernias (*gouverne-
ments* in the text) of European Russia under the Zemstvo Reform of 1864. It was
an attempt to adapt the Russian autocratic system to the needs of capitalist development.— 20, 175

38 Marx and his family were on holiday in Ramsgate from early August to 13 September 1880.— 21, 24, 35, 46, 60

39 Gorbunova asked Engels for advice concerning vocational training in Russia. She
asked him, in particular, about the ways 'to avoid, while promoting vocational
training in those industrial branches that are most adapted to big production,
the advancement of factory production with its workers totally alienated from the
land'.— 21

40 *Obshchina* (Commune)—a pre-capitalist spontaneously evolved social group of
agricultural producers, who own or control their means of production.— 22

41 *Artel*—an association of small producers in pre-revolutionary Russia engaged in
joint economic activity (carpentry, fishing, masonry, wood-cutting, agriculture,
etc.).— 22

42 The Editors are not in possession of John Swinton's letter to which Marx is replying.— 22

43 Marx met John Swinton, then responsible editor of the New York *Sun*, in Ramsgate
in August 1880. Swinton published an account of the interview Marx granted him
in *The Sun* on 6 September 1880 (see Vol. 24, pp. 583-85), and in the collection *Current Views and Notes of Forty Days in France and England*, New York, 1880.— 23, 40, 77

44 Part of this letter was published in English for the first time in: K. Marx, F. Engels,
V. I. Lenin, *The Communist View on Morality*, Novosti Press Agency Publishing
House, Moscow, 1974.— 23

45 On 18 March 1876, the German socialist Ferdinand Lingenau, who had emigrated
to the United States, bequeathed about $ 7,000, half of his fortune, to the Socialist
Workers' Party of Germany. He appointed August Bebel, Johann Philipp Becker,
Wilhelm Bracke, August Geib, Wilhelm Liebknecht and Karl Marx his executors.
After Lingenau's death on 4 August 1877 in St Louis (Missouri) they tried to have

the money bequeathed to the party transferred to its funds, and gave Sorge power of attorney. Sorge wrote to Marx on 13 August 1880 that he would have to drop the matter if he did not get hold of some money to continue with it. Bismarck ultimately managed to prevent Lingenau's legacy being credited to the Social-Democratic Party's funds.— 24, 99

[46] The reference is to the suspension, in August 1880, owing to the shortage of funds, of the publication of the French newspaper *L'Égalité*, to which Paul Lafargue had been contributing.— 24, 27

[47] The reference is to the piece on Marx's activities and works written by Hazeltine, a staff member on *The Sun*.— 24

[48] Marx's ironic reference to Douai's article in the *New Yorker Volkszeitung* sent to Engels by Sorge on 13 August 1880.— 25

[49] This letter was published in English for the first time in: Friedrich Engels, Paul et Laura Lafargue, *Correspondance*, Vol. I, Ed. Sociales, Paris, 1956.— 25

[50] Engels wrote this letter on the same sheet of paper as one to Laura Lafargue of the same date.

This letter was published in English for the first time in: Frederick Engels, Paul and Laura Lafargue, *Correspondence*, Vol. I: 1868-1886, Foreign Languages Publishing House, Moscow, 1959.— 26

[51] This probably refers to the Lafargues' plan to set up a commercial business to earn their living (see this volume, pp. 27-29).— 26

[52] The Editors are not in possession of Engels' letter to Paul Lafargue of 7 September 1880.— 27

[53] Part of this letter was quoted by Nikolai Danielson in the preface to the first Russian edition of Volume Two of *Capital*, St Petersburg, 1885.— 30

[54] The address on the envelope containing this letter was written in Eleanor Marx's hand: N. Danielson. Société du Crédit mutuel, Pont de Kazan, maison Lessnikoff, St Petersburg, Russia.— 30

[55] On 21 August (2 September) 1880, Danielson requested Marx to write an article on Russia's post-reform economy for a Russian magazine.— 30

[56] This refers to the article 'Очерки нашего пореформеннаго общественнаго хозяйства' ('Sketches of Our Post-Reform Social Economy') Danielson published in the *Slovo* in October 1880 under the pen-name Nikolai —on.— 31, 61

[57] A reference to the world economic crisis which began in 1873 and particularly affected the United States and Germany. In the late 1870s, it spread to Britain.— 31

[58] Almost all of this letter is in English, with the exception of the few paragraphs in French. It was published in English in full for the first time in: Frederick Engels, Paul and Laura Lafargue, *Correspondence*, Vol. I: 1868-1886, Foreign Languages Publishing House, Moscow, 1959.— 32

[59] The reference is to the draft rules of Grant's firm in which Paul Lafargue planned to be a partner (see Note 51).— 32

[60] Liebknecht visited Marx and Engels in London in the last ten days of September 1880. (Bebel was unable to come.) They discussed the stance of the party's printed

organ *Der Sozialdemokrat* (Zurich) during the operation of the Anti-Socialist Law. The Institute of Marxism-Leninism does not have Engels' letter to Liebknecht mentioned here.— 35, 38, 42, 50

61 This is a reply to an undated letter of Dr Ferdinand Fleckles who had enclosed a medical form to be filled in by Jenny Marx. Marx wrote it on the front of the form. Jenny's description of her illness is on the back.— 36

62 The letter to Eugen Oswald is in German, and that to the unknown correspondent, in English. The latter is the response to Kaulitz's request for a letter of recommendation for a teaching post.— 36

63 The French translation of Volume One of *Capital* was prepared by Joseph Roy. Marx made substantial changes in and additions to the manuscript. For this reason, he maintained that, like the German original, the French edition had a scientific significance of its own. In conformity with the French edition, changes were introduced into the subsequent editions of *Capital* in German, Russian and other languages.

The publication was undertaken by Maurice Lachâtre, a French journalist and publisher. The book was printed by the Lahure press in Paris. Under the contract signed by Marx and Lachâtre, *Capital* was to come out in instalments, 44 in all, 16 printed pages each. The work was printed in two instalments at a time, but was sold in series of five instalments each, which made nine series in all. Publication was begun in September 1872 and completed in November 1875.

Having received a copy of *Capital* from Marx, Swinton wrote to him on 7 December 1880: 'A thousand thanks for the great work *Capital* which I shall have bound handsomely, and keep as a treasure through life.'— 40, 42

64 Marx is probably referring to the outcome of the second Anglo-Afghan War of 1878-80. The staunch resistence of the Afghans forced Britain to abandon its plans to conquer and partition the country, and made it reach a compromise with Khan Abdur Rahman. The period also witnessed an aggravation of the situation in British-annexed Transvaal, where a Boer uprising flared up in mid-December 1880.— 40

65 A reference to the so-called local state of siege declared by Bismarck in Berlin and its environs on 28 November 1878 on the strength of Para. 28 of the Anti-Socialist Law (see Note 16) and extended to Hamburg, its environs and the adjacent Prussian territories (see also Note 198) on 29 October 1880. Under it, meetings could be held only with police permission, distribution of printed matter in public places was prohibited, persons considered politically unreliable were deported, and the right to own, carry, import and pass on arms was withdrawn or restricted.— 41, 43, 152

66 This letter was first published in English in: *Science and Society*, Vol. II, No. 2, New York, 1938.— 40

67 The *Alliance of Socialist Democracy* was founded by Mikhail Bakunin in Geneva in October 1868 as an international anarchist organisation. In 1869 the Alliance approached the General Council of the International Working Men's Association with a request to be admitted to the International. The General Council agreed to admit individual sections of the Alliance provided the latter dissolved as an independent organisation. On entering the International, Bakunin did not actually comply with this decision and incorporated the Alliance into it under the

guise of a section (called 'the Alliance of Socialist Democracy. Central Section'). Marx, Engels and the General Council fought the Alliance, exposing it as a sect hostile to the working-class movement (for details, see present edition, Vol. 23). The Hague Congress of the International (1872) dealt a severe blow at the anarchists and expelled the Alliance's leaders Mikhail Bakunin and James Guillaume from the International.— 43, 181, 190, 333, 341, 370, 408

[68] A reference to the *Programme électoral des travailleurs socialistes*, the preamble to which was dictated by Marx to Jules Guesde (see present edition, Vol. 24, p. 340). The theoretical part was followed by a minimum programme incorporating an economic and a political section. The election programme was widely discussed at workers' meetings and adopted as the official programme of the French Workers' Party (see Note 195) at its national congress in Le Havre in November 1880.— 43, 148, 342, 386, 447, 474

[69] From 1874, Charles Longuet taught French at King's College, and Jenny Longuet, German at the Clement Dun school.— 45, 61

[70] A reference to the Executive Committee of the Narodnaya Volya (People's Will) group, a revolutionary Narodnik (Populist) organisation formed in August 1879, when the secret revolutionary society Zemlya i Volya (Land and Freedom) split into Narodnaya Volya and Chorny Peredel (the Black or General Redistribution). The founders of the Narodnaya Volya were professional revolutionaries, advocates of a political campaign against the autocracy.— 44, 83

[71] Marx means the Programme of the Executive Committee of the Narodnaya Volya (St Petersburg, 22 March 1880). Marx had a copy of this edition.— 45

[72] This letter was published in English for the first time in: *The Letters of Karl Marx*, selected and translated with explanatory notes and an introduction by Saul K. Padover, Prentice-Hall, Inc., Englewood Cliffs, New Jersey, 1979.— 48, 107, 118, 159, 164, 169, 184, 198, 202, 213, 216, 225, 233, 245, 248, 253, 255, 261, 266, 270, 271, 272, 277, 290, 303, 317, 338, 339, 364, 371, 392, 398, 409, 417, 420, 424, 426

[73] In a letter of 14 September 1880 from Mantua, Achille Loria asked Marx to find him a job as a writer or journalist in London, and inquired whether Marx would take him on as secretary.— 48

[74] In late November 1879, Achille Loria sent Marx an advance copy of his book *La rendita fondiaria e la sua elisione naturale*, Milan, 1880.— 48

[75] The Editors are not in possession of the original of this letter, which is reprinted from Hyndman's book *The Record of an Adventurous Life*.— 49

[76] The controversy between the General Council and the bourgeois radical Charles Bradlaugh arose after the latter's attacks on Marx in a public lecture in London on 11 December 1871, and in his letter to *The Eastern Post* (16 December). At the General Council meeting of 19 December, Marx drew attention to the close connection between Bradlaugh's statements and the campaign of persecution unleashed against the International by the ruling quarters and the bourgeois press, which became especially fierce after the International issued the address 'The Civil War in France' in June 1871. Marx replied to Bradlaugh in a series of statements featured by *The Eastern Post* (see present edition, Vol. 23, pp. 71-73).— 52

[77] Bradlaugh nominated himself as a candidate at the elections, contributed to the press under the pen-name Iconoclast and hoped to be elected to the House of Commons in 1874 (St Stephen's in Westminster had been the seat of the House of Commons since 1547).— 53

[78] This letter was probably sent by Marx to the London bookseller Philip Stephen King (see Note 33).— 55

[79] A fragment of this letter was published in English for the first time in: K. Marx, F. Engels, *On Malthus*, People's Publishing House, Delhi, 1956.— 56

[80] In his letter of 4 December 1880, Kautsky asked Engels to comment on his book *Der Einfluss der Volksvermehrung auf den Fortschritt der Gesellschaft*, Vienna, 1880. He sent a copy to Engels in December 1880 through Bernstein. Kautsky wrote that he was coming to London for a few months in order to meet Engels and Marx personally. He arrived in London in March 1881 and met Engels on several occasions.— 56

[81] Engels is referring to the first separate German edition of *Anti-Dühring*, which appeared in Leipzig in 1878 (see present edition, Vol. 25, pp. 196-97).— 56

[82] Armchair socialists (*Kathedersozialisten*) — followers of a trend in bourgeois socialism that emerged in Germany in the 1860s-70s. In 1873, its champions (Gustav Schmoller, Adolph Wagner and Lujo Brentano) set up a society called Verein für Sozialpolitik which had its own printed organ, *Schriften des Vereins für Sozialpolitik*. Armchair socialists supported Bismarck's social policy, advocated class harmony and opposed the workers' revolutionary action.— 56, 65, 416, 449, 453

[83] By 1881, A. E. F. Schäffle had the following works printed: *Das gesellschaftliche System der menschlichen Wirtschaft*, Tübingen, 1873, in two volumes; *Die Quintessenz des Socialismus*, Gotha, 1875; *Bau und Leben des socialen Körpers*, Tübingen, 1875-78, in four volumes; *Enzyklopädie der Staatslehre*, Tübingen, 1878; *Grundsätze der Steuerpolitik*, Tübingen, 1880.— 57

[84] On page 169 of his book, Kautsky refers to Leonhard Euler's calculation, according to which the doubling of the Earth's population may theoretically occur in less than 12 years.— 57

[85] A reference to the state of siege declared on 26 September 1848 in Cologne by the Prussian authorities. Its consequence was the suppression of the *Neue Rheinische Zeitung* until 12 October 1848.— 59

[86] On Engels' advice, this poem by Georg Weerth was reprinted by *Der Sozialdemokrat* on 11 August 1881. The title, 'Ein Sozialistenfresser aus dem Jahre 1848', was to mirror that of Ludwig Börne's well-known lampoon 'Menzel der Franzosenfresser', Paris, 1837.— 59

[87] Engels is referring to the first of the two essays entitled 'Die zehn Gebote' carried by *Der Sozialdemokrat*, No. 5, 30 January 1881, which exposed the Prussian kings' policy of robbing the people, and to Eduard Bernstein's article 'Ein Gedenktag', printed under the pen-name Leo in *Der Sozialdemokrat*, No. 4, 23 January 1881, on the 88th anniversary of the execution of Louis XVI.— 59

[88] This is Marx's reply to the letter by the young English mathematician Carl Pearson of 9 February 1881. Pearson, who was at that time a supporter of the working-class

movement, believed that the situation in England favoured the dissemination of socialist ideas, and asked Marx to entrust him with the translation of Volume One of *Capital*.

The meeting scheduled for 17 February did not take place. The day before, Pearson let Marx know that the appointed time was inconvenient for him.

There is another letter from Pearson to Marx, dated 11 April 1881, from which it emerges that Marx and Pearson failed to reach an agreement concerning the translation.

Volume One of *Capital* was translated into English by Samuel Moore and Edward Aveling and appeared in print in 1887.— 60

[89] A reference to the publications of official documents by the governments of various countries, which Marx called the Blue Books after the publications of the British Parliament.— 61, 471, 472

[90] Marx is referring to the manuscript of Paul Lafargue's essay the Russian translation of which 'Движеніе поземельной собственности во Франціи' ('The Movement of Land Property in France') was published in the monthly *Ustoi* (Principles), Nos. 3-4 and 6, 1882.— 61

[91] Marx is referring to the promise of the *Слово* (*Slovo*) editors 'to return to the subject of the article' (on Danielson's article, see Note 56) 'in one of the magazine's later issues' (*Слово*, October 1880, p. 142, editorial note). However, Danielson's article was never mentioned again.— 62

[92] *Degeneration. A Chapter in Darwinism* (London, 1880), a work by Edwin Ray Lankester, appeared in Russian translation in St Petersburg in 1883 under the title *Вырожденіе. Глава изъ теоріи развитія (дарвинизма)*.— 64

[93] A copy of Janson's book was sent to Marx by Danielson, as is clear from his letter of 24 February (8 March) 1881.

The notebooks with excerpts and synopses from Russian books and other sources on Russia filled in by Marx in January-February and May-June 1881 contain excerpts from this book.— 64

[94] The address on the envelope containing this letter was written in Eleanor Marx's hand: N. Danielson, Société du Crédit mutuel, Pont de Kazan, maison Lessnikoff, St Petersburg, Russia.— 64

[95] This letter was published in English for the first time in: *International Press Correspondence*, Berlin, 1931, No. 13, II-III, Special Number.— 65

[96] This refers to Ferdinand Domela Nieuwenhuis' work *Karl Marx. Kapitaal en Arbeid* (see Note 25). The second edition of the book appeared in 1889.— 65

[97] The dedication read: 'To Karl Marx, the bold thinker, the noble fighter for the rights of the proletariat, this book is dedicated by the author as a token of respectful esteem.'— 65

[98] *Mannen van beteekenis in onze dagen* (The Outstanding Men of Our Day) — a book series published in Haarlem in 1870-82. The tenth volume of the series, edited by N. C. Balsem, contained a biography of Marx written by Arnold Kerdijk.— 65

[99] Marx's polemic with Lujo Brentano was set off by the latter's article in the Berlin magazine *Concordia*, No. 10, 7 March 1872. Brentano, who had the article pub-

lished anonymously, tried to discredit Marx as a scholar by accusing him of scientific incompetence and deliberate misquotation of the sources he used. When on 1 June 1872 *Der Volksstaat* carried Marx's reply (see present edition, Vol. 23, pp. 164-67), *Concordia* (No. 27, 4 July) responded with another article by Brentano (also anonymous) to which Marx replied in *Der Volksstaat*, No. 63, 7 August 1872 (see present edition, Vol. 23, pp. 190-97). After Marx's death, the campaign of slander launched by Brentano was taken up by the British bourgeois economist Sedley Taylor, who was exposed by Engels in June 1890 in the preface to the fourth German edition of Volume One of *Capital* and in 1891 in the pamphlet 'In the Case of Brentano versus Marx' (see present edition, Vol. 27, pp. 95-176). In the section of the pamphlet called 'Documents' Engels reproduced both of Marx's letters to *Der Volksstaat*.— 65

100 This refers to the International Socialist Congress to be convened in Switzerland on the initiative of Belgian socialists to discuss the establishment of a new International. The congress took place not in Zurich (the Zurich cantonal council forbade it), but in Chur between 2 and 4 October 1881. It was attended by delegates of socialist parties from 12 countries. The congress decided against forming a new International.

In his letter to Marx of 6 January 1881 Nieuwenhuis expressed the intention of the Dutch Social Democrats to discuss at the congress the laws to be passed immediately in the political and economic fields by the socialists should they come to power.— 66

101 Part of this letter was published in English for the first time in: Marx and Engels, *Ireland and the Irish Question*, Progress Publishers, Moscow, 1971. The end of the letter is not extant.— 67

102 Albert Regnard, a French writer and historian, wrote to Marx's daughter Jenny Longuet in connection with his articles on Irish history (they have not been found) because her contributions on Ireland to the French newspaper *La Marseillaise* in 1870 (see present edition, Vol. 21, pp. 414-41) had found recognition among the readers.— 67

103 *Scotch Covenanters* — the signers and adherents of the National Covenant, a religious and political alliance proclaimed in Scotland in 1638 after the successful uprising of 1637 against Charles I's absolutist government. Rallying round the banner of the Presbyterian (Calvinist) Church against 'Popedom', the signatories of the Covenant fought for Scotland's national autonomy. The Covenanters' war against Charles I brought forward the outbreak of the bourgeois revolution in England.— 68

104 *Ireland — English Vendée; Vendée* — a department in Western France, the centre of a largely peasant-based royalist uprising during the French Revolution. The word Vendée came to denote counter-revolution.— 68

105 *Adventurers* — in the 16th and 17th centuries, a name for members of the English commercial and financial bourgeoisie, partners in colonial and merchant companies, profiteers and bankers, who financed risky but potentially very lucrative colonial and other ventures. The name derived from the Merchant Adventurers, a trading company.— 69

¹⁰⁶ The *Long Parliament* (1640-53) — the English Parliament which was convened by Charles I and became the constituent body of the English Revolution.— 69

¹⁰⁷ The *Penal Laws* (or *Code*) were introduced by the English colonialists in Ireland in the late 17th and the first half of the 18th century under the pretext of a need to combat Catholic conspiracies and the enemies of the Anglican Church. To all practical purposes, the laws deprived the Irish, who were mostly Catholic, of all political and civil rights: restricted the right of inheritance, and of acquisition and alienation of property; introduced the practice of confiscating property; established onerous terms of lease for Catholic peasants, which aggravated their bondage to English landlords and land agents; banned Irish national schools; imposed harsh penalties on teachers, Irish Catholic priests, etc. It was not until the late 18th century that the growing national liberation movement in Ireland forced the authorities to abrogate a significant part of the penal laws.— 69

¹⁰⁸ A reference to the subsidies granted to the Irish Catholic College opened in the town of Maynooth in 1795. Pitt's government tried to use the foundation of the College to win over the Catholic clergy and the leading stratum of the Irish bourgeoisie in order to split the Irish national movement.— 69

¹⁰⁹ The *Anglo-Irish Union* came into force on 1 January 1801 and deprived Ireland of the last remnants of parliamentary autonomy (the Irish Parliament was disbanded and Irish M.P.s received a number of seats in the British Parliament, where they were in the minority).— 69, 286

¹¹⁰ The *system of national schools* — a reference to the school reform of 1831 introduced by the then Chief Secretary for Ireland Stanley (Lord Derby). Henceforth, joint schools were set up for Catholic and Protestant children and only religious subjects were taught separately.— 70

¹¹¹ Marx's letter to Zasulich, which became known to many Russian revolutionary Marxists, including Georgi Plekhanov, was preceded by several drafts, which are included in Volume 24 of the present edition.
     The letter was published in English for the first time in: Karl Marx and Frederick Engels, *Selected Correspondence*, Foreign Languages Publishing House, Moscow, 1955.— 71

¹¹² Marx is probably referring to the request that he write a book on the Russian village commune made by the revolutionary Narodnik Nikolai Morozov in December 1880 on behalf of the Executive Committee of Narodnaya Volya (see Note 70).— 71

¹¹³ Part of this letter was published in English for the first time in: Karl Marx and Frederick Engels, *Selected Correspondence*, Foreign Languages Publishing House, Moscow, 1955.— 73, 196, 250, 256, 341, 430

¹¹⁴ A reference to Engels' article 'Du sollst nicht ehebrechen' which remained unpublished. See *MEGA*₂, Bd. 1/25, S. 213-14.— 73

¹¹⁵ Engels is rewording a well-known phrase that belongs to Jeanne Antoinette Poisson, Marquise de Pompadour, usually ascribed to Louis XV, 'après nous le déluge'.— 73

¹¹⁶ Engels proceeds to critically analyse the views of A. E. F. Schäffle, which the latter set forth in the book here mentioned.— 74

117 The *Overseas Trade Society* *(Seehandlung)* — a merchant and credit company founded in Prussia in 1772. It enjoyed a number of major state privileges and granted large loans to the government, acting, in fact, as its banker and broker. In 1904, it was officially transformed into the Prussian State Bank.— 74

118 An allusion to the indecision displayed in tactical issues by the Social-Democratic leaders in Germany after the introduction of the Anti-Socialist Law (see Note 16). Their wavering was reflected in Liebknecht's speech in the Reichstag on 17 March 1879 on the introduction of the so-called local state of siege in Berlin and its environs (see Note 65), and that in the Saxon Landtag on 17 February 1880 on the elections in Chemnitz's No. 1 constituency. Liebknecht stated in the Reichstag that the Social-Democratic Party would abide by the Anti-Socialist Law, being a party of reform in the proper sense of the word, and opposed a 'violent' revolution as nonsense. In the Provincial Diet, he said that since the Social-Democratic Party of Germany was taking part in the elections to the legislative bodies, it was not a party advocating the overthrow of the government.— 75, 203

119 In February-March 1881, by decision of the Wyden Congress (see Note 418) of the Socialist Workers' Party of Germany, Friedrich Wilhelm Fritzsche and Louis Viereck visited the United States. Engels, who disapproved of the trip, wrote: '...this much is certain — no amount of American money will make good the damage that will infallibly be done if, after the manner of Fritzsche and Viereck, the emissaries again water down the party's viewpoint into a semblance of vulgar democracy and homespun philistinism' (see present edition, Vol. 47, letter to August Bebel of 18 January 1884).— 75, 99, 447

120 An attempt on William I's life was made on 2 June 1878 by the German anarchist Karl Eduard Nobiling, who fired from a sporting rifle loaded with small shot. This attempted assassination, as well as that by apprentice E. M. Hödel on 11 May 1878, served as a convenient excuse for Bismarck to demand that the Reichstag pass the Exceptional Law against the Socialists (see Note 16).— 75, 175, 209, 288, 448

121 In December 1880, the British Prime Minister Gladstone declared that he intended to submit to Parliament a new bill on the state of emergency in Ireland (see Note 123). This prompted the Left wing of the Irish Land League (see Note 139) to urge the peasants to refuse payment of land rent. The more resolute section of the revolutionary democrats believed this would be a prologue to a long-expected armed uprising.— 75

122 This may refer to the resolution passed by the House of Commons on 3 February 1881 introducing a new procedure in the British Parliament. Seeking to combat the obstructionist tactics of the Irish opposition in the House of Commons, which made it impossible to get a coercion bill for Ireland (see Note 123) passed by Parliament, Gladstone proposed a resolution granting the Speaker the right to interrupt any M.P. at any point and to expel him from the House.— 75, 84

123 The *Coercion Bills* were passed by the British Parliament several times throughout the 19th century in order to suppress the revolutionary and national liberation movement in Ireland. In early 1881, the House of Commons passed two bills introducing exceptional laws in Ireland. They declared a state of emergency there and assigned troops to evict tenants refusing to pay rent.— 75, 84, 172

[124] The *Irish Land Bill* was debated in Parliament from late 1880, but did not become law until 22 August 1881 (an Act to further amend the law relating to the occupation and ownership of land in Ireland and for other purposes relating thereto). The new Act somewhat restricted the high-handed practices of the English landlords with respect to their tenant farmers. Landlords lost the right to evict tenants provided the latter paid the rent on time, and the amount of rent payable was fixed for 15 years. Although the Land Bill gave the landlords a chance to sell land to the state at a profit, and the fixed rent remained very high, the English landlords opposed the Bill, seeking to maintain their undivided rule.— 75, 84, 86

[125] Engels is replying to Johann Philipp Becker's letter of 24 March 1881 in which the latter thanked him for the help he had received in October 1880.— 76

[126] The reference is to a meeting in the United States at the time of Fritzsche's and Viereck's stay there (see Note 119).

A report on the meeting held in Boston on 6 March 1881 was printed by *Der Sozialdemokrat*, Nos. 13 and 16, 27 March and 17 April 1881.— 77

[127] German democratic emigrants, including members of the German gymnastic clubs, took an active part in the American Civil War of 1861-65 on the side of the North. In 1861, German emigrants residing not far from St Louis joined the Northerners' detachments and prevented Governor D. Jackson from handing the town over to the South.

German gymnastic clubs — organisations of German democratic emigrants, including workers, set up in the USA by participants in the 1848-49 revolution. At a congress in Philadelphia on 5 October 1850, the gymnastic clubs joined together to form a Socialist Gymnastic Association (Sozialistischer Turnverein), which maintained contacts with German workers' organisations in America.— 77

[128] A reference to the assassination of Emperor Alexander II of Russia on 1 (13) March 1881 by decision of the Executive Committee of Narodnaya Volya. On this organisation, see Note 70.— 78, 127

[129] Most's article 'Endlich!' on the assassination of Alexander II was carried by *Die Freiheit*, No. 12, 19 March 1881. On 30 March, Most was arrested in London, tried on 4 May and sentenced in June to 16 months' imprisonment and forced labour for the written defence, in a foreign language, of a political assassination.— 78, 80, 81, 83

[130] On behalf of the board of the German Workers' Educational Society in London (see Note 8) Gottlieb Lemcke invited Engels to the opening ceremony of the Society's new club-house at 49 Tottenham Street, Tottenham Court Road, London, W.— 79

[131] This is Engels' reply to Johann Philipp Becker's letter of 30 March 1881.— 80

[132] On 30 and 31 March 1881 the German Reichstag debated the report of the Prussian government and the Hamburg Senate on the introduction of the 'local state of siege' in Berlin and Hamburg-Altona (see Note 65).— 80

[133] This letter was published in English for the first time in: *The Labour Monthly*, London, 1931, Vol. 13, No. 7.— 81

[134] The *Dogberry club* (after a character in Shakespeare's *Much Ado about Nothing*) was

a jocular name for the gatherings at the Marxs' of the family members, Engels and other friends—devotees of Shakespeare's work.—82

135 In 1874, Henri Rochefort, a French journalist, writer and politician exiled from France after the defeat of the Paris Commune, found himself in Geneva, where he contacted Russian political refugees. The Executive Committee of the Narodnaya Volya (see Note 70) sent him a letter requesting him to assist the Committee's agent Lev Hartmann in organising a propaganda campaign against the tsarist government. Judging by Marx's letter, it was this letter that Rochefort reprinted in his newspaper (the Institute of Marxism-Leninism does not have the copy of *Intransigeant* at its disposal). The publication caused Russian refugees in Geneva to voice their protest at an open meeting. The statement that they were breaking off all contacts with Rochefort appeared in *Die Freiheit* on 26 March 1881.—82

136 The trial of the Narodnaya Volya (see Note 70) members, notably Andrei Zhelyabov, Sofia Perovskaya, Nikolai Rysakov, Timofei Mikhailov, Nikolai Kibalchich and Gesya Gelfman, who took part in the assassination of Alexander II on 1 (13) March 1881, was held on 26-29 March (7-10 April) 1881. All of them, except Gelfman, were sentenced on 29 March to death by hanging and executed on 3 (15) April. In Gelfman's case, on account of her pregnancy the sentence was commuted to penal labour for life; she died in prison on 1 February 1882.—83

137 Over 3,000 people perished and more than 1,000 were injured in the earthquake on the island of Chios on 3-11 April 1881. The town of Chios and the neighbouring villages were almost totally destroyed.—83

138 The *Arms Act* (Peace Preservation Act) declared bearing arms without a permit to be a breach of the peace liable to punishment by the courts. On 18 March 1881, the operation of the Act was extended to Ireland.—84

139 The *Irish Land League*—a mass organisation set up in October 1879 by the revolutionary democrat Michael Davitt. It embraced mostly peasants and urban poor and enjoyed the support of the progressive elements of the Irish bourgeoisie. The League's agrarian programme expressed the spontaneous protest of the Irish people against the landlords' rule and national oppression. However, some of its leaders attempted to reduce its activities to the campaign for Home Rule, that is, limited autonomy of Ireland within the framework of the British Empire, and did not go so far as to demand the abolition of the English landlords' rule. In 1881, the Land League was banned by the British government but, to all practical purposes, continued to exist up to the late 1880s.—84, 286

140 Part of this letter was published in English for the first time in: Marx and Engels, *Ireland and the Irish Question*, Progress Publishers, Moscow, 1971.—85, 156, 171, 191

141 Engels is referring to the *Stenographische Berichte über die Verhandlungen des Reichstags* that included the speeches made by Ignaz Auer and August Bebel on 30 and 31 March 1881 on the subject of the 'local state of siege' in Berlin and Hamburg, and Bebel's speech on the Workers' Accident Insurance Bill delivered on 4 April 1881 (see notes 65 and 144). The shorthand report was sent by Bernstein to London before 28 April.—85

142 From mid-November 1880, Wilhelm Liebknecht served six months in the Leipzig prison for the speech he had made at a workers' meeting in Chemnitz.—86

¹⁴³ This probably refers to the Act to Consolidate and Amend the Statute Law of England and Ireland relating to Offences against the Person passed by the British Parliament in 1861.
On Most's conviction, see Note 129.— 86

¹⁴⁴ The reference is to the *Stenographische Berichte über die Verhandlungen des Reichstags. 4. Legislaturperiode. IV. Session 1881*, Vol. I, Berlin, 1881 (see Note 141). The Workers' Accident Insurance Bill was part of Bismarck's so-called labour legislation. It provided for the establishment of an Imperial Accident Insurance Bank. Two-thirds of the insurance expenses were to be incurred by the employers, and one-third, by the workers; those who earned 750 marks a year or less were to have their contributions paid by the Treasury. Bebel subjected the Bill to well-substantiated and sharp criticism and demanded that the workers' accident insurance be wholly financed by the employers. The Bill was passed by the Reichstag on 27 June 1884. Bebel's speeches were also printed by *Der Sozialdemokrat*, Nos. 16-22, 17 April-29 May 1881.
On the *state of siege*, see Note 65.— 87, 353, 386

¹⁴⁵ Engels is alluding to Robert Victor von Puttkamer's speech in the Reichstag on 30 March 1881 in which he accused the Social-Democrats of preparing to stage acts of terrorism and referred to Most's article (see Note 129), where the address 'brothers' was used on repeated occasions.— 88

¹⁴⁶ Part of this letter was published in English for the first time in: *Le Monde moderne et la femme d'aujourd'hui*, Vol. I, Paris, 1908.— 89

¹⁴⁷ Marx and his family lived not far from Maitland Park, at 41 Maitland Park Road. The street was crossed by Southampton Road, named probably after Lord Southampton.— 89

¹⁴⁸ A reference to one of the terms of the Irish Land Bill of 1881, which became law on 22 August 1881 (see Note 124).— 90

¹⁴⁹ The radical leader Georges Clemenceau criticised the government of J. Ferry when France launched a military expedition against Tunisia in April-May 1881. Clemenceau accused the government of wasting money on military ventures that only weakened France. He explained his accusations by the fact that the conquest of 'uncivilised' nations was undermining the moral prestige of the French.— 92

¹⁵⁰ This note, and Engels' letter to Sorge that follows, were printed in *The New-York Herald* as part of the interview given by Sorge to the newspaper correspondent at the request of the editors on the occasion of the Russian revolutionary Narodnik Lev Hartmann's arrival in New York from London in June 1881.— 94

¹⁵¹ *Bank Holidays* in Great Britain—the six public holidays on which banks are closed.— 95

¹⁵² The protest meeting against the Coercion Bills for Ireland (see Note 123), which took place in Hyde Park on 5 June 1881, passed a resolution which held the British government responsible for the difficult position of the Irish people, demanded that the eviction of tenants who had failed to pay their rent be stopped, the arrested leaders of the Land League (see Note 139) be released, and that the Secretary of State for Ireland William Forster, who ruthlessly suppressed the national libera-

tion movement there, resign. A long speech at the meeting was made by Charles
Stewart Parnell, who censured Forster's activities in Ireland.— 95

153 This rumour was based on an episode in the Narodnaya Volya organisation's fight
against the autocracy.

Sofia Perovskaya and Lev Hartmann, posing as husband and wife, took a flat in
the house from which a tunnel was dug to the Moscow-Kursk railway line as part
of a plan to blow up the tsar's train. The attempt, undertaken on 19 November
1879, was abortive. Perovskaya also helped with the preparations for the assassination of Alexander II, which was carried out on 1 March 1881, and was arrested
shortly afterwards.

On Perovskaya's execution, see Note 136.— 96

154 Part of this letter was published in English for the first time in: *Justice* (London),
No. 441, 25 June 1892.— 98

155 *Napoléon le petit* — a nickname given by Victor Hugo to Louis Bonaparte in his
speech at the meeting of the French Legislative Assembly in 1851; gained wide currency after Hugo's lampoon *Napoléon le Petit* appeared in print in 1852.— 100

156 *Anti-Renters* — in the 1830s and 1840s, land tenants in the State of New York who
refused to pay rent to the big landowners and demanded that the farms be sold to
them. The Anti-Renters offered armed resistance to the rent collectors. The greatest
unrest took place between 1839 and 1845. The campaign against the landowners
ended in a compromise: from 1846, they gradually began to sell land to tenants.—
101

157 Marx is probably referring to Henry George's article 'The Kearney Agitation in
California' carried by *The Popular Science Monthly* in August 1880. Marx wrote
out excerpts from it, which are still extant.

The Editors are not in possession of a copy of the *Atlantic Monthly*.— 101

158 The reference is to the Democratic Federation, an English socialist association set
up in June 1881 and headed by Henry Mayers Hyndman. Its programme closely
resembled that of the Chartists (see Note 159).

At the inaugural conference of the Democratic Federation, each participant
received a copy of Hyndman's pamphlet *England for All* in which (Chapter
II — 'Labour' and Chapter III — 'Capital') the author presented whole sections of
Volume One of *Capital* as the programme of the Federation, distorting many of
Marx's ideas and making no reference to either the work or its author.

In 1884, the Democratic Federation was transformed into the Social
Democratic Federation.— 102, 162, 251

159 *Chartism* — a political movement of British workers in the 1830s-50s advocating the
People's Charter, which contained the demand for universal suffrage and specified
the terms that would guarantee this right to the workers. Arising from the consequences of the industrial revolution, Chartism was a revolutionary form of workers' protest against capitalist exploitation, their lack of political rights and the
landlords' and big bourgeoisie's monopoly of power. The Chartist movement was
a major stage in the working-class struggle at the time preceding the emergence of
Marxism.— 102, 293

160 Between late June and around 20 July 1881, Marx and his ailing wife rested
in Eastbourne.— 104, 110, 185

¹⁶¹ Between 28 July and 22 August 1881, Engels was on holiday in Bridlington Quay (Yorkshire).— 104, 108, 126

¹⁶² In a letter of 10 June 1881, Theodor Friedrich Cuno asked Engels to help Norris A. Clowes, the *New-York Star* correspondent for Ireland.— 105

¹⁶³ In May-August 1881 Engels contributed to the printed organ of the British trade unions *The Labour Standard*, which appeared in London and was edited by George Shipton. Engels's contributions were printed anonymously nearly every week as leaders (see present edition, Vol. 24, pp. 376-418). All in all, Engels wrote 11 articles. The last one, 'Social Classes—Necessary and Superfluous', appeared in *The Labour Standard* on 6 August 1881, after which Engels terminated his work for the paper due to the mounting opportunist tendencies among its editors.— 105, 119, 197

¹⁶⁴ Between 26 July and 16 August 1881, Marx and his wife stayed with their daughter Jenny Longuet in Argenteuil not far from Paris.— 107, 115, 185

¹⁶⁵ On 26 July 1881, the French government issued a decree scheduling the elections to the Chamber of Deputies for 21 August, earlier than the date originally fixed.— 108

¹⁶⁶ Part of this letter was published in English for the first time in: *The Letters of Karl Marx*, selected and translated with explanatory notes and an introduction by Saul K. Padover, Prentice-Hall, Inc., Englewood Cliffs, New Jersey, 1979.— 110, 176, 217, 238, 374, 422

¹⁶⁷ *Code pénal*—the penal code adopted in France in 1810 and introduced in 1881 into the regions of Western and South-Western Germany conquered by the French.— 111, 445

¹⁶⁸ In the 1870s, the French journalist Victor Tissot protested at the military indemnity to Germany under the terms of the Versailles Peace of 1871 in his repeatedly reprinted books *Voyage au pays des milliards, Les Prussiens en Allemagne. Suite du Voyage au pays des milliards* and *Voyage aux pays annexés. Suite et fin du Voyage au pays des milliards*. Max Simon Nordau attacked Tissot's stand in his books *Aus dem wahren Milliardenlande. Pariser Studien und Bilder* (1st ed., Leipzig, 1878, 2nd ed., under the title *Paris. Studien und Bilder aus dem wahren Milliardenlande*, Leipzig, 1881), *Paris unter der dritten Republik. Neue Bilder aus dem wahren Milliardenlande* (1st and 2nd editions, Leipzig, 1880 and 1881).— 112

¹⁶⁹ The reference is to the 5 milliard francs which France paid to Germany as indemnity under the terms of the peace treaty after its defeat in its war with Prussia in 1870-71.— 112, 454

¹⁷⁰ The Editors are not in possession of Engels' letter to Laura Lafargue of 6 August 1881. Laura Lafargue's letter to Engels of 13 August 1881 makes it clear that she was unable to take up his invitation.— 114

¹⁷¹ Marx met Hirsch in Paris on 7 August 1881.— 115

¹⁷² In his speech at the election meeting in Batignolles (see Note 165), Albert Adrien Regnard denounced the domination of Church congregations over primary and secondary schools and advocated compulsory free secular primary schooling. Marx ironically calls him a champion of anti-clericalism ('*Kulturkämpfer*' in the

original) drawing a parallel wlith the *Kulturkampf* policy pursued by the Bismarck government in the 1870s. To suppress the clergy and weaken the Party of the Centre (see Note 225), laws were introduced that banned political agitation by clergymen, withdrew their right of supervision over the schools, etc. Bismarck's campaign was a failure. In the late 1870s-early 1880s, seeking to unite the forces of reaction, Bismarck effected a reconciliation with the Catholic clergy. Nearly all the laws passed against it at the time of the *Kulturkampf* were abrogated (see also Note 255).— 117

173 *The Labour Standard*, No. 14, 6 August 1881, anonymously printed the article by Johann Georg Eccarius 'A German Opinion of English Trade Unionism'. Eccarius regarded highly the German trade unions founded in 1868 by Max Hirsch and Franz Duncker (the so-called Hirsch-Duncker trade unions). For Engels' opinion of the article, see this volume, p. 119.— 118, 121, 123

174 The reference is to Karl Kautsky's article 'International Labour Laws' published anonymously in *The Labour Standard*, No. 15, 13 August 1881.— 119, 120, 122, 126

175 The fourteenth annual British trades union congress took place in London on 12-17 September 1881.— 119, 121, 123

176 The *Manchester School* — a trend in economic thinking which reflected the interests of the industrial bourgeoisie. Its supporters, known as Free Traders (the centre of their agitation was Manchester), advocated free trade and non-interference by the government in the economy. In the 1840s and 1850s, the Free Traders formed a separate political group, which later constituted the Left wing of the Liberal Party.— 122, 260

177 *Factories and workshops' acts* — laws regulating labour conditions in British industry. The emergence and advancement of factory legislation was a consequence of the workers' economic and political struggle against capitalist exploitation. The first laws adopted regulated the children's, adolescents', and women's labour conditions in the textile industry (early 19th century). Step by step, the operation of the factories and workshops' acts was extended to the other industries.— 122, 140

178 The *Geneva Convention* of the Red Cross of 1864 — an international document signed at the conference of 16 European states in Geneva. The Geneva Convention established principles for belligerents' treatment of the wounded and the sick, and granted the right of neutrality to the medical personnel taking care of the wounded men.— 122, 140

179 On 16 August 1881, Gambetta was to speak in Charonne (a Paris district) at the meeting of his constituents, but the assembly refused to let him take the floor.— 126, 133, 361

180 Part of this letter was published in English for the first time in: K. Marx and F. Engels, *On Literature and Art.* A selection of writings, International General, New York, 1974.— 126

181 As instructed by Eduard Bernstein, on 23 July 1881 Karl Kautsky despatched to Engels several anti-Semitic articles from German newspapers.— 126

182 Engels is referring to articles printed by the newspaper in the winter (9, 23 and 30 January and 6 February) and summer (30 June and 28 July) of 1881. On 30 June and 7 July, the 'Feuilleton' column of the newspaper also carried excerpts from

Marx's work 'On the Jewish Question' (see present edition, Vol. 3, pp. 146-74).— 126

[183] Below, Engels quotes Hirsch's letter to him of 11 August 1881.— 126

[184] Engels is referring to two of Bernstein's articles with the same title, 'Es fehlt uns an Intelligenzen', published under the pen-name Leo in *Der Sozialdemokrat*, Nos. 31 and 33, 28 July and 11 August 1881.— 127, 137

[185] On 11 August 1881, *Der Sozialdemokrat* (the 'Sozialpolitische Rundschau' column) referred to Jules Vallès as a 'brave and highly esteemed member of the Commune'. The editors mentioned Vallès' letter printed by *Le Citoyen de Paris*, in which he refused to stand for election to the French Chamber of Deputies (to which he had been nominated by two Paris districts), saying that he preferred to enter parliament not through the door but on the shoulders of the insurgent people.— 127

[186] Jules Vallès' open letter to the President of the French Republic Grévy was published in early February 1879 in the newspaper *La Révolution Française*.— 127

[187] The *New Madrid Federation* was formed on 8 July 1872 by the members of *La Emancipacion* editorial board expelled by the anarchist majority from the Madrid Federation after the newspaper had exposed the activities of the secret Alliance in Spain. An active part in the organisation and work of the New Madrid Federation was taken by Paul Lafargue. The new Madrid Federation fought against the spread of anarchism in Spain, popularised the ideas of scientific socialism, and campaigned for the foundation of an independent proletarian party there. Its printed organ, *La Emancipacion*, had Engels as one of the contributors.— 128

[188] A reference to the International Anarchist Congress, which took place in London on 14-19 July 1881. Engels' report of the congress was quoted verbatim by Bernstein in the 'Sozialpolitische Rundschau' column of *Der Sozialdemokrat*, No. 35, 25 August 1881.— 128

[189] The speakers at the Anarchist Congress used numbers rather than names (see reports on the congress printed by *Die Freiheit*, Nos. 31, 32 and 33, 30 July, 6 and 13 August 1881). The *Freiheit* report of 23 July stated that 45 delegates holding 80 mandates represented 59 federations and 320 sections.— 129

[190] *Der Sozialdemokrat* of 25 August 1881 carried this information almost verbatim in the 'Sozialpolitische Rundschau' column.— 129

[191] The reference is to the Anarchist Congress in Saint-Imier (Switzerland) convened after the Hague Congress of the First International had expelled Mikhail Bakunin and James Guillaume.— 129

[192] Engels is probably referring to his study of Marx's manuscript on the history of differential calculus, on which Marx worked in 1878-82. Marx did his first research in mathematics back in the 1860s. The extant manuscripts were published for the first time in: K. Marx, *Matematicheskiye rukopisi* (Mathematical Manuscripts), Moscow, 1968. They will be included in full in *MEGA* I/28.— 130

[193] The American physician Henry S. Tanner set a peculiar record in New York in 1880: having decided to find out how long the human organism could go without food, he fasted over a month (from 28 June to 7 August).— 133

¹⁹⁴ This refers to the election meeting held in the Paris district of Belleville on 12 August 1881, at which Léon Gambetta outlined his programme.— 133

¹⁹⁵ *Collectivists* in the French socialist movement of the 1870s-80s were the followers of Marxism who advocated collectivisation of the means of production and workers' involvement in the political struggle. Their leaders were Jules Guesde and Paul Lafargue (hence Guesdists, another and more common name for the French Marxists). Right from its formation in 1879, the Workers' Party was torn apart by fierce ideological dissent, which in 1882 led to its split (see Note 394). On the party programme, see Note 68.— 134

¹⁹⁶ Marx added these lines to his wife's letter to their daughter Jenny Longuet of 20 August 1881 (see this volume, pp. 475).— 136

¹⁹⁷ August Bebel's letter to Engels of 13 May 1881 has not been found. Engels may be referring to Bebel's letter of 13 June 1881, written in reply to Engels' letter of 28 April.— 137

¹⁹⁸ After a 'local state of siege' (see Note 65) was introduced in Leipzig in June 1881, many active socialists, Bebel and Liebknecht among them, were deported from the city. On 2 July 1881, they left Leipzig and settled down in Borsdorf close by.— 137, 336

¹⁹⁹ Engels' letter to Liebknecht and the latter's reply have not been found.— 138

²⁰⁰ On 4 April 1881, August Bebel criticised in the Reichstag the Workers' Accident Insurance Bill (see also notes 141 and 144).— 138

²⁰¹ Engels is referring to Liebknecht's speech in the Reichstag on 31 May 1881 on the Workers' Accident Insurance Bill (see Note 144): 'The historical process of evolution is infinitely stronger than the most powerful ruler. Prince Bismarck has himself experienced some interesting transformations, he honestly confessed ... that for a while he was bringing up the rear of the Free Traders, then of the Protectionist movement, and now of socialism' (see *Stenographische Berichte über die Verhandlungen des Reichstags. 4. Legislaturperiode. IV. Session 1881*, Vol. II, Berlin, 1881, p. 1455).— 138

²⁰² A reference to the speech on the Workers' Accident Insurance Bill (see Note 144) made by the German Social Democrat Georg Wilhelm Hartmann in the Reichstag on 15 June 1881, of which *Die Freiheit* (No. 26, 25 June 1881) wrote: 'Hartmann crawled on his belly before Bismarck and the Reichstag when the Bill was debated.' *Die Freiheit* quoted from Hartmann's speech referring to the *Frankfurter Zeitung*; some of the fragments deviate from the text of the official shorthand report (see *Stenographische Berichte über die Verhandlungen des Reichstags. 4. Legislaturperiode. IV. Session 1881*, Vol. II, Berlin, 1881, pp. 1757-59). Judging by the shorthand report, Hartmann stated that 'the Social Democrats gladly welcome the Bill submitted by the Imperial Chancellor' and that 'the main principle' of Social-Democracy was 'the aspiration to humanity' and 'the moral feeling of assistance to those in need'.— 138

²⁰³ The reference is to the results of the elections to the French Chamber of Deputies held on 21 August 1881, at which candidates from the French Workers' Party were standing for the first time (see Note 208).— 138

²⁰⁴ At the 1877 elections, the German Social-Democrats received about half a million votes.— 139

²⁰⁵ The Seventh International Medical Congress was held in London between 3 and 9 August 1881.— 140

²⁰⁶ The *Privy Council* — a special body under the King of England, first formed in the 13th century, consisting of secretaries of state and other officials, as well as top clergy. For a long time, it had the right to initiate legislation on behalf of the king, bypassing Parliament. In the 18th and 19th centuries, the Privy Council lost a great deal of its power. It retained only the right to accept and consider appeals concerning the colonial, ecclesiastical and administrative matters. The Privy Council comprises a number of committees, including those on scientific research, industry, medicine and agriculture. At present, the Privy Council has virtually no say in the administration of the country.— 140

²⁰⁷ On 22 September 1881, *Der Sozialdemokrat* carried a leader headed 'Die Vivisektion des Proletariats'.— 141

²⁰⁸ In October 1880, Malon, Guesde and Brousse started the newspaper *L'Émancipation* in Lyons and, on Brousse's suggestion, made a written commitment not to stand for election. In November 1880, *L'Émancipation* ceased to exist, and the editors' commitment was no longer valid. This enabled Guesde to stand at the elections of 21 August 1881 to the French Chamber of Deputies from the town of Roubaix, for which Malon and Brousse fiercely attacked him.— 142, 145, 361

²⁰⁹ Marx wrote this letter in reply to Kautsky's letter of 28 September 1881, in which he asked Marx to introduce his mother Minna Kautsky, who arrived in Paris in the autumn of 1881, to Marx's daughter Jenny Longuet, who lived in Argenteuil near Paris.— 142

²¹⁰ The Editors are not in possession of Marx's note to Jenny Longuet.— 142, 143

²¹¹ Part of this letter was published in English for the first time in: K. Marx, *Selected Works*, Vol. II, Moscow-Leningrad, 1936, New York, 1936.— 144

²¹² In a letter of 14 October 1881 posted on 20 October, Bernstein informed Engels that Lafargue had requested him in early October to hold a collection among his friends to help finance a new edition of *L'Égalité*. Bernstein asked Engels' advice on the way to treat Lafargue's request, since he felt he was not competent enough to correctly appraise the situation in the French working-class movement.— 144

²¹³ The International Socialist Congress, originally to be held in Zurich, met in Chur between 2 and 4 October 1881 (see also Note 100).— 150

²¹⁴ 27 October 1881 was the day fixed for the elections to the German Reichstag (see Note 216).— 150

²¹⁵ In a postcard dated 13 October 1881 Johann Philipp Becker wrote to Engels about the Chur Congress (see Note 100), in which he had taken part as a representative of the German workers in Switzerland.— 151

²¹⁶ At the elections to the German Reichstag on 27 October 1881 the Social Democrats won 312,000 votes and 12 seats.— 152

²¹⁷ This letter was published in English for the first time in an abridged form in: K. Marx, *Selected Works*, Vol. II, Moscow-Leningrad, 1936, New York, 1936.— 152

²¹⁸ Engels is referring to the mass demonstration in London, called by the Chartists

for 10 April 1848. It was to present a petition to Parliament for the adoption of the People's Charter. The Government prohibited the demonstration, and troops and police were brought to London to prevent it. The Chartist leaders, many of whom vacillated, called off the demonstration and persuaded the masses to disperse. The failure of the demonstration was used by the Government for an attack on the workers and repression of the Chartists.— 152

²¹⁹ This refers to Louis Bonaparte's coup d'état on 2 December 1851.— 153

²²⁰ On 17 May 1879, with the approval of the whole Social-Democratic group in the Reichstag, the Social-Democratic deputy Max Kayser defended the government project for protective customs tariffs. Marx and Engels sharply criticised Kayser because the proposal promoted the interests of big industrialists and landowners, and further condemned some of the German Social-Democratic leaders' stand vis-à-vis Kayser (see present edition, Vol. 45, pp. 259-62).— 153

²²¹ This refers to August Bebel's letter to Engels of 18 November 1879.— 154

²²² The following Social-Democrats won seats in the Reichstag at the elections of 27 October 1881: Wilhelm Blos, Johann Heinrich Wilhelm Dietz, Karl Frohme, Bruno Geiser, Karl Grillenberger, Wilhelm Hasenclever, Max Kayser, Julius Kräcker, Wilhelm Liebknecht, Moritz Rittinghausen, Karl Wilhelm Stolle and Georg Heinrich von Vollmar. August Bebel was not elected in either of the three constituencies where he had been nominated. Neither did he win at the second ballot in the Mainz constituency on 15 December.— 154, 188, 259, 454

²²³ The Rheims Congress of the French Workers' Party took place between 30 October and 6 November 1881. It was attended by 44 delegates. The Congress endorsed the National Committee (Comité national) of the French Workers' Party, set up on Malon's and Brousse's initiative in mid-October 1881 (see Note 250).

At the Rheims Congress, Malon and Brousse managed to get a decision passed recognising that the minimum programme (see Note 68) did 'not quite' live up to 'the working people's aspirations'. The Congress resolved to leave the programme in force until a new one had been adopted. This decision was spearheaded against the Marxist groups that united around L'Égalité edited by Jules Guesde.— 154, 173, 341

²²⁴ At the International Socialist Congress held in Chur (see Note 100), serious differences surfaced between the Polish socialist groups. Kautsky, who wrote to Engels about the matter on 8 November 1881, asked for his opinion concerning the stand Der Sozialdemokrat ought to take in this affair. Engels set forth his views in a letter to Kautsky of 7 February 1882 (see this volume, pp. 191-95).— 155, 166, 190, 191, 195

²²⁵ The Centre (Zentrum) — a political party of German Catholics formed in 1870-71 as a result of the unification of the Catholic groups in the Prussian Provincial Diet and the German Reichstag (its seats were in the centre of the assembly halls). It united, under the banner of Catholicism, the Catholic clergy of various social ranks, landowners, bourgeoisie and certain sections of the peasants, especially in the petty and medium-sized states of Western and South-Western Germany, and supported their separatist and anti-Prussian tendencies. Engels gave a detailed description of the Party of the Centre in his work The Role of Force in History (see present edition, Vol. 26, pp. 509-10).— 157

²²⁶ An allusion to Jenny Marx's reviews of the London theatrical scene in the *Frank-furter Zeitung*, specifically, the acting of Henry Irving: 'Aus der Londoner Theater-welt' (21 November 1875); 'Londoner Saison' (4 April 1876); 'Englische Shake-speare-Studien' (3 January 1877); 'Shakespeares Richard III in Londoner Ly-ceum-Theater' (8 February 1877), and 'Vom Londoner Theater' (25 May 1877). All the reviews appeared anonymously.— 158

²²⁷ The third German edition of Volume One of *Capital*, which appeared in print af-ter Marx's death (in 1883), was edited by Engels. By the 2nd volume Marx means here the part of his work that later made up the second and the third volumes of *Capital*.— 158, 161, 162, 434, 465

²²⁸ Part of this letter was published in English for the first time in: *The Socialist Re-view*, III-VIII, London, 1908. It appeared in English in full in *The Labour Monthly*, No. 3, London, 1933. The first half of the letter is in German, and the sec-ond, in English.— 161

²²⁹ Sibylle Hess' letter to Marx of 11 December 1881.— 164

²³⁰ Liebknecht's letter to Marx of 12 December 1881. After the 1848-49 revolution in Germany, Liebknecht was in exile first in Switzerland and then in London. He re-turned to Prussia in 1862 after an amnesty.— 164

²³¹ The first issue of the third series of *L'Égalité* appeared on 11 December 1881. Among others, it carried Guesde's programmatic article, Lafargue's article on the successes of the German Social-Democrats at the latest Reichstag elections, Guesde's report of the Rheims Congress, and Engels' speech at Jenny Marx's graveside.— 166

²³² The dedication and the letter to Roland Daniels Jun. were written by Marx on the back of his photograph taken in August 1875. The original is kept in the Karl-Marx-Haus in Trier.— 167

²³³ On 31 December 1881, Marx replied to the letters from Amalia and Roland Da-niels Jun. of 11 December 1881, in which they offered him their condolences on the death of his wife Jenny on 2 December. Marx's letters have not been found and probably did not reach their addressees.— 167, 180

²³⁴ Marx was taking a cure in Ventnor, on the Isle of Wight (the south of England), between 29 December 1881 and 16 January 1882. He was accompanied by his youngest daughter Eleanor.— 169, 171, 202, 214, 218, 224, 259, 366, 371

²³⁵ The Lafargue family had property in New Orleans.— 170

²³⁶ The reference is to the traditional annual voters' meeting in Birmingham convened by the Birmingham Liberal Association on 3 January 1882. John Bright, lead-er of the British bourgeois radicals and M.P. for Birmingham, and Joseph Cham-berlain, a public figure in the city, who spoke at the meeting, fully supported the Irish policies of Gladstone's Liberal government. Specifically, they vindicated his actions aimed at implementing the so-called Land Act of 1881 for Ireland (see Note 124).— 171

²³⁷ Probably an ironic reference to Jacob Bright, John Bright's younger brother.— 171

²³⁸ A reference to the meeting held on 3 January 1882. The official pretext for it was

a discussion of the functions of the assistant commissioners, appointed to carry out the Land Act of 1881 for Ireland (see Note 124). It was stated at the meeting that their decision to introduce a rent reduction was not objective. The landlords demanded that the government immediately consider their complaints and promulgate the law on compensation for losses they could sustain should the government sanction the rent reduction.— 172

239 Joseph Dietzgen wrote to Marx on 3 January 1882 that he was studying Hegel's works, in particular, his *Phänomenologie des Geistes.*— 172

240 When the Reichstag debated the observance of the Anti-Socialist Law in December 1881, deputies Wilhelm Blos and Wilhelm Hasenclever adopted a conciliatory stand. In its leader, *Der Sozialdemokrat*, No. 51, 15 December 1881 strongly protested that the Social-Democratic deputies in the Reichstag 'should neither wail nor complain, but brand and expose ... not enter into negotiations, but protest'. The protest was supported by the party majority outside the Reichstag and by the Social-Democratic group within it. At a special meeting at which Bebel was also present, although he was not a Reichstag deputy at the time, the members of the parliamentary group unanimously issued a declaration endorsing the general line of *Der Sozialdemokrat* as the party's printed organ. The declaration was printed by the newspaper on 16 February 1882. Both Blos and Hasenclever had signed it.— 173, 203

241 This refers to William I's rescript signed by him and Bismarck (*Erlass vom 4. Januar 1882. Deutscher Reichs-Anzeiger und Königlich Preussischer Staats-Anzeiger*, 7 January 1882). William demanded that, in future, all government acts be regarded as a constitutional expression of the King's own opinion. Referring to Art. 49 of the Prussian Constitution, which granted the King of Prussia the right to personally direct government policies, William laid down that his ministers and officials should curb any 'doubt' about the Prussian King's 'constitutional right'.— 175, 178

242 *Nihilists* — Russian intellectuals of humble origin (the 1860s). They flatly refused to accept the ruling ideology, morality and way of life. Nihilism was not a comprehensive philosophy; the only thing its proponents shared was their rejection of things as they stood. The term 'nihilism' was later applied by the reactionary press to all revolutionaries at the moments when the class struggle began to mount.— 175, 470

243 *Demagogues* in Germany were members of the opposition movement after the liberation of the country from Napoleonic rule. The name became current after the Karlsbad Conference of Ministers of the German States in August 1819, which adopted a special decision on the persecution of the demagogues.— 175

244 In June and September 1881 Count Nikolai Ignatiev, the Russian Minister of the Interior, assembled 'knowledgeable' Zemstvo representatives of his own choosing to discuss some of the practical issues of domestic policy: resettlement, consumption of alcohol, etc. In this connection, 12 Zemstvo assemblies requested that Zemstvo representatives be involved in the legislative activities not on isolated occasions but on a permanent basis, and that they be selected not by the government but by the Zemstvos themselves.— 175

245 Sorge wrote to Marx on 27 December 1881: 'Come over to us, old friend, and be-

504   Notes

come one of us! We will offer you as good a home as we can, and new surroundings
and old work will in time alleviate your sorrow and sustain you.'— 177

246 An ironic allusion to William I's flight to England at the time of the March 1848
revolution in Germany (up to 1861, William was heir to the Prussian throne and
held the title of Prince of Prussia). In England, he maintained close contacts with
the country's leading politicians.— 178

247 Marx is referring to Theodor Mommsen's, Eugen Richter's and Albert Hänel's as-
surances of their loyalty to the crown voiced at the German Reichstag sessions in
November-December 1881.— 178

248 Engels first came to England in the latter half of November 1842 to study commerce at a cotton mill in Manchester belonging to the firm of Ermen & Engels.
Engels' visit lasted until 26 August 1844.— 178

249 Marx sent a photograph of himself to Cologne for the second time probably in late
January 1882, having received Amalia Daniels' letter of 19 January. On 5 February, Roland Daniels Jun. acknowledged receipt of the photograph and explained
the confusion with the post by the fact that several persons of the same name
resided in Cologne.— 180

250 The *Comité national* (National Committee) of the French Workers' Party was set
up on the initiative of its Right-wing leaders Malon and Brousse in mid-October
1881, just before the Rheims Congress of the party (see Note 223), which endorsed
it. The National Committee was formed on the principle of equal representation of
all six federations (five persons from each) which constituted the French Workers'
Party at the time: the Federative Union of the Centre (see Note 265), the Eastern
Federative Union, the Northern Federation, the Federative Union of the South,
the Federative Union of the West, and the Algerian Federation. To all practical
purposes, only the first three federations were in existence at the time, whereas the
other three existed only on paper and their representatives, who were under Malon's and Brousse's influence, did not have legal powers. Thus, with the exception of
the five Collectivists (Guesdists), who represented the Northern Federation, the remaining 25 members of the National Committee were Malon's and Brousse's followers, which placed the party leadership into the hands of Right-wing elements.—
181

251 On the minimum programme, see Note 68. Jules Joffrin, nominated as the party
candidate at the elections to the Paris City Council, set forth his election programme in a speech made in the Monmartre district of Paris. In it, he totally ignored the theoretical part of the programme drawn up by Marx and replaced a
number of important and quite concrete points (the issue of the 8-hour day,
collective property, etc.) in its practical part by vague phrases. On 8 January 1882,
using its advantage in the National Committee (see Note 250), Malon's and
Brousse's group managed to get Joffrin's opportunistic election programme approved.— 181

252 This may refer to the note 'Russland' carried by the *Kölnische Zeitung* on 25 July
1881. The note refuted the opinion of certain European newspapers that General
Mikhail Skobelev, who visited Paris in the summer of 1881, had been instructed by
the Russian government to pave the way for a Franco-Russian alliance, open negotiations on the abolition of political émigrés' right of asylum, etc. The *Kölnische
Zeitung* stated that Skobelev's visit was a private one.— 182

253 The *Sonvillier Circular* (Circulaire à toutes les fédérations de l'Association Inter-nationale des Travailleurs. Sonvillier, 1871) was passed by the Bakuninist Jura Fed-eration at the congress in Sonvillier on 12 November 1871. It was spearheaded against the decisions of the London Conference of the International (1871) and at-tacked the activities of its General Council. It demanded the immediate convoca-tion of a general congress to revise the Rules of the International along anarchist lines. The General Council responded by issuing a private circular 'Fictitious Splits in the International' written by Marx and Engels, which exposed the Bakuninists' efforts to split the organisation (see present edition, Vol. 23).— 182

254 The mounting peasant movement in Russia in the 1860s-70s caused by the peas-ants' desperate condition forced the tsarist government to agree to slightly reduce the redemption payments. The law of 28 December 1881 reduced peasants' redemp-tion payments by one ruble for a plot per person in Russia, and by 16 per cent in the Ukraine.— 182

255 The phrase 'to go to Canossa' goes back to the humiliating pilgrimage undertaken to Pope Gregory VII at Canossa Castle (Northern Italy) in 1077 by the German Emperor Henry IV in the course of the protracted struggle between the emperors and the popes for the investiture.

In May 1872, Bismarck, who had launched a campaign against the Catholic Church that supported the separatist and anti-Prussian sentiments in Germany, stated: 'We shall not go to Canossa.' During the campaign (the *Kulturkampf*), a law was promulgated on 4 May 1874 which restricted the powers of the consis-tory (ecclesiastical court). However, in the late 1870s, when Bismarck needed the support of the Catholic Party of the Centre to combat the workers' movement and the growing influence of the German Social-Democratic Party, he abrogated nearly all the laws passed during the Kulturkampf campaign, had the principal advocates of the anti-Catholic policy resign, and made his peace with the new Pope Leo XIII. By 'the pilgrimage to Canossa' Engels is ironically referring to the abrogation of the law of 4 May 1874 effected by 233 votes to 115 in the Reichstag on 12 January 1882.— 182

256 By referring to *ultramontanes* Engels meant the Centre (see Note 225).

Particularists — members of a political movement in Germany which emerged after the establishment of the German Empire and opposed the policies of the Prus-sian government. The movement spread among the ruling classes of the petty and medium-sized South-Western German states. The top Catholic clergy, landowners and the bourgeoisie of these states resented Germany's unification under Prussian supremacy believing it to be an encroachment on their rights. As a result they cher-ished separatist aspirations, expressed their discontent with Bismarck's policy of Prussianisation of Germany, demanded autonomy from central power and im-mutability of local private rights and privileges. In the Reichstag the Particular-ists, who represented the states with a predominantly Roman Catholic popula-tion, supported the Party of the Centre.

The *Poles*, *Danes* and *Alsatians* formed independent groups in the Reichstag. They also supported the Catholic Party of the Centre. Their presence in the Reichstag was accounted for by the existence in the German Empire of national minorities discontented with the policy of enforced Germanisation. It was pursued with particular ruthlessness by Bismarck in the Polish provinces annexed by Germany in 1814-15 and in Alsace and Lorraine, which Germany received as a result of the Franco-Prussian War of 1870-71. The Danish deputies in the Reichstag represented Schleswig and Holstein, annexed by Prussia in 1867. The Poles and the Alsatians were the most powerful among the national parliamentary groups.

The *men of Progress* were members of a Prussian bourgeois party founded in June 1861. The Party of Progress demanded Germany's unification under Prussian supremacy, the convocation of an all-Germany parliament and the establishment of a strong liberal ministry accountable to the Chamber of Deputies. In 1866, a Right wing split off from the Party of Progress, a section that capitulated before Bismarck and set up a National Liberal Party (see Note 15). The vacillations in the policies pursued by the Party of Progress mirrored the instability of the merchant bourgeoisie, small industrialists, and a section of the craftsmen, on whom it relied. In 1884, the Party of Progress united with the Left wing of the National Liberal Party that had split off from it to form the German Party of Free Thinkers (Deutsche Freisinnige Partei).— 182

²⁵⁷ At the Reichstag meeting of 9 January 1852, Bismarck was forced to admit that the working masses were distrustful of the government's attempts to improve their condition.— 183

²⁵⁸ This refers to the letters Leo Frankel (18 December 1881) and Walery Wróblewski (7 December 1881) sent to Marx on the occasion of his wife's death.

At the time, Frankel was detained in the prison in Vác (Austria-Hungary), where he was placed in June 1881 on the charge of breach of the press law.

By Wróblewski's 'Polish party' in Geneva Marx had in mind a group of Polish Marxist refugees with whom Wróblewski became close in the late 1870s.— 183

²⁵⁹ In July 1878, George Howell, a former member of the General Council of the International, published a libellous article, 'The History of the International Association', in *The Nineteenth Century* monthly review. The author calumniated the history of the First International and Marx's role in it. In August of the same year, Marx published an article called 'Mr. George Howell's History of the International Working-Men's Association' in *The Secular Chronicle, and Record of Freethought Progress*, Vol. X, No. 5 (see present edition, Vol. 24, pp. 234-39).

In 1881, Howell stood for election to the House of Commons in Stafford but was voted down at the elections.— 185

²⁶⁰ Engels wrote this letter at two sittings, on 25 and 31 January 1882.

Part of this letter was published in English for the first time in: Karl Marx and Frederick Engels, *Selected Correspondence*, Foreign Languages Publishing House, Moscow, 1955.— 186

²⁶¹ An allusion to the introduction of the Anti-Socialist Law (see Note 16).— 187

²⁶² It has not been established which pamphlet of Hepner's is meant.— 188, 260

²⁶³ The new imperial judicial code came into force on 1 October 1879. Engels described it in his work *The Role of Force in History* (see present edition, Vol. 26, pp. 506-08).— 188

²⁶⁴ *Code Napoléon* — a system of bourgeois law incorporating five codes (civil, civil procedural, commercial, criminal, and criminal procedural) adopted under Napoleon in 1804-10.— 188

²⁶⁵ The *Federative Union* (full name, Union fédérative du Centre, the Federative Union of the Centre), one of the six associations constituting the French Workers' Party, had been formed by April 1880. An association of the party's organisations in Paris, it consisted of 80 groups. The Union's leadership was in the hands of the party's Right opportunist wing, the Possibilists — Brousse, Malon and Joffrin (editors of the *Prolétaire*). At the meetings of the Federative Union of the Centre on 17 and 24 January 1882, the *Égalité* editorial board and all party groups siding with the Guesdists were expelled from the Federative Union. Only 28 groups voted in favour, that is, slightly more than one-third of the groups making up the Federative Union (48 groups out of the 80 were present at the meetings mentioned above). After their expulsion from the Federative Union of the Centre, the Guesdists founded a revolutionary federation and called it the Federation of the Centre (Fédération du Centre).— 190, 332, 355, 388

²⁶⁶ The *Holy Alliance* — an association of European monarchs founded in September 1815 on the initiative of the Russian Tsar Alexander I and the Austrian Chancellor Metternich to suppress the revolutionary movement.— 191, 273

²⁶⁷ The national liberation movement for the unification of Italy ended in 1861 with the establishment of a single Italian state (only Rome, which was incorporated into the Italian state after the abolition of the Pope's secular authority in 1870, remained outside it at the time). The event paved the way for the expansion of the independent workers' movement.— 191

²⁶⁸ *Little Germany* — a plan for the unification of Germany under the Prussian aegis minus Austria.

Engels is referring here to the Austro-Prussian War of 1866, which gave birth to the North German Confederation (Norddeutscher Bund), a federative state formed in 1867 to replace the disintegrated German Confederation. The establishment of the North German Confederation was a major step towards the national unification of Germany. The Confederation ceased to exist in January 1871, when the German Empire was founded.— 191

²⁶⁹ By the Lassallean party Engels implies the General Association of German Workers, the first national German workers' organisation founded on 23 May 1863 at the congress of workers' associations in Leipzig. The main organisational documents and the programme were drawn up by Ferdinand Lassalle, who became the organisation's first president. The errors in Lassalle's propaganda strategy and in his tactics, as well as the anti-democratic structure of the Association gave rise to a strong opposition, the bulk of which joined the Eisenachers.

The *Eisenach Party* — the Social-Democratic Workers' Party of Germany set up at the General Congress of German, Swiss and Austrian Social-Democrats held in Eisenach on 7-9 August 1869. The party programme declared support for the principles of the First International, although Lassallean ideas still wielded a considerable influence in it. At the Congress in Gotha in 1875, the Eisenachers and the Lassalleans formed a single party of the working class, which called itself the Socialist Workers' Party of Germany up to 1890.— 191, 342

²⁷⁰ The *Federal Diet* (Bundestag) — the central organ of the German Confederation set up by the Vienna Congress in 1815. It comprised representatives of the German states and sat in Frankfurt-am-Main under the chairmanship of the Austrian rep-

resentative. The Federal Diet ceased to exist together with the German Confederation at the time of the Austro-Prussian War of 1866.— 191

²⁷¹ A reference to the constitution of 1860 (the so-called October diploma—
Oktoberdiplom). It gave Hungary, which formed part of the Austrian monarchy,
certain rights (the convocation of a Hungarian parliament, the use of the Hungarian language in administration, etc.) The crisis of the Austrian Empire and
mounting popular discontent led to its transformation in 1867 into the dual
Austro-Hungarian monarchy. Hungary was recognised as a sovereign part of the
state. Political consolidation promoted the development of capitalism there. In
1868, the first workers' organisations emerged in the country, the Budapest Workers' Union and the General Workers' Union (subsequently the latter became the
leading organisation of the socialist workers' movement).— 191

²⁷² A reference to the events of 1873-75, when the Bismarck government tried to provoke a war with France. The Russian government resolutely sided with France.
Thanks to the pressure being put on the German government by Russia, Austria
and Britain, Bismarck's attempt failed.— 192

²⁷³ In January 1882, Bosnia and Herzegovina, which had been occupied by Austria in
1878 under the terms of the Berlin Congress, witnessed an uprising provoked by
the Austro-Hungarian government's law of 1881 on military conscription to be
introduced in the occupied territories. The uprising reached its peak in the first
half of February 1882. The Tsarist government tried to use it to promote its own
ends.— 192

²⁷⁴ This refers to the national liberation insurrection of 1863-64 in the Polish territories belonging to Tsarist Russia. The insurrection was suppressed by the Russian
government.

The anonymous book, *Berlin und St. Petersburg. Preussische Beiträge zur Geschichte
der Russisch-deutschen Beziehungen*, Leipzig, 1880, was the work of the German political writer Julius Eckardt. Appendix 2, to which Engels refers here, deals with the
Polish insurrection of 1863-64.— 193

²⁷⁵ This refers, above all, to Walery Wróblewski and Jarosław Dombrowski. Wróblewski, appointed general, commanded one of the Commune's three armies. General Dombrowski, who first headed the defence operations at one of the key sectors
of the front, later commanded the 1st Army of the Commune and in early May
1871 was appointed commander-in-chief of its armed forces.— 193

²⁷⁶ The reference is to the programme advanced in the days of the Cracow uprising
(February 1846) by Dembowski, who voiced the interests of the peasantry and the
urban poor (to give land to those who had none, radically to improve the workers'
condition by setting up national, or 'social', workshops). The National Government formed in Cracow on 22 February issued a manifesto announcing the abolition of feudal duties and taxes. The Cracow uprising was suppressed early in
March 1846. In November, Austria, Prussia and Russia signed a treaty on the annexation of the city to the Austrian empire.— 193

²⁷⁷ Engels is referring to the 'liberal course' proclaimed by William, Prince (King
from 1861) of Prussia, in October 1858, when he assumed the regency. In actual
fact, not one of the reforms expected by the bourgeoisie was carried out. William's

policy aimed at consolidating the Prussian monarchy and Junkerdom.— 194, 208, 332, 415

278 In early February 1882, following medical advice, Marx took a trip to Algiers, where he stayed from 20 February to 2 May. On the way there, he stopped over in Argenteuil (a Paris suburb) to visit his daughter Jenny Longuet (9-16 February).— 196, 199, 202, 203, 210, 369

279 In his letter to Engels of 1 February 1882, Johann Philipp Becker proposed setting up a new international workers' organisation along the lines of the International Working Men's Association.— 196

280 Under the law proposed by the Minister of Justice Dufaure, and passed by the French National Assembly on 14 March 1872, membership of the International was punished by imprisonment.— 196

281 The reference is to the situation that emerged after the assassination of Emperor Alexander II on 1 March 1881, when Alexander III sat it out in Gatchina (the Tsar's summer residence near St Petersburg) fearing fresh terrorist acts by the secret Executive Committee of the Narodnaya Volya (People's Will) organisation.— 208

282 In the course of his visit to France in the winter of 1882, General Skobelev had a meeting with Serbian students in Paris (17 February) at which he talked about the need to emancipate the Slav peoples of Europe. As in his subsequent statements, which gave rise to a great deal of anxiety and commotion in Europe, Skobelev lashed out at Germany, describing a war with it as inevitable and urging a Russo-French alliance.— 209

283 See present edition, Vol. 35, Chapter Three, 'Money, or the Circulation of Commodities'.— 210

284 The Editors are not in possession of this letter (telegram, note).— 212, 213, 216, 221, 225, 228, 245, 251, 259, 262, 283, 311, 315, 317, 337, 338, 358, 379, 393, 394, 458, 459

285 In a letter of 24 February 1882, Jenny Longuet wrote to Marx that her sister Eleanor had turned down Prosper Lissagaray's proposal of marriage.— 219

286 This letter was first published in Russian among Marx's 16 letters from the Longuet family archive by the magazine Nachalo (Beginning), No. 5, 1899. Its translation into German was printed by the Neue Deutsche Rundschau, Vol. 2 (October 1899). The Editors are not in possession of the original letter. It was published in English for the first time in an abridged form in: The Letters of Karl Marx, selected and translated with explanatory notes and an introduction by Saul K. Padover, Prentice-Hall, Inc., Englewood Cliffs, New Jersey, 1979.— 220

287 This refers to Carl Hirsch's article 'Le Socialisme en Allemagne' in Volume 15 of La Nouvelle Revue (founded by Juliette Adam), March-April 1882, and signed 'Un socialiste allemand'.— 225, 230

288 On 25 March 1882, Engels' niece Mary Ellen Rosher gave birth to a daughter, Lilian.— 228, 234

289 Marx has in mind the 'iron law of wages', which Lassalle tried to substantiate by

reference to scientific authorities in his pamphlet *Offnes Antwortschreiben an das Central-Comité zur Berufung eines Allgemeinen Deutschen Arbeitercongresses zu Leipzig*, Zurich, 1863, pp. 15-16.

For Marx's and Engels' criticism of the Lassallean law, see present edition, Vol. 24, p. 69.

By Ricardo's and Turgot's statements on the law of minimum wages, Marx means Ricardo's *On the Principles of Political Economy, and Taxation*, 3rd ed., London, 1821, pp. 73-499, and Turgot's *Réflexions sur la formation et la distribution des richesses* (1766) in *Œuvres de Turgot*, new ed., by E. Daire, Vol. 1, Paris, 1844, p. 10. Marx's critique of Ricardo's and Turgot's ideas on this issue is contained, in particular, in *Theories of Surplus Value* (Volume Four of *Capital*) (see present edition, Vol. 30, pp. 362-67, and Vol. 32, pp. 35-54).— 230, 324

290 In the extant English original, the last paragraph is missing. In this edition, it is retranslated from the Russian publication in *Nachalo*, No. 5, 1899.— 233

291 On Marx's relations with Hyndman see Marx's letter to Hyndman of 2 July 1881 (this volume, pp. 102-03).— 234

292 An ironic reference to the sycophantic statements by the German poets Friedrich Bodenstedt and Friedrich Theodor Vischer, a Hegelian, author of a four-volume work on aesthetics. Comparing them to Horace and Virgil, Marx is alluding to the fact that those Roman poets wrote panegyrics and odes to Emperor Augustus (Octavianus).— 235

293 The reference is to the proofs of the Russian translation of Marx's and Engels' preface to the second Russian edition of the *Manifesto of the Communist Party*, a project initiated by Georgi Plekhanov, who had also done the translation. The request for the preface was made through Pyotr Lavrov. Marx and Engels wrote it on 21 January 1882, and despatched it to Lavrov on 23 January. It appeared for the first time in the magazine *Narodnaya Volya* on 5 February. The *Manifesto of the Communist Party* with this preface appeared in print in 1882 in Geneva in the *Russian Socio-Revolutionary Library* series.

Engels failed to obtain the German original of the preface from Lavrov, as the latter had left it among his papers in Paris (at the time, Lavrov was expelled from Paris on the insistence of the Russian government, and moved to London). Lavrov did not send Engels a copy of the German original until about 17 April, but earlier, on 13 April, *Der Sozialdemokrat*, No. 16, featured the preface in translation from the Russian text printed by *Narodnaya Volya*. Engels did not like the translation (see this volume, p. 244). The German original of the preface was published in *MEGA* I/25, pp. 295-96.— 235

294 Engels replies to Berthold Sparr's letter of 12 April 1882.— 236

295 6 Rose Street, Soho Square, London, W. was the address of the Social-Democratic Workers' Club, which in the 1880s had a German and an English section. The German section was the first branch of the German Workers' Educational Society in London (see Note 8) and had close contacts with *Die Freiheit*, Most's newspaper.— 236

296 Engels is referring to *Die Freiheit*'s propaganda campaign against the policies and tactics of the Social-Democratic Party of Germany and the stand taken by the So-

cial-Democratic deputies in the German Reichstag. On the eve of the Reichstag elections of 1881, Most urged his followers in Germany to do their best to prevent Bebel's and Liebknecht's election to the Reichstag (for criticism of Most's and *Die Freiheit*'s position, see this volume, p. 7).— 236

297 The reference is to the German Workers' Educational Society in London (see Note 8), which in the 1880s had its offices at 49 Tottenham Street, Tottenham Court Road, London, W.— 236, 330

298 Laura Lafargue visited Eastbourne during Marx's and his wife's stay there between late June and 20 July 1881.— 238

299 *L'Union Nationale*, a French insurance company where Paul Lafargue was employed at the time.— 240

300 This refers to the sequel to Paul Lafargue's article 'Движеніе поземельной собственности во Франціи' ('The Movement of Land Property in France'). It was published in full in Russian in the *Ustoi* (Principles) magazine, Nos. 3-4 and 6, 1882.— 240

301 The reference is to Charles V's abortive campaign of 1541 in Algeria (which at the time formed part of the Ottoman Empire) under the pretext of suppressing the pirates who had made it their base. Having suffered a crushing defeat at the hands of the Turkish troops near the town of Algiers, the Spanish troops were driven from the country's other strongholds.— 241

302 Engels learned about this from Lavrov's note of 6 April 1882.— 244

303 In early April 1882, the Social-Democratic deputy Bruno Geiser received a provocative anonymous letter from New York about preparations for an insurrection in Germany. Geiser informed the police about the letter and made a statement to the effect that the German Social-Democrats had never aimed at a revolution. The leader 'Bekennt Farbe!' in *Der Sozialdemokrat*, No. 16, 13 April 1882, sharply criticised Geiser's statement and contained a reminder that the party was indeed trying to bring forward a revolution in Germany.— 244

304 Probably a reference to one of Marx's visits to his uncle Lion Philips in Zalt-Bommel (Holland). Marx visited him between 28 February and 16 March 1861, late August-early September 1862, 21 December 1863-19 February 1864 and 19 March-8 April 1865.— 246

305 On 20 April 1882, the *Kölnische Zeitung*, No. 109, carried a report marked 'Konstantinopel' which exposed the machinations of Baron Moritz Hirsch, a notorious Austrian railway speculator to whom Turkey had granted a railway concession.— 247

306 An allusion to the poetic efforts of King Ludwig I of Bavaria, whose trivial verses, later completely forgotten, diverged from proper German grammar and provoked a great deal of ridicule.— 249

307 The Editors do not have Darwin's letter to Marx; Longuet mentioned it in Darwin's obituary carried by *La Justice* and reprinted by *Der Sozialdemokrat*, No. 18, 27 April 1882 (the note 'Darwin').— 251

308 The mounting discontent of the Irish people forced Gladstone's government to

make certain concessions, notably to repeal the emergency measures introduced in 1881 (see Note 123). On 2 May 1882, the leaders of the Irish national movement were released from prison. The Viceroy of Ireland Francis Thomas Cowper and Secretary for Ireland William Forster, both advocates of emergency measures, resigned.— 251

309 Engels alludes to the numerous terrorist acts in Ireland in 1882 provoked by the intolerable position of the tenants there: twice as many landlords, their agents, British government officials, and others were assassinated as compared with the previous years.— 252

310 Having left Algiers on 2 May 1882 on his doctor's advice, Marx travelled to Monte Carlo via Marseilles and Nice, and lived there for a month, up to 3 June.— 252, 253, 369

311 Engels stopped over in Genoa on 5-6 October 1849 on his way from Switzerland (he had emigrated there after the defeat of the Baden-Palatinate uprising) to England. He had to travel via Italy since he was liable to be arrested if he entered Germany or France.— 253

312 The newly appointed Chief Secretary for Ireland, Lord Cavendish, and the deputy of the previous secretary, Thomas Henry Burke, were assassinated on 6 May 1882 in Phoenix Park, Dublin, by members of the terrorist organisation called The Invincible, which included former Fenians (the Fenians were a secret Irish revolutionary, or republican, brotherhood, which fought for Irish independence and the establishment of an Irish republic in the 1850s-60s). Marx and Engels disapproved of the terrorist and anarchist tactics of the Fenians' epigones (see this volume, p. 247).— 254, 286

313 In the manuscript the letter is dated 10 March. This is a slip of the pen, since Engels is replying here to the question Eduard Bernstein asked about Mary-Isis in his letter of 4 May.— 256

314 The reference is to the exchange of opinions between Engels and Bernstein concerning Engels' article 'Bruno Bauer and Early Christianity' written in the second half of April 1882. It was published in Der Sozialdemokrat, 4 and 11 May.— 256

315 See present edition, Vol. 35, Chapter III.— 257

316 In his letter to Engels of 4 October 1882, Bernstein made inquiries about the Zurich businessman Louis Bamberger, who had claimed he knew Marx, Engels and Freiligrath.— 258

317 Engels is referring to Bebel's letter to Marx of 12 December 1881 in which he offered Marx his condolences on the death of his wife, Jenny. He also wrote about the difficulties being encountered by Der Sozialdemokrat and the results of the Reichstag elections of 1881, in which the Social-Democrats had done quite well.— 259

318 Engels is referring to the materials carried by Der Sozialdemokrat, Nos. 4, 5 and 9 on 19, 26 January and 23 February 1882. They gave a rebuff to Ernst Breuel's two open letters (Nos. 4 and 9, 19 January and 23 February) in which he accused the editors of bias, anarchist leanings, etc., in connection with their criticism of Wilhelm Hasenclever's and Wilhelm Blos' opportunist stand (see Note 240).— 259

319 The Echternach procession— an annual festival held on Trinity Sunday ever since the

Middle Ages in the town of Echternach (Luxembourg) as a token of gratitude for the subsidence of the St Vitus' dance, epidemic that raged there in 1374. The members of the procession do not just move forward but make more complicated forward and backward steps.— 262

320 The German playwright and literary critic Amadeus Gottfried Adolf Müllner gave pride of place in his plays to fate and predestination. Necessary romantic attributes of the so-called tragedies of fate were unlucky days, ill omens, fatal weapons, etc.; the plot usually had a tragic end.— 263

321 Presumably this refers to Engels' letter received by Marx before 20 May 1882.— 266

322 Here and below, Marx ironically alludes to Offenbach's comic opera *The Duchess of Gerolstein*; in the latter half of the 19th century, the leading part in it was played by the famous French actress and singer Hortense Schneider.— 268

323 On his way from Monte Carlo to Argenteuil Marx stopped over in Cannes between 3 and 5 June 1882.— 272

324 Garibaldi died on 2 June 1882 of bronchial catarrh.— 274

325 A joking allusion to the Old Testament dictums about dust being the serpent's meat (Genesis 3:14, and Isaiah 65:25), as well as to Darwin's book *The Formation of Vegetable Mould, through the Action of Worms, with Observations on Their Habits*, London, 1881. According to Darwin, worms help in the formation of humus by digging up the earth and passing it through their bowels.— 274

326 An ironic allusion to Adolph von Knigge's work *Ueber den Umgang mit Menschen* (Hanover, 1804) laying down the rules of human behaviour in contacts with other people. Knigge's opus abounded in superficial discourse and truisms.— 274

327 Between 6 June and 22 August, Marx stayed with his daughter Jenny Longuet in Argenteuil.— 275, 305, 369

328 After more than nine years of emigration in London Paul Lafargue returned to Paris in early April 1882.— 275, 276

329 This meeting held by the Democratic Federation (see Note 158) on 11 June 1882, in which about 40,000 people took part, was in protest at the introduction of new Coercion Bills in Ireland (see Note 123).— 276

330 The letter was published in English for the first time in the magazine *Science and Society*, Vol. II, No. 2, New York, 1938 (the first paragraph of the letter was omitted).— 278

331 In a letter of 5 May 1882, Sorge asked Engels to pay for his subscription to several newspapers (promising to send him the money later) and to look through the English translation of the *Manifesto of the Communist Party* which Engels had received previously and which Sorge intended to publish in the United States. He also asked Engels for a preface or an afterword for this publication.— 278

332 Engels ironically compares the opportunist-minded Social-Democratic deputies in the Reichstag with the bourgeois constitutionalists at the time of the 1848-49 revolution in Germany, whom democratic republicans had nicknamed 'wailers' ('Heuler').— 279

³³³ This article outlined the programme of the opportunist trend in the German So-
cial-Democratic Party after the promulgation of the Anti-Socialist Law in Germany in October 1878. Marx and Engels subjected the article to a detailed analysis and crushing critique in their 'Circular Letter to August Bebel, Wilhelm
Liebknecht, Wilhelm Bracke and Others', III. The Manifesto of the Zurich Trio
(see present edition, Vol. 24, pp. 262-69).— 280

³³⁴ The *Brimstone Gang* (Schwefelbande)—the name of a students' association at Jena
University in the 1770s, whose members were notorious for their brawls. Subsequently, the phrase became widespread. In 1849-50, a group of German petty-
bourgeois refugees in Geneva were known by this name. In 1859, the Bonapartist
agent Karl Vogt slanderously linked the activities of this 'Brimstone gang' with
Marx and his followers. Marx dealt with the matter in his pamphlet *Herr Vogt*
(present edition, Vol. 17, pp. 28-37).— 281

³³⁵ The event described by Engels took place during the Baden-Palatinate uprising in
May-July 1849, in which he was involved (see his work 'The Campaign for the
German Imperial Constitution', present edition, Vol. 10, pp. 149-239).— 281

³³⁶ The first article which appeared in *Der Sozialdemokrat* under Engels' name was the
obituary 'Jenny Marx, née von Westphalen' (No. 50, 8 December 1881; see present edition, Vol. 24, pp. 422-24). But he considered his first official contribution to
the newspaper to be the article 'Bruno Bauer and Early Christianity' (No. 19,
4 May 1882).— 283

³³⁷ The reference is to the Congress of the Federative Union of the Centre held on 14-
21 May 1882 in Paris, which confirmed the decisions to expel the editors of *L'Égalité* passed by the meetings of the Federative Union of the Centre held on 17 and
24 January (see Note 265). The note entitled 'Frankreich' in *Der Sozialdemokrat*,
No. 23, 1 June 1882 denounced the congress decision on the expulsion of the *Égalité* group. The passage mentioned in this letter appeared, in translation, in *L'Égalité*, No. 27, 3rd series, 11 June 1882. The Editors do not have the issue of the
Prolétaire with the reply to this.— 283, 341

³³⁸ Adolf Hepner, a German Social-Democrat who had emigrated to the United
States, wrote to Engels on 3 May 1882 asking for permission to reprint Marx's
and Engels' works in the USA. (For Engels' reply to Hepner on his own and Marx's
behalf, see this volume, pp. 294-95).— 284

³³⁹ On 18 May 1882, *Der Sozialdemokrat* (No. 21) featured a leader 'Die Situation in
Irland' written by Bernstein under the pen-name Leo. Engels considered it necessary to explain his stand in a letter to Bernstein. The latter passed it on to Liebknecht, who included a major part of it, without the author's permission and with
editorial comments, in the article 'Zur irischen Frage' printed by *Der Sozialdemokrat* No. 29 on 13 July 1882. Liebknecht supplied the letter with a polemical conclusion and the following editorial introduction: 'A friend of Ireland, familiar with the
country and the people as few people are, writes to us from London about his disagreement on individual points with the opinion set forth in *Der Sozialdemokrat*,
No. 21.' Engels voiced his protest at the unauthorised publication in a letter to
Bernstein of 9 August 1882 (see this volume, pp. 300-01).

Part of the original has been lost, which is why the letter is printed according to

Der Sozialdemokrat and partly to the extant original manuscript. The letter was published in English for the first time, in part, in: Marx and Engels, *On Colonialism*, Foreign Languages Publishing House, Moscow, 1959.— 285, 301

340 *Ribbonmen*—participants in the peasant movement that arose in Northern Ireland in the late 18th century. They were united in secret groups, whose emblem was a strip of green cloth.

Whiteboys—participants in the Irish peasant movement, which in the 1760s grew into a large-scale rebellion against the rule of English landlords. To make themselves unrecognisable, these men, who usually acted at night, painted their faces black and wore white shirts. In the 19th century, many of their societies merged with those of the Ribbonmen, but some continued to operate under their old name up to the end of the century.

Captain Rock—the name of the members of the various secret peasant societies that emerged and operated in Ireland between the second half of the 18th and the mid-19th century.

Captain Moonlight—the usual signature under warnings sent by the Ribbonmen's secret society to landlords.— 285

341 *Catholic Emancipation*—the abolition of restrictions on the political rights of Catholics in Ireland by the British Parliament in 1829 as a result of a mass movement. Catholics were granted the right to stand for election to Parliament and to hold certain government offices. Simultaneously, the property qualification was raised fivefold. The British ruling classes hoped this manoeuvre would bring the élite of the Irish bourgeoisie and Catholic landowners over to their side and cause a split in the Irish national movement.— 286

342 A reference to the conflict between the USA and Great Britain caused by the latter's aid to the Southern states during the American Civil War of 1861-65. The British government built and equipped warships for the Southerners, which greatly undermined the Northerners' trade by their actions. Among the vessels was the *Alabama*, a privateering ship that sank 70 Northerners' vessels. After the war, the US government demanded that the British government make full reparations for the damage inflicted by the *Alabama* and other privateering vessels to the property of American citizens. Under the decision of an arbitration court passed in Geneva on 14 September 1872, Britain was to pay $15.5 mln to the United States, which it indeed did.— 287

343 An allusion to the weekly newspaper *Die Freiheit* published in London by Johann Most, a German anarchist refugee, and edited by Karl Schneidt. The newspaper was obsessed with ultra-revolutionary rhetoric and notorious for its rude attacks against the policies and tactics of the Socialist Workers' Party of Germany and its activists.— 289

344 The reference is to the events that occurred at the congress of the Federative Union of the Centre held on 14-21 May 1882 (see Note 337).
On the *National Committee*, see Note 250.— 289

345 The *Wyden Conference* of the Socialist Workers' Party of Germany (August 1880) instructed the party leadership to set up a communication office that would establish and maintain contacts with the German Social-Democrats and the socialist parties and organisations in other countries.— 290

[346] This refers to Franz Mehring's article in the bourgeois newspaper *Weser-Zeitung* of 2 July 1882. An opponent of the Social-Democratic movement at the time, Mehring lashed out against *Der Sozialdemokrat*. He referred to Marx's and Engels' disagreement with the editorial board and stressed the paper's 'lack of tact', for which, he alleged, German workers were being constantly persecuted. By way of conclusion, Mehring promised further exposures of the newspaper. He also wrote about Marx's poor health and predicted he might be unable to complete his work on *Capital*. The *Sozialdemokrat*'s editors used the advice by Engels given here in an article against Mehring written in quite harsh terms and printed under the heading 'In eigener Sache' in No. 31, 27 July 1882.— 291, 299, 301, 377

[347] Engels is referring to his article 'Bruno Bauer and Early Christianity' published in *Der Sozialdemokrat*, Nos. 19 and 20 on 4 and 11 May 1882 (see present edition, Vol. 24, pp. 427-35).— 292

[348] In a letter of 11 May 1882, Kautsky asked for Engels' opinion on the future of the colonies, notably those in Asia, after the victory of the European proletariat. Kautsky's second letter on this subject is dated 31 May 1882.— 292

[349] This letter was published in English for the first time in: Karl Marx and Frederick Engels, *Letters to Americans. 1848-1895*. A Selection, International Publishers, New York, 1953.— 293, 466

[350] In his letter of 3 May 1882, Adolf Hepner, a German Social-Democrat who had emigrated to the United States, asked Engels for permission to publish his and Marx's works in the *Arbeiter-Library* series.— 293

[351] A reference to Johann Most's pamphlet *Kapital und Arbeit. Ein populärer Auszug aus 'Das Kapital' von Karl Marx*. 2nd edition, Chemnitz [1876]. The first edition appeared in Chemnitz in 1873. On Liebknecht's request, Marx, with Engels' help, made changes in and additions to the second edition. For Marx's appraisal of this publication, see Engels' letter to Philip Van Patten of 18 April 1883, present edition, Vol. 47.— 294

[352] A reference to the second Russian edition of Marx's and Engels' *Manifesto of the Communist Party* (see Note 293).— 295

[353] The growth of the Egyptian national movement in the early 1880s (see Note 355) led to a provisional alliance between Britain and France. On the eve of the conflict with Egypt provoked by Britain in July 1882, there were differences of opinion among French politicians: the former Prime Minister Gambetta and Freycinet, who replaced him in January 1882 (see Note 356), favoured intervention. The radical leader Clemenceau, who sought revenge on Germany, opposed the idea of an invasion, insisting that it would further aggravate the Anglo-French contradictions and thus consolidate the position of Germany.— 296

[354] *Engadine*—a Swiss mountain watering place famous for its extremely healthy climate.— 297

[355] In 1879-82, Egypt witnessed an upsurge of the national liberation movement against British and French capital which had established direct financial control over the country (in 1878, representatives of Britain and France were made ministers of the Egyptian government and given the right of veto). The insurrection of the Cairo garrison forced the Khedive of Egypt (see Note 362) to issue a constitu-

tion in September 1881. In December, Egypt acquired a parliament led by the National Party which had been founded that same year and represented a bloc of liberal landowners and merchants with the patriotically minded officers and intellectuals supported by the peasantry and petty bourgeoisie. The National Party set the country's independence as its target ('Egypt for Egyptians'). However, in the summer of 1882, having provoked a conflict with Egypt, Britain opened hostilities, which, despite the resistance of the Egyptian troops headed by Colonel Arabi, ended in a British victory. In September, they captured Cairo, and Egypt became their colony to all intents and purposes.

The public meetings of protest against the British aggression and the bombardment of Alexandria mentioned by Marx were organised in Paris by the Federation of the Centre (see Note 230) in late July 1882 with the participation of the *Citoyen* editors Henri Brissac, Jules Guesde and Paul Lafargue. The Guesdists' resolution on Egypt hailed Arabi Pasha and the National Party as worthy of the great mission they had assumed.— 298, 301, 313, 317, 319, 323, 335

356 Freycinet agreed to cooperation with Britain only in the Suez Canal zone. His proposal was turned down by the Chamber of Deputies on 29 July 1882, and his cabinet resigned.— 298

357 Marx is referring to the Quadruple Alliance, the convention of the four powers, Britain, Russia, Austria and Prussia, signed on 15 July 1840 in London. Its objective was to render military aid to the Sultan of Turkey against the Egyptian ruler Mohammed Ali to settle the Egyptian crisis of 1839-41, which arose from the rivalry of the European powers over hegemony in Egypt and the Middle East.— 298

358 Engels is referring to Johann Philipp Becker's letter of 2 August 1882, in reply to his own letter of 10 February 1882 (see this volume, pp. 196-98).— 300

359 Part of this letter was published in English for the first time in: Marx and Engels, *On Colonialism*, Foreign Languages Publishing House, Moscow, 1959.— 300

360 The reference is to the French edition of Engels' work *Socialism: Utopian and Scientific* (see Note 20) and the plans for a German edition. Bernstein wrote to Engels about the need for such an edition on 7 July 1882 (see Note 378) and asked for a short afterword on Bismarck's state socialism.— 300, 336

361 *Der Sozialdemokrat*, No. 32, 3 August 1882, published the article 'Die Socialdemokratie und die egyptische Frage', which approved of the resolution passed by the meeting convened in Paris by the Guesdists. They protested against the bombardment of Alexandria by the British and hailed Arabi Pasha and the National Party.— 301

362 *Khedive*— the title (1867-1914) of the viceroy of Egypt.— 302

363 *Fellah*— a peasant or agricultural labourer in Egypt. The fellaheen constituted the lowest exploited class of the rural population.— 302

364 The contribution Engels had promised for the feuilleton was the old English folk song 'The Vicar of Bray', which he translated into German in early September 1882; the translation, with Engels' comments on the political significance it had for Germany, was published under his name by *Der Sozialdemokrat*, No. 37, 7 September 1882 (see present edition, Vol. 24, pp. 436-38).— 302

365 On 16 September 1882, Jenny Longuet gave birth to a daughter named Jenny after her grandmother.— 303, 309, 329, 331, 372

[366] Engels spent his holiday in Great Yarmouth on the east coast of England from 11 August to 8 September 1882.— 305, 306

[367] Engels terminated his employment at the Manchester trade firm on 1 July 1869 and moved to London on 20 September 1870.— 306

[368] On 2 August 1882 Paul Brousse, S. Deynaud, Victor Marouck and Louis Mouttet resigned from the *Bataille* editorial board. The reason they gave for their split with its editor-in-chief Prosper Lissagaray was secretary J. Labusquière's announcement that he was resigning from the paper because Lissagaray was restricting his initiative, controlling his actions and keeping a check on the contributions of the above-mentioned editors, Labusquière's friends.— 309

[369] Marx and his daughter Laura stayed in Lausanne from 23 to 27 August 1882.— 310

[370] Marx stayed in Argenteuil between 26 July and 16 August 1881 and 9 and 16 February 1882.— 310

[371] On 2 August 1882, the Belgian socialist César De Paepe, suspecting Arthur Duverger, secretary of the magazine *L'Europe*, where he himself was also employed at the time, of having an affair with his wife, gravely wounded him. The jury acquitted De Paepe.— 312

[372] This refers to the speech made on 23 August 1882 by Carl Wilhelm Siemens, President of the British Association for the Advancement of Science, at the Association's 52nd congress in Southampton. It was published in *Nature*, No. 669, 24 August 1882.

The *British Association for the Advancement of Science* was founded in 1831 and still exists; the materials of its annual meetings are published as reports.— 314, 384

[373] Engels lived in Switzerland (Geneva, Lausanne, Neuchâtel and Berne) from the second half of October 1848 to mid-January 1849 and from 12 July to early October 1849. In 1849, he also visited Vevey (Canton Vaud), where he stayed from 24 July to about 20 August.— 314, 329

[374] Marx and his daughter Laura Lafargue stayed in Vevey (Canton Vaud, Switzerland) from 27 August to 25 September 1882.— 315, 317, 334, 335, 369

[375] A reference to the ceremonies held in Rome and throughout Italy on 11 June 1882 to commemorate Giuseppe Garibaldi, who died on 2 June.— 317

[376] The international congress attended by representatives of Russia, Germany, Austria-Hungary, France, Great Britain, Italy and Turkey and chaired by Bismarck was held in Berlin between 13 June and 13 July 1878. The congress ended with the signing of the Berlin Treaty revising the terms of the San Stefano preliminary treaty of 1878 that terminated the Russo-Turkish War of 1877-78 to the detriment of Russia and the Slav peoples of the Balkans. The territory of self-governing Bulgaria defined by the San Stefano Treaty was more than halved; the Bulgarian districts south of the Balkans were to form an autonomous province called Eastern Rumelia and remain under the Sultan; and the territory of Montenegro was significantly curtailed. The Berlin Treaty confirmed the article of the San Stefano Treaty that returned to Russia the part of Bessarabia lost in 1856 but it also sanctioned the occupation of Bosnia and Herzegovina by Austria-Hungary.— 319, 471, 472

377   In a letter of 11 May 1882 Kautsky asked Engels to give his opinion of the future of the colonies in Asia after the victory of the European proletariat. As for Kautsky himself, he asserted that the British proletariat and India would both benefit if India remained under Britain.— 321

378   A reference to the preparation of the German edition of Engels' work *Socialism: Utopian and Scientific* (see Note 360). As he had promised, Engels prepared the German text by making additions to and changes in it, and wrote a preface (present edition, Vol. 24, pp. 457-59). He also supplemented it by his essay 'The Mark' (ibid., pp. 439-56) on the emergence and development of landed property in Germany. The work was finished in September 1882, and the pamphlet was printed in Hottingen-Zurich at the end of the year and was on sale in early 1883 under the title *Die Entwicklung des Sozialismus von der Utopie zur Wissenschaft.*— 324, 331, 344, 352, 353, 358, 369, 390, 395, 416, 433, 454

379   The plan for a series of articles or a pamphlet about Bismarck and Lassalle was not carried out by Engels.— 324

380   Engels touches here on the Lassallean tenet about 'a fair distribution of the proceeds of labour', which found expression in the Gotha Programme. Marx analysed it in his work *Critique of the Gotha Programme* (present edition, Vol. 24, pp. 83-88).— 324

381   This refers to the merger of the two German workers' parties, the Eisenachers and the Lassalleans (see Note 269), which took place at the Gotha Unity Congress held between 22 and 27 May 1875.— 324, 343

382   At the 29 May meeting of the Gotha Congress of the Socialist Workers' Party of Germany (27-29 May 1877), Johann Most proposed that the party's central printed organ should no longer feature articles like Engels' pieces criticising Dühring. He was supported by Carl Julius Vahlteich. August Bebel suggested a compromise: *Vorwärts* was to terminate publication of Engels' articles against Dühring, which were to appear as a separate pamphlet put out by *Vorwärts* publishers. Wilhelm Liebknecht resolutely opposed Most's and Vahlteich's proposal, reminding the audience that the decision to have Engels' works published had been passed by the previous congress, that, in significance, they were second only to Marx's *Capital*, and that they were essential to promote the interests of the party. Liebknecht made an amendment to Bebel's proposal: to publish such articles in the *Vorwärts* theoretical supplement or in *Die Zukunft* magazine, or as separate pamphlets. The congress approved Bebel's proposal with Liebknecht's amendment. Parts II and III of *Anti-Dühring* were published in the supplement to the *Vorwärts.*— 325

383   A reference to two articles by Georg Heinrich Vollmar published anonymously in *Der Sozialdemokrat*, Nos. 34 and 35, 17 and 24 August 1882 under the heading 'Aufhebung des Ausnahmegesetzes?'. In the same year, they appeared in Hottingen-Zurich as a separate pamphlet entitled *Aufhebung des Sozialistengesetzes? Ein Wort zur Taktik der deutschen Sozialdemokratie* (signed 'Surtur').— 325, 332, 336, 349, 352, 357

384   Engels is referring to his translation of the English song 'The Vicar of Bray' (see Note 364), sung to a folk tune.— 326, 331

385   *Kabyles*, a branch of the great Berber people living in Northern Algeria.— 327

[386] On 15 September 1882, *La Bataille* and *Le Citoyen* carried notices of Bebel's death. On 16 September, the *Journal de Genève* reported that Bebel died in Zwickau.— 328

[387] Engels did not carry this plan through.— 332

[388] Marx and Engels repeatedly wrote about taxation in the *Neue Rheinische Zeitung* in 1848-49 (see, e. g., 'No More Taxes!!!', 'Appeal', 'The Trial of the Rhenish District Committee of Democrats', present edition, Vol. 8, pp. 36, 41 and 323-39). In 1850, Marx took up the issue of taxes in his work *The Class Struggles in France. 1848 to 1850*; it was also dealt with in Marx's and Engels' 'Address of the Central Authority to the League, March 1850' and some other works (see present edition, Vol. 10, pp. 45-145, 277-87).— 332

[389] An allusion to the notices of Marx's death printed by some German bourgeois papers in late 1881.— 335

[390] See also Note 346.— 335

[391] An allusion to the Biblical legend about the Jews' flight from Egyptian captivity.

In 1875, assisted by the Rothschild banking house in Britain and in France (Erlanger was the Rothschilds' representative in Egypt), the British Prime Minister Disraeli bought for the British government the Suez Canal shares belonging to the Egyptian Khedive.— 337

[392] On his way back from Switzerland to London, from 28 September to the first days of October Marx stayed with his daughter Jenny Longuet in Argenteuil, whence he made several trips to Paris.— 337

[393] In a letter to Engels of 28 September 1882, Laura Lafargue wrote that on 26 September, on their way from Vevey to France, she and Marx had met Johann Philipp Becker in Geneva. Bad weather drove them away the next day.— 337

[394] The reference is to the two congresses of French socialists held simultaneously in the autumn of 1882: that of the Possibilists in St-Étienne and that of the Guesdists (Marxists) in Roanne.

At the regular Congress of the French Workers' Party convened in St-Étienne on 25 September 1882, a split took place. The Marxist (Guesdist) deputies left the Congress and assembled in Roanne on 26 September, declaring themselves the Sixth Congress of the French Workers' Party. The Possibilists, who stayed in St-Étienne, rejected, both formally and essentially, the programme drawn up with Marx's participation and approved at the Congress in Le Havre in November 1880 (see Note 68), and granted the districts the right to produce their own election manifestos. In Engels' words, in the programme, approved by the St-Étienne Congress after a revision of its preamble, its 'proletarian class character has been eliminated' (see this volume, pp. 341-42). The congress expelled from the party the leaders and activists of its Marxist wing: Jules Guesde, Paul Lafargue, Émile Massard, Gabriel Deville, Fréjac and Gustave Bazin, and approved a new name for the party, Fédération française des travailleurs socialistes révolutionnaires.

The Marxist congress in Roanne, which sat up to 1 October, confirmed its commitment to the Marxist programme and retained the old name, the French Workers' Party. It had its stronghold among workers in the major industrial centres and certain groups of the Paris proletariat, mainly at big factories. The Possibilists were followed by Parisian artisans, as well as by workers in the south (Marseilles) and west (Brittany), who were still under the influence of petty-bourgeois ideas.— 339, 341, 350, 361, 406, 408

395 Marx paraphrases the beginning of a saying popular in the early Middle Ages in the European countries: 'The devil was sick, the devil a monk would be; the devil was well, the devil a monk was he'.— 339

396 *Radicals* (the 1880s and 1890s) — a French parliamentary group that had split off from the bourgeois party of moderate republicans ('opportunists'). Their leader was Clemenceau. The radicals put forward a bourgeois-democratic programme virtually abandoned by the 'parent' party: abolition of the Senate, separation of the Church from the state, introduction of progressive income taxes. In order to win voters over to its side, the group also demanded shorter working hours, disability pensions, and some other social and economic steps.— 342

397 An allusion to Vollmar's second article, 'Aufhebung des Ausnahmegesetzes?' (see Note 383).— 342

398 It has not been established just what material Engels enclosed with the letter. It may be the article 'Aus Frankreich' featured by *Der Sozialdemokrat*, No. 45, 2 November 1882.— 344

399 *Coup de Jarnac* — a treacherous blow. The expression originated with the name of one of the fighters in a duel that took place on 10 July 1547, Guy Chabot de Jarnac, who dealt his adversary a cunningly aimed surprise blow, which proved lethal.— 344

400 The reference is to the challenge to a duel sent by Prosper Lissagaray to Paul Lafargue; likening Lissagaray to the French politician and journalist Paul Adolph Granier de Cassagnac, Engels is ironically hinting at Cassagnac's scandalous press publications, which led to a number of duels and trials for libel.— 345

401 Part of this letter was published in English for the first time in *The Labour Monthly*, London, 1933, Vol. 15, No. 9.— 346

402 In August 1882, during a miners' strike at Montceau-les-Mines the anarchists staged a number of provocations, laying the blame on the strikers. The arrested men were brought to court in October.— 347, 406

403 A reference to the first Factory Act passed by the Swiss government on 23 March 1877, which came into force on 1 March 1878 as the Union Law on the Labour Conditions at Factories (das Bundesgesetz betreffend die Arbeit in den Fabriken).— 347, 364, 373

404 *Ringleader* (Haupt-Chef) — at the Cologne Communist trial in 1852, a Prussian police official, Stieber, thus called agent provocateur Cherval, seeking to ascribe to him the leading role in the Communist League and create an impression that he had contacts with Marx and the accused in the trial (see Marx's pamphlet *Revelations Concerning the Communist Trial in Cologne*, present edition, Vol. 11, pp. 407-19).— 347

405 Liebknecht was in prison from 15 October 1882; Bebel received a jail sentence to begin on 1 November 1882 and served it in the Leipzig prison until 9 March 1883.— 348, 350, 453

[406] According to the Bible, during the Jews' flight from Egyptian captivity, the weak-spirited among them, driven by hunger and privation, began to yearn for the days spent in captivity, when they were at least well fed.— 349

[407] Engels is referring to August Bebel's article 'Aufhebung des Sozialistengesetzes?' in *Der Sozialdemokrat*, No. 42, 12 October 1882, directed against two Vollmar's articles printed in *Der Sozialdemokrat* and as a separate pamphlet (see Note 383). Bebel's critique was spearheaded mostly against Vollmar's second article, in which the author advocated putsch tactics and a secret organisation of the party. Bebel denounced these tactics as unacceptable and even fatal for the party. In a letter to Engels of 1 October 1882, he explained that the imprudent language and tone of the articles like those by Vollmar could well entail unnecessary losses in the party.— 349, 357

[408] Lassalle's tenet that, with respect to the proletariat, all the other classes were 'one reactionary mass' was incorporated in the programme of the Social-Democratic Party of Germany approved at the Gotha Congress (see Note 381). For a criticism of this tenet, see Marx's work 'Critique of the Gotha Programme' (present edition, Vol. 24, pp. 88-89). In this letter, Engels uses the phrase 'single reactionary mass'.— 349, 357

[409] After Bebel's critique of Vollmar's articles published as a separate pamphlet under the pen-name 'Surtur' (see Note 383), the Right-wing Social Democrat Louis Viereck stated in his newspaper *Süddeutsche Post* that the pamphlet did not express the opinion of the party. *Der Sozialdemokrat* (No. 44, 26 October 1882) protested at Viereck's statement, stressing that the articles comprising the pamphlet were written by a party member and originally published by the party's printed organ.— 350

[410] Léon Picard's article mentioned here appeared in *Le Citoyen* on 3 September 1882 under the heading 'L'affaire de la rue Saint-Marc'. Chauvinistic in spirit, it was disclaimed by the editorial board. The article set the German refugees against the Guesdists (for details, see Engels' letter to Bernstein of 4 November 1882, this volume, pp. 359-60).— 352, 354, 360

[411] Marx stayed in the south of England in Ventnor (the Isle of Wight) between 30 October 1882 and 13 January 1883.— 353, 363, 368, 406, 419, 429, 430

[412] The Cuban revolutionaries General Antonio Maceo and two of his fellow-officers arrested by the Spanish government escaped from prison in Cadiz in August 1882 and sought political asylum in the Gibraltar fortress on British territory. On 20 August they arrived at the fortress but were instantly arrested and handed over to the Spanish police. At the House of Commons sittings of 31 October and 7 November, members of Gladstone's Liberal government (Ashley, Charles Dilke et al.) attempted to justify the Gibraltar authorities. At the same time, they denied that the government in London had anything to do with the matter.— 353, 365, 373

[413] Part of this letter was published in English for the first time in: K. Marx, F. Engels, V. I. Lenin, *On Scientific Communism*, Progress Publishers, Moscow, 1967.— 353

[414] Engels planned to write a pamphlet about Bismarck and Lassalle (see this volume, pp. 324-25, 433).— 353, 359

[415] The *Rosetta Stone*, a basalt slab found in Egypt near the town of Rosetta by an of-

ficer of Napoleon's expeditionary corps in August 1799. It had a text carved out on it in the Egyptian hieroglyphic, Egyptian demotic and Greek languages. In 1822, the hieroglyphic text was deciphered by the French scholar J. F. Champollion. The slab is kept at the British Museum in London.— 354

⁴¹⁶ The reference is to the conflict between Guesde's followers and anarchist Godard, whom they accused of taking a bribe from the French gas company. In a letter to Engels that has not survived, Bernstein probably voiced his disapproval of the Guesdists' stand in the Godard affair.

On the comparative prestige of the parties that were formed after the split of the French Workers' Party at the St-Étienne Congress, see Engels' letter to Bernstein of 28 November 1882 (this volume, pp. 386-90) in which Engels used the information contained in Lafargue's letter of 24 November.— 355, 383, 389

⁴¹⁷ Engels uses the old battle cry, 'Hie Welf, Hie Waibling!', of the two rival medieval political parties, of which one supported the Welf, and the other, the Hohenstaufen (or Waibling, from the name of their family residence and the town), dynasty. The cry sounded for the first time, or so the legend has it, during the battle at Weinsberg in 1140. Later, at the time of the struggle between the Popes and the German emperors in Italy in the 12th-15th centuries, the rivalry was between the Guelphs and the Ghibellines (the German names changed Italian-fashion).— 357

⁴¹⁸ The *Wyden Conference* — the first congress of the German Social Democrats after the promulgation of the Anti-Socialist Law (see Note 16) held on 20-23 August 1880 in Wyden Castle, Canton of Zurich (Switzerland).— 358

⁴¹⁹ The Editors are not in possession of Lafargue's letter to which Engels is referring. What is meant here is probably Brissac's and Bouis' resignation from the *Égalité* editorial board, and the political vacillations of Picard, an editor of *L'Égalité* and *Le Citoyen*.— 358

⁴²⁰ At the general elections in Italy in October 1882, socialist Andrea Costa was elected to parliament from the city of Ravenna thus becoming the first socialist deputy in the country's history.

The elections to the Norwegian parliament (Storting), in which the republicans scored an impressive victory, were held in September-November 1882.— 358, 454

⁴²¹ At the meeting held on 29 October 1882 in Constituency No. 18 in Montmartre, where Clemenceau was deputy, the working-class voters shouted him down.— 361

⁴²² In late 1882, Eduard Bernstein and Georg Heinrich von Vollmar planned to open a discussion in *Der Sozialdemokrat* with a view to introducing changes into the party programme. The Editors followed Engels' advice and confined themselves to indirect criticism of the opportunist demands contained in the Gotha programme.— 362

⁴²³ A reference to the negotiations between the *Égalité* editorial board and the Banque populaire in Paris concerning the financing of *L'Égalité*, 4th series (it appeared between 24 October and 28 December 1882).— 363, 373

⁴²⁴ The term '*dynamiters*' gained wide currency in European conservative quarters in the 1870s-80s and was applied to the revolutionary terrorists and persons who manufactured and stored explosives. *L'Égalité*, 4th series, No. 19, 11 November

1882, which reprinted the telegram from *The Standard* of 6 November, explained the recent political reprisals in France by the negotiations about the extradition of the 'dynamiters' (Russian political refugees).— 363

[425] This probably refers to the account of the National Committee report at the St-Étienne Congress (see Note 394) printed in *Le Prolétaire*. The report was spearheaded, almost in toto, against Guesde, Lafargue and other leaders of the revolutionary section of the Workers' Party of France and included a one-sided selection of fragments from Lafargue's letters to Benoît Malon. The Editors are not in possession of a copy of the issue of *Le Prolétaire* mentioned here.— 363, 394

[426] At an Electricity Exhibition in Munich (1882), the French physicist Marcel Deprez demonstrated the first experimental electric transmission line he had installed between Miesbach and Munich.— 364, 374, 449

[427] Marcel Deprez published the results of his research into electricity mostly in the journal *La Lumière Électrique* for 1881 and 1882. His works on electric power transmission appeared in the journal *Électricité* for 1881.— 364

[428] Marx is referring to the sensational news concerning the participation of Rivers Wilson, managing director of the English Public Debts Administration, and of Lord Sherbrooke as proxies and trustees of the Texas Galveston and Eagle railway joint-stock company. As a result of the M.P.s' interpellations in the House of Commons on 6 November 1882 pertaining to the incompatibility of British officials holding responsible jobs in the finances with their participation as trustees in speculative ventures, Rivers Wilson and Lord Sherbrooke were forced to divest themselves of the powers of company trustees.— 365, 376

[429] Marx alludes to the debate on events in Egypt (see Note 355) in the House of Commons on 6 and 7 November 1882.— 365

[430] The second edition of Alexander Redgrave's book *The Factory and Workshop Act, 1878*, with introduction, copious notes, and an elaborate index (London, 1879) was received by Marx from King's company. The copy, with Marx's notes, is extant.— 368

[431] In a letter of 22 August 1882, Sorge asked Engels to deal with the matter of subscription fees for *The Labour Standard*.— 368

[432] *Peter Schlemihl*—a character in Chamisso's story *Peter Schlemihls wundersame Geschichte*, who exchanged his shadow for a magic purse.— 369

[433] Marx probably referred to William Langland's allegoric poem *The Vision of William concerning Piers the Plowman, together with Vita de Do-wel, Do-bet, et Do-best, secundum Wit et Resoun*. There are three versions of the poem. A volume containing them all was published by the Early English Text Society in 1867-85. (The Society was founded by Frederick James Furnivall in 1864.)— 372

[434] On 9 June 1880, *L'Égalité* (No. 21, 2nd series) carried a report ('Le patriotisme de la bourgeoisie et les Chinois') on the meeting held on 5 May 1880 by the Paris Society of Political Economists in connection with the Chinese emigration to California. Participants in the meeting praised the cheap Chinese labour. This event was also covered by *Le Revue socialiste* (No. 9, 5 July 1880) in the article 'La Question chinoise devant les économistes', signed 'B. M.'. Its author was probably Benoît Malon.— 372

435 The manifesto of the National Council, set up as a counterbalance to the Possibilist National Committee by decision of the Roanne Congress (see note 394) on the basis of the Lyons party groups with a seat in Lyons, was printed on 5 November 1882 by *L'Égalité* (3rd series, No. 47) under the heading 'Parti ouvrier. Conseil national'.— 373

436 Engels is referring to the House of Commons' debate on the Egyptian events (see Note 355) in early November 1882.— 373

437 *Clôture* — the parliamentary procedure whereby debate is closed and the measure under discussion is brought up for an immediate vote. The *clôture* was announced on 11 November 1882. The voting was to be on the changes in parliament procedure.— 373

438 The reference is to the first of the three articles by the German Social-Democratic refugee Georg Heinrich von Vollmar carried by *Der Sozialdemokrat*, Nos. 46, 47 and 49 on 9, 16 and 30 November 1882 under the heading 'Zur Spaltung der französischen Arbeiterpartei' and signed 'V.'. The articles were a response to the piece called 'St. Étienne oder Roanne?', which appeared in *Der Sozialdemokrat*, Nos. 41, 42 and 44 on 5, 12 and 26 October 1882. The last one was signed 'Leo' (Bernstein's pen-name).— 373, 379, 386, 408

439 Engels is referring, above all, to *Dialectics of Nature* (see Note 449).— 377

440 The reference is to the legal proceedings instituted against Guesde, Lafargue and other activists of the French Workers' Party for the speeches they had made in Lyons, Roanne, Montluçon, Bézenet, and Saint-Chamond, among other places, after the Roanne Congress (see Note 394). Guesde and Bazin were summoned by the examining magistrate Édouard Piquand to the court of the first instance in Montluçon for 14 November, and Lafargue, for 21 November on the charge of instigation to civil war, assassination, burglary and arson (see Note 444), but the suspects publicly refused to appear before the jury. Lafargue, who had been staying in Paris since 7 October, was arrested by the Paris police on 12 December. In late April 1883, the jury of the town of Moulins sentenced Lafargue, Guesde and Dormoy to six months' imprisonment and a fine. Guesde and Lafargue served their sentences in the Ste Pélagie prison in Paris from 21 May 1883.— 378, 397, 401, 404, 406, 441, 445

441 Samuel Moore's mathematical research mentioned here made up a few pages of notes concerning the method of substantiating the differential calculus independently worked out by Marx (see also Engels' letter to Marx of 18 August 1881, this volume, pp. 130-32). Marx commented on Moore's notes in his letter to Engels of 22 November 1882 (see this volume, p. 380). See also Note 192.— 378, 380

442 Replying on 17 November 1882 to Engels' letters of 2-3 and 4 November, Bernstein listed the market value of the shares of the principal state-owned Prussian railways.— 379, 380

443 The *Marseilles Congress*, the first congress of the French Workers' Party, was held between 20 and 31 October 1879. In the sharp controversy that arose between the Marxists (collectivists), on the one hand, and the petty-bourgeois anarchists and Proudhonists, on the other, the Marxists headed by Jules Guesde got the upper hand. The congress passed a number of decisions of fundamental significance: on

the nationalisation of the industries and landed property; on the seizure of political power by the workers, on the establishment of a party that assumed the official name Fédération de parti des travailleurs socialistes en France (in practice called the Workers' Party). The congress approved party rules and set the task of drawing up a programme.— 379, 380, 386

444 A reference to Paul Lafargue's open letter to Édouard Piquand, the Montluçon examining magistrate, entitled 'L'affaire de Montluçon' (*L'Égalité*, 4th series, No. 26, 18 November 1882) written as a reply to the summons of 15 November to appear before the jury on 21 November (see Note 440). In it, Lafargue refused to stand for trial.— 379

445 Marx is referring to the Possibilists' party established at the St-Étienne Congress and headed by Brousse and Malon (Fédération française des travailleurs socialistes révolutionnaires) (see Note 394).— 380

446 A reference to Sheldon Amos' review of John Seymour Keay's pamphlet 'Spoiling the Egyptians' reprinted in London in 1882. The review appeared in *The Contemporary Review*, Vol. XLII, October 1882, under the heading ' "Spoiling the Egyptians": Revised Version'. Keay responded with the article ' "Spoiling the Egyptians". A Rejoinder' featured by *The Contemporary Review*, Vol. XLII, November 1882.— 381

447 Part of this letter was published in English for the first time in: Marx, Engels, *Pre-Capitalist Socio-Economic Formations. A Collection*, Progress Publishers, Moscow, 1979.— 381

448 The reference is to the split in the French workers' movement at the St-Étienne Congress in September 1882 (see Note 394). On the Marseilles Congress, see Note 443.— 384

449 Engels is referring to his manuscript *Dialectics of Nature*, specifically the article entitled 'The Measure of Motion.— Work'.

Dialectics of Nature (present edition, Vol. 25, pp. 313-588) was the culmination of profound studies carried out by Engels over a number of years. Engels wrote the items included in *Dialectics of Nature* from 1873 to 1882 with intervals, during which time he studied a vast amount of source material on major problems of the natural sciences and more or less completed ten articles and chapters and many notes and fragments, all in all, almost 200 sketches. After Marx's death, he became engrossed in work to complete and publish *Capital* and in the affairs of the international working-class movement, and had no choice but to stop work on *Dialectics of Nature*, which remained unfinished and unpublished in his lifetime (for more details about the work on and publication of the book, see present edition, Vol. 25, pp. XIX-XXV and 660-63).— 384, 395

450 Lafargue's article 'Le Ministère enchanté' was printed by *L'Égalité*, 4th series, No. 32, 24 November 1882; it sharply criticised the activities of former Finance Minister Jean Batiste Léon Say.— 385, 402

451 In 1882, Marx stayed with his daughter Jenny Longuet in Argenteuil between 6 June and 22 August and from 28 September and into the first days of October.— 385

⁴⁵² Engels intended to use these materials for a pamphlet about Bismarck and Lassalle (this volume, pp. 324-25). He did not carry out his plan.— 386

⁴⁵³ The information and quotations concerning the balance of power between the Possibilists and the Guesdists after the split in the French Workers' Party (see Note 394) were contained in Lafargue's letter to Engels of 24 November 1882.— 387

⁴⁵⁴ *Fédération du Nord* (Northern Federation), which was formed in the spring of 1880, was one of the six federations into which the French Workers' Party had been organisationally divided prior to its split (see Note 394). The Northern Federation united the party branches in Lille and Roubaix. After the split at the St-Étienne Congress, it sided with the Marxists.— 387, 408

⁴⁵⁵ The reference is to the Preamble to the Programme of the French Workers' Party drawn up by Marx (see present edition, Vol. 24, p. 340).— 387

⁴⁵⁶ Engels alludes to the stand taken by Johannes Miquel, a former member of the Communist League and later a National Liberal and minister in the Prussian government. Miquel's departure from the revolutionary stand was apparent even in his letters to Marx of 6 April and 15 August 1856. Miquel maintained that a revolution in Germany was not 'all that near' and that during it the proletariat should form a firm alliance not only with the petty but with the liberal bourgeoisie as well, and after its victory adopt tactics that would not alienate the bourgeoisie.— 388, 449

⁴⁵⁷ This refers to the St-Étienne and Roanne congresses (see Note 394).— 389

⁴⁵⁸ A reference to the exposure of the German agent provocateur Johann Karl Friedrich Elias Schmidt in Zurich. The *Sozialdemokrat* editors brought forth a pamphlet *Die deutsche Geheimpolizei im Kampfe mit der Sozialdemokratie. Aktenstücke und Enthüllungen auf Grund authentischen Materials dargestellt* (Hottingen-Zurich, 1882) that described the machinations of Schmidt and his superiors. It was reprinted there in the same year with the same subtitle under the heading *Deutsche Polizeischuftereien.*— 390, 436

⁴⁵⁹ Engels is referring to Bebel's letter of 14 November 1882 written in the Leipzig prison in reply to Engels' letter of 28 October 1882 (see this volume, pp. 349-51).— 390, 392

⁴⁶⁰ Engels is referring, above all, to Marx's unfinished work on Polish history which he was writing in 1863 and which involved the use of the book *Vom Entstehen und Untergange der polnischen Konstitution vom 3-ten May 1791*, Parts I-II, 1793 (it was published anonymously in Leipzig; its authors were J. Potocki, H. Kołłantaj and F. K. Dmochowski). The extant sketches for the work, which Marx planned to entitle *Deutschland und Polen. Politisch-militärische Betrachtungen bei Gelegenheit des Polnischen Aufstands von 1863*, and the notes he had made for it were published in: K. Marx, *Manuskripte über die polnische Frage (1863-1864)*, Amsterdam, 1961, and, in Russian and German, in: *Marx-Engels Archives*, Vol. XIV, Moscow, 1973. The mistakes that occurred in the original publication when deciphering the manuscripts were corrected in the latter.— 391

⁴⁶¹ The *Crystal Palace*—a glass-and-steel building erected for the first World Exhibition in London in 1851.— 391

⁴⁶² The polemic around Marx's theory of value was launched in *La Plebe*, No. 13, 8 October 1882, by Romeo Candelari's article 'La critica dell'economia radicale

moderna'. Candelari had several more polemical articles printed by the newspaper, among them 'De Laveleye e Rodbertus' (No. 14, 15 October 1882), which contained Laveleye's pronouncements concerning Marx's theory of value. Candelari's articles also appeared in Nos. 15, 16, 17 and 18 of *La Plebe* of 22 and 29 October and 5 and 12 November 1882. Issue No. 17 also carried Carlo Cafiero's letter to the editors called 'Polemica'.— 392

463 The reference is to the British trade union delegation headed by the editor of *The Labour Standard* George Shipton which visited France in late 1882. (On the purpose of the visit, see this volume, pp. 359-60.)— 393, 394, 396

464 *Tlingits*— a group of Indian tribes inhabiting south-eastern Alaska.

By 'once Russian America' Engels is referring to Russia's possessions in North America (Alaska), which, under the treaty of 30 March 1867, the Russian government sold to the United States for $7.2 mln.

In 1880-81, Marx wrote down a detailed synopsis of Lewis H. Morgan's book *Ancient Society or Researches in the Lines of Human Progress from Savagery, through Barbarism into Civilization*, London, 1877. It was published as 'Marx's Excerpts from Lewis Henry Morgan's *Ancient History*', in *The Ethnological Notebooks of Karl Marx*, Assen, 1972, pp. 95-241.

Morgan built his research of primitive society on studies into the gentile communities of North American Indians, including the Iroquois, a group of tribes living in the north-east of the USA.— 395

465 Georg Ludwig von Maurer's works on the agrarian, urban and state system in medieval Germany are: *Einleitung zur Geschichte der Mark-, Hof-, Dorf- und Stadt-Verfassung und der öffentlichen Gewalt*, Munich, 1854; *Geschichte der Markenverfassung in Deutschland*, Erlangen, 1856; *Geschichte der Fronhöfe, der Bauernhöfe und der Hofverfassung in Deutschland*, vols I-IV, Erlangen, 1862-63; *Geschichte der Dorfverfassung in Deutschland*, vols I-II, Erlangen, 1865-66; *Geschichte der Städteverfassung in Deutschland*, vols I-IV, Erlangen, 1869-71.— 395, 400, 408, 416, 455

466 Engels wrote these lines to Marx on Laura Lafargue's letter of 12 December 1882. Laura informed him that Paul Lafargue had just been arrested by the Paris police and, under its orders, was to be sent to Montluçon to stand for trial there.— 396

467 *Affaires véreuses cabinet* (cabinet of black affairs, or black cabinet) — a secret establishment at the postal departments of France, Prussia, Austria and some other states that opened and inspected correspondence; had existed since the time of the absolutist monarchies in Europe.— 398

468 A reference to the events in the period when the Tudors' absolutist monarchy was being established in England following the War of the Roses (1455-85). The war was caused by the conflict between the feudal lords that grouped around two rival royal dynasties, the Lancasters and the Yorks. The founder of the dynasty, Henry VII Tudor, who had defeated King Richard III of York, made an attempt to sanctify the dynasty, seeking to consolidate the monarchy and his claim to the throne, which he based on his kinship with the Lancasters. With this end in view, in 1506 he requested Pope Julius II to canonise one of the Lancasters, King Henry VI, who had been dethroned by the Yorks at the time of the War of the Roses.— 399

469 Marx probably arrived at this conclusion after reading the book by V. V.

(V. P. Vorontsov) *Sudby kapitalizma v Rossii* (The Destiny of Capitalism in Russia), St Petersburg, 1882. In the preface to the book, the author, a noted Russian writer and economist, leader of Liberal Narodism (Populism), mentioned Russian 'socialists of the Marxian school' who maintained that Russia was to follow the route of capitalist development.— 399

[470] This letter was published in English for the first time in part in: Karl Marx and Friedrich Engels, *Correspondence. 1846-1895*. A Selection with Commentary and Notes, Martin Lawrence Ltd., London, [1934] and in full in: Karl Marx and Frederick Engels, *Selected Correspondence*, Foreign Languages Publishing House, Moscow, 1955.— 399

[471] A reference to Lafargue's article 'Notre candidat' in *L'Égalité*, 4th series, No. 47, 9 December 1882.— 402, 408

[472] The *Thirty Years' War* (1618-48) — a European war in which the Pope, the Spanish and the Austrian Habsburgs and the German Catholic princes rallied under the banner of Catholicism and fought against the Protestant countries, Bohemia, Denmark, Sweden, the Republic of the Netherlands and a number of German states. The rulers of Catholic France — rivals of the Habsburgs — supported the Protestant camp. Germany was the principal battleground and the chief object of plunder and the belligerents' aggressive claims. The war ended with the signing of the Westphalian Peace Treaty, which fixed Germany's political fragmentation.— 404, 448

[473] The *Sachsenspiegel* (Saxonian mirror) — a medieval German law code explaining the local (Saxonian) common law.— 404

[474] A reference to a postcard from Johann Philipp Becker to Engels of 13 December 1882. For Engels' reply, see this volume, pp. 405-07.— 404

[475] Engels is referring to Marx's lengthy studies of writings on the commune and forms of communal property, and the Russian village commune in particular, as part of his research into land rent and agrarian relations in general. Specifically, somewhat earlier Marx had made a thorough study of Kovalevsky's book *Communal Land Ownership: the Causes, Course and Consequences of Its Disintegration* (1879), from which he copied out passages on the character of the commune and its place and socio-economic role at different times and among different peoples.— 408

[476] This refers to the Socialist Republican Alliance founded in Paris in October 1880 by a group of amnestied Communards. Among them were noted and influential figures in the working-class and democratic movement, former members of the International Working Men's Association and its General Council. The members of the Alliance declared themselves socialists, but refused to be committed to any doctrine whatsoever. In early 1881, the Alliance fell apart.— 408

[477] The reference is to Sergei Podolinski's article 'Il socialismo e l'unità delle forze fisiche', which was first published in 1881 in *La Plebe*, Anno XIV, Nuova serie, No. 3, pp. 13-16, and No. 4, pp. 5-15, and then reprinted by the German journal *Die Neue Zeit*, Jg. 1, 1883, pp. 413-24, and 449-57, under the heading 'Menschliche Arbeit und Einheit der Kraft'.— 410

[478] In a letter to Engels of 21 December 1882 Laura Lafargue wrote that she was un-

easy about Jenny Longuet's health and that the latter should consult a doctor.— 413, 417

[479] *Weitlingianism* — the doctrine of utopian egalitarian communism advocated by Wilhelm Weitling that gained some currency among German craftsmen. In the early 1840s, it had had a certain progressive role, but later, since it rejected the need for active political struggle on the part of the proletariat and advocated sectarian, conspiratorial methods, it began to act as a brake on the evolution of the German workers' class awareness. The reactionary features of Weitling's doctrine, which gradually acquired a religious, Christian colouring, became more and more apparent with the passage of time. Neglect of the laws of history and dogmatism typical of the doctrine led to scientific methods and the need for a bourgeois-democratic stage in the revolution in Germany being ignored, and to excessive stress on the role of personality in history.— 413

[480] At that time, Bebel was doing a 4-month jail sentence in the Leipzig prison (he was allowed to go and stay at home on 2-9 January 1883).— 414

[481] On the eve of the Austro-Prussian War of 1866, Bismarck made it understood to Napoleon III that, in exchange for France's neutrality, he would not hinder expansion of its territory at the expense of Belgium, Luxembourg and the German lands lying between the Rhine and the Moselle. On 6 August 1866, the French government demanded that Bismarck pay the promised compensation, insisting that the frontiers be changed back to those of 1814, the Prussian garrison withdrawn from Luxembourg, and the latter's annexation by France be ensured. But Bismarck resolutely rejected these demands and responded to them on 19 March 1867 by making public the Prussian secret alliance with the South German states of Baden and Bavaria concluded back in 1866.

Referring to Bismarck's behaviour at that time, Engels implies his negotiations of 19 November 1882 with the Russian Foreign Minister Girs, who was asking for Germany's assistance for Russian policies in the East. After the negotiations, the German press featured notes and official articles on the alliance concluded by Germany and Austria-Hungary back in 1879.— 415

[482] This refers to Rodbertus' *Briefe und Socialpolitische Aufsätze*, published by Dr. Rudolf Meyer (vols I-II, Berlin [1882]). In a letter to Engels of 14 November 1882, Bebel jokingly noted that Meyer was full of praise for Marx and Engels, flattered probably by his 'good reception' in London in 1879-80, but that they had to share the 'glory' with 'the five cardinals who had honoured him in the same manner'.— 416, 449

[483] A reference to Dr F. Bayshawe's letter to James M. Williamson dated 4 January 1883, 5 Warrior Square, St Leonards on Sea (see this volume, p. 420).— 419

[484] A reference to Paul Lafargue's letter to Engels of 6 January describing the state of Jenny Longuet's health, August Bebel's letter of the same date, in which he set forth his ideas about the impending crisis in the German economy, and Adolph Hepner's letter with the request for a new preface to the *Manifesto of the Communist Party*.— 421, 424

[485] By all indications, Eleanor Marx failed to find a copy of Marx's Algerian photo, and he had to send Mrs Williamson a photo taken in 1875 (see this volume, pp. 166-67).— 423

⁴⁸⁶ The reference is to the sales of the second German edition of Volume One of *Capital* published in 1872 by Otto Meissner in Hamburg.— 423, 425

⁴⁸⁷ Liberal M. P. and former Chartist Joseph Cowen justified the British invasion in Egypt (see Note 355) in his speech in Newcastle on 8 January 1883.— 423

⁴⁸⁸ Marx is probably referring to the events of 1847. On 28 March 1847, the *Deutsche-Brüsseler Zeitung*, No. 25, carried an article about corn speculation written, presumably, by Ferdinand Wolff, a member of the Communist League whose brother was a corn profiteer.— 425

⁴⁸⁹ Marx's New Year wishes to Mrs Williamson were written on the back of a photo of his taken in 1875 (see this volume, pp. 166-67).— 429

⁴⁹⁰ Jenny Longuet died on 11 January 1883.— 429, 430, 434, 450, 458, 461

⁴⁹¹ Engels is referring to the speech made by the Social-Democratic deputy Karl Grillenberger at the Reichstag meeting on 14 December 1882. It was spearheaded against Minister of the Interior Robert Victor von Puttkamer, who tried to justify the need for the introduction of a state of siege in several regions of Germany in connection with the Anti-Socialist Law (see Note 16), insisting that Social Democracy was undermining the sanctity of the family and advocating free love. The reference is also to the *Sozialdemokrat* articles dealing with Grillenberger's speech, 'Aus Grillenberger's Rede über die Handhabung des Sozialistengesetzes' (Nos. 1 and 2, 1 and 4 January); 'Zum Kapitel von der freien Liebe. Etwas für Herrn von Puttkamer zum Vorlesen im Reichstage' (No. 2, 4 January); 'Puttkamer und die "Heiligkeit" der Familie' (No. 3, 11 January); 'Zum Kapitel von der freien Liebe. Den Herren v. Puttkamer und v. Nostiz Wallwitz gewidmet' and 'Von der patentierten Ehre' (No. 9, 22 February 1883).— 431, 455

⁴⁹² A phrase from Frederick William II's instructions of 14 August 1748 for the major-generals of cavalry.— 431

⁴⁹³ An allusion to Prussia's annexation of the formerly independent states — Hanover, Nassau and the Electorate of Hesse, as well as the free city Frankfurt am Main — as a result of the Austro-Prussian War of 1866 and the unification of Germany.— 432

⁴⁹⁴ During his stay in London in May 1882, Paul Singer discussed with Engels the attitude the Social-Democratic Party should take to Bismarck's policies, which probably compelled Singer to modify his stand.— 433

⁴⁹⁵ Engels compares Kautsky's book *Der Einfluss der Volksvermehrung auf den Fortschritt der Gesellschaft* (1880), which defended the 'sound core' of Malthus' theory, with his own pamphlet *Die überseeische Lebensmittel-Konkurrenz*, which was an off-print from *Staatswirthschaftliche Abhandlungen* (Serie II, Heft IV und V, 1881).— 434

⁴⁹⁶ Engels is referring to Hegel's idea of the objectively existing dialectical contradiction in things and processes, which Dühring attacked in his book *Kritische Geschichte der Nationalökonomie und des Socialismus.*— 434

⁴⁹⁷ In the first part of his work *Die überseeische Lebensmittel-Konkurrenz* (Leipzig, 1881) (see Note 495), Kautsky makes use of the information on the forms of agriculture in Canada supplied by Rudolf Meyer to the Viennese newspaper *Das Vaterland.*— 437

498   A reference to the first article, entitled 'Hetärismus', from the series of Kautsky's articles *Die Entstehung der Ehe und Familie* in the Darwinist journal *Kosmos* (Stuttgart, Jg. VI, Bd. XII, October 1882-March 1883). The second article was called 'Die Raubehe und das Mutterrecht. Der Clan', and the third, 'Die Kaufehe und die patriarchalische Familie'. In 1883, they were published as a separate edition under the general heading of the series.— 437, 450, 451

499   The *Hutzwang* (enforced partition) — under the law of ancient Germans, the duty of all members of the commune to remove the fences around their land plots for the period between the harvest and the sowing so that the land could be used as communal pasture in the meantime.— 438

500   Engels may be referring to the letter to the French Minister of Justice signed by Lafargue and Guesde and printed by *L'Égalité* on 16 February 1883. The letter was entitled 'Deux noveaux prétendants'. In an ironic manner, Guesde and Lafargue demanded a milder punishment for themselves, equal to that reserved for royalty, for, considering the morals of the French monarchs, was anybody able to vouch that the accused did not have royal blood in their veins?— 441

501   Engels had first despatched this letter to be approved by Schorlemmer but by an oversight must have omitted to address it, and it was returned to the author. It was sent by Engels to Bernstein alongside with another letter, that of 27 February-1 March 1883 (see this volume, pp. 445-50).— 442

502   A reference to the Copenhagen Congress of the Socialist Workers' Party of Germany, which took place from 29 March to 2 April 1883; originally, the congress was to be held in Zurich.— 442, 450

503   A reference to Bernstein's letter to Engels of 24 February 1883.— 445

504   On 8 March 1883, *Der Sozialdemokrat* reported that the publication of *L'Égalité* was about to be stopped, as the owner of the printing press had cancelled his contract with the editorial board.— 445

505   Viereck and Fritzsche stayed in London in the second half of January 1881 on their way to the United States (see Note 119).— 446

506   This refers to the programme approved at the Unity Congress in Gotha on 22-27 May 1875 (see also Note 381).— 447

507   In February 1883, the German socialist Moses Oppenheimer was proved guilty of secret contacts with the bourgeois press and embezzlement of party funds.— 447

508   Eduard Bernstein wrote to Engels on 24 February 1883 that as far as he knew, Georg Schumacher in Solingen was agitating for the *Süddeutsche Post* and urging the workers to read that newspaper and not *Der Sozialdemokrat*. Replying on 7 March to this letter by Engels Bernstein wrote that the things said about Schumacher were not true.— 450

509   Engels alludes to the oath taken by Liebknecht in the Saxon Landtag in November 1879, and by August Bebel in July 1881.— 454

510   The *Deutsch-Amerikanische Arbeiter-Library* series initiated by Hepner opened with Bebel's pamphlet *Unsere Ziele*, which Hepner published in 1883 in New York under another title, *Die Ziele der Arbeiterbewegung*, having first made a number of changes.— 455

511 Engels' telegram to Sorge of 14 March 1883 was published in the *New Yorker Volkszeitung* without Engels' knowledge (the editors added the word 'afternoon') to create the impression that the telegram had been addressed to the newspaper. For the telegram that Engels did send to the paper, see present edition, Vol. 24, p. 462.

Engels voiced his protest at the editors' high-handedness in a letter to the *New Yorker Volkszeitung* of 18 April 1883 (see present edition, Vol. 24, p. 472).— 457

512 This letter was published in English for the first time in: F. Engels, *On the Death of Karl Marx*, Cooperative Publishing Society of Foreign Workers in the USSR, Moscow, 1933, and F. Engels, *The Fourteenth of March 1883*, Lawrence, London, 1933.— 458, 459, 460

513 Jenny Marx died on 2 December 1881.— 458, 461

514 Marx visited Johann Philipp Becker in Geneva on 26 September 1882 before his departure from Switzerland.— 460

515 This letter was published in English for the first time in: F. Lessner, *Sixty Years in the Social-Democratic Movement*, The Twentieth Century Press, London, 1907.— 463

516 Engels included the full text of the telegram from the students of the Petrovsky Academy of Agriculture in Moscow in his article 'On the Death of Karl Marx' printed by *Der Sozialdemokrat*, 3 and 17 May 1883 (see present edition, Vol. 24, pp. 473-81).— 464

517 In a letter of 16 March 1883, Theodor Cuno asked Engels to confirm that Marx was called Mohr by his family. Cuno wanted to mention it in his article about Marx. Hepner, however, asserted that Marx had never had such a nickname and that mentioning it could only 'harm' the party.— 466

518 The Communards were amnestied in July 1880.— 469

519 A reference to the mounting political tension in Ireland in the late 1870s-early 1880s engendered by the campaign for Home Rule and by the people's protest action against the landlords (see notes 124 and 139).— 471

520 Probably a reference to 4 August 1789, when, pressed by the mounting peasant movement, the French Constituent Assembly solemnly removed feudal duties and taxes, which had by that time been abolished, to all practical purposes, by the insurgent peasants. However, the laws that were later promulgated abrogated only the personal duties without redemption fees. The abolition of all feudal duties without redemption payments was not carried out until the time of the Jacobean dictatorship by the law of 17 July 1793.— 473

534

NAME INDEX

A

Abercorn, James Hamilton, 1st Duke of (1811-1885) — English statesman, Conservative; Lord Lieutenant of Ireland (1866-68 and 1874-76); opposed the adoption of the Land Bill of 1881 for Ireland.— 172

Abdul Hamid II (1842-1918) — Turkish Sultan (1876-1909).— 248

Adam, Juliette (née *Lamber*) (1836-1936) — French writer and journalist, founder and director of the *Nouvelle Revue* (1879-86).— 225, 230

Aksakov, Ivan Sergeyevich (1823-1886) — Russian writer, Slavophile; criticised the domestic policy of tsarism (the 1850s-60s); a champion of pan-Slavism and great power chauvinism (the 1870s-80s).— 194

Aleko Pasha (*Vogorides, Alexandros*) (c. 1823-1910) — Bulgarian-born Turkish statesman and diplomat, counsellor of the Embassy in London (1856-61), ambassador to Vienna (1876-78), governor of Eastern Rumelia (1879-84).— 373

Alexander II (1818-1881) — Emperor of Russia (1855-81).— 80, 175, 288

Alexander III (1845-1894) — Emperor of Russia (1881-94).— 78, 175

Allsop, Thomas (1795-1880) — English democrat, Chartist; was persecuted on suspicion of being an accomplice in Orsini's attempt on the life of Napoleon III in 1858; later collaborated with Marx in helping refugees of the Paris Commune.— 114

Alphand, Jean Charles Adolphe (1817-1891) — French state official, engineer; directed reconstruction works in Paris from 1854 and was in charge of the city water supply from 1878.— 337

Amos, Sheldon (1835-1886) — English lawyer, barrister in Egypt from the early 1880s, judge in the Court of Appeal (local tribunal) in Alexandria (1882).— 381

Arabi Pasha, Ahmed Arabi el Husseini (c. 1839-1911) — Egyptian politician and military figure; headed the national liberation movement (1879-82); a leader of the National Party; War Minister

and from 1893); a founder and leader of the German Social-Democrats; friend and associate of Marx and Engels.— 10-12, 35, 77-79, 87-88, 99, 137-39, 154, 173, 188, 259-61, 266, 279, 280-83, 289, 291, 294, 325, 326, 328, 330, 333, 334, 349-51, 353, 357, 386, 390, 414-17, 421, 433, 442, 453-55, 469

Bebel, Julie (1843-1910) — August Bebel's wife.— 417, 458

Becker, Elisabeth (d. 1884) — Johann Philipp Becker's wife.— 159

Becker, Johann Philipp (1809-1886) — prominent figure in the international working-class movement; brushmaker; took part in the German and Swiss democratic movements in the 1830s and 1840s and in the 1848-49 revolution; prominent figure in the First International in the 1860s, delegate to all its congresses; editor of *Der Vorbote* (1866-71); friend and associate of Marx and Engels.— 7-9, 23, 38, 50, 76, 80, 151-52, 159-60, 196, 197, 299, 311, 314, 404, 405, 407

Beesly, Edward Spencer (1831-1915) — British historian and politician, bourgeois radical, positivist, professor at London University (1860-93); defended the International and the Paris Commune in the English press (1870-71).— 89, 118

Bennigsen, Rudolf von (1824-1902) — German politician, advocate of Germany's unification under Prussia's supremacy; President of the National Association (1859-67); from 1867 leader of the Right-wing of the National Liberal Party, which defended the interests of the big industrial bourgeoisie; deputy to the German Reichstag (1871-83 and 1887-98).— 373

Bernstein, Eduard (1850-1932) — German Social-Democrat from 1872; editor of *Der Sozialdemokrat* (1881-90); came

out with a revision of Marxism after Engels' death.— 8, 58-59, 73-75, 85-87, 126-29, 137, 144-51, 152-55, 165-66, 172-74, 186-90, 203-08, 210, 244, 247-48, 250-52, 256, 260, 285, 291, 300-02, 323-26, 331-34, 335, 341, 345, 346-48, 352, 353-58, 359-62, 364, 365, 373, 377, 379, 380, 386, 389, 390, 395, 407-08, 413, 430-36, 442, 445-48, 450, 459

Beust, Adolf — German physician, Friedrich von Beust's son, Engels' relative.— 26, 30, 35, 36, 39, 244, 326

Beust, Friedrich von (1817-1899) — Prussian army officer, member of the committee of the Cologne Workers' Association (1848); an editor of the *Neue Kölnische Zeitung* (September 1848-February 1849); later a teacher; took part in the foundation of the International's section in Zurich in 1867.— 30, 76, 89, 290

Bevan — Charles Roesgen's wife.— 346

Bismarck (in full *Bismarck-Schönhausen*), *Otto Eduard Leopold, Prince von* (1815-1898) — statesman of Prussia and Germany, diplomat; Prime Minister of Prussia (1862-71 and 1873-90) and Chancellor of the German Empire (1871-90), author of the Anti-Socialist Law (1878).— 4, 11, 40, 43, 53, 73-75, 78, 80, 83, 112, 146, 175, 178, 182, 183, 187, 191, 192, 208, 209, 256, 261, 282, 324, 327, 348, 350, 359, 386, 415, 433, 441, 454

Blanc, Jean Joseph Charles Louis (1811-1882) — French petty-bourgeois socialist, historian, member of the Provisional Government and President of the Luxembourg Commission in 1848; pursued a policy of conciliation with the bourgeoisie; emigrated to England in August 1848; a leader of the petty-bourgeois refugees in London; deputy to the National Assembly (1871), opposed the Paris Commune.— 53, 408

tor; Liberal M. P., Civil Lord of the Admiralty (1880-84).— 83

Braun, Heinrich (1854-1927) — German Social-Democrat, journalist; contributed to *Die Neue Zeit* (1883-88), took part in the publication of several other journals, later reformist.— 321

Brentano, Ludwig (Lujo) (1844-1931) — German economist; one of the major representatives of armchair socialism.— 65

Breuel, Ernst — German Social-Democrat, was banished from Hamburg under the Anti-Socialist Law; refugee in Copenhagen from the early 1880s; criticised the stand of the *Sozialdemokrat*'s editors in 1882.— 259

Bright, Jacob (1821-1899) — English politician, bourgeois radical, M.P., John Bright's brother.— 171

Bright, John (1811-1889) — English manufacturer and politician, a leader of the Free Traders and founder of the Anti-Corn Law League; M. P. (from 1843); leader of the Left wing of the Liberal Party from the early 1860s, held several ministerial posts.— 53, 171, 473, 474

Brimont — French Bonapartist, Charles Bradlaugh's acquaintance in Paris.— 53

Brissac, Henri (1823-1906) — participant in the French working-class movement, socialist, journalist; member of the Paris Commune, General Secretary of the Executive Committee, then of the Committee of Public Safety, banished to New Caledonia after the suppression of the Commune; returned to France after the 1880 amnesty, member of the French Workers' Party, an editor of *L'Égalité* in 1882; Guesde's supporter.— 358, 389

Brousse, Paul Louis Marie (1844-1912) — French physician; socialist;

participant in the Paris Commune; lived in emigration after its suppression, sided with the anarchists; joined the French Workers' Party in 1879; a leader and ideologist of the Possibilists, an opportunist trend in the French socialist movement.— 11, 141, 145-47, 149, 154, 155, 173, 181, 190, 282, 289, 309, 333, 339, 341, 342, 345, 350, 374, 380, 406-07, 456

Brown, John (1800-1859) — American farmer; a prominent leader of the revolutionary wing of the abolitionist movement; took an active part in the armed struggle against the slave-owners in Kansas (1854-56); attempted to organise a revolt of black slaves in Virginia in 1859; was tried and executed.— 77

Brown, Willard — American socialist, journalist, Marx's acquaintance in the 1880s.— 99, 170

Brunswick, Charles Frederick August William of (Braunschweig, Karl Friedrich August Wilhelm von) (1804-1873) — Duke of Brunswick from 1823, overthrown in early September 1830, emigrated; tried to return to power with the help of a number of European states; maintained contacts with democratic émigrés in the 1840s-50s; published the *Deutsche Londoner Zeitung.*— 258

Brunswick, Ferdinand, Duke of (1721-1792) — general in the Prussian service; during the Seven Years' War (from November 1757) commander of the Prussian and Allied troops, which fought against the French and Austrian armies.— 158

Bückler, Johann (1777-1803) — German robber, nicknamed Schinderhannes (Hannes the Skinflint).— 206, 281

Burke, Thomas Henry (1829-1882) — British statesman, permanent Irish Under-Secretary from 1869 to 1882; killed by members of the Irish terrorist organisation 'The Invincibles' on 6 May 1882.— 254, 288

Bürkli, Karl (1823-1901) — Swiss socialist, economist and journalist; took part in the 1848-49 revolution in Germany; an organiser and leader of the First International in Zurich, delegate to the Geneva (1866) and Secretary of the Lausanne (1867) congresses of the International; a founder and leader of the Swiss co-operative movement.— 177, 181, 189, 197, 209

Burleigh, Bennet (1839-1914) — English journalist, one of the first directors of the Central News information agency (founded in 1870).— 37, 38

Burns, Lydia (*Lizzy, Lizzie*) (1827-1878) — Irish working woman, Engels' second wife.— 104

Burns, Mary Ellen — see *Roscher, Mary Ellen*

C

Caesar (*Gaius Julius Caesar*) (c. 100-44 B. C.) — Roman general, statesman and writer, author of *Commentarii de bello Gallico.*— 382

Cafiero, Carlo (1846-1892) — participant in the Italian working-class movement, member of the First International; pursued the General Council's line in Italy in 1871; one of the leaders of the Italian anarchist organisations from 1872, abandoned anarchism at the end of the 1870s; published a summary of Volume One of Marx's *Capital* in Italian (1879).— 392

Caird, James (1816-1892) — Scottish agriculturist, Liberal M. P. (1857-65), author of works on the land question in England and Ireland.— 31

Calonne, Charles Alexandre de (1734-1802) — French statesman, Controller-General of Finance (1783-87); a leader

of the counter-revolutionary émigrés during the French Revolution.— 73

Candelari, Romeo — Italian journalist, contributed to the *Plebe* in the 1880s.— 392

Carlos I — see *Charles V*

Cartesius, Renatus (*Descartes, René*) (1596-1650) — French philosopher, mathematician and naturalist.— 384

Cassagnac — see *Granier de Cassagnac, Bernard Adolphe*

Casthelaz — Maurice Casthelaz's mother.— 219, 240

Casthelaz, Maurice — French physician and pharmaceutist, Marx's acquaintance.— 219, 222, 224, 226, 233, 240, 246

Catherine II (1729-1796) — Empress of Russia (1762-96).— 205

Cavendish, Frederick Charles, Lord (1836-1882) — English statesman and politician, Liberal M. P. from 1865; appointed Chief Secretary for Ireland in May 1882; killed by members of the Irish terrorist organisation 'The Invincibles' on 6 May 1882.— 254, 288

Cavour, Camillo Benso, conte di (1810-1861) — Italian statesman, head of the Sardinian Government (1852-59 and 1860-61), pursued a policy of unifying Italy under the supremacy of the Savoy dynasty relying on the support of Napoleon III; headed the first government of united Italy in 1861.— 191

Cazot, Théodore Joseph Jules (1821-1913) — French statesman, moderate bourgeois republican, lawyer; opposed the Second Empire regime, was in prison from 1851 to 1859; General Secretary of the Ministry of Foreign Affairs of the Government of National Defence (1870), deputy to the National Assembly (from 1871), Minister

took part in the English working-class movement.— 301

Dechend, Hermann Friedrich Alexander (1814-1890) — German statesman, Chairman of the Bank of Prussia (from 1864), then of the Reichsbank (1875-90), member of the State Council (from 1884).— 257

Deinhardt, C.— a Munich engineer.— 442, 443

Delachaux — a doctor and surgeon in Interlaken (Switzerland).— 253, 254

Demuth, Helene (Lenchen, Nim, Nym) (1820-1890) — housemaid and friend of the Marx family.— 92, 96, 113, 115-16, 124, 132, 136, 164, 170, 174-75, 200, 215, 224, 284, 285, 297, 299, 315, 316, 319, 328, 331, 340, 345, 372, 397, 417, 426, 440, 456, 458, 462, 465, 475

De Paepe, César Aimé Désiré (1841-1890) — Belgian socialist, compositor, subsequently physician; one of the founders of the Belgian Section of the International (1865); member of the Belgian Federal Council; delegate to the London (1865) Conference, the Lausanne (1867), Brussels (1868) and Basle (1869) congresses and to the London (1871) Conference of the International; following the Hague Congress (1872) supported the Bakuninists for some time; a founder of the Belgian Workers' Party (1885).— 146, 312

Deprez, Marcel (1843-1918) — French physicist and electrician; worked on the problem of electric energy transmission.— 364, 374, 449

Derby, Edward Geoffrey Smith Stanley, 14th Earl of Derby (1799-1869) — British statesman, Tory leader, Prime Minister (1852, 1858-59 and 1866-68).— 70

Détroyat, Pierre Léonce (1829-1898) — French journalist and writer, naval officer; Bonapartist; took part in the Crimean (1853-56) and Franco-Prussian (1870-71) wars; owner and editor of several newspapers in the 1870s-80s; Émile de Girardin's relative.— 53

Deville, Gabriel Pierre (1854-1940) — French socialist, active member of the French Workers' Party, journalist; author of a popular exposition of the first volume of Marx's Capital, and also of a number of philosophic, economic and historical works, delegate to the International Socialist Workers' Congress (1889), abandoned the working-class movement in the early 20th century.— 199, 282, 297, 386-87, 389, 402, 413

Dietz, Johann Wilhelm (1843-1922) — German publisher; Social-Democrat, founder of the Social-Democratic publishing house, deputy to the Reichstag from 1881.— 437

Dietzgen, Joseph (1828-1888) — German Social-Democrat, tanner; delegate to the Hague Congress of the International (1872).— 172

Dilke, Ashton Wentworth (1850-1883) — British politician, journalist and traveller, bourgeois radical, owner and editor of the Weekly Dispatch from the early 1870s, M. P. (1880-83).— 83, 211, 214

Dilke, Sir Charles Wentworth, Baronet (1843-1911) — British politician and writer; a leader of the Radical wing of the Liberal Party, Under-Secretary for Foreign Affairs (1880-82), president of the local government board (1882-85).— 83, 211, 365, 373

Disraeli, Benjamin, 1st Earl of Beaconsfield (1804-1881) — British statesman and author, a Tory leader; Chancellor of the Exchequer (1852, 1858-59 and 1866-68) and Prime Minister (1868 and 1874-80).— 53, 83, 90

deputy to the Legislative Assembly (1850-51); later Bonapartist; notorious for his lack of principles in politics.— 53, 472

Gladstone, William Ewart (1809-1898) — British statesman, Tory and later Peelite, leader of the Liberal Party in the latter half of the 19th century; Chancellor of the Exchequer (1852-55 and 1859-66), Prime Minister (1868-74, 1880-85, 1886 and 1892-94).— 40, 53, 54, 75, 80, 82-84, 86, 90, 121, 172, 185, 251, 286, 288, 319, 353, 365, 373

Godard — French anarchist, journalist.— 355, 383, 389

Goethe, Johann Wolfgang von (1749-1832) — German poet.— 110, 126, 230, 260, 268

Gorbunova (in the second marriage *Kablukova*) *Minna Karlovna* (1840-1931) — Russian statistician and economist, Narodnik writer; studied abroad the organisation of vocational training for a few years and corresponded with Engels in connection with this in 1880; studied female domestic crafts in Moscow Gubernia in the 1880s; contributed to the journal *Otechestvenniye Zapiski.*— 17-18, 19, 20, 21

Gorchakov, Alexander Mikhailovich, Prince (1798-1883) — Russian statesman and diplomat; envoy to Vienna (1854-56); Foreign Minister (1856-82).— 83

Goschen, George Yoachim, Viscount of Hawkhurst from 1900 (1831-1907) — British statesman and politician; German by birth; at first Liberal; M. P. from 1863, member of Government several times, author of a number of works on economics.— 381, 424

Gould, Jay (1836-1892) — American millionaire, railway owner and financier.— 63

Graham, Sir James Robert George (1792-

1861) — British statesman, Whig and later Peelite; Home Secretary (1841-46), First Lord of the Admiralty (1830-34 and 1852-55).— 365

Grant — English manufacturer.— 27-29, 33

Granier de Cassagnac, Paul Adolph Marie Prosper (1843-1904) — French journalist and politician; known for his duels and sharp polemics.— 345

Green, Lisa.— 96

Grévy, François Jules Paul (1807-1891) — French statesman, moderate republican; President of the Republic (1879-87).— 117, 127

Grillenberger, Carl (1848-1897) — German fitter, editor, head of a Nuremberg printing house; member of the German Social-Democratic Workers' Party from 1869, publisher and editor of Social-Democratic newspapers in Nuremberg; organised the distribution of the *Sozialdemokrat* in South Germany; deputy to the German Reichstag (1881-97); member of the Party leadership (1884-90); an opportunist in the 1880s.— 431, 455

Grimaldi — dynasty of Monaco princes; has reigned from the 14th century up to the present (with an interval from 1793 to 1814).— 273

Grimaldi, Lamberto (died c. 1494) — Prince of Monaco (1457-c. 1494).— 273

Guesde, Jules (Mathieu Jules Bazile) (1845-1922) — prominent figure in the French and international working-class movement; republican at the beginning of his career; sided with the anarchists in the first half of the 1870s; later a founder of the French Workers' Party (1879) and exponent of Marxism in France; leader of the revolutionary wing of the French socialist movement for many years.— 43, 44, 128, 145-50,

154, 173, 181, 183, 190, 199, 282, 289, 294, 297, 333, 346, 350, 355, 360, 362, 363, 370, 378, 380, 383, 385, 386, 387, 389, 397, 401, 402, 406, 441, 445, 474

Guizot, François Pierre Guillaume (1787-1874) — French historian and statesman, Orleanist; Foreign Minister (1840-48), Prime Minister (1847-48); virtually determined the home and foreign policy of France from 1840 to the February 1848 revolution; expressed the interests of the big financial bourgeoisie.— 100

Gumbel, Abraham — German Social-Democrat, refugee in France in the early 1880s; bank clerk in Paris (1883); author of letters to the editors of the *Sozialdemokrat*, in which he criticised the paper's position on the split in the French Workers' Party.— 430, 431

Gumpert, Eduard (d. 1893) — German physician resident in Manchester, a friend of Marx and Engels.— 24, 114, 117

H

Hales, John (b. 1839) — British trade unionist; weaver; member of the General Council of the International (1866-72) and its Secretary (1871-72); delegate to the London Conference (1871) and the Hague Congress (1872) of the International; headed the reformist wing of the British Federal Council from the beginning of 1872; expelled from the International in 1873.— 52

Hänel, Albert (1833-1918) — German politician, professor of history of state law, leader of the Party of Progress group in the Reichstag (1867-93 and 1898-1903), then sided with the Party of Free Thinkers.— 178

Hanssen, Georg (1809-1894) — German economist; author of a few books on

the history of agriculture and agrarian relations.— 403

Harney, George Julian (1817-1897) — prominent figure in the English labour movement; a Chartist leader (Left wing); editor of *The Northern Star, Democratic Review, Red Republican* and *Friend of the People*; lived in the USA (1862-88); member of the International; was on friendly terms with Marx and Engels.— 77, 93, 293

Harry — see *Longuet, Henri*

Hartmann, Georg Wilhelm — German worker; member of the General Association of German Workers; from 1875 one of the two chairmen of the Executive Committee of the Socialist Workers' Party of Germany; deputy to the Reichstag (1878-81).— 82, 138

Hartmann, Lev Nikolayevich (1850-1908) — Russian revolutionary, Narodnik (Populist); took part in a terrorist act of the Narodnaya Volya (People's Will) group against Alexander II in 1879, following which emigrated to France; representative of the Narodnaya Volya group abroad; left London for the USA at the end of 1881.— 82, 92-94, 95, 96, 138, 278, 320, 376, 381, 391, 395, 400, 404, 413, 422, 470

Haschert, Lina — Carl Hirsch's wife.— 292

Hasselmann, Wilhelm (1844-1916) — one of the leaders of the Lassallean General Association of German Workers (1871-75).— 10, 43, 431

Hatzfeldt, Sophie, Countess von (1805-1881) — friend and supporter of Ferdinand Lassalle.— 12

Hatzfeldt-Wildenburg, Edmund, Count von — Sophie von Hatzfeldt's husband.— 15

Hegel, Georg Wilhelm Friedrich (1770-1831) — German philosopher.— 131, 296, 354

League; Secretary of the Parliamentary Committee of the Trades Union Congress (1871-75); opposed revolutionary tactics.— 155, 185

Hugues, Clovis (1851-1907) — French poet, journalist and politician; was close to radicals; supporter of the Paris Commune; deputy to the National Assembly from 1881.— 408

Hume — English physician in London.— 240

Hyndman, Henry Mayers (pseudonym *John Broadhouse*) (1842-1921) — British socialist, reformist; founder (1881) and leader of the Democratic Federation, transformed into the Social-Democratic Federation in 1884.— 49-50, 82, 102-03, 162, 228, 234, 251, 348, 423

Hyndman, Mathilda (d. 1913) — Henry Mayers Hyndman's wife from 1876.— 49, 50, 82, 103

I

Ignatiev, Nikolai Pavlovich, Count (1832-1908) — Russian diplomat and statesman, ambassador to Turkey (1864-77), Russia's representative at the signing of the San Stefano Peace Treaty (1878); Minister of the Imperial Domains (1881-82), then Minister of the Interior.— 194, 363

Irving, Henry (1838-1905) — famous English producer and actor; played in a number of Shakespeare's tragedies.— 82, 104, 158

J

Jaclard, Charles Victor (1840-1903) — French socialist, Blanquist, journalist, physician and mathematician; member of the International and of the Paris Commune, following the suppression of the Paris Commune

emigrated to Switzerland and then to Russia; after the 1880 amnesty returned to France, where continued to take part in the socialist movement.— 116

Janson, Yuli Eduardovich (1835-1893) — Russian statistician and economist, professor at St Petersburg University, head of a statistical department of the Petersburg City Council (from 1881); author of a few works on the theory and history of statistics.— 64.

Jeffrey — American engineer and inventor.— 96

Jenny — see *Longuet, Jenny*

Jervis — Lafargue's partner in publishing business in England in the early 1880s.— 28-29, 33, 34

Joffrin, Jules François Alexandre (1846-1890) — French socialist, mechanic; an organiser of the Mechanics' Syndicate in Paris; took part in the Paris Commune; after its suppression refugee in England (1871-81); member of the French Workers' Party, a leader of its Possibilist wing, member of the Paris City Council from 1882.— 173, 181, 183, 190, 362

Johnny — see *Longuet, Jean Laurent Frédéric*

Jollymeier, Jollymeyer — see *Schorlemmer, Carl*

Jonas, Alexander (d. 1912) — German-born American socialist, journalist, editor-in-chief of the *New Yorker Volkszeitung* from 1878.— 422

Jourde, François (1843-1893) — French socialist, bank employee; member of the French Section of the International; member of the Central Committee of the National Guard and of the Paris Commune; head of the Finance Commission; banished to New Caledonia after the suppression of the Commune; escaped in 1874; returned to France in 1880.— 408

Julius II (1443-1513) — Pope (1503-13).— 399

Jung — see *Vezin, Jane Elisabeth*

Juta, Johann Carl (1824-1886) — Dutch merchant, Marx's brother-in-law, husband of Marx's sister Louise.— 65

K

Kablukov, Nikolai Alexeyevich (1849-1919) — Russian economist and statistician, Narodnik (Populist); professor at Moscow University.— 64

Kapell, August (b. 1844) — German Social-Democrat, carpenter, Lassallean; member of the General Association of German Workers in the 1860s-early 1870s; a founder and leader of the General Association of German Carpenters; deputy to the Reichstag (1877-78), was banished from Hamburg under the Anti-Socialist Law (1880); later abandoned political activity.— 282

Karl von Hohenzollern, Prince (1801-1883) — son of King Frederick William III of Prussia.— 434

Katkov, Mikhail Nikiforovich (1818-1887) — Russian revolutionary journalist, editor of *Moskovskiye Vedomosti* (1850-55 and 1863-87).— 194

Kaub — Karl Kaub's wife.— 116

Kaub, Karl — German worker, a refugee in London and after 1865 in Paris; member of the German Workers' Educational Society in London; member of the Central (November 1864 to 1865) and the General (1870-71) Council of the International, participated in the London Conference of 1865.— 115, 116

Kaufmann, S. F. — German refugee in London, member of the German Workers' Educational Society in London in the 1880s.— 72

Kaulitz — notary in Brunswick, G. Kaulitz's father.— 37

Kaulitz, G. — German Social-Democrat, refugee in London, Engels' acquaintance.— 37, 39

Kautsky, Karl (1854-1938) — German Social-Democrat, journalist, economist and historian, editor of *Die Neue Zeit* (1883-1917); associated with Marxists in the 1880s; author of several theoretical works on Marxism; an ideologist of Centrism in the German Social-Democratic Party and the Second International.— 56-58, 77, 81, 86, 95, 99, 120, 122, 126, 129, 138, 140-43, 150, 155, 165-66, 174, 190-95, 211, 248, 292, 299, 302, 320-23, 325, 348, 376-77, 434, 435-38, 451-53

Kautsky, Louise (née *Strasser*) (1860-1950) — Austrian socialist, Engels' secretary from 1890; delegate to the Zurich Congress of the Second International (1893); Karl Kautsky's first wife.— 377

Kautsky, Minna (1837-1912) — German writer, author of a few novels on social themes; Karl Kautsky's mother.— 82, 141, 142-44

Kayser, Max (1853-1888) — German journalist; member of the Social-Democratic Workers' Party of Germany; deputy to the Reichstag (1878-87), belonged to the right wing of the Social-Democratic group.— 153, 311, 431-32

Keay, John Seymour (1839-1909) — big English bank official in India (1862-82), Liberal; took part in the political life of India and England.— 381

Kegel, Max (1850-1902) — German journalist and poet; joined the Social-Democratic Workers' Party in 1869; contributed to various workers' press organs (the 1870s-80s) and was imprisoned for this several times during the operation of the Anti-Socialist Law; founder and editor of the Social-Democratic journals *Nußknacker* and *Wahre Jakob* (the 1880s); author of the party anthem.— 128, 137

Kerdijk, Arnold (1846-1905) — Dutch public figure and journalist, Liberal, close to armchair socialism.— 65

Kiepert, Johann Samuel Heinrich (1818-1899) — German geographer and cartographer, professor at Berlin University from 1859, compiled a number of geographic atlases.— 207

Kindlinger, Nikolaus (1749-1819) — German historian.— 403

King, Philip Stephen — bookseller in London, corresponded with Marx from 1867.— 19, 367, 378

Koch, Robert (1843-1910) — German scholar, a founder of modern microbiology; discovered the pathogens of tuberculosis and cholera in the 1880s.— 262

Kolkmann — bookseller in London.— 378

Kollár, Jan (1793-1852) — Slovak poet and philologist, a leader of the national movement, advocated the unity of the Slav peoples within the framework of the Austrian Empire (Austro-Slavism).— 194

Korvin-Krukovskaya (Jaclard), Anna Vasilyevna (1843-1887) — Russian revolutionary, member of the Russian Section of the First International; took part in the Paris Commune; Charles Victor Jaclard's wife.— 116

Kotzebue, August Friedrich Ferdinand von (1761-1819) — German writer and journalist, extreme monarchist.— 111

Kovalevsky, Maxim Maximovich (1851-1916) — Russian sociologist, historian, ethnographer and lawyer; politician, Liberal; author of a number of works on the history of the primitive communal system.— 45, 295

Kraus, Bernard (1828-1887) — Austrian physician, founder and publisher of the *Allgemeine Wiener medizinische Zeitung* (1856-87).— 6

Kryloff, Wanda.— 346

Kunemann (born c. 1828) — German physician in Monte Carlo, who treated Marx in May and early June 1882.— 254, 262-64, 267, 270, 273, 275

L

Labouchere, Henry (1831-1912) — British politician, diplomat and journalist, Liberal M.P.; an owner of the *Daily News* from the late 1860s.— 54

Lafargue, Laura (1845-1911) — Marx's second daughter; was active in the French working-class movement; translated into French many of Marx's and Engels' works; Paul Lafargue's wife from 1868.— 23, 25, 26, 30, 35, 96, 114, 118, 164, 170, 175, 186, 200, 215, 216, 222, 228, 238, 240, 244, 245, 252, 262, 277, 296, 297, 299, 303, 304, 309, 312, 315, 318, 320, 328, 329, 331, 336, 337, 338, 339-41, 344-46, 352, 363, 369, 396-99, 401, 402, 406, 413, 417, 421, 439-41, 456-57, 465

Lafargue, Paul (1842-1911) — prominent figure in the French and international working-class movement; member of the General Council of the International (from 1866); a founder of the French Workers' Party (1879); follower and associate of Marx and Engels, husband of Marx's daughter Laura from 1868.— 12, 15, 23, 25-30, 32-35, 38, 43, 61, 64, 99, 106, 118, 128, 144-45, 147, 148, 150, 155, 170, 174, 181, 183, 186, 190, 200, 220-22, 224, 240, 244, 251, 266, 271, 275, 276-78, 282, 291, 297, 299, 332, 340, 343-50, 351-52, 354, 356, 357, 358, 361, 363, 369-70, 374, 375, 378, 379, 383, 385, 387-91, 396, 398, 399, 401, 402, 404, 406,

413, 421, 424, 426, 441, 445, 456-57, 465

Laffitte, Jacques (1767-1844) — French banker and liberal politician, headed the government in the early period of the July monarchy (1830-31).— 73

Lagrange, Joseph Louis (1736-1813) — French mathematician and mechanic.— 380

Landor, Walter Savage (1775-1864) — English poet, writer and critic; was suspected of being an accomplice in Orsini's attempt on the life of Napoleon III in 1858.— 83

Langland, William (c. 1330-c. 1400) — English poet.— 371

Lankester, Sir Edwin Ray (1847-1929) — English biologist, professor from 1874.— 64, 82, 262, 461

Lassalle, Ferdinand (1825-1864) — German writer and lawyer; participated in the democratic movement in the Rhine Province (1848-49); founder of the General Association of German Workers (1863); an initiator of the opportunist trend within the German Social-Democratic movement.— 12, 15, 82, 146, 158, 191, 230, 294, 324, 325, 332, 343, 354

Laura — see *Lafargue, Laura*

Laveleye, Émile Louis Victor, baron de (1822-1892) — Belgian historian and vulgar economist.— 157, 392

Lavrov, Pyotr Lavrovich (1823-1900) — Russian philosopher, subjective sociologist and journalist, an ideologist of the revolutionary Narodism (Populism); emigrated in 1870; member of the International and of the Paris Commune, edited the journal *Vperyod!* (1873-76) and the newspaper *Vperyod* (1875-76).— 124-25, 184-86, 201, 211-12, 218, 235, 244, 271, 284, 295, 464

Law, Harriet (1832-1897) — a leading fig-

ure in the atheist movement in England; member of the General Council (June 1867 to 1872) and of the Manchester Section of the International (1872); published the *Secular Chronicle* (1876-79).— 54

Leibniz, Gottfried Wilhelm (1646-1716) — German philosopher and mathematician.— 380, 384

Lem(c)ke, Gottlieb (c. 1844-1885) — member of the German Workers' Educational Society in London.— 79

Lenchen — see *Demuth, Helene*

Leonhardt, Gerhard Adolf Wilhelm (1815-1880) — German lawyer and statesman, Minister of Justice in Hanover (1865-66) and Prussia (1867-79).— 189

Lessner, Friedrich (1825-1910) — German tailor; member of the Communist League; took part in the 1848-49 revolution; defendant at the Cologne Communist trial (1852); refugee in London from 1856; member of the German Workers' Educational Society in London; member of the General Council of the International (1864-72) and of the British Federal Council (1872-73); friend and associate of Marx and Engels.— 52, 463

Liebknecht, Natalie (1835-1909) — wife of Wilhelm Liebknecht from 1868.— 137

Liebknecht, Wilhelm (1826-1900) — prominent figure in the German and international working-class movement, took part in the 1848-49 revolution, member of the Communist League and of the International, deputy to the North German Reichstag (1867-70), deputy to the German Reichstag from 1874 (with intervals); one of the founders and leaders of the German Social-Democratic Party; friend and associate of Marx and Engels.— 3, 4, 12, 24, 35, 38, 40, 42, 50, 78, 80, 86, 99, 138, 164, 188, 261, 301, 304, 328, 334, 336, 348, 351, 370, 373, 442, 447, 455, 458, 469-70, 473

Lilienthal, F. W.— German physician, refugee in New York (the 1880s), was close to socialists.— 278, 368

Lingenau, Johann Karl Ferdinand (c. 1814-1877) — German-born American socialist, bequeathed his money to the German Social-Democratic Party.— 99

Lissagaray, Prosper Olivier (1838-1901) — French journalist; took part in the Paris Commune, adhered to the bourgeois-democratic 'new Jacobins' group, emigrated to England after the defeat of the Commune; author of the *Histoire de la Commune de 1871* (1876), returned to France in 1880, published *La Bataille* (1882-83, 1888-93), a newspaper which opposed Guesde and Lafargue, leaders of the French Workers' Party.— 116, 134, 150, 289, 309, 343, 346, 356

Littré, Maximilien Paul Emile (1801-1881) — French philosopher, philologist and politician.— 473

Longuet, Charles (1839-1903) — prominent figure in the French working-class movement, journalist, Proudhonist; member of the General Council of the International (1866-67, 1871-72), Corresponding Secretary for Belgium (1866), delegate to the Lausanne (1867), Brussels (1868) and Hague (1872) congresses and the London Conference (1871); member of the Paris Commune (1871), later joined the Possibilists, member of the Paris City Council (the 1880s-90s), husband of Marx's daughter Jenny from 1872.— 19, 23, 44, 47, 52-55, 61, 81, 84, 90, 92, 96, 98, 107, 108, 109, 111, 135, 136, 157, 199, 200, 202, 212, 219, 220, 224, 230, 232, 285, 295, 303, 309, 310, 313, 316, 327, 330, 340, 364, 369, 375, 408, 424, 426, 457, 469-74, 475

Longuet, Charles (Caro) (September 1873-July 1874) — son of Jenny and Charles Longuet, Marx's grandson.— 156

Longuet, Edgar (1879-1950) — son of Jenny and Charles Longuet, Marx's grandson.— 3, 61, 81, 89, 90, 95, 96, 107, 110, 135, 158, 160, 164, 165, 219, 225, 230, 240, 296, 303, 316, 327, 340, 426, 470

Longuet, Felicitas — Charles Longuet's mother.— 111, 113, 303

Longuet, Henri (Henry, Harra, Harry) (1878-1883) — son of Jenny and Charles Longuet, Marx's grandson.— 23, 61, 81, 89, 90, 95, 107, 108, 110, 111, 135, 136, 158, 160, 164, 165, 219, 225, 230, 240, 250, 256, 303, 316, 327, 340, 371, 417, 464, 470, 475

Longuet, Jean Laurent Frédéric (Johnny) (1876-1938) — son of Jenny and Charles Longuet, Marx's grandson.— 23, 61, 81, 85, 89, 90, 95, 96, 98, 107, 108, 109, 110, 115, 158, 160, 164, 165, 199, 219, 225, 230, 231, 232, 240, 250, 296, 303, 308, 312, 316, 318, 320, 328, 340, 353, 372, 378, 379, 417, 421, 424, 426, 475

Longuet, Jenny (née *Marx*) (1844-1883) — Marx's eldest daughter, prominent figure in the international working-class movement, wife of Charles Longuet from 1872.— 23, 61, 67-70, 81-85, 89-92, 95-96, 97-98, 106, 109, 110, 111, 113, 116, 117, 134-35, 142, 143, 156-59, 160, 164-65, 169, 199, 212, 217, 218-19, 220-21, 223-25, 230, 232, 240, 250, 255, 259, 265-66, 271-72, 276, 277, 278, 284, 289, 296, 303, 309, 310, 311, 315-17, 328, 329, 330, 331, 338, 340, 345, 402, 413, 417, 419, 420, 421, 424-26, 429, 430, 434, 458, 461, 469-75

Mohammed (*Mahomet, Muhammed*) (c. 570-632) — founder of Islam.— 242, 247, 425

Molière (real name *Jean Baptiste Poquelin*) (1622-1673) — French dramatist.— 164

Mommsen, Theodor (1817-1903) — German historian, author of works on the history of Ancient Rome.— 178

Moore, Samuel (1838-1911) — English lawyer, member of the International, translated into English the first volume of Marx's *Capital* (in collaboration with Edward Aveling) and the *Manifesto of the Communist Party*, friend of Marx and Engels.— 3, 26, 30, 35, 98, 166, 175, 215, 306, 307, 319, 378, 380

Morley, Samuel (1809-1886) — English industrialist and Liberal politician, M. P. (1865, 1868-85).— 54, 359

Most, Johann Joseph (1846-1906) — German anarchist, joined the working-class movement in the 1860s, deputy to the German Reichstag (1874-78), emigrated to England in 1878 after the promulgation of the Anti-Socialist Law; founder (1879) and editor of the *Freiheit*; as an anarchist, expelled from the German Socialist Workers' Party in 1880, emigrated to the USA in 1882 where continued his anarchist propaganda.— 7, 10, 39, 42, 43, 59, 75, 78, 80, 81-83, 86, 105, 141, 187, 260, 289, 325

Müllner, Amadeus Gottfried Adolf (1774-1829) — German poet, playwright and literary critic.— 263, 437

Murhard, Franz (*Francis*) — German refugee in the USA.— 46-47

N

Napoleon I Bonaparte (1769-1821) — French statesman and gener-

al, first Consul of the French Republic (1799-1804), Emperor of the French (1804-14 and 1815).— 188, 273, 327, 402

Napoleon III (*Charles Louis Napoleon Bonaparte*) (1808-1873) — nephew of Napoleon I; President of the Second Republic (December 1848 to 1851), Emperor of the French (1852-70).— 53, 100, 191, 200, 210, 454

Necker, Jacques (1732-1804) — French banker and politician, several times Director General of Finance in the 1770s and 1780s, attempted to carry out reforms.— 73

Newton, Sir Isaac (1642-1727) — English physicist, astronomer and mathematician, founder of classical mechanics.— 380

Nicholls — an acquaintance of the Engels family in London.— 25

Nicholls, Sarah — an acquaintance of the Engels family in London, daughter of the above.— 25

Nieuwenhuis, Ferdinand Domela (1846-1919) — prominent figure in the working-class movement in Holland, a founder of the Dutch Social-Democratic Party, M. P. from 1888, delegate to the international socialist workers' congresses of 1889, 1891 and 1893, went over to anarchism in the 1890s.— 16, 65-67, 166-67, 365

Nikitina, Varvara Nikolayevna (née *Gendre*) (1842-1884) — Russian journalist, lived in Italy from the late 1860s, later in France, contributed to several French periodicals.— 157

Nim, Nym — see *Demuth, Helene*

Nobiling, Karl Eduard (1848-1878) — German anarchist, made an attempt on the life of William I (1878) which served as a pretext for the introduction of the Anti-Socialist Law.— 175, 288

Nordau, Max Simon (real name *Südfeld*) (1849-1923) — German-born French writer and journalist.— 112, 114

Norgate — bookseller in London.— 103

Novikova, Olga Alexeyevna (1840-1925) — Russian journalist, lived in England for a long time, was in fact a diplomatic agent of the Russian government under Gladstone's administration in the 1870s.— 319

O

O'Connell, Daniel (1775-1847) — Irish lawyer and politician, leader of the Liberal wing in the national liberation movement.— 69, 286, 288

O'Donovan Rossa, Jeremiah (1831-1915) — a leader of the Fenian movement, published *The Irish People* (1863-65); was arrested in 1865 and sentenced to life imprisonment, amnestied in 1870, emigrated to the USA where he headed the Fenian organisation, retired from political life in the 1880s.— 287

Offenbach, Jacques (1819-1880) — French composer, a founder of the classical operetta.— 268

Oldenburg, Heinrich — German Social-Democrat, journalist.— 365

Oldrini, Alessandro — Italian-born French socialist, fought on the side of France in the Franco-Prussian war (1870-71), lived in France in the 1870s-early 1880s, exiled from France in late 1882.— 345

Oppenheimer, Moses — German Social-Democrat, was proved guilty of secret ties with the bourgeois press and embezzlement of Party funds (1883).— 447

Oswald, Eugen (1826-1912) — German journalist, democrat, took part in the revolutionary movement in Baden (1848-49), emigrated to England after the defeat of the revolution.— 36-37

P

Palmerston, Henry John Temple, 3rd Viscount (1784-1865) — British statesman, first Tory, from 1830 Whig, Foreign Secretary (1830-41 and 1846-51), Home Secretary (1852-55) and Prime Minister (1855-58 and 1859-65).— 251, 319, 365

Parker, Sarah — Engels' housemaid.— 135

Parnell, Charles Stewart (1846-1891) — Irish politician and statesman, Liberal, bourgeois nationalist, M. P. from 1875, Home Rule Party leader from 1877, a founder and leader of the Irish Land League (1880-81).— 84, 86, 95, 471

Parnell, Miss. — 98

Parsons, William (c. 1570-1650) — English statesman, took part in the colonisation of Ireland, big Irish landowner, Lord Chief Justice of Ireland (1640-48), Privy Councillor from 1623, M. P.— 68

Pauli, Ida — Philipp Viktor Pauli's wife.— 92

Pauli, Philipp Viktor (1836-after 1916) — German chemist, Carl Schorlemmer's friend, was on intimate terms with Marx and Engels, was in charge of a chemical plant in Rheinau, near Mannheim (1871-80).— 92

Pearson, Carl (1857-1936) — English mathematician, biologist and philosopher, professor at University College in London from 1884; champion of socialist ideas and the working-class movement.— 60

Peel, Sir Robert (1788-1850) — British

statesman, moderate Tory, Prime Minister (1834-35 and 1841-46), repealed the Corn Laws in 1846.— 69, 365

Pelletan (1846-1915) — French bourgeois politician, journalist, editor-in-chief of the *Justice* from 1880, associated with the Left-wing Radicals.— 471

Péreire, Isaac (1806-1880) — French banker, Bonapartist, deputy to the Corps legislatif; together with his brother Émile Péreire, founded the joint-stock bank *Crédit Mobilier* in 1852; it went bankrupt in 1867 and was liquidated in 1871; author of works on credit.— 73

Péreire, Jacob Émile (1800-1875) — French banker, adhered to the Saint-Simonists (1825-31), later a Bonapartist, a founder (1852) and director of the *Crédit Mobilier*.— 73

Perovskaya, Sofia Lvovna (1853-1881) — Russian revolutionary, prominent figure in the *Narodnaya Volya* (People's Will) secret society, executed for involvement in the assassination of Alexander II.— 96

Philips, Antoinette (Nannette) (c. 1837-1885) — Marx's cousin.— 246

Phillips, Wendell (1811-1884) — American public figure and politician, orator, a leader of the revolutionary wing in the abolitionist movement, advocated revolutionary methods in the struggle against the Southern slaveholders, joined the working-class movement in the 1870s, favoured the formation of an independent workers' party in the USA, joined the First International in 1871.— 77-78

Picard, Léon — French socialist, journalist, member of the French Workers' Party, an editor of the *Égalité* in the early 1880s.— 352, 354, 358, 361, 389

Pickering — English physician in Cannes.— 273

Piquand, Édouard — French lawyer, examining magistrate in Montluçon in the early 1880s.— 397

Pitt, William (1759-1806) — British statesman, a Tory leader, Prime Minister (1783-1801 and 1804-06).— 69

Plon-Plon — see *Bonaparte, Prince Napoléon Joseph Charles Paul*

Plutarch (c. 45-c. 127) — Greek moralist, writer and philosopher.— 273, 382

Podolinski, Sergei Andreyevich (1850-1891) — Ukrainian public figure, politician, scientist, Darwinist, one of the first propagandists of Marx's economic theory in the Ukraine; emigrated to Austria in 1871, later to France, lived in Switzerland from the 1880s; had contacts with Russian revolutionary émigrés, an initiator of putting out socialist literature in Ukrainian in Vienna (1879); was personally acquainted with Marx and Engels, and regularly corresponded with them.— 410, 411, 412-13

Poliakov, Samuil Solomonovich (1837-1888) — railway entrepreneur and financier in Russia.— 248

Pollaky, Ignatius Paul — owner of a private police bureau in London in the early 1880s, contributed to the *Foreign Police Gazette*.— 390

Prendergast, John Patrick (1808-1893) — Irish historian, Liberal, author of works on the history of Ireland.— 68

Proudhon, Pierre Joseph (1809-1865) — French writer, petty-bourgeois socialist, economist and sociologist, a founder of anarchism.— 44, 93, 100, 177, 193, 472

Pumps — see *Rosher, Mary Ellen*

Puttkamer, Robert Victor von (1828-

1900) — Minister of the Interior in the German Empire (1881-88), initiated the persecution of Social-Democrats at the time of the Anti-Socialist Law.— 88, 431, 455

Pyat, Félix (1810-1889) — French journalist, playwright and politician, democrat; took part in the 1848 revolution, emigrated to Switzerland in 1849 and later to Belgium and England; opposed independent working-class movement, using the French Section in London, conducted a slander campaign against Marx and the First International; deputy to the National Assembly (1871), member of the Paris Commune (1871); emigrated to England after the suppression of the Commune, returned to France after the 1880 amnesty, published the newspaper *Commune* (September-November 1880).— 43, 116

R

Raciborski, Adam (1809-1871) — Polish physician, took part in the 1830-31 insurrection in Poland, emigrated to France after the suppression of the insurrection.— 437

Rackow, Heinrich — German Social-Democrat, emigrated to London in 1879, a tobacco shop owner, member of the German Workers' Educational Society in London.— 7

Radford, Ernest — English lawyer, acquaintance of the Marx family, Dolly Maitland's husband.— 82, 104, 475

Rae, John (1845-1915) — English economist and sociologist, contributed to the *Contemporary Review* in the 1880s, author of *Life of Adam Smith*.— 162, 185

Ranke, Johannes (1836-1916) — German physiologist and anthropologist, professor at Munich University.— 417

Rasch, Gustav (d. 1878) — journalist, lawyer, took part in the 1848-49 revolution, emigrated to Switzerland and then to France after the suppression of the revolution, member of the German Social-Democratic Party from 1873.— 206

Redgrave, Alexander — factory inspector in England.— 56, 368

Redpath — see *Redgrave, Alexander*

Regnard, Albert Adrien (b. 1836) — French radical journalist and historian, took part in the Paris Commune, emigrated to England after its suppression, returned to France after the 1880 amnesty.— 67-69, 117

Reinhardt, Richard (1829-1898) — German poet, refugee in Paris; Heinrich Heine's secretary, friend of Marx and Engels.— 170, 172, 285

Rendstone — Marx's acquaintance.— 134

Reynaud — French physician in Argenteuil.— 111, 112, 113

Reynaud — wife of the above.— 111, 112, 113

Ricardo, David (1772-1823) — English economist.— 16, 93, 100, 230

Richard III (1452-1485) — King of England (1483-85).— 399

Richter, Eugen (1838-1906) — German Left-wing liberal politician, leader of the Party of Progress, member of the North German Reichstag (1867) and of the German Reichstag (1871-1906), a founder and leader of the Party of Free Thinkers (Deutsche Freisinnige Partei), opposed Bismarck, favoured free trade, fought Social-Democracy.— 178

Roby, Henry John (1830-1915) — English school teacher, author of a Latin grammar; partner in the Manchester firm of Ermen & Roby (1874-94), Liberal M. P. (1890-95).— 307

first who defended and popularised the Marxian economic teaching in Russia.— 45, 64

Siemens, Carl Wilhelm (1823-1883) — German electrical engineer, businessman; lived in London from 1859 where he was in charge of the London branch of the German Siemens & Co., President of the British Association for the Advancement of Science in 1882 and member of other scientific societies, author of works on heat and electricity.— 92, 314, 384

Simon, John (1816-1904) — English physician, medical inspector in the Privy Council.— 140

Simon, Jules François Simon Suisse (1814-1896) — French statesman, idealist philosopher, moderate bourgeois republican, deputy to the Constituent Assembly (1848-49), member of the Government of National Defence, Minister of Public Education in it and in Thiers' government (1870-73), deputy to the National Assembly (1871), inspired the struggle against the Commune, Chairman of the Council of Ministers (1876-77).— 140

Singer, Paul (1844-1911) — prominent figure in the German working-class movement and in the Social-Democratic group in the Reichstag, active member of the Marxist wing in the Second International, member of the Board of the Socialist Workers' Party of Germany from 1887, its Chairman from 1890; deputy to the Reichstag from 1884 and Chairman of its Social-Democratic group from 1885.— 260, 261, 433

Skaldin — see *Yelenev, Fyodor Pavlovich*

Skobelev, Mikhail Dmitrievich (1843-1882) — prominent Russian general, took part in military expeditions to Central Asia (1873, 1875-76 and 1880-

81) and in the Russo-Turkish war (1877-78).— 209, 235

Smith, Adam (1723-1790) — Scottish economist.— 16

Soetbeer, Georg Adolf (1814-1892) — German economist and statistician.— 257

Solari, Jean — Swiss socialist, journalist, editor of the *Précurseur* in the early 1880s.— 405

Songeon — French democrat, member of secret workers' revolutionary societies in Paris during the 1848 revolution, émigré in London in the 1850s, Chairman of the Paris City Council in the 1880s.— 317, 318

Sophocles (c. 497-406 B. C.) — Greek dramatist.— 230

Sorge, Adolph (d. 1907) — Friedrich Adolph Sorge's son, mechanical engineer, lived in the USA up to 1895; worked as an engineer in Baku oilfields in 1895-98, later moved to Germany.— 99, 161, 162, 177, 237, 280, 368

Sorge, Friedrich Adolph (1828-1906) — German teacher, took part in the 1848-49 revolution in Germany; emigrated to the USA in 1852 where he organised American sections of the International, secretary of the General Council, delegate to the Hague Congress (1872), General Secretary of the General Council in New York (1872-74), a founder of the Socialist Workers' Party of North America (1876-77), friend and associate of Marx and Engels.— 24, 25, 42-47, 94, 98-101, 161-63, 177, 237, 278-80, 304-05, 368-70, 457, 460

Sorge, Katharina — Friedrich Adolph Sorge's wife.— 177

Soulié, Melchior Frédéric (1800-1847) — French revolutionary romantic writer and dramatist, republican;

B. C.) — Roman author of comedies.—
147

Terry, Ellen Alicia (1847-
1928) — English dramatic actress,
famous performer of Shakespearean
roles.— 104

Theisz, Albert Frédéric Jules (1839-
1881) — metal-worker, prominent figure in the French working-class movement, Proudhonist, member of the
Paris Commune, emigrated to England after the suppression of the Commune, member of the General Council
of the International (1871).— 44

Thierry, Jacques Nicolas Augustin (1795-
1856) — French liberal, historian of
the Restoration.— 414

Thiers, Louis Adolph (1797-
1877) — French historian and statesman, Prime Minister (1836 and 1840),
head of the Orleanists after 1848,
Chairman of the Council of Ministers
(1871), organised the suppression of
the Paris Commune (1871), President
of the Republic (1871-73).— 52

Tissot, Victor (1845-1917) — French writer and journalist, lived in Switzerland
up to 1874, later in France; contributed to the *Gazette de Lausanne et Journal
Suisse* from 1868 and edited it during
the Franco-Prussian war, an editor of
the *Figaro* in 1891-93.— 112

Trouchu, Louis Jules (1815-
1896) — French general and politician, Orleanist, took part in the conquest of Algeria (the 1830s-40s), the
Crimean (1853-56) and Italian (1859)
wars; head of the Government of National Defence, commander-in-chief of
the Paris armed forces (September
1870-January 1871), sabotaged the defence of the city, deputy to the National Assembly (1871).— 469

Tupper, Martin Farquhar (1810-
1889) — English writer, author of
Proverbial Philosophy.— 96

*Turgot, Anne Robert Jacques, baron de
l'Aulne* (1727-1781) — French economist and statesman, Physiocrat, Controller-General of Finance (1774-
76).— 73, 230

Tussy — see *Marx, Eleanor (Tussy)*

V

Vallés, Jules Louis Joseph (1832-
1885) — French writer, politician and
journalist, republican; was imprisoned
several times for his struggle against
the Second Empire; member of the
First International and of the Paris
Commune, member of the Commission
of Education and Foreign Relations;
edited the *Cri du Peuple* (1871), was
close to the Blanquists and Proudhonists; emigrated to England after
the suppression of the Commune; edited
the *Cri du Peuple* in France from October 1883.— 127

Vezin, Jane Elisabeth (1827-
1902) — English actress, performed
Shakespearean roles, acquaintance of
the Marx family.— 176

Viereck, Laura — Louis Viereck's wife.—
99, 141, 442

Viereck, Louis (1851-1921) — German
publisher and journalist, a leader of the
Right wing in the Socialist Workers'
Party of Germany at the time of the
Anti-Socialist Law; deputy to the
Reichstag (1884-87); dismissed from
all responsible Party posts by decision of the 1887 St Gallen congress;
emigrated to America in 1896 and
withdrew from the socialist movement.— 75, 77, 93, 99, 139, 141, 259,
279, 350, 430, 431, 442-44, 445-47,
449, 450

Virchow, Rudolf (1821-1902) — German
naturalist, founder of cellular pathol-
ogy; politician, a leader of the Party of

1842) — Jenny Marx's father, Privy Councillor in Trier.— 158

Wilhelm — see *Liebknecht, Wilhelm*

William I (1743-1821) — Elector of Hesse-Cassel (1803-07 and November 1813 to 1821).— 273

William I (1797-1888) — Prince of Prussia, King of Prussia (1861-88), Emperor of Germany (1871-88).— 78, 175, 178, 234-35, 441

William II (1859-1941) — King of Prussia and Emperor of Germany (1888-1918).— 208

Williams — bookseller in London.— 103

Williamson — James M. Williamson's wife.— 423

Williamson, James M. — English physician in Ventnor, treated Marx from November 1882 to early January 1883.— 366, 371, 372, 375, 392, 399, 419, 420, 429

Willich, Johann August Ernst (1810-1878) — Prussian officer who left the service on political grounds, member of the Communist League, participant in the Baden-Palatinate uprising of 1849, one of the leaders of the sectarian group that split away from the Communist League in 1850, emigrated to the USA in 1853, took part in the American Civil War on the side of the North.— 281, 329

Wilson, Charles Rivers (1831-1916) — big English state and colonial official, head of the English Public Debt Administration (1874-94), Minister of Finance in the national government of Egypt (1878-79).— 365, 376, 381

Windthorst, Ludwig (1812-1891) — German politician, Minister of Justice in Hanover (1851-52 and 1862-65), deputy to the Reichstag and a leader of the Party of the Centre.— 189

Wishart of Pittarow, Jeanie — see *Westphalen, Jeanie von*

Wolf — see *Longuet, Edgar*

Wolff — German merchant, brother of Ferdinand Wolff.— 425

Wolff, Ferdinand (*Red Wolff*) (1812-1895) — German journalist, member of the Brussels Communist Correspondence Committee in 1846-47, member of the Communist League, an editor of the *Neue Rheinische Zeitung* in 1848-49, left Germany after the 1848-49 revolution, supported Marx during the split in the Communist League (1850), later withdrew from political life.— 425

Wolseley, Garnet Joseph (1833-1913) — English general, commanded English troops in Egypt in 1882.— 313, 317, 327

Wróblewski, Walery (1836-1908) — Polish revolutionary democrat, a leader of the Polish liberation insurrection of 1863-64, general of the Paris Commune, emigrated to London after the suppression of the Commune, sentenced to death in absentia, member of the General Council of the International and Corresponding Secretary for Poland (1871-72), delegate to the Hague Congress (1872), actively fought the Bakuninists, headed the Polish revolutionary society *Związek Ludu Polskiego* in London in 1872, advocated the idea of the Polish-Russian revolutionary union, returned to France after the amnesty, maintained contact with Marx and Engels.— 183, 311, 314

Y

Yelenev, Fyodor Pavlovich (pseudonym *Skaldin*) (1827-1902) — Russian writer, journalist, liberal; Secretary of the Editorial Commissions for the Prepara-

INDEX OF LITERARY AND MYTHOLOGICAL NAMES

INDEX OF QUOTED
AND MENTIONED LITERATURE

WORKS BY KARL MARX AND FREDERICK ENGELS

Marx, Karl

Capital. A Critique of Political Economy. Vol. I, Book One: The Process of Production of Capital (present edition, Vol. 35)
— Das Kapital. Kritik der politischen Oekonomie. Erster Band, Buch 1: Der Produktionsprocess des Kapitals. Hamburg, 1867.— 16, 44, 56, 103, 140, 162, 163, 189, 257, 294, 298, 310, 369
— Das Kapital. Kritik der politischen Oekonomie. Bd. I, Buch 1: Der Produktionsprocess des Kapitals. Zweite verbesserte Auflage. Hamburg, 1872.— 225, 423, 425
— Капиталъ. Критика политической экономіи. Сочиненіе Карла Маркса. Переводъ съ нъмецкаго. Томъ первый. Книга I. Процессъ производства капитала. С.-Петербургъ, 1872.— 45
— Das Kapital. Kritik der politischen Oekonomie. Herausgegeben von Friedrich Engels. Erster Band. Buch 1: Der Produktionsprocess des Kapitals. Dritte vermehrte Auflage. Hamburg, 1883.— 158, 161, 162, 225, 347, 359, 368, 423, 425, 434
— Le Capital. Traduction de M.J. Roy, entièrement revisée par l'auteur [Vol. 1.], Paris [1872-75].— 40, 41
Capital. A Critique of Political Economy. Vol. II, Book Two: The Process of Circulation of Capital (present edition, Vol. 36)
— Das Kapital. Kritik der politischen Oekonomie. Zweiter Band, Buch 2: Der Cirkulationsprocess des Kapitals. Hamburg, 1885.— 16, 158, 161, 465
Capital. A Critique of Political Economy. Vol. III, Book Three: The Process of Capitalist Production As a Whole (present edition, Vol. 37)
— Das Kapital. Kritik der politischen Oekonomie. Dritter Band, Theile I-II.

The Condition of the Working-Class in England. From Personal Observation and Authentic Sources (present edition, Vol. 4)
— Die Lage der arbeitenden Klasse in England. Nach eigner Anschauung und authentischen Quellen. Leipzig, 1845.— 190, 294

Cotton and Iron (present edition, Vol. 24). In: *The Labour Standard*, No. 13, July 30, 1881.— 140, 197

Dialectics of Nature (present edition, Vol. 25).— 348, 350, 377

Draft of a Speech at the Graveside of Karl Marx (present edition, Vol. 24)
— Discours de Frédéric Engels. Under the general heading: Obsèques de Karl Marx. In: *La Justice*, No. 27, 20 mars 1883.— 465

A Fair Day's Wages for a Fair Day's Work (present edition, Vol. 24). In: *The Labour Standard*, No. 1, May 7, 1881.— 140, 197

The French Commercial Treaty (present edition, Vol. 24). In: *The Labour Standard*, No. 7, June 18, 1881.— 140, 197

Jenny Marx, neé von Westphalen (present edition, Vol. 24)
— Jenny Marx, geb. v. Westphalen. In: *Der Sozialdemokrat*, Nr. 50, 8. Dezember 1881.— 282

Karl Marx's Funeral (present edition, Vol. 24)
— Das Begräbniß von Karl Marx. In: *Der Sozialdemokrat*, Nr. 13, 22. März 1883.— 465

The Mark (present edition, Vol. 24)
— Die Mark. In: F. Engels, *Die Entwicklung des Sozialismus von der Utopie zur Wissenschaft*. Hottingen-Zürich, 1882.— 331, 390, 395, 399, 403, 407, 409, 410, 416, 432, 454

Outlines of a Critique of Political Economy (present edition, Vol. 3)
— Umrisse zu einer Kritik der Nationalökonomie. In: *Deutsch-Französische Jahrbücher*, Paris, 1844.— 58

Preface to the First German Edition of 'Socialism: Utopian and Scientific' (present edition, Vol. 24)
— Vorwort. In: F. Engels, *Die Entwicklung des Sozialismus von der Utopie zur Wissenschaft*. Hottingen-Zürich, 1882.— 331, 358

Social Classes — Necessary and Superfluous (present edition, Vol. 24). In: *The Labour Standard*, No. 14, August 6, 1881.— 140, 197

The Socialism of Mr. Bismarck (present edition, Vol. 24)
— Le socialisme de M. Bismarck. In: *L'Égalité*, 2ᵉ Série, Nos. 7 et 10, 3 et 24 mars 1880.— 149

Socialism: Utopian and Scientific (present edition, Vol. 24)
— Socialisme utopique et socialisme scientifique. Traduction française par Paul Lafargue. Paris, 1880.— 15, 300, 331, 335-36, 352, 369
— Le socialisme utopique et le socialisme scientifique. In: *La Revue socialiste*, Nos. 3, 4, 5, 20 mars, 20 avril et 5 mai 1880.— 15, 300

— Die Entwicklung des Sozialismus von der Utopie zur Wissenschaft. Hottingen-Zürich, 1882.— 300, 324, 331, 334, 335, 336, 344, 352, 358, 390, 432, 433, 454

Trades Unions (present edition, Vol. 24). In: *The Labour Standard*, Nos. 4 and 5, May 28 and June 4, 1881.— 140, 197

Two Model Town Councils (present edition, Vol. 24). In: *The Labour Standard*, No. 8, June 25, 1881.— 140, 197

The Vicar of Bray (present edition, Vol. 24)
— Der Vikar von Bray. Aus dem Englischen von Friedrich Engels. In: *Der Sozialdemokrat*, Nr. 37, 7. September 1882.— 302, 326, 331

The Wages System (present edition, Vol. 24). In: *The Labour Standard*, No. 3, May 21, 1881.— 140, 197

The Wages Theory of the Anti-Corn Law League (present edition, Vol. 24). In: *The Labour Standard*, No. 10, July 9, 1881.— 140, 197

A Working Men's Party (present edition, Vol. 24). In: *The Labour Standard*, No. 12, July 23, 1881.— 140, 197

Marx, Karl, and Engels, Frederick

The Alliance of Socialist Democracy and the International Working Men's Association. Report and Documents Published by Decision of the Hague Congress of the International (present edition, Vol. 23)
— L'Alliance de la Démocratie Socialiste et l'Association Internationale des Travailleurs. Rapport et documents publiés par ordre du Congrès International de la Haye. Londres-Hambourg, 1873.— 129, 375

Circular Letter to August Bebel, Wilhelm Liebknecht, Wilhelm Bracke and Others (present edition, Vol. 24).— 279, 281

Fictitious Splits in the International. Private Circular from the General Council of the International Working Men's Association (present edition, Vol. 23)
— Les prétendues scissions dans l'Internationale. Circulaire privée du Conseil Général de l'Association Internationale des Travailleurs. Genève, 1872.— 129

Manifesto of the Communist Party (present edition, Vol. 6)
— Manifest der Kommunistischen Partei, London, 1848.— 100, 278, 293, 422, 425
— Манифестъ коммунистической партіи. Переводъ съ нѣмецкаго изданія 1872. Съ предисловіемъ авторовъ. Женева, 1882.— 184, 295

To the Meeting in Geneva Held to Commemorate the 50th Anniversary of the Polish Revolution of 1830 (present edition, Vol. 24)
— Do meetingu w Genewie, zwołanego na pamiątke 50-ej rocznicy Rewolucyi Polskiej 1830. In: *Sprawozdanie z międzynarodowégo zebrania zwołunego w 50-letnią rocznicę listopadowégo powstania przez redakcyje Równości w Genewie. Genewa, 1881.— 195

Preface to the 1872 German Edition of the 'Manifesto of the Communist Party' (present edition, Vol. 23)

— Vorwort. In: Marx, K., Engels, F. *Das kommunistische Manifest*. Neue Ausgabe mit einem Vorwort der Verfasser. Leipzig, 1872.— 422, 425

Preface to the Second Russian Edition of the 'Manifesto of the Communist Party' (present edition, Vol. 24).— 244

— Предисловіе, написанное К. Марксомъ и Ф. Энгельсомъ къ предпринятому 'русск. соц.-револю́ц. библіотекой' переводу *Манифеста коммунистической партіи*. In: *Народная воля*, № 8/9, 5 февраля, Спб., 1882.— 184, 244, 247, 425

— Vorrede zu der zweiten russischen Auflage des *Manifestes der Kommunistischen Partei*. In: *Der Sozialdemokrat*, Nr. 16, 13. April 1882.— 247

Review, May to October [1850] (present edition, Vol. 10)

— Revue, Mai bis Oktober. London, 1. November 1850. In: *Neue Rheinische Zeitung. Politisch-ökonomische Revue*, Nr. 5-6, 1850.— 189

WORKS BY DIFFERENT AUTHORS

Amos, Sh. ' "Spoiling the Egyptians": Revised Version.' In: *The Contemporary Review*, Vol. XLII, October 1882.— 381

The Arabian Nights.— 219

Auer, I. [Speech in the Reichstag on 30 March 1881.] In: *Stenographische Berichte über die Verhandlungen des Reichstags. 4. Legislaturperiode. IV. Session 1881. Band I. 25. Sitzung am 30. März 1881*. Berlin, 1881.— 85, 86

Bachofen, J. J. *Das Mutterrecht. Eine Untersuchung über die Gynaikokratie der alten Welt nach ihrer religiösen und rechtlichen Natur*. Stuttgart, 1861.— 453

Bancroft, H. H. *The Native Races of the Pacific States of North America*. Volume I. *Wild Tribes*. New York, 1875.— 394, 438

Bax, E. B. *Leaders of Modern Thought. XXIII—Karl Marx*. In: *Modern Thought*, Vol. III, No. 12, December 1, 1881.— 163, 165, 184

Bazin, G. *À Monsieur le commissaire de police*. In: *L'Égalité*, 4ᵉ Série, No. 38, 30 novembre 1882.— 391

B[ebel, A.] *Aufhebung des Sozialistengesetzes?* In: *Der Sozialdemokrat*, Nr. 42, 12. Oktober 1882.— 357

Bebel, A. *Polizei-Orgien in Berlin unter dem Belagerungszustand*. In: *Der Sozialdemokrat*, Nr. 11, 14. März 1880.— 10

— [Speech in the Reichstag on 31 March 1881.] In: *Stenographische Berichte über die Verhandlungen des Reichstags. 4. Legislaturperiode. IV. Session 1881. Band I. 26. Sitzung am 31. März 1881*. Berlin, 1881.— 85, 86, 87

— [Speech in the Reichstag on 4 April 1881.] In: *Stenographische Berichte über die Verhandlungen des Reichstags. 4. Legislaturperiode. IV. Session 1881. Band I. 29. Sitzung am 4. April 1881*. Berlin, 1881.— 85, 86, 87, 433

— *Unsere Ziele. Eine Streitschrift gegen die 'Demokratische Correspondenz'*. Leipzig, 1870.— 454, 455

— *Die Ziele der Arbeiterbewegung*. Nach der sechsten Auflage vom Jahre 1877 kritisch revidirt und herausgegeben von Ad. Hepner. New York, 1883.— 454, 455

[Bernstein, E.] *Bekennt Farbe!* Signed: Leo. In: *Der Sozialdemokrat*, Nr. 16, 13. April 1882.— 244
— *Entweder — oder!* Signed: Leo. In: *Der Sozialdemokrat*, Nr. 51, 15. Dezember 1881.— 173, 203
— *Ein Gedenktag.* Signed: Leo. In: *Der Sozialdemokrat*, Nr. 4, 23. Januar 1881.— 59
— *Es fehlt uns an Intelligenzen.* Signed: Leo. In: *Der Sozialdemokrat*, Nr. 31 und 33, 28. Juli und 11. August 1881.— 127, 137
— *Die Situation in Ireland.* Signed: Leo. In: *Der Sozialdemokrat*, Nr. 21, 18. Mai 1882.— 301

Bible.— 70
    The Old Testament.— 274, 349
    The New Testament.— 251, 278, 395

Bismarck, O. von [Speech in the Reichstag on 9 January 1882.] In: *Stenographische Berichte über die Verhandlungen des Reichstags. V. Legislaturperiode. I. Session 1881/82. [Band I.] 20. Sitzung am 9. Januar 1882.* Berlin, 1882.— 183

Bracke, W. *Der Lassalle'sche Vorschlag. Ein Wort an den 4. Congreß der socialdemokratischen Arbeiterpartei. (Einberufen auf den 23. August 1873 nach Eisenach.)* Braunschweig, 1873.— 294
— *'Nieder mit den Sozialdemokraten!'*, Braunschweig, 1876.— 294

Brentano, L. *Wie Karl Marx citirt.* In: *Concordia*, Nr. 10, 7. März 1872.— 65
— (anon.) *Wie Karl Marx sich vertheidigt.* In: *Concordia*, Nr. 27, 4. Juli 1872.— 65

Bürkli, K. *Abschüttelungs halber.* In: *Arbeiterstimme*, 7. und 14. Januar 1882.— 177
— *Demokratische Bank-Reform. Oder: Wie kommt das Volk zu billigerem Zins? Sieben Fragen und Antworten über die Reorganisation der Kantonalbank.* Zürich, 1881.— 209, 210

Caesar, G. J. *Commentarii de bello Gallico.* In: *Die Geschichtschreiber der deutschen Vorzeit in deutscher Bearbeitung.* Bd. 1: *Die Urzeit.* Hrsg. v. G. H. Pertz, J. Grimm u. a. Berlin, 1847-1849.— 382

Cafiero, C. *Polemica.* In: *La Plebe*, Num. 17, 5 Novembre 1882.— 392

Candelari, R. *Ancora sulla teoria del valore secondo Marx.* In: *La Plebe*, Num. 18, 12 Novembre 1882.— 392
— *Carlo Marx.* In: *La Plebe*, Num. 15, 22 Ottobre 1882.— 392
— *La critica dell'economia radicale moderna.* In: *La Plebe*, Num. 13, 8 Ottobre 1882.— 392
— *De Laveleye e Rodbertus.* In: *La Plebe*, Num. 14, 15 Ottobre 1882.— 392
— *Il Salario.* In: *La Plebe*, Num. 17, 5 Novembre 1882.— 392
— *La teoria del valore secondo Marx.* In: *La Plebe*, Num. 16, 29 Ottobre 1882.— 392

Chamisso, A. von. *Salas y Gomez.*— 439

Cieszkowski, A. *Du Crédit et de la circulation.* Paris, 1839.
— *Prolegomena zur Historiosophie.* Berlin, 1838.— 177, 189

Colins, J. G. *L'économie politique. Source des révolutions et des utopies prétendues socialistes.* Tome I-III. Paris, 1856-1857.— 100

[Danielson, N. F.] *Очерки нашего пореформеннаго общественнаго хозяйства.* Signed: Николай—онъ. In: *Слово,* Спб., октябрь 1880.—31, 61, 62, 64

Dante, Alighieri. *La Divina commedia.*—291

Darwin, Ch. *The Formation of Vegetable Mould, through the Action of Worms, with Observations on Their Habits.* London, 1881.—274

Die deutsche Geheimpolizei im Kampfe mit der Sozialdemokratie. Aktenstücke und Enthüllungen auf Grund authentischen Materials dargestellt. Hottingen-Zürich, 1882.— 390, 436

Deville, G. *Il y a cinq ans.* In: *L'Égalité,* 4ᵉ Série, No. 27, 19 novembre 1882.—387
— *Le travail.* In: *L'Égalité,* 4ᵉ Série, Nos. 57 et 58, 19 et 20 décembre 1882.—413

[Dozon, A.] *Български народни пѣсни. Chansons populaires bulgares inédites.* Paris, 1875.— 207

Dühring, E. *Kritische Geschichte der Nationalökonomie und des Socialismus.* Zweite, theilweise umgearbeitete Auflage. Berlin, 1875.—434

[Eccarius, J. G.] *A German Opinion of English Trade Unionism.* In: *The Labour Standard,* No. 14, 6 August 1881.—118, 120, 121, 123

[Eckardt, J.] *Berlin und St. Petersburg. Preussische Beiträge zur Geschichte der Russisch-Deutschen Beziehungen.* Leipzig, 1880.—193

Epicurus [Letter to Menoeceus].—462

Fielding, H. *The History of the Adventures of Joseph Andrews and His Friend Mr. Abraham Adams.*—329

The Financial Reform Almanach. For 1882. London.—211

Fitzgibbon, G. *Ireland in 1868, the Battle-Field for English Party Strife; its grievances, real and factitious; remedies, abortive or mischievous.* London, 1868.—70

Freeman, Ed. A. *History of Europe.* London, 1876.—417

Friedrich II. *Aus der Instruction für die Generalmajors von der Cavallerie (14. August 1748).* In: *Die Werke Friedrichs des Großen,* Bd. 6: Militärische Schriften, hrsg. von Gustav Berthold Volz, deutsch von Friedrich v. Oppeln-Bronikowski. Berlin, 1913.—431

George, H. *The Kearney Agitation in California.* In: *The Popular Science Monthly,* Vol. XVII, August 1880.— 101
— *Progress and Poverty: an inquiry into the cause of industrial depressions and of increase of want with increase of wealth. The Remedy.* New York, 1880.—93, 99-101

Die Geschichtschreiber der deutschen Vorzeit in deutscher Bearbeitung. Bd. 1: *Die Urzeit.* Herausgegeben von G. H. Pertz, J. Grimm, u. a. Berlin, 1847-1849.—382

Goethe, J. W. von. *Das Göttliche.*—230
— *Faust.*—110
— *Der Fischer.*—126
— *Reineke Fuchs.*—95

— *Der Schatzgräber.*— 260
— *Zahme Xenien.*— 268

Grillenberger, K. [Speech in the Reichstag on 14 December 1882.] In: *Stenographische Berichte über die Verhandlungen des Reichstags. V. Legislaturperiode. II. Session 1882/83. Band I. 28. Sitzung am 14. Dezember 1882.* Berlin, 1883.— 454

Guesde, J., et Lafargue, P. *Le Programme du Parti Ouvrier.* Paris, 1883.— 43, 44

Hales, J. *To the Editor of 'The Eastern Post'.* In: *The Eastern Post,* No. 158, 7 October 1871.— 52
— *International Working Men's Association.* In: *The Eastern Post,* No. 171, 6 January 1872.— 53

Hanssen, G. *Die Aufhebung der Leibeigenschaft und die Umgestaltung der gutsherrlich-bäuerlichen Verhältnisse überhaupt in den Herzogthümern Schleswig und Holstein.* St. Petersburg, 1861.— 403

Hartmann, G. W. [Speech in the Reichstag on 15 June 1881.] In: *Stenographische Berichte über die Verhandlungen des Reichstags. 4. Legislaturperiode. IV. Session 1881. Band II. 61. Sitzung am 15. Juni 1881.* Berlin, 1881.— 138

Hegel, G. W. F. *Werke.* Vollständige Ausgabe durch einen Verein von Freunden des Verewigten: Ph. Marheineke, J. Schulze, Ed. Gans, Lp. v. Henning, H. Hothe, C. Michelet, F. Förster. Bd. I-XVIII.
— *Band II. Phänomenologie des Geistes.* Zweite unveränderte Auflage. Berlin, 1841.— 172, 296
— *Band III. Wissenschaft der Logik. Erster Theil. Die objective Logik.* Erste Abtheilung. *Die Lehre vom Seyn.* Zweite unveränderte Auflage. Berlin, 1841.— 131
— *Band VIII. Grundlinien der Philosophie des Rechts oder Naturrecht und Staatswissenschaft im Grundrisse.* Zweite Auflage. Berlin, 1840.— 354
— *Band IX. Vorlesungen über die Philosophie der Geschichte.* Zweite Auflage. Berlin, 1840.— 354

Heine, H. *Reisebilder.*— 430
— *Zur Beruhigung.*— 187

[Hirsch, C.] *Le Socialisme en Allemagne.* Signed: Un socialiste allemand. In: *La Nouvelle Revue,* t. 15, mars-avril 1882.— 225, 230

[Höchberg, K., Bernstein, E., und Schramm, C. A.] *Rückblicke auf die sozialistische Bewegung in Deutschland.* Kritische Aphorismen von * * *. In: *Jahrbuch für Sozialwissenschaft und Sozialpolitik.* 1. Jg. 1. Hälfte, Zürich-Oberstrass, 1879.— 279, 281, 292, 448

Hyndman, H. M. *England for All.* London, 1881.— 102, 103, 162, 163

[Janson] Янсонъ, Ю. Э. *Сравнительная статистика Россіи и западно-европейскихъ государствъ.* Спб., 1877.— 64

Joffrin, J. *A M. Jules Guesde, rédacteur de l'Égalité.* In: *Le Prolétaire,* No. 171, 7 janvier 1882.— 181, 183

Kautsky, K. *Der Einfluss der Volksvermehrung auf den Fortschritt der Gesellschaft.* Wien, 1880.— 56, 434

— *Die Entstehung der Ehe und Familie.* In: *Kosmos.* Zeitschrift für Entwickelungslehre und einheitliche Weltanschauung. IV. Jahrgang. XII. Band. Oktober 1882-März 1883. Stuttgart, 1882.— 437, 450-52

— (anon.) *International Labour Laws.* In: *The Labour Standard,* No. 15, August 13, 1881.— 119, 120, 122, 123, 126, 140

— (anon.) *Der Staatssozialismus und die Sozialdemokratie.* Signed: Symmachos. In: *Der Sozialdemokrat,* Nr. 10, 6. März 1881.— 73

— *Die überseeische Lebensmittel-Konkurrenz* (Separatabdruck aus den *Staatswirthschaftlichen Abhandlungen,* Serie II, Heft IV u. V). Leipzig, 1881.— 434, 437

— (anon.) *Der Vetter aus Amerika, eine Erzählung für Landleute, erbaulich zu lesen* [s. l., s. d.].— 138, 141

— (anon.) *Die Vivisektion des Proletariats.* In: *Der Sozialdemokrat,* 22. September 1881.— 141

Kayser, M. [Speech in the Reichstag on 17 May 1879.] In: *Stenographische Berichte über die Verhandlungen des Deutschen Reichstags.* 4. Legislaturperiode. II. Session 1879. Bd. II. 47. Sitzung am 17. Mai 1879. Berlin, 1879.— 153

Keay, J. S. *Spoiling the Egyptians: A Tale of Shame, Told from the Blue Books.* London, 1882.— 381

— *'Spoiling the Egyptians'. A Rejoinder.* In: *The Contemporary Review,* Vol. XLII, November 1882.— 381

Kerdijk, A. *Karl Marx.* Haarlem, 1879. In: *Mannen van beteekenis in onze dagen.*— 65

Kiepert, H. *Karte von Böhmen, Maehren und Oesterreich.* Berlin, 1866.— 207

Kindlinger, N. *Geschichte der Deutschen Hörigkeit insbesondere der sogenannten Leibeigenschaft.* Berlin, 1819.— 403

Knigge, A. *Ueber den Umgang mit Menschen.* In drei Theilen. Achte verbesserte Auflage. Hannover, 1804.— 274

Kollár, J. *Sláwy dcera. Lyricko-epická báseň w pěti zpěwjch.* Úpelné wydánj. W Pešti, 1832.— 194

Lafargue, P. [Public reply to the examining magistrate M. Ed. Piquand.] In: *L'Égalité,* 4ᵉ Série, No. 26, 18 novembre 1882: *L'Affaire de Montluçon.*— 379

— *Le droit au rire.* In: *L'Égalité,* 4ᵉ Série, No. 29, 21 novembre 1882.— 406

— *Le Ministère enchanté.* In: *L'Égalité,* 4ᵉ Série, No. 32, 24 novembre 1882.— 385, 398, 402

— *Notre candidat.* In: *L'Égalité,* 4ᵉ Série, No. 47, 9 décembre 1882.— 398, 402, 408

— *Prêtres et commerçants.* In: *L'Égalité,* 4ᵉ Série, No. 58, 20 décembre 1882.— 413

— Лафаргъ, Поль. *Движеніе поземельной собственности во Франціи.* In: *Устои,* №№ 3-4 и 6, мартъ, апрѣль и іюнь 1882.— 61, 64, 240

Langland, W. *The Vision concerning Piers the Plowman.*— 371

Lankester, E. Ray. *Degeneration. A Chapter in Darwinism.* London, 1880.— 64
— Ланкестеръ, Э. Рей. *Вырожденіе. Глава изъ теоріи развитія (дарвинизма).* С.-Петербургъ [1883].— 64

Liebknecht, W. [Speech in the Reichstag on 31 May 1881.] In: *Stenographische Berichte über die Verhandlungen des Reichstags.* 4. Legislaturperiode. IV. Session 1881. Bd. II. 53. Sitzung am 31. Mai 1881.— 138

Loria, A. *La legge di popolazione ed il sistema sociale.* Siena, 1882.— 299
— *La rendita fondiaria e la sua elisione naturale.* Milano, Napoli, Pisa, 1880.— 298
— *La teoria del valore negli economisti italiani.* Bologna, 1882.— 299

Malon, B. *Les Débuts du Parti ouvrier.* In: *La Revue socialiste,* No. 11, 5 août 1880.— 43

M[alon], B. *Histoire critique de l'économie politique.* Lugano, 1876.— 392

Malon, B. *Histoire du socialisme depuis ses origines probables jusqu'à nos jours.* Lugano, 1879.— 147, 155, 386
— *Histoire du socialisme depuis les temps les plus reculés jusqu'à nos jours ou efforts des réformateurs et des révoltés a travers les ages.* Tome I-II. Paris, 1882-1883.— 155

[Marx, Jenny.] *Aus der Londoner Theaterwelt.* In: *Frankfurter Zeitung und Handelsblatt,* 21. November 1875.— 158
— *Englische Shakespeare-Studien.* In: *Frankfurter Zeitung und Handelsblatt,* 3. Januar 1877.— 158
— *Londoner Saison.* In: *Frankfurter Zeitung und Handelsblatt,* 4. April 1876.— 158
— *Shakespeares 'Richard III.' im Londoner Lyceum-Theater.* In: *Frankfurter Zeitung und Handelsblatt,* 8. Februar 1877.— 158
— *Vom Londoner Theater.* In: *Frankfurter Zeitung und Handelsblatt,* 25. Mai 1877.— 158

Maurer, G. L. von. *Einleitung zur Geschichte der Mark-, Hof-, Dorf- und Stadt-Verfassung und der öffentlichen Gewalt.* München, 1854.— 336, 395, 400, 408, 416, 455
— *Geschichte der Dorfverfassung in Deutschland.* Bd. I-II. Erlangen, 1865-1866.— 395, 400, 408, 416, 455
— *Geschichte der Fronhöfe, der Bauernhöfe und der Hofverfassung in Deutschland.* Bd. I-IV. Erlangen, 1862-1863.— 109, 400, 403, 408, 416, 455
— *Geschichte der Markenverfassung in Deutschland.* Erlangen, 1856.— 336, 395, 400, 408, 416, 455
— *Geschichte der Städteverfassung in Deutschland.* Bd. I-IV. Erlangen, 1869-1871.— 395, 400, 408, 416, 455

Meitzen, A. *Der Boden und die landwirthschaftlichen Verhältnisse des Preussischen Staates nach dem Gebietsumfange vor 1866.* Bd. I-IV. Berlin, 1868-1871.— 403

Meyer, R. *Der Emancipationskampf des vierten Standes.* Bd. I-II. Berlin, 1874-1875.— 157
— *Politische Gründer und die Corruption in Deutschland.* Leipzig, 1877.— 449

Mirabeau, H. G. *Histoire secrète de la cour de Berlin, ou Correspondance d'un voyageur français, depuis le 5 juillet 1786 jusqu'au 19 janvier 1787.* Tome premier, 1789.— 290, 434

Molière, J.-B. *Bourgeois gentilhomme.*— 164

[Most, J.] *Endlich!* In: *Freiheit,* Nr. 12, 19. März 1881.— 78, 80, 81

Most, J. *Kapital und Arbeit. Ein populärer Auszug aus 'Das Kapital' von Karl Marx.* [Chemnitz, 1873.]— 294

— *Kapital und Arbeit. Ein populärer Auszug aus 'Das Kapital' von Karl Marx.* Zweite verbesserte Auflage, Chemnitz [1876].— 294

Müllner, A. *Die Schuld.*— 437

Nieuwenhuis, F. D. *Karl Marx. 'Kapitaal en Arbeid'.* s' Hage, 1881.—16, 65

[Nikitina, V. N.] *Le catholicisme socialiste en Allemagne.* Signed: B. Gendre. In: *La Justice,* No. 687, 2 décembre 1881.— 157

Nordau, M. *Aus dem wahren Milliardenlande. Pariser Studien und Bilder.* Bände I-II. Leipzig, 1878.— 112

— *Paris. Studien und Bilder aus dem wahren Milliardenlande.* Zweite vermehrte Auflage. Bände I-II. Leipzig, 1881.— 114

O'Connell, D. *Memoir on Ireland addressed to the Queen.*— 69

O[ldenburg,] H. *Die Grundlage des wissenschaftlichen Sozialismus.* In: *Jahrbuch für Sozialwissenschaft und Sozialpolitik.* Erster Jahrgang. Zweite Hälfte. Zürich-Oberstrass, 1880.— 365, 373

Picard, L. *L'affaire de la rue Saint Marc.* In: *Le Citoyen,* 3 septembre 1882.— 352, 354, 360, 361

Plutarchos. *Leben des Marius.* In: *Die Geschichtschreiber der deutschen Vorzeit in deutscher Bearbeitung.* Bd. 1: *Die Urzeit.* Hrsg. v. G. H. Pertz, J. Grimm. Berlin, 1847.— 382

— *Vitae parallelae.*— 273

[Potocki, I., Kołłątaj, H., Dmochowski, F. K.] *Vom Entstehen und Untergange der polnischen Konstitution vom 3ten May 1791,* Th. I-II. 1793.— 391

Prendergast, J. P. *The Cromwellian Settlement of Ireland.* London, 1865.— 68

Proudhon, P. J. *Système des contradictions économiques, ou Philosophie de la misère.* T. 1-2. Paris [1846].— 177

Puttkamer [R. V. v.] [Speech in the Reichstag on 13 December 1882.] In: *Stenographische Berichte über die Verhandlungen des Reichstages.* V. Legislaturperiode. II. Session 1882/83. Band I. Berlin, 1883.— 431, 455

Rae, J. *The Socialism of Karl Marx and the Young Hegelians.* In: *The Contemporary Review,* Vol. XL, October 1881.— 162, 185

Ranke, J. *Grundzüge der Physiologie des Menschen mit Rücksicht auf die Gesundheitspflege und das praktische Bedürfnis des Arztes.* Leipzig, 1868.—417

Redgrave, A. *The Factory and Workshop Act, 1878,* with introduction, copious notes, and an elaborate index. Second edition. London, 1879.—56, 368

Ricardo, D. *On the Principles of Political Economy, and Taxation.* Third edition. London, 1821.—230.

Rodbertus-Jagetzow [J. K.] *Briefe und Socialpolitische Aufsätze.* Herausgegeben von Dr. R. Meyer. Bände I-II. Berlin [1882].—416, 434, 449.

Rodbertus [-Jagetzow, J. K.] *Sociale Briefe an von Kirchmann. Dritter Brief: Widerlegung der Ricardo'schen Lehre von der Grundrente und Begründung einer neuen Rententheorie.* Berlin, 1851.—416.

Roscoe, H. E., und Schorlemmer, C. *Ausführliches Lehrbuch der Chemie.* Bd. I-III. Braunschweig, 1877-1882.—446

Šafařík, P. J. *Slowanský Národopis.* W Praze, 1849.—206, 207

Saling's Börsen-Papiere. Zweiter (finanzieller) Teil. Siebente Auflage. *Saling's Börsen-Jahrbuch für 1883/84. Ein Handbuch für Bankiers und Kapitalisten.* Berlin, 1883.—359

Samter, A. *Social-Lehre. Ueber die Befriedigung der Bedürfnisse in der menschlichen Gesellschaft.* Leipzig, 1875.—101

Sax, E. *Die Hausindustrie in Thüringen.* Wirthschaftliche Studien. I. Theil. Das meininger Oberland. Jena, 1882.—323

[Schäffle, A.] *Die Quintessenz des Socialismus. Von einem Volkswirth.* Separatabdruck aus den *Deutschen Blättern.* Gotha, 1875.—73, 74

Schramm, C. *Karl Bürkli und Karl Marx.* In: *Arbeiterstimme,* Nr. 52 und 53, 24. und 31. Dezember 1881.—177, 181, 189

S[chramm], C. A. *Zur Werttheorie.* In: *Jahrbuch für Sozialwissenschaft und Sozialpolitik.* Erster Jahrgang. Zweite Hälfte. Zürich-Oberstrass, 1880.—16

Serraillier, A. [Speech at the meeting of the General Council of the IWMA on 2 January 1872.] In: *The General Council of the First International. 1871-1872.* Moscow, 1968.—53

Shakespeare, W. *Much Ado about Nothing.*—82
— *Othello.*—312

Siemens, C. W. [Speech at the 52nd Congress of the British Association for the Advancement of Science.] In: *Nature,* No. 669, Vol. XXVI, 24 August 1882.—314, 384

Simon, J. *State Medicine.* In: *Nature,* No. 616, Vol. XXIV, 18 August 1881.—140

[Skaldin] Скалдинъ, *Въ захолустьи и въ столицѣ.* С.-Петербургъ, 1870.—109

Soetbeer, A. *Edelmetall-Produktion und Werthverhältnis zwischen Gold und Silber seit der Entdeckung Amerika's bis zur Gegenwart.* Gotha, 1879.—257

Sophocles. *Antigone.*—230

[Spence, Th.] *The Nationalisation of the Land in 1775 and 1882. Being a lecture delivered at Newcastle-on-Tyne, by Thomas Spence, 1775.* Reprinted and edited, with notes and introduction by H. M. Hyndman, 1882. London, Manchester, 1882.—228

Stiebeling, G. C. *Lesebuch für das Volk. Eine Kurzgefaßte und leichtverständliche Darstellung des Wichtigsten aus Naturlehre und Menschen-Kunde.* New York, 1882.—369
— *The People's Reader. A sketch of man's physical, political, mental and social development in the past, present and future.* New York, 1882.—369

Tacitus, C. *Germania.* In: *Die Geschichtschreiber der deutschen Vorzeit in deutscher Bearbeitung.* Bd. 1: *Die Urzeit.* Hrsg. v. G. H. Pertz, J. Grimm u. a. Berlin, 1847-1849.—382, 383, 394

Terentius, Afer Publius. *Andria.*—147

Thierry, A. *Histoire de la conquête de l'Angleterre par les Normands, de ses causes, et de ses suites jusqu'à nos jours, en Angleterre, en Écosse, en Irlande et sur le continent.* Tome I-III. Paris, 1825.—414

Tissot, V. *Les Prussiens en Allemagne. Suite du voyage au pays des milliards.* Paris, 1876.—112
— *Voyage au pays des milliards.* Paris, 1875.—112.
— *Voyage aux pays annexés. Suite et fin du Voyage au pays des milliards.* Paris, 1876.—112

Turgot [A. R. J.] *Réflexions sur la formation et la distribution des richesses.* In: *Œuvres de Turgot.* Nouv. éd. par Eugène Daire. T. 1. Paris., 1844.—230

Vallès, J. *Letter to J. Grévy.* In: *La Revolution Française,* février 1879.—127

[Vollmar, G. H.] *Aufhebung des Ausnahmegesetzes?* In: *Der Sozialdemokrat,* Nr. 34 und 35, 17. und 24. August 1882.—325, 332, 336, 342, 349, 350, 357
— *Aufhebung des Sozialistengesetzes? Ein Wort zur Taktik der deutschen Sozialdemokratie.* Signed: Surtur. Hottingen-Zürich, 1882.—352

V[ollmar, G. H.] *Zur Spaltung der französischen Arbeiterpartei.* In: *Der Sozialdemokrat,* Nr. 46, 47 und 49; 9., 16. und 30. November 1882.—373, 379, 386, 408

[Vorontsov] Воронцовъ, В. П. *Судьбы капитализма въ Россіи.* Спб., 1882.—399

W[eerth], G. *Heute Morgen fuhr ich nach Düsseldorf.* In: *Neue Rheinische Zeitung,* Nr. 44, 14. Juli 1848.—59
— (anon.) *Ein Sozialistenfresser aus dem Jahre 1848.* (Aus dem Feuilleton der *Neuen Rheinischen Zeitung.*) In: *Der Sozialdemokrat,* Nr. 33, 11. August 1881.—59

Westphalen, Ch. H. Ph. von. *Geschichte der Feldzüge des Herzogs Ferdinand von Braunschweig-Lüneburg. Nachgelassenes Manuskript von Christian Heinrich Philipp Edler von Westphalen.* Bd. I-II. Berlin, 1859.—158
— *Geschichte der Feldzüge des Herzogs Ferdinand von Braunschweig-Lüneburg.* Zusammengestellt aus Materialien seines Nachlasses und des Kriegs-Archivs des Herzogs Ferdinand, und hrsg. von F. O. W. H. v. Westphalen. Bd. I-VI. Berlin, 1871-1872.—158

Wilhelm I. *Erlaß vom 4. Januar 1882.* In: *Deutscher Reichs-Anzeiger und Königlich Preußischer Staats-Anzeiger*, 7. Januar 1882.— 175, 178

DOCUMENTS

An act to further amend the law relating to the occupation and ownership of land in Ireland and for other purposes relating there to (Irish Land Bill).— 68

Agricultural Returns of Great Britain for 1881, with Abstract Tables for the United Kingdom, British Possessions, and Foreign Countries. London, 1882.— 367

Agricultural Returns of Great Britain for 1882, with Abstract Tables for the United Kingdom, British Possessions, and Foreign Countries. London, 1883.— 367

Agricultural Statistics, Ireland. General Abstracts Showing the Acreage under the Several Crops, and the Number of Live Stock, in Each County and Province for the Year 1880-1881. Dublin, 1881.— 367

Agricultural Statistics, Ireland, General Abstracts Showing the Acreage under the Several Crops, and the Number of Live Stock, in Each County and Province for the Year 1881-1882. Dublin, 1882.— 367

Arms Act (Peace Preservation Act).— 84

Association Internationale des Travailleurs. Statuts et règlements. Londres, 1866.— 342

Das Bundesgesetz betreffend die Arbeit in den Fabriken (vom 23. März 1877), n. d.— 347, 364, 373

Cinquième congrès national ouvrier socialiste de Reims. Compte rendu analytique. In: *Le Prolétaire*, Nos. 162 et 163, 5 et 12 novembre 1881.— 155

Circulaire à toutes les fédérations de l'Association Internationale des Travailleurs. Genève, 1871.— 182

Code civil.— 188

Code pénal, ou code des délits et des peines, Cologne, 1810.— 111, 445

Coercion bills.— 75, 84, 172

Factories and Workshop Acts.— 122, 140

Gesetz gegen die gemeingefährlichen Bestrebungen des Sozialdemokratie. In: *Reichs-Gesetzblatt*, Nr. 34, 1878.— 11, 38, 40, 49, 50

Gewerbeordnung, die deutsche, in ihrer durch das Innungsgesetz erlangten neuesten Gestalt, mit den Einführungsgesetzen für Württemberg, Baden, Bayern und Elsaß-Lothringen, den Abänderungen und Ergänzungen der Novellen und dem Gesetz über die eingeschriebenen Hülfskassen vom 7. April 1876, nebst den Ausführungs-Verordnungen des Bundesrathes. 3. Auflage. Köln, 1882.— 347, 364

Irish Land Bill 1881.— 75, 84, 86, 90

Offences against the Person Act. Passed in 1861.— 86

Parti ouvrier. Conseil national. In: *L'Egalité*, 3ᵉ Série, No. 47, 5 novembre 1882.— 373

Programme électoral des travailleurs socialistes. In: *L'Egalité*, 2ᵉ Série, No. 24, 30 juin 1880.— 148, 149, 181, 342

Программа партии Народная воля.— 45

Reports from Her M's Consuls. Part IV.— 19

Reports of the Commissioners Appointed to Inquire into the State of Popular Education in England. 1861.— 17

Reports of the Commissioners of Her Majesty's Inland Revenue on the Inland Revenue. London, 1874-1882.— 368

Report of the Commissioners on Education in Ireland, 1826.— 70

Reports of the Inspectors of Factories to Her Majesty's Principal Secretary of State for the Home Department, for the half-year ending 31 October 1877-1881. London, 1882.— 367

Reports of Reformatory and Industrial School.— 17

Der Sachsenspiegel.— 404

Statistical Abstract for the United Kingdom in Each of the Fifteen Years. No. 28. From 1866 to 1880. London, 1881.— 368

Statistical Abstract for the United Kingdom in Each of the Last Fifteen Years. No. 29. From 1867 to 1881. London, 1882.— 368

Stenographische Berichte über die Verhandlungen des Reichstags. 4. Legislaturperiode. IV. Session 1881. Band I. 25., 26. und 29. Sitzungen am 30., 31. März und 4. April 1881. Berlin, 1881.— 85, 86, 87

Stenographische Berichte über die Verhandlungen des Reichstages. V. Legislaturperiode. I. Session 1881/82. [Band I.] Von der Eröffnungssitzung am 17. November 1881 bis zur Schlußsitzung am 30. Januar 1882. Berlin, 1882.— 188, 203

[Ukase re the reduction of redemption payments.] In: *The Times,* No. 30403, January 13, 1882.— 182

ANONYMOUS ARTICLES AND REPORTS PUBLISHED IN PERIODIC EDITIONS

The Eastern Post, No. 168, December 16, 1871; *Mr Bradlaugh and the Communists.*— 52

— No. 169, December 23, 1871: *International Working Men's Association.*— 53

— No. 173, January 20, 1872: *Mr Bradlaugh and the International.*— 52

L'Égalité, 2ᵉ Série, No. 21, 9 juin 1880: *Le patriotisme de la bourgeoisie et les Chinois.*— 372

— 3ᵉ Série, No. 1, 11 décembre 1881.— 166
— " " No. 2, 18 décembre 1881.— 166
— " " No. 4, 1 janvier 1882: *Allemagne.*— 173; *Paris.*— 173
— " " No. 27 11 juin 1882.— 283, 289
— 4ᵉ Série, No. 53, 15 décembre 1882: *L'Arrestation de Lafargue.*— 404
— " " No. 54, 16 décembre 1882: *L'Affaire de Montluçon.*— 404

Freiheit, Nr. 26, 25. Juni 1881: *Socialpolitische Rundschau. Deutschland.*— 138
— Nr. 13, 26. März 1881: *Socialpolitische Rundschau. Schweiz.*— 80
— Nr. 31-33, 30. Juli, 6. und 13. August 1881: *Congress. Bericht.*— 129
— Nr. 13, 1. April 1882: *Deutschland.*— 236

The Statist, Vol. VII, No. 153, January 29, 1881.—62-63

Le Temps, No. 7773, 6 août 1882: *Allemagne.*—304

The Times, No. 30165, April 11, 1881: *Cork, April 10.*—84
— No. 30390, December 29, 1881: *Money-Market and City Intelligence.*—170
— No. 30395, January 4, 1882: *Mr Bright and Mr Chamberlain at Birmingham.*—171; *Irish Landlords and the Government.*—171
— No. 30712, January 9, 1883: *Mr Cowen at Newcastle.*—423

INDEX OF PERIODICALS

Le Citoyen Français — see *Le Citoyen*

Le Citoyen International — see *Le Citoyen*

La Commune — a daily edited by Félix Pyat and published in Paris in September-November 1880.—43

Concordia. Zeitschrift für die Arbeiterfrage — a journal of big industrialists and armchair socialists, founded in 1871 and published in Berlin up to 1876.—65

The Contemporary Review — a bourgeois-liberal monthly published in London since 1866.—162, 185, 381

The Daily News — a liberal daily of the industrial bourgeoisie, published in London from 1846 to 1930.—54, 83, 121, 216, 464

Deutsche Jahrbücher für Wissenschaft und Kunst — see *Hallische Jahrbücher für deutsche Wissenschaft und Kunst*

Deutsch-Französische Jahrbücher — a German-language yearly published in Paris under the editorship of Karl Marx and Arnold Ruge; only the first issue, a double one, appeared in February 1844. It carried a number of works by Marx and Engels.—58, 177

The Eastern Post — an English workers' weekly published in London under this title from 1868 to 1873, and under various titles up to 1938; organ of the General Council of the International from February 1871 to June 1872.—52-53

L'Égalité — a French socialist weekly, founded by Jules Guesde in 1877; an organ of the French Workers' Party from 1880 to 1883. It was published in six series, each with its own subtitle. The first three series were published weekly (113 issues in all). The 4th and 5th series appeared daily (56 issues in all). Only one issue of the 6th series appeared in 1886.—24, 27, 41, 144, 146, 149, 150, 155, 166, 173, 183, 190, 197, 200, 219, 221, 237, 238, 266, 278, 282, 283, 304, 332, 340, 347, 351, 353, 356, 357, 358, 361, 362, 370, 372, 373, 374, 379, 383, 384, 386, 387, 390, 391, 393, 394, 396, 402, 404, 407-08, 413, 441, 445

L'Émancipation. Organe Quotidien du Parti Ouvrier — a French socialist daily published in Lyons from 31 October to 24 November 1880 under the editorship of Benoît Malon.—145, 361

L'Étendard Révolutionnaire. Organe anarchiste hebdomadaire — a French anarchist daily published in Lyons from 30 July to 8 October 1882.—375

L'Exploité de Nantes — a French workers' newspaper published in Nantes in 1882.—387

The Financial Reform Almanach — a yearly published in London and Liverpool from 1865 to 1904.—212

ic and social reforms, and voiced the interests of the petty and middle bourgeoisie. In 1880 Charles Longuet became its editor.—45, 61, 84, 96, 111-12, 157, 158, 219, 230, 328, 330, 334, 335, 344, 345, 364, 373, 408, 426, 465, 470

Kölner Zeitung—see *Kölnische Zeitung*

Kölnische Zeitung—a German liberal daily published in Cologne from 1802 to 1945.— 10, 59, 114, 182, 235, 247, 248, 313, 330, 353, 394, 396

Königlich privilegirte Berlinische Zeitung von Staats- und gelehrten Sachen—a daily published in Berlin from 1785; also called *Vossische Zeitung* after its owner Christian Friedrich Voss.—112

The Labour Standard. An Organ of Industry—a trade union weekly published in London from 1881 to 1885. Engels was its contributor in 1881.— 105, 118, 119-21, 123, 126, 140, 197, 278, 305, 359, 442

Die Laterne—a satirical Social-Democratic weekly published in Brussels from 15 December 1878 to 29 June 1879 under the editorship of Carl Hirsch.—173

La Liberté—a conservative evening daily published in Paris from 1865 to 1944; in 1866-72 it belonged to Émile Girardin, supported the policy of the Second Empire.—52

Modern Thought—a monthly journal on problems of religion, politics, ethics, science and literature published in London from 1879 to 1884.—163, 165, 184

[Narodnaya Volya] *Народная Воля*—a Russian illegal newspaper of the terrorist Narodnik organisation of the same name. It was published from October 1879 to October 1885, the printing being carried out by underground printing shops in various cities of the country. 12 issues appeared in all. Up to 1 March 1881 its editors were Nikolai Morozov and Lev Tikhomirov and later Hermann Lopatin and others.—236, 244

Nature. A Weekly Illustrated Journal of Science—a journal published in London since 1869.—140

Neue Rheinische Zeitung. Organ der Demokratie—a daily published in Cologne under the editorship of Marx from 1 June 1848 to 19 May 1849 (with an interval between 27 September and 12 October 1848); an organ of the revolutionary proletarian democrats during the 1848-49 revolution in Germany; Engels was one of its editors.—12, 59, 466

Neue Rheinische Zeitung. Politisch-ökonomische Revue—a journal published by Marx and Engels from December 1849 to November 1850, theoretical organ of the Communist League.—189

Neue Zeit—a journal of the German Social-Democrats published in Stuttgart from 1883 to October 1890 once a month, and then, up to the autumn of 1923, weekly

SUBJECT INDEX

Working-class movement in France — 11,
43-45, 61, 134, 138, 141, 144-50, 153,
154, 157, 191, 192, 333, 343, 344, 347,
355, 356, 360-61, 386, 387, 406, 474
See also *Proudhonism*
Working-class movement in Germany — 8, 9,
38, 42, 49, 139, 140, 151-53, 156, 157,
188, 193, 194, 203, 279, 431, 448
See also *German Social-Democracy*; *Lassalleanism*
Working-class movement in Hungary — 191
Working-class movement in Italy — 191,
197, 358
Working-class movement in the Netherlands — 65, 197

Working-class movement in Portugal — 197
Working-class movement in Romania — 197
Working-class movement in Serbia — 197
Working-class movement in Spain — 128
Working-class movement in Switzerland —
143
*Working-class movement in the United States
of America* — 77, 78, 143, 279, 284, 294,
356
Working day — 157, 388, 473, 474

Z

Zoology — 377